Eternal City

Eternal City

Rome in the Photographs Collection of the
Royal Institute of British Architects

edited by
Marco Iuliano
Gabriella Musto

SKIRA

Cover
George Everard Kidder Smith
*Staircase adjacent to the Palazzo
dei Conservatori,
Piazza del Campidoglio*, 1954
Architectural Press Archive
RIBA Collections

Art Director
Marcello Francone

Design
Lugi Fiore

Editorial coordination
Vincenza Russo

Editing
Anna Albano

Layout
Barbara Galotta

Translations
Paul Metcalfe for Scriptum,
Rome

First published in Italy in 2018
by Skira editore
Palazzo Casati Stampa
via Torino 61
20123 Milano
Italy
www.skira.net

© 2018 Ministero dei beni
e delle attività culturali
e del turismo
© 2018 The authors for their
texts
© 2018 Skira editore, Milano

Printed and bound in Italy.
First edition

ISBN: 978-88-572-3919-4

Distributed in USA, Canada,
Central & South America by
ARTBOOK | D.A.P. 75, Broad
Street Suite 630, New York, NY
10004, USA.
Distributed elsewhere in the
world by Thames and Hudson
Ltd., 181A High Holborn,
London WC1V 7QX,
United Kingdom.

**Eternal City. Rome in the Photographs Collection
of the Royal Institute of British Architects**

Rome, Monument to Vittorio Emanuele II
Sala Zanardelli
28 June – 28 October 2018

*Research Project,
Exhibition
and Catalogue by*
Marco Iuliano
Gabriella Musto

*for the Royal Institute
of British Architects*
Valeria Carullo

Steering Committee
Wouter Bracke
Valeria Carullo
Edith Gabrielli
Marco Iuliano
Stephen Milner
Gabriella Musto
Richard Pare
François Penz
Nicholas Ray

in association with

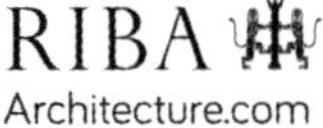

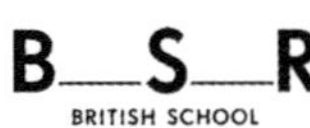

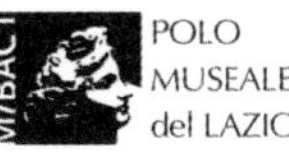

Polo Museale del Lazio
Edith Gabrielli, *director*

Director's Staff
Stefano Brachetti
Simonetta Facchini
Luca Gabioli
Stefania Properzi

Communications Office
Marco Sala, *director*

*Department of Exhibitions
and Loans*
Mario Di Bartolomeo, *director*
Mario Nissolino
Alessandra Spanedda
Carolina Vigliarolo

*Photographic Archive
and Laboratory*
Lia Di Giacomo, *director*
Maria Castellino
Maximiliano Massaroni
Massimo Taruffi
Gianfranco Zecca

Office for Audiovisual Material
Maria Antonietta Curione,
director

Office for Archives and Protocol
Sara De Angelis, *director*
Daniele Iori
Mauro Lambardi
Claudio Lopez
Fabrizio Lupardini
Silvia Micarelli
Gabriella Micci

Office for Financial Control
Daniela Baroni, Daniela Santilli,
Lucilla Torre, *supervisors*
Nazzareno Brusca
Gennaro Di Matteo
Albertina Liguori
Francesco Loscrì
Angela Pia Manicone
Maximiliano Massaroni
Daniele Palomba
Nicoletta Piancastelli
Alessandra Sbarra
Alessia Vignali

**Monument to Vittorio
Emanuele II**
Gabriella Musto, *director*

Technical Department
Liliana Cristiano
Luigi Papa
Gianni Pittiglio

Administrative Department
Rosa Lavia
Daniela Abbate

Personnel of the security,
access and reception section

Organisation and Production
Polo Museale del Lazio

*Communications
and Press Office*
Civita

Exhibition Installation
Studios s.r.l.

General Direction of Works
Gabriella Musto

Exhibition Layout
Gabriella Musto
Martha Magrini Sissa

Graphics
Martha Magrini Sissa

Health and Safety Consultant
Fabrizio Pompozzi

Technical Secretariat
Roberto Faraone

*Head of Accident
Prevention and Safety*
Alessandro Bernoni,
Sintesi S.p.a.

*Support in Security,
Access and Reception*
ALES S.p.a.

Acknowledgements
Tim Benton, Sophie Briard,
Daniele Carrer, Edoardo
Cecconi, Umberto Cecconi,
Cathy Dembsky, Giovanni
Fanelli, Valeria Ferraro, Stefano
Fittipaldi, Michela Gatti,
Beatrice Gelosia, Giovanni
Greco, Barbara Iuliano, Angelo
Maggi, Jonathan Makepeace,
Alberto Mazza, Jane
Moscardini, Daniel Naegele,
Stefania Peterlini, Alessandra
Petretto, Antongiulio
Sangiuliano, Valerie Scott,
Annalisa Sonzogni, Luciano
Striani, Suzanne Waters,
Anthony Wilkinson

The fresco Veduta di Roma *(1413–14, also known as* Pianta di Roma) *painted by Taddeo di Bartolo in the arched entrance to the ante-chapel of the Palazzo Pubblico in Siena shows the Rome of the period, namely the early fifteenth century, with no apparent discontinuity between classical and medieval monuments: the Colosseum in the centre and Palazzo Senatorio in the foreground.*

Silvia Maddalo and other scholars have devoted time and attention to identifying Taddeo's sources. Importance thus appears to attach, for example, to the gold seal of the Holy Roman Emperor Louis IV (datable to 1328), which also presents this circular, all-inclusive view. Another possible source of the monuments chosen for reproduction is the Mirabilia Urbis Romae, *already a very popular guide at the time. Attention should also be drawn to the links with developments in geography and cartography, not least in connection with the rediscovery of Ptolemy's* Cosmographia. *In this sense, Taddeo's view of Rome has parallels with a miniature of the* Très riches heures du Duc du Berry *by Paul, Jean and Hermann de Limbourg (1411–12) and with a wash drawing in Fazio degli Uberti's* Dittamondo *(1447).*

Greater importance appears to attach here, however, to the location of Taddeo's fresco and its connection with other significant representations than to the buildings shown or the cultural parallels. The Veduta *is in fact part of a series painted by the artist in the ante-chapel, the place that housed the offices of the Consistory, Siena's ruling council. In order to emphasise its political role, Taddeo added nearby the virtues essential to the correct use of power, including Justice, Magnanimity, Fortitude and Prudence, as well as a gallery of exemplary figures that contributed by their deeds to the rise of Rome, such as Cato, Gaius Mucius Scaevola and Scipio. Rome, not only ancient Rome but also the medieval city of the time, was evidently associated with a series of political and moral values that Siena, which claimed to be its legitimate heir in many respects, continued to uphold.*

Let us now take a great leap forward into the second half of the seventeenth century and precisely to the year 1665, when the Roman publisher De Rossi brought out the first volume of the Nuovo teatro delle fabriche, et edificii, in prospettiva di Roma moderna, sotto il felice pontificato di n.s. Alessandro VII. *Two more then appeared by 1669 to form a compact and well-organised trilogy. The first two volumes illustrate the edifices built, restored and enlarged by order of Pope Alexander VII, and the third those connected with his immediate successor Clement IX. The author of the engravings in all three was Giovanni Battista Falda from Piedmont, who arrived in Rome at the age of 14 and began to produce engravings for De Rossi before entering the service of the Chigi family a few years later.*

The three books of the Nuovo Teatro, *and indeed the fourth and fifth volumes too, were certainly regarded for far too long as no more than illustrated souvenirs of Rome. It was Richard Krautheimer that revealed the political implications of Falda's series and hence the real aims of Alexander VII in one of his many important books. Like Gregory XIII and Sixtus V, Alexander was intent on presenting the image of modern Rome with its buildings, churches and gardens in accordance with a unified plan of urban expansion. This operation was made all the more necessary by the severe crisis, both economic and political, that characterised his reign and the city as a whole at the end of the seventeenth century.*

There are 250 years — and of course a host of other things too — between Taddeo di Bartolo and Giovanni Battista Falda. We have chosen these two artists and these two works deliberately out of all the other possibilities in order to highlight a common factor, namely the historical image of Rome. While this phenomenon also characterises other cities, Italian or otherwise, from Florence and Venice to London and Paris, what counts here is Rome's truly original if not indeed unique ability to take on connotations, overtones or at least nuances of a political character with every new representation.

The image of Rome captured by British photographers of the past and the present: this is essentially the subject of Eternal City.

The motivations and drives underlying and informing the shots taken by the photographers featured in the exhibition are examined in the catalogue by various authors, including the Director of the British School at Rome. These motivations and drives are indeed quite varied and there is hardly any need to go over them again one by one here.

As Director of the Polo Museale del Lazio, and hence responsible for the Pantheon, Castel Sant'Angelo, the Vittoriano and forty-three other monuments of great national and international importance, I am naturally and indeed necessarily in some respects interested in the general substance of this exhibition. Not least because the Polo is the organ of the Italian state responsible in academic and administrative terms for fostering knowledge and access to the cultural heritage in the Lazio region as a whole, starting of course with Rome, its most important city.

Observation of Rome in a broader perspective, the perspective of history in the long term, immediately reveals, however, connections also between this exhibition, though indisputably contemporary and equally indisputably original, and a substantial number of other undertakings that have marked the city's life over the centuries and indeed millennia, which of course include Taddeo di Bartolo's Veduta di Roma *and Giovanni Battista Falda's* Nuovo teatro delle fabriche.

Edith Gabrielli
Director of the Polo Museale del Lazio

Over the centuries the place of Rome within the British social imagination has been mediated through a vast range of artistic practices. Whilst exposure to the cultural inheritance of classical antiquity may have animated the commissioning practices of the young nobility during the Grand Tour, the increasing sophistication of print technology saw the emergence of mass-produced engravings and lithographs. Adapting traditional practices to new technologies, the photographing of Rome by the British has a long and illustrious history which can be used to chart the evolution of photographic technology itself from its earliest manifestation as daguerreotype, salted paper print, and photo-mechanical printing to the most sophisticated contemporary digital forms. The Roman photographic campaigns of the likes of Robert Macpherson (1814–1872), Father Peter Paul Mackey (1851–1935), and Thomas Ashby (1874–1931) not only focused attention on Rome's ancient topography and architectural monuments but also sought to capture something of the city's everyday life and the juxtaposition of the old and new as the city was transformed by new building projects. The set piece veduta *beloved of the grand tourist began to give way to more personalised glimpses of the city as photographers moved from the well-trodden paths of the recommended routes to examine the city's previously unrecorded corners and hidden byways. The Eternal City of classical antiquity and Roman Catholicism gave way to a softer city of personal reflection and curiosity. These earlier photographs are now of increasing importance in understanding 'Roma com'era' prior to the urban redevelopment of the 1920s and 1930s and beyond. British photography also played an important part in assessing the impact of World War II on the city's urban fabric. The Royal Air Force (RAF) took a whole series of aerial photographs of war-torn Rome and John Bryan Ward-Perkins (1912–1981), Director of the Allied Sub-commission for Monuments and Fine Arts and subsequently Director of the British School at Rome, collected together an archive of over 1000 photographs of damaged monuments and works of art from across the whole Italian peninsula, including Rome. Yet the current exhibition derives from another important and large-scale British archive containing significant*

Roman material, namely the photographic collection of the Royal Institute of British Architects (RIBA). Alongside early photographs, it contains the work of a number of leading British post-war photographers who undertook work in Rome and are featured in the present exhibition. Unlike the pioneering work of the earlier period, these works have received less exposure and critical attention. The present exhibition seeks to redress the balance. In the pages which follow, scholars and experts with different backgrounds tackle a difficult, interdisciplinary subject, moving back and forth between architecture and the visual arts. Marco Iuliano gives an overview of the project and introduces architectural photography in Rome, while Gabriella Musto reflects on the historical perception of the Vittoriano and its contemporary role; Richard Pare furnishes a scholarly analysis of the origins of photography in Rome, whilst Owen Hopkins and François Penz respectively consider the impact of the city on the imagination of architects and film-makers. Valeria Carullo explores the richness of the RIBA photographs collection before we come to the catalogue section, which is complemented by essays by Paolo Mascilli Migliorini, Nicholas Ray, Antonello Alici, Carla Molinari and Tom True. A detailed bibliography by Jemma Street completes the book.

Whilst the early humanists of the Italian Renaissance claimed to be walking in the footsteps of the ancients, this exhibition invites us to walk in the footsteps of more modern practitioners of Rome's many layered urban spaces, practitioners from Britain carrying cameras. Simultaneously ancient and modern, the emotive power of the Eternal City lies in its ability to provoke strong subjective responses in its beholder due to the depth of its historical memory. And every beholder comes away changed by the encounter.

Stephen J. Milner
Director, British School at Rome

Alessandra Giovenco
Archivist, British School at Rome

Contents

Marco Iuliano

Rome after Photography

'It occurs to me that some few facts respecting the state of photography in Rome may not be without interest to those of you readers who take a delight in this beautiful branch of Art; and as many of my photographic acquaintance have frequently expressed a wish that I would publish the method I adopted for making negatives during a four month's residency in the Eternal City, I have thought it best to forward a familiar letter on the subject for insertion in your journal — should you deem the communication of sufficient importance.'[1]

This is the simple beginning of the account of the experiments carried out in Rome by Richard Wheeler Thomas published in London by *The Art Journal* in 1852. A chemist and amateur photographer active between 1852 and 1879, Thomas mentioned some of the haunts of the Roman photographers — 'I need hardly say that their places of rendezvous are the Lepre and Caffè Greco' — and some of his contemporary colleagues, including Giacomo Caneva, Eugène Constant, Frédéric Flachéron and a certain Mr Robinson.

Many other names can certainly be added to Thomas's list, especially those of James Anderson (1813–1877) and Robert Turnbull Macpherson (1814–1872), two British photographers who took up permanent residence in Rome at the birth of the new medium. The multinational group of pioneers that gathered at the Caffè Greco saw a predominance of French and British alongside professionals from every corner of pre-unification Italy, when the long exposure times required at the dawn of photography made sculpture and architecture the most suitable subjects for exploration. The works photographed at first ranged from the statues in the Vatican to antiquities, the latter being the object of systematic series such as those commissioned by John Henry Parker (1806–1884).[2] The presence of visitors from the United Kingdom was consolidated in 1901 with the founding of the British School at Rome, whose library and archives include rare prints, photographs and books on the topography of Rome as a result, in particular, of the efforts of Thomas Ashby (1874–1931), the director from 1906 to 1925.[3]

Rome is a city that has always fired the collective imagination. Between memories of antiquity and modern experimentation, it had been an ideal subject for painters and engravers since the Renaissance. Developed when Italy was on the point of achieving unification, photography helped to enhance the aura that already enveloped Rome in previous centuries. While the first nineteenth-century photographs present a picturesque city and are practically indistinguishable from the views of painters and engravers in terms of subjects and framing, the new medium developed quickly along its own fascinating trajectory.[4] William Henry Fox Talbot spoke about its technical evolution in the opening chapter of *The Pencil of Nature*, written when he was "a wanderer in classic Italy".[5] Experimentation in the following years resulted in first the birth and later the disappearance of daguerreotypes, negatives on paper, calotypes and albumen prints. The latter, introduced by Louis Désiré Blanquart-Evrard in 1850, became the method of reproduction most frequently used until the early twentieth century.[6]

In their group outings, the first painter-photographers set up their cameras in the same places, thus often making it hard to attribute the photos taken. The emblematic staircase of Trinità dei Monti seen from Via dei Condotti and the even more iconic Forum were essentially photographed with only slight variations.[7] Some of the more unusual shots linger on the retina longer than others, for example the horizontal line of the upper section of the Temple of Hercules Victor in the daguerreotype by Joseph-Philibert Girault de Prangey (1842), the paper negatives of Flachéron (1851) and the panoramic view of Rome from Villa Medici by Alfred-Nicolas Normand (c. 1851).[8]

Together with Silvio Negro e Nicola Pietrangeli, principal curators of the exhibition on photography in Rome from 1840 to 1915 held at Palazzo Braschi in 1953, Piero Becchetti was the most prolific pioneer of studies in this area. Driven by an uncommon passion combined with impeccable scientific rigour, he published a number of books and studies on photography, stereoscopy and early pioneers such as Macpherson, Caneva, Anderson and the D'Alessandri brothers. More recently, the municipal Archivio Fotografico of Rome, which possesses an interesting collection of early images of the city, has helped to enhance awareness of an exceptional period in the history of photography that is finally beginning to receive the public recognition and attention it deserves.[9]

Architectural photography did not yet exist as a discipline when the systematic collection and arrangement of images began in Rome. The English photographer and curator Richard Pare (b. 1948), founder of one of the first collections of architectural photography for the Canadian Centre for Architecture (CCA) in Montreal and a pioneer in this field of study, tells us that the first item of the CCA collection, purchased from a New York antique dealer in 1974, was indeed a photograph of the Capitoline Hill by Robert Macpherson.[10] This fact confirms the indisputable primacy of Rome in any collection of architectural photography. Pare continues: 'As far as I am aware the CCA collection was the first to take a conscious attitude to the idea of the art of architectural photography; one of the tenets was that it had to be a good photograph to warrant consideration. Exceptions were made for images such as a rare recording of a significant structure since demolished or subjects difficult of access, or temporary constructions such as fortifications and siege works, and the great exhibitions from the Crystal Palace onwards. People would bring pictures for consideration and often they were of little interest, even though they would say that a particular picture was very rare. The riposte was that rarity was not enough. It also expanded rapidly once I was able to set aside the work on the Court House project, growing from the first picture acquired in 1974, to around 48.000 images over the succeeding 15 years.'[11]

Robert Elwall embarked on a similar operation at the Royal Institute of British Architects (RIBA) in London, on the other side of the Atlantic, in 1981. His interest focused, however, not on the individual image but on the photographic archive as a whole, as reflected by the huge number of over 1.7 million prints and negatives in the RIBA collection. In any case, the professional commitment of the first two curators of architectural photography led to the creation of some of the world's most important collections of this nature, rivalled only by the Prints and Photographs Collection of the Library of Congress in Washington, the collection of the Avery Architectural and Fine Arts Library in New York and very few others. Elwall's own words make it clear, however, that as recently as 2009, "despite its importance in shaping our perception of the world around us, the study of architectural photography is still in its infancy. Interaction between architecture and photography has been and remains undervalued both in the architectural and photographic communities."[12]

In the RIBA collection the first phase in the history of photography is represented in the exhibition by the images of the Anderson family, first James and then his eldest son Domenico (1854–1938), and a few other items, especially an album entitled *Roma* that belonged to Lady Eyre, resident at number 27 Piazza di Spagna, consisting of large-format albumen prints as was customary at the time.[13] Between the two world wars, Ralph Deakin (1888–1952), Rome correspondent of *The Times* and a keen amateur,[14] photographed everything that struck his fancy and marked many of the vantage points used on a map of the national agency of tourism (ENIT) still held by the RIBA. It is interesting to note the contrast between Deakin's lyrical vision of the city, characterised by the interplay of light and shadow, and the photographs of the frenzied demolition and construction work carried out on Fascist Rome taken in the same period for the *Architects' Journal* and *Architectural Review*, the two major organs of professional information for British architects, and now held in the Architectural Press Archive.

For most of the twentieth century, architectural magazines had their own official photographers, a practice recently discontinued due to the financial costs involved. It was instead often necessary to borrow images from abroad for articles on architectural works outside the UK. This is why some of the items in the

Architectural Press Archive are marked on the back with the stamps and names of the foreign institutions and photographers involved, which would otherwise be hard to identify.

The images of Rome in the Architectural Press Archive taken by non-British photographers include views of Saint Peter's Square and Castel Sant'Angelo at night taken by Spartaco Appetiti (active 1926–1978), Luigi Moretti's Casa del Girasole by Alberto Cartoni (1898–1976), and la Rinascente department store by Franco Albini and Franca Helg by Oscar Savio (1912–2015). The representations of the Capitol Square and the views of the city by the American photographer George Everard Kidder Smith (1913–1997) are also of great interest.[15] The British photographers connected with the Architectural Press and active also in Rome include Marion Johnson (1912–1980), better known by her pen name Georgina Masson, and Bruno de Hamel (active in the 1960s), who took the photographs of the British embassy in Rome designed by Basil Spence.

In this highly varied panorama, architecture magazines played a key role both in fostering debate and in building up the store of collective imagery. As has been pointed out, the history of modern architecture in the United Kingdom is characterised by a series of predominant theories, each of which is represented in a publication by means of a specific vocabulary and specific graphics. Importance attaches in this sense to the *Architectural Review* in the 1930s and 1940s, *Architectural Design* in the 1960s, and more recently *AA Files*, the magazine of the Architectural Association in London.[16] The most intense debate took place on the pages of the first two publications from the post-war period up the 1960s. It is no coincidence that many of the photographs on show originated precisely in these two cultural spheres, even though few were actually published. A key role in all this was played by Monica Pidgeon, editor of *Architectural Design* from 1946 to 1975 and an active figure in British and international architecture,[17] and Ivy de Wolfe, real name Hazel Hastings, the wife of Hubert De Cronin Hastings, editor of the *Architectural Review*. Original analyses with very different results thus intersected in Rome in the 1960s and gave rise to a very dynamic experimentation, albeit in opposite spheres: mainly private in the case of Pidgeon but public for Hastings, who took the photographs for *The Italian Townscape* (1963), a book based on the

research of Gordon Cullen and written by her husband Hubert under the name of Ivor de Wolfe. Some of these photographs appeared in the *Architectural Review* in June 1962. In any case, both Pidgeon and Hastings capture a city very different from the idealised collective image and much closer to the perception of the urban structure actually experienced. This was also due to technical developments that made it possible to take a series of shots in quick succession.

While the introduction to *The Italian Townscape* proves slightly confused as regards the stated aims, it is followed by 461 photographs of Italian locations, landscapes, towns, villages and architectural details, once again with a primary focus on Rome. The opening image is indeed an unusual view of the equestrian statue of Marcus Aurelius on the Campidoglio. The concluding section instead clarifies the concept of townscape and the couple's interest in Italy, and can be regarded as a sort of caption encompassing the author's numerous Italian photographs: 'Townscape deals with foils, focal points, fluctuation, vistas closed and vistas open, truncation, change of level, perspective, silhouette, intricacy, anticipation, continuity, space, enclosure, exposure, the precint, profile. […] Closeness instead of openness. End of the by-law traffic artery. The occupation of the streets by those who are *on* it at the expense of its thoroughness. This the Italians always well understood and matched their understanding with their acts, though in recent years the scooter has undone some of the good work. The theme-song of this philosophy, it's a long lane that has no turning, was incorporated into the folklore of the race a long time ago, but we are an unconscionable time a-learning. Why? Because we have no humility. We think we are good but we aren't good. A bird's-eye-view of town planning in this century reveals the richness of our resources and the poverty of imagination that has the disposing of them.'

Evidence of the rapid growth of architectural photography is provided in the early 1960s by Eric de Maré (1910–2002), a trained architect and professional photographer who wrote one of the first books on this subject, combining technical aspects with interesting theoretical ideas.[18] Eric de Maré was a contemporary of Edwin Smith (1912–1971), among the most renowned British professional photographers, who actually preferred Sicily to Rome, with which he had a less than idyllic relationship, regarding the city as eternal only in its noise. We are reminded of the preference Ruskin expressed for the stones of Venice over over the ruins of Rome, albeit for different reasons.[19] Smith visited Rome on various occasions in the 1950s and '60s for different publishing projects and took a large number of sophisticated photographs in line with the traditional approach to its urban iconography. While well-acquainted with the nineteenth-century images, which he probably studied carefully before his visits to the city, Smith also took some highly original photographs.

As mentioned above, apart from some photographs published in architectural magazines and *The Italian Townscape*, most of the images exhibited remained in the photographers' own archives. Another exception is the work of the cited Georgina Masson, for works like Aubrey Menen's *Rome Revealed* (1960), a large-format book of a popularising historical nature. The last chapter is illustrated by a large number of black and white photos, most of which were taken by Masson, who was living in Rome at the time.[20]

In the late 1960s and then again in the 1970s, the photographer and historian Tim Benton (b. 1945) took a large number of photographs in black and white for publication with a particular focus on the Renaissance, the Monument to Vittorio Emanuele II, interwar architecture and the EUR district. Benton did not prepare his visits to Rome but roamed around the city with no particular plan, guided by instinct and his interests with only the red and blue guides of the Touring Club Italiano in his pocket.[21] His photographs are a far cry from those criticised by Tom Picton in a well-known article entitled 'The Craven Image', published in two issues of *The Architects' Journal* in 1979.[22] The first part was a fierce attack on the perfect images of architecture produced at the time, reflecting a superficial society: 'Arid and soulless and pompous photographs too often, on the evidence of the buildings, accurately portray an arid and soulless and pompous profession.' The second instead is made up of interesting interviews with various photographers then active, including Richard Einzig, Henk Snoek, John Donat, Martin Charles and John Brandenburger, which provide invaluable detailed documentation and insight into the culture of British professional photography in the late 1970s.

More recently, two of the best-known British photographers, namely the above-mentioned Richard Pare and Richard Bryant (b. 1947), have worked on parallel lines to present a more contemporary image of Rome with all its evident contradictions. Their photographs record both the irreverent marks made on the patina of the ancient city and the new architectural icons, represented with technical perfection, often detached and isolated from their urban surroundings. While contemporary works, especially those of Richard Meier, Zaha Hadid and Renzo Piano, certainly generate a new image of Rome, they have only a partial impact on the construction of new social realities. The city and its extended outskirts now become a simple backdrop in a reversal that recalls a recent photograph taken by Léonie Hampton (b. 1978), the photographer featured in the 2017 Rome Commission, a project launched in 2003 whereby a different figure is commissioned every year to photograph Rome with complete freedom of action. One of the images in Hampton's *Mend* shows the dome of Saint Peter's as the distant, unattainable background to the wild vegetation of a semi-slum area on the outskirts, a paradigmatic example of the city's countless speculative building projects. The effective visual and aesthetic discontinuity suggests a rift also in social and cultural terms.

As readers may have realised by now, most of the texts and the photographs of Rome in this catalogue focus on a period that has been investigated to a lesser extent, both in Italy and in other countries, precisely because its historicisation is still under way. As pointed out, there is already an extensive literature of meticulous works on the dawn of photography in Rome, recently and significantly extended to cover the interwar period, but much less on the image of the city, and hence on the city itself, after 1945.[23] A different degree of attention is also focused in the same period on its social and photojournalistic history at the national and international level in the years of the *dolce vita*.[24]

This is most probably due to the place occupied by Rome in the cultural debate of British architecture in the post-war period, which appears to be marginal until the end of the 1970s, confined to the past, to the meditations of Colin Rowe in 'Mannerism and Modern Architecture' (*AR*, May 1950) and to a series of articles on particular buildings in architectural magazines. Bernard Rudofsky discussed the EUR district, with splendid photographs of the areas abandoned after the war, closed to the public and characterised by a surrealistic setting, before the redevelopment of a few years later in connection with the Rome Olympics of 1960 (*AR*, July 1951). *Architectural Design* published a map with twenty-seven works of modern architecture in Rome, compiled by the magazine in collaboration with Bruno Zevi and Carlo Pouchain, in July 1960. It was, however, the *Architectural Review* that published works of ancient, modern and contemporary architecture with the greatest frequency, including the Trevi Fountain (*AR*, August 1978), the Pantheon (*AR*, April 2004), the new Museo dell'Ara Pacis (*AR*, January 2006) and the Maxxi (*AR*, July 2010), places partially connected with the major established tourist attractions — the Colosseum, Piazza Navona, Piazza di Spagna, Villa Borghese, the Forum, Saint Peter's and the Pantheon[25] – but also mapping out new itineraries for visitors.

A turning point appears to have been reached, however, in 1978. *Roma interrotta*, an exhibition designed to rekindle debate on contemporary urban planning after years of building speculation and intellectual inertia, opened in Trajan's Market.[26] The same year saw the publication of *Collage City* (by Colin Rowe and Fred Koette; Cambridge, MA: MIT Press, 1978), one of the four books — together with Aldo Rossi's *L'architettura della città* (Padova: Marsilio, 1966), *Learning from Las Vegas* by Robert Venturi, Denise Scott Brown and Steven Izenour (Cambridge, MA: MIT Press, 1977) and *Delirious New York* (New York: Oxford University Press, 1978) by Rem Koolhaas — that guided contemporary architecture in the years after World War II. With the obvious exception of *Delirious New York*, Rome occupied an important place in all of these works.[27]

Colin Rowe is one of the intellectuals that have had a major influence on architecture in Britain and elsewhere. Ever since his well-known article 'The Mathematics of the Ideal Villa' (*AR*, March 1947), Rowe has always regarded history as a continuum, an oscillation between ancient and contemporary. In the immediate post-war period, James Stirling, a student of his at Liverpool University, demonstrated his ability to apply his mentor's precepts to architectural design, using a deep understanding of history as material to plan the future.[28] Both Stirling and Rowe, the pupil and the master, took part in *Roma interrotta*, albeit in two different groups.

As pointed out by Thomas Muirhead, Freud drew attention in *Civilization and its Discontents*, one of Rowe's favourite books, to the similarity between the complex stratification of Rome and the unconscious. While the way in which we 'dig up' and make use of this knowledge is certainly a subjective matter, its existence is indisputable. It represents what we are. Even if we did not create it, we can reorganise it through the vocabulary of architecture developed over centuries: 'The courtyard in its infinite variants, the axis, the grid, the street, the piazza and the piazzetta. By knowing these models and re-elaborating them we can design anything, understand everything: Le Corbusier's Villa Stein or Palladio's Villa Malcontenta draw on the same sources. There are universal truths and it is the business of architects to address them.'[29]

Rowe knew Rome very well. Having moved from England to Cornell University in the United States, where he had been teaching since the 1960s, he spent part of the academic year in the university's Roman branch in Palazzo Massimo alle Colonne. He also discussed the city repeatedly in his private correspondence. Reflecting on the growing problems that Rome began to present with the advent of globalisation, he spoke in a letter of July 1988 about its small *centro storico*, which he compared with other highly exclusive places in world capitals like New York, London and Paris. Twenty-five years after *The Italian Townscape*, the scenario appears to have altered radically and the historian comments scathingly on the mismanagement of the great legacy: 'So it's the usual story about Rome. It's horrible; it's crude; it's a collection of mountain villages pretending to be a city; it's a lot of old warehouses grotesquely described as palaces; but, though it's impossible, there seems to be no escape from it. The Upper East Side? Pony Street? Cadogan Whatever It May Be Called? The Rue de Varennes? None of these add up to the squalid, and hideously paved presence of that little *centro storico*. There is no polish in Rome. Repeat: it's just crude; and this causes me to think of Russell Hitchcock, years ago, in New Haven. The last granddaughter of the Vanderbilt had died; and Russell looked at the pic (she was nothing to talk about, Mrs. Twombly) and snorted: "Just imagine, so much tenu and no looks". So I think that Mrs. Twombly must have been a bit like Rome; and the only explanation for Rome must be in terms of tenu, absolutely not in terms of looks.'[30] No trace remains in these words of the nineteenth-century idyll. While the reconciliation between the city imagined and the one actually experienced, albeit in somewhat harsh tones, confirms the primacy of Rome, its management is unequivocally condemned at the same time. What is basically lacking is the idea of a town, to borrow the title of a well-known book, again focused on Rome,[31] by Joseph Rykwert, a British architectural historian of Polish origin. A negative vision of the contemporary world appears to emerge from the reading of both authors. Despite the intellectuals' merit of clearly identifying the problem, their extremely critical tendency usually fails to contribute towards its solution and serves at best to fuel a debate often confined to the cultural élite.

Returning to the sphere of photography, we shall end with the disenchanted words written in 1859, just twenty years after the invention of photography, by Oliver Wendell Holmes: 'There is one Coliseum or Pantheon; but how many millions of potential negatives have they shed [...] Every conceivable object of Nature and Art will soon scale off its surface for us. Men will hunt all curious, beautiful, grand objects as they hunt the cattle in South America, for their skins, and leave the carcasses as little of worth.'[32]

These are reflections and tensions that recur periodically, that have not halted creativity but perhaps even helped to stimulate it over the years. Holmes is indeed an emblematic case in this connection, as he was soon to make a crucial contribution to stereoscopy, the illusion of three-dimensional vision generated by viewing a pair of photographs.

Rome remains a place of the imagination rather than a real one, a construct of images that continue to condition our way of seeing, interpreting and representing the city. Images that do not easily fade, that remain in the memory: from the prints by Dupérac to those by Piranesi, from the photographs by the Caffè Greco pioneers to picture postcards.[33] It is all born out of the desire to possess an object which represents Rome, a tangible memory to bring delight to ourselves first and, then, to others. Pasolini was right — the Eternal City belongs to tourists.[34]

[1] Richard W. Thomas, 'Photography in Rome', in *The Art Journal*, 14, May 1852, pp. 159–160; p. 159.

[2] Karin Einaudi, 'The Fototeca Unione Archive and Archeological Photography', in *Visual Resources*, vol. II, nos. 1-2-3, pp. 7–17.

[3] In addition to his activities as an archaeologist, scholar, collector of maps and photographer, Ashby also contributed to the debate on Rome in the *Town Planning Review*, the world's oldest periodical in this sector, published by the Liverpool University Press since 1910. The photographic archives of the British School at Rome include those taken by Ashby and comprise about 100,000 items, some of which are rare, like the prints of Macpherson and Father Mackey. See, for example, Alistair Crawford, 'Robert Macpherson 1814–72, the foremost photographer of Rome', in *Papers of the British School at Rome*, vol. LXVII, pp. 353–403, and Robert Coates-Stephens, *Immagini e memoria: Rome in the photographs of Father Peter Paul Mackey, 1890–1901*, London and Rome: British School at Rome/ British Academy, 2009. The professional photographer Robert Eaton (1819–post 1871) was also in Rome around 1850–55 but did not take up permanent residence.

[4] The inventions of Louis Daguerre and Henry Fox Talbot (1839) followed the first photographic image ever created with a camera obscura, the renowned view of rooftops taken by Nicéphore Niépce around 1826/27 from the window of Le Gras, his estate in the village of Saint-Loup-de-Varennes. Niépce's photograph is now in the Harry Ransom Center of the University of Texas at Austin, to which it was donated by the historian of photography Helmut Gernsheim.

[5] See William Henry Fox Talbot, *The Pencil of Nature*, London: Longman, Brown, Green and Longmans, 1844, p. 5. The chapter in question is entitled 'Brief Historical Sketch of the Invention of the Art'.

[6] For the technical developments, see the essay by Richard Pare in this catalogue. For further aspects, see also Richard Pare, *Photography and Architecture: 1839-1939*, Montreal: Callaway Editions / Canadian Centre for Architecture, 1982, pp. 14–16.

[7] For a careful analysis of the complex subject of viewpoints, see Giovanni Fanelli, *Per una storia dell'iconografia fotografica del Foro Romano nell'Ottocento*, Paris, printed by the author, 2009.

[8] Respectively: John A. Pinto, *City of the Soul: Rome and the Romantics* (New York, Morgan Library & Museum, 17 June – 11 September 2016), New York: The Morgan Library & Museum, The Foundation for Landscape Studies; Hanover, NH: The University Press of New England, 2016, pp. 80–81, 82–83; Anne Cartier-Bresson, Anita Margiotta (eds.), *Roma 1850. Il Circolo dei pittori fotografi del Caffè Greco* (Rome, Musei Capitolini, Palazzo Caffarelli, 29 November 2003 – 25 January 2004; Paris, Maison Européenne de la Photographie, 11 February – 18 April 2004), Milan: Electa, 2003, p. 116.

[9] Maria Francesca Bonetti, 'La Mostra della fotografia a Roma dal 1840 al 1915: collezionisti, studiosi e conoscitori intorno al 1953', in *Rivista di Studi di Fotografia*, n. 6, 2017, pp. 50–70; Piero Becchetti, *La fotografia a Roma dalle origini al 1915*, Rome: Colombo, 1983. Becchetti's personal collection is held in Rome at the Istituto Centrale per il Catalogo e la Documentazione. See the bibliography at the end of this work for details of the studies and articles on the other photographers and the exhibitions organised by the Archivio Comunale.

[10] Richard Pare, *op. cit.*, p. 6. The cover photograph is a view of the Forum by Auguste-Rosalie Bisson.

[11] Conversation with Richard Pare, spring 2018. For the Court House project, see *Court House: a photographic document*, New York: Horizon Press, 1978.

[12] Communication from Robert Elwall, summer 2009. The formation of collections was accompanied by a succession of exhibitions, conferences and books on architectural photography. Pare opened the series with the above-mentioned *Photography and Architecture: 1839–1939* (1982). Cervin Robinson and Joel Herschman extended the temporal span up to the 1980s five years later with *Architecture Transformed: a history of the photography of buildings from 1839 to the present* (Cambridge, MA: MIT Press, 1987). The subject is examined with scholarly tools and rigour by Robert Elwall in *Building with Light: the international history of Architectural Photogra-*

phy (London: Merrell Publishers, 2004) and Giovanni Fanelli in *Storia della fotografia di architettura* (Rome-Bari: Laterza, 2009). In *Photographic Architecture in the Twentieth Century* (Minneapolis, MN: University of Minnesota Press, 2014), Claire Zimmerman instead discusses how the medium has gone beyond its original function of representation to influence the perception and design of architecture. Finally, the exhibition *Image Building* at the New York Parrish Museum (New York: DelMonico Books-Prestel, 2018) and its catalogue are the most recent evidence of interest in the discipline.

[13] Before the founding of the British School at Rome, the city was already the key stage of the Grand Tour for architects, who were often the guests of Italian academies. The Royal Academy was in fact not founded in London until 1768 and the Royal Institute of British Architects (originally the Institute of British Architects) until 1834. See Frank Salmon, 'British Architects, Italian Fine Arts Academies and the Foundation of the RIBA, 1816–43', in *Architectural History*, vol. 39 (1996), pp. 77–113. The postcard (not illustrated at first) was introduced in 1873 and became popular in the last quarter of the nineteenth century.

[14] See the biographical sketch of Deakin at the end of this volume.

[15] The Cartoni and Appetiti archives are now in the Archivio Fotografico Cicconi, Rome. The Savio archive is instead in Rome at the Macro; see Luca Massimo Barbero (ed.) *Roma '50-'60. Guida alle architetture nelle fotografie di Oscar Savio*, Milan: Electa, 2011. The Kidder Smith archive is at the IUAV in Venice; see Angelo Maggi, 'The Visual Transmission of European Architecture by George Everard Kidder Smith', in Rubén A. Alcolea and Jorge T. Mingo (eds.), *Inter-photography and architecture*, Navarra: Servicio de Publicaciones Universidad de Navarra, vol. 3, 2016, pp. 140–51.

[16] Andrew Higgott, *Mediating Modernism. Architectural Cultures in Britain*, London and New York: Routledge, 2006, p. 1; Christine M. Boyer, 'An Encounter with History: the postwar debate between the English journals of *Architectural Review* and *Architectural Design* (1945–1960)', proceedings of the conference 'Team 10 – Between Modernity and the Everyday', Faculty of Architecture TU Delft, 5–6 June 2003, pp. 135–63 (www.team10online. org); see also Jessica Kelly, 'Vulgar Modernism: J. M. Richards, Modernism and the Vernacular in British Architecture', in *Architectural History*, vol. 58, 2015, pp. 229–59.

[17] Peter Murray, *Leading Lady: Monica Pidgeon, editor of Architectural Design, 1946 to 1975*, in "Architectural Design", vol. 80, no. 2, March/April 2010, pp. 106–109.

[18] *Eric De Maré: Photography and Architecture*, Penguin Books: London, 1961. The De Maré archive is held by the Architectural Association; see Andrew Higgott, *Eric de Maré: Photographer, Builder with Light*, London: Architectural Association Publications, 1990.

[19] See Robert Ewall, *Evocations of Place. The Photography of Edwin Smith*, London, Merrell/RIBA: 2007, pp. 109–23; p. 114. Ruskin,

who visited Italy for the first time in 1840–41, regarded the Italian Renaissance as a repudiation of the Gothic.

[20] Aubrey Menen, *Rome Revealed,* London: Thames and Hudson, 1960. Some of the nocturnal photos in the book are by Appetiti (pp. 127 and 150–51), whose work is also held in the Architectural Press Archive of the RIBA. Georgina Masson (Marion Johnson)'s work is held in the American Academy in Rome; cf. Alessandra Capodiferro, Cornelia Lauf (eds.), *Georgina Masson: 1912–1980*, Milan: Charta, 2003.

[21] Conversation with Tim Benton, spring 2018.

[22] Tom Picton, 'The Craven Image or the apotheosis of the architectural photograph', in *The Architects' Journal*, vol. 170, n. 30, 25 July 1979, pp. 175–90 (part 1); vol. 170, n. 31, 1 August, pp. 225–42 (part 2); quotation on p. 190.

[23] See the recent essay by Glenda Furini and Guido Gambetta, 'Le fotografie di Rodrigo Pais come documentazione dello sviluppo urbano di Roma nella seconda metà del Novecento', in Maria Antonietta Crippa, Ferdinando Zanzottera (eds.), *Fotografia per l'Architettura del XX secolo in Italia. Costruzione della storia, progetto, cantiere*, Cinisello Balsamo: Silvana Editoriale, 2018, pp. 195–199.

[24] For the representation of architecture in post-war Italy in the RIBA archives, see Robert Elwall, Valeria Carullo, *Framing Modernism: Architecture and Photography in Italy 1926–1965*, London: Estorick Collection of Modern Italian Art, 2009.

[25] Listed in decreasing order by number of visitors; see Annamaria S. de Rosa, 'Place, identity and social representation of historic capital cities. Rome through the eyes of six visitors from six countries', in Annamaria S. de Rosa (ed.), *Social Representations in the 'Social Arena'*, London and New York: Routledge, 2013, pp. 311–64; p. 340.

[26] Léa-Catherine Szacka, '"Roma Interrotta": Postmodern Rome as the Source of Fragmented Narratives', in Dom Holdaway, Filippo Trentin (eds.), *Rome, Postmodern Narratives of a Cityscape*, London and New York: Routledge, 2016, pp. 155–209; see also the essay by Owen Hopkins in this catalogue.

[27] Alberto Ferlenga, 'Uno di Quattro', in Mauro Marzo (ed.), *L'architettura come testo e la figura di Colin Rowe*, Venice: Marsilio, 2010, pp. 171–78. For Venturi and Rome, see Frederick Fisher, Stephen Harby, *Robert Venturi's Rome*, London and Novato, CA: Oro Editions, 2017.

[28] Cfr. Marco Iuliano, Francesca Serrazanetti (eds.), *James Stirling. Inspiration and Process in Architecture*, Milan: Moleskine, 2015, pp. 10-26.

[29] Thomas Muirhead, 'Colin Rowe, theorist and Gold Medallist, dies', in *The Architects' Journal*, vol. 210, n. 18, 1999, p. 20.

[30] Letter to Dorothy Rowe, 29 July 1988, in Daniel Naegele, *The Letters of Colin Rowe: Fifty Years of Correspondence*, London: Artifice 2015, p. 296. Rowe had also complained on other occasions about Italian *laissez-faire*, indicating it as one of the country's endem-

ic problems, when an unbearable traffic was making its appearance; see the letter to Pat Miller, 24 September 1970, p. 181.

[31] 'Nowadays if we think of anything as "symbolic" it is practically always an object or action which can be taken at a single view.' Joseph Rykwert, *The Idea of a Town: The Anthropology of Urban Form in Rome, Italy, and The Ancient World* (1963) (cons. ed. London: Faber, 1976, preface).

[32] Quoted in Claire Zimmerman, 'Reading the (Photographic) Evidence', in *Journal of the Society of Architectural Historians*, vol. 76, n. 4, December 2017, pp. 446–48; p. 446.

[33] '[…] modes of representation are not significantly altered when new techniques are discovered, but they perpetuate pre-existing conventions'. James Ackerman, 'On the origins of architectural photography, in Kester Rattenbury (ed.), *This is not architecture: media constructions*, London and New York: Routledge, 2002, pp. 26–36; pp. 34–35.

[34] 'Romans are either illiterate or cynical. They know nothing of their traditions except for an empty figure of speech. To the common people the ruins are just so much rubble, to the middle classes they are tiresome things seen day after day but of which, on certain occasions, they must feel they must be proud. To make up for this there are the tourists. The Eternal City belongs to them'; quoted in William Klein, *William Klein: Rome*, Paris: Editions du Seuil (cons. ed. London: Thames and Hudson, 2009, p. 25).

Resident in Rome from the 1950s and deeply aware of its social reality, Pasolini passed a scathing and challenging judgement that certainly cannot be extended to all the city's inhabitants. The rhetorical image built up through Pasolini's words on Rome is not so far removed from the recent cinematographic reading presented by Paolo Sorrentino in *The Great Beauty* (2013), where Rome is the magnificent setting for a dissolute, worldly society incapable of relating to the greatness within which a decadent everyday life takes place.

Gabriella Musto

Reflections on the Vittoriano:
Stories of Distorted Images and Augmented Reality

Visiting Rome is not a mere set of itineraries but an authentic cultural, historical, political, social and architectural experience.

A trip to Rome means immersion in mythic places recounted by artists, poets and writers of every era and country. It is impossible to set foot on its stones without attempting to capture fleeting images in its streets and alleys, in places of memory or imagination, where human material melds and mingles with the mystery of architecture that triumphs over time and a natural landscape that survives, despite the cement, midway between an already contemporary dimension and the decadent tang of corners that still remain incredibly bucolic.

Rome has a thousand faces, reflected in the Tiber and the gold of its domes at sunset, distinct identities that are sometimes contradictory and sometimes superimposed, deposited in layers to construct a closely-knit fabric of tales and events that is incredibly hard to represent. Rome has a great soul that includes countless others, the myriad souls of all those who have visited, inhabited and recounted it over the centuries. Because everyone can talk about Rome, even those who have never been there. The true mystery of this evocative city lies, however, in the knowledge that no one has ever been truly able to capture it other than in an idea that is no sooner born than it vanishes.

Rome is mythic. One characteristic of myth is the fact of being meta-historical, with no space or boundaries. This makes it unquestionably immortal and radically different from reality. While the transmutation of the Eternal City into myth is a process studied and analysed by many critics of the present and the past, what interests us here is not so much the myth in itself as the way in which it has been fuelled, constructed and probably also distorted by the power of images.

As from the end of the eighteenth century, visitors on the Grand Tour endeavoured to capture the uninhibited, timeless beauty of Rome in their notebooks and sketches, countless fragments of description built up over the years into a grand mosaic. Rome is a rite and an exorcism for everyone that has been there. Thousands of travellers have been exposed to its poignant enchantment while wrestling at the same time with their own angels and demons, as its streets cannot be walked without out visitors being enthralled and transformed, without them yearning to retain images crystallised even in a single sketch, photograph or notebook, to establish order in the all-embracing maze of archaeological, baroque and neorealist images.[1]

As critics of contemporary photography are well aware, however, the power of images, both visual and narrative, consolidates a form of indirect knowledge in the mind, one that has become almost real in the case of Rome. The Eternal City described by Goethe or splendidly limned by artists like Canaletto and Turner — as in the latter's *Modern Rome – Campo Vaccino* (1839), an incredible masterpiece that captures a timeless, magical atmosphere poised between history, architecture and the bucolic world — has lived and will live forever, constructing a precise image of Rome in the collective consciousness. Just as the idea of the Rome of the last century lives on in the imagination without replacing those of the Renaissance and the eighteenth and nineteenth centuries.

The archaeological and romantic Rome of the photographs of the Anderson and Alinari dynasties, the dim, melancholy Rome of the films of Dino Risi, the Rome of the *dolce vita* as seen by Fellini, Visconti and Lattuada, the *Mamma Roma* of Pasolini, expressed as the 'elegy of a winding course of bodies and camera between the slums and the open fields a few yards away',[2] the 'open city' jaggedly portrayed by Rossellini; the Rome of corruption captured by photojournalists or seen from the sarcastic, contemporary vantage point in Sorrentino's *The Great Beauty*.

These and countless others are the cult icons of the Eternal City. Of all the forms of representation handed down through time, however, it is probably photography that has succeeded best of all in capturing the great theatre of these places,[3] as perhaps only cinema and literature have been able to do. To quote Gabriele Basilico, one of the greatest masters of contemporary photography, 'I think that writing in general, above all narrative, is capable of evoking, describing and reinventing a place better than an image can. This awareness has become a very important guiding idea for me. The analytical power of writing deepens and expands the time of perception and the imagination, whereas the symbolic and stratified value contained in a photograph often has to be decoded for its message to be fully understood.'[4] This observation, made precisely by a photographer, indirectly suggests the pitfalls involved in the construction of a story in images.

Together with cinema, the icons borrowed from photography have been the dimensions through which the image of this city has been nourished and grown, following a process of great power that can seldom be distinguished for other places. It will therefore be interesting to use photographic documentation and partly cinema too in a journey through the distorted images and augmented reality that have moulded a certain by now international idea of the Eternal City, not just a name but a place capable of conjuring up myths, stories and legends even miles away.

The point to be made is that documentation in the form of images captures and recounts but inevitably corrupts at the same time.

The camera investigates and reveals the truth, endowing the contingent with certainty, but is at the same time a tool that can, if suitably handled, lead to the construction of an idea that is perhaps plausible but not necessarily true.[5] A photograph is a representation of reality and at the same time its most persuasive form of simulation.

The question is whether and how far what we would now call the mass-media and social image have influenced the knowledge of Rome and its cultural places, distorting the real identity of certain spaces and con-structing one solely out of historical and sociological conditioning.

The different ways in which a photo can be read can also give rise to different interpretations of the objective reality. Over the years, photography on the one hand and cinema on the other have constructed a reality that we could describe today as augmented, an idea or model of the Eternal City that is sometimes accentuated and in any case embedded in a past that no longer exists. The same process can also be observed in many respects in the case of one of Rome's most contradictory and evocative landmarks, namely the Monument to Vittorio Emanuele II or Vittoriano, its own mausoleum and museum, detested by Romans just as much as it is loved by foreigners, perhaps because the latter are sufficiently detached from the history of Italy not to be burdened by its weight.

We are again concerned with a myth, this time of a building, the Vittoriano, regarded both as an architectural failure and a glorious symbol of its era in the course of its eventful history. Public opinion today encompasses extreme and opposite views of this edifice, still regarded as a place detached from the context to which it belongs. Not because of any failure of appropriation but because its scale, its urban and environmental impact, and its surfeit of symbolism and meaning make it appear laborious and extraneous, only apparently integrated into the urban landscape and context.

Examination of the phenomenon and the critical fortunes or misfortunes of this eclectic building, which is also the fruit of the most interesting Italian technological experimentation of the early twentieth century, is a highly complex undertaking.

The Vittoriano is unquestionably a unicum created as a monument to Vittorio Emanuele II, the first king of Italy, and above all to the people's love for their finally unified homeland. As a result of extraordinary and unexpected historical developments, it was to broaden its already manifold and complex meaning by becoming the place of commemoration for the fallen, from World War I to the Nasiriya bombing of 2003. When bombs exploded in 1969 on the tomb of the unknown warrior, it was clear that the Vittoriano had been identified as a symbol of monarchism and the subsequent dictatorial culture of Fascism, with which it had remained strongly associated.

The process of political association with the Fascist regime began when Mussolini chose it together with

Palazzo Venezia as the place representing his power, unquestionably because of the obvious neoclassical architectural characteristics that were so in line with the contemporary model of the Third Rome taken by the Duce as his political ideal.

The countless photographs and metres of film produced in that period by the Istituto Luce featured the image of the Vittoriano in a propaganda campaign that necessarily made it a Fascist icon.[6]

Many today are indeed convinced that the Vittoriano was actually built by order of Mussolini, thus revealing how little they know of history and of the political manipulation imposed on the building, which has paid the price of all this for years. The misunderstanding of a multiple identity never given a single clear and comprehensible thrust has made the edifice unknown to the majority and odious to many. It is therefore obvious that any rehabilitation of the monument's image must necessarily entail real knowledge in an attempt to construct an identity of present-day relevance.

'Who are you?' This question opens the surrealistic dialogue between Alice and the caterpillar in Lewis Carroll's famous novel.[7] Disturbed by the extraordinary sight of a little girl, something evidently out of place in his enchanted world, the caterpillar asks Alice who she is. The grotesque character cannot recognise or place the image of Alice among those known to him. The concepts of beauty and ugliness are inverted in the writer's universe, full of references and metaphors, where the perception of reality is distorted and transformed in the constant dynamics of paradox. His message is clear. We are afraid above all of what we do not know and what we do not recognize because it is alien to our system of pre-established rules. The Other, being feared, is therefore perceived and regarded as ugly.

On beholding the Vittoriano, many today wonder what it is. Unable to discern an identity for this historical work of architecture, they wonder what purpose it serves.

We have talked about oddness, ugliness and monstrosity for centuries, and been fascinated at the same time by these departures from the norm.

Photography has addressed the same subjects too on a large scale with aims that are purely aesthetic but also have ethical if not indeed social and anthropological implications. Suffice it to consider some shots by Lewis H. Hine and the work of Charles Eisenmann on circus monsters and sideshow freaks.

In architecture, the debate on beauty, understood as the picturesque and the sublime, reached its peak in the very years when the first stones of the cumbersome monument were laid. The concept of beauty in ruins, a paradoxical reversal of the perfect Renaissance building, shook and revitalized architecture in the eighteenth and nineteenth centuries.[8] As Luciano Patetta writes, 'Beauty was no longer the sole value of art but accompanied by others like newness, oddity, exceptionality, astonishment and dread, which aroused intense emotions and a state of tension, thus generating greater aesthetic enjoyment. And since these values belong to the sphere of the sublime, the sublime became the highest of aesthetic aspirations.'[9]

In addition to the picturesque, the concept of sublime beauty was also rooted in the gigantic and the disproportionate. The spaces of the architecture abandoned the proportion obsessively pursued by humanism and the sublime in architecture began to be identified with awe-inspiring hugeness, frightening but moving at the same time with the sense of grandeur aroused. Etienne Louis Boullée and Charles-Nicolas Ledoux were among the masters who produced architecture mostly on paper but constructed new models for this pursuit of the sublime.[10] From the very first drawings, the sublime was taken as the paramount model for the Vittoriano. The aim was to move the feelings of the people by presenting the beauty of newly-born Italy in an architectural symbol.

As is known, in architecture and in the specific case of monuments, the disproportionately large has always belonged to the associated typological models. In the case of the Vittoriano, however, the expression attained is so lofty that we cannot but ascribe it also to the themes of contemporary international architecture developed by Piranesi, Lodoli, Milizia and others in Italy, and by Boullée and Ledoux among others in France.[11]

This pursuit of the sublime through sheer scale was to characterise the building from the outset or rather from the initial competition, remembered in history for the surrealistic if not lunatic entries submitted and the impossibility of choosing either a first or second prize winner.[12] The marble edifice is thus characterized today precisely and above by its disproportionate bulk in the urban skyline. Commemorating the sovereign's demise and celebrating the birth of newly unified Italy at the same time in a perfect synthesis of life and death, the monument was to stand out with almost overwhelming vigour in the new urban layout.

Issue no. 40 of the magazine *Perspecta* included an interesting article on the subject of the monstrous and the sublime, concepts applied simultaneously to the Vittoriano from the outset. Sublime beauty, touching the heartstrings of a community that basically accuses the building of responding in its disproportionate scale to the aesthetic sensory violence, but also 'massive, hard-edged and blazingly bright', an object that cannot be fitted into the context and image of Rome.[13]

As Kirk points out in the article, the word *monumental* derives from the Latin verb *monere*, meaning *to remember* but also *recommend* and *persuade*, while the word *monstrous* comes from *mostrare*, meaning *to show*. The Vittoriano flaunts itself in its hugeness and prominence: 'High on the spur of the hill, it rises squarely above the roofs of everything around it, emphatically redrawing with a horizontal bar line the skyline of the city once characterized by curved church domes.'[14]

Everything in the Vittoriano was designed to achieve the maximum impact and create the image of a sometimes shocking presence perceived by many as extraneous to its city, somehow unknown and alien, just as Alice appeared to the caterpillar.

In line with the new international trends exemplified by the Walhalla in Regensburg, designed by Leo von Klenze in 1819 and completed in 1842, the disproportionate and gargantuan became the guiding aesthetic principles of new edifice built by order of Giuseppe Zanardelli, the first minister of the interior of the newly unified Italy, in accordance with the wishes expressed by the political class as a whole in 1882.

In response to the clear architectural programme laid down for the Vittoriano practically ad hoc by the royal commission specially set up for the project,[15] work commenced in 1885 to the winning design submitted for the second competition by Giuseppe Sacconi, who was to stick to his composition and carry it through despite the incredible difficulties of a technical, economic and political nature that subsequently arose.[16] The hard work involved and the weight of the social and political expectations certainly had an adverse effect on the already delicate health of the architect from the Marche region, who died at the age of 51 in 1905, six years before the inauguration of the monument in 1911.[17] The architects Pio Piacentini, Manfredo Manfredi and Gaetano Koch took over the work on his death and brought about a by no means negligible shift in compositional approach towards rhetorical celebration.

The tomb of the unknown warrior was built inside the monument in 1921 to commemorate the thousands who fell in the horrors of the Great War. Already overladen with symbols in the iconography of the decoration of the steps of the façade on Piazza Venezia, the edifice thus took on further significance as a glorification of the most complex events in the history of Italy in the late nineteenth and early twentieth century: the wars of independence, national unification and World War I. Symbolic imagery thus came to predominate definitively over the albeit sophisticated compositional system of the building, which ended up as a stage for expression of the ethical and moral but above all political aims of a country still in search of a new identity. The end result was indeed very different from what Sacconi intended, ultimately reflecting 'the stylistic impasse in which the young Italy found itself, seeking a national style of its own and obtaining in the end nothing other than a cold and pompous reworking of ancient models'.[18] It was in 1927 that the last phase of building saw the installation of the splendid four-horse chariots on top of the propylaea.

Another original sin of the Vittoriano — described as 'venial' by Camillo Boito, one of the founding fathers of the principles for the protection and preservation of cultural heritage[19] — was the wholesale demolition and destruction carried out on the Capitol hill for the purposes of construction. The violence thus concretely unleashed for the erection of the monument certainly shook the population, who experienced this and other acts of destruction as a brutal imposition and a form of political tyranny. The series of photographs taken during the demolition work to clear the way for the Via del Mare and Via dei Fori Imperiali so as to preserve the historical memory of the places erased in the name of modernity were of little or no avail.[20] As Settis observed in a recent book on the conflict between architecture and democracy, 'The city expands … devouring its ancient heart (the historical centre) and the surrounding countryside at the same time.'[21]

While the photographic image of the demolition and construction work is once again the 'theatrical' story of contingent events, what the spectator[22] experiences is a feeling of loss before what is perceived not as birth and construction but as death and destruction.[23] These are the scars left in the memory of Romans. This is the task that faces the Vittoriano every day in its quest for real historical interpretation.

With the advent of Fascism and ensuing political exploitation, the process of dissociation was completed and the original identity of the Vittoriano definitively gave way to its new image.

An aesthetic of the sublime understood also as awesome (frighteningly great, transcending the human dimension) was thus saddled with the still more burdensome weight of history and the resulting architectural document is today largely misunderstood and interpreted subjectively all too often on the basis of a story told by the media in images.

The photographs that crystallize and accelerate this process over the years often show the white edifice with no human figures on its magnificent terraces: a vantage point for viewing the city that remained empty as time went by, a rhetorical building with no real function other than that of celebrating itself and the history whose memory it rigidly encapsulates.

Some shots of the 1930s show small groups of people, priests and soldiers on the sharp edges of the monument.[24] The sacrality of the place is such as to permit no real possibility of immersion and admit no function other than that of celebration. Thus it was at least until the bombs of 1969 and the subsequent decision to close the Vittoriano to the public. Its slow and complicated ongoing process of rehabilitation began in 2000, when President Ciampi[25] decided to reopen it and restore it to the people.

Nor can we forget the photographs taken during the years of closure, which capture the hush fallen on the Vittoriano. The desolating absence of people on the steps and the silence of the fountains, without the water on which their existence and function depends, seem to accentuate the urban impact of this document of realist symbolism, enhancing the whiteness of the *botticino* marble and heightening the sense of abeyance and expectation. 'Photographs and drawings can paradoxically become as important as the building, perhaps even more, and the image, subject to the interpretation of others, can therefore replace reality without too much difficulty.'[26] The mausoleum's only remaining form of life was the uninterrupted cycle of military ceremonies connected with the Altar of the Homeland and the tomb of the unknown warrior. This condition, born out of the continuity of military operations, certainly helped to avoid the edifice being wholly divorced from the life of the city but also and just as certainly to endow its image with greater rigidity and severity. Once again, the mutation of this condition into the media image was to affect the construction of a new identity for the monument. This was the period in which the Vittoriano began to be called the 'typewriter' or 'wedding cake', a grim phase of denigration that even led around 1980 to the birth of a movement calling for it to be demolished or left to fall into ruins.[27]

This period of closure and oblivion marked the monument's most critical phase of detachment from reality and the peak of its unpopularity, above all with the Roman population. As stated above, it was President Ciampi that brought this phase of official decline to an end with his decision to break the spell and finally allow the building to resume its function by reopening the monument to the public.

Today the Vittoriano appears to be reconciled with social preconceptions and is recognized as a special object, an architectural backdrop and a clearly recognizable and distinctive component of Rome's skyline, an authentic architectural landmark, the north of an imaginary compass that always leads citizens and tourists towards the centre of the city.

Paradoxically enough, it was on the Internet that the rehabilitation of the monument's image first began, that the Vittoriano was clearly identified as one of the key icons of Rome in thousands of photos of the Eternal City posted on the virtual platform, where the marble edifice is not only a scenic setting but also a dynamic protagonist in the life of its city.

In the age of the mass reproduction of images, the Vittoriano is undergoing semantic renewal, divided into distinct facets that join together in a single identity. If it is true that the Altar of the Homeland is the home and temple of Italians and therefore a sacred place for all citizens, it can also be a place of art and culture at the same time, a space where citizens can celebrate the most important ethical and moral values of the nation but which they can also visit as a container of art and museum of itself. The exhibitions, performances and events that take place today on its terraces are all indicative of the throbbing life lived every day on the marble slabs visited by tourists from all over the world.

Talking about the identity of the Vittoriano thus means knowing and understanding the path that has led from its creation through countless rebirths all the way to the present, a trajectory that includes more of the most important pages in Italy's contemporary history than many other places in Rome. This complex history is told not only through all the distorted media images that have invested the Vittoriano with a sort of augmented reality but also through all the portraits that have instead endeavoured to capture its soul.

More than any other medium of representation, photography has traced the history of the Vittoriano, recounting its sublime and terrible beauty through all the vicissitudes that have fuelled and enhanced its complex myth, one that has greatly delayed real collective recognition of the building's identity and its effective acceptance and integration into the urban context.

Today, many years after its construction, it is necessary to rise above historical preconceptions and begin to address the question on which recognition of the monument hinges. 'I think that photography makes it possible, within certain limits, to reorganize the chaos that is before our eyes, which is a common and repetitive aspect of the contemporary urban landscape … The aim I have set myself for a long time now is to free my vision from moralism, ideology and the lurking nightmare of prejudice. It is not therefore a matter of aesthetic judgment but, if anything, an effort to grasp a new physical reality, the image of which always seems to elude the eye.'[28] As Basilico says, it is not a matter of aesthetic judgment but of identifying a new reality. Understanding the true identity of the Vittoriano does not necessarily involve an aesthetic judgment but rather reinterpreting its historical, sociological and political significance today in the light of a necessary and already accomplished critical detachment from the past.

The Vittoriano is a container. In other words, its function remains the one for which it was designed but enriched with layers of meaning built up over the years. The Vittoriano today is the container of the country's morality, the container of forms of artistic expression of the late nineteenth and early twentieth centuries. It bears witness to the changes that have taken place in the architectural, aesthetic and technological spheres. The extraordinary machinery housed in its depths include the original pumps of the fountains installed in 1911, the automatic mechanism of the railings and the life-size pantograph. The Vittoriano houses some of the most interesting examples of 19th-century aesthetics, some of the most spectacular decorative works produced in the last few centuries, not only the sculpture but also the sophisticated mosaics that adorn the ceiling of its upper portico.[29] Finally, the Vittoriano is also the container of the urban landscape, one of the first complexes built for observation of the city with an extraordinary system of terraces looking out over Rome.

The Monument to Vittorio Emanuele II is displaying unexpected potential in terms of attraction and has learned to work through its twin facets, symbolic identity on one hand and museum complex on the other, two lives that coexist and can support one another with no denial or attempt at predominance.

The Vittoriano unquestionably bears witness to the key events in the recent history of Italy, a history with which we must now be reconciled so as to preserve its architectural legacy as well as its purest values, some of which are still to be regained.

[1] '[The] principal characteristic of the view is the intentional representation of objects, not imaginary or optionally real but necessarily existent in their objectual givenness as referents taken as the model of the image, through which, thanks to the representative conventionality of Renaissance perspective, the viewer, with an act of extreme pride in his cultural awareness and free will, imposes cognitive order and rule on the chaos of the world outside, and also makes it visible precisely through the strategies of representation adopted, his dominion over the natural or urban environment in which his action takes place, opening up the season of realistic and truthful knowledge and allowing the possibility of essentially visual communication.' Marina Miraglia, 'La "veduta" fotografica come forma rappresentativa privilegiata della scena urbana e dell'architettura', in Carlo Cresti (ed.), *Fotografia e architettura – Quaderni semestrali*, Florence: Angelo Pontecorboli Editore, 2004, p. 23.

[2] Stefano Boeri, 'Movimenti dello sguardo', in Uliano Lucas (ed.), *Storia d'Italia – Annali 20 – L'immagine fotografica 1945-2000*, Turin: Einaudi, 1979.

[3] 'Photography has been, and is still, haunted by the ghost of Painting. […] Yet it is not (it seems to me) by Painting that Photography touches art, but by Theater.' Roland Barthes, *Camera Lucida. Reflections on Photography*, trans. Richard Howard, New York: Hill and Wang, 1981, section 13. It is the theatre of life (and death) that is captured and presented by the photographic image.

[4] Gabriele Basilico, *Architetture, città, visioni. Riflessioni sulla fotografia*, ed. Andrea Lissoni, Milan: Bruno Mondadori, 2007, p. 132.

[5] 'First of all, I did not escape, or try to escape, from a paradox: on the one hand the desire to give a name to Photography's essence and then to trace an eidetic science of the Photograph; and on the other the intractable feeling that Photography is essentially (a contradiction in terms) only contingency, singularity, risk: my photographs would always participate, as Lyotarc says, in "something or other": is it not the very weakness of Photography this difficulty

in existing which we call banality? Next, my phenomenology agreed to compromise with a power: *affect*. […] As *Spectator*, I was interested in Photography only for "sentimental" reasons; I wanted to explore it not as a question (a theme) but as a wound: I see, I feel, hence I notice, I observe, and I think.' Roland Barthes, *op. cit.*, section 8.

[6] 'In those years, totalitarianism imposed a photographic approach aimed exclusively at glorification of the regime and the description of an empire whose *raison d'*être was to be found in rhetoric and monumentality.' Gabriella Musto, 'Un architetto dietro l'obbiettivo: l'archivio fotografico di Giuseppe Pagano', in Alfredo Buccaro, Gaetana Cantone, Francesco Starace (eds.), *Storie e teorie dell'architettura dal Quattrocento al Novecento*, Pisa: Pacini Editore, 2008, p. 240. Readers are also referred in the extensive literature to Piero Bevilacqua, *Il paesaggio italiano nelle fotografie dell'Istituto Luce*, Rome 2002; and 'Architettura e città negli anni del fascismo in Italia e nelle colonie', in *Architettura & Arte, Quaderni semestrali ¾*, Florence: Angelo Pontecorboli Editore, 2004.

[7] Lewis Carroll, *Alice's Adventures in Wonderland*, 1865, chapter 5.

[8] For the debate on the sublime, see the essays selected by Luciano Patetta in *Storia dell'architettura. Antologia critica*, Milan: Etaslibri, 1975, and especially his own 'Sublime e poetica del Pittoresco', pp. 189–92.

[9] Luciano Patetta, *op. cit.*, p. 189.

[10] 'Our buildings, and above all our public buildings, must be in a certain sense poems. The images they offer to our senses must arouse feelings in us similar to their content. […] Architecture is an art of the imagination and pure invention. […] Let us observe an object. The first feeling we have obviously arises from the impression it makes on us. I call this *character*, the effect that arises from this object and makes a certain kind of impression on us.' Étienne-Louis Boullée, c. 1790, in Étienne-Louis Boullée, *Architettura. Saggio sull'Arte*, Padua: Marsilio, 1967, pp. 7–24.

[11] 'Architecture is to building as poetry is to the humanities; it is the dramatic enthusiasm of a craft and can only be spoken of with exaltation […] Buildings of great size have no need of decoration to assert themselves; the details are lost when seen at a distance; they must be seen from close up, annihilated by the overwhelming mass that predominates. […] Unity, the hallmark of beauty, consists in the relationship between mass and detail or ornamentation with no interruption of the lines, which prevent the eye from being distracted by noxious superfluity. […] Decoration is the expressive characteristic of greater or lesser simplicity conferred upon every building. It makes the surfaces living and immortal.' Claude-Nicolas Ledoux, *L'Architecture considerée sous le rapport de l'art, des moeurs et de la législation*, Paris, 1804.

[12] See Carlo Dossi, *I mattoidi al concorso pel Monumento a Vittorio Emanuele*, Milan, 1883.

[13] See the photographs in the *Urban Landscapes* section of the catalogue: nos. 125 and 126.

[14] Terry Kirk, 'Monumental Monstrosity, Monstrous Monumentality', in *Perspecta*, no. 40, 2008, p. 13.

[15] Camillo Boito, 'Il Monumento Nazionale a Vittorio Emanuele', in *Nuova Antologia*, vol. LXIV, August, pp. 640–662.

[16] See Pier Luigi Porzio (ed.), *Il Vittoriano. Materiali per una storia*, 2 vols., Rome: Fratelli Palombi Editori, 1986.

[17] See Primo Acciaresi, *Giuseppe Sacconi e l'opera sua massima. Cronaca dei lavori del Monumento Nazionale a Vittorio Emanuele II*, Rome: Tipografia dell'Unione editrice, 1911.

[18] Catherine Brice, 'L'immaginario della Terza Roma. I concorsi per il Monumento a Vittorio Emanuele II', in Pier Luigi Porzio (ed.), *op. cit.*, pp. 22–23.

[19] 'All that remained was therefore to find the vast area required for the grand monument, to knock down buildings and clear the site. Sanitation benefitted. The part of the slope down towards Piazza Venezia and the nearby streets was crammed with filthy, stinking slums and hovels squashed together and piled up on one another. […] Hence the need to demolish part of the convent, a building of little artistic and historical interest, from which the few details worth preserving were easily removed. Hence the need to destroy the so-called tower of Paul III, containing some decorative wall paintings worthy of preservation and already connected by means of a long overhead walkway to Palazzo Venezia and the basilica of San Marco. A sin but a venial one.' Camillo Boito, *Questioni pratiche di Belle Arti*, Milan, 1893, p. 245.

[20] 'As the bulldozers advanced, the archaeologists of the Ripartizione X Antichità e Belle Arti del Governatorato took constant care to "preserve through a series pf photographs the memory […] of the buildings of historical interest that were disappearing". Special measures were taken by the Governatorato in the period 1930–36 to commission photographers like the D'Amico brothers, Filippo Reale, Michele Valentino Calderisi, Angelo Sallustri and Cesare Faraglia to take shots of a "specifically technical" character.' Anita Margiotta, 'Le fotografie delle demolizioni degli Anni Trenta alle pendici del Campidoglio', in Claudio Parisi Presicce, Alberto Danti (eds.), *Campidoglio. Mito, memoria, archeologia*, Rome: Campisano editore, 2016, p. 127.

[21] Salvatore Settis, *Architettura e democrazia*, Turin: Einaudi, 2017, p. 130.

[22] 'The *Operator* is the Photographer. The *Spectator* is ourselves, all of us who glance through collections of photographs—in magazines and newspapers, in books, albums, archives […] And the person or thing photographed is the target, the referent, a kind of little simulacrum, any eidolon emitted by the object, which I should like the call the *Spectrum* of the Photograph, because this word retains, through its root, a relation to 'spectacle' and adds to it that rather terrible thing which there is in every photograph: the return of the dead.' R. Barthes, *op. cit*, section 4.

[23] Interest attaches to the photographic collection of the Archivio del Ministero dei Lavori Pubblici, which includes most of the documentation regarding the initial demolition work on the Capitoline hill towards Piazza Venezia (c. 1885). See Pier Luigi Porzio (ed.), *op. cit.*

[24] See the photographs in the *Urban Landscapes* section of the catalogue: nos. 145, 168, 170.

[25] Settis recalls that it was Carlo Azeglio Ciampi, in a speech delivered as president of the Republic at Palazzo Quirinale on 5 May 2003, who described article 9 on the protection of the historical, artistic and natural heritage of the nation as the 'most original of the Italian constitution'. See Salvatore Settis, *op. cit.*, p. 11. In this reference to contemporary history, Settis highlights Ciampi's acute perceptiveness in recognizing the historical, artistic and natural heritage as a crucial ingredient of democracy, equality and liberty, and confirming the honesty of the vision that had led to his decision, a few years before the speech at the Quirinale, to restore the monument to the Italian people.

[26] G. Basilico, *op. cit.*, p. 136.

[27] See in this connection Susanna Nirenstein, 'L'Altare della Patria è stato condannato ma niente demolizioni', in *la Repubblica*, 28 January 1986.

[28] G. Basilico, *Architettura, città, visioni*, op. cit., pp. 144–45.

[29] For the decorations of the monument, see Simona Antellini, *Il Vittoriano. Scultura e decorazione tra classicismo e liberty*, Rome: Artemide, 2003.

Richard Pare

Tradition and Innovation.
Early Photographs of Rome

In the last days of Pope Eugenius IV, two of his servants — the learned Poggius and a friend — ascended the Capitoline Hill, reposed themselves among the ruins of columns and temples, and viewed from that commanding spot the wide and various prospect of desolation. The place and the object gave ample scope for moralising on the vicissitudes of fortune, which spares neither man nor the proudest of his works, which buries empires and cities in a common grave; and it was agreed that in proportion to her former greatness the fall of Rome was the more awful and deplorable.

Pope Eugenius IV (1383–1447), lived in early Renaissance Rome and the incident, recorded by the humanist scholar Poggio Bracciolini, is reported by Edward Gibbon in *The History of the Decline and Fall of the Roman Empire*.[1] The story shows how even in the fifteenth century there was the same rapt fascination with the ruins of a long dead empire that persists to this day. Within a few years Leon Battista Alberti was in Rome, sent by an enlightened patron, to study the relics and establish the revival of the classical orders.

To begin to think about photography in Rome we must go back to these foundations, even to Vitruvius, whose *Ten Books on Architecture* had such a great influence in Renaissance times almost 1,500 years later. The mantle passes from Alberti, onwards to Andrea Palladio and in turn led to the traditions of the *vedutisti*.

In British thought the idea of the classical world in architecture was later introduced by Inigo Jones who also went to Rome to study the classical remains around the turn of the seventeenth century. He translated those forms into his own practice as had Alberti before him. From then onwards we see the rise of the Grand Tour and aristocratic travellers returning to their Palladian estates with prints and pictures by Giovanni Battista Piranesi, Giovanni Paolo Panini, Canaletto and Hubert

Robert to mention the most prominent. These pictures, many composed of at least partly archaeological fictions, are all in a completely different realm to what the photographer could present. Painters romanticised the image through selective compositional devices, the introduction of landscape elements and classical figures engaged in pastoral activities. Over time the canonical vantage points of the ravaged remains of ancient Rome became established; the city's ascent as the bastion of Catholicism in the Vatican assured the continuing fascination. Rome, therefore, was a central subject for photography from the outset: photographers simply took up this basic repertory of standard views and continued to adhere to the traditions of the already established vantage points. However, it did not take long for the differences of photographic representation to be recognised, and this had the effect of defining new ways of approaching the classical subjects. Photographers began to express the individuality of photographic representation as a virtue to be exploited for its own sake.

The years that followed the announcement of photography in 1839 were turbulent times in Italy. Mazzini had established the Giovine Italia in 1831 and the movements towards revolution and independence were gathering force throughout these years. The Pope, Pius IX, fled Rome in 1849 and, in the same year, the French army landed in Civitavecchia on its way to Rome. It was not until 1860 that Garibaldi started the campaign with his band I Mille, raised in Sicily, when by chance one of the greatest French photographers, Gustave Le Gray, was in Palermo on his way to Egypt, and recorded the barricaded streets with a large view camera.[2] During those turbulent decades the country was still made up of independent states and a loose agglomeration of provinces, until the formal creation of the Kingdom of Italy in 1861. Rome, instead, remained 'outside' Italy until the Porta Pia breach, 20 September 1870, the final event of Unification.

Some of this unrest is reflected in images of the defensive earthworks in front of the city gates in Rome that appear in the photographs of Robert Macpherson, who, among others, was recording the garrisoned status of the city at that time. For the most part the city looks unchanging in these early images, untroubled by the political events swirling around it. Ox carts and herds of goats are seen in Piazza del Popolo and graze on areas of open ground in the heart of the city. The first photographers working in Rome devised new ways of seeing, translating structures that had been part of a mythic vision of the city since time immemorial.

In those years the population of the city was relatively small having stabilised at around 200,000 inhabitants for several hundred years after the collapse that followed the sacking by the Visigoths in 410 AD; at its zenith at the height of the Roman empire the population was over a million. This sense of abandonment and diminished might in the contracted city is powerfully conveyed in early photographs and the streets and piazzas still retained an urban integrity that was left in much the same state as it had continued for centuries. Rome would only begin to change significantly after 1870 and, even then, quite slowly until the introduction of motorised transport in the twentieth century, which changed the urban landscape forever. The modern visitor to Rome can recapture a shadow of this tranquil aspect in the early hours of the morning in those parts of the city that in recent years have been closed to traffic, but the sense of empty streets and peaceful mornings that imbues many of the pictures from the early decades has been lost in the age of mass tourism.

Confronting such an extended idea of time, one that is inescapable in such an environment, brings its own challenges to the artist. Whether in the graphic tradition of the *vedutisti* or more recently in photography — still not 180 years old — the artist must grasp the thread of time and weave the fibres together to create a vision that reveals the central body of the subject, clothing the idea and setting it forth in such a way that others, the audience, can bring their own interpretations: each beholder enriching the picture through the pleasures of the imagination.

The singular difference between the earlier methods of representation and photography is of course the means of capture. The pre-photographic realm relied on artistic invention in a completely different way from that of the photographers. Photography demands that aspects of selectivity and position be approached with the complete image understood and ready to be grasped in the moment. Before photography an image was achieved by an accumulation of gestures and each image inevitably had its own extended frame of time within it, from the conception of the image until it is brought to completion. This cumulative and selective approach vanished at a stroke in the photographer's world. The attitude to time in a photograph was transformative: photography has the ability to seize a fragment out of time and spin from that moment a position for the image in relation to the subject, which could then be translated once again in the mind of the observer. This shifting between the subjective and objective response has always seemed to me to be one of the glories of photography.

The earliest years of photography have left us images of surpassing beauty and sensibility. The ability to seize a subject for the first time in a photograph must have been extraordinarily exhilarating. To stand with a camera in front of a subject renowned for centuries, making pictures in a manner that before had only been dreamed of, must have had a dynamic effect on the pioneers. Though quite soon these early experimenters were to be eclipsed in production, if not ability, by the proliferation of commercial enterprises producing images in thousand copies.

As soon as the techniques of photography became more straightforward and plates could be reliably mass produced in industrial quantities, the whole balance of the early support for photography shifted from the dedicated artist professional to a commercial enterprise. For it must be remembered how difficult it was to produce a satisfactory result in the early years. As the medium evolved the technical challenge was changing almost daily as different methods were set out and adjusted, leading to endlessly variable solutions with a significantly different appearance in the resulting image. Over this short history, the initial half century — easily encompassed during the lifetime of a single practitioner — it could have been necessary to learn the technical requirements of daguerreotype, calotype, waxed paper, collodion wet plate, dry plate and then, eventually, those that followed the introduction of flexible film in 1888.

Somewhat later, but in less than seventy years from the origins of photography, a viable colour process arrived in 1907.[3] Each of these steps, just a few of the many, made for significant differences in the making and distribution of photographs. Each step forward in technical development offered new possibilities in the artistic realm, and the early practitioners were inevitably pushing the limits, often achieving the most transformative results, still superlative in the vision that they set before us. No doubt some of this is derived from the kind of lyric beauty which these early exponents captured, of uncrowded streets and from a time when Rome was still an essentially pre-industrial culture.

The realm of the image for almost all photographs in the first decades was limited to a single frame defined by the focal length of the lens in relation to the format of the negative or the size of the camera back. From the very beginnings of photography the magnificence of description that was so perfectly exemplified in the daguerreotype set the bar high for the early experimenters. These necessarily small and precious images (they rarely exceed 165 × 215 mm, each one unique) had a jewel-like quality and a capacity for resolution that seemed hyper-real. They were the perfect objects to hold in the hand, an aspect that gives a very different connection to the image to that of one hung on a wall. Daguerreotype was an intractable, unforgiving medium, requiring a nigh impossible, and yet at the same time, ideal set of conditions for a successful result in the uncontrolled environment of the city. The necessary equipment and facilities for the preparation and processing of the images had to be kept close to hand and deployed with speed and fluency. The single great collection of surviving daguerreotypes that includes a significant number of images of Rome is the remarkable set of 153 plates compiled by Alexander Ellis who both commissioned others and made images himself between 1841–45. Among the pictures that survive in this collection of Italian views are thirteen sequential plates taken by Achille Morelli from the tower of the Capitol in June of 1841 constituting a 360-degree panorama of the city, almost certainly the first time anything of this kind had been attempted.[4] The entire group are considered to be the earliest surviving photographs of Italian subjects. Ellis was quickly followed by Girault de Prangey who was in Rome the following year,[5] making daguerreotypes from the summit of Trajan's column

and in the garden's of the Villa Medici,[6] but he was to do most of his work around the shores of the Mediterranean and the Roman pictures are among the smaller groups in the set.

The daguerreotype rapidly became obsolete once the negative working processes invented by William Henry Fox Talbot became sufficiently advanced, the greatest advantage being the ability to make multiple prints of any given image. Talbot's negative working method on a coated sheet of paper was announced more or less simultaneously with that of Daguerre. The ascendancy of paper over the silvered copper plate of a daguerreotype initially took longer to establish but by the mid-1840's Calvert Jones, an early practitioner and a friend of Talbot, was adjusting his camera to make panoramic assemblages from multiple negatives. The endless variability in the resulting prints is one of the pleasures of early photography. It is a misnomer to define the results as black and white photography as there is an endless degree of variation in print colour. According to the methods employed, images are preserved in every tint from a cold blue to golden and reddish tones, achieved with different chemical processes and stabilising baths of precious metals. Some were simple, cyanotype, others much more complex involving solutions of metals like gold and platinum.

Early paper photographs have a luminosity and sense of surface derived from the fibres in the paper that offer a distinctive beauty that has rarely been equalled in the warmth and sensuousness of these characteristics. The paper process improved quickly until it too was superseded by the arrival of the technically challenging wet collodion process. The sense of hallucinatory detail present in the daguerreotype was approached again in these glass negatives. In collodion the rendering of detail in the image was a given and the idea of ever larger prints became the next objective. (It remained virtually impossible to enlarge images with any degree of consistency until the introduction of electric lamps). This meant that the camera had to be able to accommodate large sheets of glass or waxed paper with all the associated problems of light loss through the greater depth of the camera which would require very small apertures to retain any significant depth of field which in turn demanded longer exposure times (Tommaso Cuccioni produced images as large as a meter wide by a half meter high). But a perfectly achieved wet-plate collodion negative gave such supreme descriptive resolution in the final print that when deployed by the early masters of photography it became an attribute that lent a sense of direct observation, as if replacing and surpassing the experience of the thing itself. The idea of the photographic representation of the subject had already become so powerful that many buildings are now described by historians through the filter of the photographer's eye. They replaced the idea of verisimilitude of the steel engraving and etchings that had preceded them almost completely, and the usefulness to scholars of those prints slipped away leaving the purely aesthetic aspects of those works paramount, or for the lesser works, oblivion. Some stood higher, Piranesi; many others fell into obscurity. This sudden ascendancy of the new medium was particularly evident in Rome, where the photographic recording of the city was well established by the mid-1840s.

The photographer's challenge was very different to that of the earlier image makers. After taking on the received canonical views photographers began to invent ways of representation that were purely photographic in conception. Nowhere is this better illustrated than in Rome. Sites in the city that had been on the pilgrimage route, and those established through the Grand Tour, remain the chief subjects in the mass of commercially produced images, largely driven in the making by the need to generate sales. The turnover in print sales was considerable and in 1877 Vilhelm Bergsoe described 'a little boy dashing down from one of the lofty studios holding in his hand the small wooden box which contains the glass negative placed over the paper. Breathlessly he hurtles out into the sunlight and sits down boldly in the middle of the square holding the photograph up to the sun, rotating it all the while. None of the passers-by sees anything unusual in this performance and five minutes later the image is fixed.'[7] This was presumably a popular portrait photographer with a studio under a skylight on the top floor of a building. There were also gentlemen amateurs, like Giacomo Caneva; a shadowy figure, Frédéric A. Flachéron; and De Prangey and Ellis who intended to apply their work to scholarly ventures, none of which were ever completed.[8]

The early photographers were grappling with the limits of relatively primitive optics and the circle of illumination cast by the lenses of the day was often little larger than the field of the back of the camera when the lens and objective were aligned on the central axis of the camera. Later, as lens design improved, it became possible to project an optical cone larger than the camera back and the use of camera movements begins. This had a strong, though still largely unexamined, visual effect on issues of composition and continues to be one of the most valuable tools given to a photographer to govern the composition of an image. The limited circle of illumination is the chief reason why many early photographs are presented with an arched top to the image. To raise the lens mount often presented a situation where the coverage was not sufficient to provide even illumination to the corners of the image. The solution was to cut rounded corners which was deemed less distracting than having the printed image fall off to black. Camera movements make it possible to shift the vanishing point in an image and to adjust the angles and perspective recession in planar surfaces — all these have a significant effect on the appearance of the final print. The photographer was freed from a rigidly centrifugal geometric arrangement of perspective.

Did the population actually vanish because of the lengthy exposures? Or was it relatively easy in these years in Rome to wait and choose quiet hours, to achieve a result with little human activity, thus eliminating the problems of blurred motion in areas with heavy foot traffic and vehicles (the afternoon rest has been posited as one of the reasons for the empty streets).[9] Occasionally a few indications of occupancy tell us something of the business of the city, ironmongery hangs on the exterior of a shop built into the walls of the theatre of Marcellus, watering pots rest on the edge of the basin of a fountain at the Pincio, washed linen is set out to bleach in the sun on the railings of the Forum, then as now flower stands are present at the foot of the Spanish Steps. Yet there is very little evidence of people or traffic moving through the streets. Calvert Jones photographed the Colosseum in 1846, with the recurring trope of the English gentlemen standing with commanding ease in the foreground. But these were arranged situations and it is hard to imagine that a photographer appearing on the street would not attract a curious crowd in a more populous city. We know for example that Roger Fenton was pursued by people wanting to have their portrait made in the midst of the military campaign in the Crimea during 1855.

In Rome these were difficult years, the political instability and the decline of the Papal States led to a high percentage of unemployment which resulted in great poverty and lawlessness in the city, visitors were advised caution, and to beware of thievery and disease, the summer months were still rife with malaria arising from the undrained Pontine marshes, and there were far fewer visitors in the city than in more peaceful times. It was not until after 1870 that the population began to recover and Rome, as the newly established administrative capital of the country, began to prosper once again. John Henry Parker, later director of the Ashmolean Museum in Oxford, was the first to make use of photography for documentary record of the city's historic monuments. He set up the British and American Archaeological Society of Rome, and an extensive programme of documentation of antiquities commenced that inevitably recorded some of the remaining earthworks in the series of pictures traversing the still complete walls of the city. These, sometimes, create confusion between archaeological excavation and military preparedness. The Society listed in its catalogue of 1879 more than 3,300 images commissioned chiefly from Italian photographers.[10] Though small in format they are still fascinating images and the analytical approach gives them an added sense of immediacy. In these pictures the city is still quiet, there are only a few people depicted, bullock carts stand idle by the roadside and human presence is indicated more in absence than presence, by washing hung out to dry in the sun and the haphazard intersections of those living in the city. But the archaeological value of the work continues to be manifest, the pictures recorded the state of the city as it was and since then much has been lost in the rapid expansion and modernising of the city. There are images in several collections showing Papal excise officers on duty at the gates. But there appears to be almost nothing comparable in Rome to the immediacy of the large-scale pictures by Gustave Le Gray in Palermo.

Most of the photographers we are now aware of were professionals running their studios as businesses, producing views in substantial numbers for an increasing tourist market. In later editions of his catalogue, always printed on a single sheet, Robert Macpherson lists as many as 450 images, the majority views of Rome and environs. These were purchased by wealthy travellers who returned with them to England, where the pictures were mounted in albums or kept in folios. Assembling such an extensive gallery of images at a time when the process was difficult and intractable was a major undertaking and because it required a great deal of technical skill as well as artistic ability to achieve superior results it was possible for the early practitioners to make a good living in the periods of relative calm in the city.

In the 1850s, Britain was a politically stable nation, relatively unruffled by the insurrections that swept over much of the rest of Europe, an industrial giant at the beginning of the industrial age and the United Kingdom was in the midst of consolidating and expanding an empire. The great wealth that flowed in contributed to the rise of a substantial leisure class able to travel abroad in luxurious circumstances at the same time as poverty-stricken millions, driven out of work by that same industrialisation were emigrating to America in search of a better life. In these years before the unification the market for photographs appears to have been dominated by British tourists, a situation fully exploited by Macpherson and James Anderson. Both ran what appear to have been highly lucrative operations in these years. Perhaps this was because the United Kingdom was relatively stable at this time and avoided the revolutionary upheavals that streamed across Europe in the 1840s and 1850s.[11] But the community of expatriates in Rome has always been significant and there were collectors from the United States such as the architects Henry Hobson Richardson[12] and Richard Morris Hunt,[13] who compiled substantial collections of photographs. Citizens of other European states would have had less freedom and inclination to travel to Italy during times of political uncertainty at home than did the British traveller.

The public's hunger for photographic interpretations of the history of civilisation reached its peak with the ascent of the stereo card and lantern slide companies that produced millions of views of every conceivable subject around the globe. By 1897 the American firm of Underwood and Underwood was printing 25,000 images a day. These companies went into sharp decline after the rise of the newsreel and the printed magazines which replaced them. The most prominent of these, Gaumont Pathé and the National Geographic were in their turn to be eclipsed by the arrival of television though the latter continues to publish. The studios that had been able to sustain themselves by the business of selling photographic prints gradually closed and the prints they provided for decades were replaced by the humble postcard, still with images of the same canonical sites that had been repeated for generations, and until recently displayed on revolving stands in the doorways of every souvenir shop in Rome. The images made by the pioneering photographers in the city were forgotten until recently, while the third great wave in the collecting of photography only began in the late 1970s. The importance of these early works has been rediscovered, reconsidered in terms of the historical record and as works of art in their own right.

It is the early years that in many ways represent the pinnacle of achievement: in Italy the first decades up to 1870 are often referred to as the heroic years, when the language of photography was in its infancy. That aspect of the birth of a completely new and unparalleled way to take on the description of the city coupled with an artistic intelligence and constructed on the accumulation of centuries of practice, led to a flowering of the art of photography in Rome in the second half of the nineteenth century that we are now in the position to be able to appreciate in a manner that would have given great satisfaction to the luminaries of that time working in the medium. It is an extraordinary legacy derived from indefatigable engagement and creative endeavour by pioneering photographers.

The sense of revelation must have been remarkable for both the practitioners and the audience. That sense of discovery still remains and the fascination with the idea, as Garry Winogrand put it, of wanting to see what the subject would look like as a photograph, still remains undiminished in the mind of photographers. Now we grapple with subjects that are familiar — everything imaginable has now been seen through the lens and can be disseminated universally at the click of a button, the current deluge of imagery still has not diminished the desire in photographers to find new and potent ways to set forth the essence of a subject. The continual desire to deal with the inevitability of the idea of time in photography is, I think, what makes the pursuit of photographic methods of interpreting the world the most compelling reason to be engaged with the medium. It still has the potential to span every aspect of humanity and the continuing urge to record the whole range of human endeavour and experience makes the pursuit one without end and the goal unachievable. The same humanistic impulse drives the subject of architecture in photographs. Rome proved to be a fertile ground for these early experiments in the translation of history into images.

In a city such as Rome, where the layerings of centuries and the rise and fall of civilisations make the presence of a single being seem insignificant in the longer reach of time, it is inevitable that the artists' vision is infused by the long tradition of image making that precedes the moment of engagement. But in a curious inversion of the fatalism of the idea, one can take comfort from Henri Cartier-Bresson's celebrated dictum that we can never recover the moment that has past and it will never repeat itself. We can only photograph what we know, but we can push at the edges of our cognisance by challenging our comprehension. To reach for greater reverberation in the way a subject is rendered through the accumulation of experience. As if the picture is a challenge to transcend history.

Working in photography now when the whole aspect of the medium is in the greatest state of flux since 1839 depends on the same sense of timeliness as it ever did, and it has always appeared to me that the best pictures require a vital sense of the contemporaneous moment. In taking architecture as subject this is more straightforward in new structures because there is an inevitable connection to the now. But the same attitude can imbue subjects wound into history. There are ways to set up that compositional tension that makes a picture stand or fall. The boundary of the frame is the most photographic of tools in the matter of composition, an essential consideration established as soon as a photographer stood behind a camera. A picture can be changed as radically by what is included within as by what is left outside the frame. Cartier-Bresson's succinct and aphoristic statements on the idea of photography apply just as much to static subjects as they do to other, more animated images. 'The decisive moment' is as applicable to architecture as a subject as it is to capturing a man jumping across a puddle; though perhaps not in such a hyper reflexive manner as in that ability to organise the chaos of daily existence. It is equally applicable that the right time for a picture of a building is not only at that moment when the sun illuminates a given façade in a manner that sharply defines the surface texture and relief, a kind of image that has dominated the architectural press for decades. Buildings continue to exist in all weathers and seasons and some attention to this aspect of illumination and aspect is equally important. Frequently conditions appear to be far from ideal but one must find a way to work, particularly when there are time constraints or it is not possible to return under more favourable conditions. There are ways of exposing the structure that depend on completely other aspects of illumination; I am reminded of the simplicity and clarity of the serial approach of Bernd and Hilla Becher whose lifetime engagement with the exposition of typologies made such a profound difference to the way we regard industrial structures.

As a photographer, my most recent stay in Rome took me to the EUR, a district which I had never visited before. The place itself is encumbered by Mussolini's grandiosity and neo-imperialist aspirations. My curiosity was piqued long ago by the apparition of the water tower, a landmark of the district still, which appears in the opening sequences in *L'eclisse* (1962), the last part of Michelangelo Antonioni's superlative trilogy of films on modernity and its discontent[14]. Monica Vitti's character opens the curtains to reveal the modernist tower in the flat light of dawn, after an uneasy night culminating in her walking away from a relationship, a sequence that precipitates the unfolding narrative of the film. That same water tower is now bristling with antennae destroying the simplicity and strangeness of the form. The area is still a magnet for tension and I found evidence of the increasing factionalism in the political realm in the form of strident graffiti and electioneering posters. This, layered onto the neo-imperialist structures of the late 1930s, created an atmosphere with an uneasy portent for the future.

Most of us pass through life using our eyes simply as negotiating devices to see us safely to our destination. Or placing ourselves in front of something of note, we look but don't see. Unless we pay special attention it is easy to be caught in the inevitability of the flow of time, and pass by, without noticing the transformations occurring before unseeing eyes. I seek out the longer time frame, meandering with purpose, loitering with intent, through the cities and spaces where I find myself, wherever it may be. With that necessary sense of heightened regard, alertness rewarding the photographer with moments of revelation gathered in by a process that still seems near miraculous, when the elements of an image align. This is the true magic of photographs, the ability to capture the most evanescent phenomena, be it the brief play of light across a surface or the startling *mise en scène* of an incident plucked out of life on the streets, or stones that have stood for centuries and are revealed in a moment never to be repeated.

[1] Edward Gibbon, *The History of the Decline and Fall of the Roman Empire*, vol. 4, chapter LXXI, par. 1, London: Strahan & Cadell, 1776-1789.

[2] Gustave Le Gray, *A practical treatise on photography, upon paper and glass*, London: T. & R. Willats, 1850.

[3] The Lumière Brothers Autochrome plate was introduced in 1907.

[4] Held at Victoria and Albert Museum, London. See also note 8.

[5] Joseph-Philibert Girault de Prangey daguerreotype in the collection of Metropolitan Museum of Art, *Ponte Rotto*, exhibited at the MET in *Paradise of Exiles: Early Photography in Italy*, 13 March – 13 August 13 2017.

[6] Illustrated in Christie's, *A photographic Grand Tour Important Daguerreotypes by Joseph-Philibert Girault de Prangey*, New York: Christie's, 2010.

[7] Quoted in *Rome in early photographs, the age of Pius IX: photographs 1846-1878 from Roman and Danish collections*, exhibition catalogue (Copenhagen, Thorvaldsen Museum, 1977), translated by Ann Thornton, Copenhagen: The Thorvaldsen Museum, 1977.

[8] The Ellis plates ended up in the Science Museum in London where they were deposited by his son in 1880, they are now at the Victoria and Albert Museum. The Girault de Prangey plates were essentially unavailable except to a few scholars. The plates were dispersed at auction by Christie's in two sales in 2004 and 2010.

[9] *Rome in early photographs*, cit.

[10] The most extensive collection of these images is to be found in the Collection of the Kelsey Museum of Archeology at the University of Michigan. The original archive was destroyed by fire.

[11] This sense of the predominance of British tourists in the city in these years is based on the substantial quantities of photographs, often still in the original folios, that appeared in the British market more than a century later in the 1980s.

[12] Richardson's collection takes up 55 linear feet in the Francis Loeb Library at Harvard University. James S. Ackerman, 'On the origins of architectural photography', in Kester Rattenbury (ed.), *This is not architecture: media constructions*, London and New York: Routledge, 2002, pp. 26–36.

[13] Hunt's collection, now housed at the Library of Congress, consists of around 30,000 images.

[14] Jacopo Benci, 'Michelangelo's Rome: Towards in Iconology of L'Eclisse', in Richard Wrigle (ed.), *Cinematic Rome*, Leicester: Troubador Publishing Ltd., 2008, pp. 63–84.

Owen Hopkins

Rome in the British Architectural Imagination:
Inigo Jones, John Soane, James Stirling

[...] The cloud-capped towers, the gorgeous palaces,
The solemn temples, the great globe itself —
Yea, all which it inherit — shall dissolve.

Prospero in *The Tempest* by William Shakespeare

In these famous lines, Prospero describes the unnamed island in *The Tempest* — a place of illusion, mysticism and the imaginary, where architecture takes on the role of the fantastical. The play is believed to have been written in 1610–11, less than a decade after the accession of James I to the throne in England and with it the establishing of the new Stuart dynasty and an age of transformation. The architectural historian Christy Anderson has argued that these lines can be read as a reference to the masques of the Stuart court whose mythological or historical subjects were played out against elaborate and often highly architectural stage sets.[1] Yet, they might also be read as a reference to Rome, a city that up to that point only existed in the imagination for the vast majority of English men and women, but which nonetheless — or indeed because of that fact — was already arousing fascination.

Looking back more than 400 years later, there are few cities that have captured the British imagination quite as powerfully as Rome.[2] 'All roads lead to Rome', as the proverb says, and this has been the case for architects perhaps more than any other creative discipline. It is, moreover, no surprise that the first concerted forays by Englishmen to Rome in the sixteenth and early seventeenth centuries paved the way for the emergence of architecture as a creative and intellectual discipline, distinct from stone masonry and the craft of building. From the early years of the eighteenth century it became de rigueur for aspiring architects to visit Rome, and Italy more broadly, to learn directly from the buildings of the ancients, and immerse themselves in the culture that had built up around them. Almost every significant architect practising from 1750–1840 spent time in Rome, with three to four years the average. It is hard to imagine from our era quite how much of a revelation this experience would have been for young architects who had up to this point understood Roman architecture only through prints and casts.

The Grand Tour continued well into the nineteenth century, when before the advent of the railways, the journey was little changed from the convoluted and dangerous expeditions made by the pioneer tourists at the beginning of the seventeenth century. As the railways and then jet travel annihilated the distances between Britain and Rome, as a new modern Rome added yet another historical layer onto the rich palimpsest, and as the advent of photography allowed its sights to be captured into images to be held in an album or dispersed, our relationship with Rome was inevitably modified. For centuries Rome represented an ideal to be aspired for, if never reached, but in the mid-nineteenth century this began to change.

The choice of a Gothic rather than Roman design for rebuilding of the Palace of Westminster in 1836 is usually seen as representing a watershed in Rome's decline in importance, with classical and imperial ideals replaced with a newly imagined, native Gothic past.[3] While both cultural and political factors played their part, the broader backdrop for this shift was the industrial revolution, which was already overturning all existing social, economic and aesthetic certainties. Ultimately it was the condition of modernity, rather than the Gothic Revival, that saw Rome's horizons surpassed, with attention turned towards how to build the future, rather than emulate the past. Yet as that notion of the future turned sour in the last few decades of the twentieth century, the very palimpsestic nature of the city, of accumulated layer upon accumulated layer, which so contrasted with the modernist tabula rasa, became an ideal once more for all its complexities and multivalent architectural and urban riches. Writing in an explanation of his 2014-2015 *The Roman Singularity* created while living in Rome, the architectural designer, Adam Nathaniel Furman, goes even further. For him, Rome is 'the contemporary city par-excellence, an urban version of the internet, in which subjective experience merges with an abundant profusion of historical artifacts. It is a place where the analogical-whole history of society, architecture, politics, literature and art coalesce into a space so intense and delimited that they collapse under the enormity of their own mass into a singularity of human endeavour, in which time is suspended as a dimension and everything is simultaneous, coextensive, feeding off of everything else in a city-scale feast of endlessly creative auto-cannibalism.'

The result, Furman argues, is to 'almost force it [Rome] to be perpetually radical about the present'.[4]

It is this final comment that provides the starting point for this essay, which will look at how three architects from three distinct moments of British architectural history were inspired by Rome in quite different ways to create architectural visions that were radical in their own presents. The first is Inigo Jones (1573–1652), architect to the Stuart court, and one of the first to have visited Italy and studied remains of Roman and Renaissance buildings at first hand. Jones is traditionally credited with introducing a Roman form of classical architecture into Britain as a way of aggrandising the new Stuart dynasty which he served. The real story, however, is rather more complicated: Rome was not a model that could be simply transplanted into Britain, both for the difficult associations it engendered with Catholicism and the papacy, and also the endurance of native styles. The result was a mediated version of Roman architecture, through the work of Palladio and Serlio as is well known, but also through Anglo traditions.

While Jones's visit to Italy at the beginning of the seventeenth century made him something of a pioneer, John Soane (1753–1837) followed a path that was already well trodden. Soane was part of the neoclassical generation of architects who would be allowed by the direct experience of ancient architecture to look beyond the texts that had informed the previous Palladian architects. Their interest was in what was there in ruined form, which they studied and measured, but also in the imaginative and creative possibilities of the ruin itself, which were so important in the formation of Soane's unique architectural vision.

James Stirling (1924–1992) was the most celebrated British architect of the second half of the twentieth century, who in the late 1970s appeared to transition effortlessly from modernist to postmodernist. The reality was that the traits and characteristics, which defined his postmodern phase were there from the beginning, instilled in part through the influence of his friend and mentor Colin Rowe. Rowe's ideas on the city reached something of summation in his book, *Collage City*, written with Fred Koetter, and published in 1978, in which the authors rejected the totalising strictures of orthodox modernist planning in favour of fragmentation, layering, collision and contamination, which characterised the most successful cities. Of particular interest here is Stirling's proposal for the *Roma interrotta* (Rome Interrupted) exhibition of 1978 in which a number of architects were invited to speculatively redraw Giambattista Nolli's famous 1748 map of Rome. While influenced by Rowe's ideas, the overt grandiosity of Stirling's proposal uses Rome's status as the apotheosis of the pre-modern city in a powerful critique, perhaps even parody, of the modernist planning that had compromised so many cities across the world.

Running through each of these three case studies is a series of tensions. In the case of Jones, there is a clear tension between classical architecture and Rome; they are not synonymous and his choice of Palladio as mediator of the ancients was an important one. More broadly, there is the tension arising in the way Rome's complex historical layers exist simultaneously: ancient next to Renaissance, Mannerist next to Baroque, nineteenth-century next to modern, and any permutation therein. Which of these Romes, so to speak, are architects drawing inspiration from? The answer, as I hope the essay will illustrate, is that every architect creates their own version of Rome, shaped by their impressions, sensations and knowledge of the city, while reflecting prevailing trends and fashions of their particular moment. Rome is perpetually remade by every visitor.

Inigo Jones
Thou art not, Penshurst, built to envious show,
Of touch, or marble, not canst boast a row
Of polish'd pillars or a roofe of golde:
Thou hast no lantherne, whereof tales are told;
Or stayre, or courts; but standst an ancient pile.[5]

Written in 1616, Ben Jonson's *To Penshurst* encapsulates the still powerful hold of the medieval house over the early Stuart psyche. Jonson contrasts the modest beauties of the originally fourteenth-century Penshurst Place in Kent with what he sees as 'proud, ambitious heaps' of more recent decades. Interestingly, Jonson's critique is about style — and materials. 'Pillars' and 'lanthernes' are condemned as heartily as 'marble' and 'golde'. Jonson's target is usually seen as the great Elizabethan 'prodigy' houses of the previous generation. However, in his sights may also have been an even more recent, and arguably more novel, building: the Queen's House in Greenwich, begun in 1616 to the designs of Inigo Jones, and the first authentically classical building in Britain.

If Jonson was in part thinking of Queen's House when he wrote those words, then his animosity towards it would not have been solely architectural, but personal too. Jonson and Jones notoriously quarrelled when working together in devising and staging the masques that took place at the Stuart court. Masques were a kind of pageant show during which members of the court, including royalty, acted out scenes from mythology and distant history, usually accompanied by music and dancing. Jonson wrote the words of about two-dozen masques, while the responsibility for the creation of the sets for these performances was the job of Jones. Given the often fantastical nature of the subjects, designing these temporary sets acted as a kind of test-bed for Jones to explore a range of architectural ideas and styles, including and most importantly, classical architecture.

Despite what is still sometimes assumed, the British Isles had not been cut off from the dissemination of Renaissance architectural treatises during the sixteenth century, many of which had reached its shores. Nor had Englishmen interested in architecture been unable to visit Italy, though this was still unusual. John Shute was among the first to do so, spending time in Rome studying its architecture, and later publishing *The First and Chief Groundes of Architecture* (1563) — the first architectural treatise to be written in English.

While the combination of the circulation of treatises and travel to Italy clearly paved the way for the rise of classical architecture in Britain, it did not make it inevitable.[6] That it was slow to take hold, moreover, was not the result of lack of knowledge or understanding, rather of deliberate decisions about how to build. For example, the Triangular Lodge in Northamptonshire, built in the mid 1590s by Sir Thomas Tresham, shows no influence of classical architecture whatsoever, yet its designer owned copies of the major Renaissance treatises: Palladio, Serlio *et al.*[7] As the architectural historian Alice T. Friedman has noted, even though these works were familiar to an aristocratic English audience, what they contained was 'intentionally suppressed in favour of a decorative and narrative style heavily influenced by Flemish, French, and German designs' that could be used to convey the 'complex messages of Elizabethan political ideology'.[8] It was, furthermore, no coincidence that the first building to break from the mould was Hardwick Hall in Derbyshire, designed in the early 1590s by Robert Smythson, whose patron was a woman, Elizabeth Shrewsbury, better known as 'Bess of Hardwick', who was not bound by the same codes of display as a male courtier.[9]

While to some eyes, classical architecture represented order, rationality and the elevation of architecture into a intellectual pursuit, to others, its connotations were rather different: luxurious, foreign and tainted by its association with Rome. For the puritan preacher, John Gordon, it was still not possible to forget that 'the first three hundred yeeres the true Christians who worshipped one onely God […] had been persecuted by Pagan Rome, even so the worshippers of this true adoration have beene cruelly persecuted during the three hundred years of the first period, by Rome disguised with a Christian maske'.[10] Because of this and other multitudinous sins, Rome, according to Gordon, was the 'great whore of *Babilon*'.[11]

Gordon's views of Rome were at the extreme end of the scale, and clearly for someone like Inigo Jones, it was quite the reverse. Yet, this should not disguise the fact that when the old Banqueting House burnt down in 1619, the decision to rebuild it in a classical style was not without risk. The very reasons it was chosen — to set it apart from the rest of Whitehall Palace, and indeed the rest of the city; to stand as an expression of the power and status of the Stuart dynasty; and maybe even have expressed some European connection when Charles, James I's son, was seeking the marriage of the Spanish Infanta – made it a bold and potentially controversial choice.

As far as the architect was concerned, Jones had been appointed Surveyor of the King's Works in 1615 after returning from Italy the previous year. During his two years away, Jones had visited Rome, Naples, Vicenza and Venice, among other cities, absorbing their architecture both ancient and more recent. Hugely influential in informing Jones on what and how he saw were Barbaro's edition of Vitruvius and Palladio's *I quattro libri dell'architettura* whose distillation of Roman architecture into a system of rules, propositions and principles was a major influence, as it has been for countless architects since. Palladio's architecture was also of great interest to Jones, who acquired a number of his original drawings and even met his pupil, Vincenzo Scamozzi.[12]

Jones' travel combined with close and often critical reading of architectural treatises gave him a deeper knowledge of classical architecture than perhaps any other Englishman in history up to that point. Moreover, after him, the classical became the normative architectural style in Britain for over two centuries. However, just as we should not assume the emergence of classical architecture in Britain in the early seventeenth century as inevitable, we should not when looking at a work such as the Banqueting House see its subsequent triumph as a similarly forgone conclusion. Some may have seen the Banqueting House as the first part of a new Whitehall Palace, but for the vast majority of observers it was a new and singular imposition.

The simplistic characterisation of Jones as some kind of classical pioneer disguises the continuities with tradition present even in a building as seemingly radical as the Banqueting House. At first glance it is as if a Roman building has been transplanted into London. The calm and deliberate arrangement of the façade, the rusticated base level, and two storeys of superimposed orders — Ionic and then Composite above with a slight central emphasis created through the combination of half and three-quarter columns — are all distinctly Palladian features, derived from Roman precedent, and quite different from the English architectural tradition. On close inspection, however, elements that Jones could have scarcely seen in Italy announce themselves. The building's proportions are not quite as stipulated in *I quattro libri*, though it is possible that Jones noticed deviations from these ideals in Palladio's own buildings. More significantly, the austere Portland-stone façade we see today is the result of restoration by Sir John Soane (1753–1837); originally the façade used several different types of stone to create a more polychromatic effect. Also, the placement of garlands between the Composite capitals creating a frieze level above has no obvious Roman precedent, and on a visual level suggests continuities with the highly decorated Elizabethan and Jacobean styles.

Unsurprisingly, Jones himself was highly conscious of the marked difference between seeing a building in the flesh and doing so on paper — and the Banqueting House very much bears this out. On paper it is a straightforwardly Roman building filtered through the lens of Palladio. In the flesh it is rather more complex, and of course, in Jones's day sat within the very un-Roman context of the Tudor Whitehall Palace.

Inside, the Banqueting House is a slightly different story. The open, rectangular interior, with columns around its perimeter, is closely inspired by Vitruvius' description of the Egyptian Hall, which was depicted by Palladio in the second book of *Quattro libri*. Decorating the ceiling are a series of paintings commissioned from the artist Peter Paul Rubens (1577–1640) glorifying James I as the new Solomon and celebrating the still new Stuart court. In purely architectural terms, there are few elements that suggest continuity with British architectural tradition, yet when combined with Rubens' paintings we see in a very clear way how the building takes over the job of the masques; the abstract art of architecture combining with the literal and allegorical art of painting. Fittingly, the paintings' installation meant that the space could in fact no longer be used to hold masques; the soot from candles used to light them was detrimental to the paintings.

The case of the Banqueting House makes clear that the emergence of classical architecture in Britain should not be considered as a case of one style or mode of architecture replacing another, but of continuity and dialogue between the influence of Roman architecture and British traditions. Intriguingly, for Jones this dialogue extended to an apparently indigenous structure — Stonehenge — which, prompted by James I, was the subject of speculative theories concerning the history of Roman architecture in Britain. Seduced by its geometry, Jones postulated that Stonehenge was a Roman temple, dedicated to the god of the sky, Caelus. He took detailed measurements and created views of the monument apparently 'restored', which were published posthumously in 1655.

However fanciful Jones' formulations appear now, and perhaps, for some, appeared so at the time, they demonstrate the profound impact of Rome and what it represented that began to build in Britain in the first decades of the seventeenth century. Soon, hundreds of aspiring architects and many others besides would follow in Jones' footsteps and make the journey to Rome and see its monuments at first hand in a way that he himself had actually half-predicted: 'The magnificence of that stately [Roman] Empire, is at this day clearly visible in [...] the ruins of their Temples, Palaces, Arches Triumphal, Aqueducts, Thermae, Theatres, Amphitheatres, Cirques, and other secular, and sacred structures.'

History affords only contemplation, whereby their great actions are made conceivable alone to reasoning, but the ruins of their buildings demonstration, which obvious to sense, are even yet as so many eye-witnesses of their admired achievements.[13]

John Soane

At 5.30am on 18 March 1798, John Soane set off on the long journey to Italy. So important did Soane consider his two years away that he marked the day of his departure for the rest of his life. Other than his brief stop in Paris, we know relatively little about Soane's journey to Italy, but fortunately rather more about what he did there and where he visited: arriving in Rome before heading south to Naples, Pompeii and Paestum, and then north to Mantua, Parma, Vicenza, Padua and Venice among other places. In Italy, Soane was able to study at first hand the buildings that he had known up to that point only from images and written accounts, and as for so many others on the Grand Tour this experience would stay with him for the rest of his life.

Aspiring architects usually embarked on their Grand Tour at the end of pupillage, usually around the age of twenty-one. Two to three years was the typical duration, although longer was not unusual; Charles Robert Cockerell, for example, managed to extend his Grand Tour to no less than seven years. While the aristocratic Grand Tourist was typically as interested, if not more so, in the opportunities for socialising and revelling in the freedom of being away a very long way from home, as in education, architects were for the most part focused on accumulating knowledge and experiences that would aid them through their careers. That said, many architects were also well aware that a proportion of the young gentlemen they met and socialised with might also be future clients. Money inevitably played

a large part in determining the type of experience an architect might have while away. Soane was fortunate to have the backing of the King's Gold Medal scholarship, as it was unlikely that as someone of his relatively lowly social background would have had the personal funds to support himself. Nevertheless, he still returned home in debt. Robert Adam, in contrast, arrived flush with cash and lived accordingly, even employing a servant, unlike his compatriot, Robert Mylne, who was so hard up that he had to undertake part of the journey to Rome on foot.

Once in Rome, architects were able to spend considerable time inspecting ruins at first hand: taking measurements, surveying, producing drawings of what they saw and comparing them to what they knew from books. Often this meant climbing rickety ladders to look in detail at capitals or entablatures. Ladders were easy to come by in Rome, but were harder and more expensive to find elsewhere. Getting up close to ruins and being systematic in how they recorded them revealed the many inaccuracies and inconsistencies that existed in publications, such *Les édifices antiques de Rome dessinés et mesurés très exactement* (1682) by Antoine Desgodetz, which had previously been held up as an almost sacred document because of its assumed accuracy. It also became obvious the extent to which Desgodetz and others had been quite restrictive in what they chose to depict, thus presenting an incomplete and distorted picture of what actually existed. Experiencing Rome with one's own eyes, even if some ruins were inevitably of more interest than others, it was impossible not be affected and take account of everything one saw.

The depictions of ancient buildings contained in works by Desgodetz and others typically showed them in their imagined original, un-ruined states. Seeing the ruins for themselves made architects very much aware of how speculative these reconstructions were; while they were portrayed as objective, in reality they were anything but. One consequence was a trend for showing buildings actually as ruins by the likes of Robert Adam and his sometime collaborator, Charles-Louis Clérisseau. In their famous depictions of the Diocletian's palace at Split, published in *Ruins of the Palace of the Emperor Diocletian at Spalatro in Dalmatia* (1764), Adam and Clérisseau appeared far more interested in topography and setting the ruin in some of indistinct or half-imagined moment of time than in archaeological accuracy. Rather than seeing the ruin as a fragment of a whole that could be reconstructed, the ruin became the end in itself, dislocated from time and place and available to be appropriated by architects in wholly new ways.[14]

That architects could, on the one hand, with systematic measurement and accurate depiction concern themselves with an almost scientific investigation of ruins, yet, on the other, indulge their imaginations in allowing room for invention and even fantasy, was a paradox not lost on those at the time, not least Soane. Although visible in the work of many architects, this paradox is explored most fully in the work of the great architectural visionary, Giovanni Battista Piranesi. His reputation as draughtsman and printmaker able to convey in dramatic fashion both the appearance and feeling engendered by the experience of a ruin crossed geographic borders, and it was on the recommendation of the architect, Sir William Chambers, first Treasurer of the Royal Academy, that Soane sought him out.

Soane met Piranesi in 1798, the year of his death, and was given four prints by the old man, all of Roman subjects: *The Pantheon*, *The Arch of Constantine*, *The Arch of Septimius Severus* and *The Tomb of Caecilia Metella*. Later in his career when Professor of Architecture at the Royal Academy, Soane recommended to his students that 'Piranesi alone will afford a mine of information to the studious inquirer, and from his overflowing much may be gleaned […]'.[15] Yet, later in his lectures, Soane censured Piranesi for his disregard of archaeological accuracy in favour of drama and fantasy: 'That men, unacquainted with the remains of Ancient Buildings, should indulge in licentious and whimsical combinations is not a matter of surprise, but that a man, who had passed all his life in the bosom of Classic Art, and in the contemplation of the majestic ruins of Ancient Rome, observing their sublime effects and grand combinations, a man who had given innumerable examples how truly he felt the value of the noble Simplicity of those buildings, that such a man, with such examples before his eyes, should have mistaken Confusion for Intricacy, and undefined lines and forms for Classical variety, is scarcely to be believed; yet such was Piranesi.'[16]

Nevertheless, in later life Soane assembled a major collection of Piranesi's work and himself admitted that the spaces he created at his home in Lincoln's Inn Fields evoked the Italian's dramatic images.[17]

Although Soane described the Pantheon in his Royal Academy lectures as 'the glory of the ancient and the admiration of the modern world', it was experience of ruins that had a far deeper hold on his psyche.[18] This had taken root early in his trip. On 1 August 1778, he wrote to a friend, Mr Wood, from Rome, describing: 'I need not tell you my attention is entirely taken up in the seeing and examining the numerous and inestimable remains of Antiquity, as you are no stranger to the zeal and attachment I have for them and with what impatience I have waited for the scenes I now enjoy […]'.[19] While Rome remained for Soane, as it did for others, the city around which the experience of the Grand Tour revolved, the place that perhaps most captivated his imagination was Hadrian's villa at Tivoli, just outside Rome. Quite unlike the monuments he encountered in the Forum in Rome, here Soane discovered a series of ruined vaults and domes, only partially excavated and covered by vegetation. At Tivoli, Soane also saw the ruined Temple of Vesta — a distinctive circular temple that became his favourite building from antiquity, appearing multiple times in his museum, and providing the model for the Tivoli Corner of the Bank of England.

Soane cut his Grand Tour short when he got word of a possible commission from the Earl of Bristol, previously the Bishop of Derry, whom he had met in Rome. Alas for Soane, the commission came to nothing and while travelling across the Alps he lost his luggage including his notebooks and drawings. Despite this unhappy end to his trip, the Grand Tour and his experience of Rome in particular had been hugely formative for Soane in his architectural career. Years later when lecturing at the Royal Academy, he recommended his students visit Italy having undertaken a thorough education at home, and so 'complete his studies by visiting foreign countries. Thus prepared, the young architect may be reasonably expected […] to receive every possible advantage to be derived from the study of the extensive remains with which Rome and the Campagna, as well as many others parts of Italy, abound.'[20]

One of the over 1,000 drawings produced to illustrate a lecture on the Corinthian in fact shows a 'Student measuring a Capital of the Temple of Jupiter Stator (Castor and Pollux), Rome'.[21] However, with the arrival of Napoleon's troops in Italy in 1796, travel became more difficult and later impossible.[22] Recognising the importance of the first-hand direct experience of ancient architecture he had enjoyed, shortly after becoming Professor of Architecture Soane began to create a museum of architecture at the back of his house in Lincoln's Inn Fields, close to the Royal Academy, which students would be able to visit and where they could inspect fragments and casts, including fittingly one of the capital of the Temple of Castor and Pollux.

In 1807, Soane, then living in 12 Lincoln's Inn Fields, bought No. 13 so as to create a new double-height museum space on the houses' stable block at the rear of the site. Soane's collection of casts was not unique at the time; other architects had their own collections.[23] Soane's vision, however, was always more totalising, and with the sale of his country estate, Pitzhanger Manor, in 1810 his collection of casts, antiquities, painting, sculpture and drawing was for the first time brought together under one roof. An atmospheric watercolour by Joseph Michael Gandy shows the 'Dome Area' at the heart of the museum around this time. We look across the central void with a hidden light source below, bathing the collection of casts and fragments in Soane's famous *lumière mystérieuse*. The scene, and indeed the space itself, is deeply Piranesian: the dramatic light effects, the exaggerated perspective, the indication of spaces beyond the ones we see, the way fragments appear almost to defy gravity.[24] To the right, we see Soane himself leaning forward and directing the viewer's gaze towards a model of the Temple of Vesta at Tivoli.

As a result of a series of subsequent changes by Soane, the 'Dome Area' at Sir John Soane's Museum is now rather different to how Gandy depicted it in 1811. Yet the overriding effect remains largely similar. There are many ways of interpreting the space, but few that do not relate directly to Soane's experience of the Grand Tour. That he lost his luggage on his return journey is an interesting pointer, because the consequence was that all of Soane's experiences of Rome from that point on only existed in his memory, and importantly not on paper. There they may have remained if Soane had not acquired the means in later life to assemble his extraordinary collection of casts, create an architectural frame in which to place them, and so re-spatialise his memories of the Grand Tour for the benefit of himself, his students and others who visit the museum. To step into the 'Dome Area' is to peer inside Soane's mind. Each cast or fragment corresponds to a memory — whether real or imagined — of a building in Italy, and at the same time, because it is a cast, has an indexical link to what it refers: they are both the memory and the thing remembered.

Soane's experience of Rome during the Grand Tour did not just provide source material or inspiration for what he designed, it shaped how he understood architecture itself. Experiencing the buildings of antiquity in ruins, rather than on paper, was not just about what an architect saw, but how: their scale, the effects of light and shadow, the feeling of the passage of time and of the weight of history, all of which Piranesi had so dramatically captured. For Soane, it was not enough to simply present his collection of fragments in a straightforward way, they had to be activated by an evocation of the experience of seeing them as ruins in situ — and this is the effect even now of wandering around his museum. As Gandy wrote in a letter from Rome of 1796, 'We are apt to praise and form greater ideas of ruins than we would perhaps have had of the buildings when whole'.[25]

James Stirling

The mid-1970s were relatively fallow years for James Stirling. After bursting onto the international architecture stage with the Engineering Building at the University of Leicester in the early 1960s, followed by the Faculty of History at Cambridge University and the Florey Building at Queen's College, Oxford — the buildings that comprise his so-called 'red trilogy' — commissions had begun to dry up. Nevertheless, he remained one of the world of architecture's most charismatic and best known figures, and a fearless intellectual force. It was no doubt for these reasons that he was one of twelve architects invited to participate in a speculative project-exhibition to re-draw Giambattista Nolli's 1748 great map of Rome: 'Roma interrotta'.

The project was initiated by Incontri Internazionali d'Arte (International Art Meetings), a small, not for profit organisation normally focused on contemporary art.[26] This project marked a rare foray into the world of architecture. Rather than being staged in an art gallery, the project took place in Trajan's Market, an important though still relatively overlooked archaeological site, so it was embedded in Rome's dense urban history, both conceptually and physically.

Nolli's map, properly titled 'Nuova Topografia di Roma' (New Topography of Rome), was commissioned by Pope Benedict XIV to record the city in a clear and objective way. The map is split into twelve equal segments, with Nolli systematic in his use of hatch marks to denote solids, white or light shades of grey to indicate open spaces, giving the map an immediate legibility. Surrounding the map were two allegorical scenes: on the left portraying ancient/pagan Rome and on the right, modern/Christian Rome.[27] The architects were each given one of the twelve segments of Nolli's map to reinterpret, thus laying an additional synchronic-urban dialogue on top of that already contained in Nolli's map, an aspect of the project that was accentuated in the way the two maps were displayed.

The architectural historian, Léa-Catherine Szacka, has noted that the obvious intellectual inspiration for the project was the work of the Anglo-American architectural theorist, Colin Rowe, principally his interests in speculations on alternative histories/futures and his critique of modernist planning.[28] Rowe was, moreover, a longtime friend and former tutor of Stirling whose ideas had proved influential on the architect's thinking about the city across his career and in the 'Roma interrotta' project specifically.

Rowe had first come to attention with the publication of his now seminal essay 'The Mathematics of the Ideal Villa' in 1947, in which he compared and charted common principles between the work of Le Corbusier and Palladio. Soon after he returned to Liverpool University where his teaching sought to introduce students, such as Stirling, to architects like Palladio, the Mannerists and more recent figures such as the rationalists Terragni and Cattaneo. His ambition was to reintroduce history into contemporary architectural theory and debunk modernism's claims of somehow sitting outside history.

Rowe developed his critique of the Modern Movement and in particular modernist planning after his move to Cornell University in the early 1960s, culminating in the above-mentioned hugely influential book, *Collage City* (1979), co-written with Fred Koetter. Here, developing arguments he had made in previous articles, Rowe took the hammer to what he saw as the faux-scientific rigour of modern architecture and planning, its naive idealism, its overt precision and claims of rationality, objectivity and even universality. Instead, he proposed an urbanism of 'bricolage', of layering, fragmentation and multivalency that characterised the pre-modern city. Rome was in many ways the archetype of his 'collage city'. While he admired seventeenth-century Rome, a 'complete city with the assertive identity of its subdivisions' with its 'collision of palaces, *piazze* and villas', for Rowe 'imperial Rome is, of course, far the more dramatic statement. For, certainly with its more abrupt collisions, more acute disjunctions, its more expansive set pieces, its more radically discriminated matrix and general lack of "sensitive" inhibition, imperial Rome, far more than the city of the High Baroque, illustrates something of the "bricolage" mentality at its most lavish — an obelisk here, a column from there, a range of statues from somewhere else, even at the level of detail the mentality is fully exposed; and, in this context, it is amusing to recollect how the influence of a whole school of historians (Positivists, no doubt!) was, at one time, strenuously dedicated to presenting ancient Romans as inherently nineteenth century engineers, precursors of Gustave Eiffel, who had, somehow, and unfortunately, lost their way.

So Rome, whether imperial or papal, hard or soft, is here offered as some sort of model which might be envisaged as alternative to the disastrous urbanism of social engineering and total design.'[29]

Although not a designer, Rowe was one of the invitees to the 'Roma interrotta' project.[30] His project naturally stayed very close to ideas contained in *Collage City* (1978): a subtle yet complex interweaving of sometimes apocryphal or even entirely fictitious events, memories, ideas and buildings into the historic fabric. Stirling's proposal was rather more dramatic: eventually replanning his whole area by placing in it his own built and unbuilt projects. Combining the monumental with the playful, he altered a vista from a Baroque palace, so that rather than looking towards a statue of Garibaldi, it terminated with a statue of Stirling himself leaning on a column.[31]

For Stirling, the project was both a reflection and a critique of a long tradition of 'megalomaniacal' urban planning: 'Megalomania is the privilege of a chosen few. Piranesi who made his plan in 1762 was surely a megalomaniac frustrated architect (MFA), as also Boullée, Vanbrugh, Soane, Sant'Elia, Le Corbusier, etc., and it is within this distinguished company as an MFA architect that we make our proposal. The megalomaniac architect is most frustrated with regard to projects designed but not built, so the initial decision was to revise Nolli's plan incorporating all our unbuilt works. Soon we were trying to incorporate the entire oeuvre, and in order to sustain a momentum a rigorous method was necessary. Therefore the selection of projects, is limited to those appropriate to aspects of context and association either to the circumstances of 1748, or to JS projects at the time they were designed — sometimes to both. […]

A selection had to be made of existing buildings and places essential to preserve/integrate/intensify, and this, along with contextual, associational, topographical, prototypical, typological, symbolic, iconographical and archaeological considerations, has helped integrate JS projects.

This "contextual - associational" way of planning is somewhat akin to the historic process (albeit timeless) by which the creation of built form is directly influenced by the visual setting and is a confirmation and a complement to that which exists. This process may be similar to that of "Collage City" (and the teaching of Colin Rowe), and the working method of a few architects (e.g.: O. M. Ungers), and stands in comparison to the irrationality of most post-war planning — supposedly "rational", but frequently achieving a reversal of natural priorities.'[32]

As well as acknowledging the project's debts to Rowe, Stirling's mention of Piranesi and his *Campo Marzio dell'Antica Roma* plan of 1762 is also important. While Nolli's plan was largely unprecedented in the accuracy and legibility of its analysis and rendering, Piranesi's roughly contemporary plan was far more speculative in its interpretation of the architectural and archaeological evidence to create an almost imaginary view of what ancient Rome might have looked like. Similarly, Stirling's plan in its wild speculation is deliberately and exaggeratedly subjective, in stark contrast to the claims of objectivity of modernist planning. In many respects it has gone beyond the realistic propositions of *Collage City* to create a city that is literally collaged, with Nolli's plan treated like an image onto which elements from elsewhere have been cut out and set on top. All is rendered flat. In any other city, this would be a wholly preposterous act, a one liner with little meaning, but because, as Stirling notes, Rome has over the years been the subject of so many grand visions — realised and unrealised — he is able to claim connection to a historic lineage, lending even further weight to his critique of the hypocrisy of modernist planning. In his reworked Nolli plan, Stirling is seemingly appropriating Rome for his own ends, but in doing so in such an overtly grandiose and subjective way he exposes — and in many ways parodies — the folly and hubris of trying to overcome a city whose existence is bound up in the interrelation of the physical and imaginary. Rome, Stirling implies, always resists.

For those British architects who have ventured to Rome over the centuries — architects like Jones, Soane, Stirling, and even twenty-first-century travellers like Furman — the city they find appears almost like a dream, simultaneously real and imaginary. Rome is a place where history and the past are manifest, and whose colossal weight rests heavy on all who roam its streets and explore its ruins. Yet because of the sheer size and nature of this burden, which is perpetuated not only through its physical existence but drawings, prints and photography, there is conversely the possibility of liberation, of not being dragged down in its histories, but of traversing them, revelling in them, even subverting them. In bringing together three quite different case studies, this essay has aimed to show that each architect visitor remakes Rome for themselves. Rome is not just a physical entity but, as the example of these three architects illustrate, exists in the mind's eye of all who visit it, affirming its claim to be truly the city of the imagination.

[1] The idea of beginning the essay with this quote from Shakespeare's *The Tempest* (Act 4, scene 1, l. 150–53) is borrowed from Christy Anderson, 'Gorgeous Places and Solemn Temples: Inigo Jones and the New Ideas of Architecture', in Michèle-Caroline Heck, Frédérique Lemerle, Yves Pauwels (eds.), *Théorie des arts et création artistique dans l'Europe du Nord du XVIe au début du XVIIIe siècle*, Villeneuve d'Ascq: Université Charles-de-Gaulle-Lille 3, 2002, p. 155.

[2] Venice is Rome's only rival in this regard.

[3] Frank Salmon notes that there were actually a number of significant neoclassical buildings built after the Palace of Westminster, but they have often been ignored in the historiography. See Frank Salmon, *Building on Ruins: The Rediscovery of Rome and English Architecture*, Aldershot: Ashgate, 2000, p. 20.

[4] Quote from Adan Nathaniel Furman's website for *The Roman Singularity* (http://theromansingularity.blogspot.co.uk/p/about.html).

[5] Ben Johnson's *To Penshurst* (1616) quoted by Christy Anderson, *op. cit.*, p. 157.

[6] *Ibid.*

[7] Christy Anderson, *op. cit.*, p. 164.

[8] Alice T. Friedman, 'Did England Have a Renaissance? Classical and Anticlassical Themes in Elizabethan Culture, in *Studies in the History of Art*, 27, 1989, pp. 96 and 97.

[9] Alice T. Friedman, *op. cit.*, p. 103.

[10] John Gordon, *The Union of Great Britain* (1604), pp. 41–42, quoted by Vaughan Hart, 'Imperial Seat or Ecumenical Temple? On Inigo Jones's Use of "Decorum" at St Paul's Cathedral', in *Architectura*, vol. 25, no. 2, 1995, pp. 194–96.

[11] John Gordon, *England and Scotlands Happiness* (1604), p. 45 quoted by Vaughan Hart, *op. cit.*, p. 200.

[12] For a full account of Jones's journey in Italy, see Giles Worsley, *Inigo Jones and the European Classicist Tradition*, New Haven, CT, and London: Yale University Press for the Paul Mellon Centre for Studies in British Art, 2007, pp. 19–30.

[13] Inigo Jones, *The Most Notable Antiquity of Great Britain: Vulgarly Called Stone-Heng, on Salisbury Plain, Restored,* (1655) quoted by John Newman, 'Inigo Jones and the Politics of Architecture', in Kevin Sharpe and Peter Lake (eds.), *Culture and Politics in Early Stuart England*, Stanford, CA: Stanford University Press, 1994, p. 255.

[14] See Frank Salmon, *op. cit.*, pp. 27–46.

[15] David Watkin (ed.), *Sir John Soane: The Royal Academy Lectures*, Cambridge: Cambridge University Press, 2000, Lecture III, p. 86.

[16] David Watkin, *Sir John Soane: Enlightenment Thought and the Royal Academy Lectures*, Cambridge: Cambridge University Press, 1996, Lecture VIII, p. 603.

[17] See John Soane, *Crude Hints Towards an History of My House in Lincoln's Inn Fields*, unpublished manuscript, London, 1812.

[18] David Watkin, *op. cit.*, 1996, Lecture XII, p. 653.

[19] Arthur T. Bolton, *The Portrait of Sir John Soane (1753–1837), set forth in letters from his friends (1775–1837)*, London: Butler & Tanner, 1927, p. 16.

[20] The quote is from Soane's twelfth lecture quoted by Frank Salmon, *op. cit.*, p. 63.

[21] The drawing was produced by Henry Parke.

[22] While Italy was out of bounds, this did not stop travel entirely. Charles Robert Cockerell, for example, headed to Constantinople, Athens and the Peloponnese, Malta and Sicily before finally reaching Italy in 1814 after Napoleon's abdication. No doubt his extensive, first-hand experience of different places and cultures shaped his distinctively eclectic architectural sensibility.

[23] Frank Salmon, *op. cit.*, p. 74.

[24] See MaryAnne Stevens, Margaret Richardson (eds.), *John Soane Architect: Master of Space and Light*, exhibition catalogue (London, Royal Academy of Arts, 11 September – 3 December 1999), London: Royal Academy of Arts, 1999, p. 160.

[25] Quoted by Frank Salmon, *op. cit.*, p. 26.

[26] Léa-Catherine Szacka, '"Roma Interrotta": Postmodern Rome as the Source of Fragmented Narratives', in Dom Holdaway, Filippo Trentin (eds.), *Rome, Postmodern Narratives of a Cityscape*, London and New York: Routledge, 2016, p. 157.

[27] *Ibid.*, pp. 156–57.

[28] *Ibid.*, pp. 160–61.

[29] Colin Rowe, Fred Koetter, *Collage City*, Cambridge, MA: MIT Press, 1983, pp. 106–107.

[30] The complete list is Costantino Dardi, Romaldo Giurgola, Michael Graves, Antoine Grumbach, Léon Krier, Robert Krier, Paolo Portoghesi, Aldo Rossi, Colin Rowe, Piero Sartogo, James Stirling and Robert Venturi with Denise Scott Brown. Léa-Catherine Szacka, *op. cit.*, p. 155.

[31] Mark Girouard, *Big Jim: The Life and Work of James Stirling*, London: Chatto and Windus, 1998, p. 203.

[32] James Stirling, 'Nolli Sector IV – James Stirling', in *Architectural Design*, vol. 49, no. 3–4, 1979.

François Penz

Cinéroma

Dear Marco,*

A year ago when we discussed this article, it sounded like a very good idea… like most of your ideas. But as time progressed I felt more and more like Jean-Luc Godard, not that I am comparing myself to him, who was commissioned by Freddy Buache to make a film about the city of Lausanne — the film is entitled *Lettre à Freddy Buache* (1982) and tells of the difficulty in making such a film. The transcript of the letter starts as follows — in French as it is difficult to translate — but I know that your French is good enough:

Lettre à Freddy Buache à propos d'un court-métrage
sur la ville de Lausanne

Mon cher Freddy .
Je vais essayer de te . te parler de . de ce court-métrage
sur la . sur la ville de Lausanne .
Sur, toujours sur. Je voudrais essayer de . même pas
de parler de la . là je te parle . pour te guider tu vois .
Je pense qu'ils . qu'ils seront furieux parce qu'ils
diront que c'est . on avait commandé, on a donné
de l'argent pour .
pour un film sur . et ça c'est un film de .
il arrive pas encore à la sur-face .
Il est encore . au fond . au fond des choses . et toi
et moi on .
on est trop vieux et le . et le cinéma va est .
va mourir bientôt, très jeune . sans avoir
donné tout ce qu'il a pu donner alors il faut .
il faut aller vite au fond des choses il y a urgence .

It is written in the form of a poem where the repetition and the punctuation do matter. This short film was a commission by the city of Lausanne to commemorate the 500 years of the birth of the city. Freddy Buache, one of the founder of the Swiss cinémathèque, was instrumental in getting Godard involved. The idea was to create a film that would depart from the traditional promotional city video. Freddy Buache was keen to commission a film that would have pride of place in any cinémathèque — and in effect two films were commissioned, the other one by Yves Yersin, a Lausanne based filmmaker, a longer film. Godard, who is a Swiss citizen, knows Lausanne well — and had recently settled back in the near-by town of Rolle in 1977. So he was keen to make this film. That's the background to this project.

On the face of it the commission was a failure. Godard, who never shies away from controversy, states from the outset, with his own voice-over that 'they will be furious to have given money for a film that hasn't surfaced / materialised'. And indeed the city of Lausanne were unhappy — a case of self-fulfilling prophecy. But in the event the film was shown in Cannes in 1982 — to critical acclaim — and made the front pages of *Le Monde* and *France-Soir* — Lausanne got its money's worth of publicity after all and the controversy subsided. In 1985 Deleuze will also devote a short paragraph to the film in the time-image[1] — it will have made it in the pantheon of film criticism, although the film remains relatively unknown, I very much doubt people would have heard of it. But overall what Godard proposed is an interesting exercise; it is a film about filmmaking or rather a film about non-film making or the difficult of making a film about a city — he even accuses the city of Lausanne of dishonesty for having commissioned such a film — that it would take five light-years to do it justice! Something that was reflected in the choice of music, Ravel's *Boléro* a famously unresolved piece of music!

Godard, the auteur by excellence, is not only the voice in the film but he is also staging himself. He is essentially speculating and interrogating himself — and Freddy Buache — on how best to depict Lausanne. In its form this short film is a good example of what I would call an essay in the mould of Montaigne's literary essays — a way of engaging in a kind of informal, even disorderly speculations — it is a frank, intimate and interior voice — a spontaneous flow of subjective responses, conjectures and opinions around the problem at hand — this is a precious and rare example of a filmic essay about a city.

Now back to the Rome project. I will not accuse you of unfairness — I took on the commission, and so I must proceed. But it is indeed a tall order to write about films about Rome in a book and an exhibition essentially devoted to the Rome photographs in the RIBA collection — quite a responsibility to be the only flag bearer of the illustrious Roman cinematic enterprise; going back to Godard, I feel, at this stage, that I can only fail. Of course, I am aware that there are a great many scholarly books about Rome in films. Indeed, I have acquired some and borrowed others — they are all here on my desk, staring at me, many unopened.

Part of the difficulty is that I am not from Rome, I am not Italian, although my wife, Fabia, is (thank God for that!) but my Italian is not very good as you know, although I pretend to understand it — at least Godard was well acquainted with Lausanne and spoke the language. I feel I start even further back than he did. Of course I am not making a film so it ought to be easier — and after all I have written a fair amount about cities and films — urban cinematics,[2] city symphonies[3] and cinematic urban geographies. But a lot of my city film research treats film as metadata and data mining. For example, for the work we did in Battersea in London,[4] I put forward the idea of a 'cinematic urban archaeology' approach where accumulated layers of moving-image material (fiction, documentaries, and amateur movies) over decades have been deposited over parts of a city and do constitute a form of invisible archaeological layers — and yet always present if only we know where to look. However, the issue is that such a retrospectively 'longitudinal' cinematic studies requires time and a team of researchers — for Battersea we studied close to 700 films over two years. It would be wonderful to undertake such a project in Rome. We briefly discussed this idea, but even in a very restricted form, time was far too short.

The issue of being an outsider to a city is in itself interesting when it comes to filmmaking. Thom Andersen in *Los Angeles Plays Itself* (2003) speculates that 'the directors who did the most to make Los Angeles a character in movies and then a subject were outsiders, like Wilder, or tourists. They weren't interested in what made Los Angeles like a city; they were interested in what made Los Angeles unlike the cities they knew'. He also goes on to note that we can distinguish between two different class of movie tourists 'Just as there are highbrows and lowbrows, there are high tourists and low tourists. Just as there are highbrow directors and lowbrow directors, there are high tourist directors and low tourist directors. Low tourist directors generally disdain Los Angeles. They prefer San Francisco and the coastline of northern California. More picturesque'.

I find this to be a useful distinction and I might start by thinking of myself as a highbrow 'Roman ciné-tourist'. Andersen goes on to say that 'Continental European directors are usually high tourists, so they appreciate Los Angeles, even the tacky stuff we hate, like the Sunset Strip. In *The Outside Man* by Jacques Deray, a Parisian hit man stranded in Los Angeles discovers a city of parking lots, motels, bus stations, coffee shops, strip bars, and real estate opportunities. It's all quite ugly, I suppose, but it adds up to a precise portrait of the city in 1973, just as I remember it'.

In my view one of the best analysis of Roman films is by David Bass[5]. He also does distinguish amongst different categories of tourist filmmakers but is less generous than Andersen towards outsiders. 'Outsiders' films of Rome violently warp the city's topography and present stereotypes of its culture and physical constitution. Such films are intimately tied to the phenomenon of tourism: filming on location is a form of visit, the plot concerns the exploits of outsiders visiting the city, and viewing represents a form of "armchair tourism"'.[6] Bass thoroughly resents outsider filmmakers denying Rome its topography: 'Unwittingly an epicentre for jump-cutting, the Trevi Fountain finds itself in *Roman Holiday* implicitly placed next to the Via Condotti 600 yards away. Such "postcard" movies warp and fold the city, ignoring and destroying swathes of urban context, to create a film-city of "attractions" selected from the real city's obliging scenic reserve. The city of attractions is a lazy tourist's dream: a collection of desirable wonders, visitable without hot slogs through potentially boring, dangerous, "non-places" in between'.[7]

By contrast Bass praises the insiders' films such as *Bicycle Thieves* (Vittorio De Sica, 1948), *Roma ore undici* (Giuseppe De Santis, 1951), *Sciuscià* (Vittorio De Sica, 1946) and *Umberto D* (Vittorio De Sica, 1952) arguing that 'if the film cartolina remakes the city in the service of the film, folding it to maximise the intake of touristic sights, then insiders' films of resistant urban context are made in the service of the existing city, their actions guided and squeezed by its intransigent topography and the character of its areas'.[8]

Bass is right to point out that in the film cartolina genre, parts of Rome remained invisible 'folded away in the interstices of its montage'. But we also have to remember that *Roman Holiday* (William Wyler, 1952) and *Three Coins in the Fountain* (Jean Negulesco, 1955) were hugely successful productions that not only made Rome a global cinematic city but helped the US studios weather the industrial transformations of the postwar era, in particular the advent of television. As Shandley argued, Rome would save Hollywood.

The success of *Roman Holiday* is not only due to Audrey Hepburn and Gregory Peck as marketable stars, but very much because of Rome itself as 'Wyler and Paramount had succeeded in convincing critics that they had created an authentic travelogue film experience, one that was ahead of the trends of the time'.[9]

Shandley further points out that the technical imperatives dictated by the use of the Cinemascope experiment, subordinated all other aspects of *Three Coins in the Fountain's* production and in a fashion not dissimilar to the ways in which the new motion picture medium was deployed in the late nineteenth and early twentieth century in the service of colonialist ethnographic enterprises; the film sets out to capture Rome with its new medium — and in the process showed many of the same locations deployed in *Roman Holiday* — and as the original review in *Newsweek* put it, '*Three Coins in the Fountain* is "pleasant for travelers who'll miss Rome this summer"'. In many instances, Negulesco resorts to making the story secondary to the settings, the Roman background becoming the narrative foreground to exploit the features of the new wide screen format. The Spanish steps, the Colosseum, the Mouth of Truth and many of the Roman tourist spots became the stars; it was a far cry from the Italian neo-realist tradition of the late 1940s and it 'made Rome look like the best place on earth to cut loose for a few days, just a few years after the world took pity on the Romans with their stolen bicycles and handmade shoeshine boxes and pawn shops filled with bed linen and socks'.[10]

Perhaps the film that most struck a chord and occupies the no man's land between the neo-realist visions and the American tourist travelogues, is Fellini's *La dolce vita* (1960). A hugely controversial film at the time, it became most remembered for its night-time Trevi Fountain scene a moment that 'would stand for decades as one of the most erotic scenes ever presented in the cinema — a reverie, a dream come to life, a true coupling of object and subject, divine and mortal, masculine and feminine, fantasy and reality. Ekberg, undulant and ample and alluring, and Mastroianni, bladelike and dashing [...] it carried echoes of a work of art that stood not a mile away: Michelangelo's *Creation of Adam* on the ceiling of the Sistine Chapel, another immortal depiction of the divine and the human almost but not quite touching'.[11] So influential was *La dolce vita* that it caught the global collective imagination as far as Tokyo with Nigel Coates's Caffè Bongo (1986), which was based on a reading on Fellini's vision — its overtly layered composition intended to express Japan's new ability to connect with faraway places.[12]

Having myself been to Rome three times for short visits, I am well acquainted with the familiar tourists spots and can start to connect with the city through personal experience, although this differs from the idea of cinema spectatorship as a travel experience, as reported in the case of *Roman Holiday* and *Three Coins in the Fountain* for an American audience in the 1950s. We have to recognise that as 'tourists spectators' experiencing a foreign location from the comfort of our cinema's armchair, we are experiencing second hand the original locations and actions. Although the immersive experience of film may give us the illusion of being in its diegetic space, we experience what Barthes calls the 'two bodies' effect 'I must be in the story (there must be verisimilitude), but I must also be elsewhere: a slightly disengaged image-repertoire, that is what I must have [...]'[13]

However, in my view, this disembodied experience may vary greatly with the experience of familiar locations, as remarked by Corbin: '[...] watching your own neighbourhood on-screen would simulate tourism, even though your individual experience of that film might have more perceptual and emotional layers than the experience of watching a film set in a foreign locale'. Christie concurs and states that 'As a resident of the area portrayed in the film, however, I have a more intimate and affective relationship with what it portrays. These are streets and locations that I know well, and walk and cycle through almost daily. My relationship is not that of a British viewer of *My Darling Clementine*, or of any film set in a place I have never visited, but that of a native, or at least resident'.[14]

A personal connection to the locality is key to our film's perception and this is why Bass is so enraged by the obliteration of 300 meters of city separating two places across a cut in *Three Coins in the Fountain*, something that I would be hard pushed to notice even if I tried. Even such relatively minor topographical edits can become a huge distraction to a local spectator — opening a wide affective and perceptual gap between the insider spectator and the outsider one. I have experienced a related phenomenon recently while visiting Japan. I have a good knowledge of Japanese cinema that gave me an instant connection to the country — what could be described as a sense of *déja vu* — it gave me a sense of familiarity with some sights of Tokyo — same for some domestic interiors. I remembered the same feeling while visiting New York for the first time, the films of Woody Allen and Scorsese were a good preparation.

But while recently visiting Japan, we stayed in a *ryokan*, a traditional Japanese inn, featuring tatami-matted rooms and communal baths where visitors are invited to wear kimonos. This sounded like a good idea since I am currently engaged in a research project aiming to generate a novel understanding of deeply rooted societal differences in the usage of architecture, experience of space and everyday activities through a comparative study of Western cinema with Chinese and Japanese films.[15] However, my Western body was totally unprepared for the level of discomfort offered by the tatami-mats — and four nights sleeping in the *ryokan* made me more aware, in my own body, through aches and pains, of the deep cultural differences. Furthermore, I have started re-watching Japanese films with a fresh eye, feeling a strong connection with the interiors of Ozu's films in particular, cringing and admiring in equal measure when the characters go peacefully to sleep. Similarly I feel a much closer relationship with city

location shots, although I couldn't claim noticing any topographical jumps — I have gained a direct experience and acquaintance with street furniture, pavements, street signs, cars, trains and metro stations. I have bodily experienced such spaces and places — in effect I have built a set of personal memories that gets re-activated when I now see a Japanese film. It is a particularly strong feeling — of course because it is recent — but also because the culture is so different, it made a strong impression and impact.

This is of course not so strange — and recent research has shown that the hippocampus is associated both with mental map making of the external environment and with storing new memories.[16] People with damage to the hippocampus, such as amnesia patients, lack the ability to form new memories. We are equipped with a 'GPS brain mechanisms' that links spatial experiences with memories. And there cannot be any forms of memory recall if no first-hand spatial experience is associated with a place in the first instance. I can only speculate at this stage that my own experience with Japan is linked to this mechanism as I have not found any research extending the so-called GPS brain theory to films. To summarise I am proposing that watching a city film can be a three-way process: we see a film and gain a knowledge of a city; we then visit this city and experience a form of *déja vu*; we then watch the film again and the experience of having seen the place acts as a memory recall that gives a much stronger emotional connection to both the film and the city.

As mentioned before, my association with Rome is tenuous, so I only have a weak affective connection to the city — and although I may think of myself as a highbrow 'Roman ciné-tourist' I am still in the position of an outsider. However, I have a strong emotional link to the Vespa as I have owned one for fifteen years and ride it very regularly. The Vespa gives me a personal involvement to a film such as *Dear Diary* and many others, it acts as a memory trigger and is the right vehicle for me to navigate Rome in the movies, no pun intended. Sadly the Vespa film is not a genre commonly discussed, although it could be argued that it is related to the road movie, a perfectly respectable genre that involves characters going on a road trip, usually far away from home — more often than not crossing the USA — although *Il sorpasso* (Dino Risi, 1962), partly set in Rome, could just about be counted as one of them.

And yet there are hundreds of Vespa films — as recounted in the exhibition catalogue of *The Vespa and the Movies* exhibition, staged at the Piaggio Museum in Pontedera in 2010, proudly acknowledging 'the long list of international movie stars seen on the world's most famous scooter over the years, in films ranging from *Quadrophenia* to *Absolute Beginners*, *American Graffiti*, *The Talented Mr. Ripley*, *102 Dalmatians* and the blockbuster *Transformers*. In the photos, in the films and on the sets, the Vespa was the "travelling companion" of stars like Raquel Welch, Ursula Andress, Geraldine Chaplin, Joan Collins, Jayne Mansfield, Virna Lisi, Milla Jovovich, Marcello Mastroianni, Charlton Heston, John Wayne, Henry Fonda, Gary Cooper, Anthony Perkins, Jean-Paul Belmondo, Nanni Moretti, Sting, Antonio Banderas, Matt Damon, Gérard Depardieu, Jude Law, Eddie Murphy, Owen Wilson, Nicole Kidman and many others'.[17]

Interestingly the Vespa, created in 1946, first appears in the 1950 film *Sunday in August – Domenica d'agosto* (Luciano Emmer), a movie that creatively weaves together the story of Romans escaping the city on a hot Sunday afternoon towards the beaches of Ostia. Eight minutes into the film, a group of Vespas is seen overtaking cyclists, all racing towards the beaches, a scene that speaks of freedom and anticipation, the heat almost palpable, like a small and noisy army, the Vespas lead the charge with their characteristic sound being the 'fanfare for Italy, which through hard work is recapturing her right to live'.[18] Piaggio had introduced the Vespa as a utility vehicle for a recovering Italian post-war society and it was as unprepared as anyone for the immense success of its vehicle.

Roman Holiday played its part in this success: 'It featured gelato and wine and an open-air market and streets crowded with picturesque faces and the most glorious Vespa ride through and around it all, still an iconic image of freewheeling liberty and swank style decades later'.[19] The Vespa scenes played by Gregory Peck and Audrey Hepburn turned into unforgettable icons, contributing to the success of Wyler's romantic comedy. The 1952 Vespa 125 used in the film — also known as 'Farobasso' because its headlight is placed on the front fender — became a fantastic advertisement for Piaggio and is said to have been worth 100,000 sales […] clearly audiences had been inspired to do the same.[20]

Vespa scenes abound in Roman films and Jude Law in *The Talented Mr. Ripley* (Anthony Minghella, 1999) is often quoted — but further in the film a more intriguing scene sees Matt Damon and Gwyneth Paltrow on an olive-green scooter circling the cobbled streets of Rome — a closer inspection reveals that they are riding a 1951 Lambretta with a broken headlamp hanging from the handlebar. Those are the sort of details that attract my attention — real anorak stuff! But one of the most touching Roman Vespa scene is in Gianni Di Gregorio's *Mid-August Lunch* (2008), when Di Gregorio and Viking, his white-haired friend, run through the empty winding alleys of Trastevere during Ferragosto, heading for the Tiber in search of fish. An everyday tale of a middle-age man having to entertain his 93-year-old mother and three other elderly ladies during Italy's biggest summer holiday, Ferragosto. Di Gregorio 'escapes' on the Vespa for a few moments, only to return later to provide the lunch. It is utterly whimsical, nothing much happens, and the disruption of the Vespa scene makes the ordinary all the more palpable.

But the king of the Roman Ferragosto Vespa tale is the majestuous *Dear Diary*. Bass describes the film in the following term: 'Nanni Moretti's *Dear Diary* (1993) features the director marking Rome's boundaries, visiting the commonly disdained garden suburbs and modern megastructures that encircle the city. As he wanders around on his Vespa, a motoflâneur of the suburbs, his curiosity and enthusiasm for the ordinary uncover things to stimulate the imagination in the outskirts. Underneath Moretti's whimsical enthusings, there is still a darker side to the periphery. At the end of his *vagabondaggi*, Moretti makes a pilgrimage to the seaside location where Pasolini was murdered by the kind of boys from the *borgate* about whom he made his first films.'[21]

The joy of Moretti, the *motoflâneur,* is communicative and watching the film I found it difficult not to fully identify with his character. Moretti expresses this sense of freedom as follows: '*Dear Diary* with a great feeling of freedom, pleased with myself, wanting to do it my way. In the first episode, drifting through the streets on a Vespa in a deserted Rome, followed only by a jeep on which there were the camera operator and director of photography. It was a joy. I felt as free as when I made my first short films. Even the style is affected; something new here is that the camera moves continuously […]

there are changes where I used to prefer static shots and a certain type of internal montage.[22]

In the film he speculates to make a movie only made of buildings: 'La cosa che mi piace più di tutte è vedere le case, vedere i quartieri. E il quartiere che mi piace più di tutti è la Garbatella. E me ne vado in giro per i lotti popolari. Anche quando vado nelle altre città l'unica cosa che mi piace fare è guardare le case. Bello sarebbe un film fatto solo di case: panoramiche su case. Garbatella 1927, Villaggio Olimpico 1960, Tufello 1960, Vigne Nuove 1987, Monteverde 1939'.

I always found this statement very touching — it is as if *Dear Diary* is the realisation of Benjamin's dream but for Rome: 'Couldn't an exciting film be made from the map of Paris? From the unfolding of its various aspects in temporal succession? From the compression of a centuries-long movement of streets, boulevards, arcades, and squares into the space of half an hour? And does the *flâneur* do anything different?'.[23]

… what else would we want and need? Pure film and pure architecture in movement. And so, dear Marco, I started from Lausanne and ended up in Rome, it simply proves that indeed all roads lead to Rome.

Cordialmente,
François

* Marco Iuliano

[1] Gilles Deleuze, *Cinema 2: The Time Image*, London: Athlone, 1989, p. 187.
[2] François Penz, Andong Lu (eds.), *Urban Cinematics: Understanding Urban Phenomena Through the Moving Image*, Bristol and Chicago: Intellect, 2012.
[3] Stavros Alifragkis, François Penz, 'Dziga Vertov's Man with a Movie Camera: Thoughts on the Computation of Style and Narrative Structure', in *Architecture and Culture* 3, no. 1, March 1, 2015, pp. 33–55.
[4] François Penz, Aileen Reid, Maureen Thomas, 'Cinematic Urban Archaeology: The Battersea Case', in François Penz and Richard Koeck (eds.), *Cinematic Urban Geographies*, New York: Palgrave Macmillan, 2017.
[5] David Bass, 'Insiders and Outsiders – Latent Urban Thinking in Movies of Modern Rome', in François Penz, Maureen Thomas (eds.), *Cinema & Architecture: Méliès, Mallet-Stevens, Multimedia*, London: British Film Institute, 1997, pp. 84–99.
[6] *Ibid.*, p. 85.
[7] *Ibid.*, p. 86.
[8] *Ibid.,* p. 88.
[9] Robert R. Shandley, *Runaway Romances: Hollywood's Postwar Tour of Europe / Robert R. Shandley*, Philadelphia, PA: Temple University Press, 2009, p. 45.
[10] Shawn Levy, *Dolce Vita Confidential: Fellini, Loren, Pucci, Paparazzi and the Swinging High Life of 1950s Rome*, London: Weidenfeld & Nicolson, 2016, p. 113.
[11] *Ibid.*, pp. 299–300.
[12] Nigel Coates, *Narrative Architecture*, Chichester, West Sussex, and Hoboken, NJ: John Wiley & Sons, 2012, p. 113.
[13] Roland Barthes, *The Rustle of Language / Roland Barthes*, translated by Richard Howard, Berkeley, CA: California University Press, 1989, p. 347.
[14] Ian Christie, '"Merely Local": Film and the Depiction of Place, Especially in Local Documentary', in François Penz, Richard Koeck (eds.), *op. cit.*, p. 86.
[15] See www.cinemusespace.arct.cam.ac.uk.
[16] See http://brainworldmagazine.com/meet-brains - gps-hippocampus/.
[17] See www.piaggiogroup.com/en/archive/press/piaggio-opening-vespa-and-movies-exhibition.
[18] Carsten Nielsen, 'La "Vespa" nell'opinione estera', in *Piaggio*, no. 2, 1949, p. 6.
[19] Shawn Levy, *op. cit.*, p. 113.
[20] See www.bbc.com / culture/story / 20131122-the - vespa - motoring-with-style.
[21] David Bass, *op. cit.*, p. 91.
[22] Eleanor Andrews, *Place, Setting, Perspective: Narrative Space in the Films of Nanni Moretti*, Vancouver: Fairleigh Dickinson University Press, 2014, p. 22.
[23] Walter Benjamin, *The Arcades Project.*, trans. Howard Eiland and Kevin McLaughlin, Cambridge, MA: The Belknapp Press of Harvard University Press, 1999, p. 83.

Filmography
My Darling Clementine, John Ford, 1946
Sciuscià, Vittorio De Sica, 1946
Ladri di biciclette, Vittorio De Sica, 1948
Domenica d'agosto, Luciano Emmer, 1950
Roma ore undici, Giuseppe De Santis, 1951
Umberto D, Vittorio De Sica, 1952
Roman Holiday, William Wyler, 1953
Three Coins in the Fountain, Jean Negulesco, 1955
La dolce vita, Federico Fellini, 1960
Il sorpasso, Dino Risi, 1962
Lettre à Freddy Buache, Jean-Luc Godard, 1982
Caro diario, Nanni Moretti, 1993
The Talented Mr Ripley, Antony Minghella, 1999
Los Angeles Plays Itself, Thom Andersen, 2003
Pranzo di Ferragosto, Gianni Di Gregorio, 2008

*Valeria Carullo**

The Robert Elwall Photographs Collection at the Royal Institute of British Architects

In August 1835, after several experiments, the pioneer of British photography William Henry Fox Talbot succeeded in capturing the first image on paper ever produced by means of a camera obscura. It showed a window of his home at Lacock Abbey in Wiltshire. The subject of the first photograph obtained with the negative/positive technique, which was to supplant the daguerreotype invented in France, was therefore architectural.[1] The previous summer had seen the founding in London of the Institute of British Architects, which then became the Royal Institute of British Architects (RIBA) in 1837. Born as a professional body to set and ensure professional and ethical standards amongst architects, the institute was also intended as a cultural association from the very outset. One of its primary aims was therefore the creation of a library for its members, to which end it urged from the start to donate architectural items such as books, manuscripts, prints and drawings.[2] In the meantime, photography began to establish itself as one of paramount media of architectural representation by virtue of its precision and speed of execution by comparison with drawing and engraving. Architects were quick to realise its advantages and began as early as the second half of the nineteenth century to have their own works photographed and to collect photographs of historical buildings and archaeological sites. The RIBA thus began to build up a collection of photographs not only from British professionals but also from visiting foreign architects, especially Honorary and Corresponding Members. The growth of the library and collections was such that the institute was obliged to move twice in fairly quick succession, first in 1845 and then in 1859. (Non-members were also permitted to use the library as from 1854.) Evidence of the constant growth of the photographic collection is provided by the creation in 1883 of a special section of

the Library Management Committee to decide on the best method of classifying the items and having them bound in volumes. A key moment in the history of the collections came in 1930 with the appointment as chief librarian of Edward J. 'Bobby' Carter (1902–1982), known as Bobby, who initiated the reorganisation and modernisation of the library. The lack of adequate space for the collections was one of the reasons for the decision taken by the RIBA the same year to move from the premises on Conduit Street (an eighteenth-century building renovated in the mid-nineteenth) to a new home specifically designed for the purpose. The winner of the competition held in 1931 was George Grey Wornum (1888–1957), whose building on Portland Place is still the main headquarters of the RIBA.

Its inauguration in 1934, which marked the centenary of the founding of the institute, was celebrated with a major exhibition entitled *International Architecture 1924–1934*, which enjoyed great success with the public and went on to tour other cities. While also including drawings and models, it consisted primarily of photographs and was followed during the 1930s by other shows of similar format. These formed the basis of an extensive collection of images of modern architecture,[3] further expanded with photographs donated by British and foreign architects during the decade by request of a special committee set up in 1935.

The library remained open during World War II but some of its most valuable items were temporarily entrusted to the National Library of Wales in Aberystwyth. While the appointment of the first curator of drawings shortly after the war in 1954 indicates the importance attached to this medium, it was not until the 1980s that photographs were accorded similar acknowledgement. After years of relative indifference on the part of the RIBA towards this area of its collections, which was essentially regarded as possessing only documentary value, the way was paved for a radical change in course by the appointment of Robert Elwall (1953–2012) as the first curator of the Photographs Collection in 1981. Having read history at Oxford and gone on to specialise as a librarian, Elwall was keenly aware not only of the importance of the photographic material held by the RIBA but also of the leading role played by photography from the very outset in the dissemination of ideas and promotion of knowledge. Elwall embarked on the reorganisation of the existing collection and endeavoured at the same time to acquire the archives of major British photographers of architecture who had ceased their activities. Further major additions to the collection came about through the acquisition by the RIBA of entire archives of architects. By the end of the 1990s, the collection had increased considerably both in size and in reputation but still lacked adequate premises for its protection and preservation. Elwall succeeded in persuading the institute, which was engaged at the time in transferring the Drawings & Archives Collection to new premises,[4] to invest also in an air-conditioned store for the Photographs Collection in Portland Place, which was completed in 2002. Two years later, Elwall launched a project for the digitisation of the library as an integral part of his commitment to making the collections available to the widest possible audience. He worked tirelessly in the following years to this end and to promote the study and appreciation of architectural photography. His extraordinary contribution includes exhibitions organised with his team at the RIBA and in other venues, presentations and conferences in the United Kingdom and other countries, and an incredible number of publications that demonstrate the depth and breadth of his knowledge. Among these, *Building with Light: The International History of Architectural Photography* is internationally regarded as one of the key books on the relationship between photography and architecture. His contribution to the discipline and to the RIBA was acknowledged in 2012, when the collection was named after him.

The Robert Elwall Photographs Collection is today one of the world's most extensive and comprehensive of its kind, with over 1.6 million architectural images. Nor is the collection confined the British professional world alone, as approximately one third of the material is international in character. The photographs include not only buildings but also associated spheres like urban and rural landscape, gardens, design and social history as well as portraits of architects, artists and known figures. Every type of photographic format is represented in the collection, from negatives, prints and albums to photomechanical reproductions, slides and digital images. While the earliest item, a salt paper print of the Bodleian Library in Oxford (William Henry Fox Talbot, 1843), dates from the dawn of photography, the most recent are digital prints by contemporary photographers. The collection can be divided into a number of main areas, which overlap in some cases:

- Nineteenth-century holdings
- Photographers' archives
- Photographic archives of architects
- The archive of the *Architectural Press*
- Albums
- Portraits
- Inter-War Collection
- RIBA Press Office Collection
- CEMA Collection
- Small collections and individual photographs

As stated above, the collection of nineteenth-century items commenced in the third decade after the birth of the RIBA, when photography began to be recognised by architects as one of the most effective forms of representation for their own work and for the historical buildings that constituted a great source of inspiration for the eclecticism in vogue at the time. The medium also made it possible to document the urban areas undergoing transformation, especially in connection with the slum-clearance schemes that characterised the major European cities in the second half of the nineteenth century. Finally, in addition to serving as an aid in surveying and restoration, it also provided material for the growing souvenir market for tourists and travellers, above all in the countries historically included in the Grand Tour. As we have seen, donations of photographs to the RIBA came not only from British but also from foreign architects like the Frenchmen Rohault de Fleury, Mathieu Prosper Morey and Antoine-Nicolas Louis Bailly, Honorary and Corresponding Members of the RIBA, the German Leo von Klenze and the American Richard Morris Hunt, both winners of the RIBA Gold Medal, respectively in 1852 and 1893.[5] The nineteenth-century architecture of the United States is well represented in the collection thanks in part to contributions from British winners of the RIBA Godwin Bursary, a grant for study in Europe or America, and in part to donations from visiting American architects like William Ware, a founding member of the American Institute of Architects (AIA). The highly interesting material presented by Ware to make the most important contemporary works of his country known to his British colleagues include a remarkable group of rare photographs of Central Park in New York taken during its construction around 1860. Great interest also attaches to the views of the building of the new Louvre in Paris taken by the great French photographer Édouard Baldus and donated to the RIBA by Frederick Richard Wilson in 1857, a year after being awarded its RIBA Silver Medal.[6] The nineteenth-century holdings were also greatly expanded from the 1980s through the purchases made by Robert Elwall during his first decade as curator[7] as well as the acquisition of the archives of architects like Herbert Baker — who designed the Bank of England in London (1925–1939) and New Delhi (1911–1931) together with Edwin Lutyens — Geoge Devey and others, all collectors of nineteenth-century photographs. Major recent acquisitions include the collection's first nineteenth-century negative, a calotype of the Taj Mahal by the Scot John Murray, three salt prints of Egyptian monuments photographed around 1850 by the Frenchman Maxime du Camp during his travels in Egypt and the Middle East with Gustave Flaubert, and the above-mentioned view of the Tower of the Five Orders of the Bodleian Library, Oxford, taken by William Henry Fox Talbot around 1843.

In addition to Great Britain, the United States, France and Europe in general, the countries represented in this vast area of the collection also include some that were British colonies in the nineteenth century, like Canada, Australia and above all India, and some with a rich archaeological heritage, like Egypt. The country most extensively documented, however, is probably Italy, seen by British architects both as a fundamental source of inspiration for their works with its classical and Renaissance architecture, and as a romantic and picturesque place to visit. The authors of the numerous images include Italian photographers like the Alinari brothers and Carlo Naya as well as non-Italians like Giorgio Sommer and James Anderson. During the nineteenth century, Italy exerted a particular attraction for photographers, many of whom moved there from other countries and contributed to the formation of an international community characterised by exchanges of both technical and artistic ideas. Italian photographers benefitted in particular during the 1840s from the presence of foreign colleagues, from which they learned the new techniques of the daguerreotype and calotype.

There are, however, few photographs in the collection of nineteenth-century Italian architecture. An exception is the material donated to the RIBA in 1867 and 1869 by two Italian architects, Luigi Poletti and Giuseppe Poggi, which was later placed in an album including some of the major donations received in the 1850s, 60s and 70s. There are over five hundred albums in the collection, which include not only numerous collections of nineteenth-century photographs but also images of twentieth-century architecture. In addition to containing souvenir shots of buildings visited during journeys, the album served in fact as a portfolio for photographers and architects alike to present their work to potential clients and colleagues. The interest in some cases lies not only in the quality of the material included in the album but also in the annotations made by its owner. To give just a few examples, the countless gems in this area of the collection include an album of large-sized prints of the Hagia Sophia take in the late nineteenth and early twentieth century; a series of extraordinary views of the Century of Progress Exposition in Chicago (1933–34); a complete series of rare photos of the renowned Art Déco interiors of the French liner *Normandie*; and an album of platinum prints of Leighton House, London (1866–1879), with the wonderful Moorish interiors created for its owner, the Victorian artist Lord Leighton. Considerable documentary value attaches to albums like the one compiled by the architects John and Kenneth Brown (father and son), who travelled through the Netherlands, Germany and other European countries in the mid-1930s to examine their recent works of modern architecture. Though lacking the quality of the work of professional photographers, these small contact prints not only provide information of a documentary nature but also insight into the two architects' interests and sources of inspirations.

This type of in-depth study is made even easier by the possession of the entire photographic archives of an architect or architectural firm, which generally include both material regarding their works and material used for study and creative inspiration. Fascinating discoveries are often made in the latter field, making it possible to reconstruct otherwise undocumented sources. Obviously enough, the photographic archives donates to the RIBA over the years are mainly those of British architects. Unlike archives of drawings, however, they often include material of an international character, as it has always been comparatively easy for the architects to obtain photographs from other countries and sometimes to exchange shots with foreign colleagues. After those of Herbert Baker and George Devey mentioned above, two of the major archives of the first half of the twentieth century are of particular importance for the light they shed on the enormous contribution made by central European architects to British architecture in the two post-war periods. We refer to the archives of the Hungarian Ernö Goldfinger (1902–1987) and the Russian Berthold Lubetkin (1901–1990), who both moved to London in the 1930s after spending the previous decade in Paris. In that period Great Britain became a refuge for architects and artists opposed to or fleeing from the totalitarian regimes of their own countries. Some of them, including Goldfinger and Lubetkin, remained there also during and after World War II, consolidating their careers and exerting a considerable influence on British modern architecture. Others, like Walter Gropius and Marcel Breuer, spent only a few years there before moving definitively to the United States, which appeared to offer greater opportunities. The years spent in the United Kingdom did, however, involve work with some of the most interesting British architects.[8] Gropius collaborated with Edwin Maxwell Fry (1899–1987), who later worked on Chandigarh with Le Corbusier together with his wife and fellow architect Jane Drew (1911–1996). Breuer formed a partnership with F. R. S. Yorke (1906–1962), an active champion of the Modern Movement in Britain (also as a writer) and founder of the renowned Yorke Rosenberg Mardall firm with the Slovakian Eugene Rosenberg (1907–1990) and the Finn Cyril Mardall (1909–1994) after World War II. The entire archives of Maxwell Fry and Jane Drew was entrusted to the RIBA and the works of Yorke, of Rosenberg and of the partnership are well represented in the photographic collection. The major archives of the second half of the twentieth century include in particular those of Powell & Moya and Ahrends Burton &

Koralek, both of which developed important projects in the fields of culture and education, of Denys Lasdun (1884–1963), whose best-known building is perhaps the iconic National Theatre in London, and of Leslie Martin (1908–2000), architect, educator and one of the most influential figures in post-war British architecture.

Some of the most important photographic archives in the collection are of figures who worked in the field but not as professional architects. One is Monica Pidgeon (1913–2009), editor of the journal *Architectural Design* for over thirty years and a talented photographer. Another is Hubert de Cronin Hastings (1902–1986), owner and (periodically) editor in chief of the monthly *Architectural Review* and the weekly *Architects' Journal*. Hastings and his wife Hazel (1902–?) were both keen photographers and the collection includes a considerable number of pictures taken by them in Europe under the pseudonyms of Ivor and Ivy de Wolfe. Moreover, the *Architectural Review* underwent major transformation under Hastings in terms of graphic design and content during the 1930s. In becoming the standard bearer of modern architecture, it adopted photography as its primary means for the communication of the new ideas and gave it pride of place in terms of layout.

It was precisely the *Architectural Review*, together with its sister publication the *Architects' Journal*, that provided the RIBA with what is by far the largest photographic archive in the collection, namely the Architectural Press Archive (from the name of the publisher). Acquired from the present publisher Emap in 2004, it comprises over 500,000 images dated from the period from the late 1920s to the early 1980s. International in its scope, it is still being catalogued but is already amply represented in the RIBA image database, a subject to be discussed below. Its value for research in the fields of architecture and photography is enormous not only for the quantity and variety of the material included but also for the wealth of annotations made on the backs of the photos by photographers, architects, editors and printers. Divided in accordance with various criteria, mostly by building type, it also includes independent sections like *Pre-War* (architecture between the two world wars), *AP Books* (the Architectural Press also published books as well as the periodicals), one on architects and *Manplan*, the name of the survey of British architecture and town planning carried out by the *Architectural Review* over 1969 and 1970. Characterised by its polemical spirit, this dispassionate, critical examination of the successes and failures of the post-war urban transformations was illustrated not by the customary professionals but by the leading photojournalists and street photographers of the time. One of these was Tony Ray-Jones (1941–1972), one of the great talents of his generation, who took the photos for the issue on housing shortly before his premature death at the age of 31. Another section of the Architectural Press Archive that deserves particular mention is the collection of glass plate negatives covering the work of Dell & Wainwright, official photographers of the *Architectural Review* from 1930 to 1946. Deeply influenced by the New Photography school, Mark Oliver Dell and Herbert Lionel Wainwright created a characteristic style of their own, perfectly suited to the representation of the modernism, which was ultimately to transform the British architectural photography.

While the RIBA collection holds most of the architectural photographs of Dell & Waiwright through the Architectural Press Archive, it does not possess their complete archives. It has succeeded, however, over the years, above all through the efforts of Robert Elwall, in securing the archives of the leading British professional photographers of the twentieth century, including John Maltby (1910–1980), founder of one of the most long-lived firms, Henk Snoek (1915–1980), Colin Westwood (1920–2004), John McCann (b. 1926) and John Donat (1933–2004). Among other things, Donat had the merit of contributing to an important phase in the history of British architectural photography during the 1970s through the introduction of an approach strongly influenced by photojournalism and documentary photography. The archive of Edwin Smith (1912–1971), one of the greatest British photographers of the twentieth century in the field of the built environment and the landscape, was bequeathed to the RIBA in 2002 by his widow, the writer Olive Cook. Particularly interested in historical architecture and extraordinarily gifted in conveying the sense of place, Smith was known above all for his work in the UK but also worked frequently in other European nations and especially Italy, a country he found especially fascinating. More recently, the RIBA has also acquired the extensive archives of Martin Charles (1940–2012), active for several decades in the field of architectural photography. All of the above reflects an important image of the profession in the UK during the twentieth century in addition to providing invaluable documentation both of the buildings and of the changes in the urban fabric and landscape of the nation.

The above-mentioned Inter-War Collection is instead broadly international in character, comprising a series of rare, large-sized photographs that document the various architectural movements of the period, from Art Déco to the International Style. Encouraged by the success of the exhibition *International Architecture 1924–1934*, held in 1934 to inaugurate its new headquarters, the RIBA went on to organise others of a primarily photographic nature during the decade. In order to build up a large stock of images of contemporary architecture as a source of material for these exhibitions, it set up a special committee to urge British and foreign architects to donate photographs of their work, even indicating the desired measurements. While the exceptional and extensive collection built up as a result of this initiative comprises a great variety of subjects, it becomes more interesting still if we consider the inclusions and exclusions, which obviously depended on the support of the committee members for the different architectural movements of the period. This collection is again organised by type rather than, for example, geographical areas (these include not only Europe, North America and the Commonwealth but also countries like Israel, Japan and the Soviet Union).

Also based on items for public display is the CEMA Collection, which consists of about 900 photographs of standard format mounted on pasteboard. It was created by the RIBA in 1944 with funding from the Centre for the Encouragement of Music and the Arts (CEMA)[9] to supply visual material for hire and use in the frequent debates of the period on contemporary architecture. While the CEMA Collection, covering the years up to 1959, does not therefore present the same variety or ambition as the Inter-War Collection, it does offer fascinating insight into a key moment in the development of modern architecture in Great Britain. Again created by the institute, the RIBA Press Office Collection comprises the photographic material used by the press office from around 1950 to 1975. Like the others already mentioned, this is again organised by type within two sections, national and international architecture, which are in turn divided into modern and historical works. As might be expected, the Press Office Collection presents a great variety of content and is based on photographs that all possessed great topical relevance at a certain moment in the period covered. Finally, the Photographs Collection also includes a vast series of portraits of architects, again international in character, and other small collections of various origins as well as a huge number of individual photographs or small groups of photos received as donations or purchased, including the growing collection of prints by contemporary photographers like Richard Bryant, Hélène Binet and Paolo Rosselli.

The RIBA Collection thus includes the works of great photographers and great architects as well as buildings that have altered the course of the history of architecture. Equal importance attaches, however, to all the other photographs of the built environment and the landscape, the ones that recount the context, the development of the architectural culture and ideas. One of the delights that the RIBA Collection has to offer is precisely the occasional discovery of previously unknown architectural work, underestimated photographers and extraordinary images. Not to mention the endless stimuli for research and countless ways of relating past, present and future. How are we to expand and develop such a collection? Many things have changed since the advent of the digital era and must unquestionably be taken into account. For curators, one of the priorities is to safeguard the physical material and the other to keep constantly up-to-date on the methods of storing digital files. In both cases, the aim is to make the RIBA Collection accessible to contemporary users and preserve it for the future generations. Access to the RIBA library and its collections is free of charge and open to all. Visitors include students, architects, historians of architecture, restorers and media professionals but also ordinary citizens interested, for example, in discovering the history of the building, the neighbourhood or the town in which they live. Moreover, access to a constantly growing proportion of the collections is ensured all over the world by the online image database RIBApix.[10] Protection, digitisation and access are therefore indispensable activities for the extraordinary resource that is the RIBA Photographs Collection, as they should be ideally for all the collections and archives based on the precious but fragile support of photography.

* Curator, the Robert Elwall Photographs Collection, RIBA British Architectural Library

[1] As is known, the daguerreotype and the Fox Talbot calotype were invented within a few months of one another in 1839.

[2] The first donation, of money, was made by Charles Barry, the architect of the Houses of Parliament.

[3] The splendid Inter-War Collection, as it is now known, comprises over 3,000 images and is one of gems of the Photographs Collection.

[4] The Drawings & Archives Collection, housed in Portman Square as from 1971, was moved to new premises and offices inside the Victoria & Albert Museum in 2004.

[5] The RIBA Gold Medal has been awarded by the RIBA, with royal approval, to an architect, architectural firm or other figure since 1848 in recognition of the contribution made to architecture during their entire career.

[6] The Royal Silver Medal has been awarded every year since 1836 for the best student design project.

[7] Including in particular the collection of photographs of French and German medieval architecture built up by the Architectural Photographic Association (founded in 1857), which played a crucial part in making architects aware of the usefulness of the new medium but proved very short-lived, as it ceased to exist in 1868.

[8] Foreign architects could only practice their profession at the time in partnership with British colleagues.

[9] The Centre for the Encouragement of Music and the Arts was the precursor of the present-day Arts Council, a government agency for the promotion and funding of the visual arts, the performing arts and literature.

[10] www.ribapix.com.

Catalogue

The following photographs of Rome,
selected from the thousands held by
the Royal Institute of British Architects,
are divided into five complementary sections:
Antiquity, Modernity, Simultaneity, Urban
Landscapes and Atmospheres. Each is introduced
by a text that is to be understood as a possible
interpretation of the choices made. Obviously,
in many cases that certain images could be
placed in more than one section. The selection
of the photographs and their arrangement
in sequences suggested by visual analogies
are intended to stimulate appraisal through
the construction of a timeless narrative.

Roman antiquities may be one of the most popular subjects of all time. In drawings from life and reproductions, they are models to be studied even when contemporary images and icons tend to be produced elsewhere, in New York, London, Beijing or Dubai. In such a shift of those places that iconise reality, photographs of the ancient remains of Rome — such as those of Pompeii or Leptis Magna — are intrinsically part of our contemporary images, part of the contemporary world. They certify our lifestyle, the quality of the places we frequent and in which life is lived. They are the representation of various emotions of the beautiful, sometimes of the sublime, and have been since ancient times. And this is probably why, among the genres whereby photography most often returns to the previous iconographic tradition, Roman antiquity is one of the most stable, from the choice of viewpoints to the inevitable sets of images, which have formed collections of photographs since the second half of the nineteenth century. An example is provided by James Anderson, who moved from England to Rome in the late 1830s. Having started out as a painter of watercolours, he opened one of the leading photographic studios in the city, which became his permanent home.[1]

It is therefore not only artistic photographs but also collections, like those of Anderson, Alinari, Brogi and Sommer, that created the shared idea, the common way of seeing Rome, the expectations of those setting out on their journey and the memories of those returning home. A history of architecture in images, with prints and photographs as the points of reference, visual documents of the present day, the evolution of the archaeological heritage, and the cultural approach to the subject of antiquity.

In *Le Antichità Romane* (1756), Giambattista Piranesi had already represented Rome's monuments with the eye of an architect and antiquarian,[2] one trained during his early years in the city to pick up the traces and details of the ruins while collaborating with Vasi on the Nolli Map (1748).[3] He therefore saw and sought to show, as explained in his long and scholarly captions, the variety of decorative forms and devices, the fragment as an indication of the whole, laden with the same evocative energy as the immense ruins. This grandeur, as exemplified by the Baths of Caracalla, not only represents a physical dimension capable of generating emotion, the hallmark of antiquity, but is also the exclusive characteristic of Rome (as the Greece of Paestum was later to be), lying inside the stones and the forms, still perceptible in its ruins.

The subjectivity of Piranesi's images was translated into a collective emotion in the 101 views of ancient Rome (1819–1823) of Luigi Rossini and Bartolomeo Pinelli.[4] This was to be for the last time. Devoid of Piranesi's educational intent, the prints develop a pure narrative of the pleasure of the emotions in the remnants of Rome, images of a now pictorial and picturesque journey that established more sophisticated viewpoints and ways of seeing. Not therefore the melancholy of bygone greatness but the sense of disorientation and fascination instilled by the ruins in their present state. This role was soon to be taken over by photography, which quickly assumed the character of industrial mass production, like the earlier print-making but to a far greater extent. The transition from the print to the photograph brought support and freedom. The earlier medium was freed from the constraint of documentation, no longer required to compete in terms of narrative precision, a role taken over by the faster and more modern technique. At the same time, engraving took up the task of subjectivity, no longer capturing the place alone but also its emotive dimension and subjective evocation of the exotic.

This marks the break. Examination of the sedate photographic image of ancient Rome developed in the second half of the nineteenth century reveals the gap in all its technical aspects. The use of saturated tones and scenes often devoid of human figures were not so much stylistic choices as imposed by the long exposure times required. Moreover, James Anderson and the first foreign photographers prior to Italy's unification established a new standardisation of recurrent viewpoints, which were in turn the viewpoints exported for travellers and became the mass viewpoint by virtue of the sheer number of copies and their dissemination. The 'lowly' medium of the photograph, less noble than the oil painting, watercolour and engraving, was not averse to the speed of reproduction in countless copies. It no longer produced objects of furnishing but forms of communication. In this sense, if we shift the argument for a moment into the contemporary world, the capacity for real-time narrative of the digital era is the true competitor of the analogical photographic series in strictly numerical terms. And this is perhaps why our critical approach is increasingly (and rightly) coming to accord priority to the matrix, a feature shared by engraving and photography, rather than reproducibility.

And then there is the growing popularity of archaeology, which began to compete with the other subjects that emerged precisely because of photography, such as street scenes, everyday life, the documentation of urban transformations, and especially the celebration and representation of progress and achievement through new architectural works.

These are all aspects that must be taken into account, above all in relation to the constant evolution of the heritage of Roman antiquity, the object of excavation and exhibition ever since the fifteenth century. The age of photography thus documented major discoveries connected with post-unification demolition in the heart of the medieval city and later construction work on the capital of Fascist Italy. The broad span of time thus includes at least two epoch-making moments and milestones with a direct impact on the organisation and image of the monumental area: the building of the Monument to Vittorio Emanuele II, or 'Vittoriano', visible from everywhere in Rome like the dome of Saint Peter's, by Giuseppe Sacconi between 1885 and 1911; and the construction of the Via dell'Impero through the Forum in 1932.[5] We thus have a before and an after, which does not constitute a new reading of antiquity, strangely enough, and is not specifically characterised by the new architecture and the contemporary era. While the Vittoriano now emerges in the panorama of the Forum as a sort of background in the photographic composition, the question of the relationship between ancient and modern is not even addressed in these new images. The Forum is in fact gradually revealed as something different, less agricultural and less haphazard, to the point of 'striking a pose' when the evolution of urban planning in the capital took heroic cognisance of the past and presented it as a different scenario.

The simultaneously fortuitous and everyday nature of the encounter with antiquity is not, however, only a chronological fact that we can follow in the images of the Flavian Amphitheatre (Colosseum), the Forum, the Arch of Septimius Severus and the Column of Marcus Aurelius, all recurrent subjects in this collection. A new and different representation of antiquity was in fact established, no longer related in any way to the iconographic tradition of engraving but presented as a familiar place with the same character as the modern and if anything less heroic than it. This is the true hallmark of the modern vision, the epic challenge of the future. Photography now narrates, documents, and makes clearly comprehensible. It now constitutes a shareable memory for the traveller, evidence

of a completed itinerary and, at the same time, documentation of a fleeting and therefore dating state of reality. Meanwhile reality, even the immutable reality of the monuments of the past, undergoes rapid transformation, altering contexts and documents of stone, some restored, some more neglected, and some vanished. It is in the latter sense that we can read this part of the photographic collection of the Royal Institute of British Architects, as a guide to the transformation of the ancient city. It is no coincidence that in very few of all these photographs Rome is presented as picturesque or that human figures are few and far between in a sacralised range of ancient monuments to discover, visit and study. Monuments located among monuments of other ages all the way up to the Servian Walls are now engaged in dialogue with the contemporary reality of the Termini railway station. Fragments of a city are now reassembled in photographic documents, infused with the aura that makes them an essential part of a dedicated collection, an inexhaustible source of study for architecture.

Paolo Mascilli Migliorini

[1] Piero Becchetti, 'Una dinastia di fotografi romani: gli Anderson', in *Archivio Fotografico Toscano*, y. II, no. 4, 1986, pp. 56–67.
[2] Giovanni Battista Piranesi, *Le Antichità Romane*, Rome: Stamperia di Angelo Rotili, 1756.
[3] Mario Bevilacqua, *Nolli Vasi Piranesi. Immagine di Roma Antica e Moderna: rappresentare e conoscere la metropoli dei Lumi* Rome: Artemide 2004); Mario Bevilacqua, *Roma nel secolo dei lumi. Architettura, erudizione, scienza nella pianta di G.B. Nolli 'celebre geometra'*, Naples: Electa Napoli, 1998.
[4] Luigi Rossini, *Le Antichità Romane divise in cento tavole*, Rome: Scudellari, c. 1823.
[5] See Rossella Leone and Anita Margiotta, *Fori Imperiali: demolizioni e scavi. Fotografie 1924/1940*, Milan: Electa, 2007; Rossella Leone, Anita Margiotta, Fabio Betti, and Angela Maria D'Amelio (eds.), *Via dell'Impero: demolizioni e scavi. Fotografie 1930/1943*, Milan: Electa, 2009.

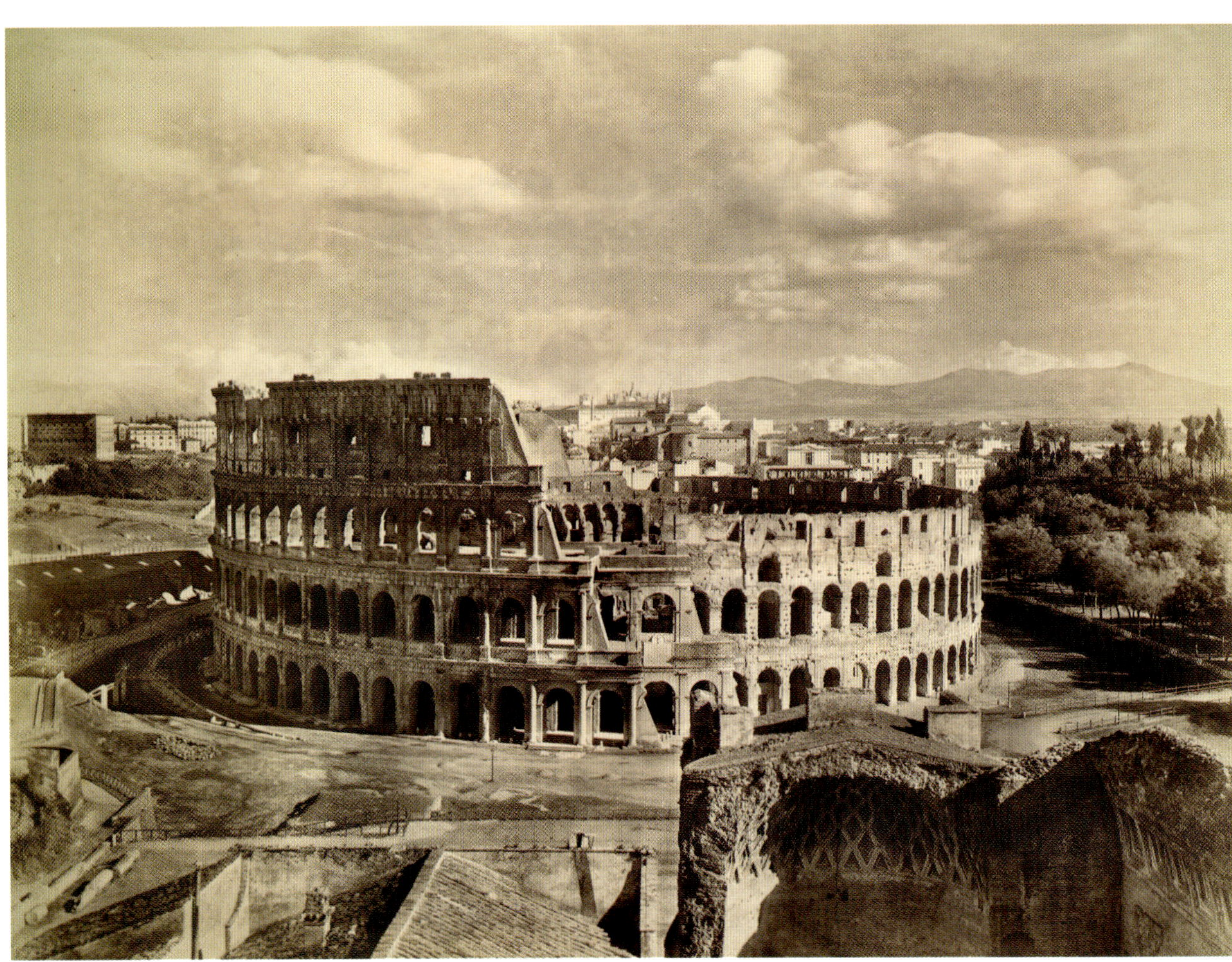

1. James Anderson
*Flavian Amphitheatre
(Colosseum)*, c. 1860

2. Unknown photographer
*Flavian Amphitheatre seen
from the Domus Aurea,*
1860s–1870s

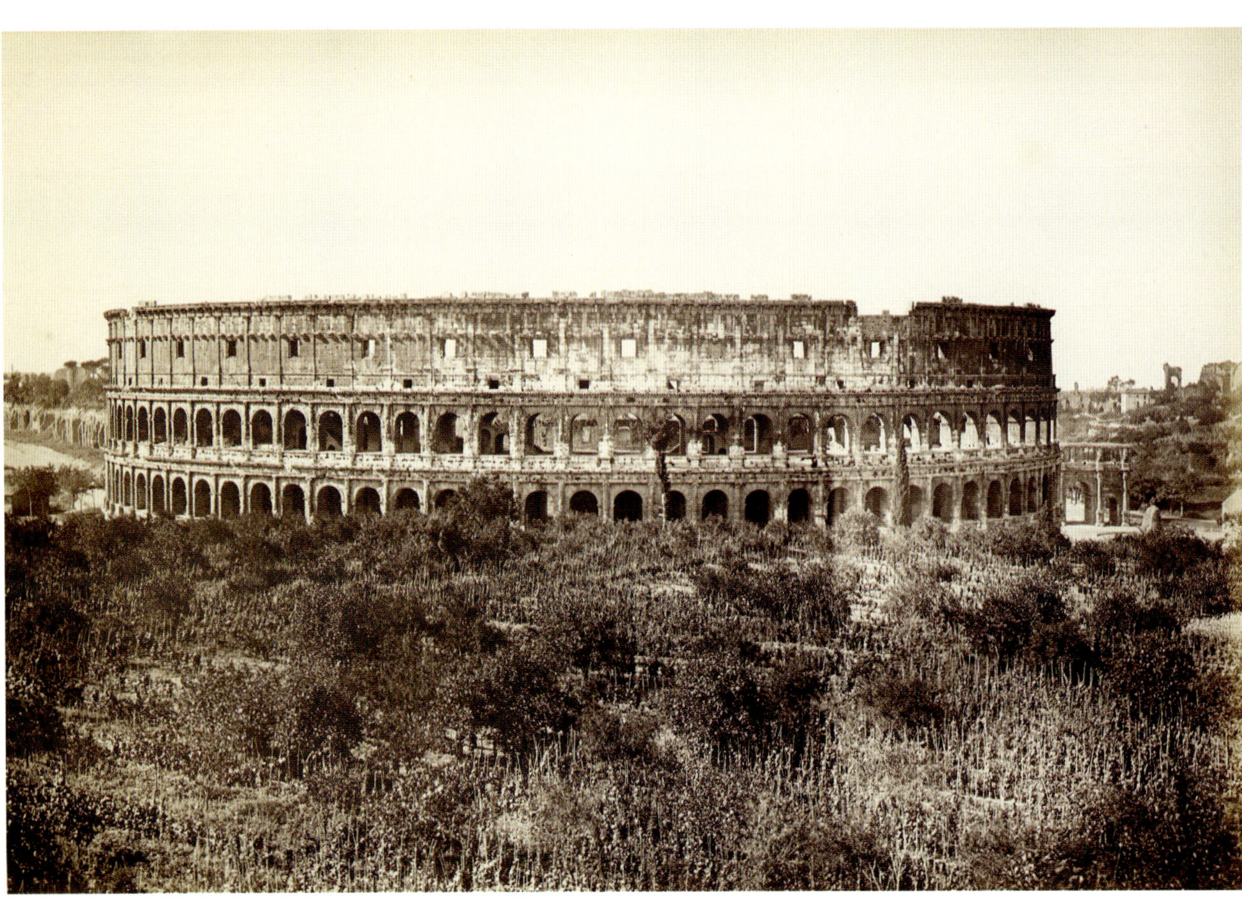

3. Enrico Verzaschi
Roman Forum, after 1860

4. Enrico Verzaschi
Roman Forum, after 1860

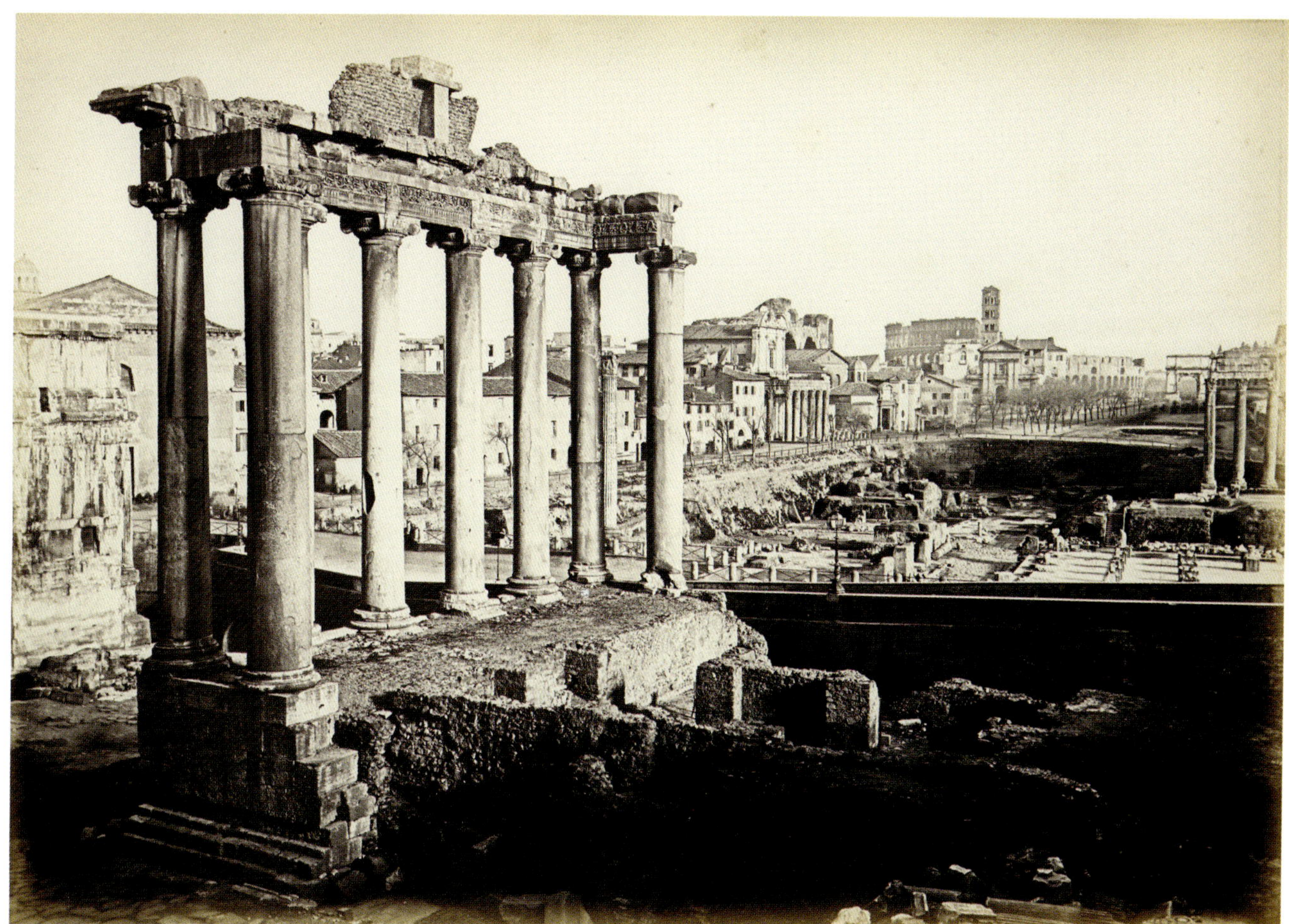

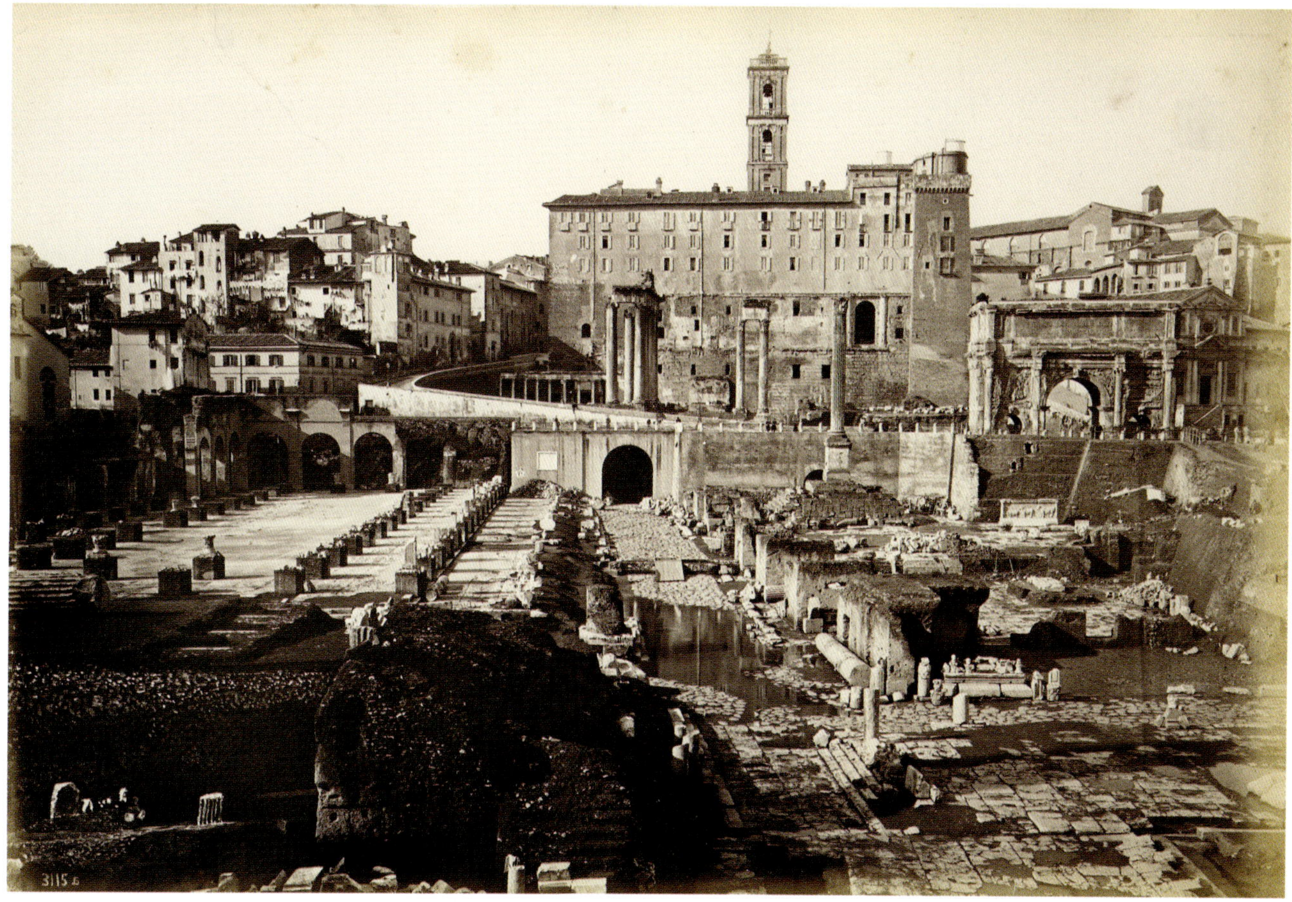

5. Stabilimento Fotografico
Domenico Anderson
Friezes in the Roman Forum,
early twentieth century

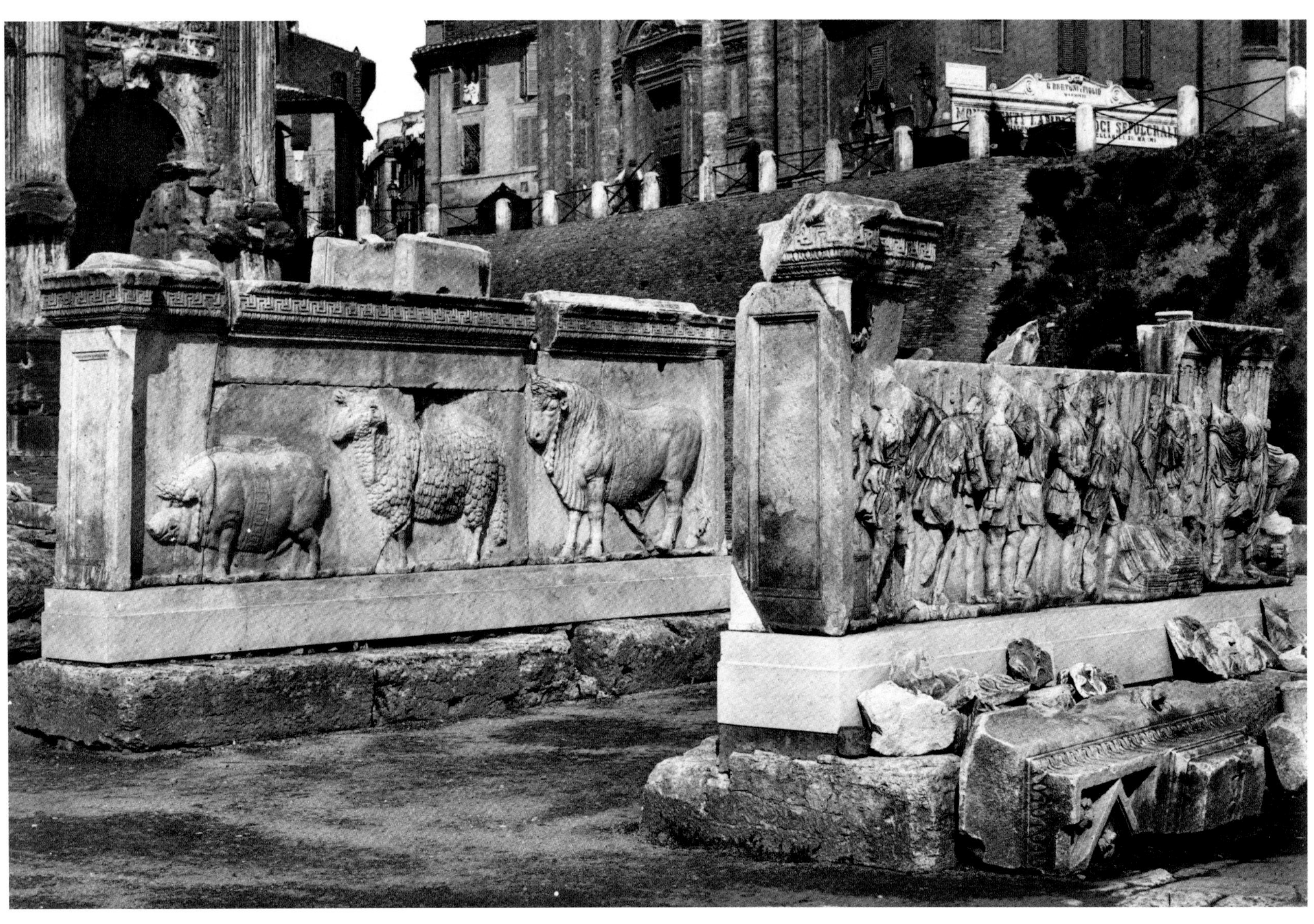

6. Stabilimento Fotografico
Domenico Anderson
Arch of Septimius Severus,
Roman Forum,
early twentieth century

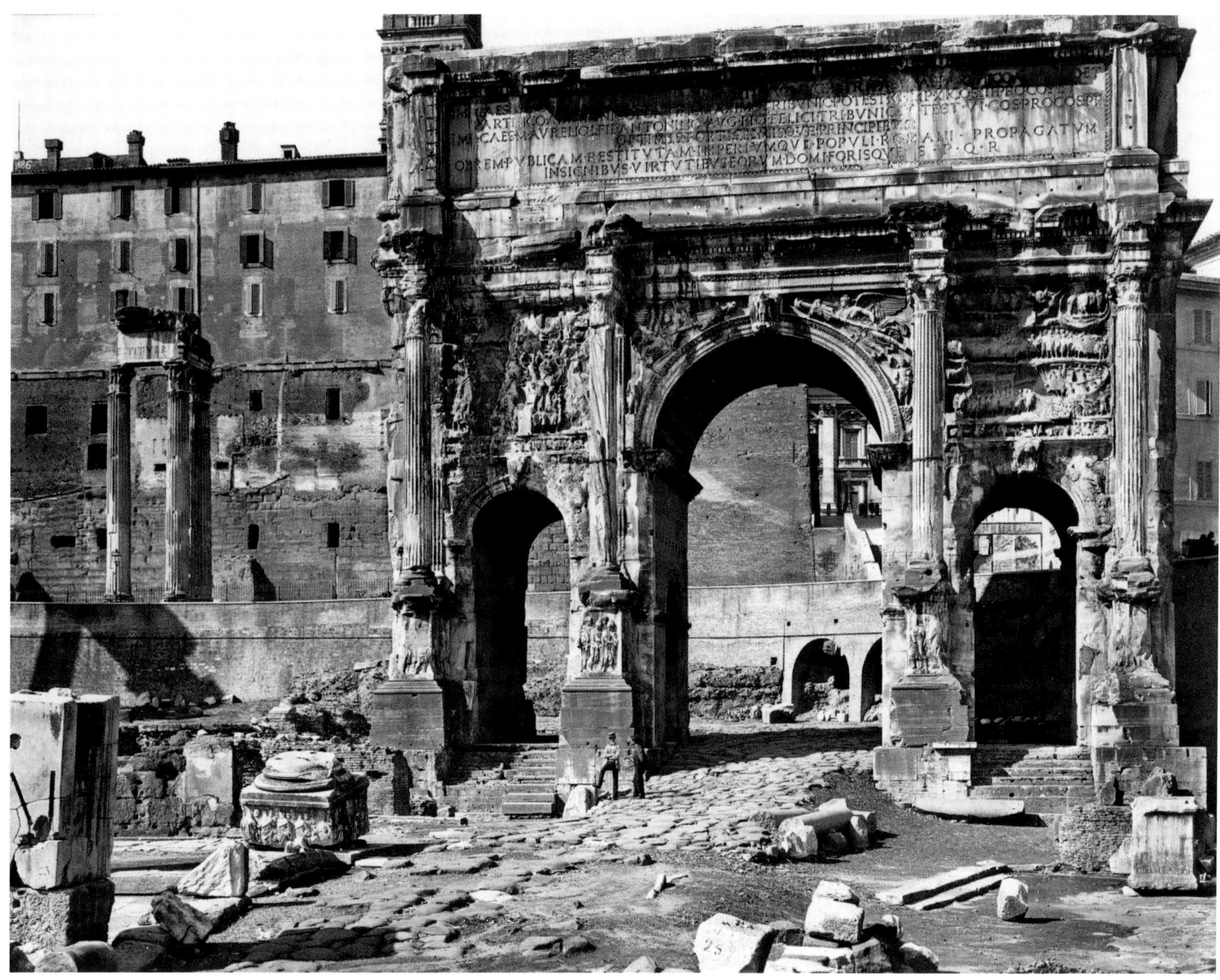

63

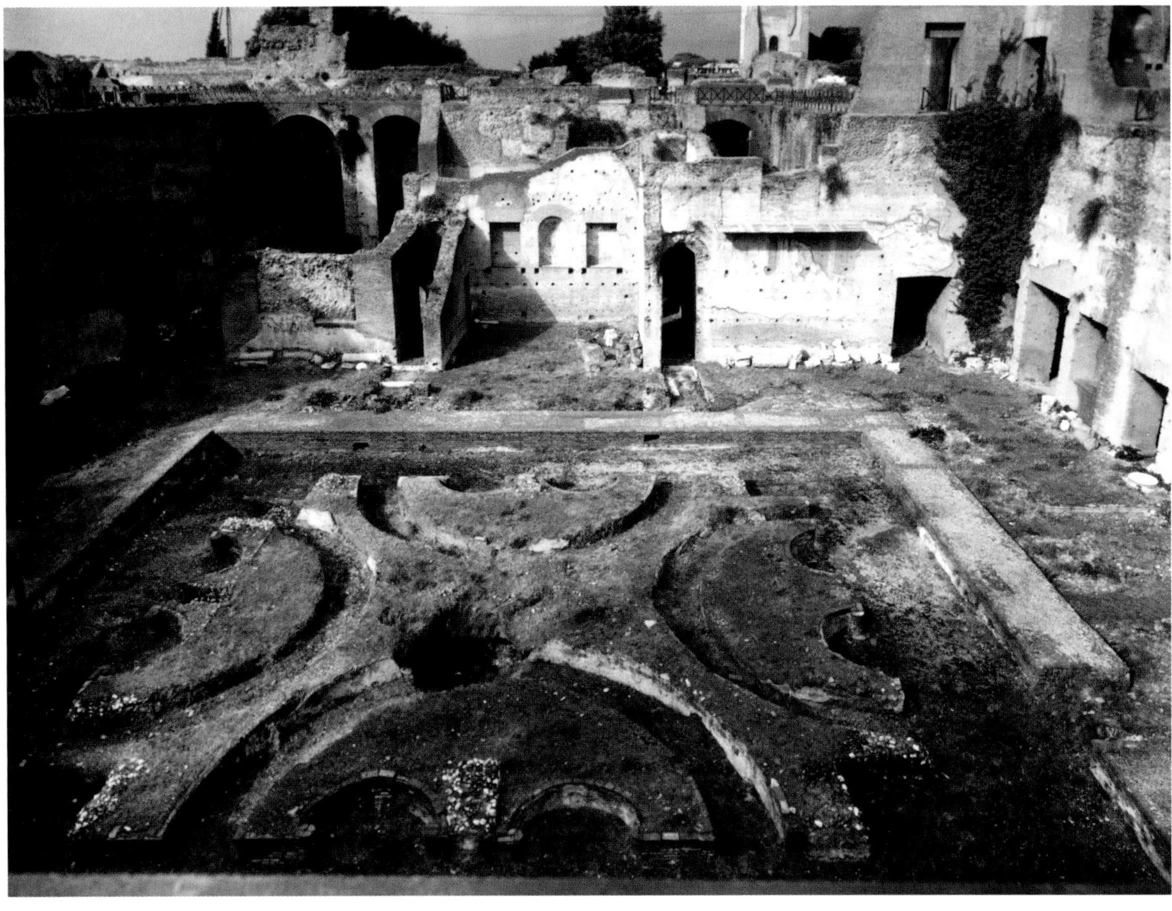

7. Unknown photographer
*Ruins of the House of Augusta,
Palatine Hill*, 1950s

8. Edwin Smith
*Roman Forum, with the Arch
of Septimius Severus
in the foreground*, 1970

9. Ralph Deakin
*Atrium of Vesta's House,
with the Basilica of Maxentius
on the left, Roman Forum,*
1930s

10. Edwin Smith
Roman Forum, 1963

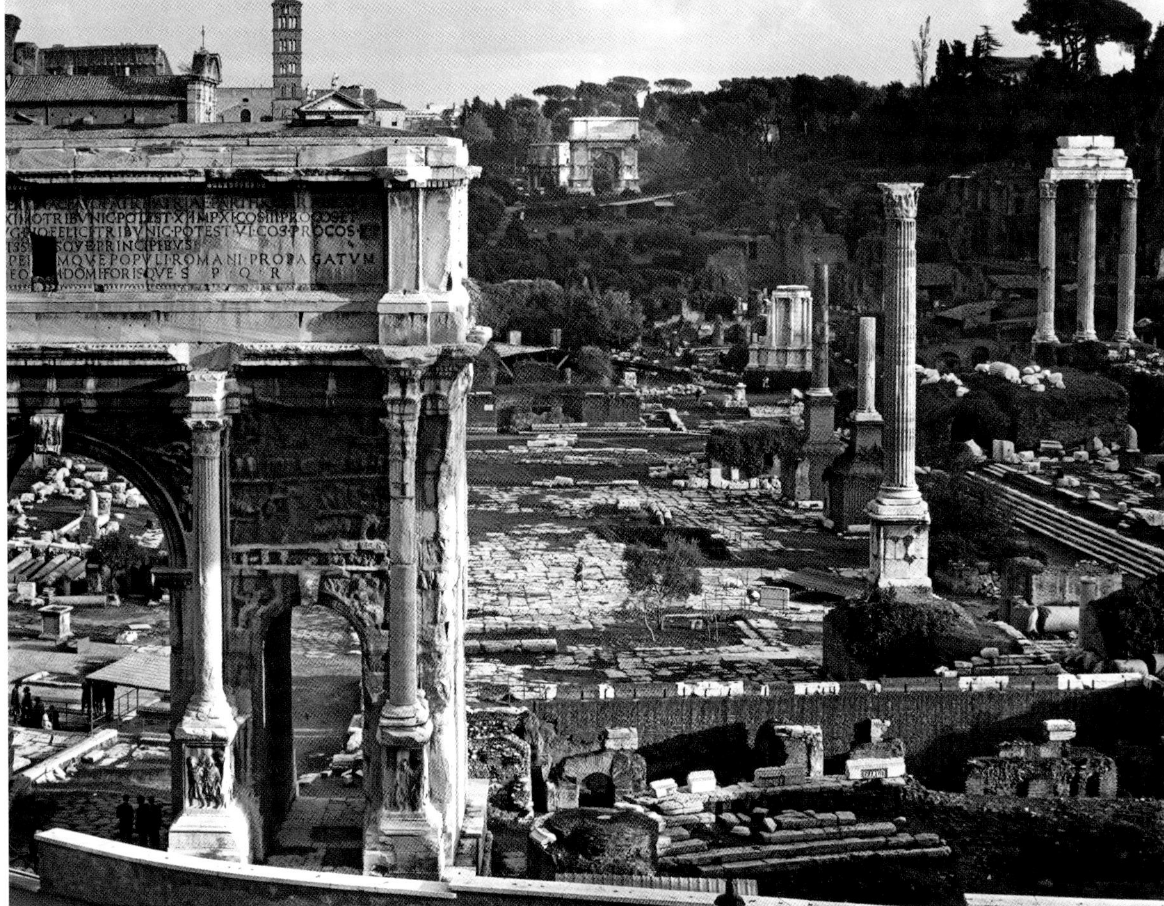

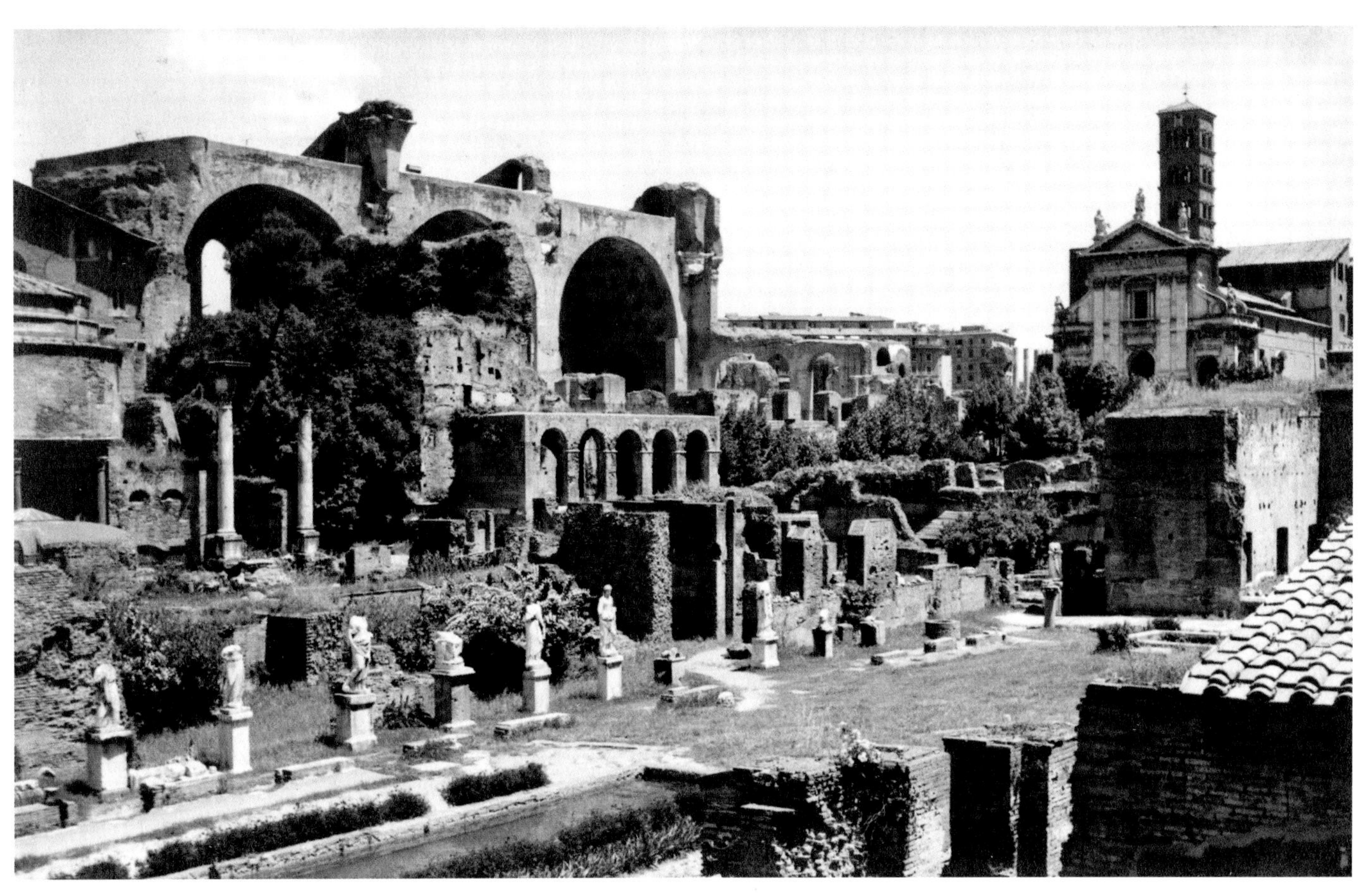

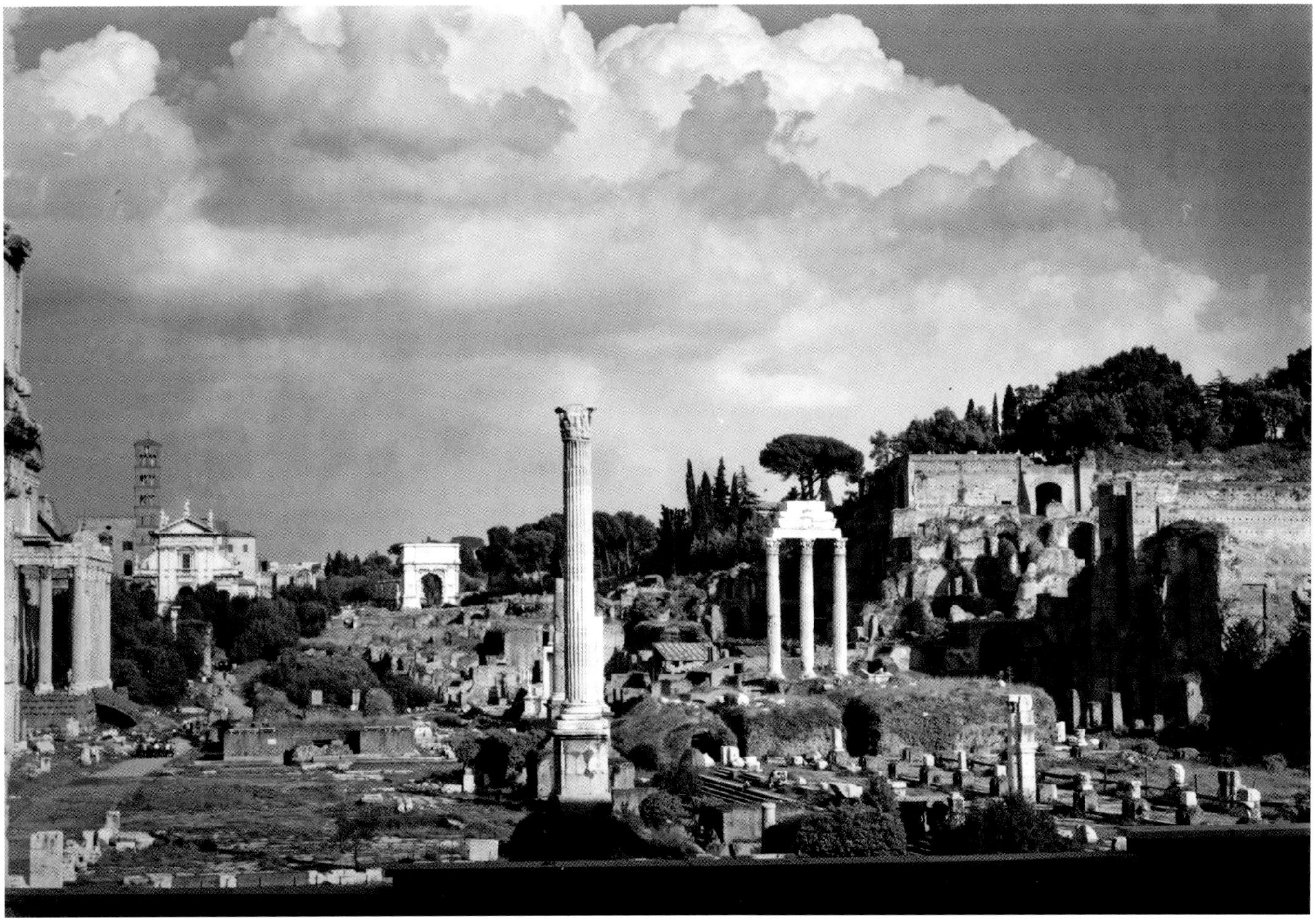

11. Edwin Smith
*Tomb of Marcus Vergilius
Eurysaces, Porta Maggiore,*
1970

12. Ralph Deakin
Temple of Portunus, 1930s

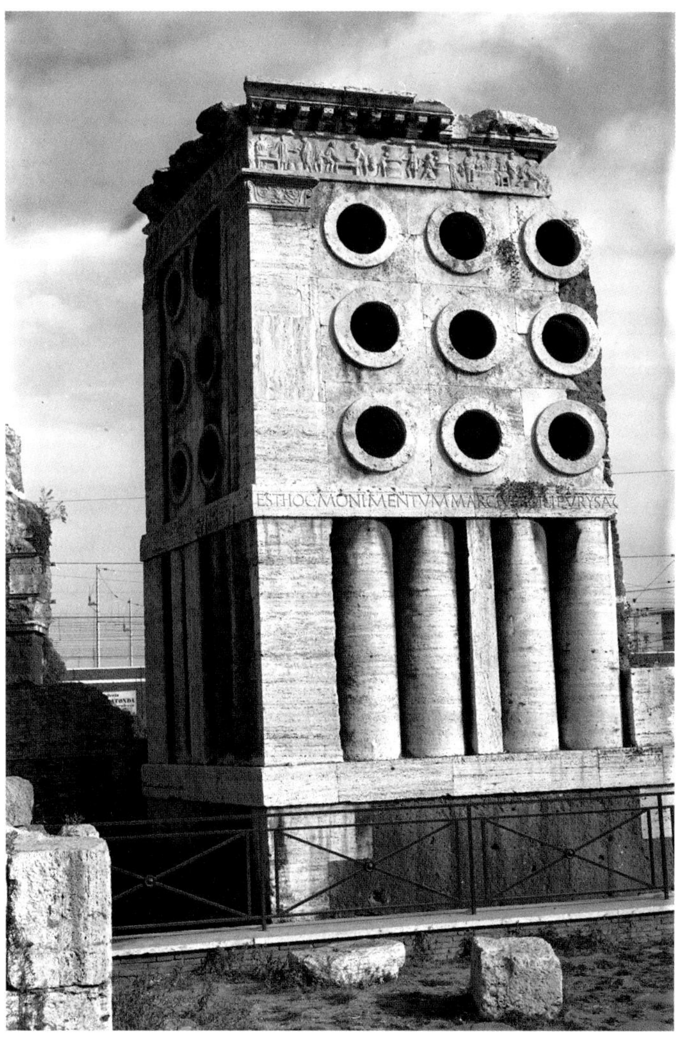

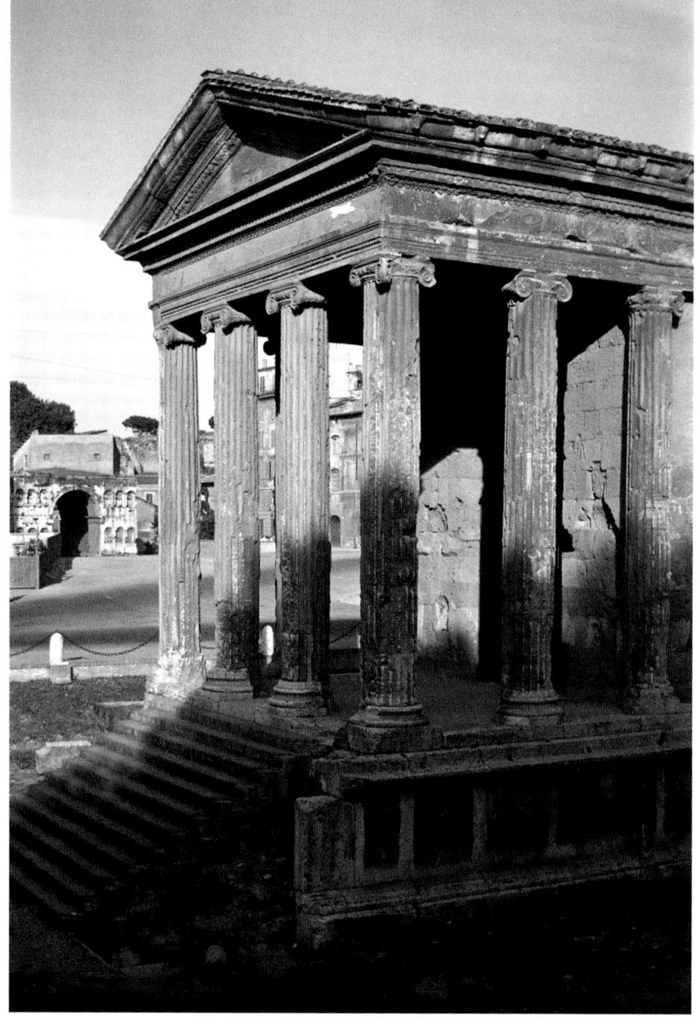

13. Edwin Smith
*Temple of Hercules Victor
and Temple of Portunus*, 1962

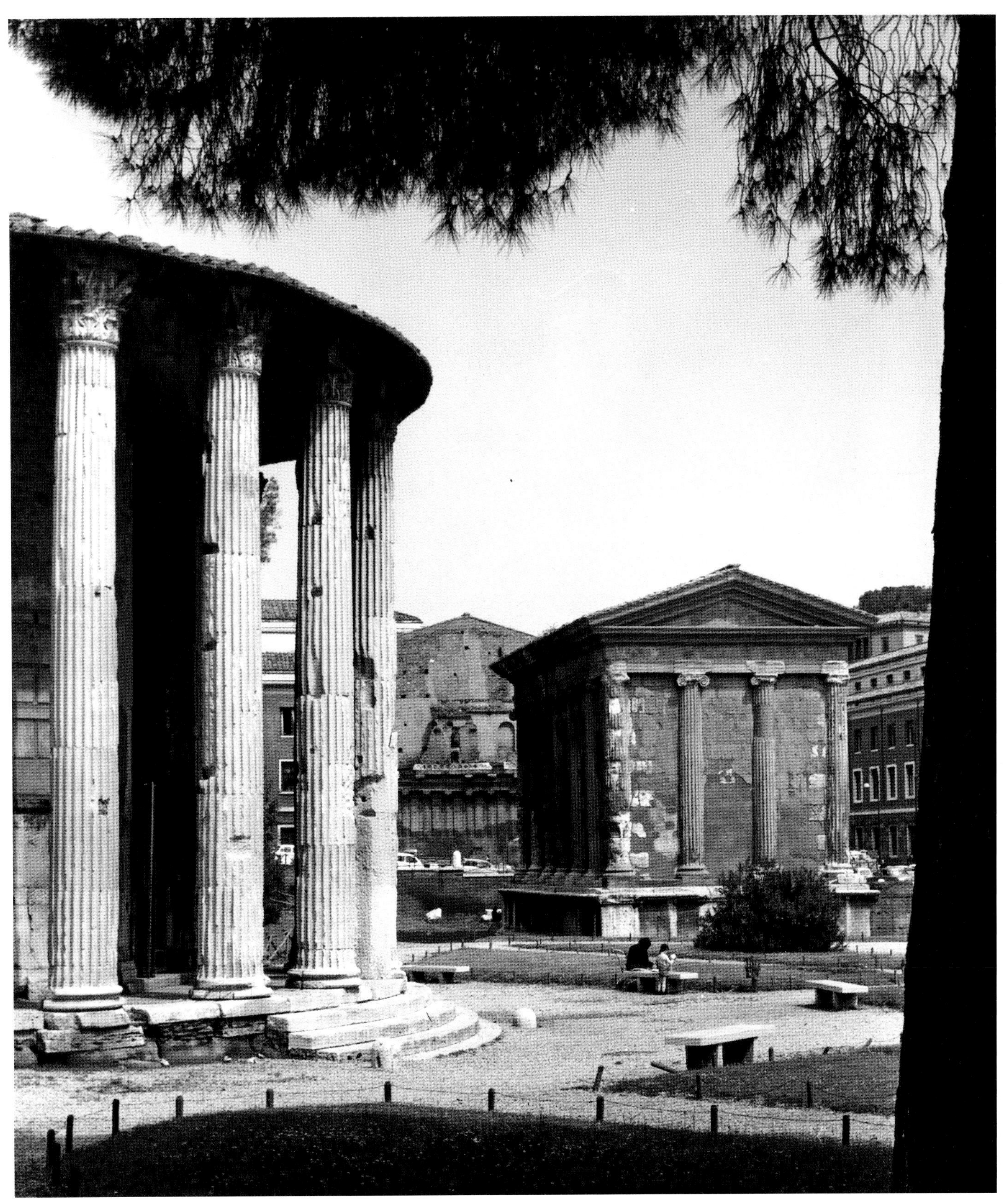

14. Edwin Smith
*Arch of Septimius Severus,
Roman Forum, 1970*

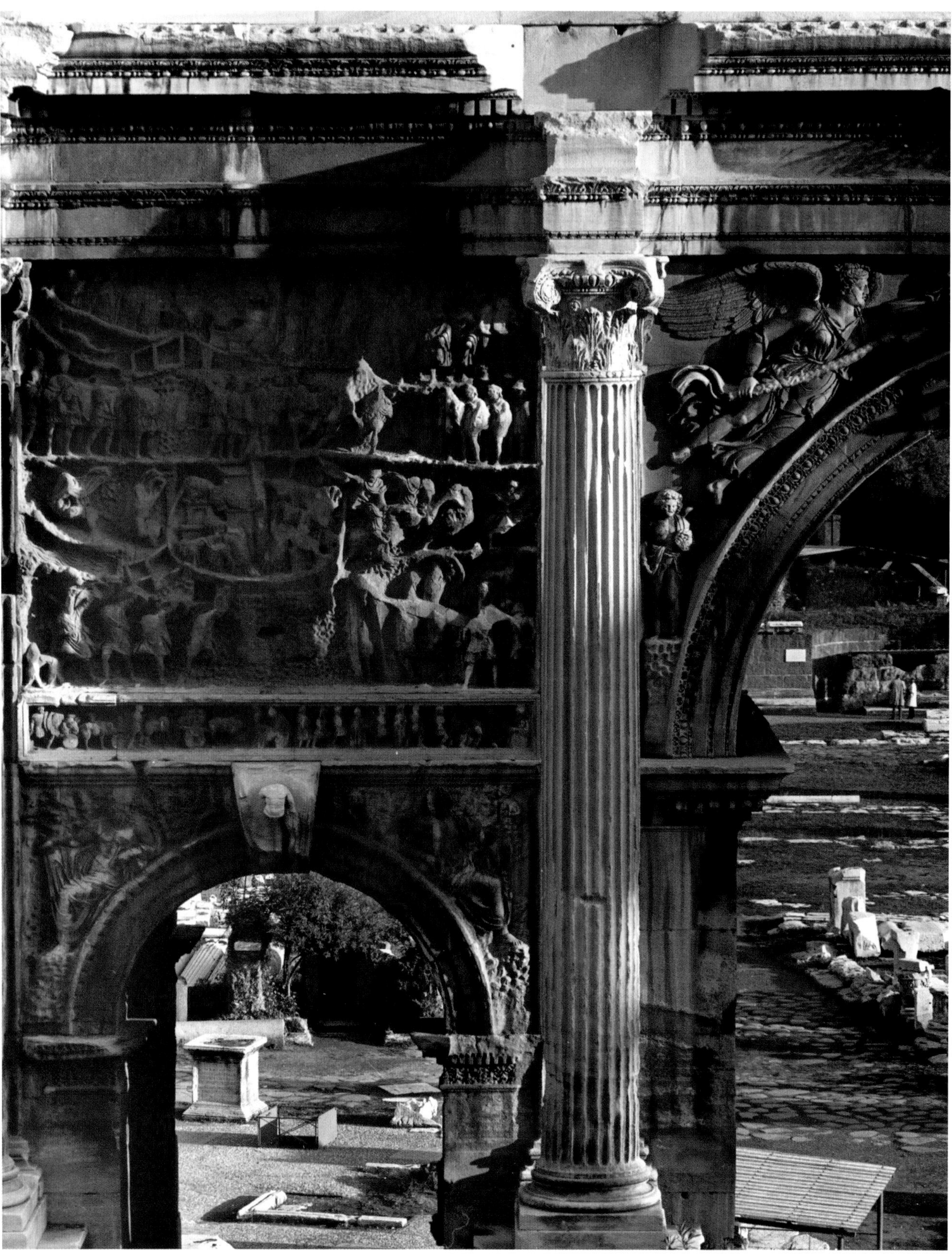

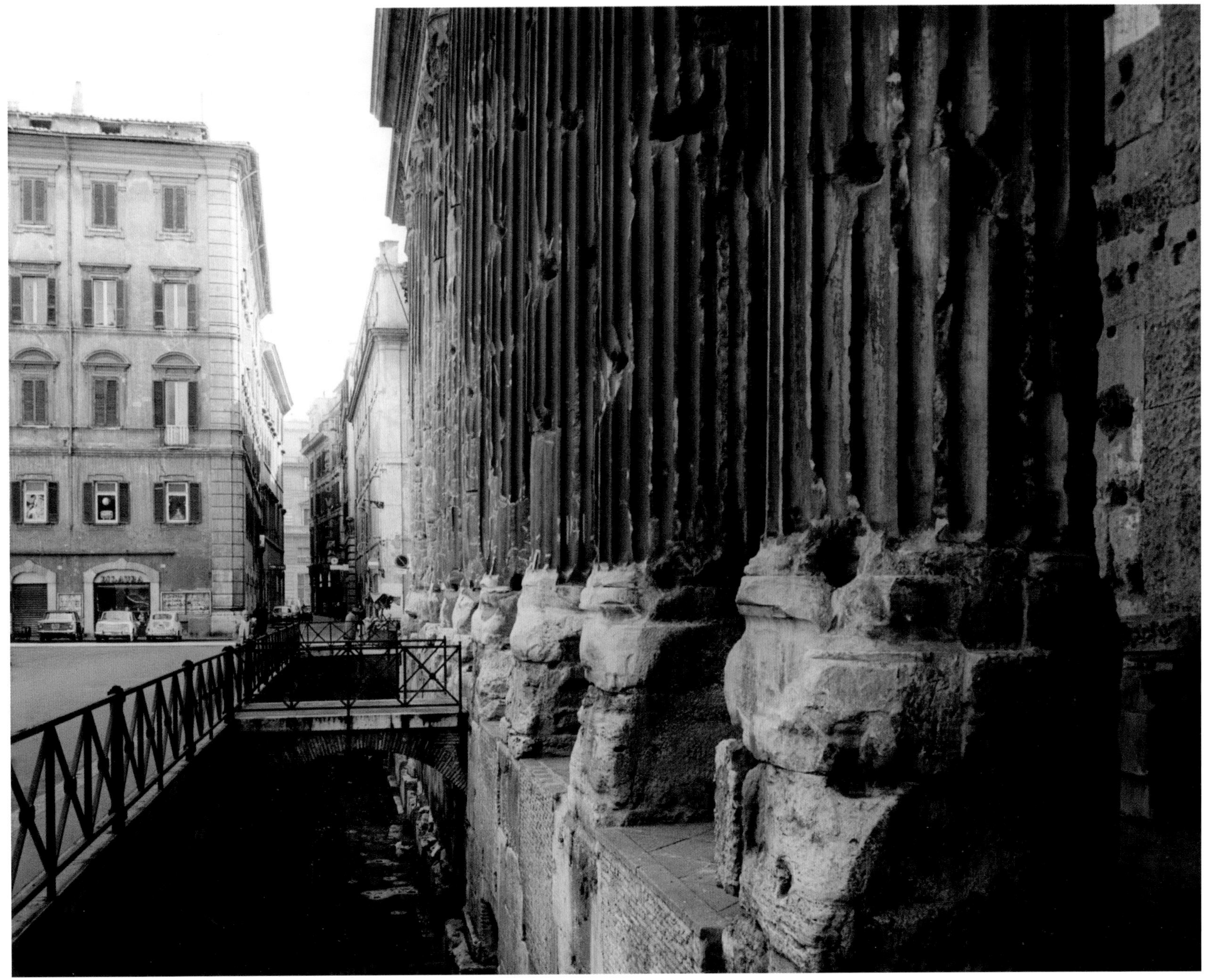

15. Edwin Smith
Temple of Hadrian,
Piazza di Pietra, 1963

16. Edwin Smith
Pantheon, 1963

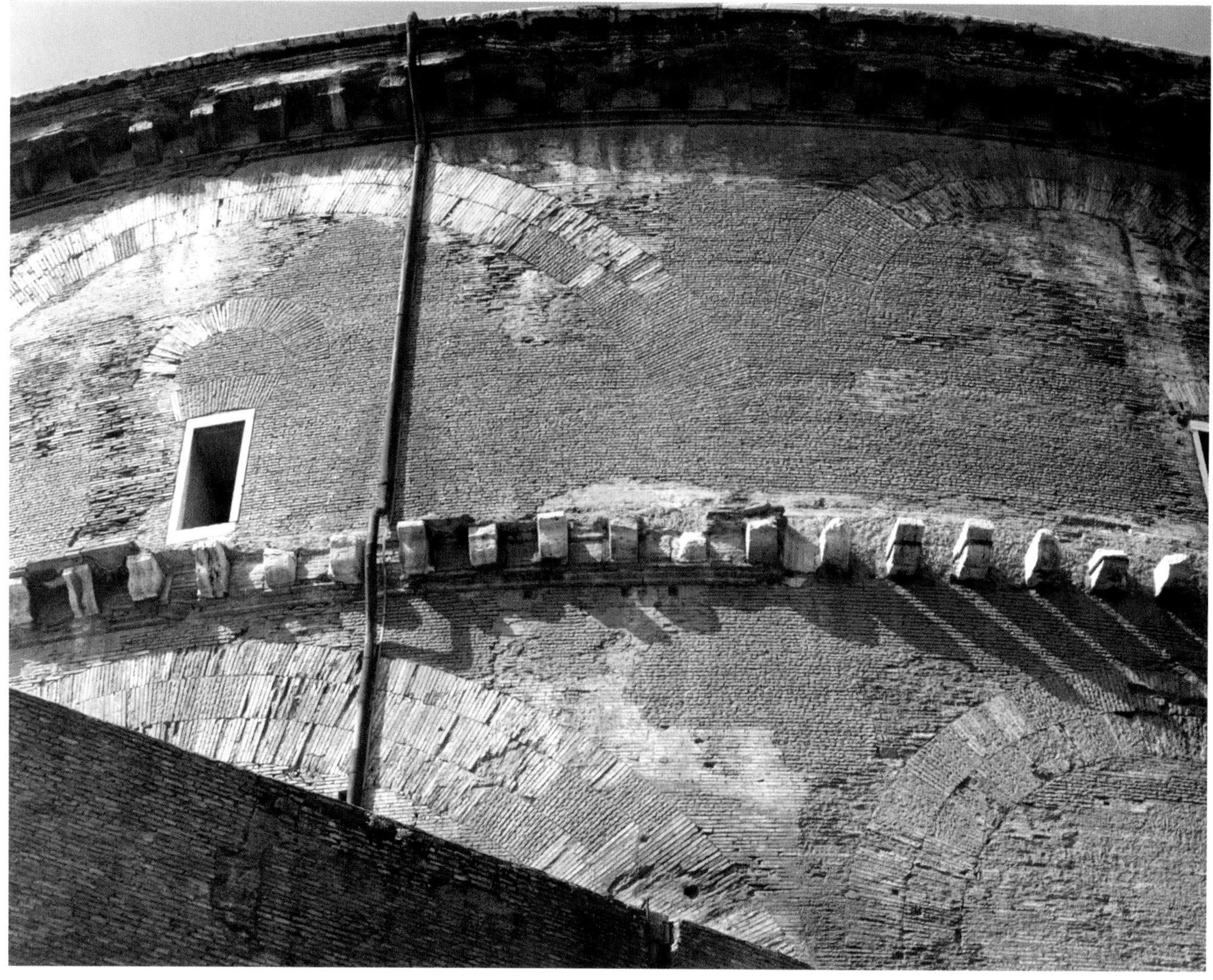

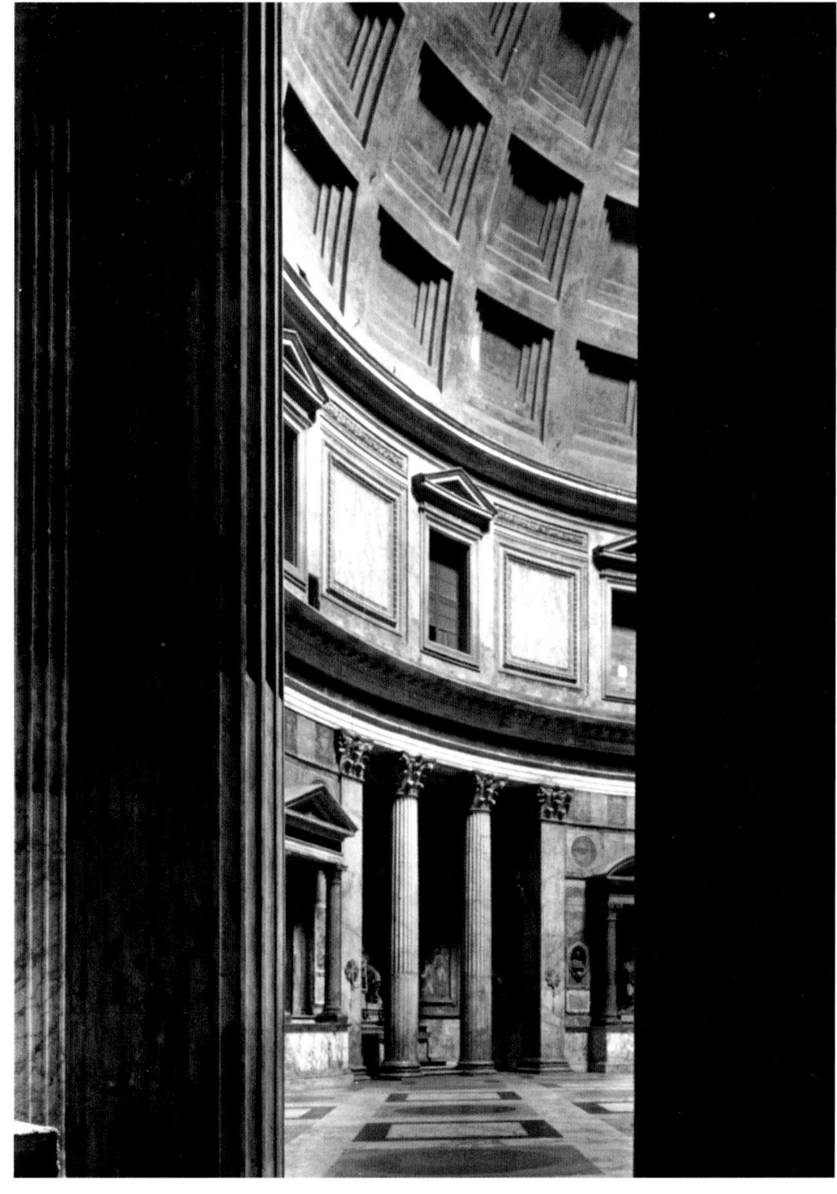

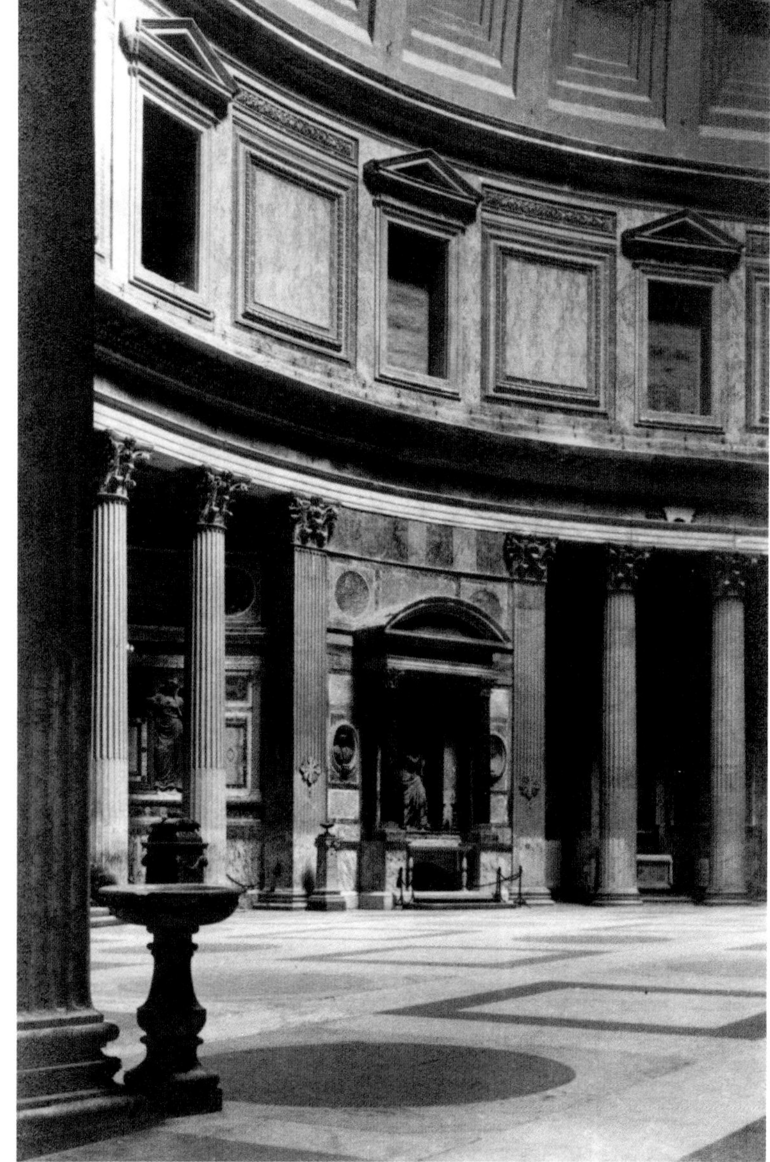

19. Edwin Smith
*Fragments of the colossal
statue of Constantine the Great,
Palazzo dei Conservatori, 1954*

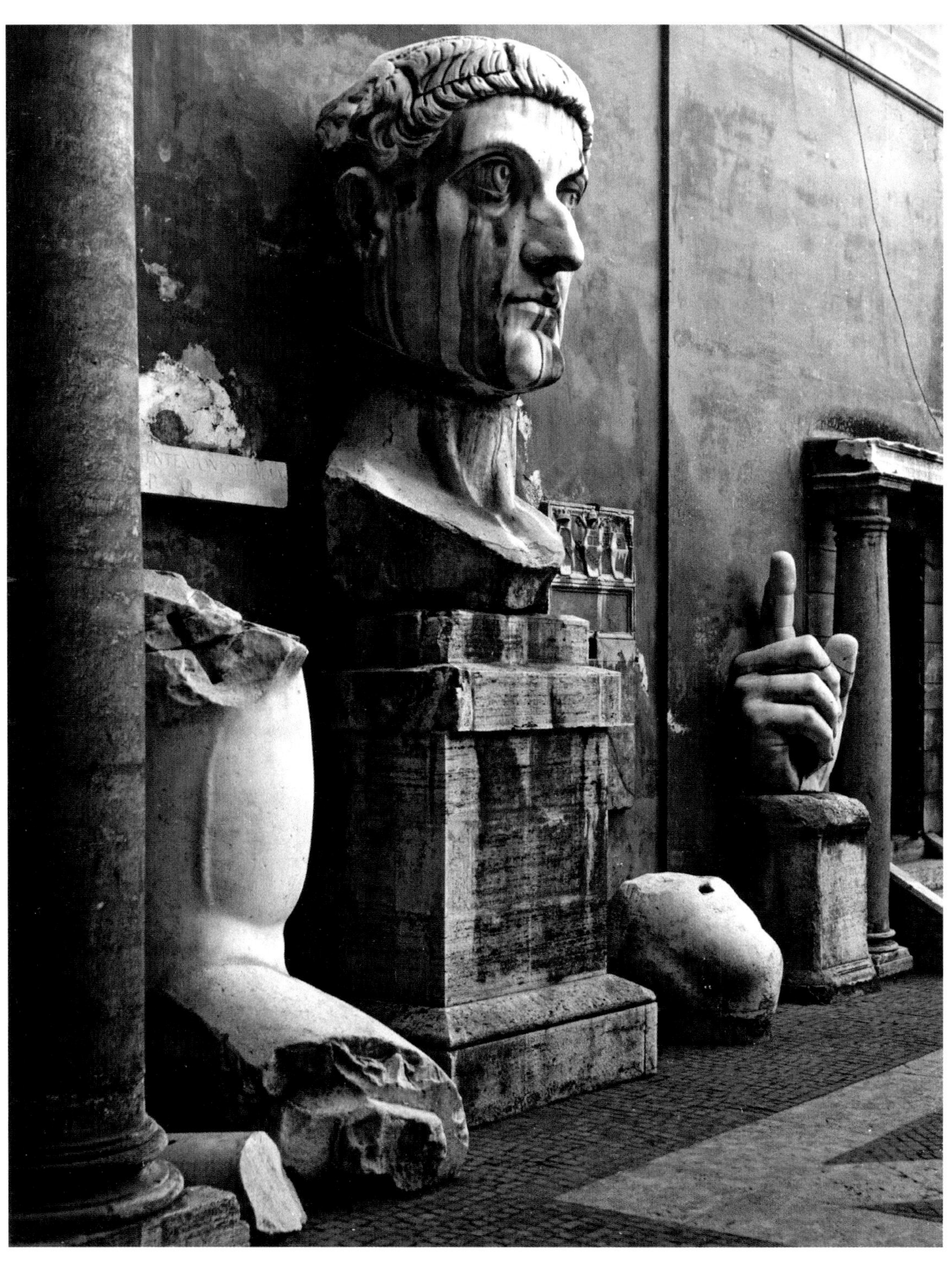

20. Edwin Smith
*Fragments of the colossal
statue of Constantine the Great,
Palazzo dei Conservatori, 1954*

21. Unknown photographer
*Fragments of the colossal
statue of Constantine the Great,
Palazzo dei Conservatori, 1950s*

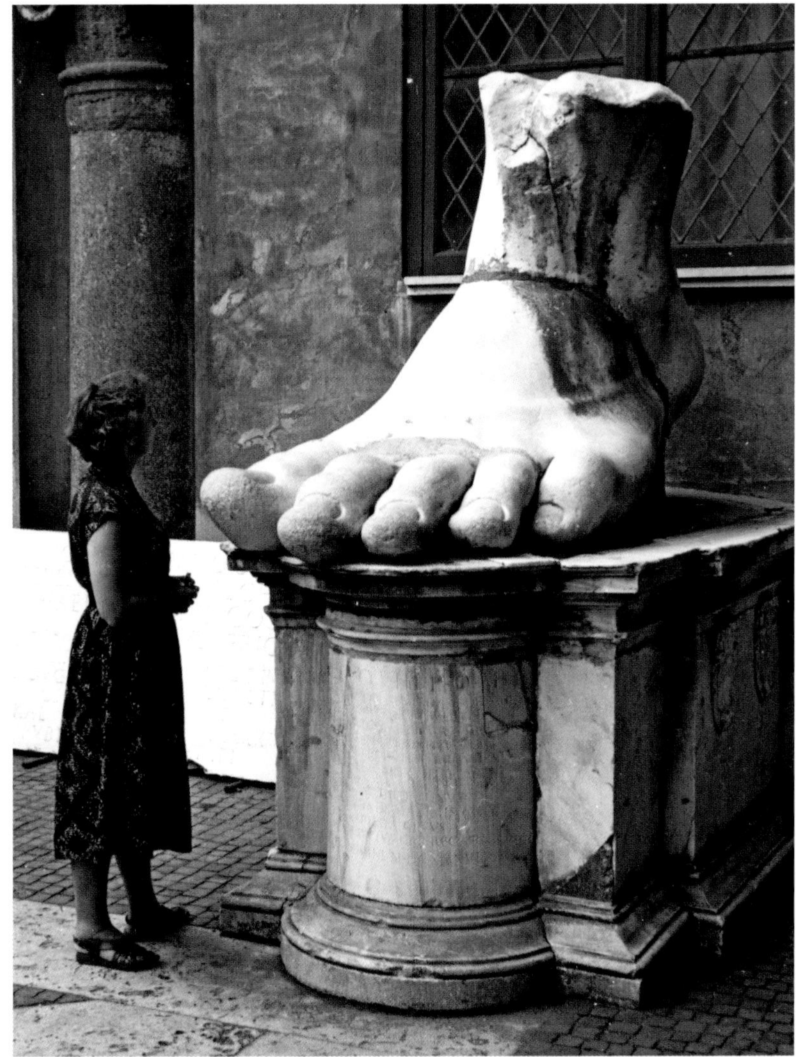

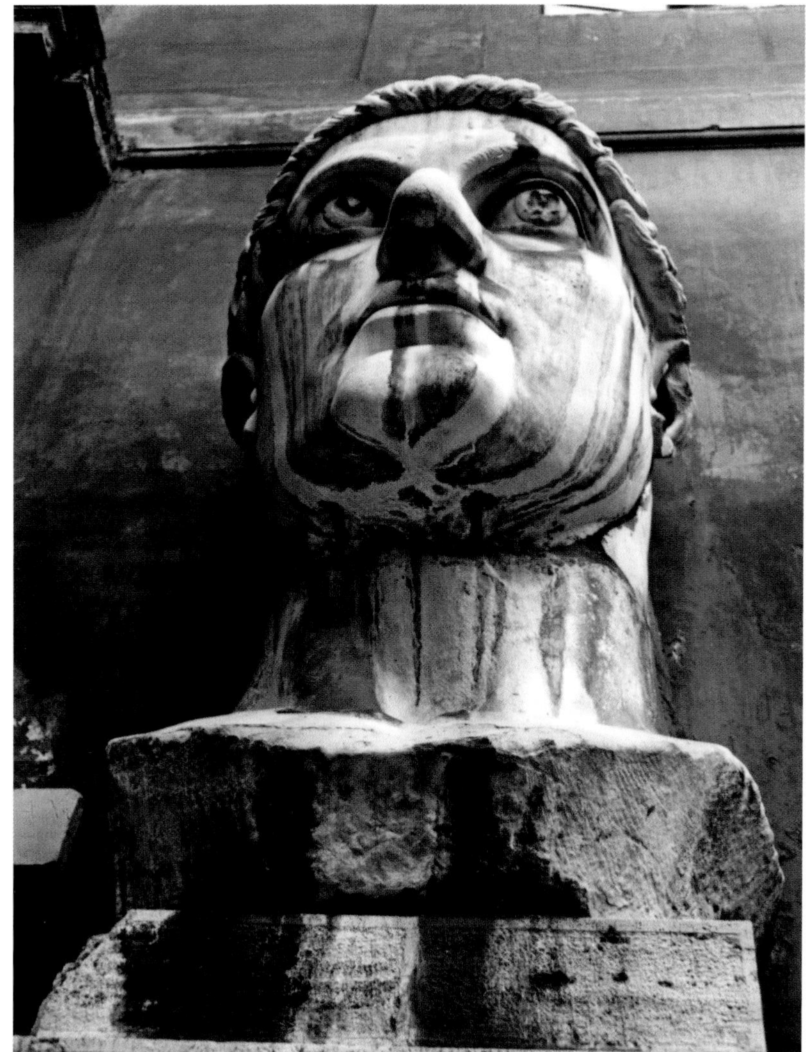

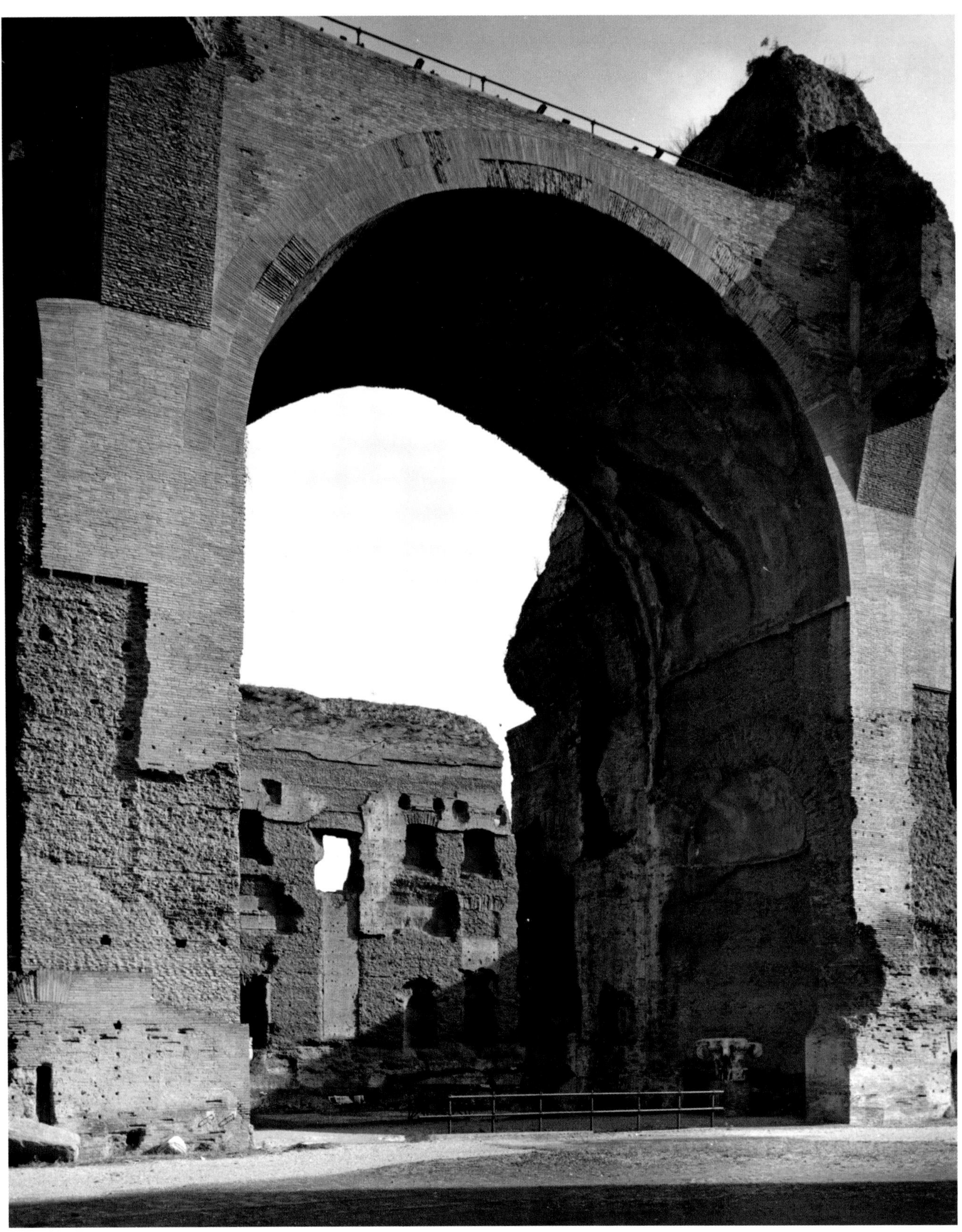

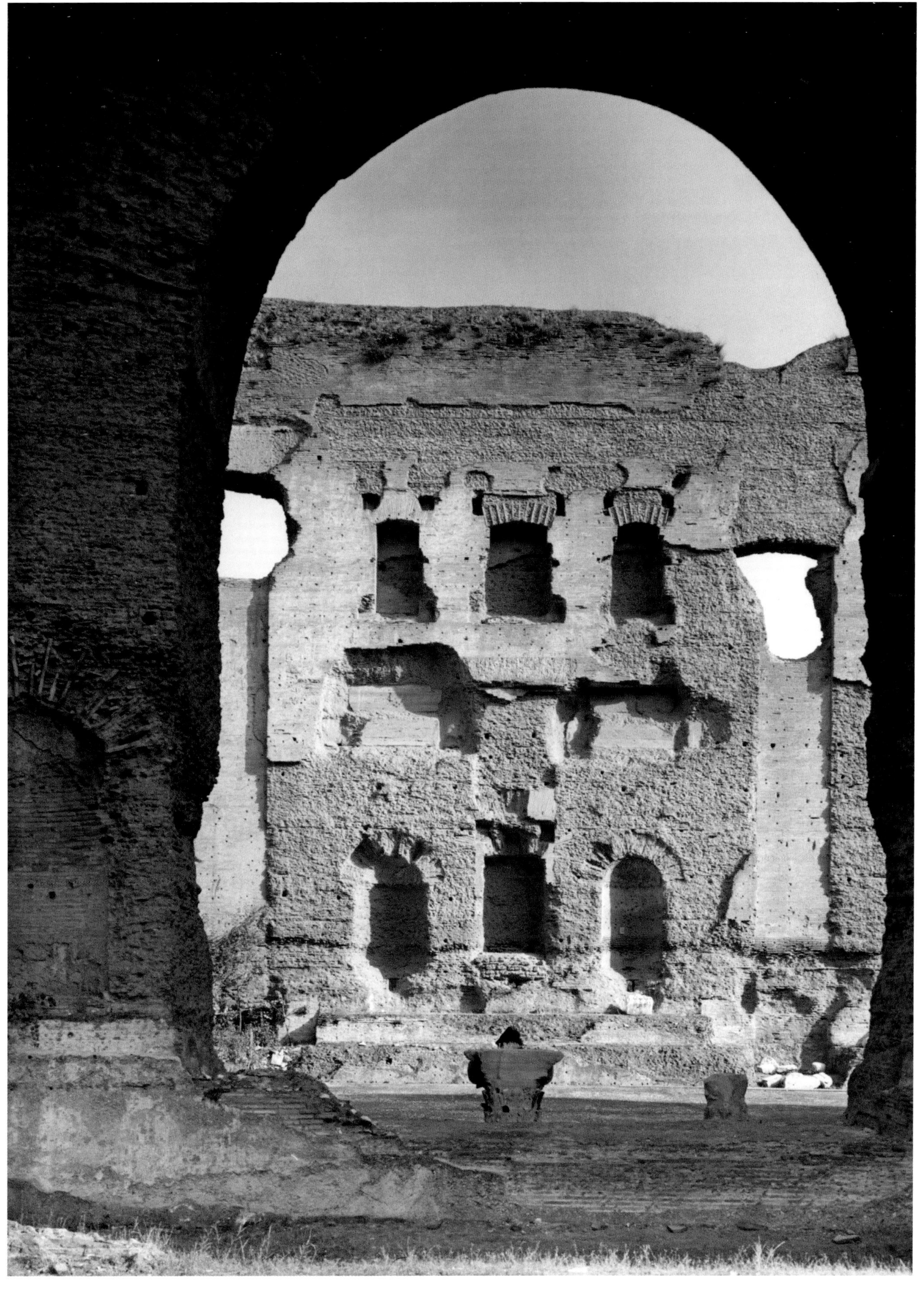

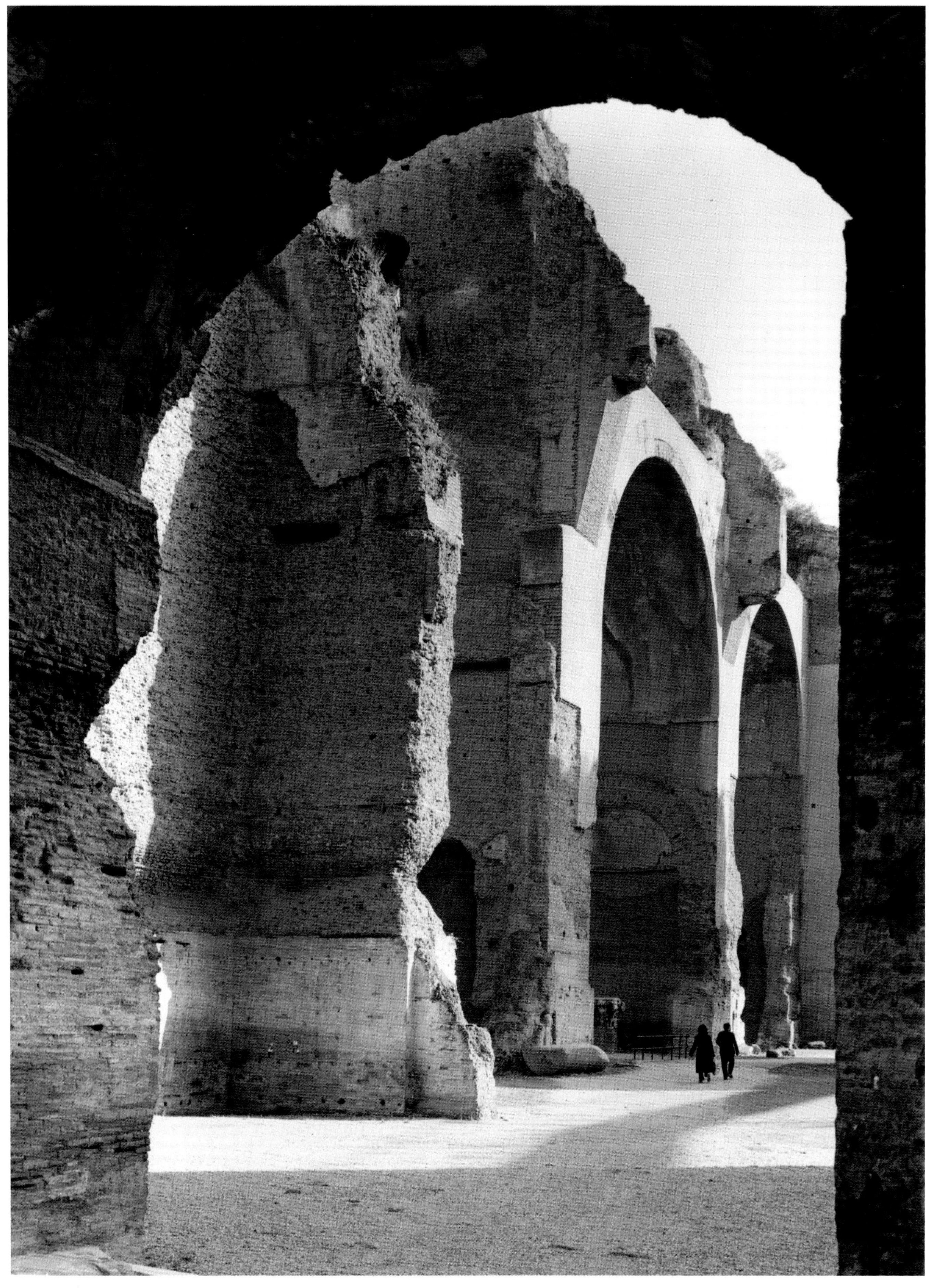

24. Edwin Smith
Baths of Caracalla, 1970

25. Monica Pidgeon
Basilica of Maxentius, 1961

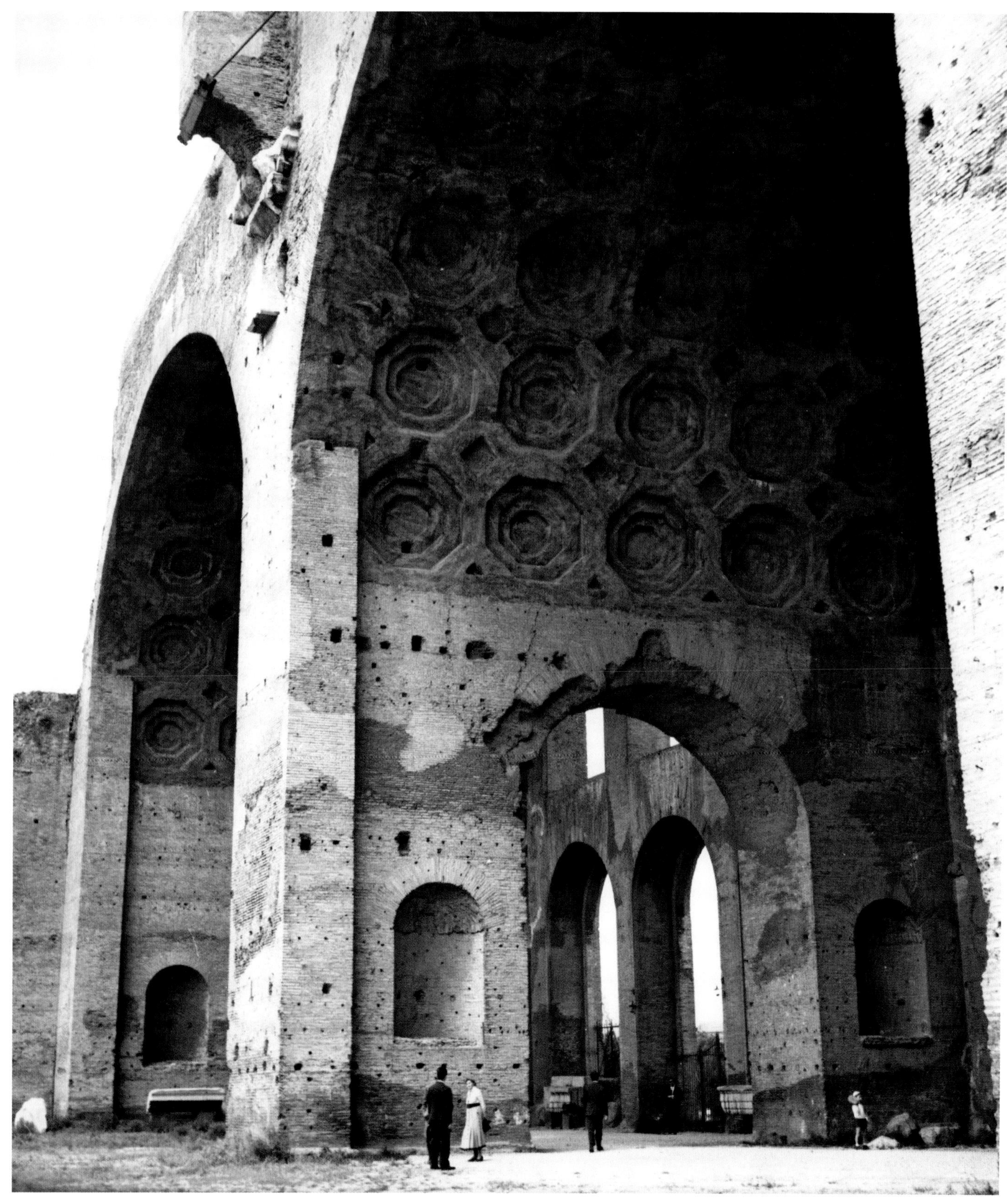

26. Edwin Smith
Baths of Diocletian, 1970

27. Ralph Deakin
*Remains of the Palace
of Caligula, Palatine Hill*, 1930s

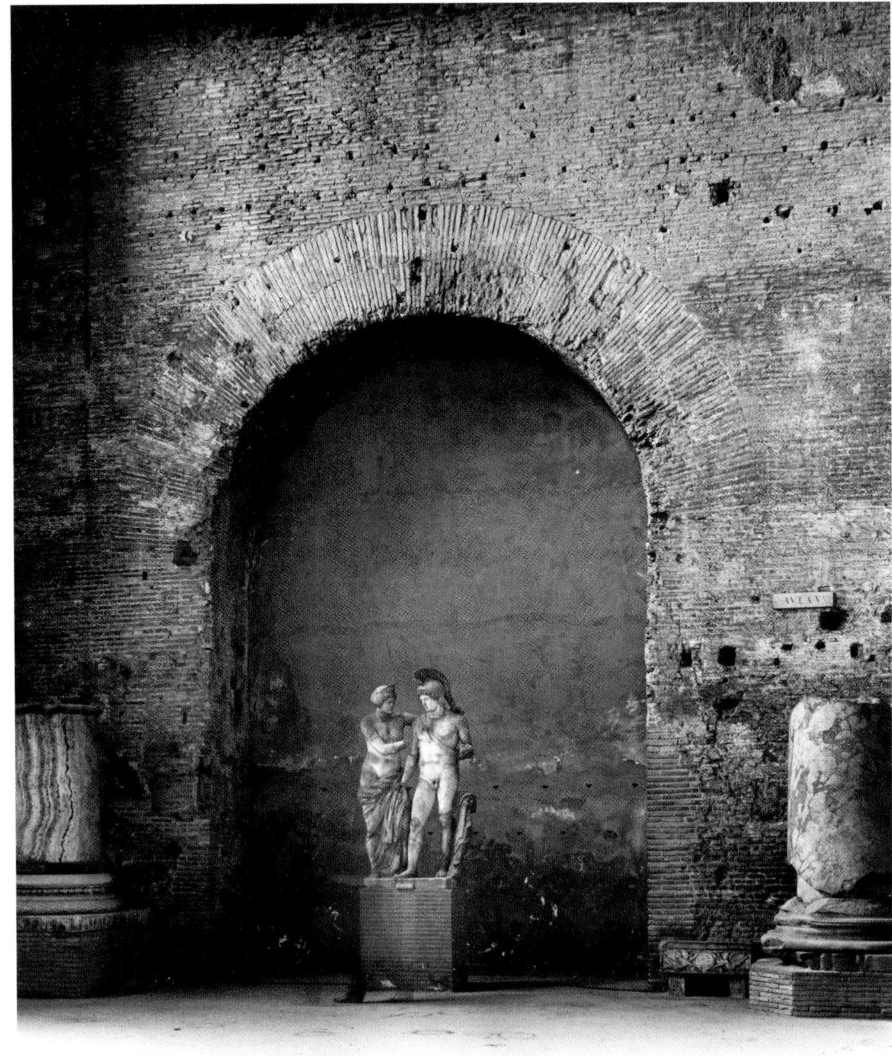

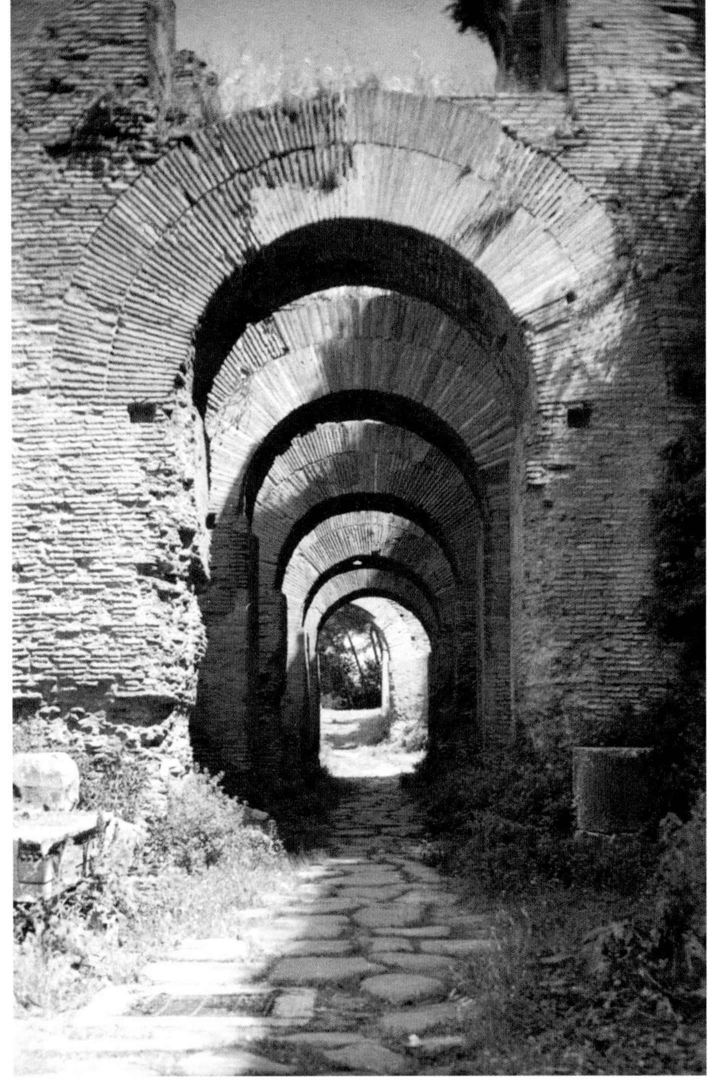

28. Ralph Deakin
Arch of Drusus, Via Appia,
1930s

29. Edwin Smith
*Tabularium, Roman
Forum*, 1970

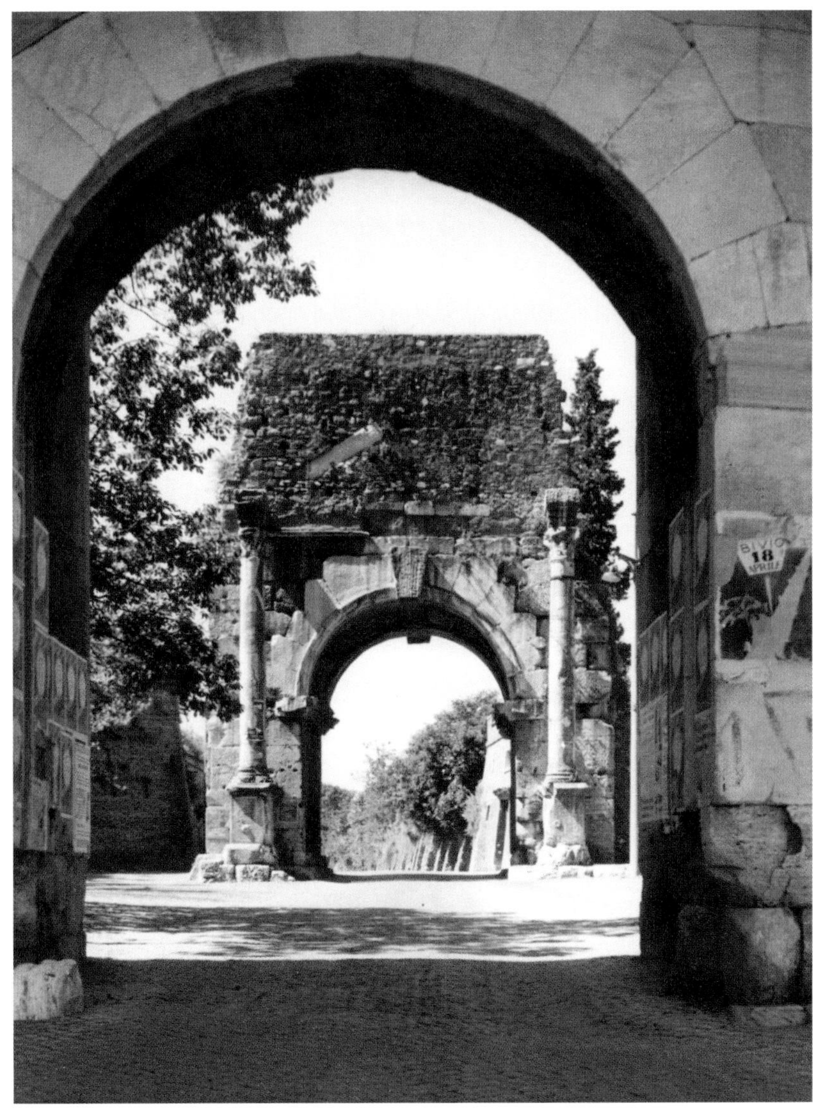

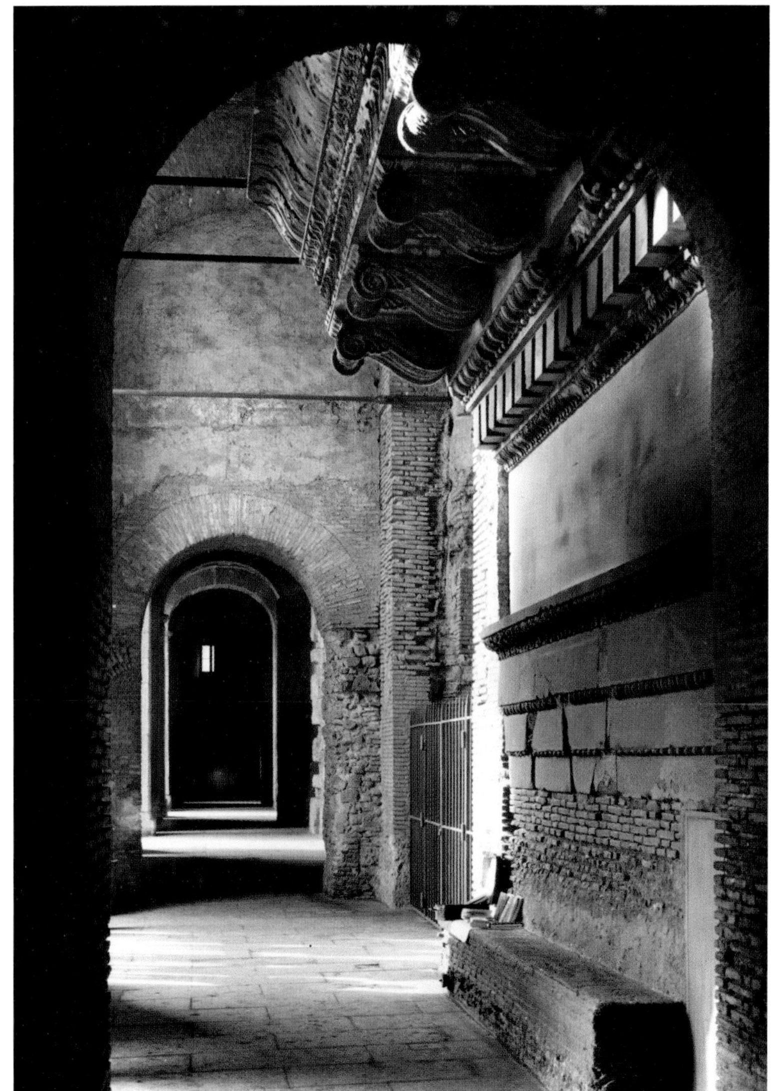

30. Photographer unknown
*Remains of the Temple of Mars
Ultor, Forum of Augustus,
in the Convent of Santa Maria
Annunziata ai Monti, 1930s*

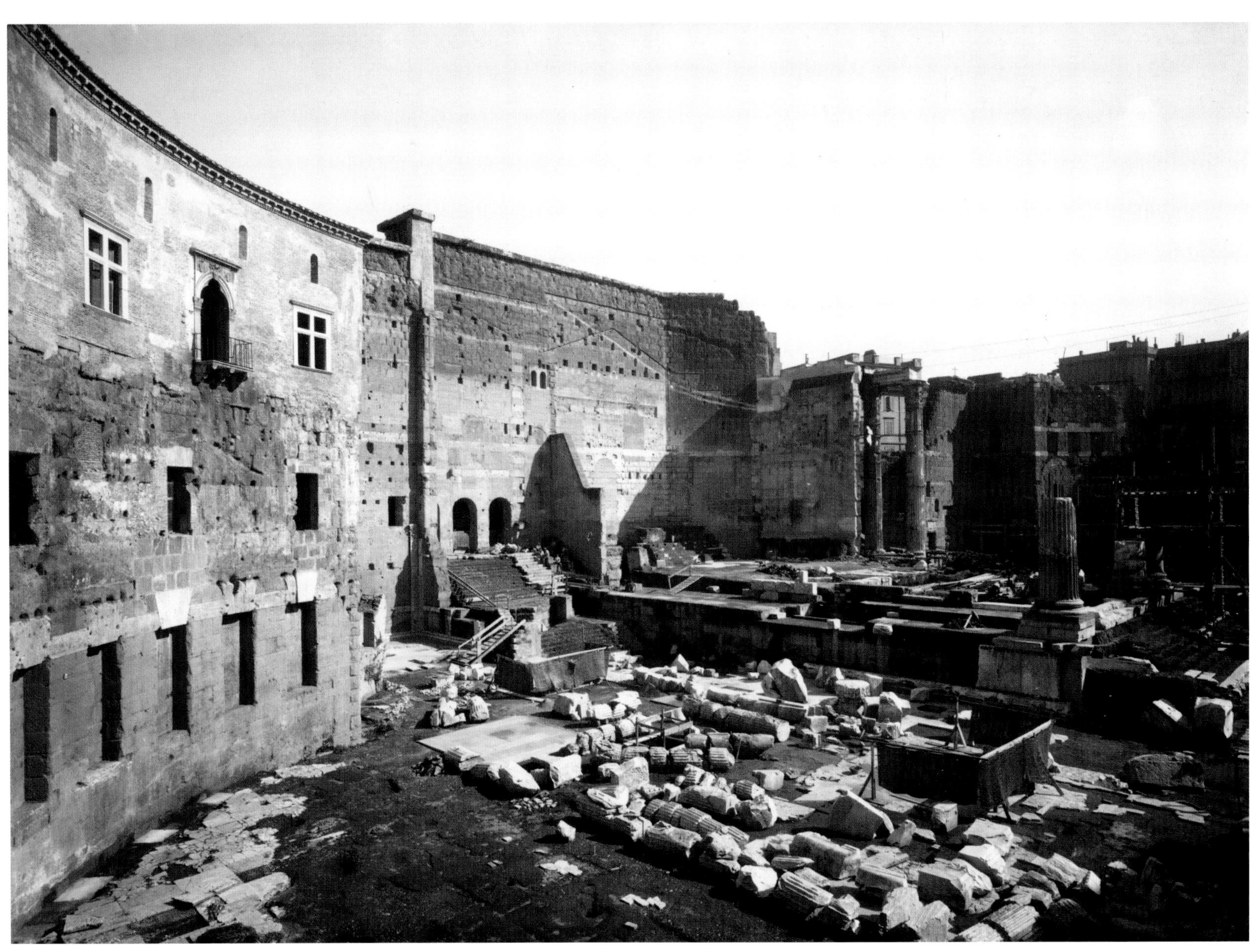

31. Photographer unknown
*Temple of Venus and Roma,
Roman Forum after the 1932
fitting out*, 1930s

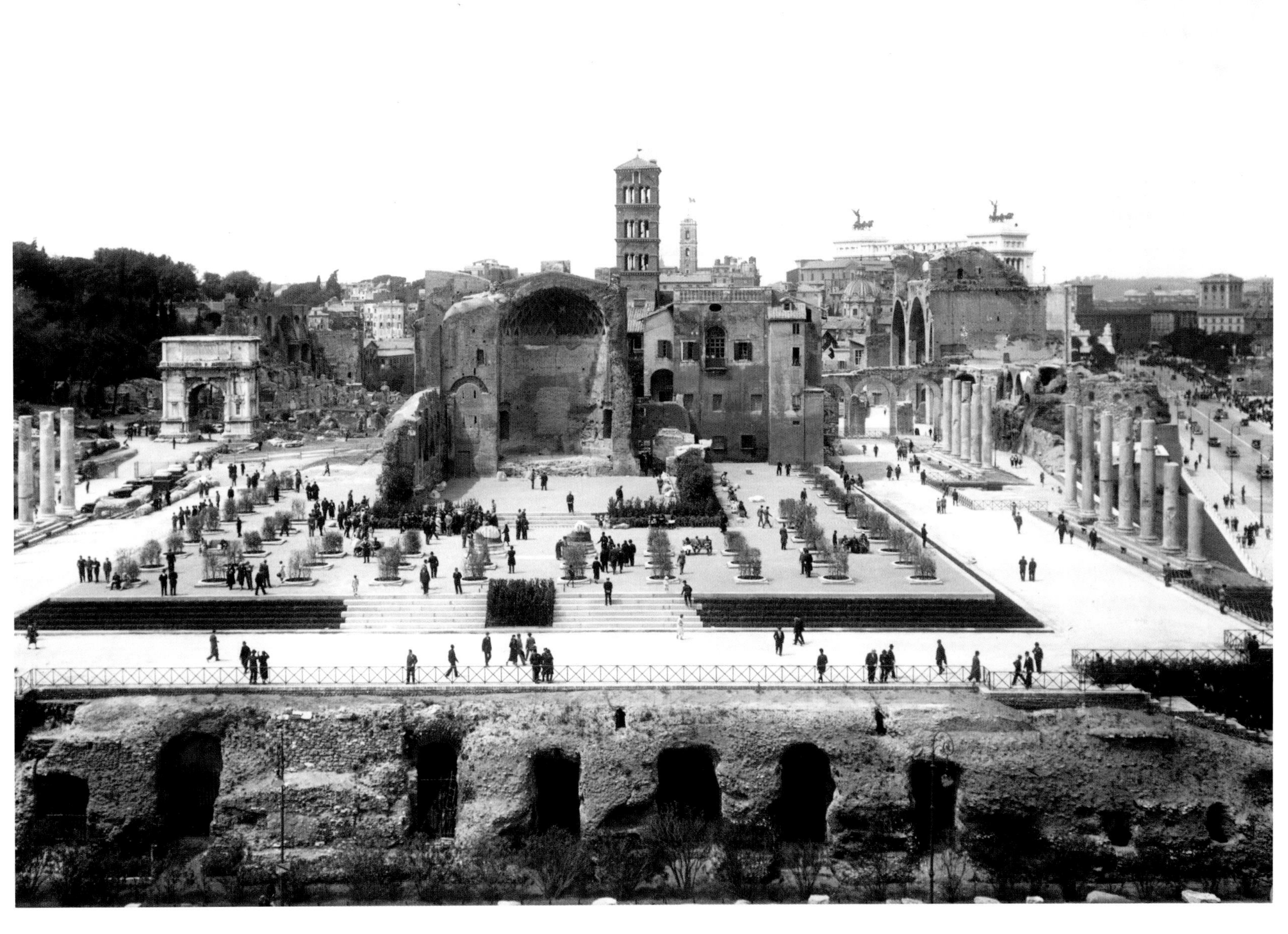

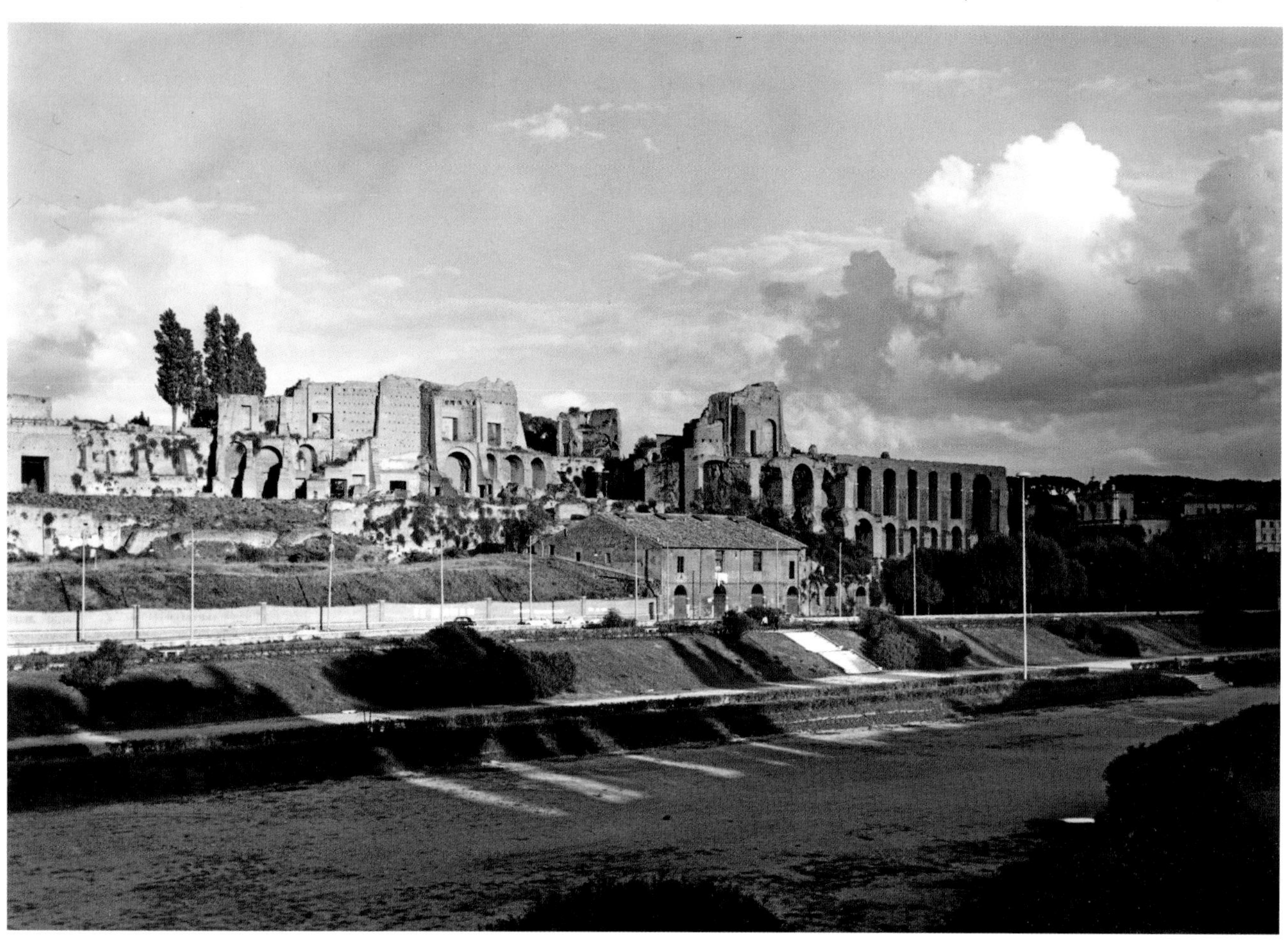

32. Edwin Smith
*Circus Maximus,
with the Palatine Hill
in the background*, 1970

33. Edwin Smith
*Temple of Venus and Roma,
Roman Forum*, 1970

34. Ralph Deakin
*Flavian Amphitheatre
(Colosseum)*, 1930s

35. Ralph Deakin
Roman Forum, 1930s

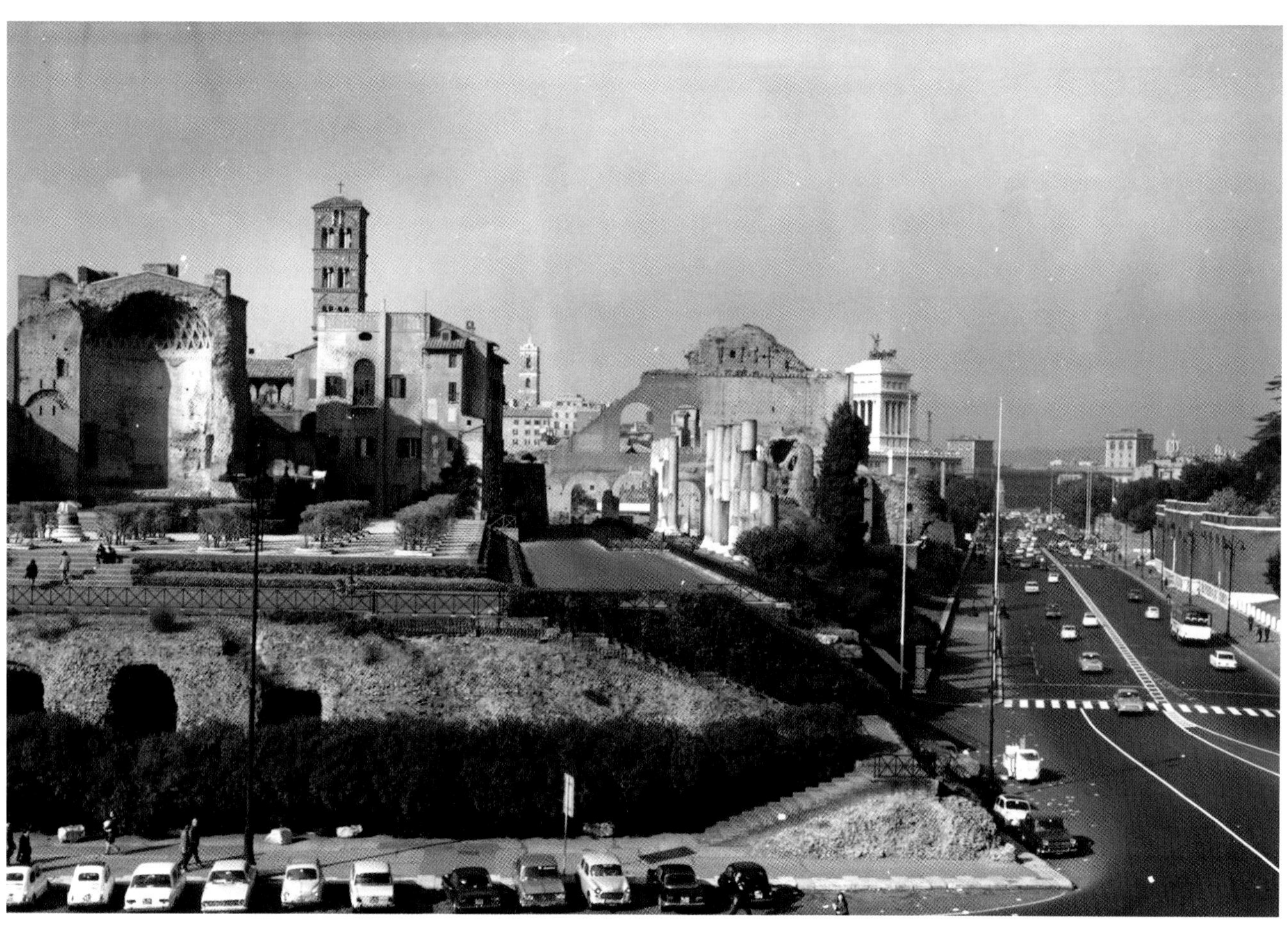

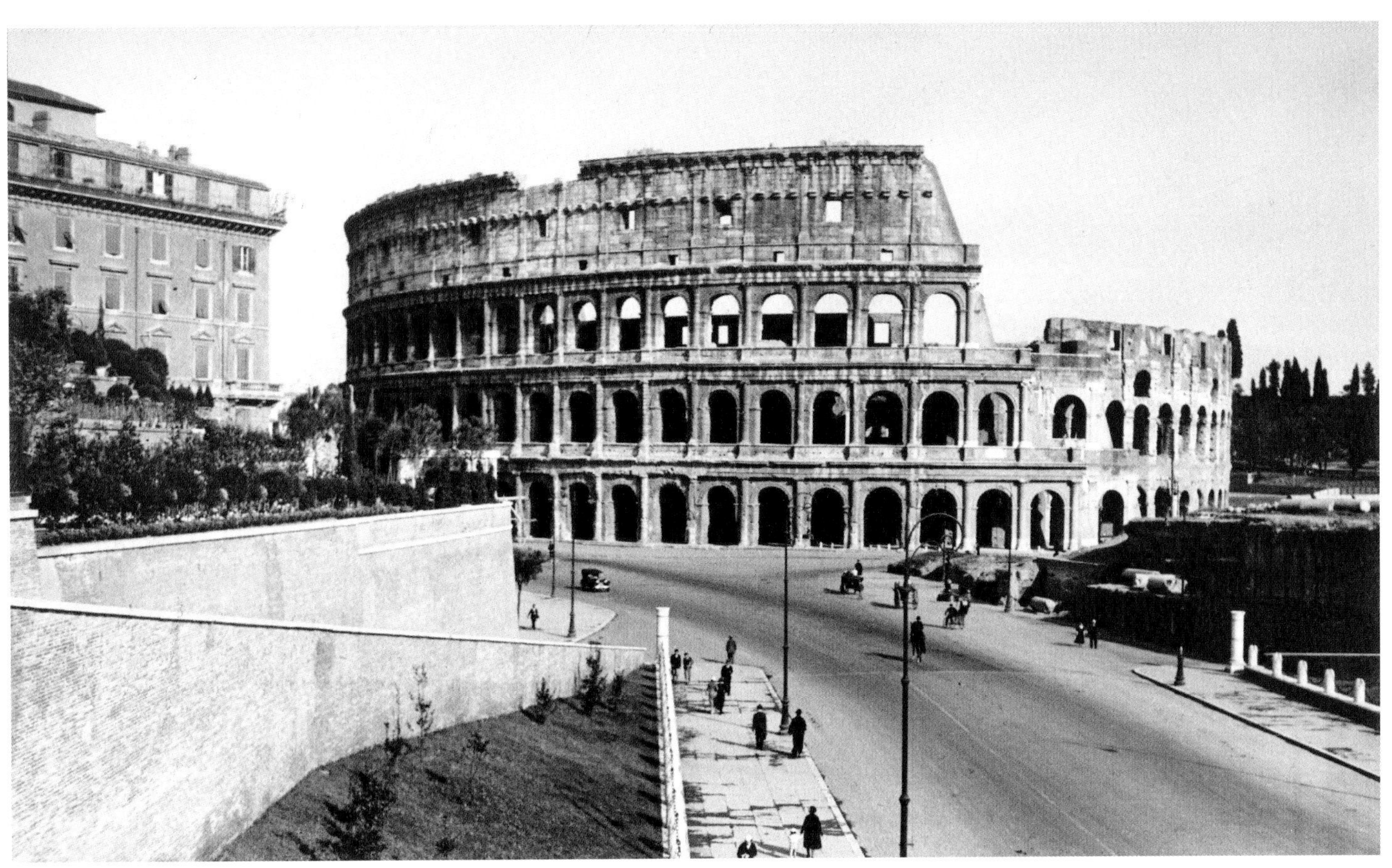

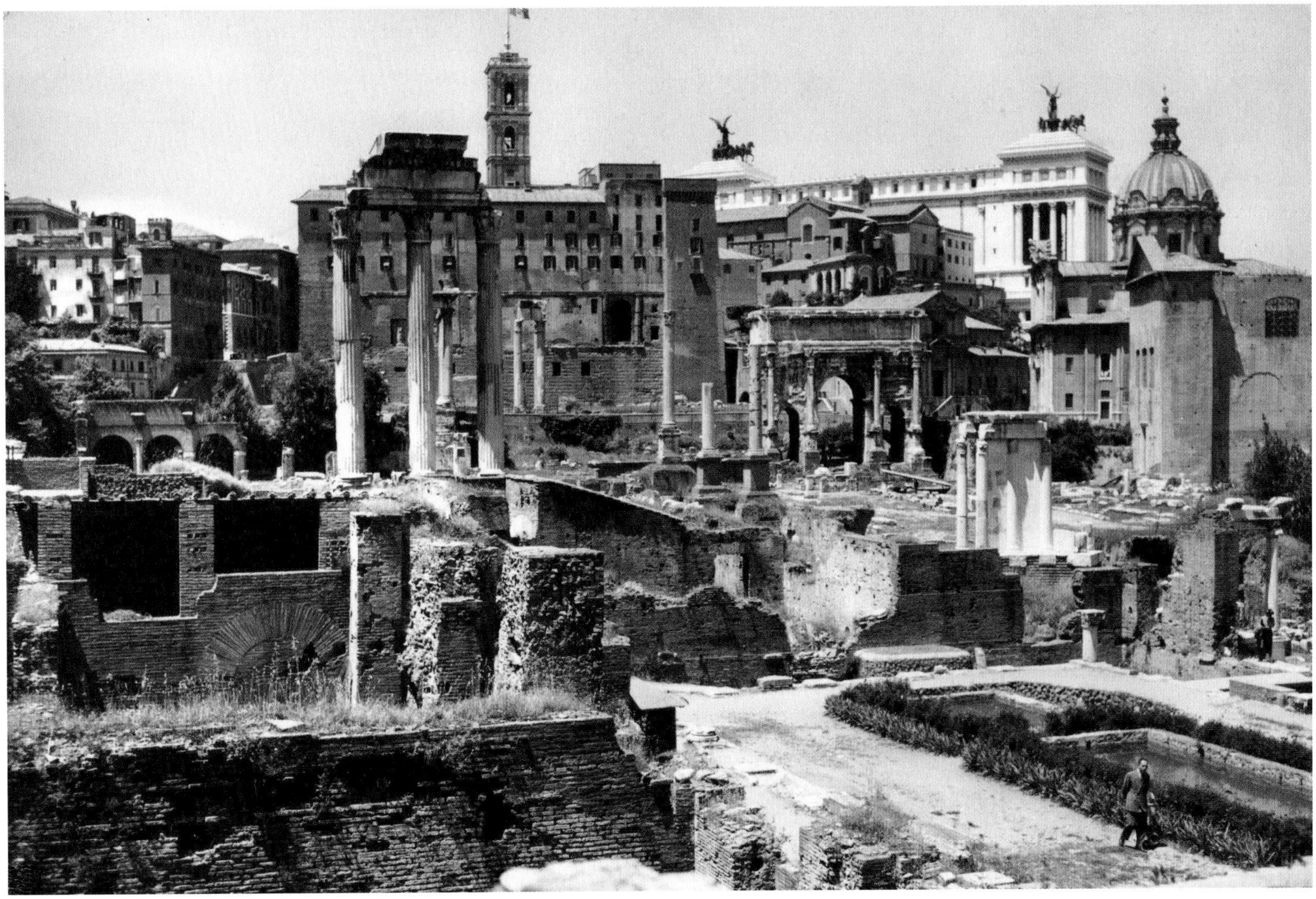

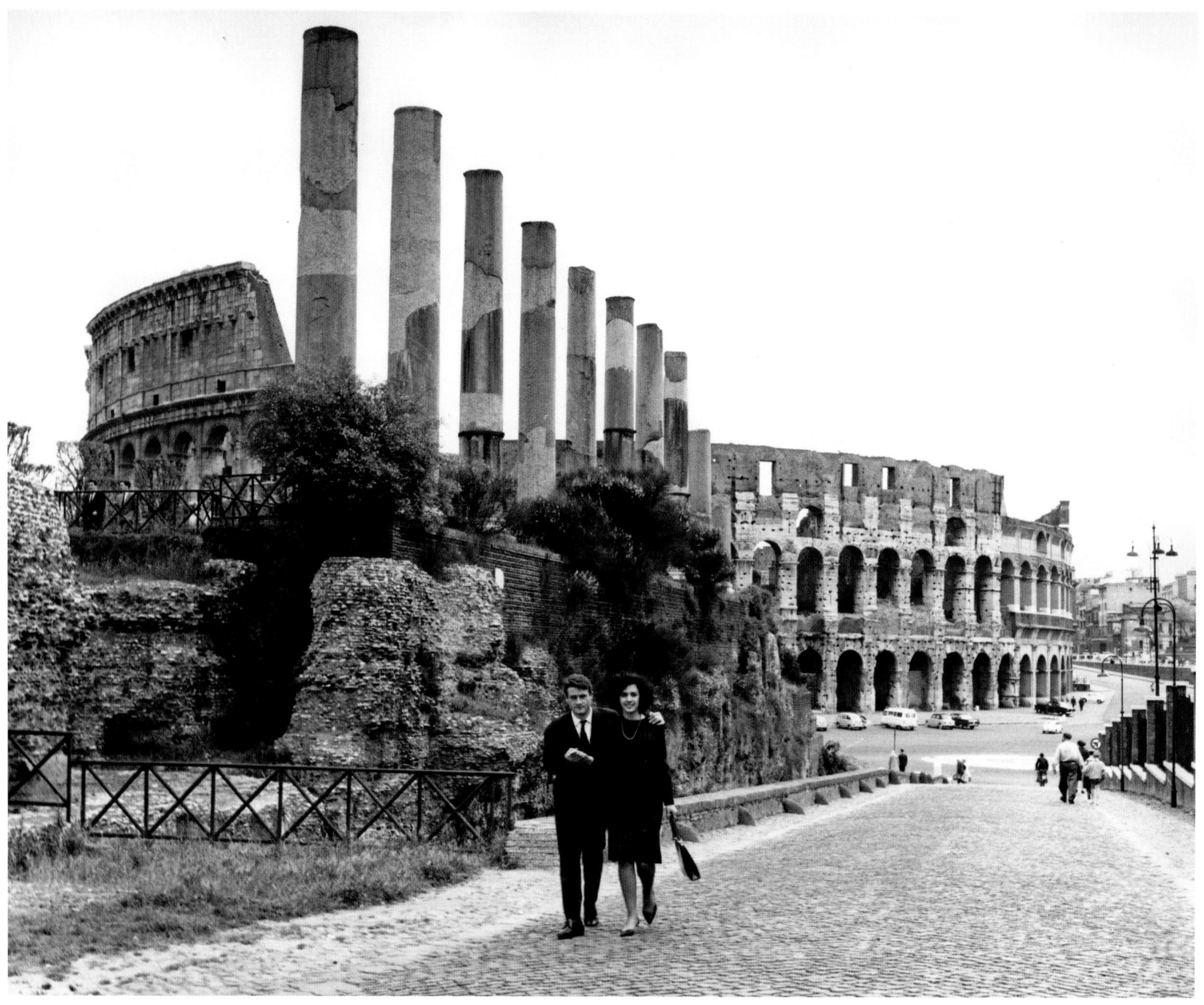

36. Monica Pidgeon
*Flavian Amphitheatre
(Colosseum) from
the north-west*, 1961

37. Monica Pidgeon
Temple of Vespasian,
Flavian Amphitheatre, 1961

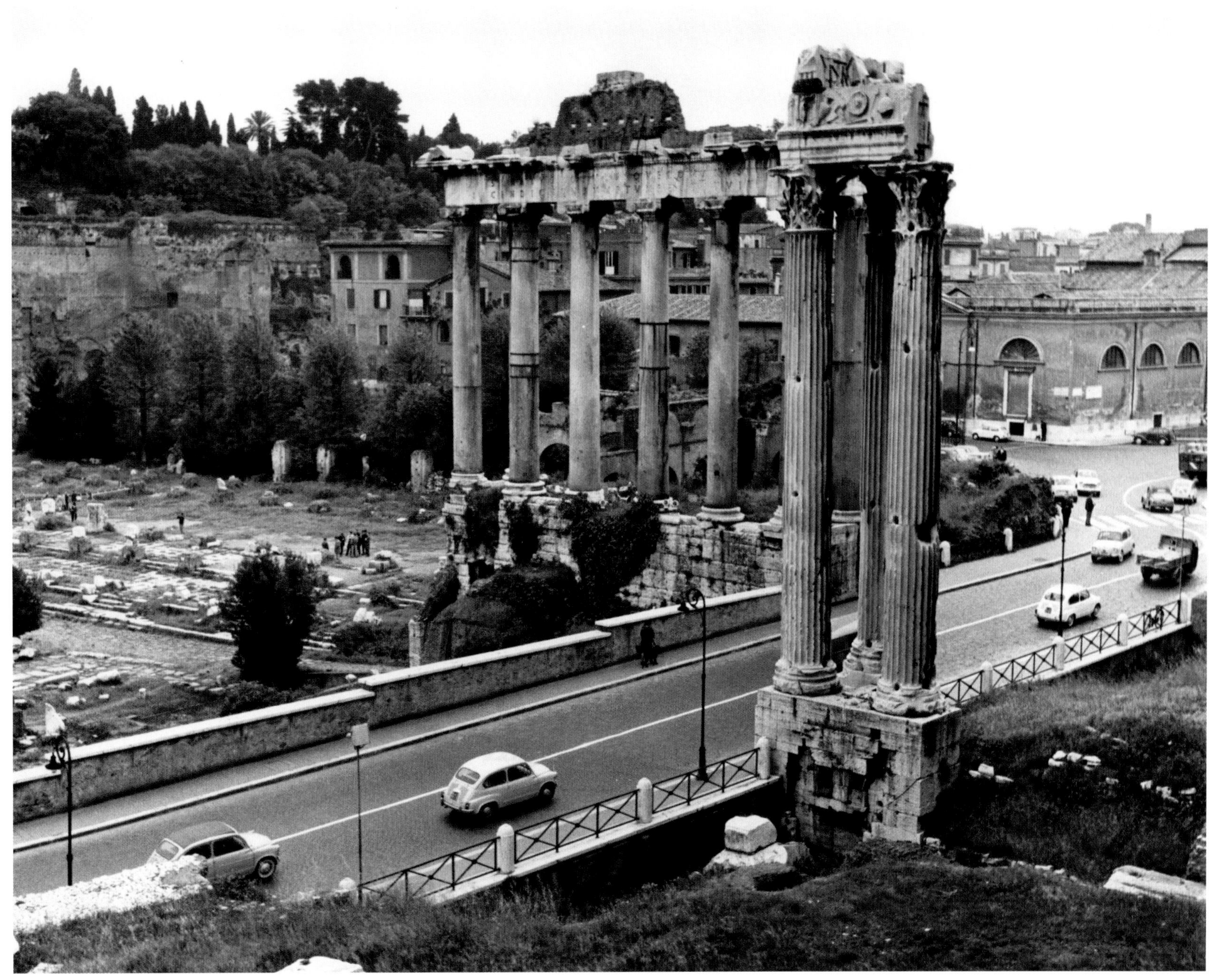

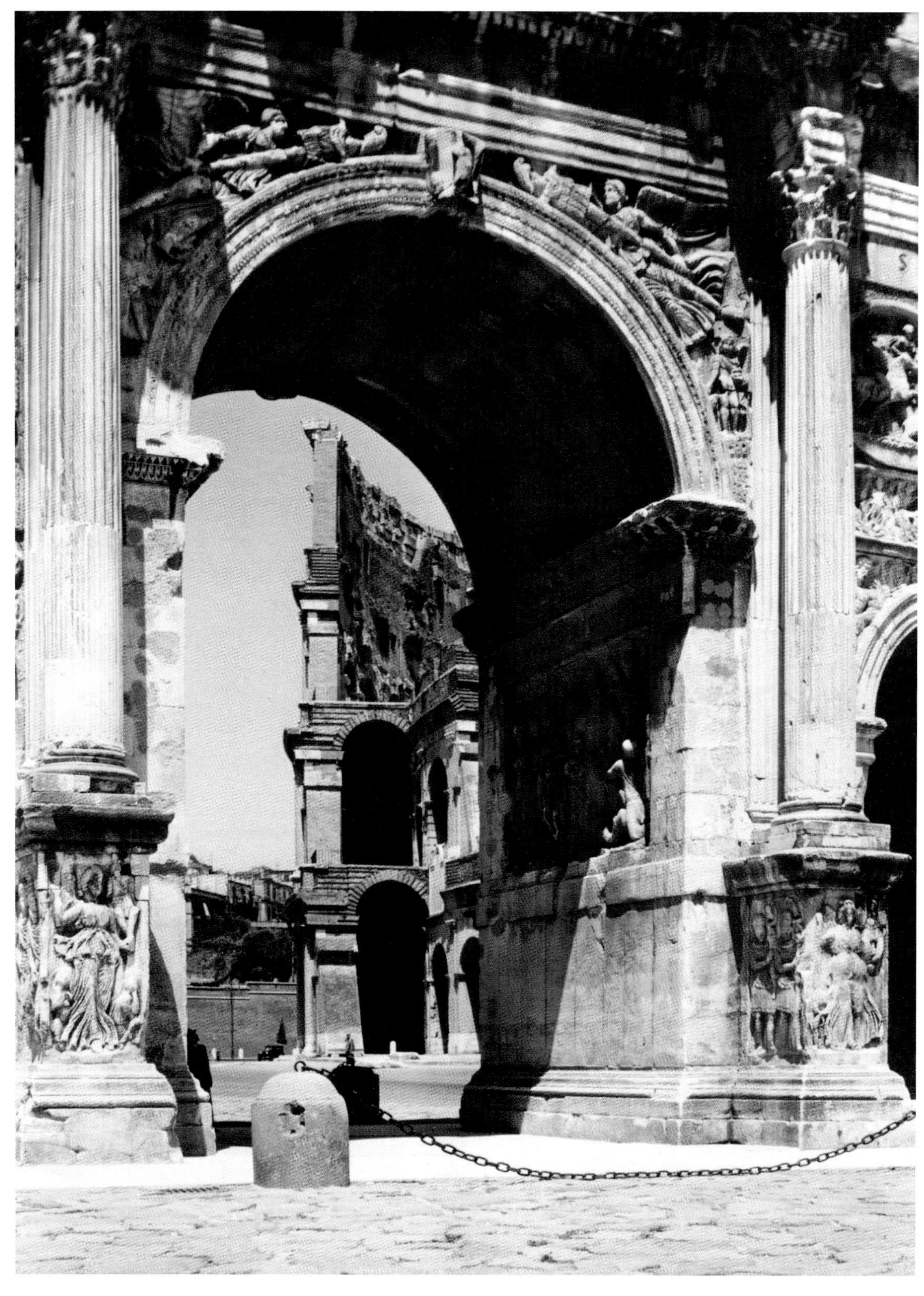

38. Ralph Deakin
Arch of Constantine,
with a glimpse of the Flavian
Amphitheatre (Colosseum),
1930s

39. Unknown photographer
Detail of Flavian Amphitheatre,
1950s

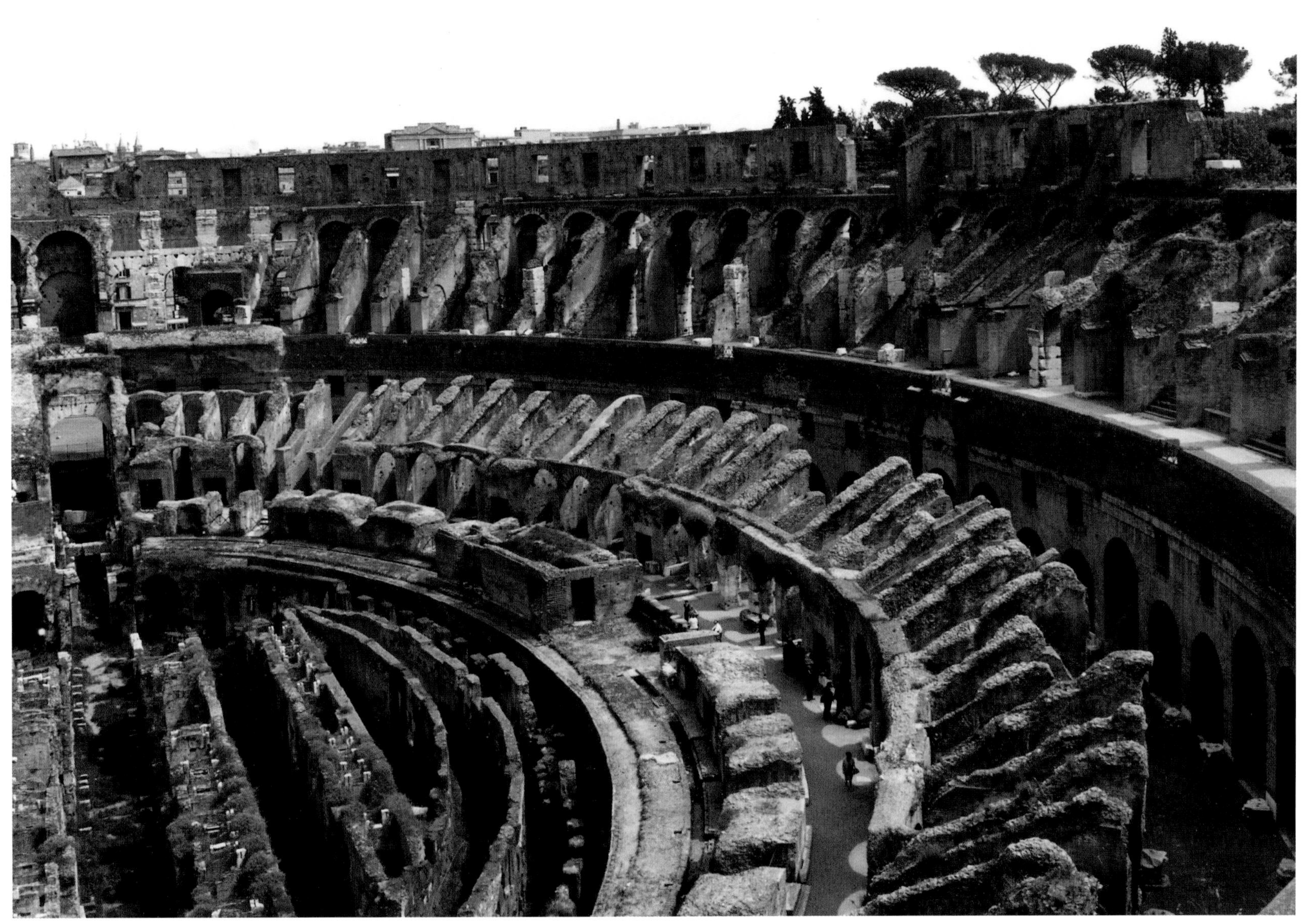

40. Stabilimento Fotografico
Domenico Anderson
*Interior of the Flavian
Amphitheatre (Colosseum),*
early twentieth century

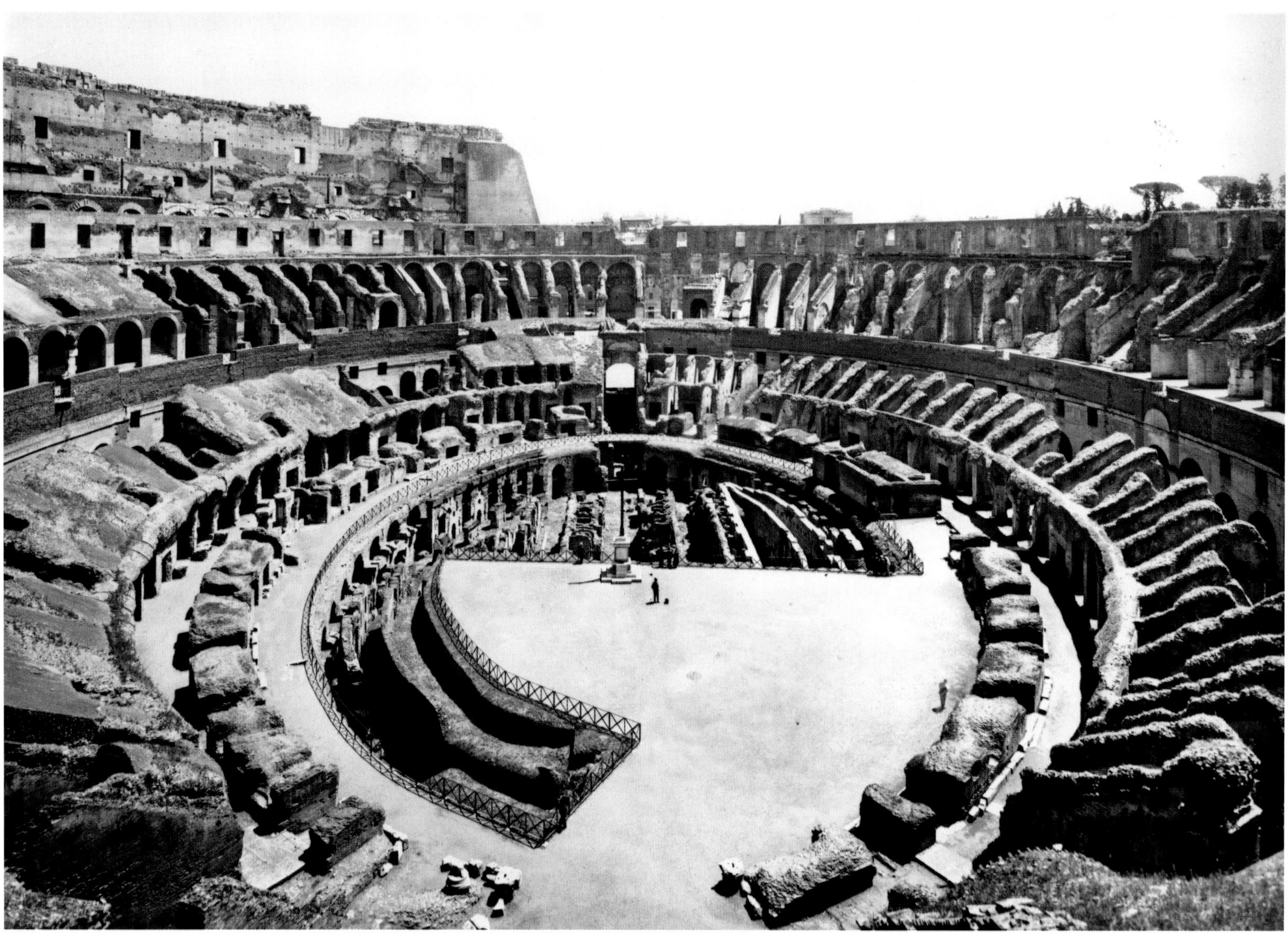

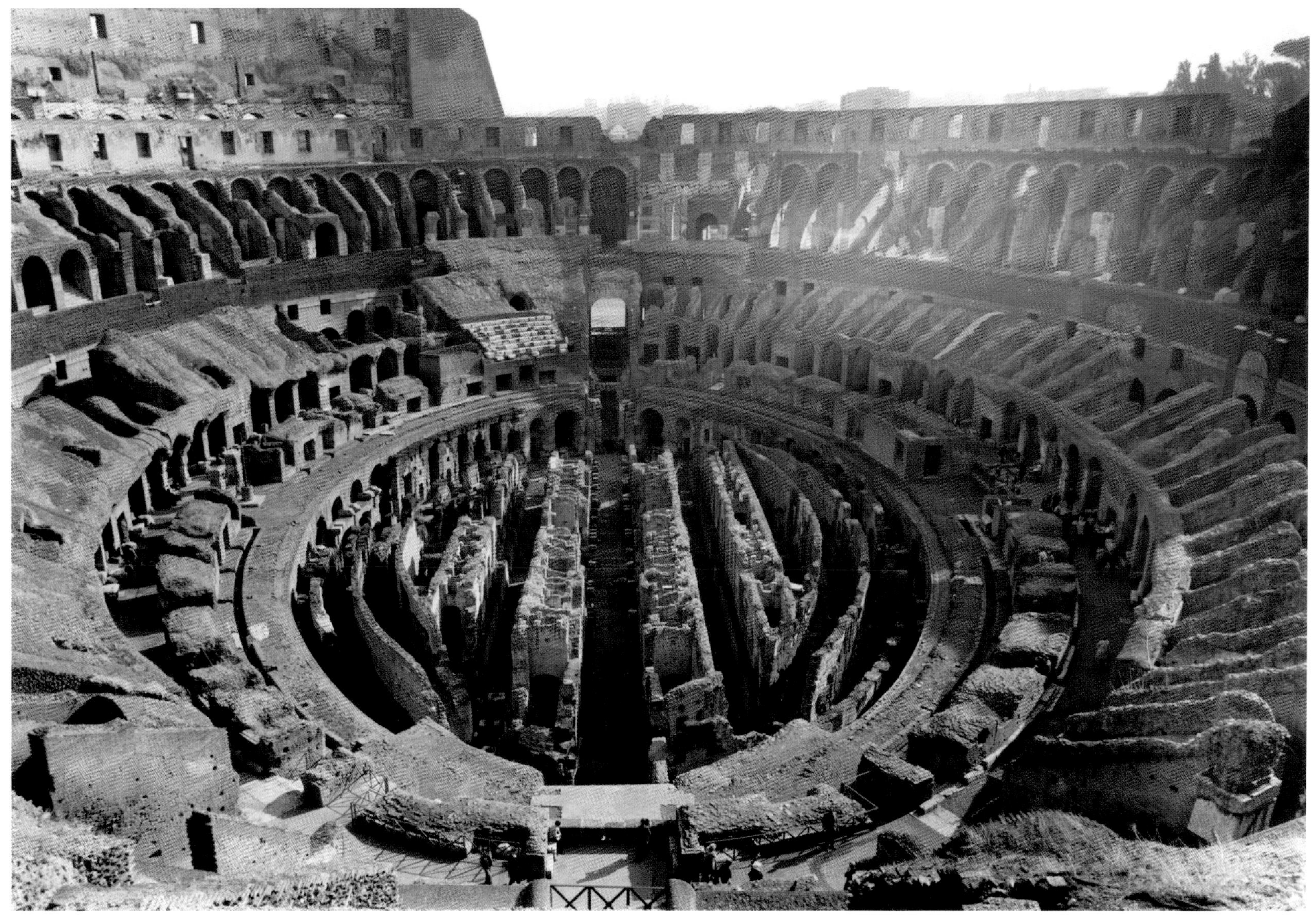

41. Edwin Smith
*Interior of the Flavian
Amphitheatre*, 1970

Imagine a young architectural student arriving in Rome, at the Stazione Termini, in the 1960s. What preconceptions does he bring with him (for 80% of British architectural students were male at that time)? What did he expect, what did he encounter, how did he react?

Rome, the Eternal City, was surely a city of continuities: from the antique past through the Renaissance and Baroque period, to its (dimly understood and perceived) modern manifestation. And architectural history for him at that date had two components. Firstly, in the interpretation of Sigfried Giedion and Nikolaus Pevsner, it was essentially an evolving history of space. But following the perceptions of Wittkower's *Architectural Principles in the Age of Humanism*, and his pupil Colin Rowe in his 'Mathematics of the Ideal Villa', what really counted was the consistency of architectural form, and the manipulation of geometry: interpretations validated by Christian Norberg-Schulz's *Intentions in Architecture*.[1] So our enthusiastic student went to Santa Maria Maggiore not to inspect its architectural motifs but to stand on its steps and gaze down the axis established by Sixtus V; he visited Santa Maria della Pace not to study Pietro da Cortona's façade but to examine Bramante's solution to the 'corner problem'.

The first surprise was surely Stazione Termini itself. No doubt he had thought it was just a station that was a 'terminus', and was embarrassed to discover that its name referred to the site of some remains of the Diocletian baths.[2] But more disconcerting than this first reminder, of history in the presence of the modern, was his experience of the space itself: the platforms disgorging on to a monumental cross-axis, and then the sinuous canopy, echoing the shape of the preserved Servian walls, catapulting arriving passengers into the bustling city. Turning to look back on the façade, he saw beyond an inventive game of scale — nine window stripes on a building that clearly was not nine floors high. This was a kind of modernism, designed in the late 1940s, for which no one had prepared him: a visceral manipulation of the emotions in the handling of space, and a shocking flirtation with ambiguous form. He knew something of Nervi — indeed he intended a pilgrimage to the Palazzetto dello Sport. But that was an example of how rigorous structural efficiency becomes a sculptural artefact, and its circular geometry ensured it was a 'figure', like the Pantheon. It could safely be placed amongst the 'lessons of Rome' that Le Corbusier had observed. This canopy and façade suggested another starting point for architecture,

accommodating to context, and derived from an understanding of how a building might be experienced rather than how it might obey some pre-determined rules of form.

Undeterred, he starts to study the Baroque. He is aware of only one writer, Sacheverell Sitwell, who had written at any length about the style of which Britain had few coherent examples, but he was a member of an eccentric literary family.[3] Maybe the handling of the wall planes on baroque façades could be studied formally? Analytical drawings of the development of churches since the Gesù were duly prepared — Santa Susanna and the rest — and he felt himself to be a pioneer, since Anthony Blunt was yet to publish his own interpretation.[4] As he shaded his eyes to identify the differences between clusters of pilasters, half-round columns, three-quarter columns and fully disengaged columns, did he anticipate that another way of conceiving architecture was on its way, one that sought to privilege the experience of phenomena in a more personal and rounded way? And did he realise that, ten years before, the young Robert Venturi had been reading Rome in a completely different way, seeing complexity and contradiction in the composition of Mannerist and Baroque buildings, and understanding the way that Moretti or Brasini could be understood as inheritors of that tradition?

In short, he did not. He would have done well to have looked at some contemporary images of Rome, and perhaps taken more notice of the lessons of 'Townscape' promoted in the monthly *Architectural Review*. In time he would grow to realise that photographers, like topographical artists in the eighteenth and nineteenth centuries, both subscribed to inherited conventions and developed their own characteristic style. Two-point, not three-point, perspective was *de rigueur* — so when he abandoned his own Voigtländer to adopt a more sophisticated camera it had to be a Nikon with a perspective control lens. Subsequently he would gaze intently at the photographs of professionals to check the parallax, and see whether they included people in relation to space, as did John Donat (1933–2004); or sought to evacuate the frames of the traces of human activity in order to privilege form; or included clues as to inhabitation, to suggest rather than portray the relationship between the settings and the action that could be anticipated. He could not fail to notice one characteristic, however, and that led him to question some of his architectural preconceptions. Photographers of the city sought to capture, in most instances, its character and atmosphere. Sunshine and shadow (aided by red filters), reflections

and silhouettes, figured as strongly as
architectural motifs. Could similar concerns
be a starting point for architecture itself?
Could form be the result of a concern for
place, rather than of the rational
manipulation of geometry to meet analysable
human needs, and aesthetic preconceptions?
Might discontinuities be privileged over
continuities? If so, where would he find
examples to sustain that thesis?

In Rome itself, it would turn out, even if
the re-balancing swiftly turned to caricature.
Rowe's *Collage City* superseded the
'Mathematics of the Ideal Villa' and his
'Roma Interrotta' succeeded the comfortable
continuities to which he had become
accustomed.[5] Nolli's map, manipulated
by a new generation of architects bored
with the previous orthodoxy, was to become
a self-conscious mapping of a heterodox,
self-conscious post-modernism. Naturally,
in catering without difficulty to radical
discontinuities, Rome paradoxically
reasserted itself as the city of continuities:
how could it not do so?

And what came after these disjunctions?
New reappraisals, and a collection of
representative artefacts. During the 1950s
architects learned from Aldo Rossi to love
the aedicule, but during the 1980s and 1990s
they were able to look again at the stripped
neo-classicism of EUR. With the passage
of time, its fascist associations could be
discounted, and the differences 'between
Pagano and Piacentini, Michelucci and
Terragni, Argan and Bartolini', which
as early as 1941 Gio Ponti had been accused
of smoothing over, could be forgotten.[6]
Stripped classicism could be stripped of its
associations. At the same time, as other cities
had done, Rome could begin to collect
representative examples of international
architects' work: Meier and Hadid, as well
as Renzo Piano.

Perhaps our student retains some vestige
of his 'formal' training in the 1960s? Or
maybe he has come to a similar conclusion as
the thoughtful Rafael Moneo, who had spent
two years in the early 1960s at the Spanish
Academy in Rome: there are occasions
when free composition is required,
and others when the architect has a duty
to choose carefully from the substantial
repertoire provided by the canon of
architectural history. Neither
autobiographical consistency, nor a striving
after those dynamic effects that the newest
technology can achieve, should justify
sculptural inventiveness in every instance:
the city is not simply landscape.

That is not to say that landscape does not
help to fashion the city, sometimes in a
profound way. Michelangelo's simultaneously
modest yet monumental group of buildings
on the Capitoline — part conversion, part
screen, part new construction — acts as a
threshold to that memorable valley, fashioned
by the hills around: the Forum itself.
Each addition to the complex of buildings,
and their weathering over time, contributes
to its atmosphere, and the white Monument
to Vittorio Emanuele II does not inflict
serious damage. Rome is robust, he realises.
And the city has always been re-read by
each generation in its own way, continuously
relevant, providing exemplary timeless
precedents for everything purporting
to be new.

Nicholas Ray

[1] Rudolf Wittkower, *Architectural Principles in the Age of Humanism*, London: The Warburg Institute, 1949; Colin Rowe, 'The Mathematics of the Ideal Villa', in *Architectural Review*, March 1947, republished 1976 in *The Mathematics of the Ideal Villa and Other Essays*, London and Cambridge, MA: MIT Press); Christian Norberg-Schulz, *Intentions in Architecture*, London and Cambridge, MA: MIT Press, 1968.
[2] More precisely to the so-called *Botte di Termini*, a cistern demolished in nineteenth century.
[3] Sacheverell Sitwell, *Southern Baroque Revisited*, London: Weidenfeld & Nicolson, 1967.
[4] Anthony Blunt, *Guide to Baroque Rome*, New York: Harper & Row, 1982.
[5] Colin Rowe, Fred Koetter, *Collage City*, London and Cambridge, MA: MIT Press, 1978; Colin Rowe, 'Roma Interrotta', in *Architectural Design Profile*, vol. 49, no. 3-4, 1979. Even Norberg-Schulz changed his own position: Christian Norberg-Schulz, *Genius Loci*, New York: Rizzoli, 1979.
[6] Giuseppe Pagano, 'Potremo salvarci dalle false tradizioni e dalle ossessioni monumentali?', in *Costruzioni Casabella*, 157, January 1941, pp. 2–7.

42. Stabilimento
Fotografico Vasari
Termini Station, 1950

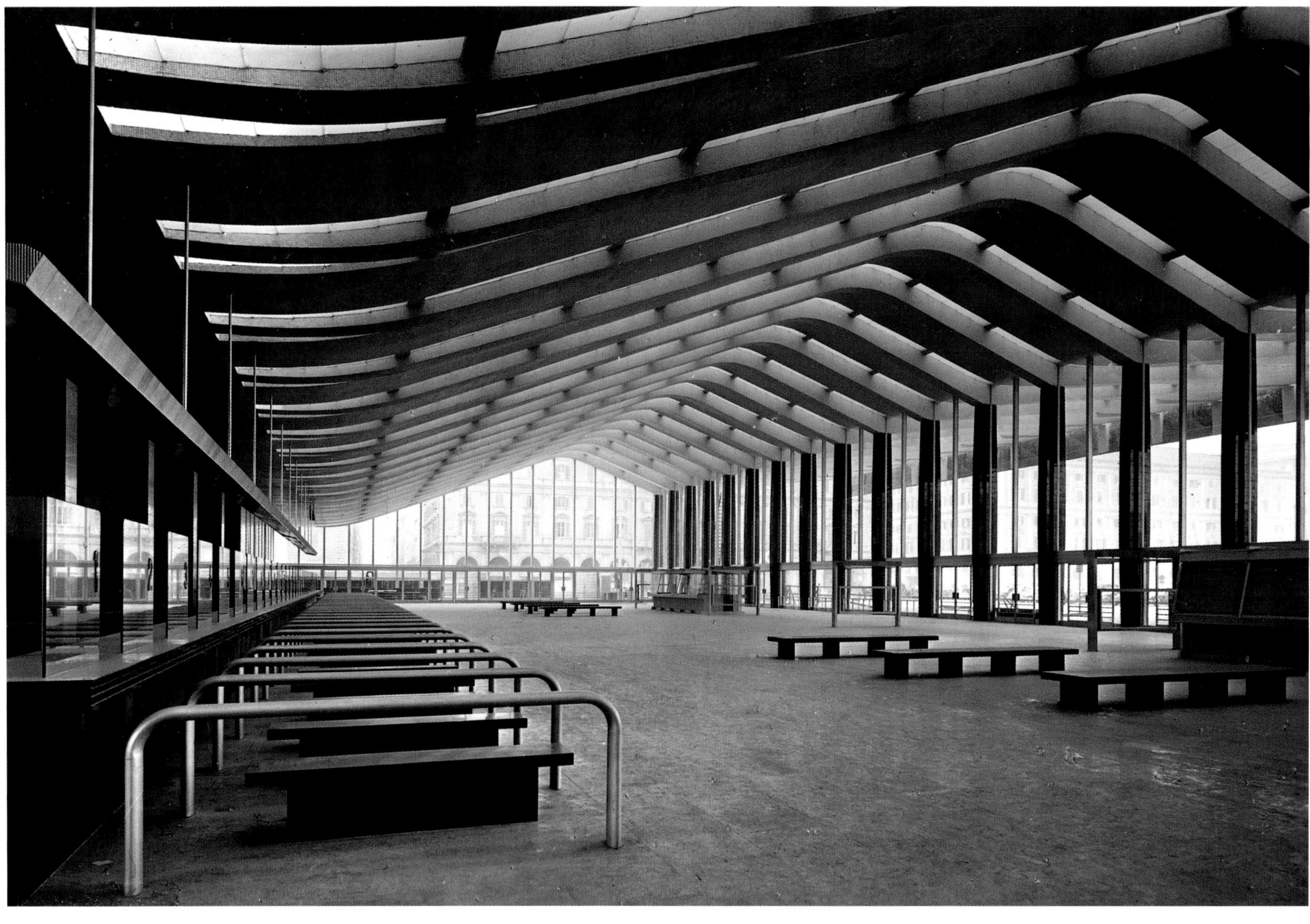

43. Marion Johnson
Termini Station, 1951

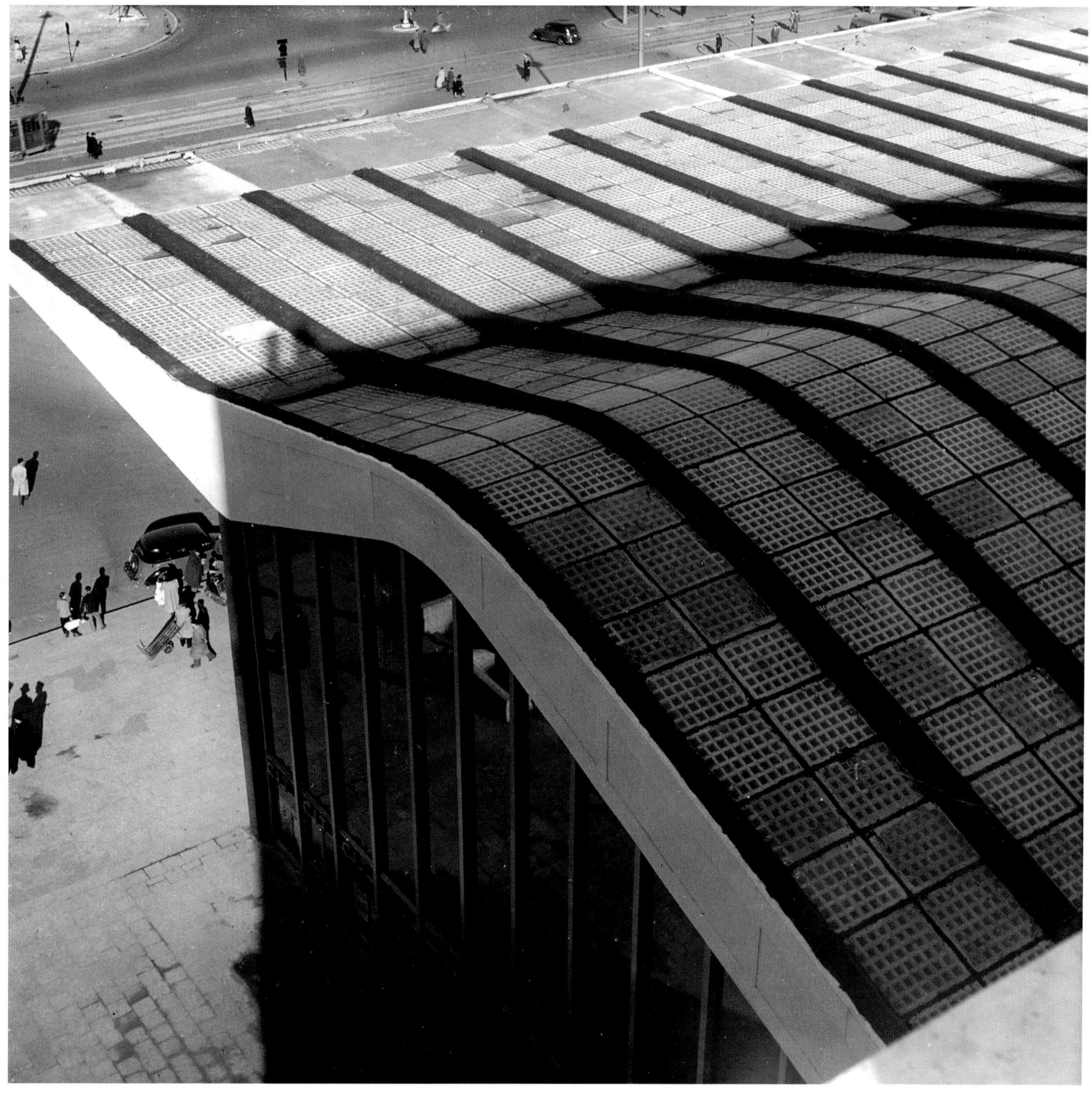

44. Marion Johnson
Termini Station, 1950

45. Marion Johnson
Termini Station, 1950

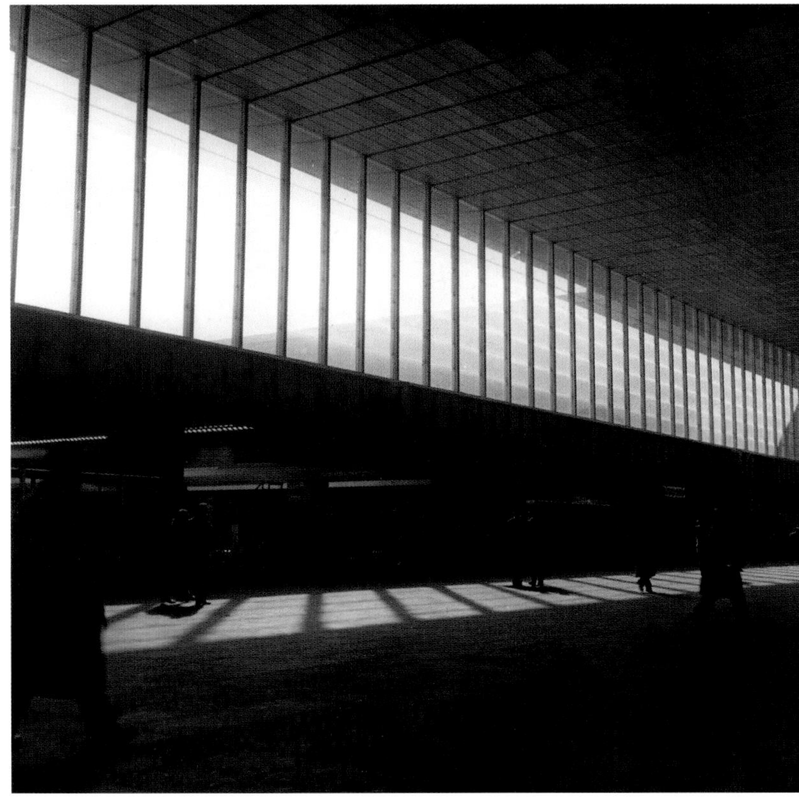

44. Marion Johnson
Termini Station, 1950

45. Marion Johnson
Termini Station, 1950

46. Marion Johnson
Termini Station, 1950

47. Marion Johnson
Termini Station, 1951

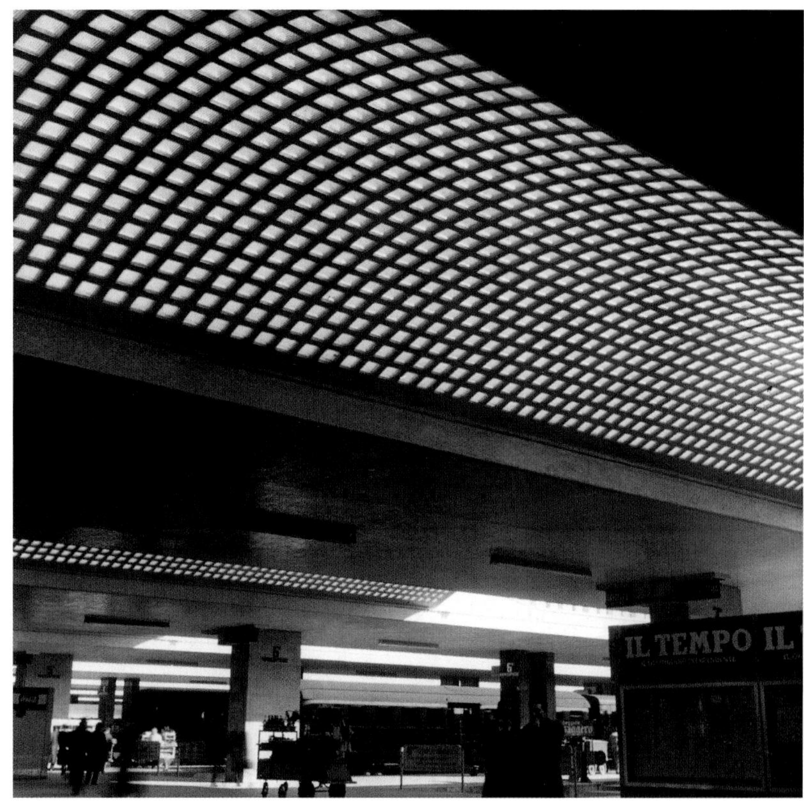
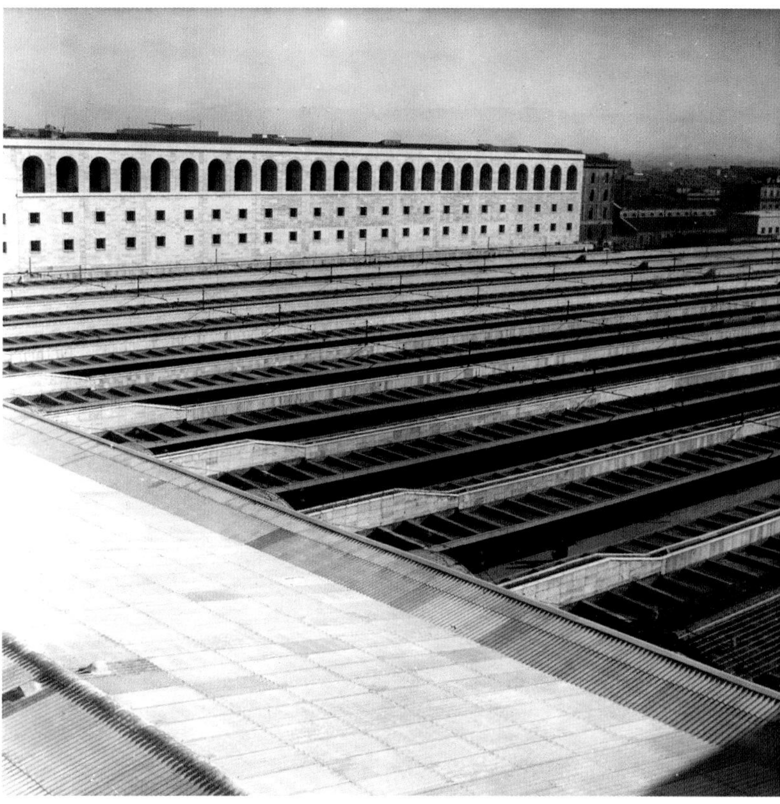

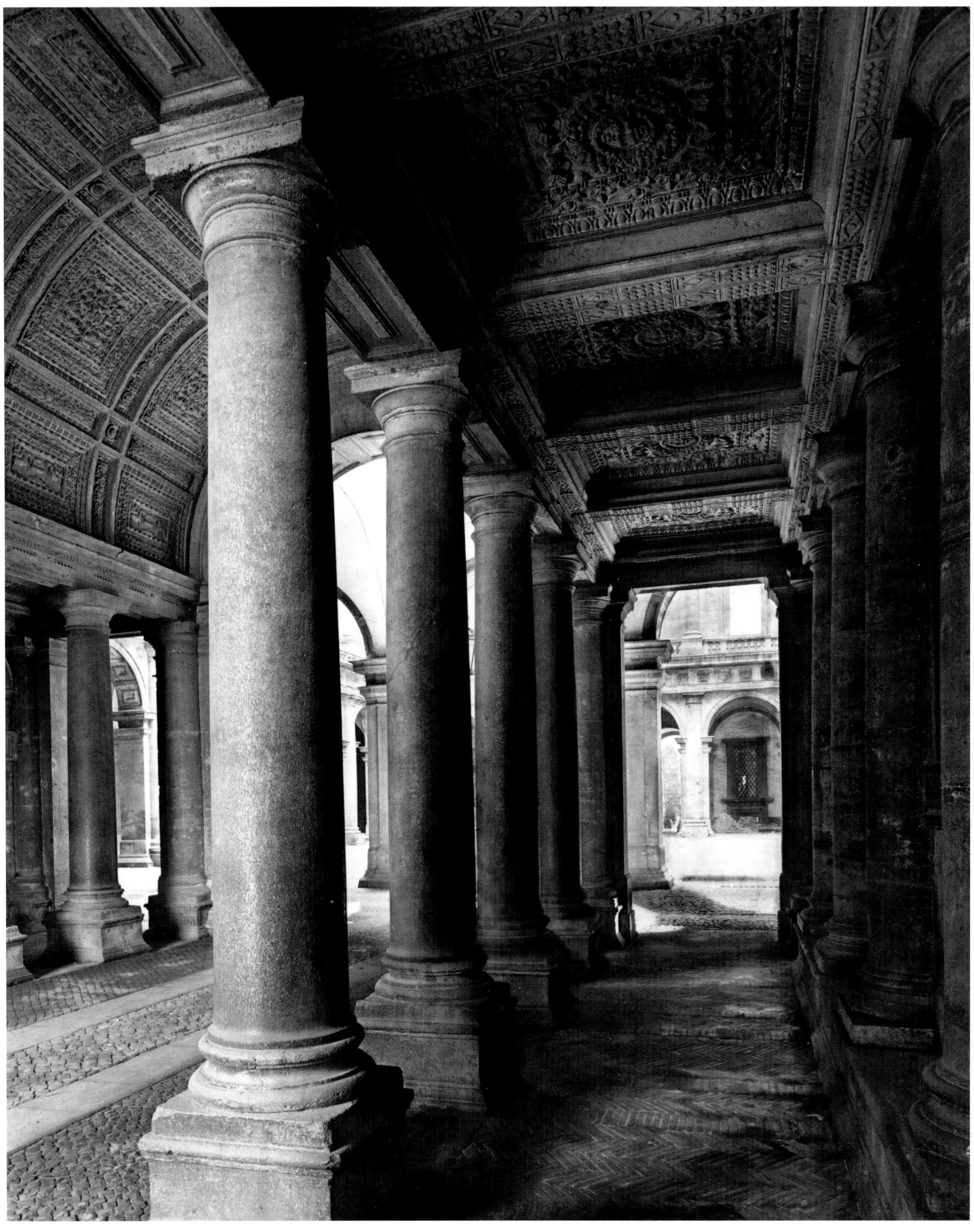

48. Stabilimento Fotografico
Domenico Anderson
Palazzo Farnese,
early twentieth century

49. Stabilimento Fotografico
Domenico Anderson
Palazzo Massimo alle Colonne,
early twentieth century

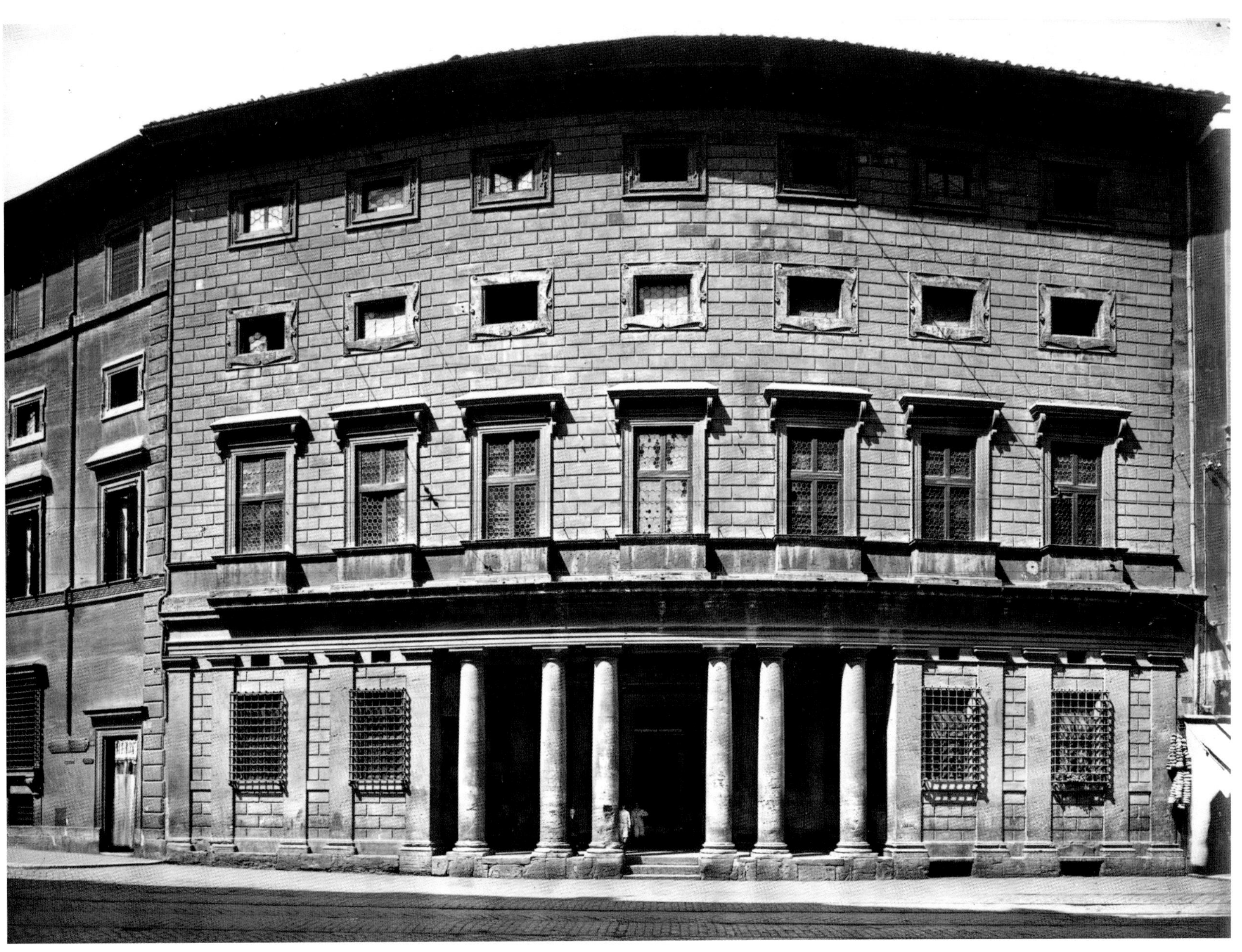

50. Edwin Smith
*Tempietto, San Pietro
in Montorio*, 1966

51. Edwin Smith
Sant'Ivo alla Sapienza, 1962

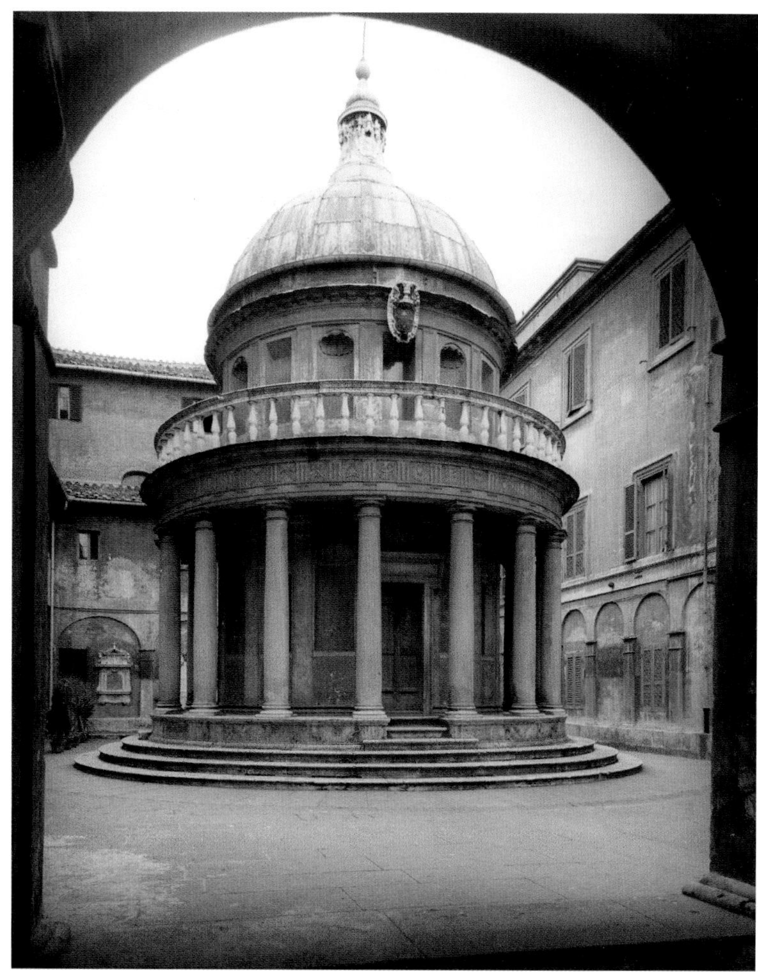

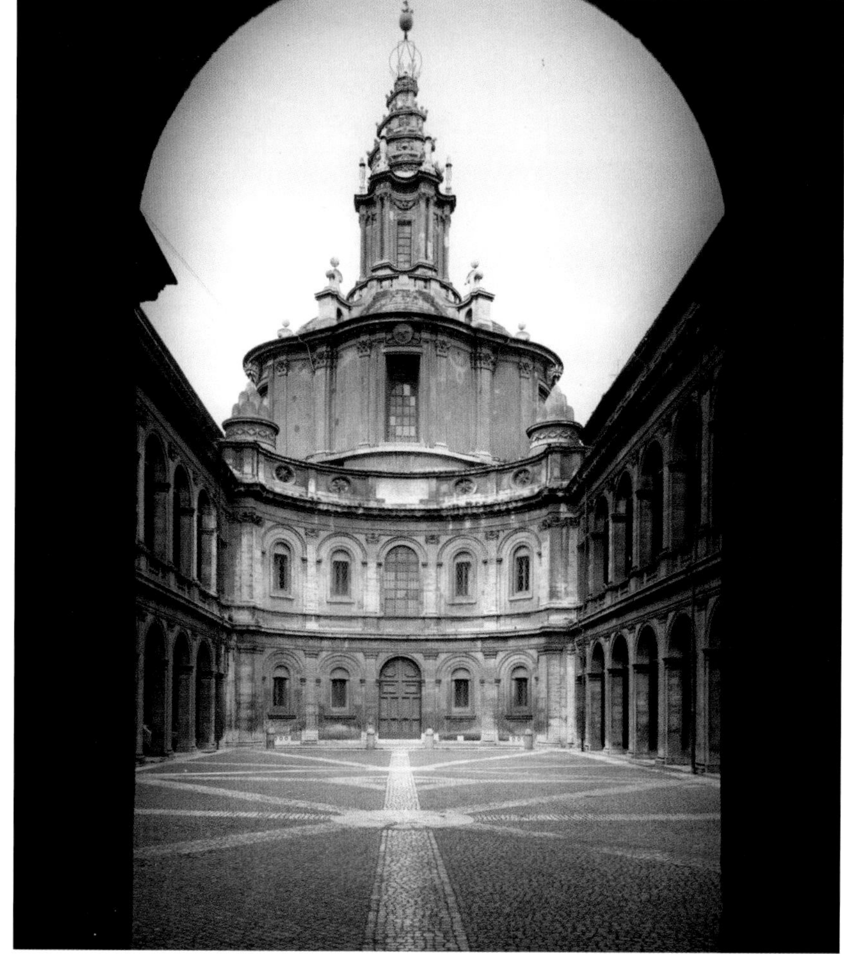

52. Stabilimento Fotografico
Domenico Anderson
*Model of the dome
of Saint Peter's Basilica*,
early twentieth century

53. Stabilimento Fotografico
Domenico Anderson
Dome of Saint Peter's Basilica,
early twentieth century

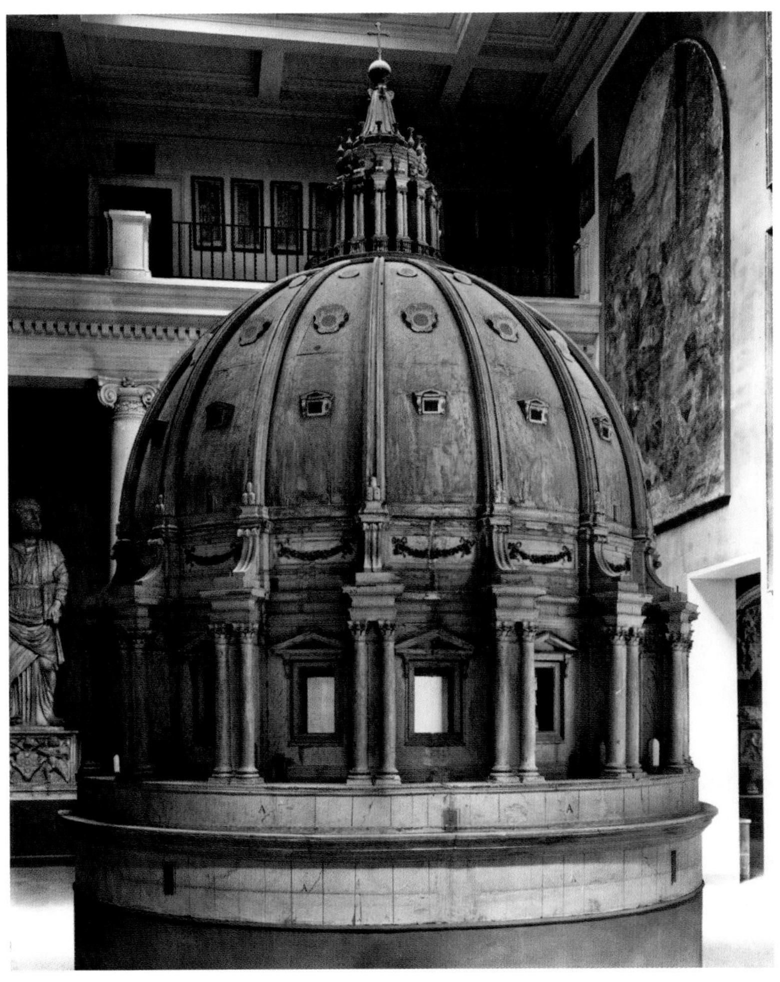

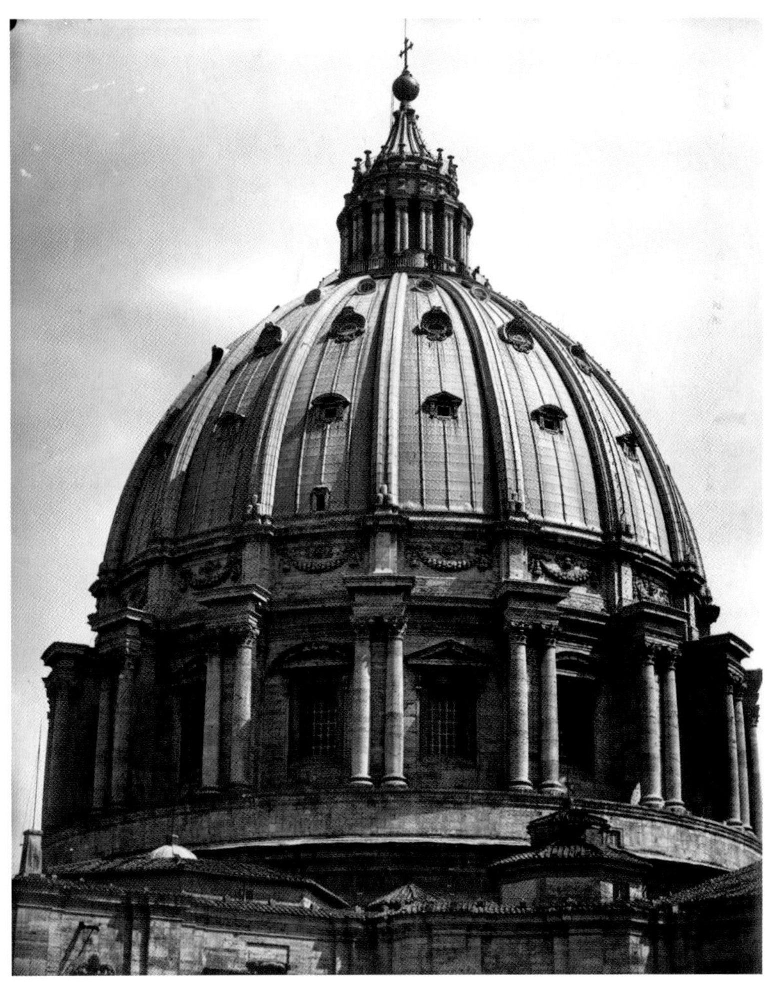

54. Edwin Smith
Sala dei Parati Piemontesi,
Palazzo del Quirinale, 1963

55. Ralph Deakin
Chiesa Nuova, or Santa Maria
in Vallicella, 1930s

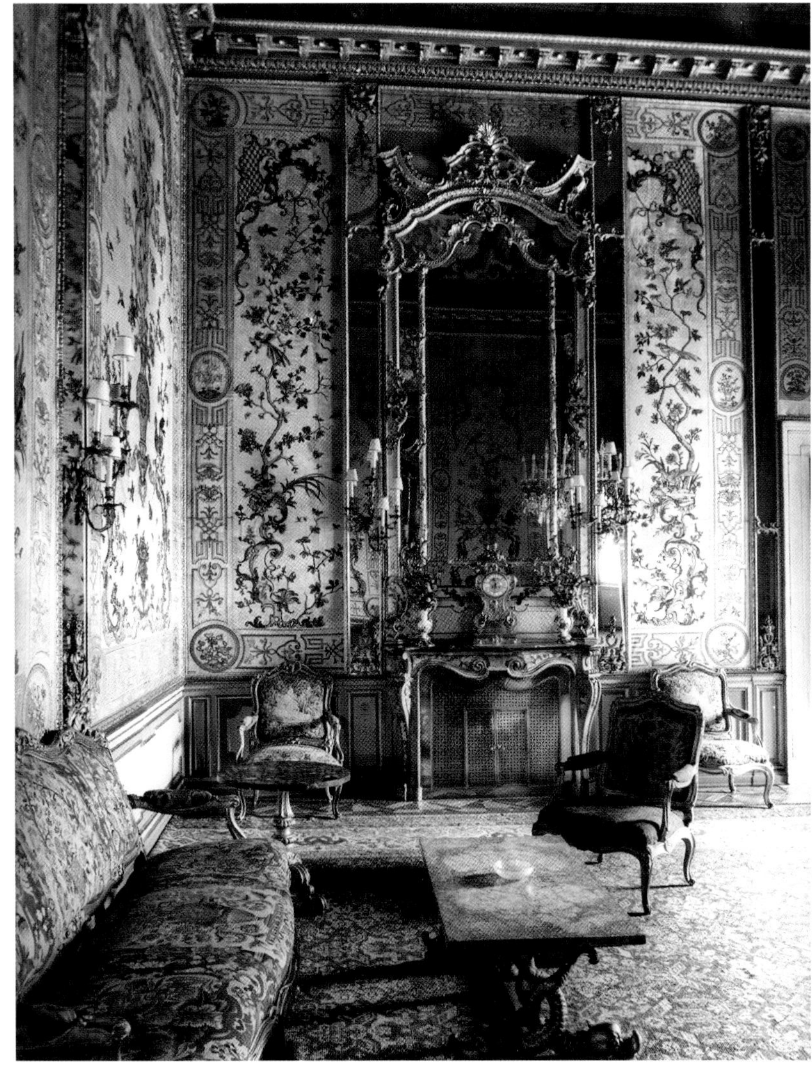

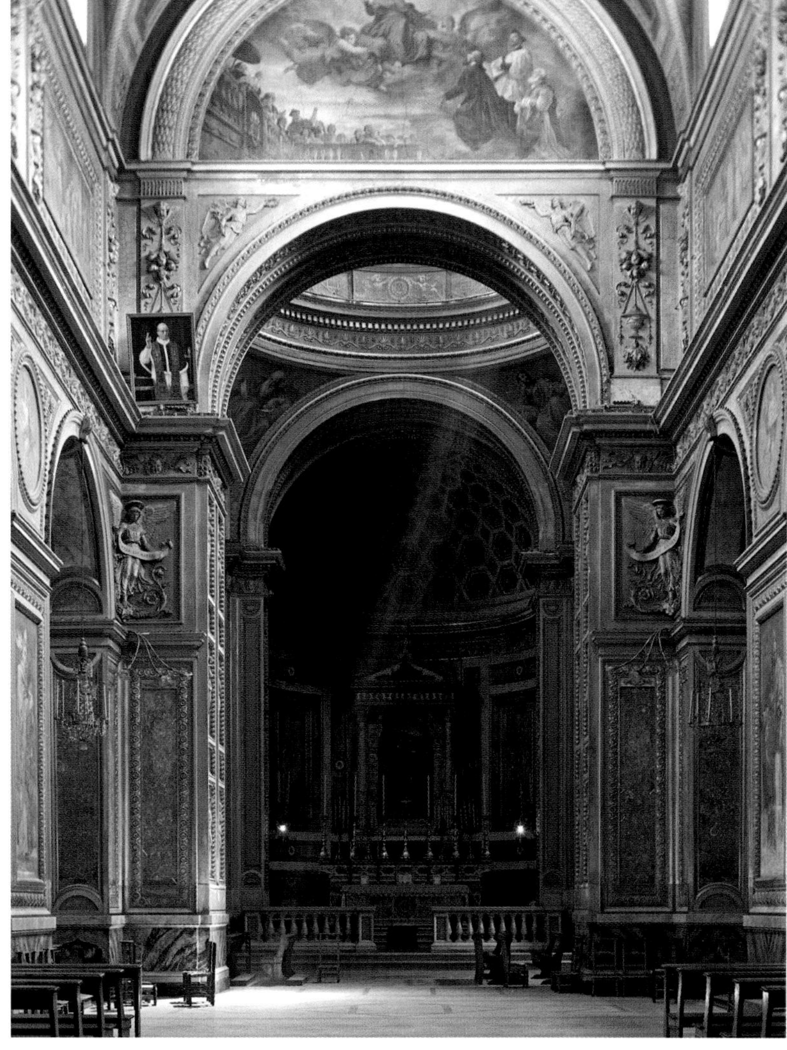

56. Stabilimento Fotografico
Domenico Anderson
Saint Peter's Basilica,
early twentieth century

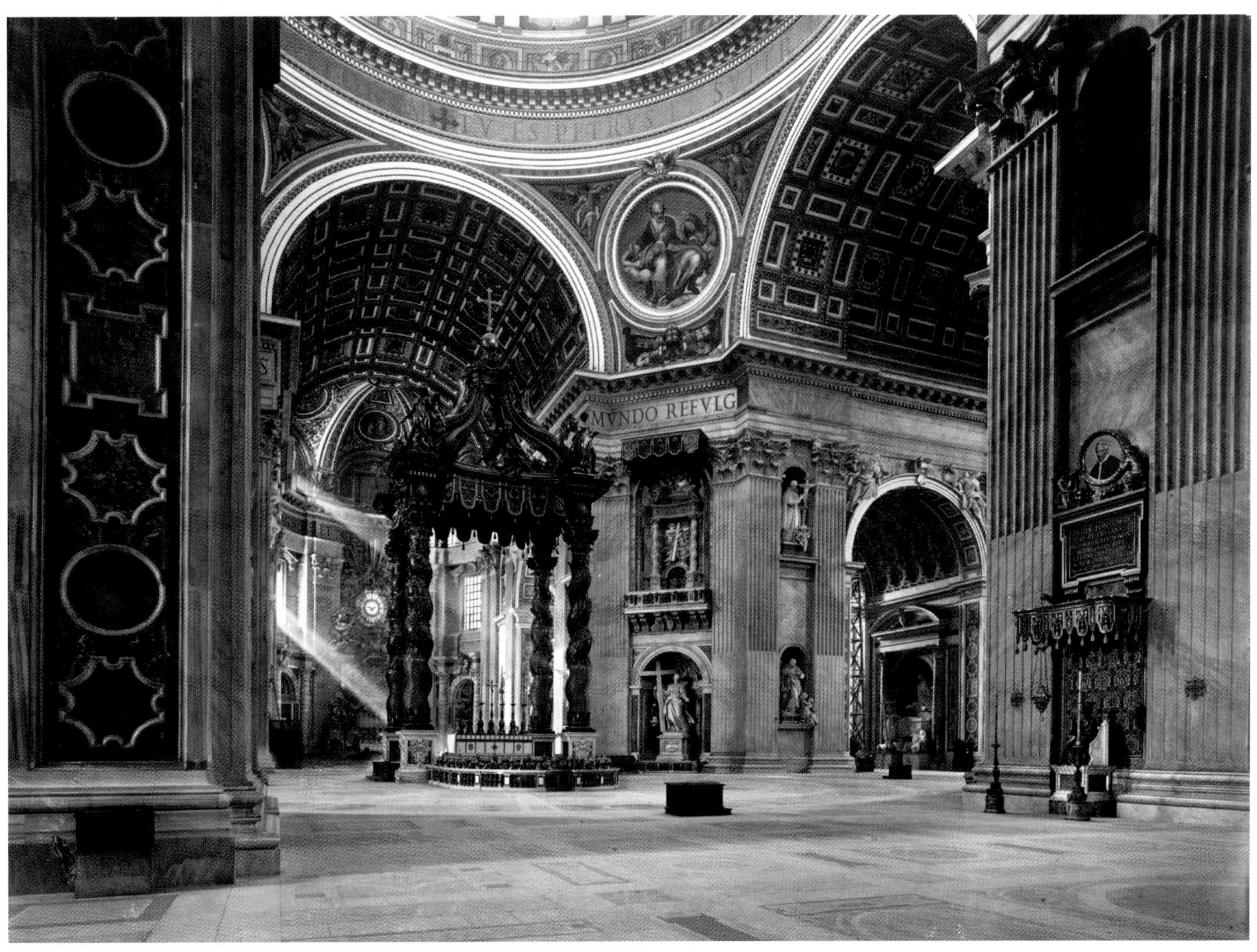

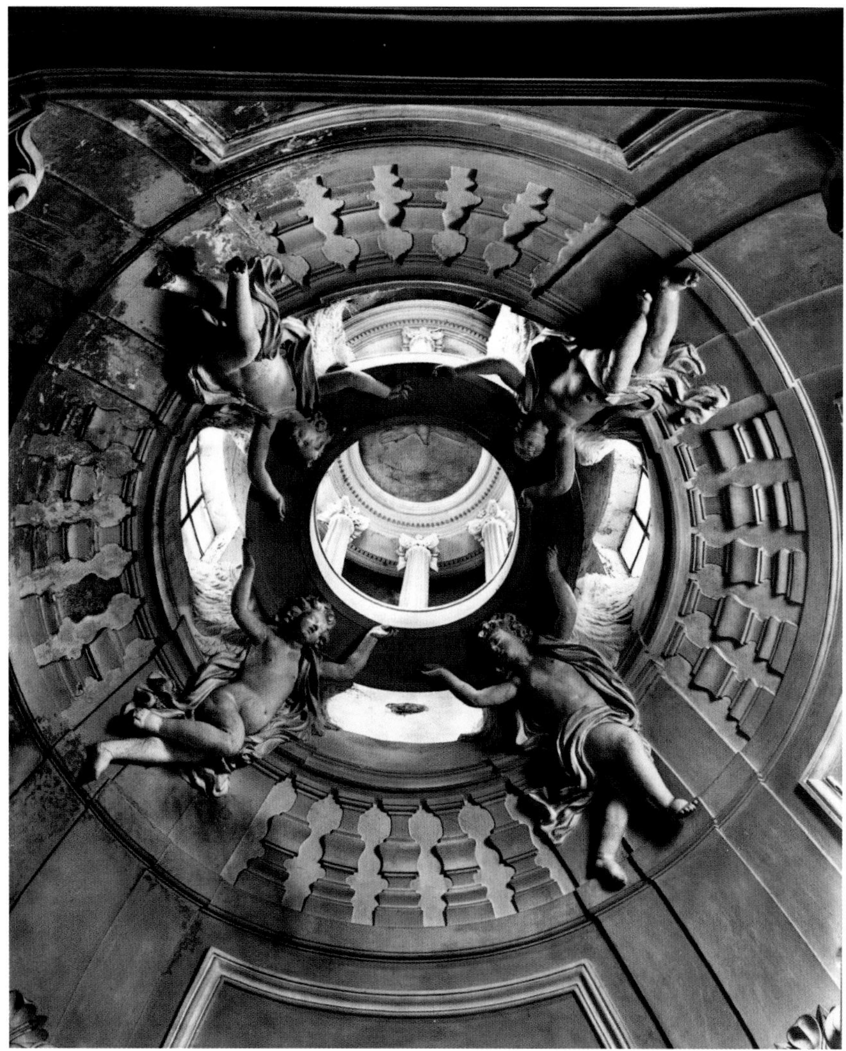 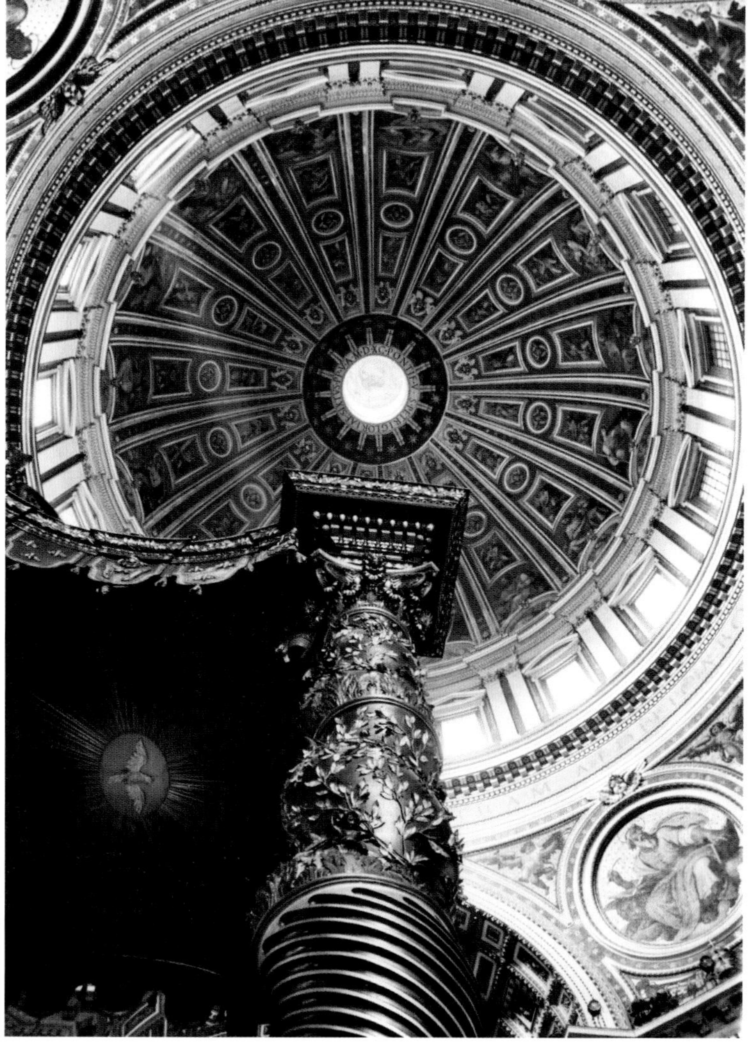

57. Stabilimento Fotografico
Domenico Anderson
Dome of the Avila Chapel,
Santa Maria in Trastevere,
early twentieth century

58. Edwin Smith
Dome and baldacchino,
Saint Peter's Basilica, 1970

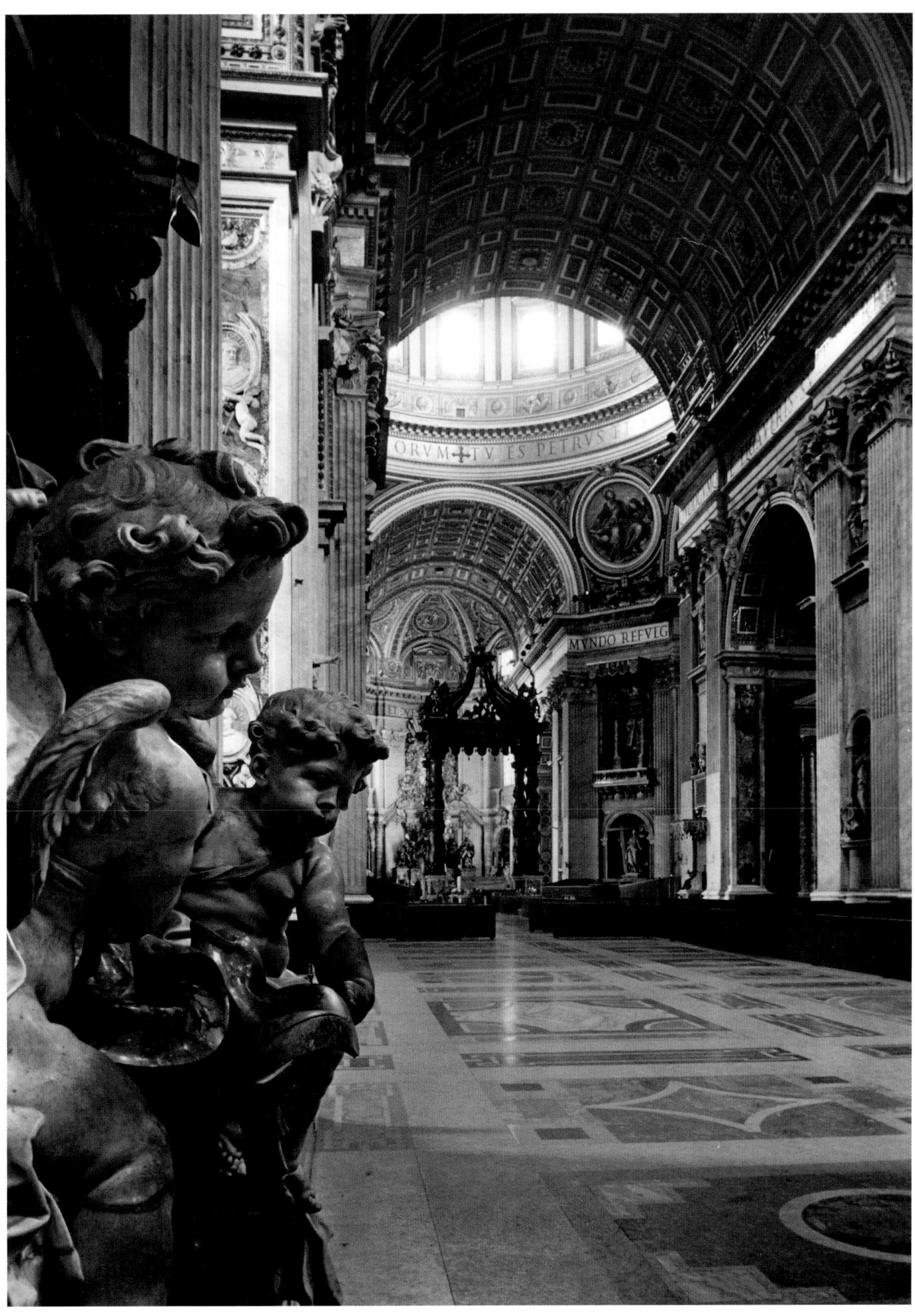

59. Edwin Smith
Saint Peter's Basilica, 1970

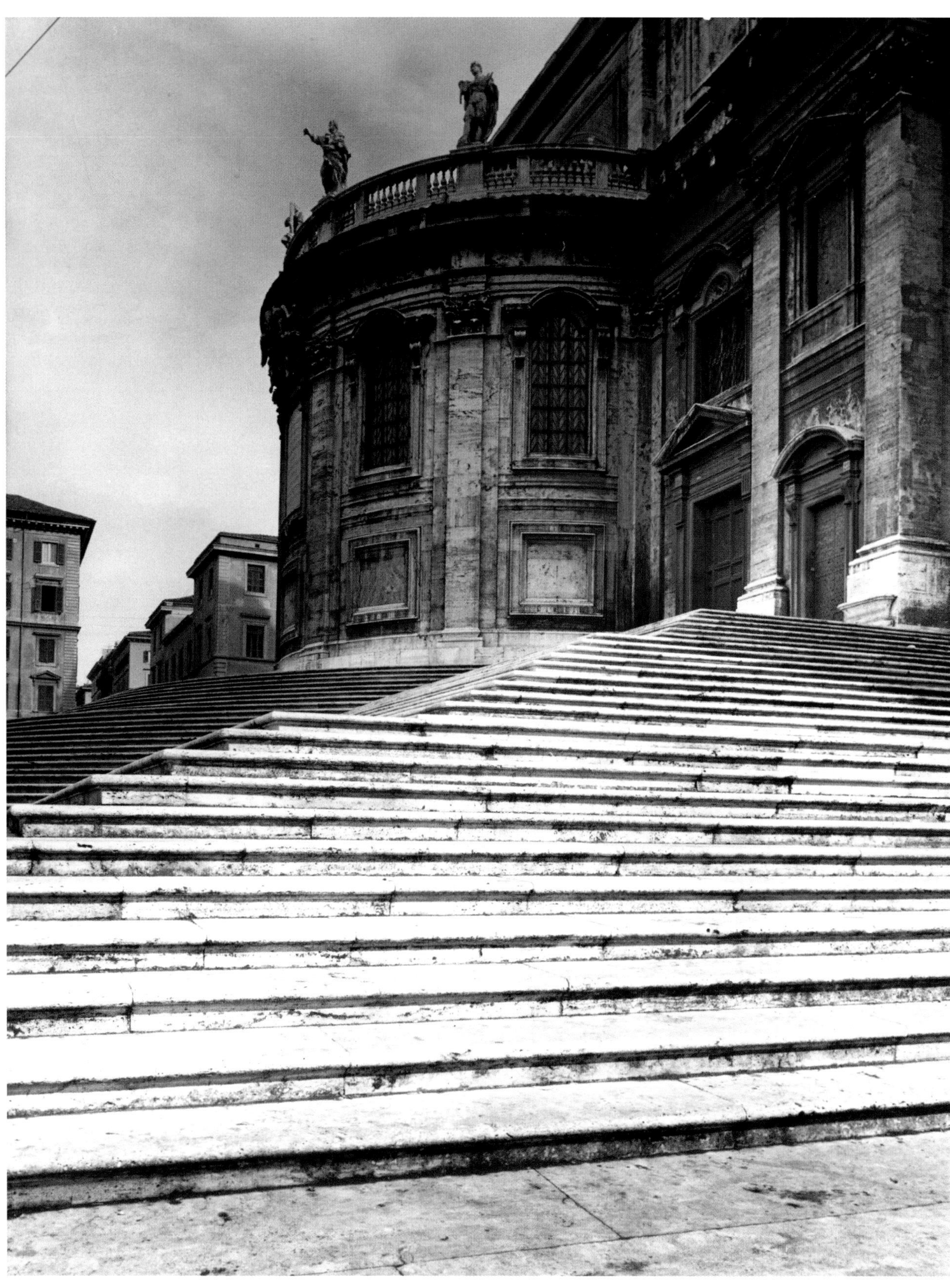

60. Edwin Smith
Santa Maria Maggiore, 1970

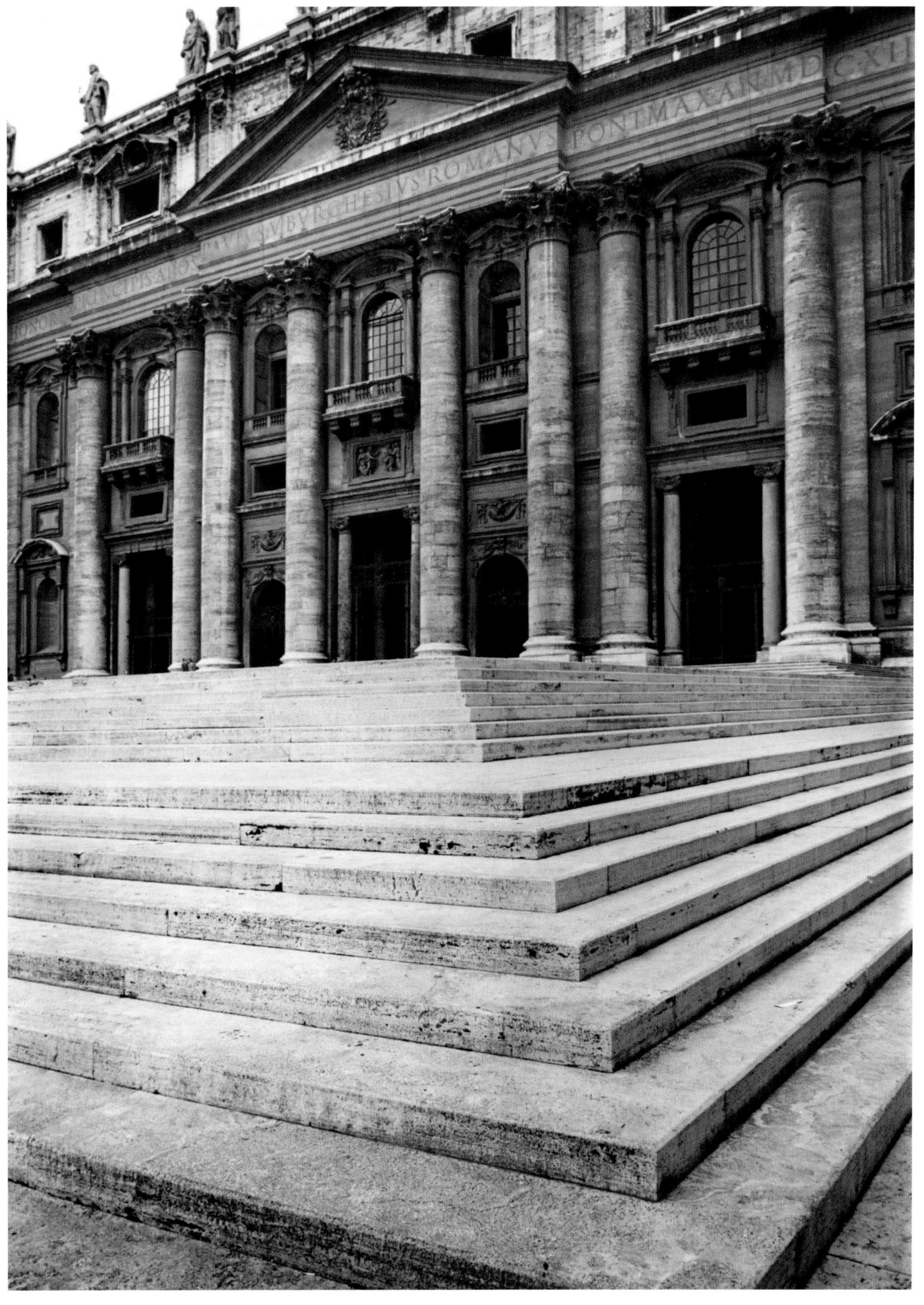

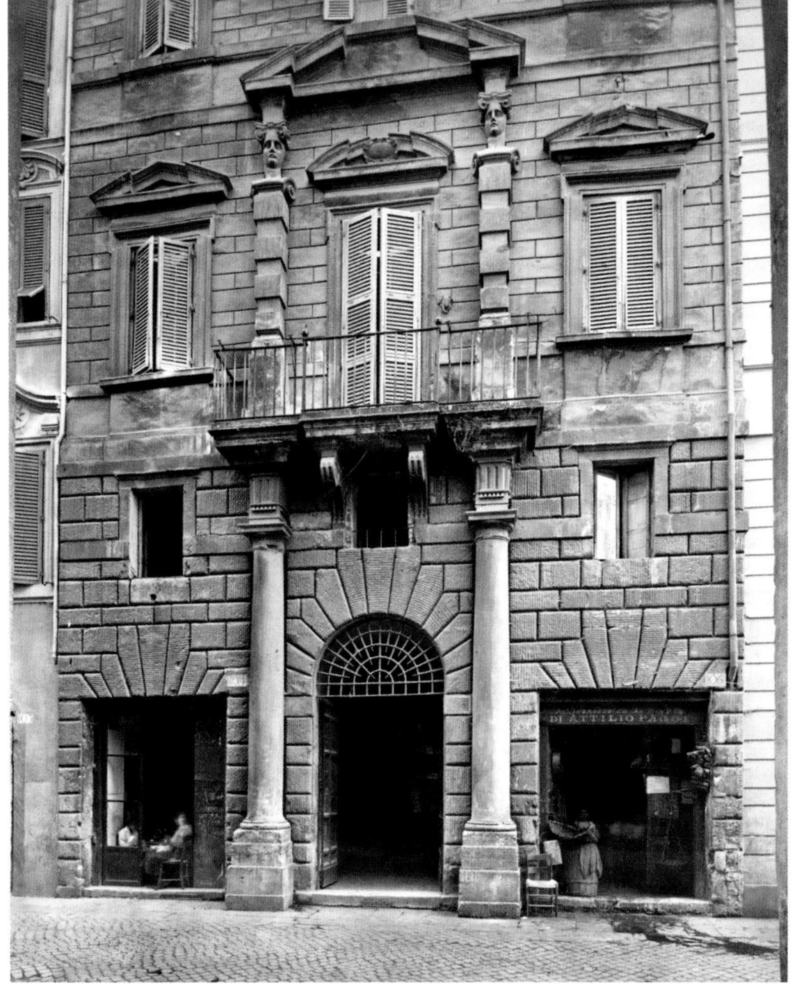

62. Stabilimento Fotografico
Domenico Anderson
Palazzo in Via Monserrato,
early twentieth century

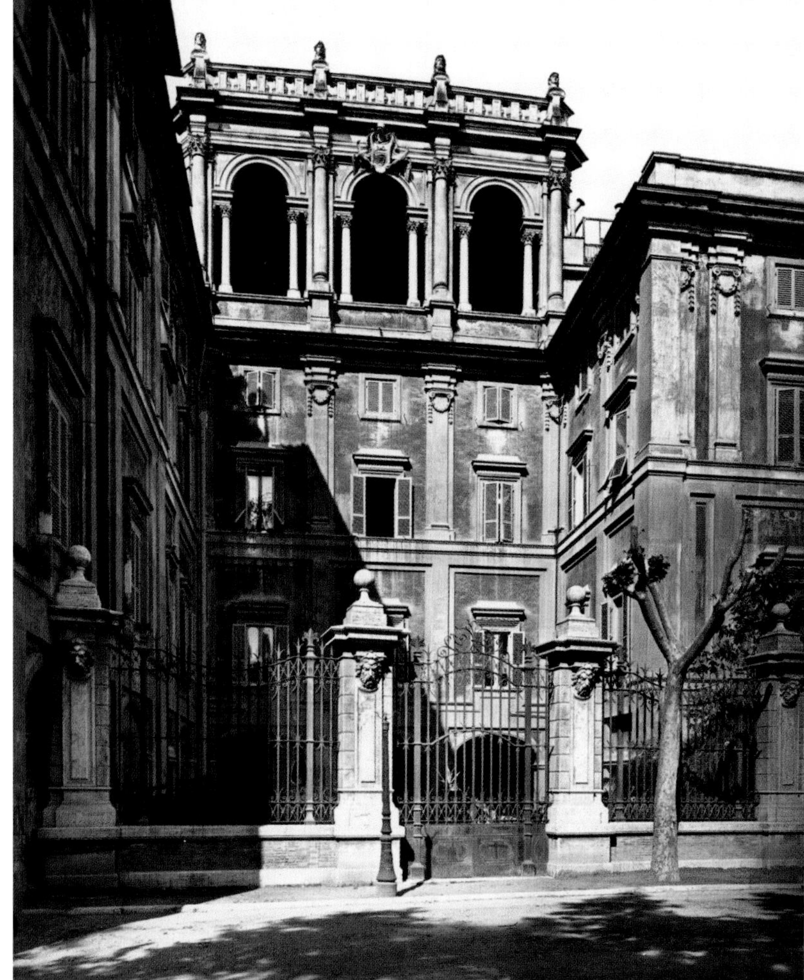

63. Stabilimento Fotografico
Domenico Anderson
Palazzo Falconieri,
early twentieth century

64. Stabilimento Fotografico
Domenico Anderson
*Sant'Agnese in Agone,
Piazza Navona*, early
twentieth century

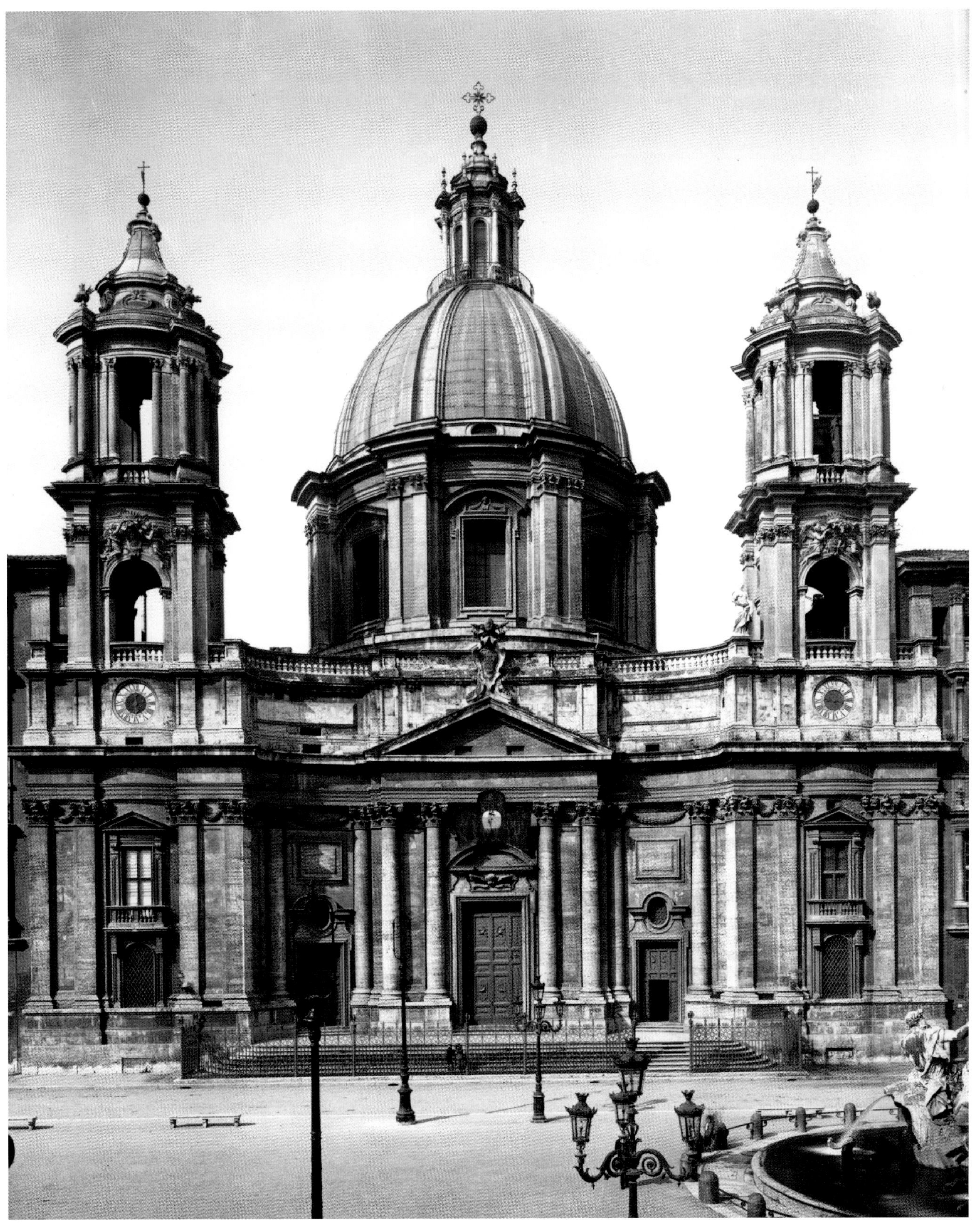

65. Stabilimento Fotografico
Domenico Anderson
Sant'Andrea delle Fratte,
early twentieth century

66. Stabilimento Fotografico
Domenico Anderson
San Carlo alle Quattro Fontane,
early twentieth century

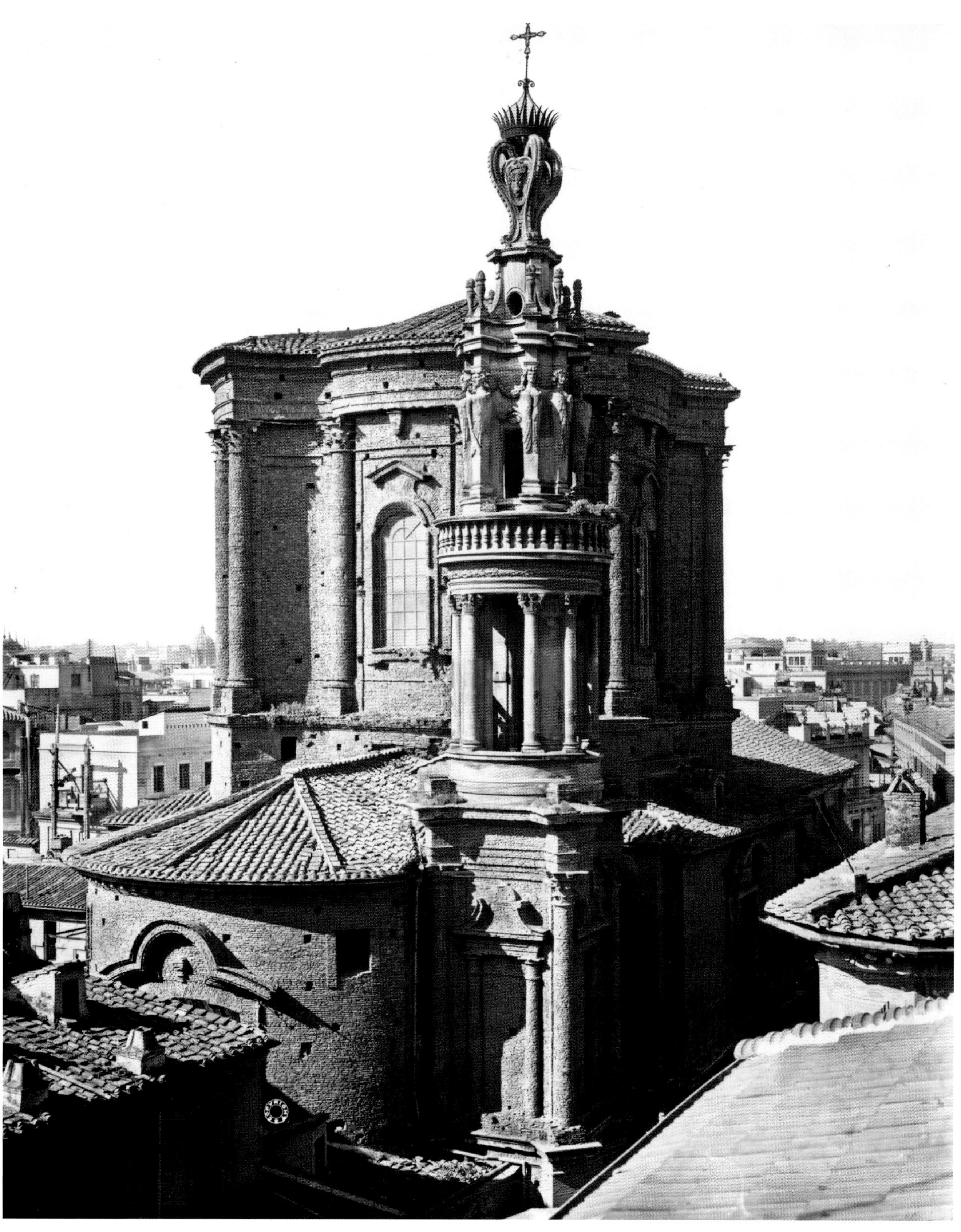

65. Stabilimento Fotografico
Domenico Anderson
Sant'Andrea delle Fratte,
early twentieth century

66. Stabilimento Fotografico
Domenico Anderson
San Carlo alle Quattro Fontane,
early twentieth century

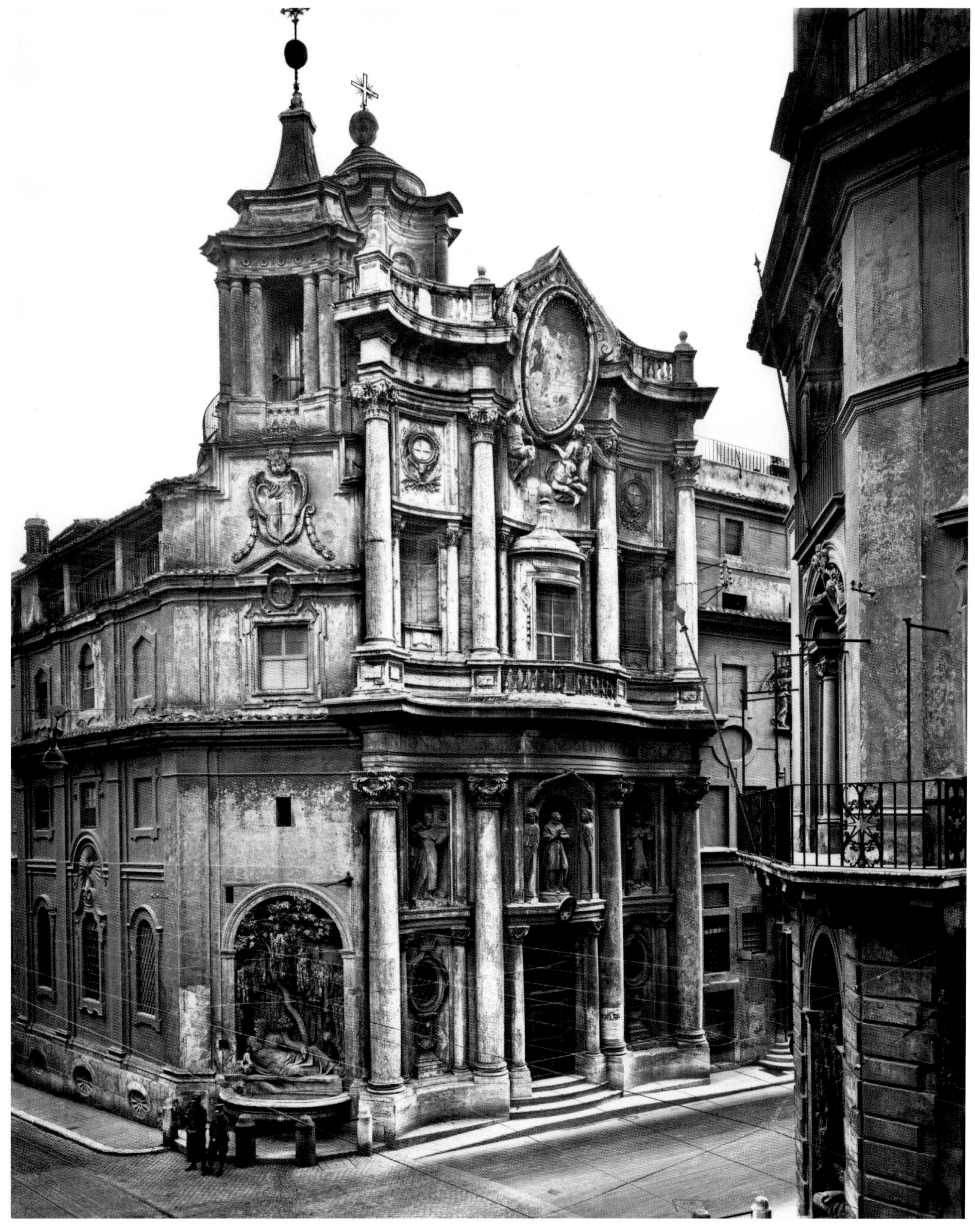

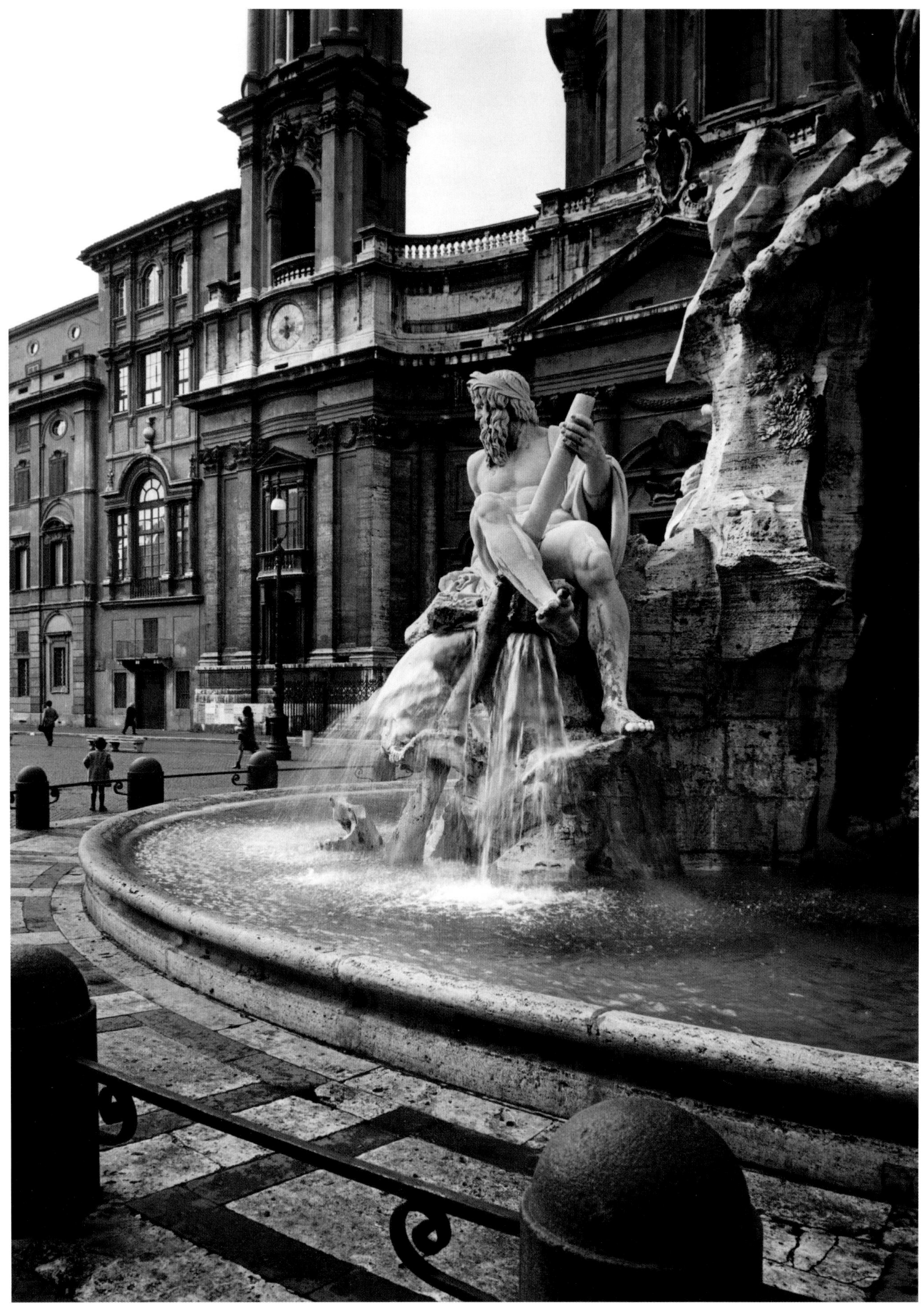

67. Edwin Smith
Fountain of the Four Rivers,
Piazza Navona, 1970

68. Edwin Smith
Fontana della Barcaccia,
Piazza di Spagna, 1962

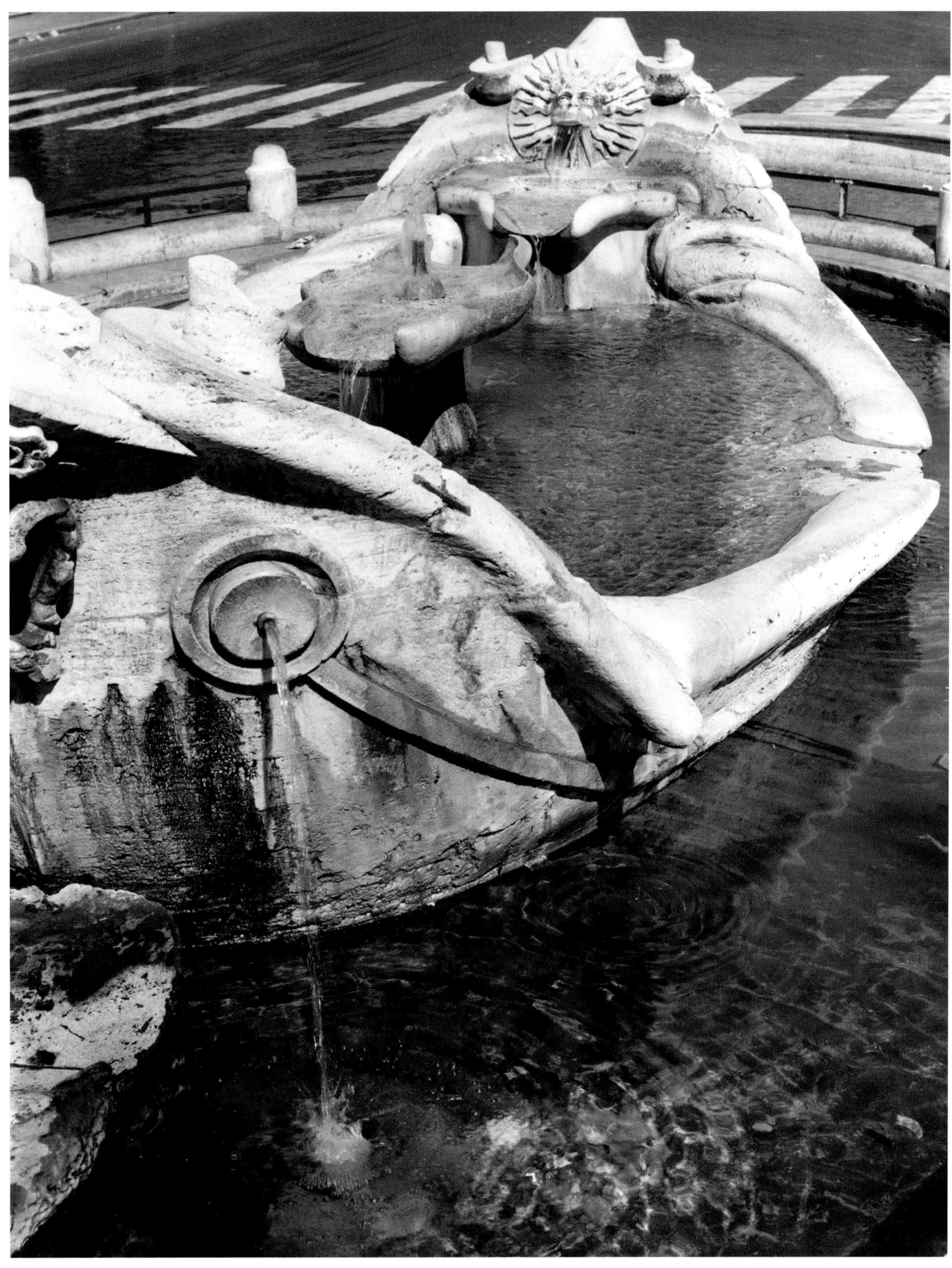

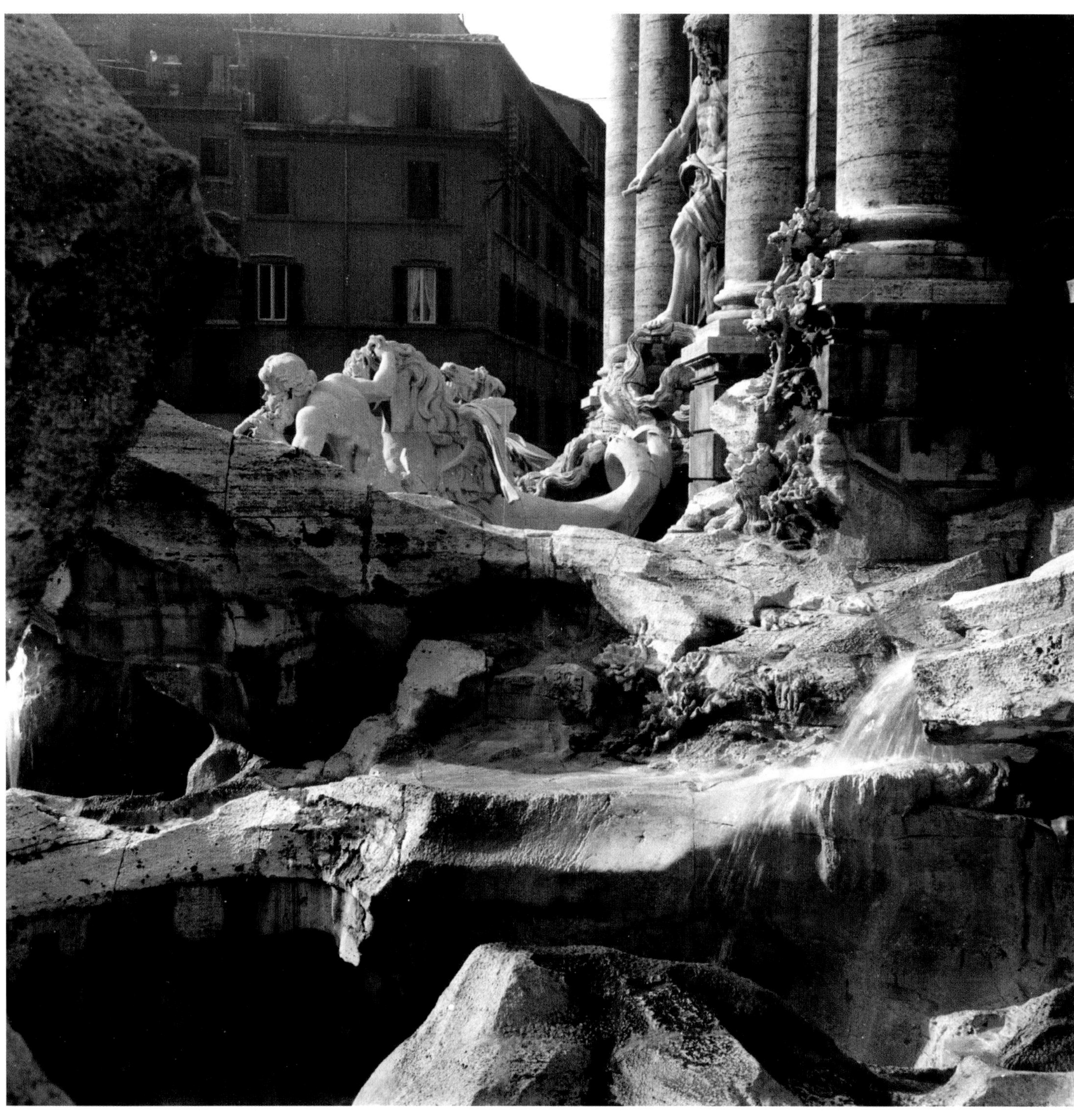

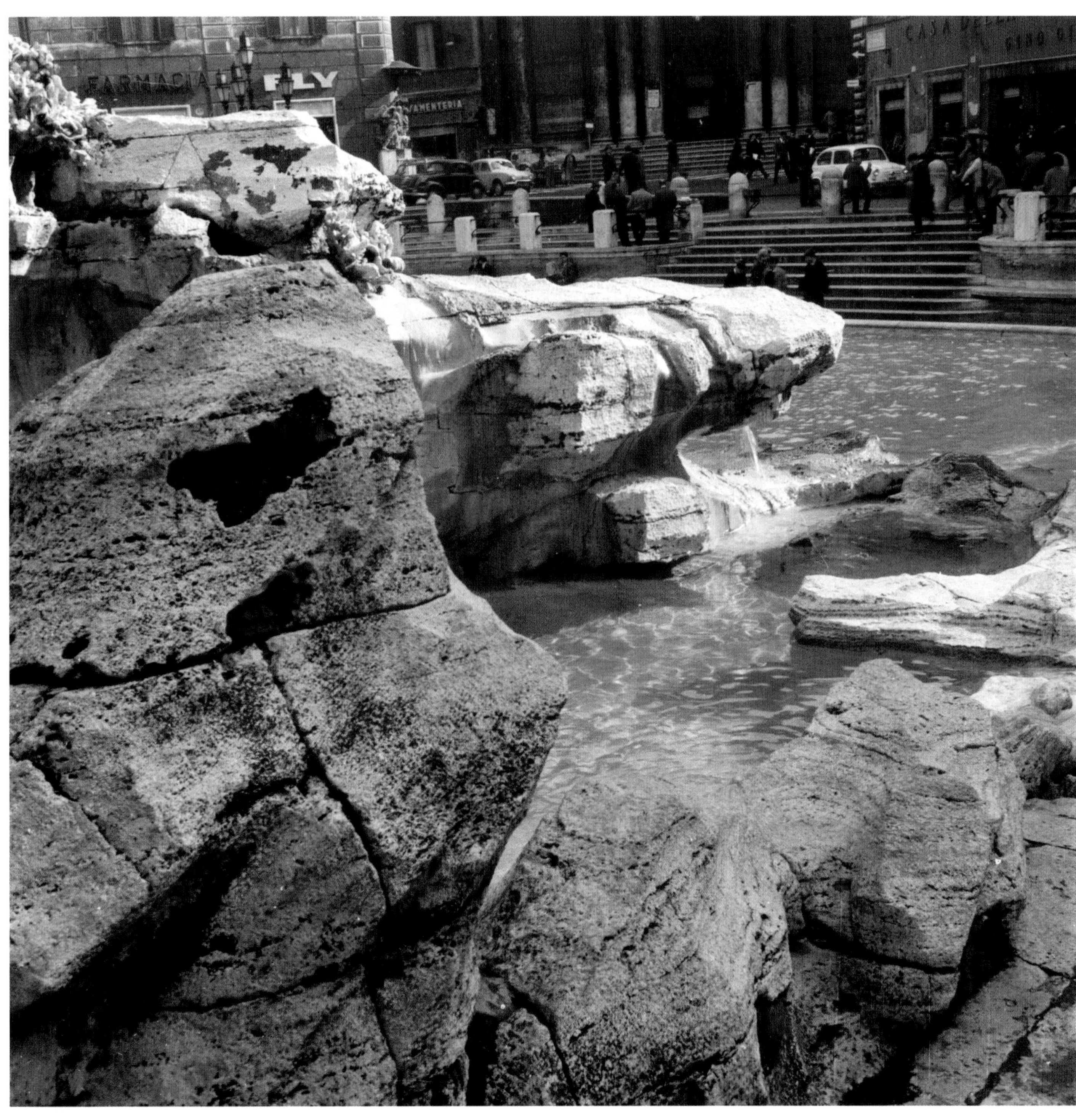

70. Ivy de Wolfe
Trevi Fountain, 1961

71. Tim Benton
*Fencing Academy,
Foro Italico*, 1976

72. Stabilimento Fotografico
Domenico Anderson
*Industrial school for the
daughters of post office
employees, Garbatella*, 1936

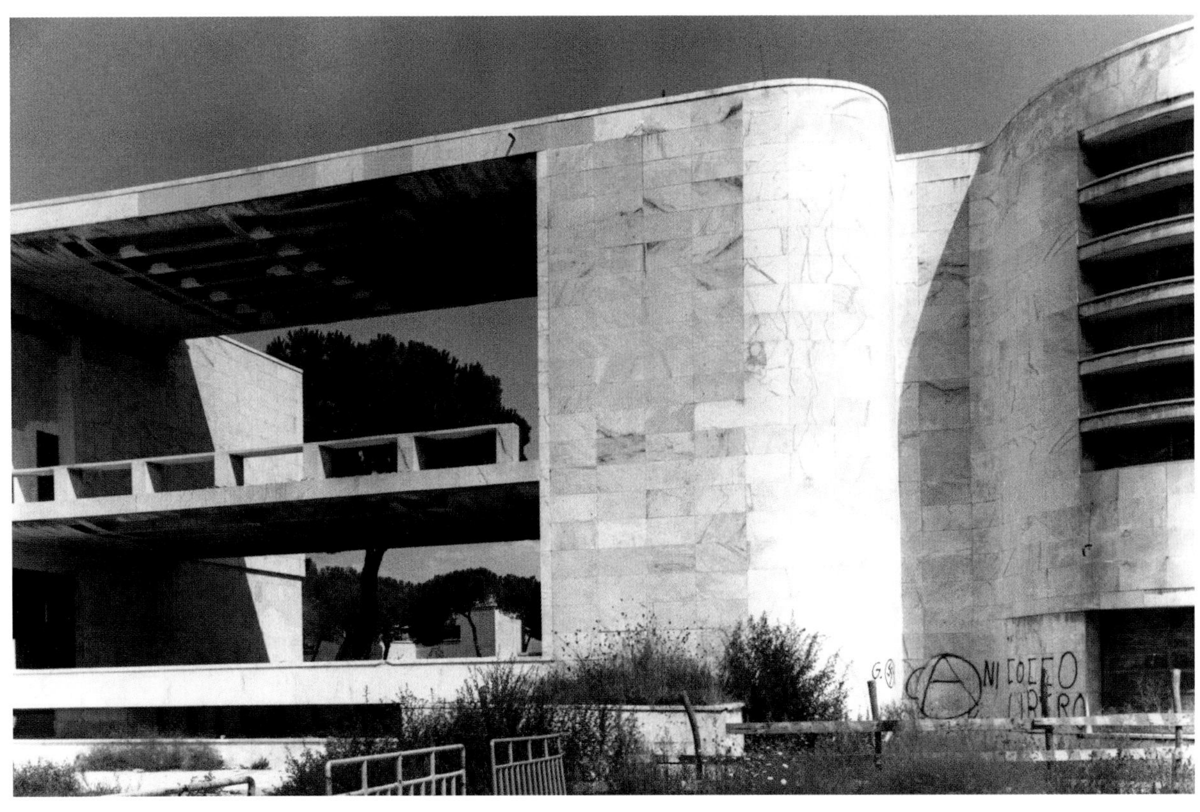

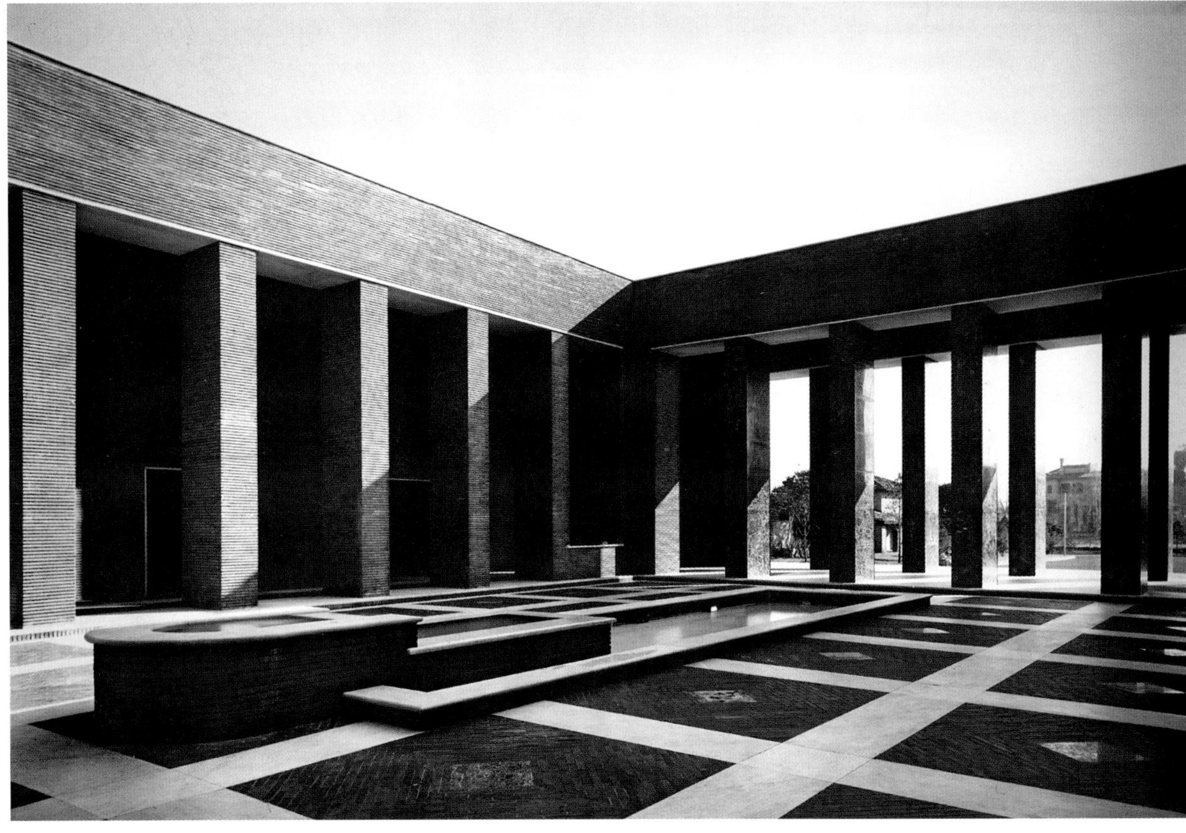

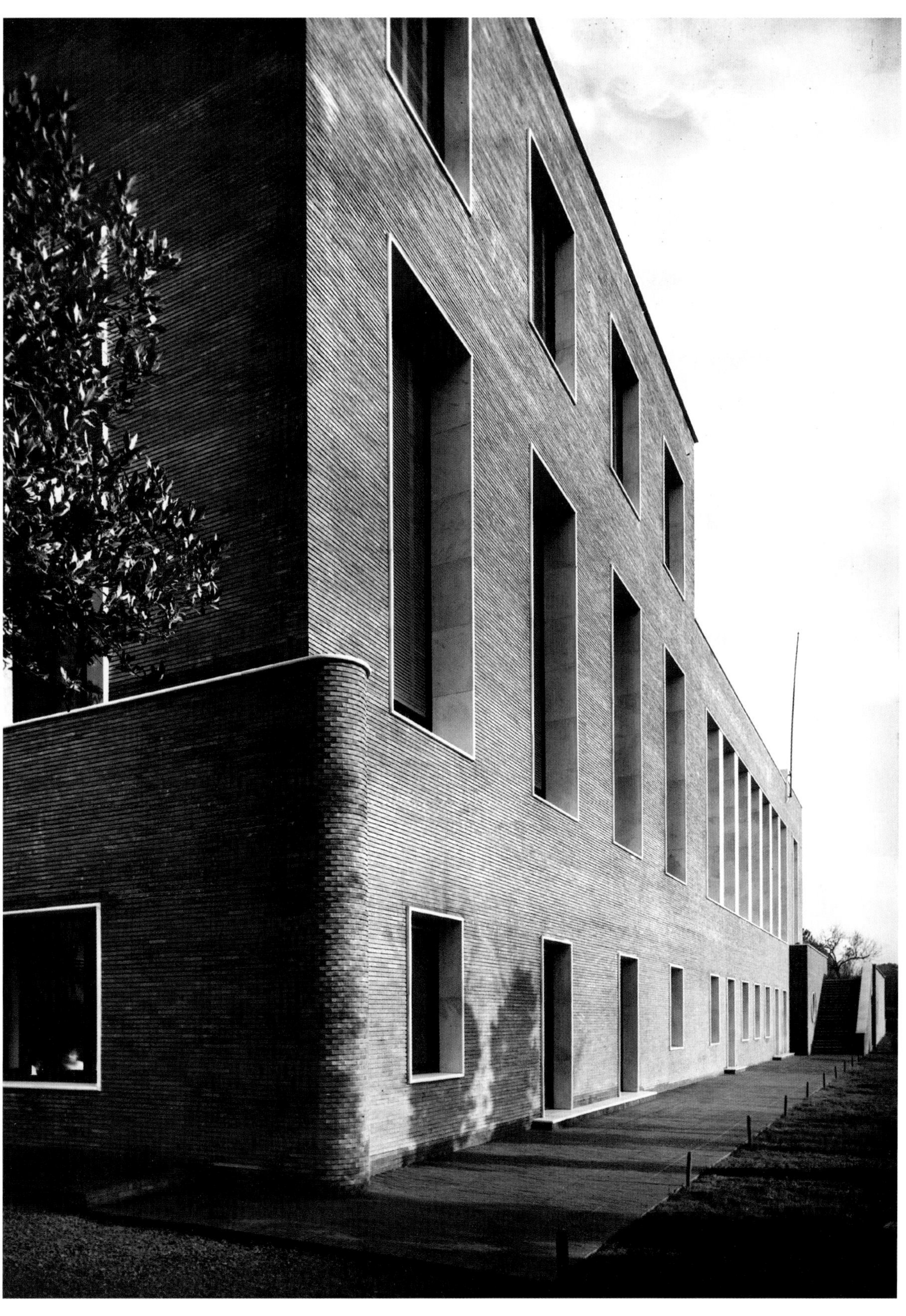

73. Stabilimento Fotografico
Domenico Anderson
*Industrial school for the
daughters of post office
employees, Garbatella, 1936*

74. Tim Benton
*Portico of the Santi
Pietro e Paolo Basilica,
EUR*, 1976

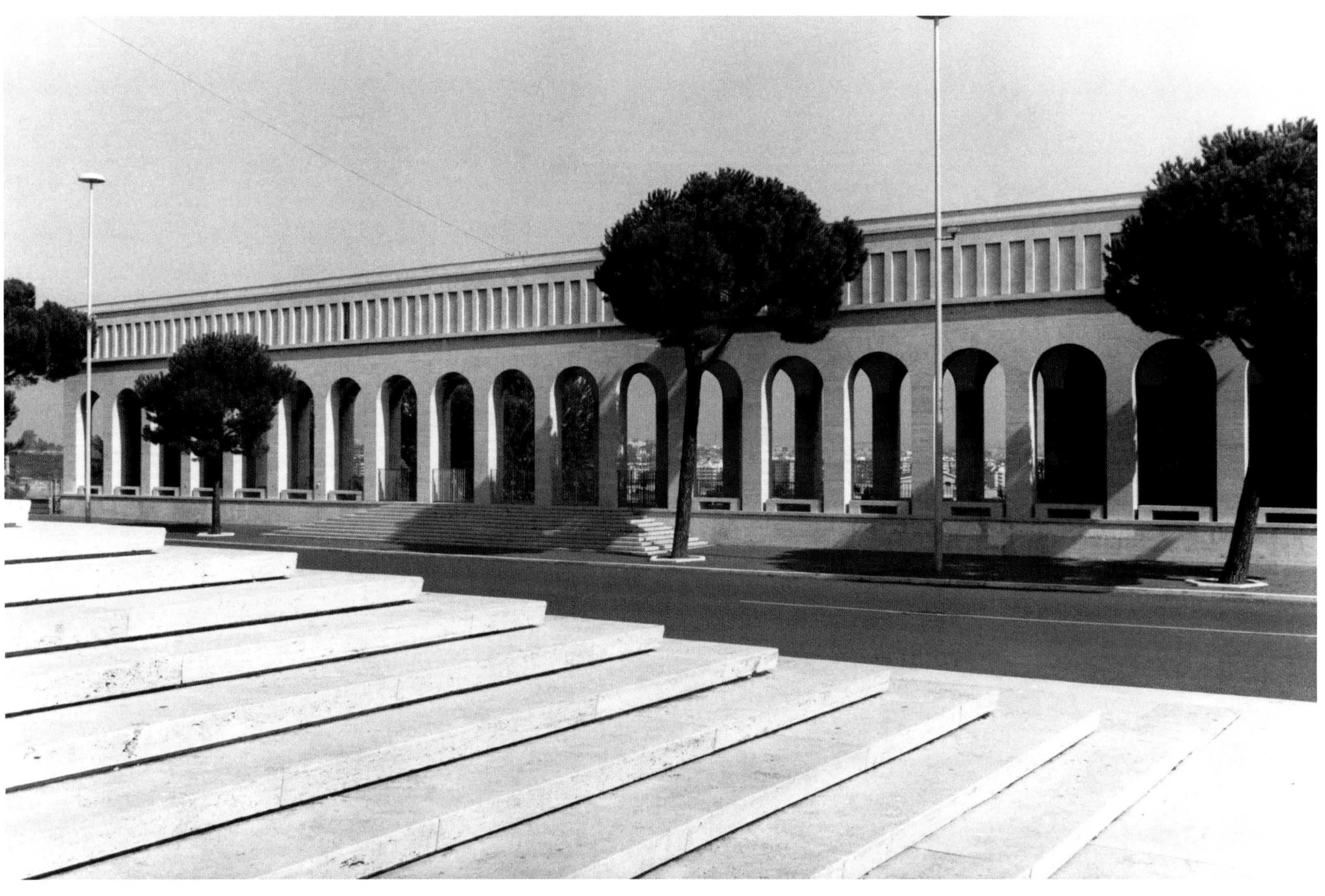

75. Tim Benton
*Palazzo della Civiltà Italiana,
EUR*, 1976

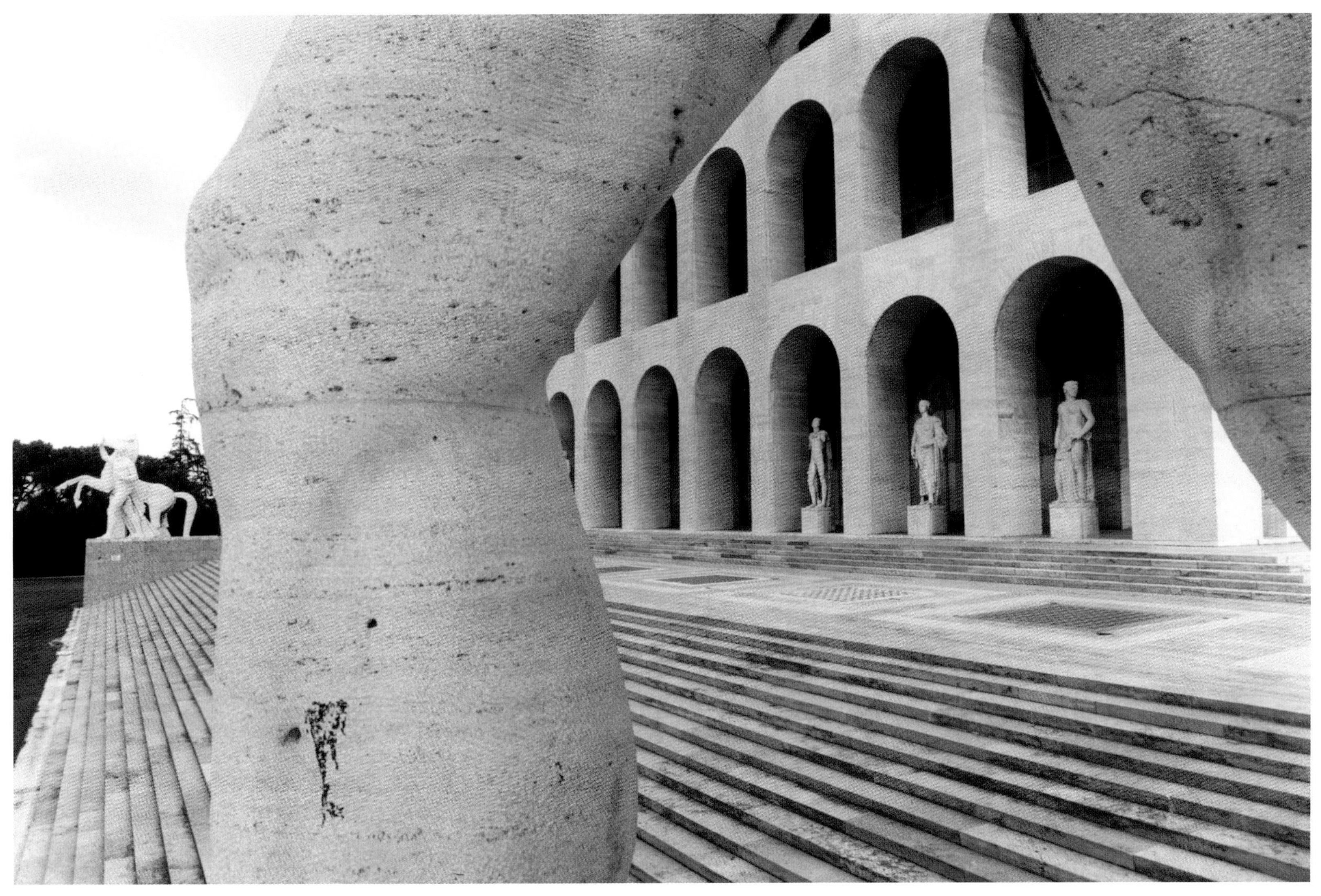

76. George Everard Kidder Smith
*Palazzo dello Sport under
construction, EUR*, 1954

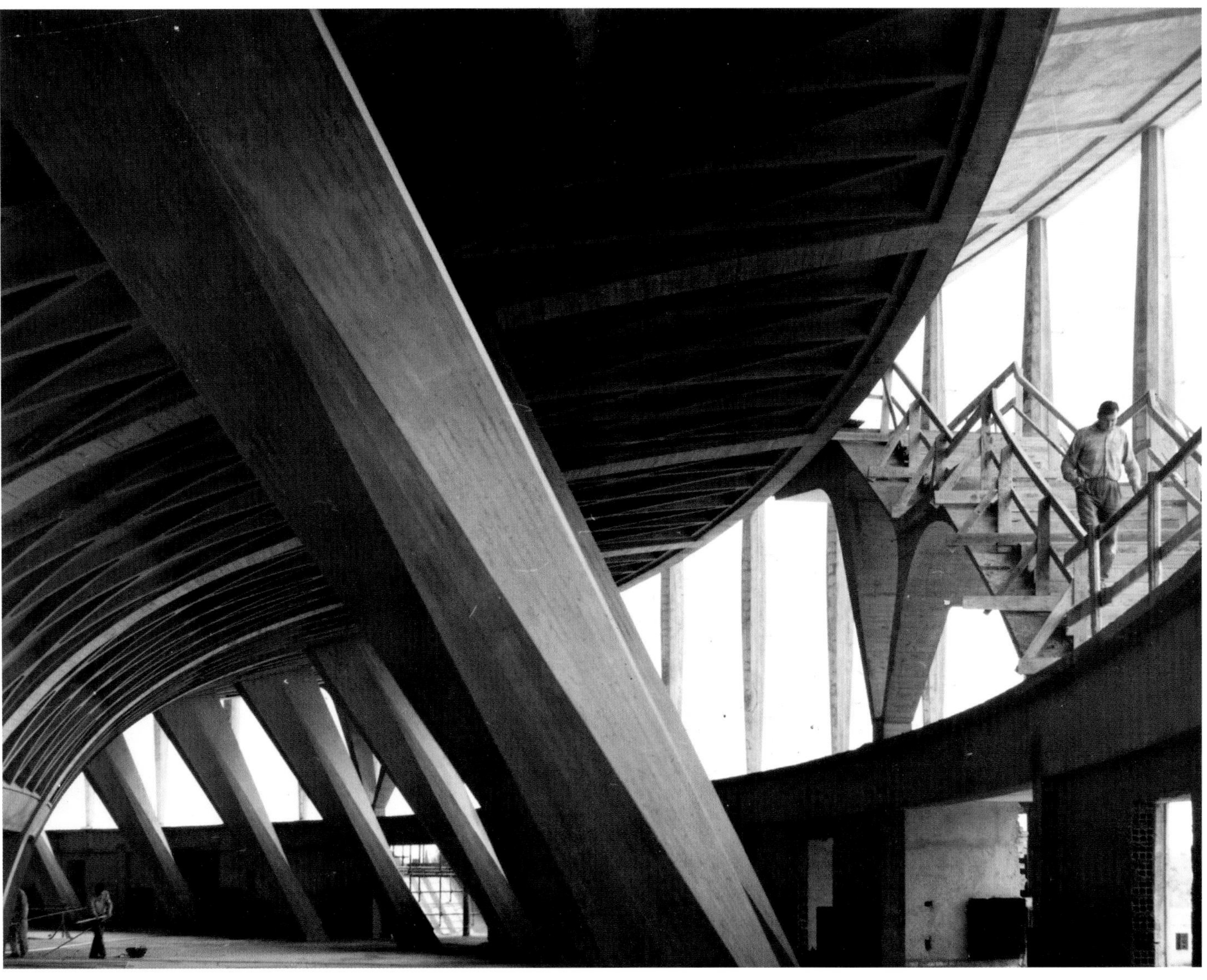

77. Edwin Smith
Palazzetto dello Sport, 1970

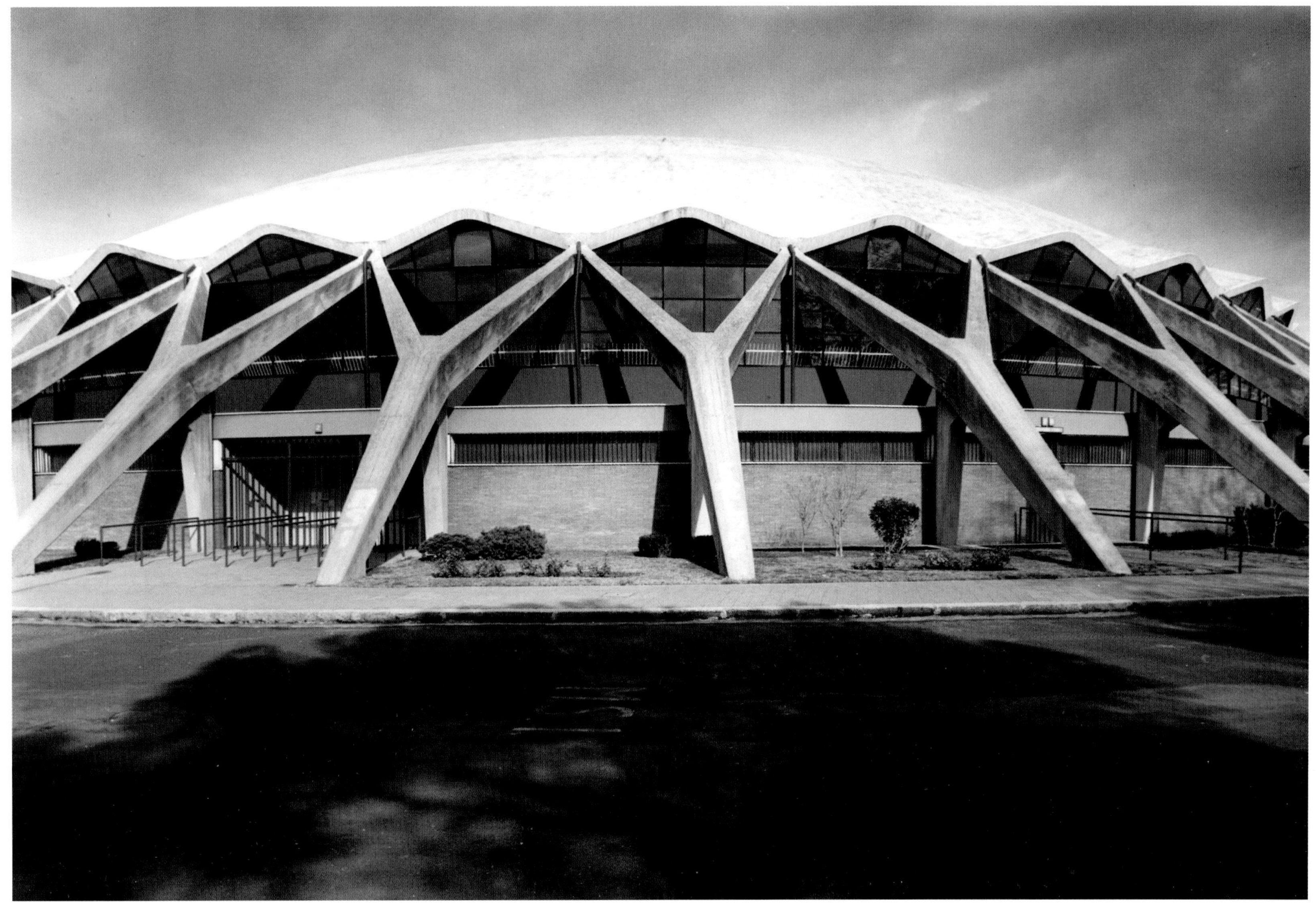

78. Oscar Savio
Staircase, la Rinascente, 1961

79. Oscar Savio
Staircase, la Rinascente, 1961

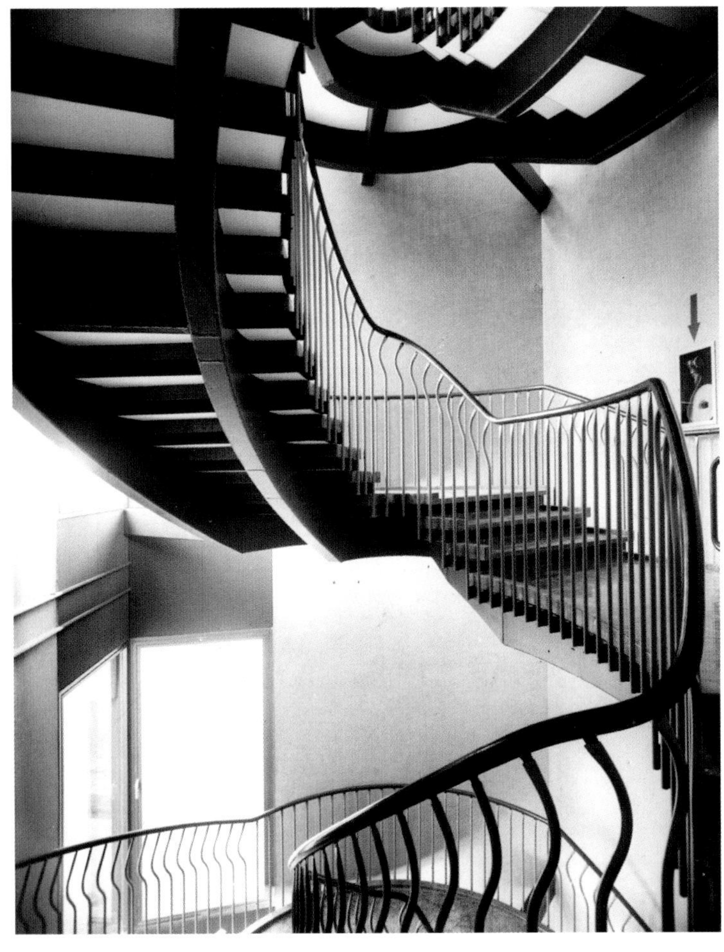

78. Oscar Savio
Staircase, la Rinascente, 1961

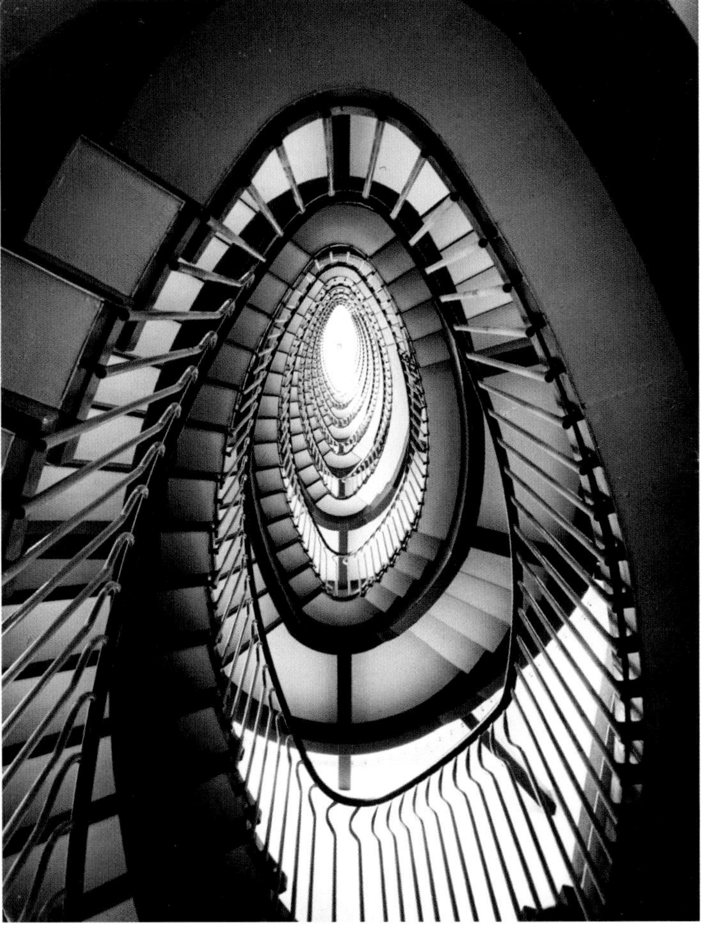

79. Oscar Savio
Staircase, la Rinascente, 1961

80. Alberto Cartoni
Casa del Girasole, 1950

81. Alberto Cartoni
Casa del Girasole, 1950

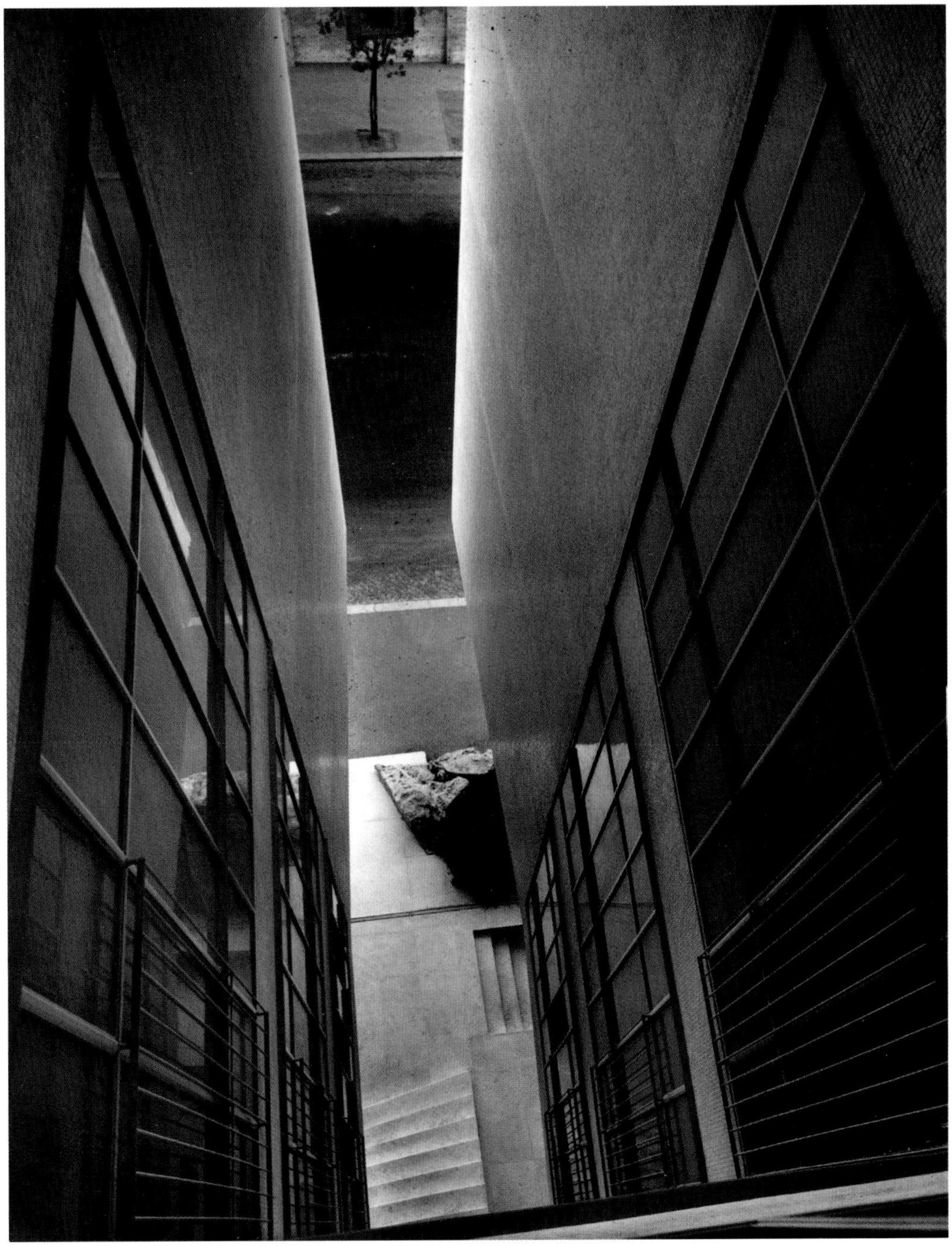

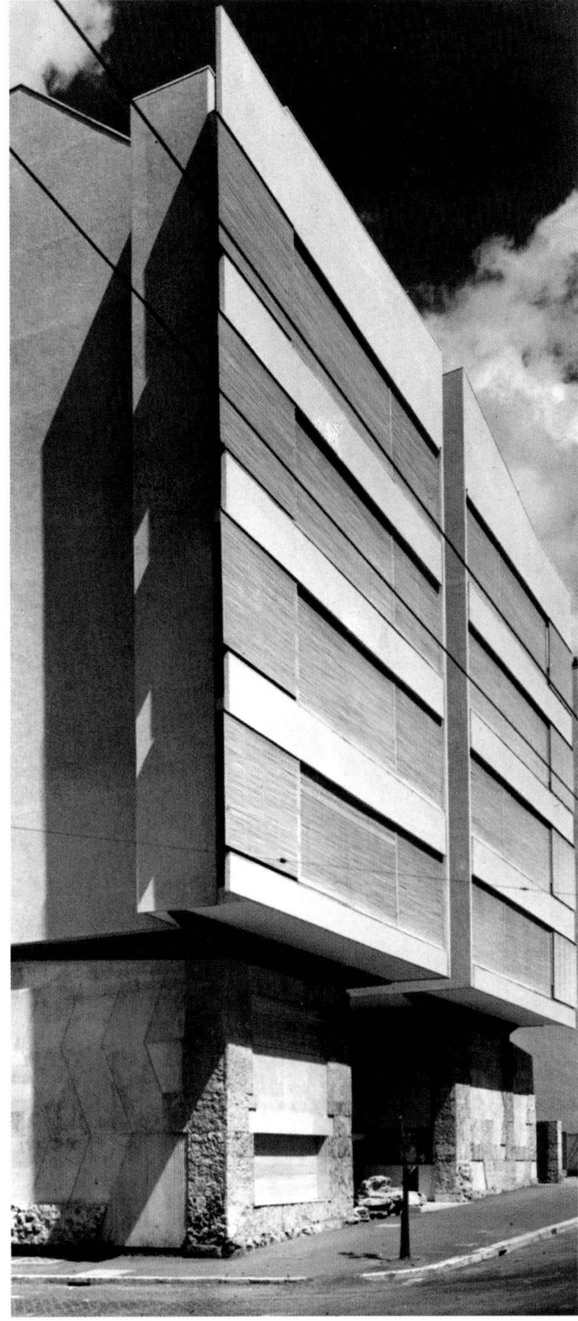

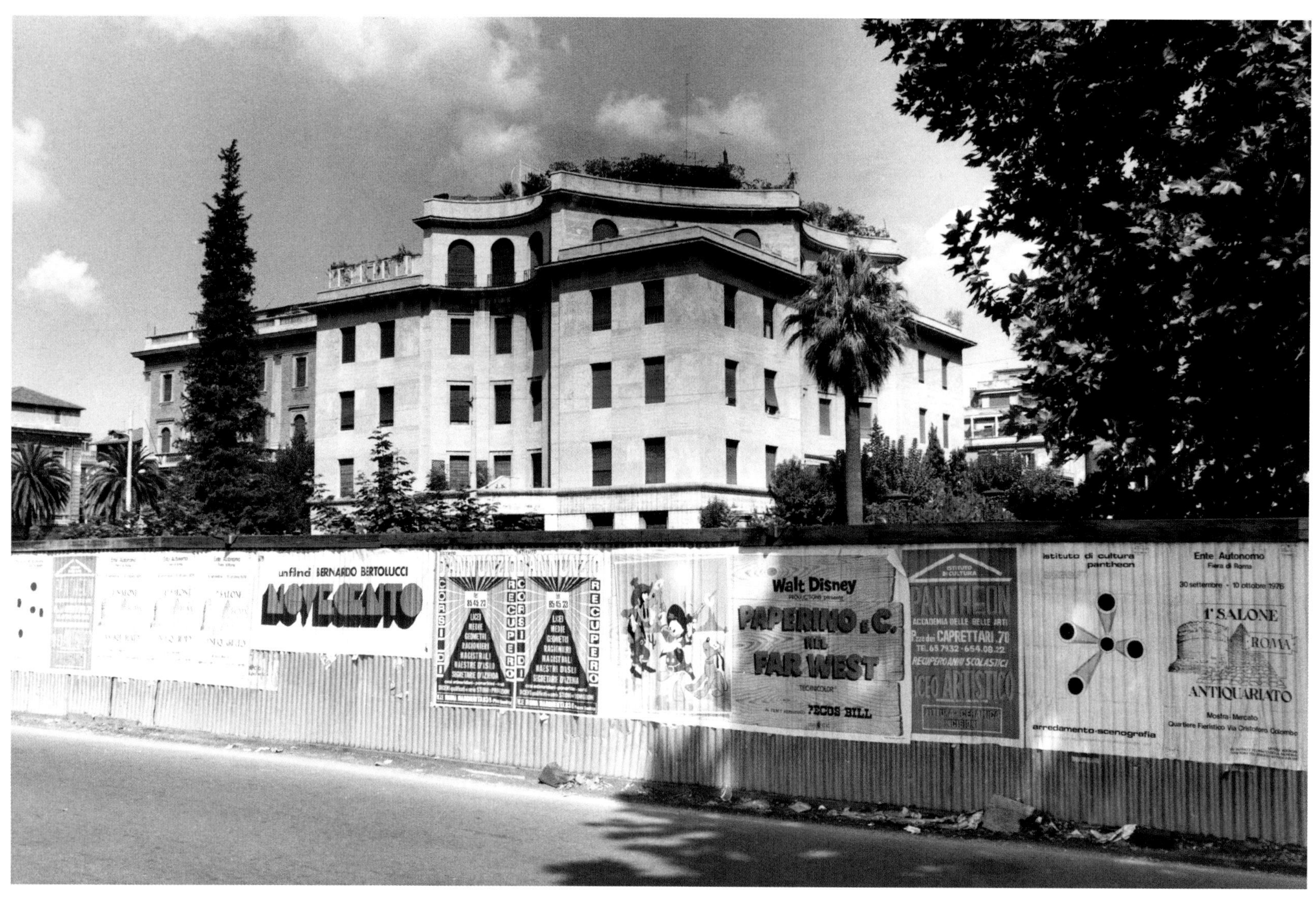

82. Tim Benton
Palazzina Nebbiosi, lungotevere
Arnaldo da Brescia, 1976

122

83. Ludovico Canali
*Multi-purpose office building
between Via Campania
and Via Romagna*, 1966

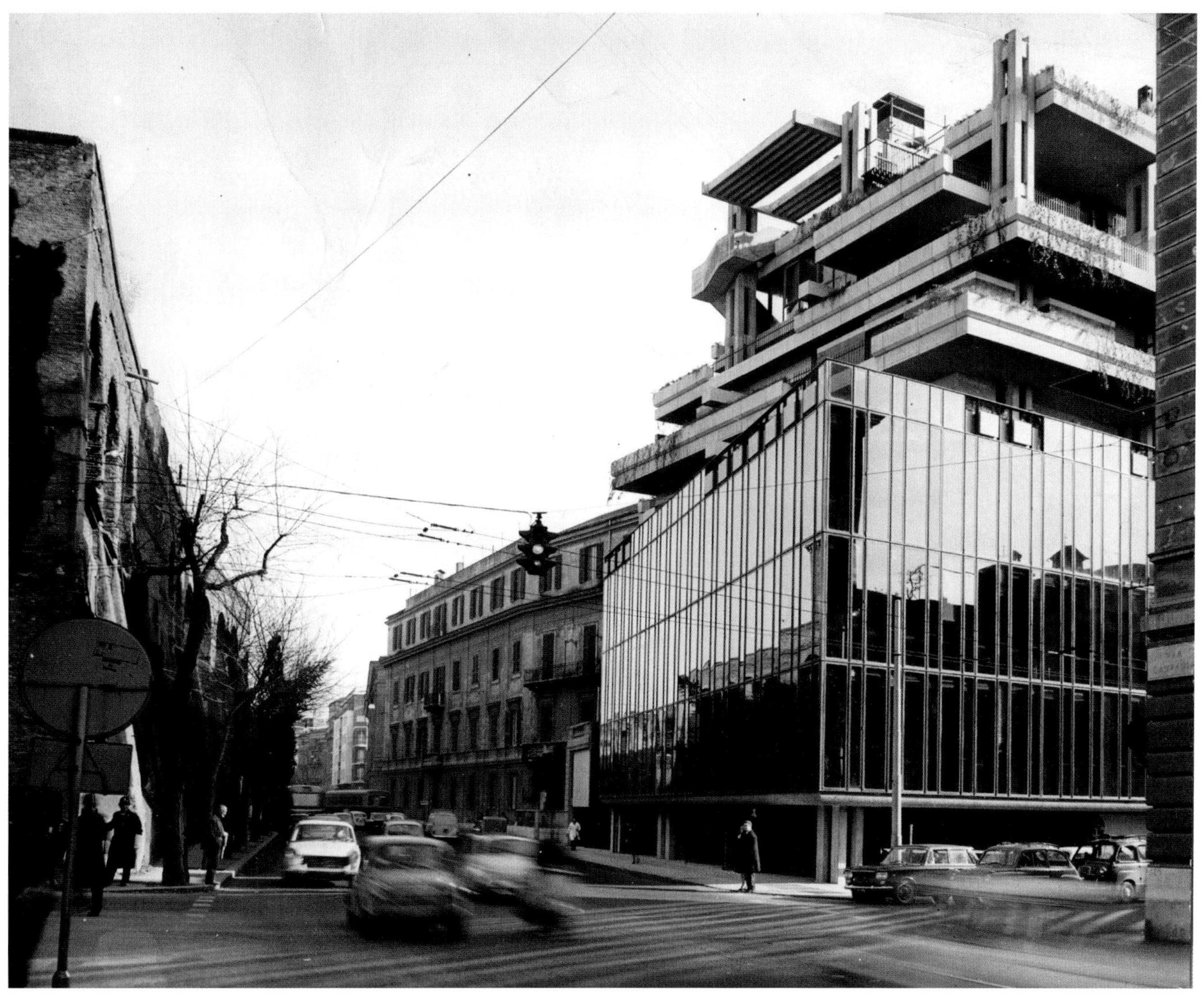

84. Ralph Deakin
*Monument to Vittorio Emanuele
II, or 'Vittoriano', 1930s*

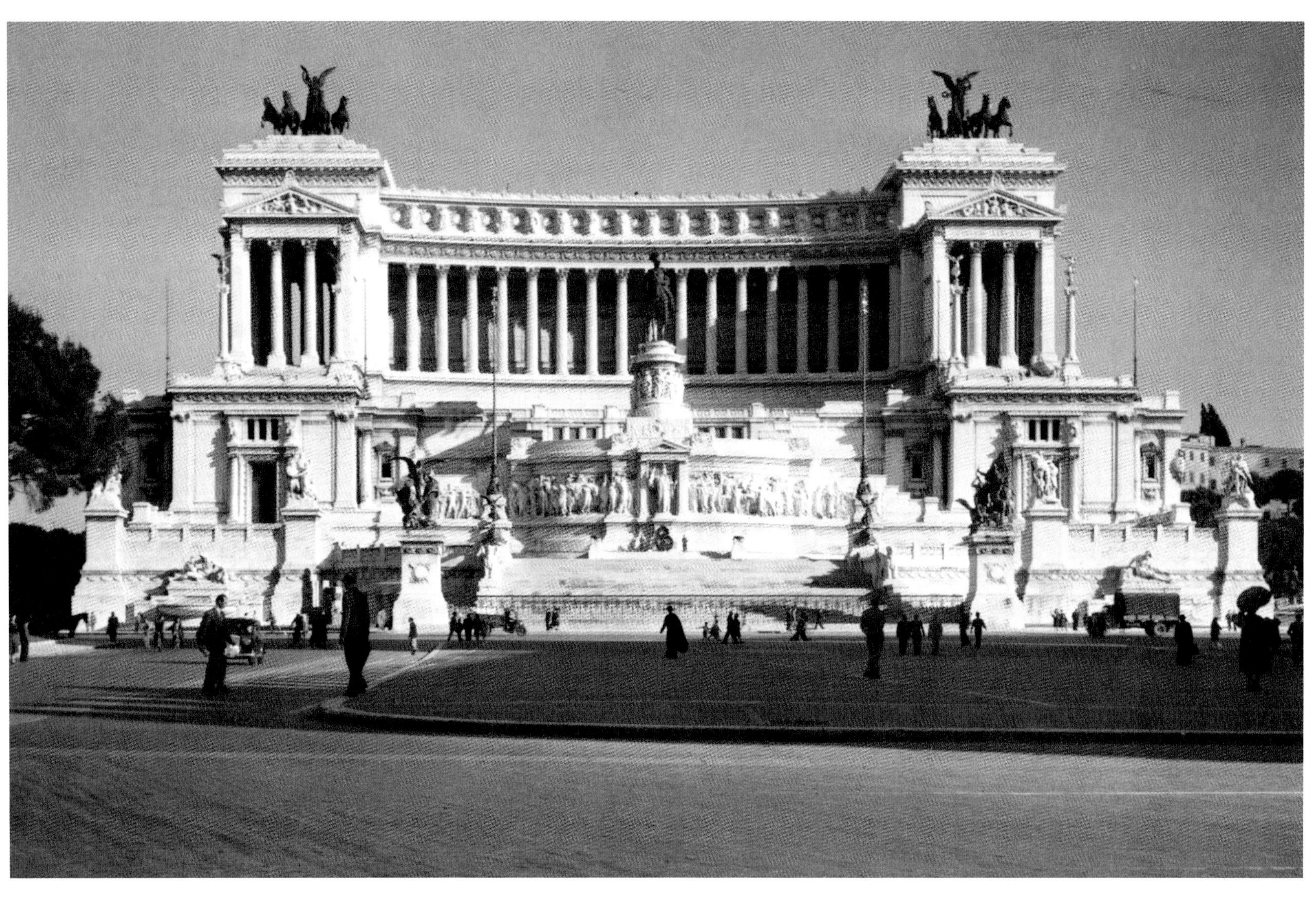

85. Bruno De Hamel
*Chancery Building,
British Embassy*, 1971

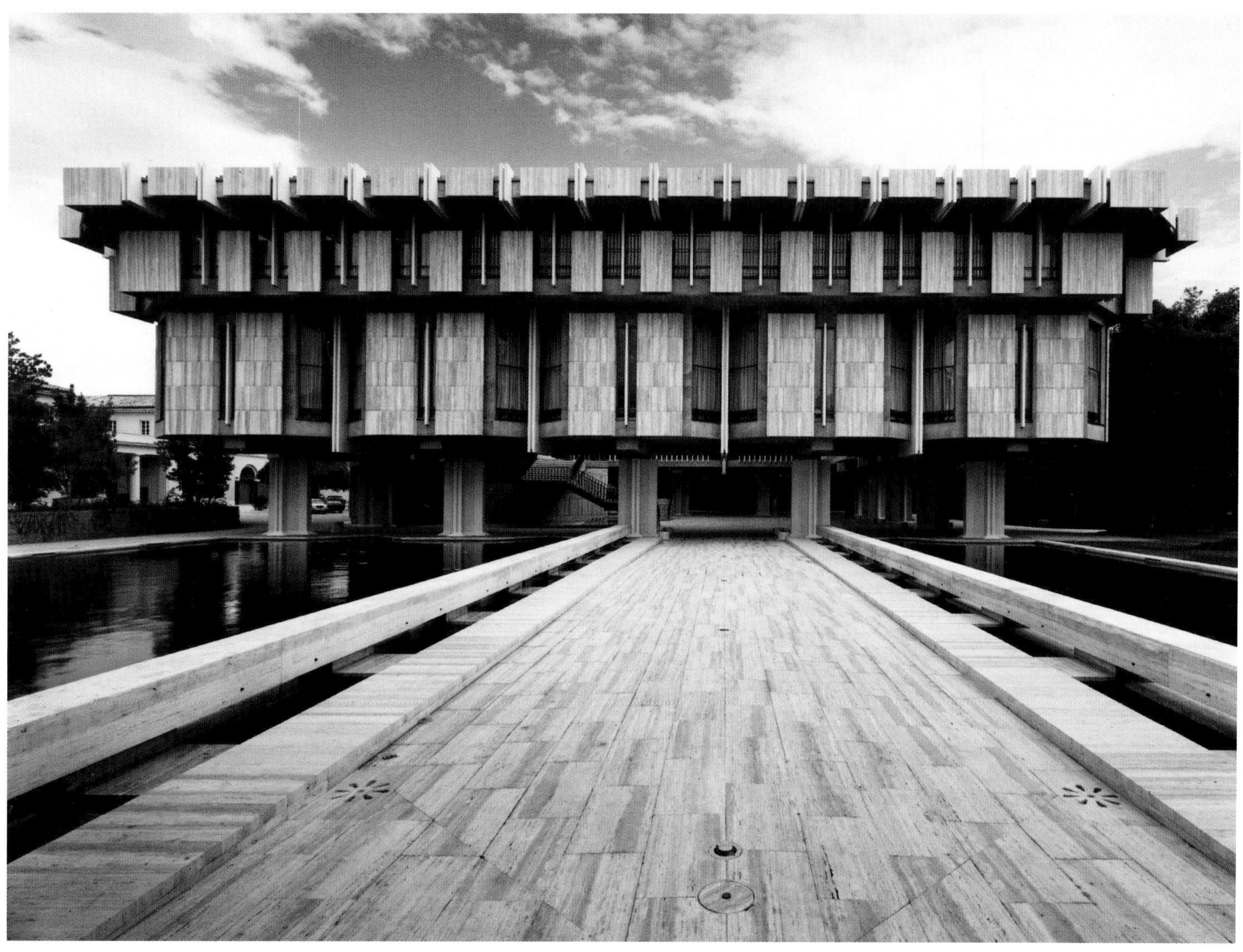

86. Edwin Smith
*Palazzo Nuovo, Piazza
del Campidoglio*, 1954

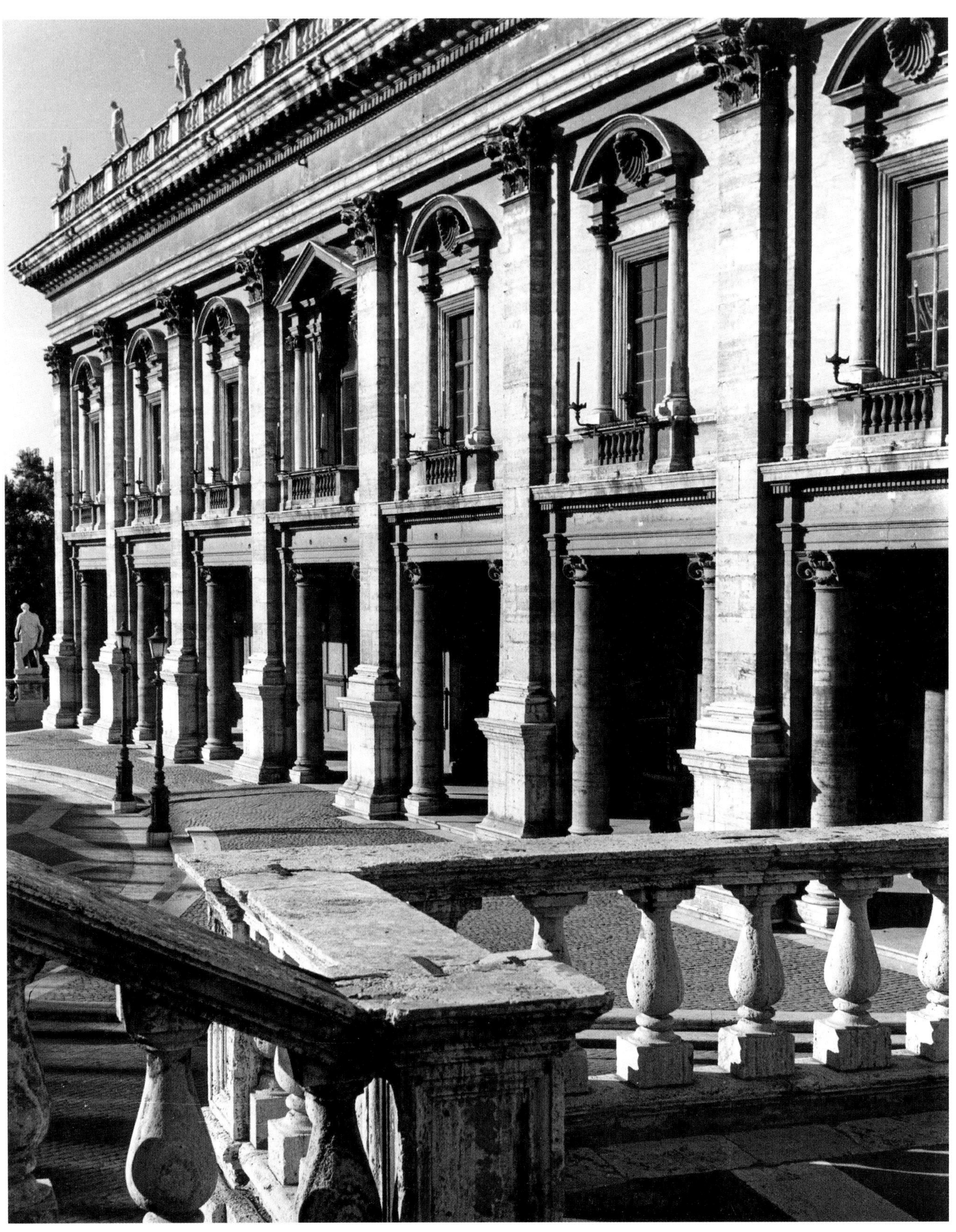

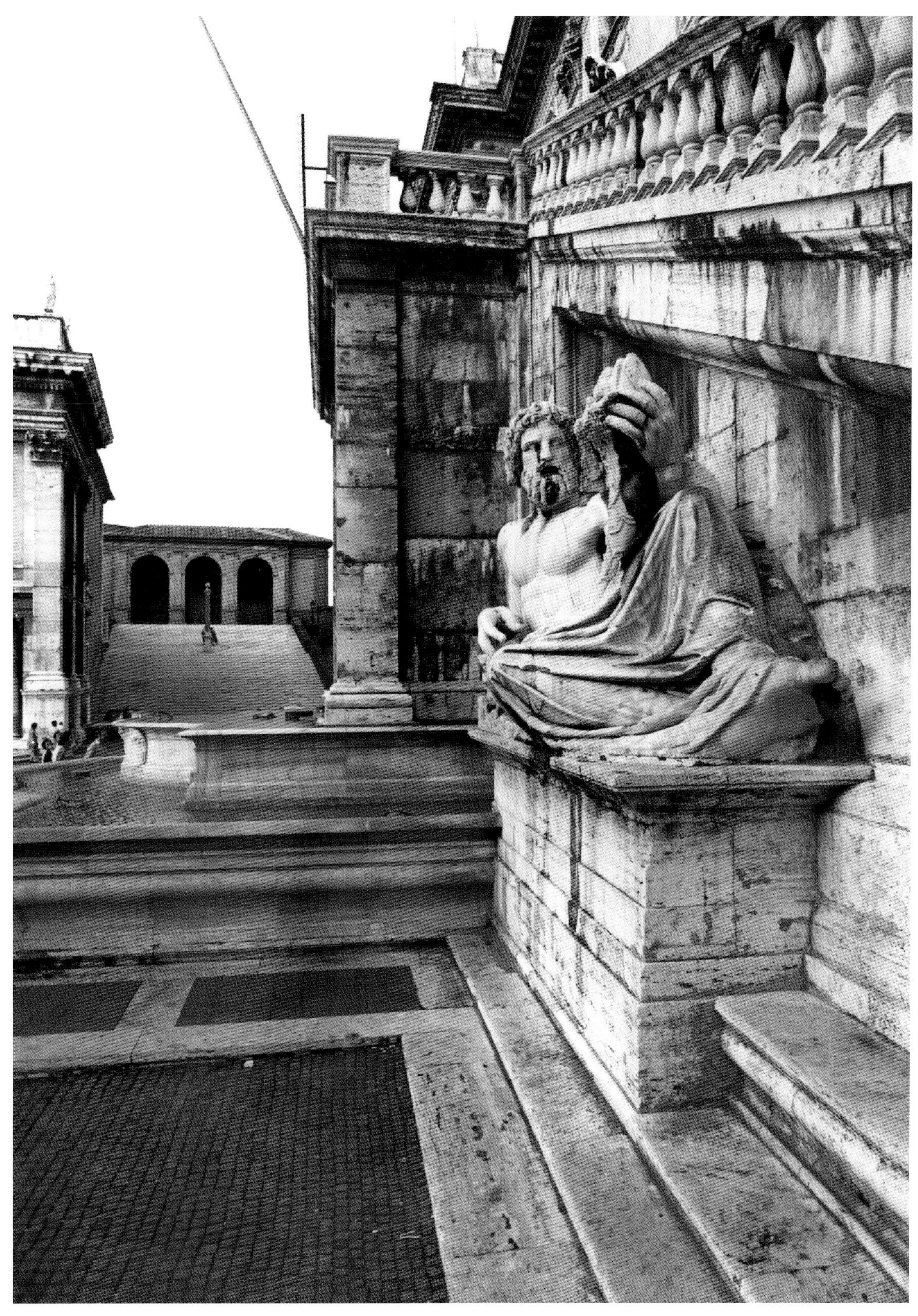

87. Tim Benton
Staircase, Palazzo Senatorio,
Piazza del Campidoglio, 1976

How is Rome seen today by visitors and by the people who live their everyday lives there? Theirs are images and impressions that reflect one another and reveal a dual city, one that displays both the fascination and the burden of its long history, that continues to attract but can only be lived to the full at the cost of great energy.

Contemporary Rome is a multipolar, multiethnic city that presents ever-differing facets in its extraordinary stratification of people and places. Built up in disorderly and contradictory fashion around its historical nucleus, between planned districts and widespread unauthorised building, the capital has proved impervious to the models of urban planning with the complicity of a political class incapable of governing its potential and dynamism. It has thus long remained predominantly tied to its ancient framework of consular roads, a network unable to ensure adequate connections between the different parts. Hence the social conflict that reveals differing priorities in the long wait for an efficient transport system.

Authoritative historians and observers have expressed common feelings of defeat or regret in reconstructing the most recent stages in Rome's history. Leonardo Benevolo speaks of a 'continuous, unstoppable ruin' condemned to 'endless atonement in abandonment or chaos for the splendours of an overly glorious past' at the risk of a 'metamorphosis of monuments and ruins into insignificant objects in the turmoil of a nondescript city'.[1] Claudia Conforti points out how 'an idea of architecture combined with an idea of the city has given way to architecture that is confined to the problem of housing and urban planning that tends to overlap with politics'.[2] Vittorio Vidotto has clearly shown how the planning scheme of the early 1960s failed 'as a tool to shape the new city and solve the problems of the old'.[3] Italian writers and journalists have also voiced criticism and above all conveyed a sense of failure by comparison with other capital cities.

A different note is struck by foreign travellers, who have in any case been responsible for shaping Italy's image and fostering its mythic dimension for centuries. Attention must also be drawn to the part played by the foreign academies located in some of the city's most beautiful spots, like Valle Giulia, the Pincio, the Gianicolo, the Aventine and Trastevere. These form a small archipelago that has established a special dialogue with the city over the years, hosting authoritative scholars who have examined Rome from a whole variety of viewpoints ranging from archaeology to the discovery of its contemporary dimension.

For this reason it is interesting to go on following their tracks, which blaze new trails within the historical city and on its outskirts scattered in the countryside, eliminating temporal differences.

The collection of contemporary photographs held by the Royal Institute of British Architects thus reveals the course of more recent construction work born out of special events, like the 1960 Olympics, and distributed — again somewhat haphazardly — over the vast urban territory, alternating controversial surgical operations in the old centre with high-quality grafts in culpably neglected peripheral areas.

On the one hand, new cultural buildings like Renzo Piano's Auditorium Parco della Musica, home of the Accademia di Santa Cecilia, Zaha Hadid's Museo delle arti del XXI secolo (Maxxi), and Odile Decq's Museo di Arte contemporanea di Roma (Macro); on the other, works of radical transformation, like Richard Meier's Museo dell'Ara Pacis and Juan Navarro Baldeweg's Biblioteca Hertziana. These operations have offered priceless opportunities to introduce citizens to the languages of contemporary art and architecture, which have succeeded in transcending their narrow disciplinary confines to become a shared heritage, not least with the creation of a specific directorate of the Ministry of Culture. The months that it took to construct the Auditorium and the Maxxi, followed by the long queues of visitors, above all youngsters on school trips, have remained memorable in the annals of Rome. The new educational policy thus launched has made Rome internationally competitive, as have the new stations of the underground line running through the fragile underbelly of the ancient city, the wholly renovated Tiburtina railway station, and indeed the new churches built on the outskirts to celebrate the Holy Year of 2000.

The new focal points thus created in the urban landscape, offering an opportunity for rediscovery and redevelopment of rundown sections of the city, have gradually become part of the most cultured itineraries and are now established points of reference for high-quality tourism. Confirmation is provided by the event *Open House Roma* with the exponential increase in the number of places featured and of visitors.

One example is the Flaminio district. The site of the 1960 Olympics with the renowned works by Pier Luigi Nervi and the Olympic Village of Vittorio Cafiero, Adalberto Libera, Amedeo Luccichenti, Vincenzo Monaco and Luigi Moretti, this has become a bustling cultural hub with the addition of the Auditorium and the Maxxi as well as the recent Ponte della Musica bridge by Buro Happold, joining it to the Foro Italico sports complex. The circuit thus created runs through most of twentieth-century Rome, bounded by the nearby Museo di Villa Giulia, the Galleria Nazionale di Arte Moderna and the foreign academies of Valle Giulia. Though still awaiting completion, the new Tiburtina station project has also achieved its aim of revitalising a very rundown area, as recently attested by new works like the Bnl-Bnp Paribas building by studio 5+1AA.

The RIBA photographs on show make these new realities visible. Their authors present an image of the city that displays both known and unknown facets simultaneously, and do so with highly realistic acumen. On the one hand, they focus on the monumental city, both ancient Rome and its celebration and revisitation under the Fascist regime, from the Pantheon to Ponte Milvio, the Tiber embankments, and the EUR district. There is also space for the spectacle of the baroque city, explored in the sumptuous interiors of buildings, in the contrast between the dense urban fabric and the reassuring skyline of domes. Signs of the present day are superimposed on the patina of time with graffiti that deface ancient marble and mosaics, indicating a certain degree of indifference and neglect of the everyday landscape. The wire mesh and scaffolding of unfinished construction sites framing monuments and the abandonment of the Ponte Rotto, overgrown with vegetation, are emblematic in this sense.

Other eyes guide us in the discovery of new centralities where the patina gives way to the freshness of experimentation with new technologies that establish an effective dialogue with history. A whole series of photographs observe the effects of fluid shapes of concrete alternating with Nervi's ageless patterns, linger on zoomorphic metal shapes that suggest a modern landscape of domes, explore the transparent sheets of glass and the rugged travertine stone framing history, as in the case of the Ara Pacis, and gauge the effect of the white sails that stand out like gems in the drabness of the Tor Tre Teste district.

Richard Pare and Richard Bryant compose a sophisticated narrative in their different approach to the Eternal City. Accentuating its qualities and contrasts, they show us all the fascination of Rome's two sides: the slightly scruffy, common, everyday face against a backdrop of domes and monuments, and the face of extraordinary works of architecture, both ancient and contemporary. Exploring the layers of the historical city in a simultaneous and timeless reading, the photographers capture the glowing range of colours and an all-enveloping light that continues to assert Rome's extraordinary identity despite its countless contradictions.

Antonello Alici

[1] Leonardo Benevolo, *Roma dal 1870 al 1990*, Rome-Bari: Laterza, 1992, p. VIII.
[2] Claudia Conforti, 'Roma, Napoli, Sicilia', in F. Dal Co (ed.), *Storia dell'architettura italiana. Il secondo Novecento*, Milan: Electa, 1997, pp. 176–241; 223.
[3] Vittorio Vidotto, *Roma contemporanea*, Rome-Bari: Laterza, 2001, p. 300.

88. Richard Pare
*Statue of the Nile, Fountain
of the Four Rivers,
and Sant'Agnese in Agone,
Piazza Navona*, 1985

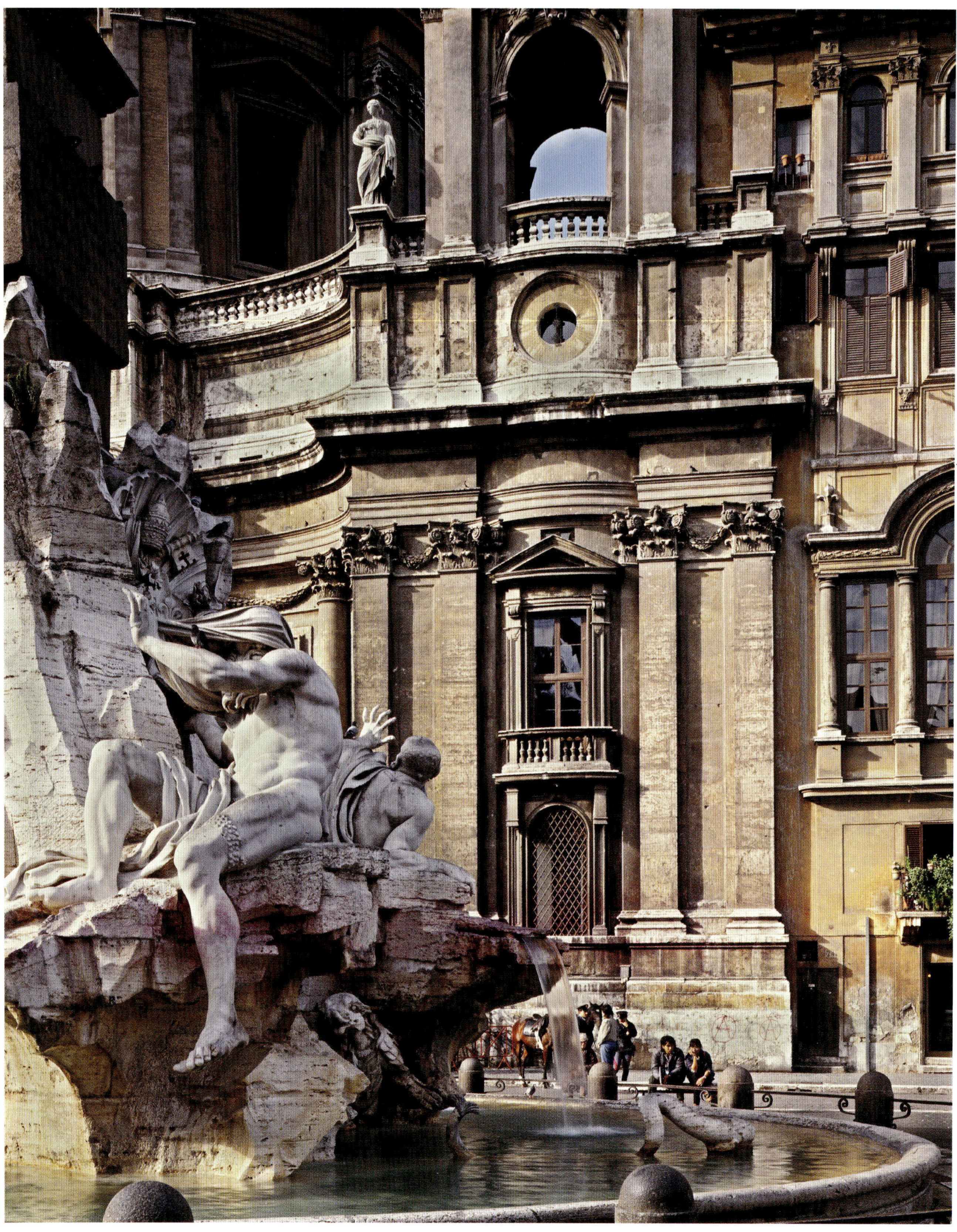

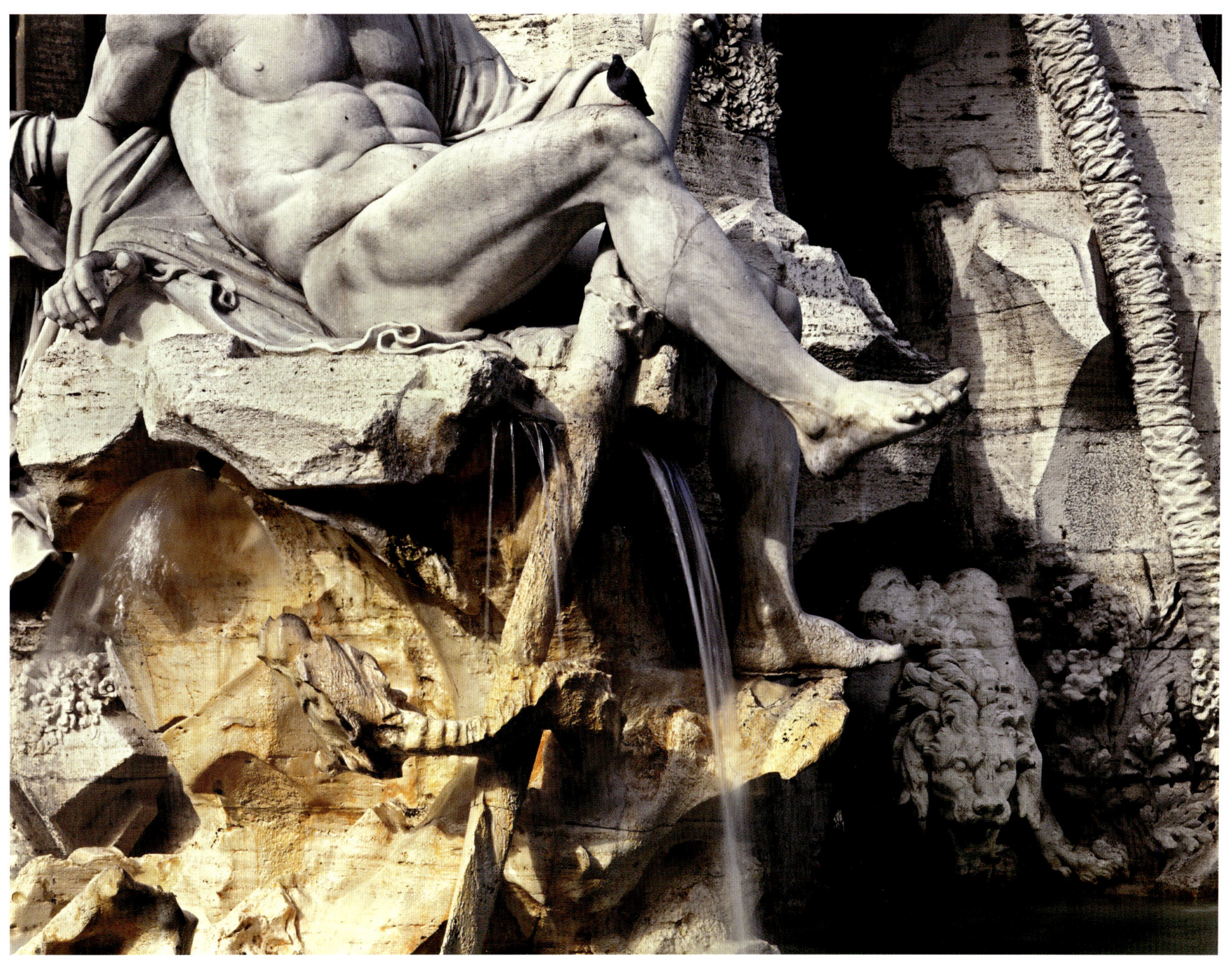

89. Richard Pare
*Statue of the Ganges,
Fountain of the Four Rivers,
Piazza Navona, 1985*

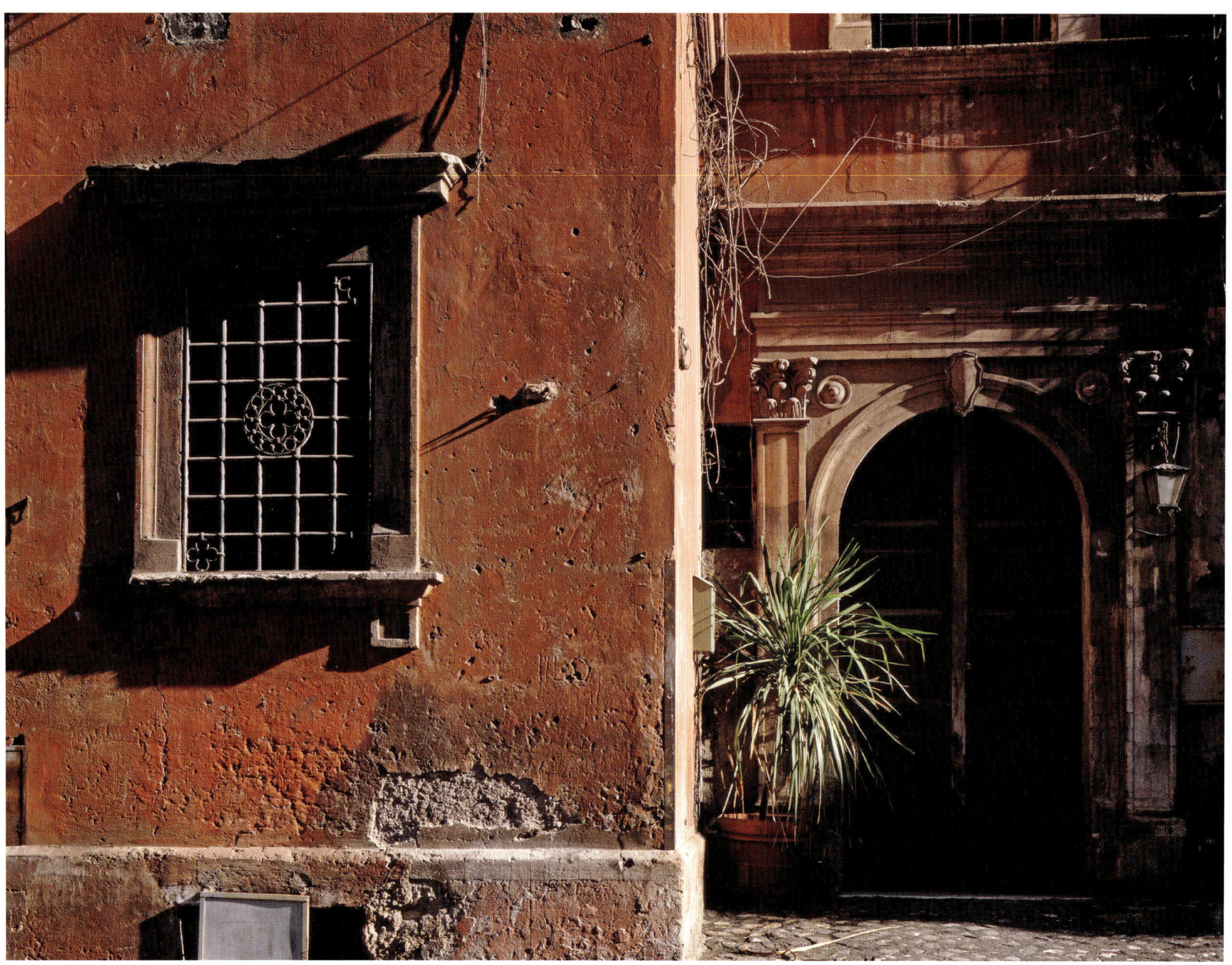

90. Richard Pare
14 Piazza dei Mercanti,
Trastevere, 1985

91. Richard Pare
Spanish Steps, towards
Trinità dei Monti, 1985

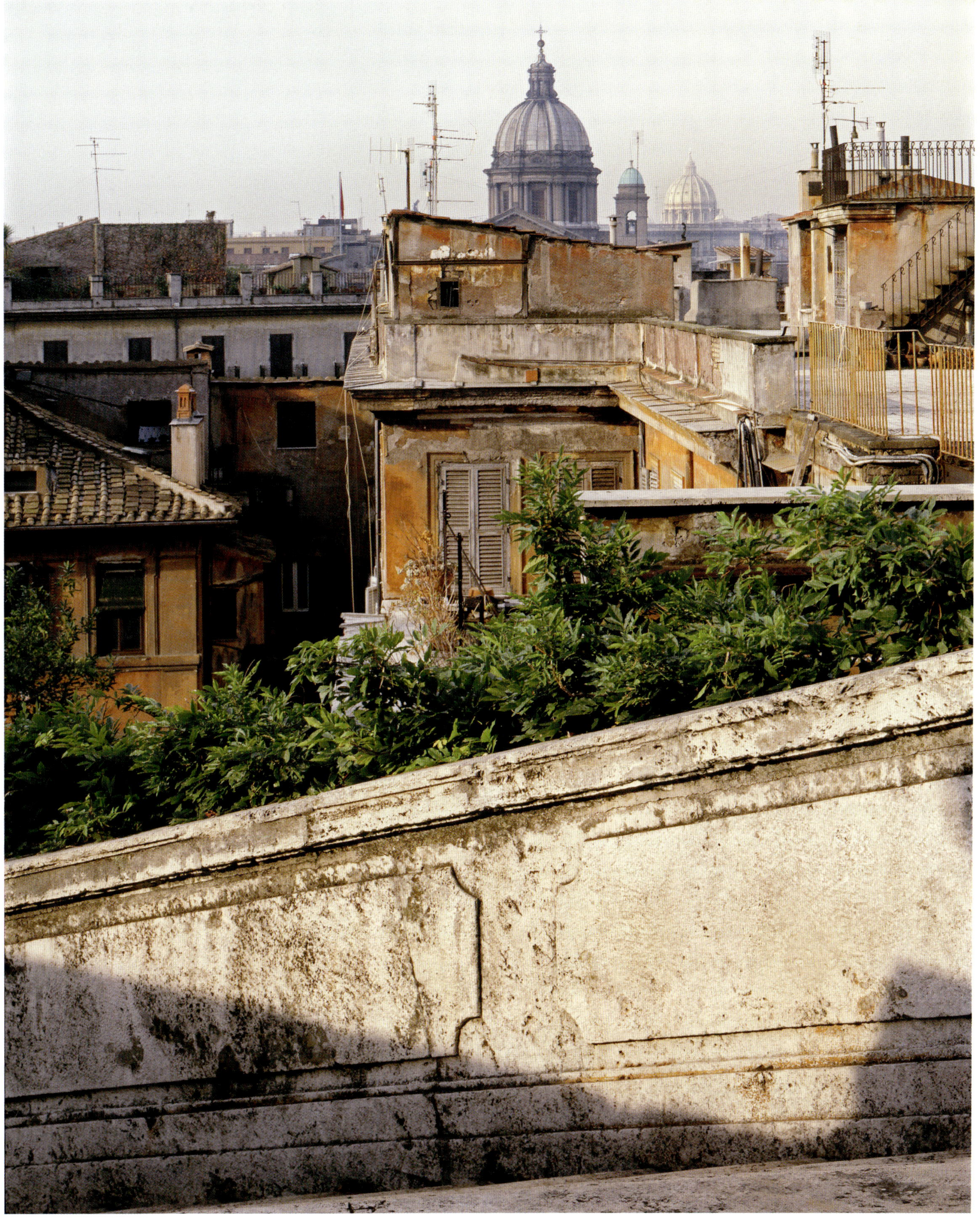

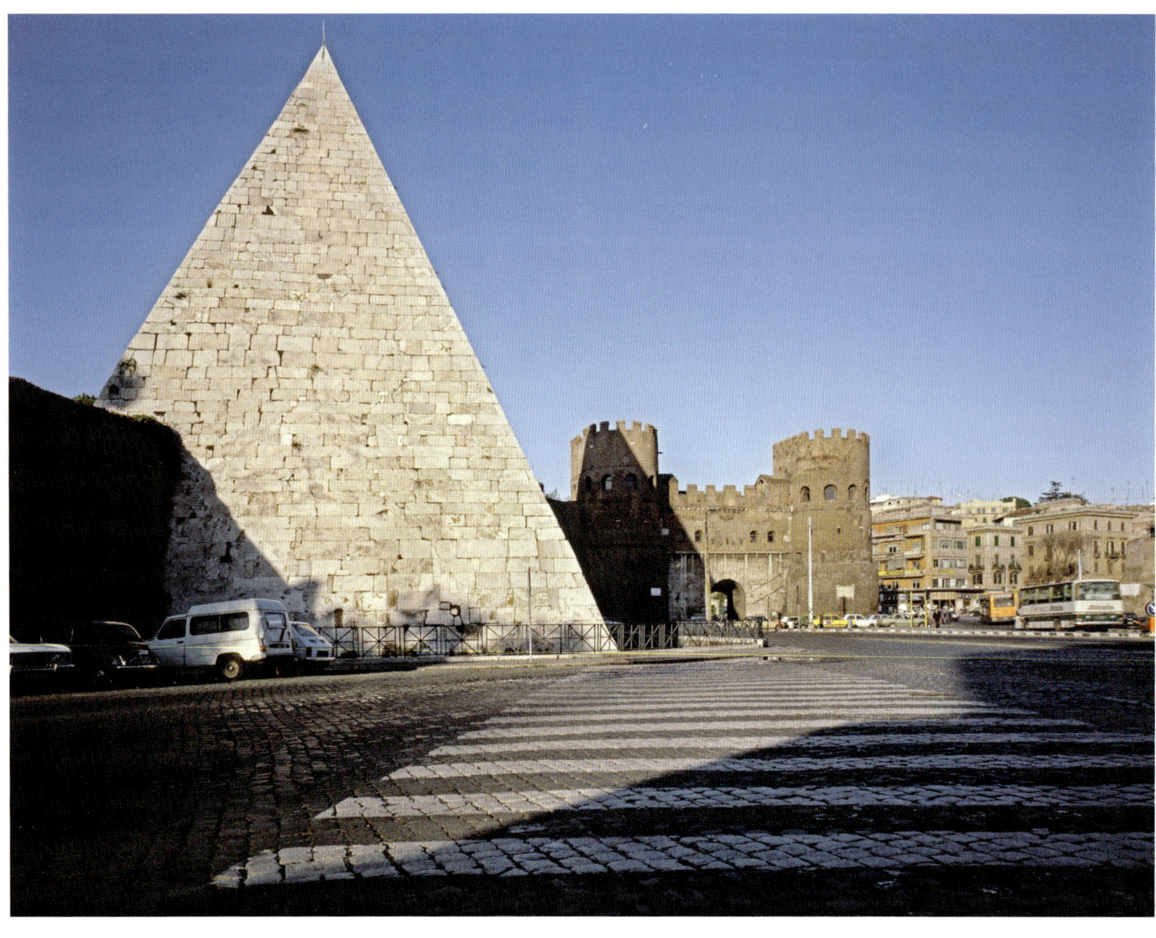

92. Richard Pare
Pyramid of Caius Cestius, 1985

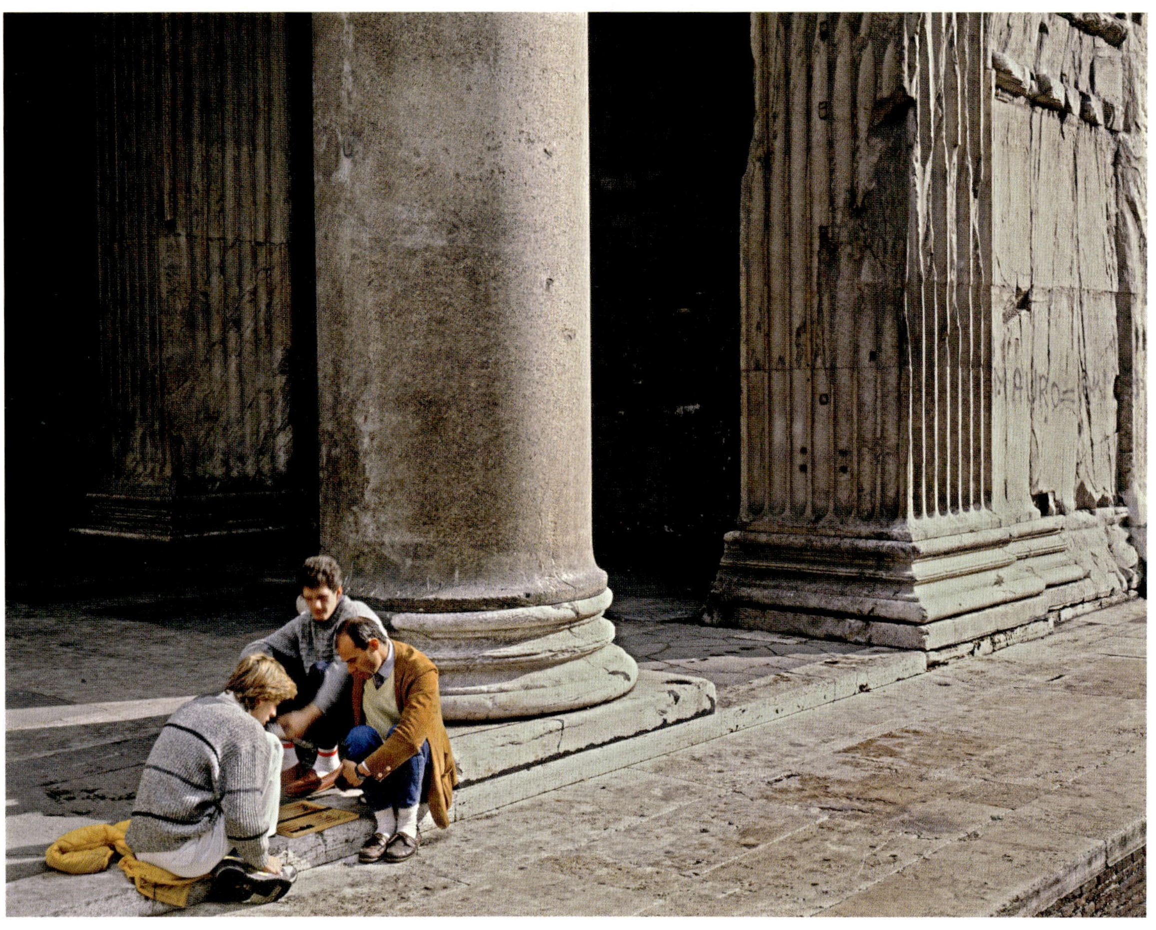

93. Richard Pare
Pantheon, 1985

94. Richard Pare
Arco del Ponte Rotto, 1985

95. Richard Pare
Pincio gardens, 1985

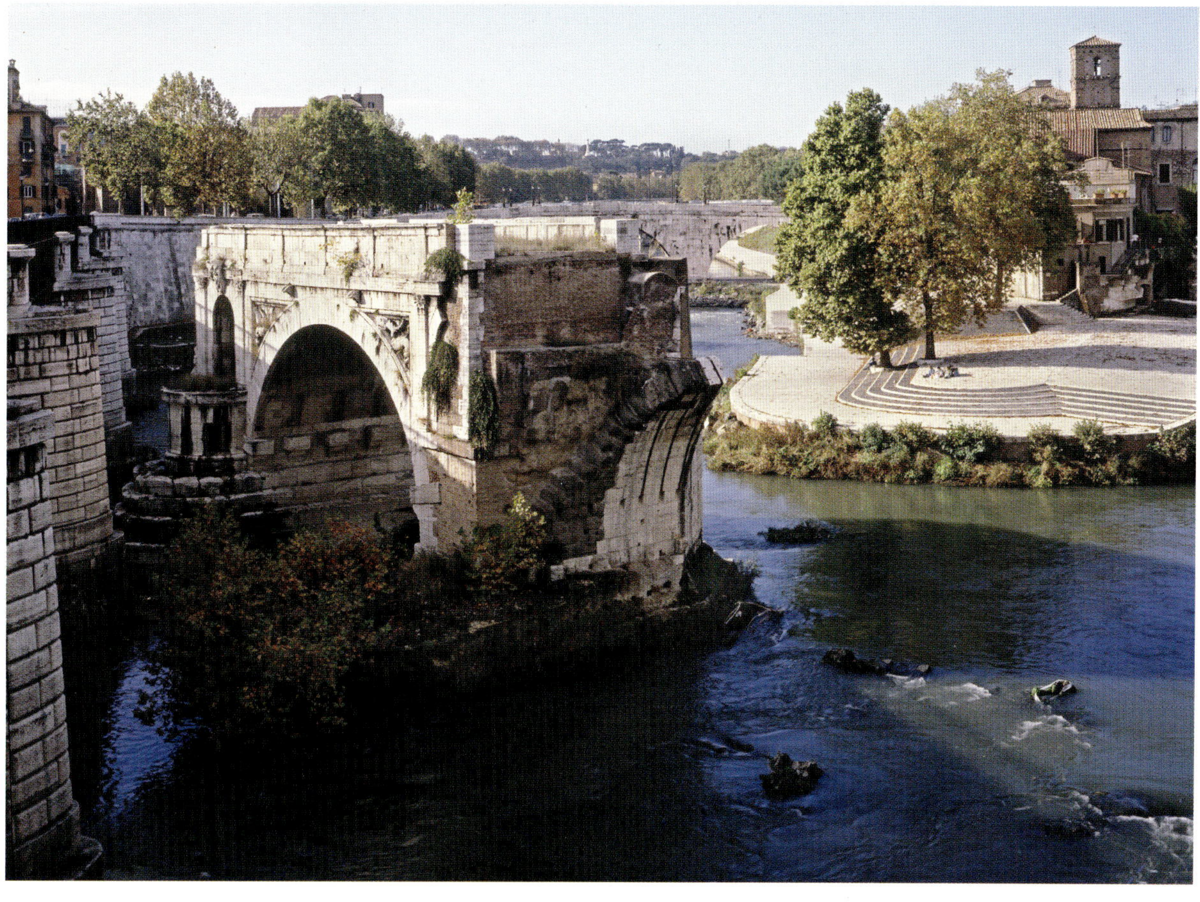

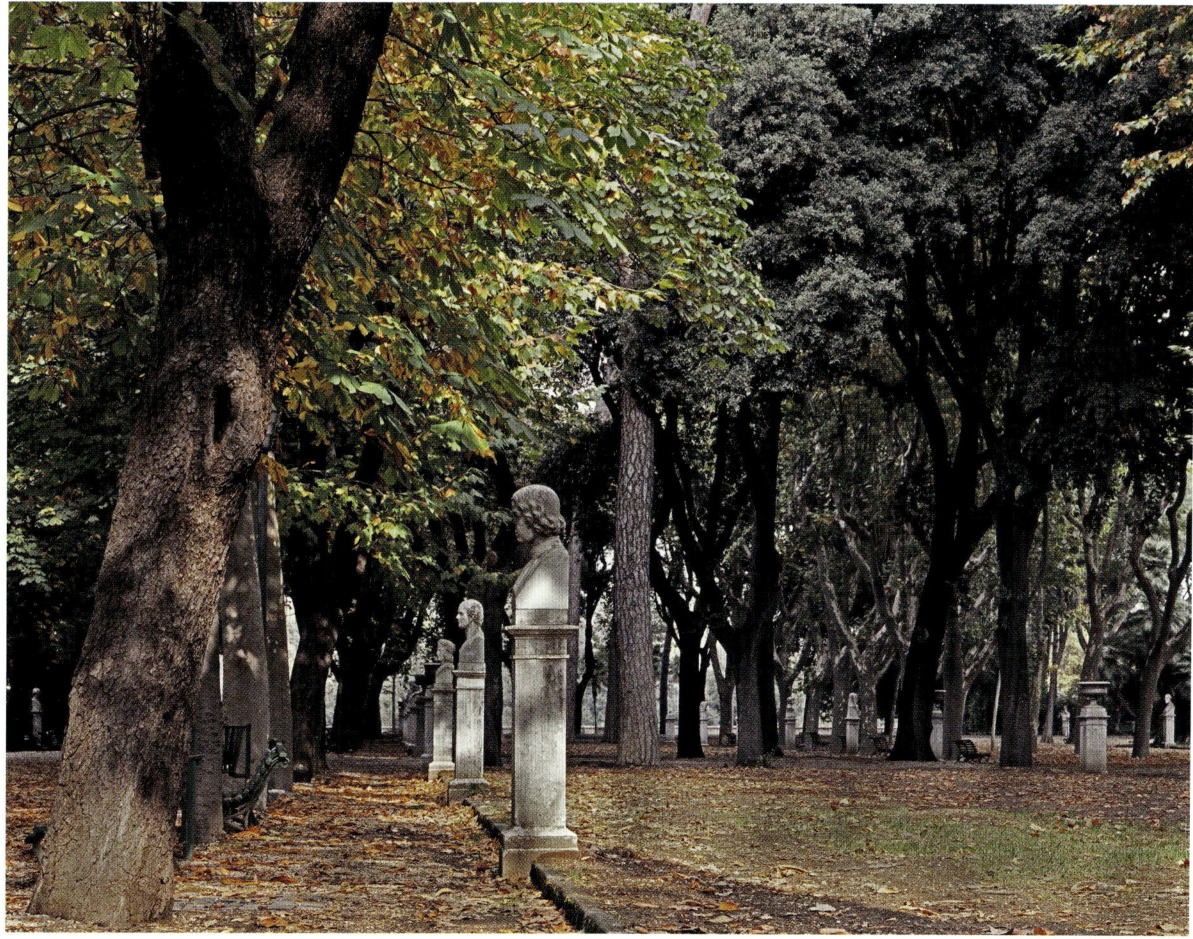

96. Richard Pare
Isola Tiberina, 1985

97. Richard Pare
EUR, c. 2000

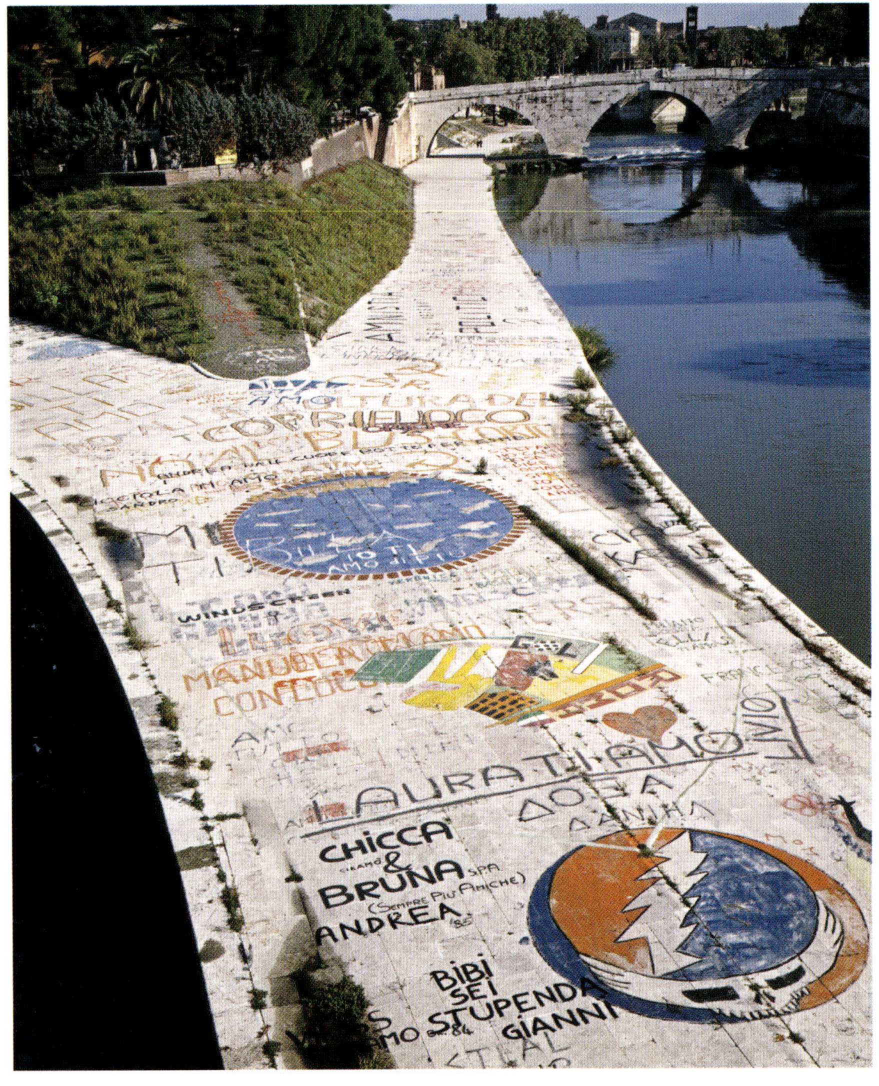

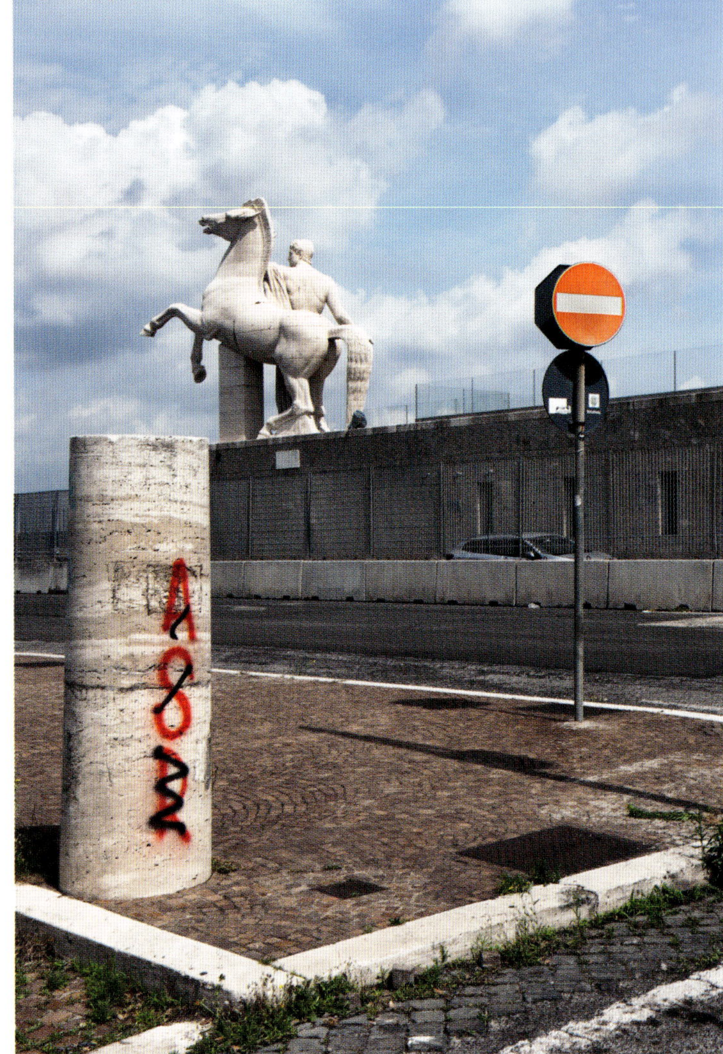

98. Richard Pare
Palazzo della Civiltà Italiana,
EUR, 1985

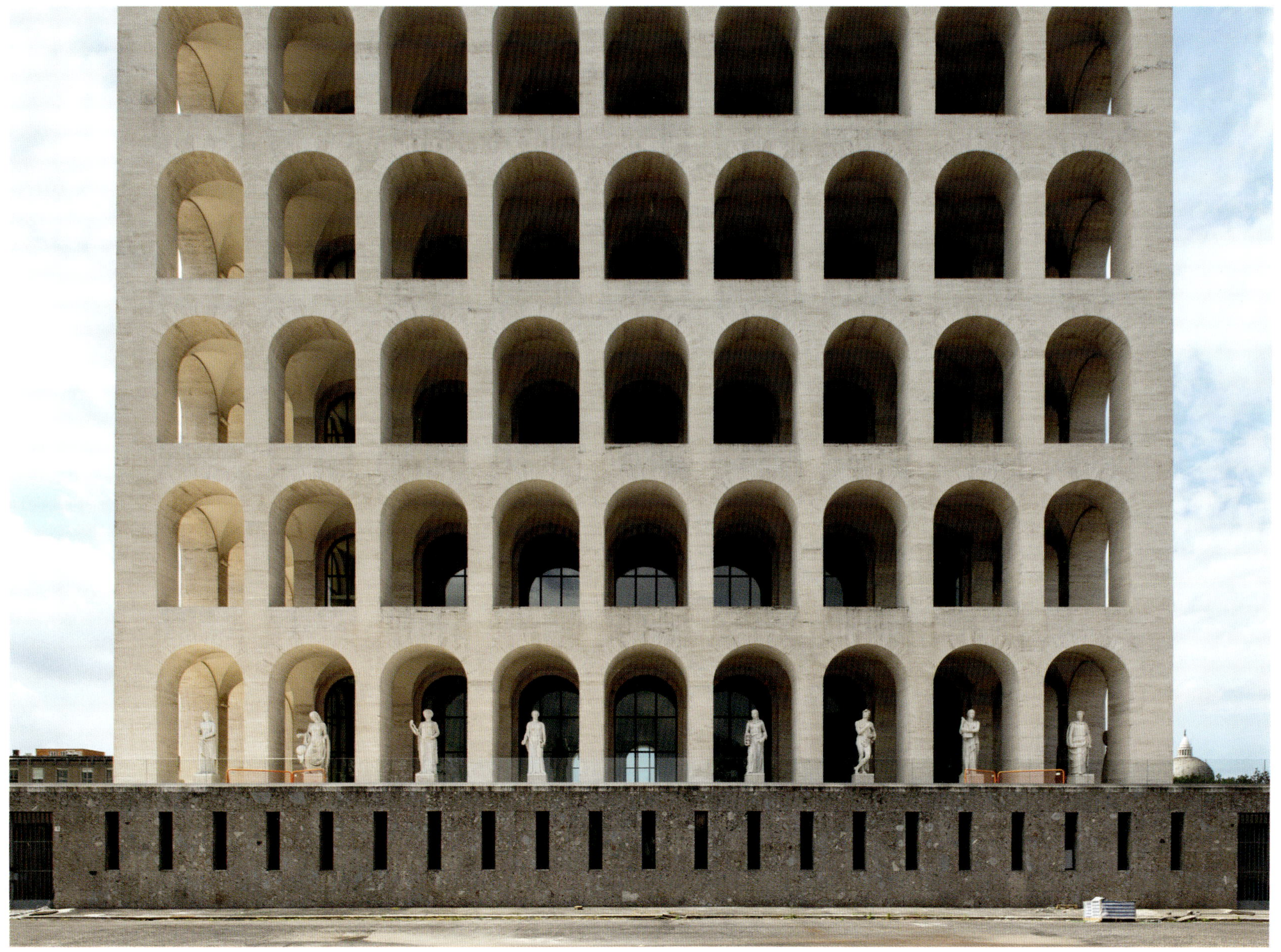

99. Richard Bryant
Palazzetto dello Sport, 2009

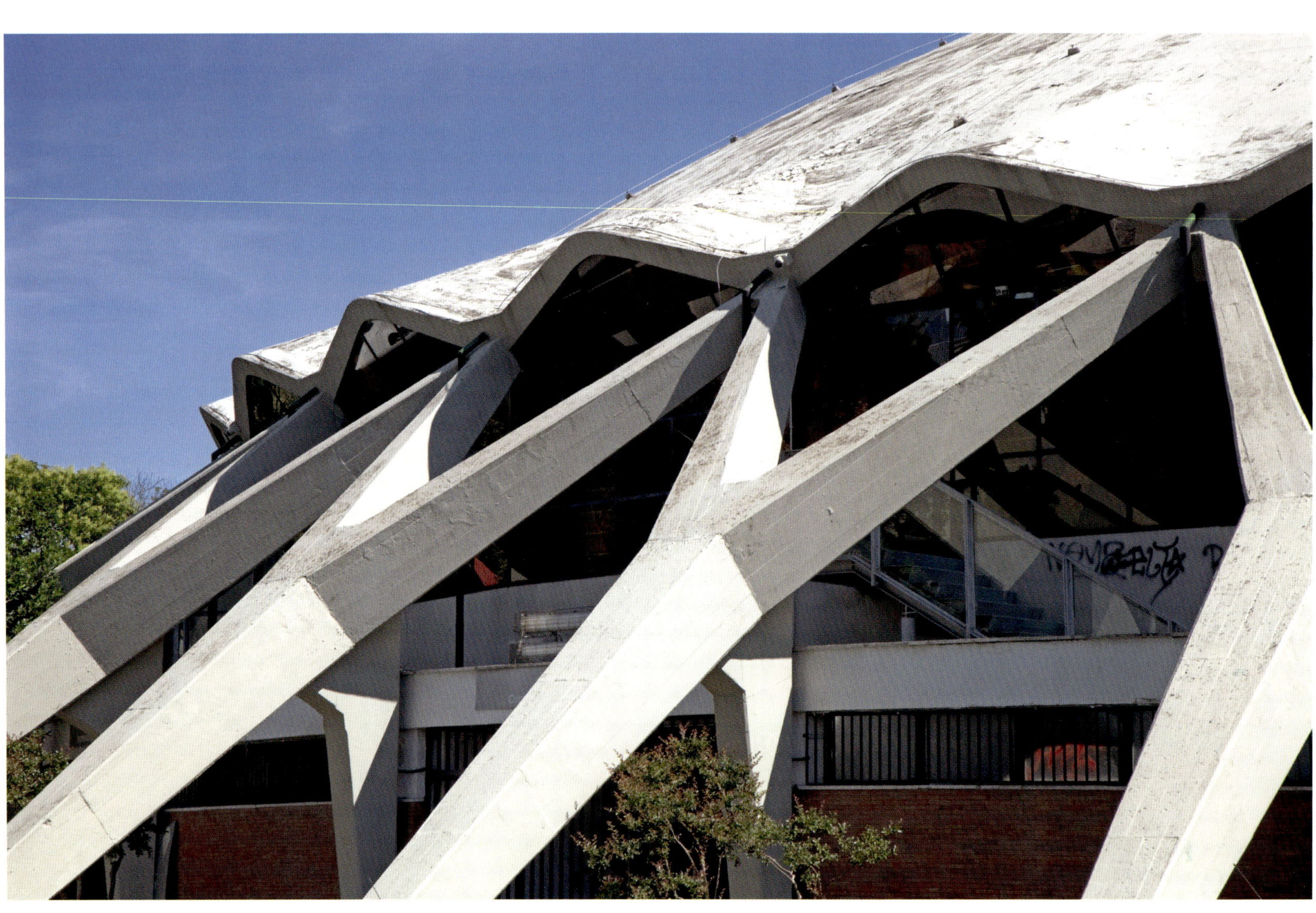

100. Richard Bryant
Ara Pacis Museum, Rome, 2009

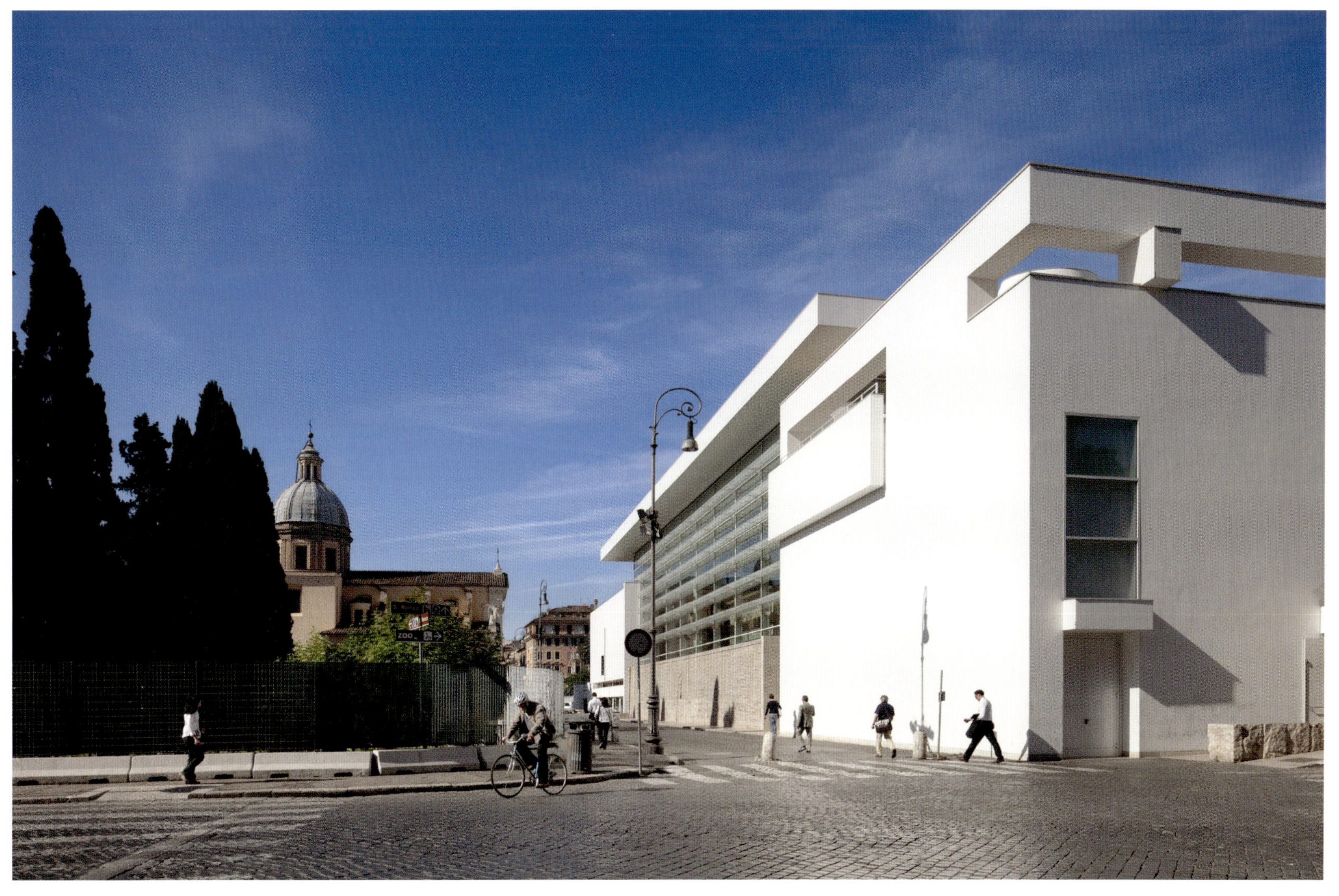

101. Richard Bryant
Parco della Musica, 2002

102. Richard Bryant
Parco della Musica, 2002

103. Richard Bryant
Parco della Musica, 2002

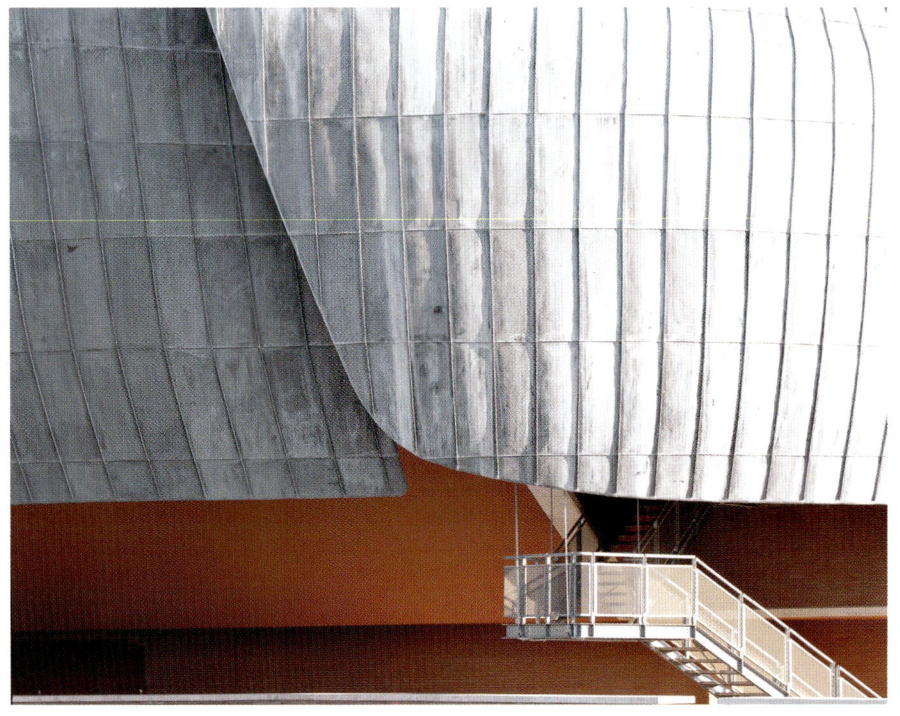

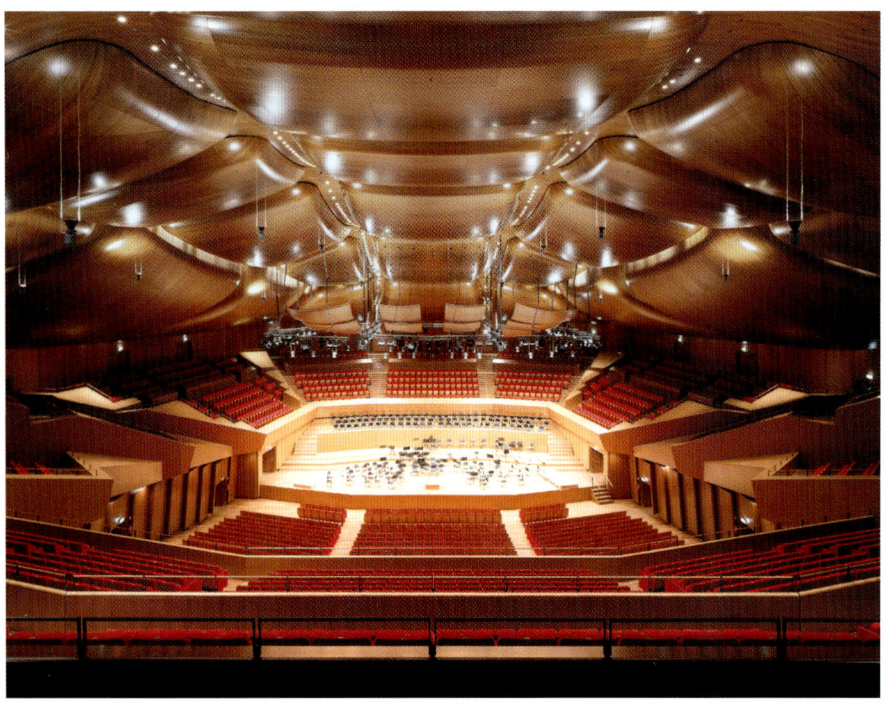

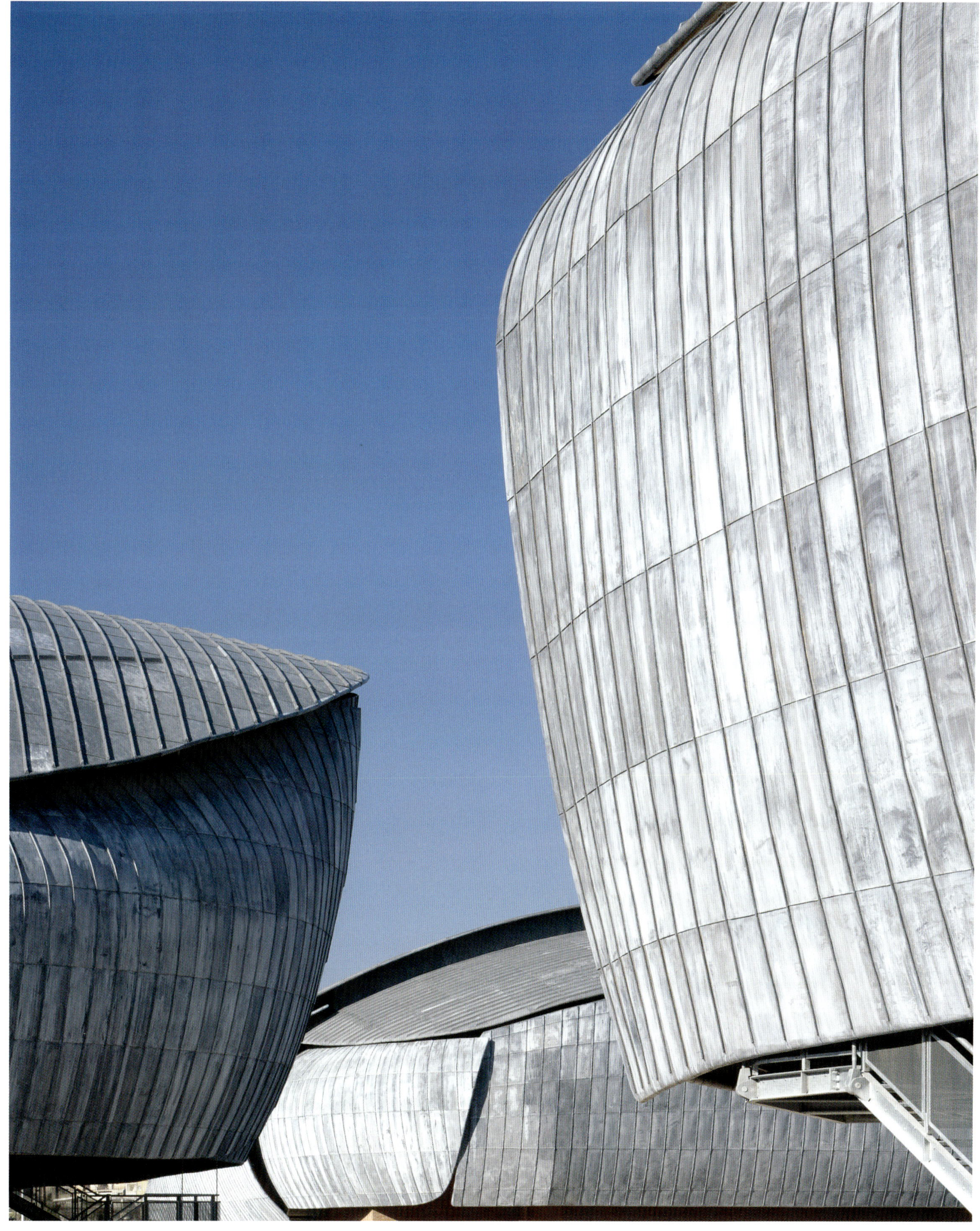

104. Richard Bryant
Parco della Musica, 2002

105. Richard Bryant
*Chiesa del Dio Padre
Misericordioso,
Tor Tre Teste, 2003*

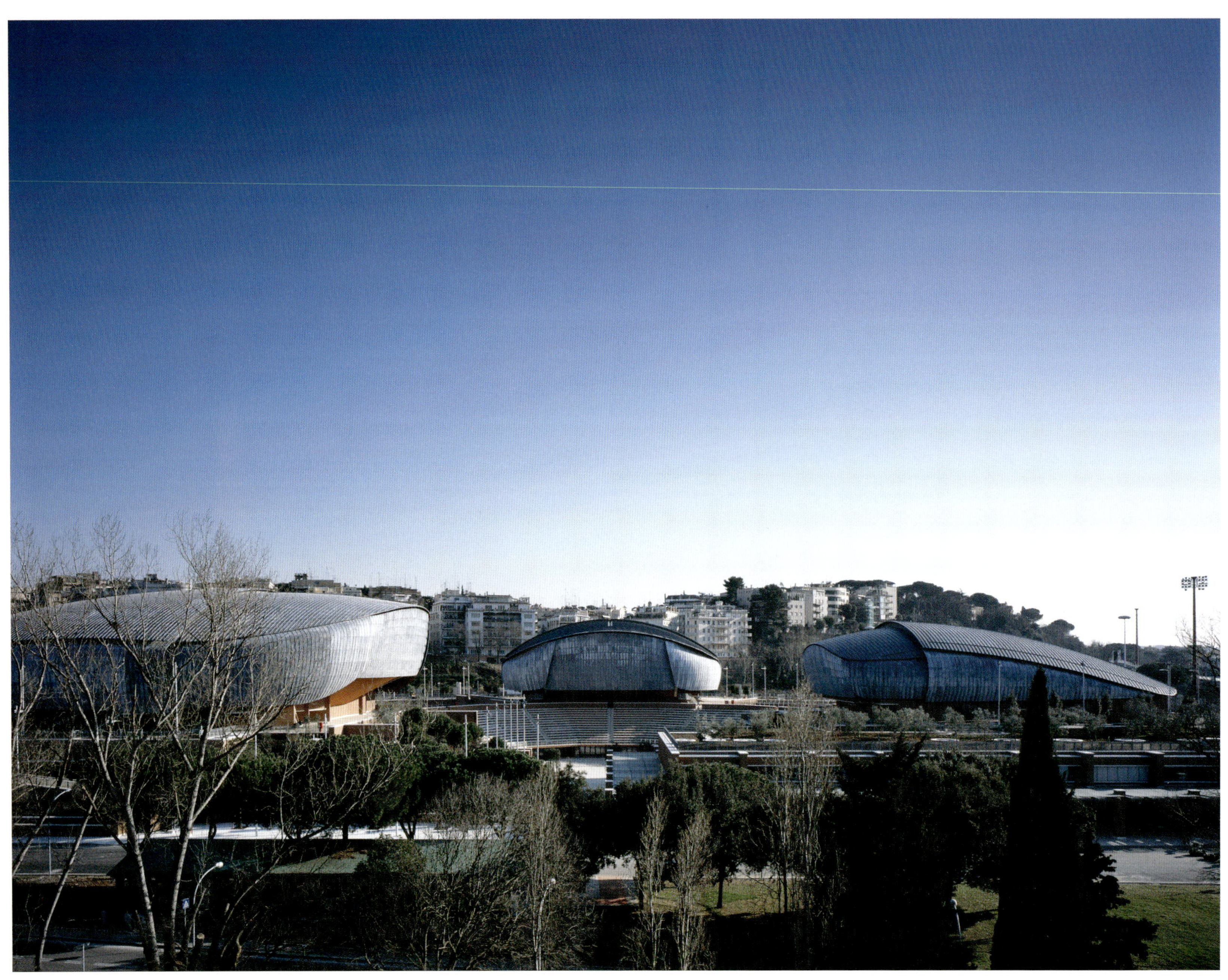

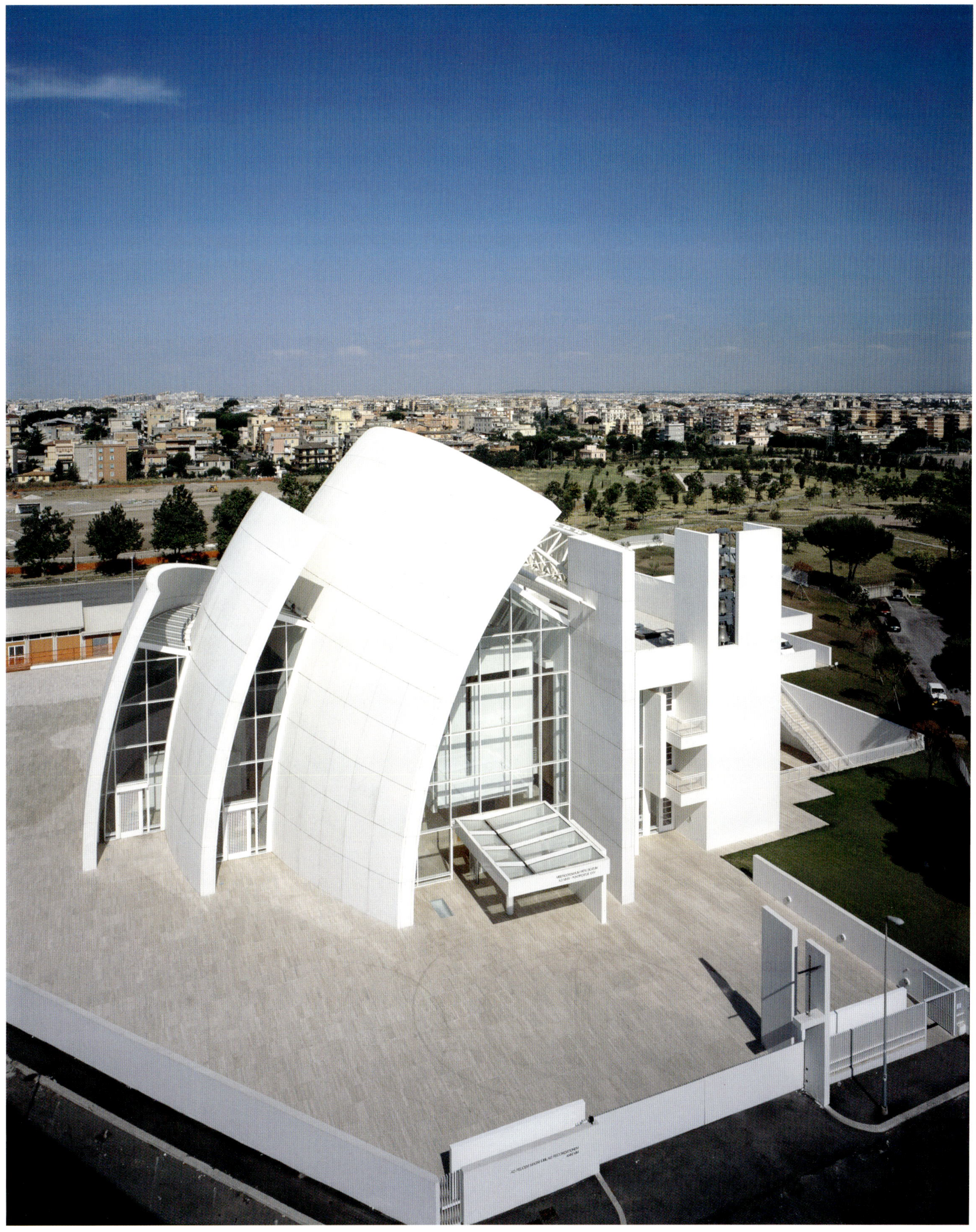

106. Richard Bryant
Chiesa del Dio Padre
Misericordioso,
Tor Tre Teste, 2003

107. Richard Bryant
Chiesa del Dio Padre
Misericordioso,
Tor Tre Teste, 2003

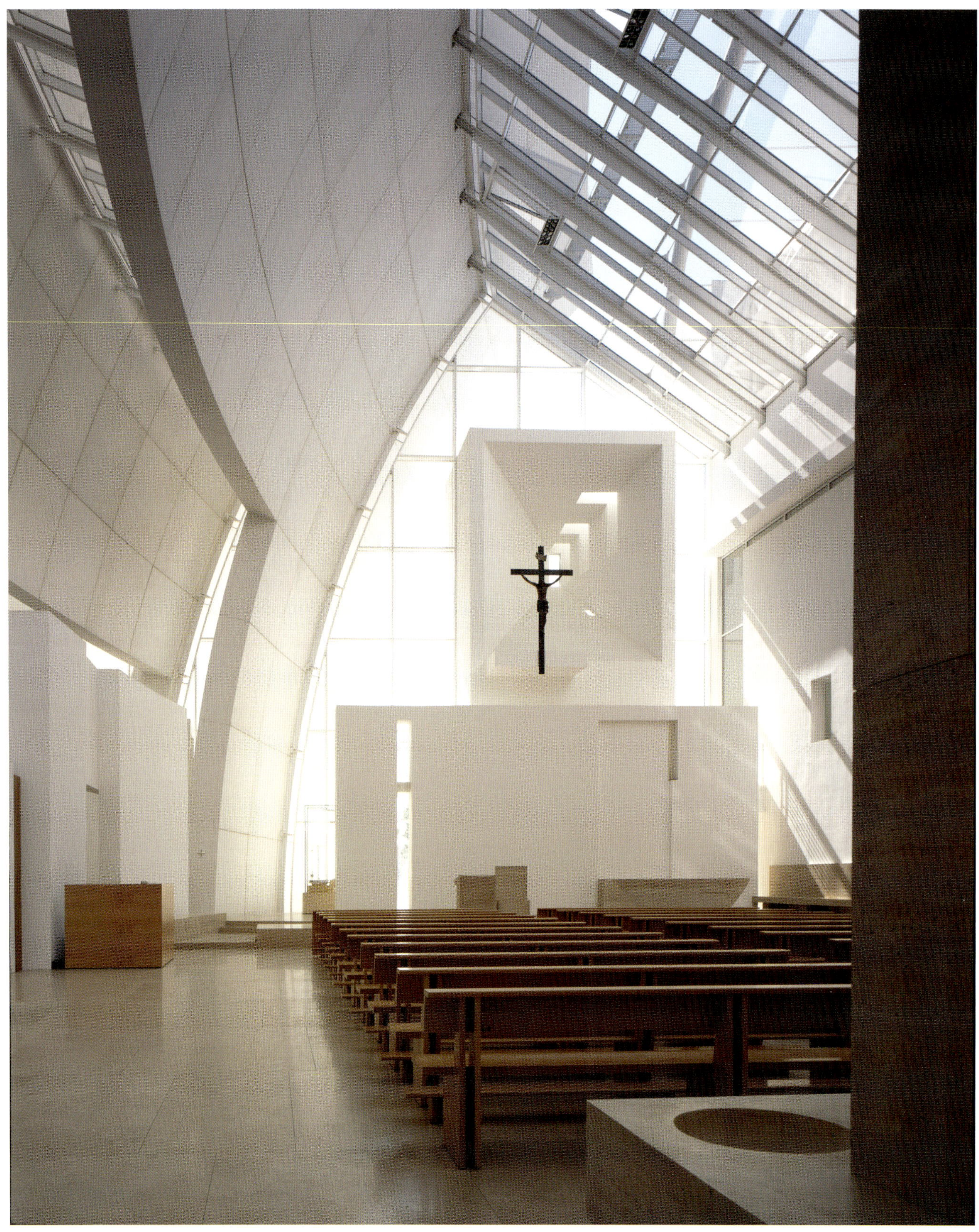

106. Richard Bryant
Chiesa del Dio Padre
Misericordioso,
Tor Tre Teste, 2003

107. Richard Bryant
Chiesa del Dio Padre
Misericordioso,
Tor Tre Teste, 2003

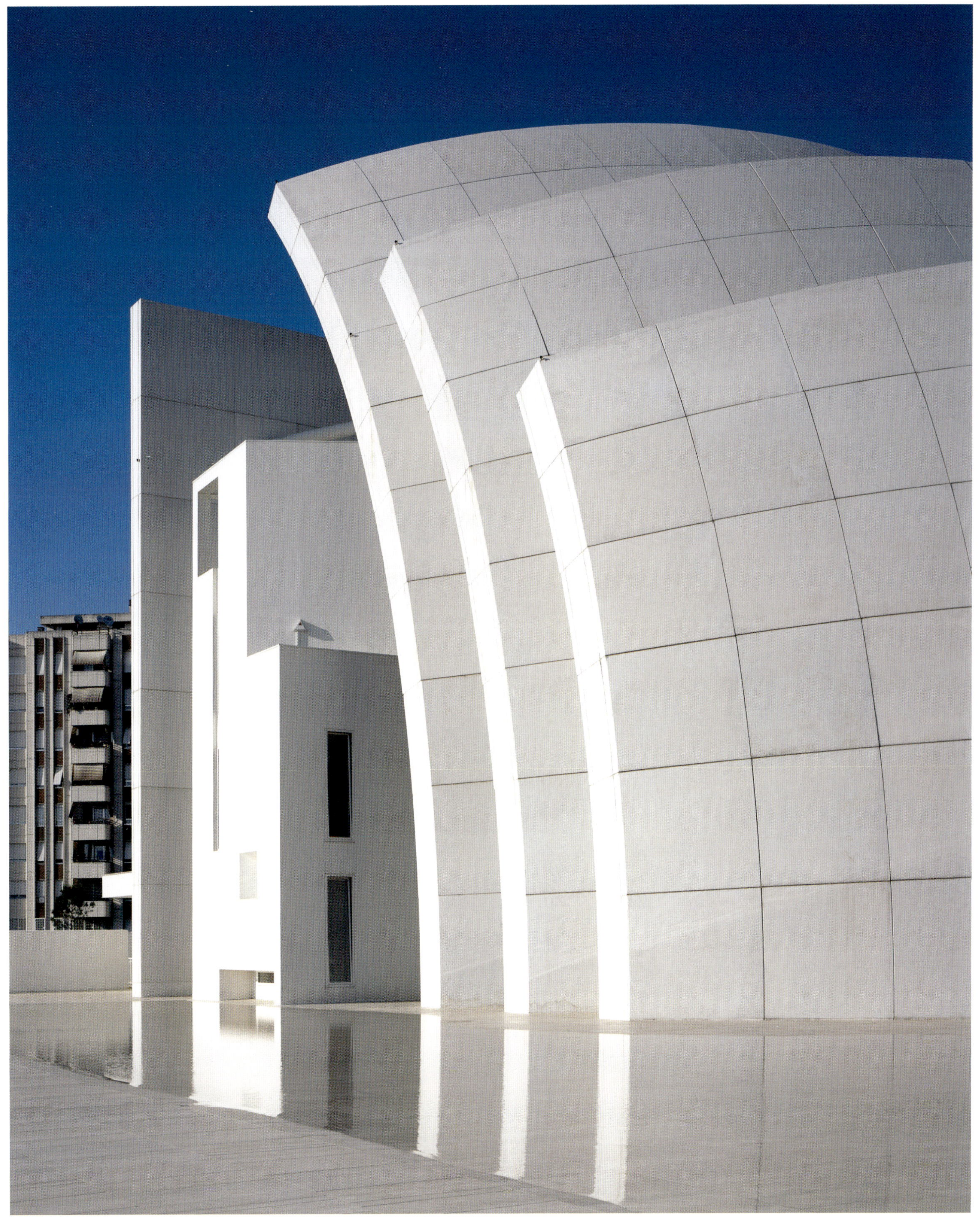

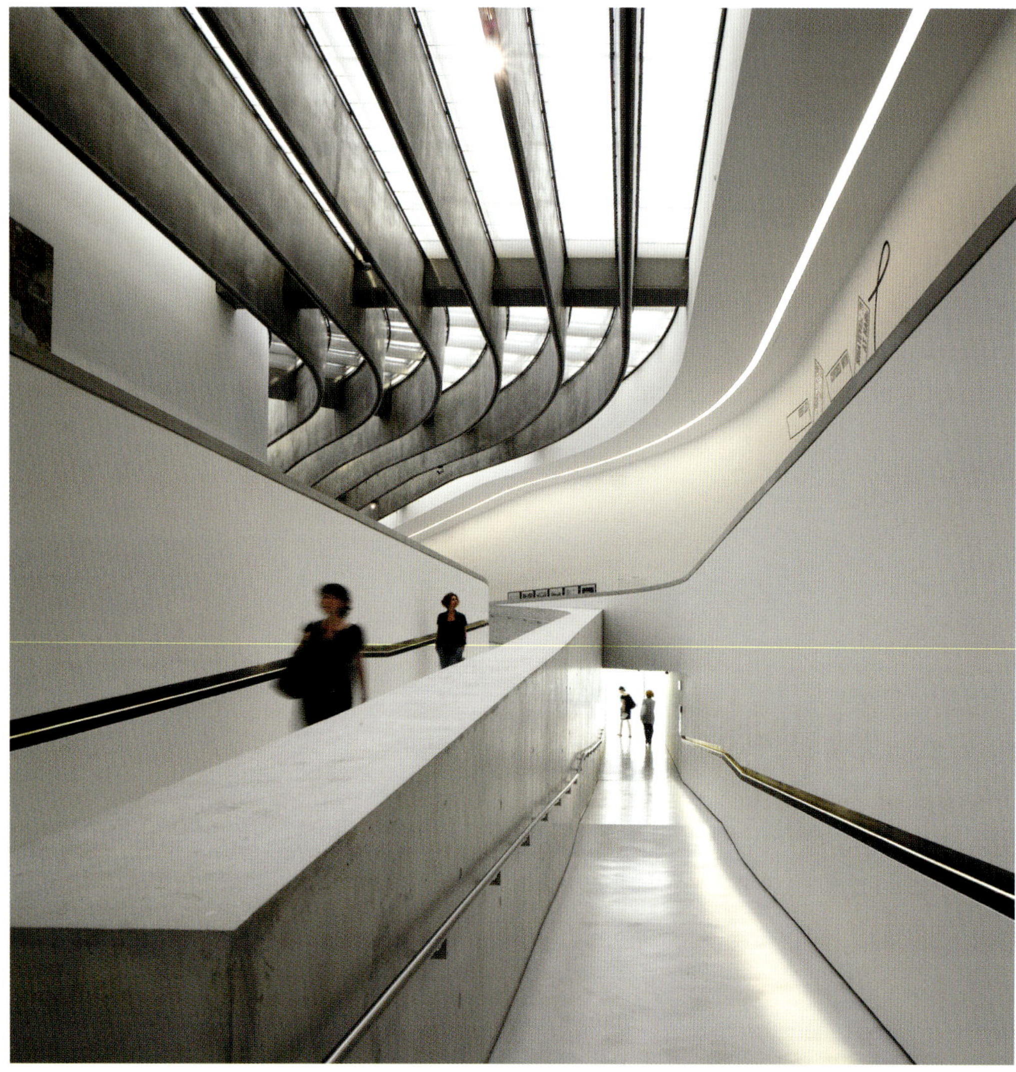

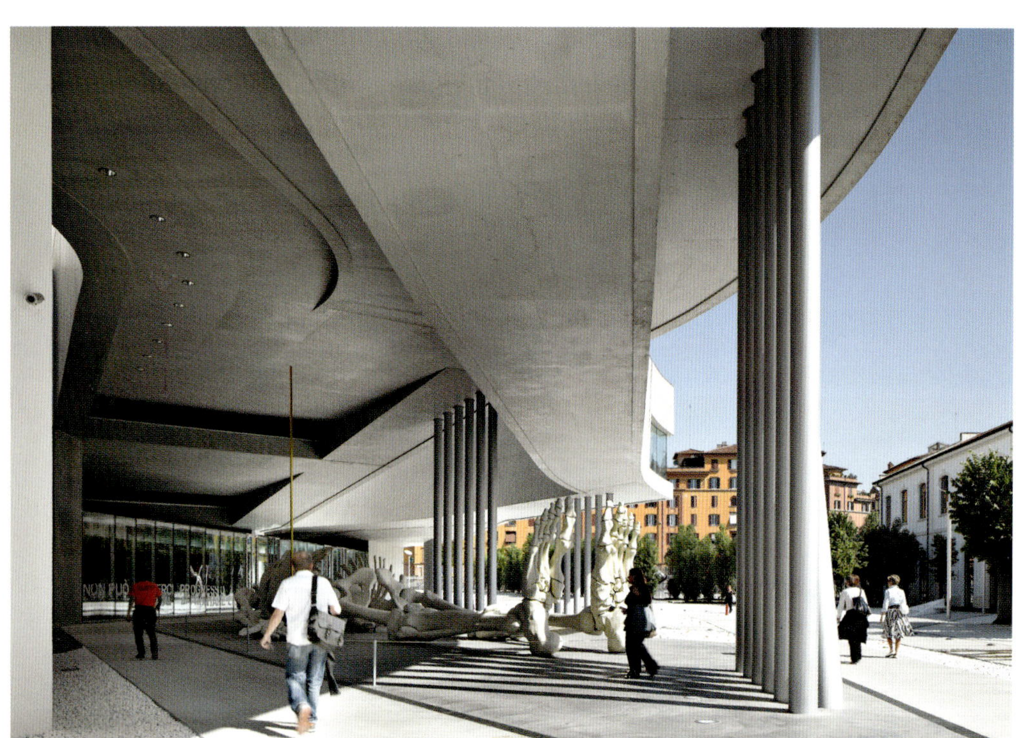

108. Richard Bryant
*MAXXI, National Museum
of 21st Century Arts*, 2009

109. Richard Bryant
*MAXXI, National Museum
of 21st Century Arts*, 2009

146

110. Richard Bryant
*MAXXI, National Museum
of 21st Century Arts, 2009*

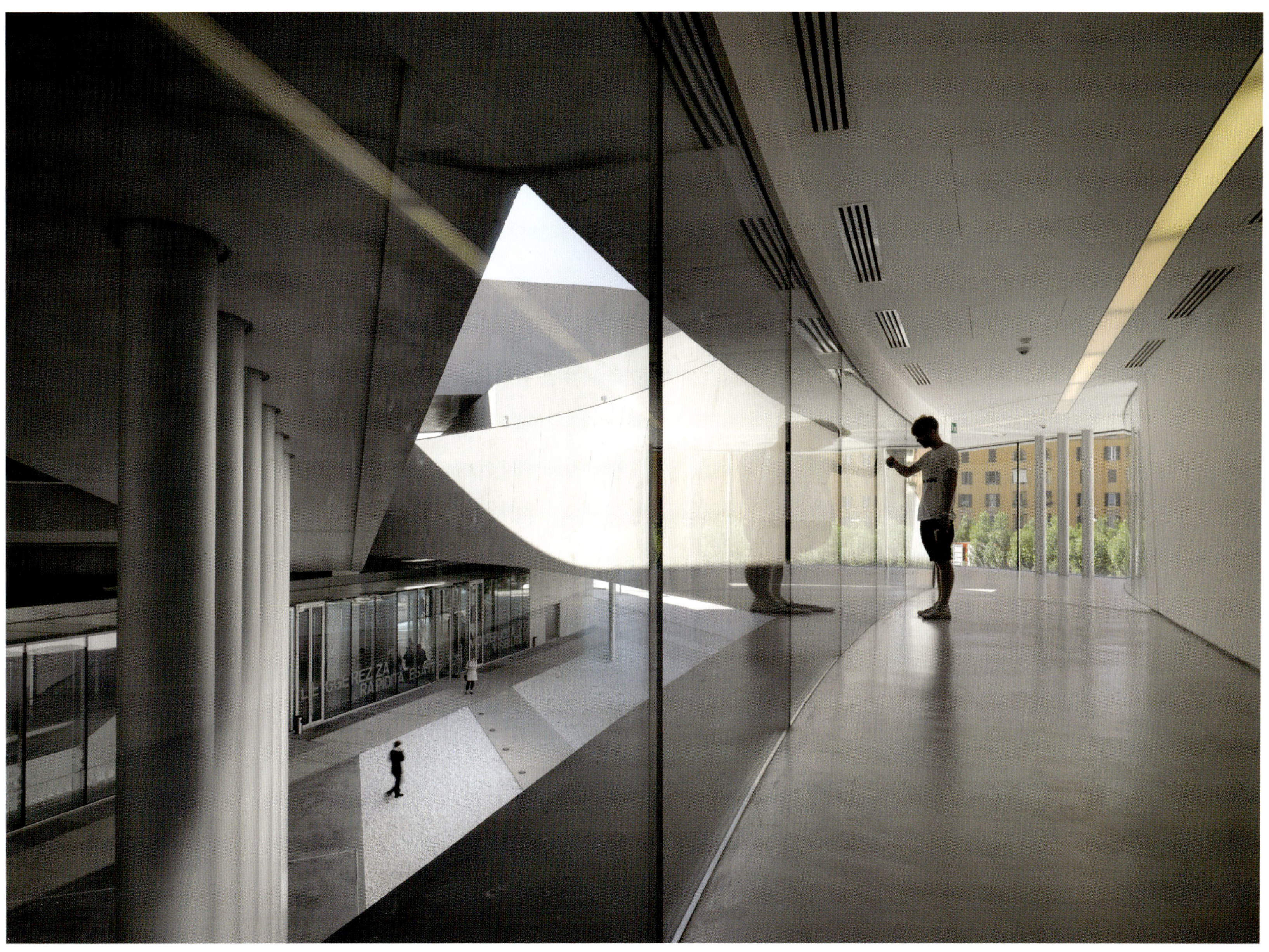

Urban Landscapes

The representation of Rome in the modern and contemporary era has contributed to the creation of a singular visual memory connected with the city. The image of its urban landscape is made clearly distinguishable not only by reproductions of its characteristic monuments, as often happens in other contexts too, but also through its views.

Various figures contributed even before the birth of photography to this process of recognisability, of the construction, dissemination and sedimentation of a specific image, including painters like Nicolas Poussin, Joseph Wright of Derby and Jacob Philipp Hackert. In views of ruins, the surrounding countryside, corners of the city and architectural works in chiaroscuro, Rome is poised midway between the reality and the imagination.

In this perspective, we cannot fail to smile at how disappointed Dickens was on his arrival to find a city completely at odds with his expectations: 'We entered the Eternal City, at about four o'clock in the afternoon, on the thirtieth of January, by the Porta del Popolo [...]. There were no great ruins, no solemn tokens of antiquity, to be seen; they all lie on the other side of the city. There seemed to be long streets of commonplace shops and houses, such as are to be found in any European town; there were busy people, equipages, ordinary walkers to and from; a multitude of chattering strangers. It was no more my Rome: the Rome of anybody's fancy, man or boy; degraded and fallen and lying asleep in the sun among a heap of ruins: than the Place de la Concorde in Paris is. A cloudy sky, a dull cold rain, and muddy streets, I was prepared for, but not for this: and I confess to having gone to bed, that night, in a very indifferent humour, and with a very considerably quenched enthusiasm.'[1] Dickens travelled the roads and countryside around Rome in an effort to bring his personal experience into line with the idea of the city built up in advance on the basis of secondary sources.

In any case, the mass reproduction of stereotypes still works today to build up collective images that often precede and in some respects influence real experience, transforming the journey into one of verification rather than discovery.

In the case of Rome, the creation of such a sharply defined character of representation, sometimes more pervasive than the reality itself, can be traced back to two fundamental aspects. The first is the continuity of the physical and environmental characteristics of the landscape, leading to a reiteration of compositional themes encountered first in painting and then also in photography.

The second is the strategic role of photographs and their circulation in connection with tourism, which led to the selection of a series of specific subjects that were constantly repeated, thus facilitating recognisability. When we consider the early dissemination of photographs of Rome, attention should be brought to the close connection not only between painting and photography but also between photography and tourism. Photography flourished in the Eternal City due to the increasing demand of pilgrims, travellers and tourists for souvenir images, previously sold in the form of paintings and engravings. Halfway through the nineteenth century, it was a group of painter-photographers who frequented the Caffè Greco[2] that enthusiastically promoted the new technique, combining their pictorial training with photographic experimentation and thus establishing an indivisible link between the disciplines from the very outset.

Rome formed an essential stage of the Grand Tour from the seventeenth century onwards, offering the ideal setting for the reproduction of classical and conventional views in response to the demand of customers, whose taste had been moulded by years of artistic production limited to a selection of standardised subjects.

This tourism was indeed primarily shaped by the pages of the few publications in circulation at the time. In this context, guide books became an indispensable aid for most of the travellers eager to learn while on the move, visiting the places recommended along the suggested routes. As a result, the demand for images to illustrate the Roman adventure also tended towards stable repetition. While conforming to the choice of the items represented, the words and pictures stimulated subjective emotions. Rome offered a contrast of sacred and profane, lofty art and rusticity, the sublime and the picturesque. The views condensed all these juxtapositions, encompassing both objective reality and the imagination.

In the variety of photographs from the collection of the Royal Institute of British Architects, these themes are evident and sublimated, albeit in completely different ways, in the work of Edwin Smith and of Ivy de Wolfe. The former exploited the different planes, forms and perspectives of urban spaces (and voids), reinterpreting some of the traditional iconographic themes. In many of his works the landscape is already shifted into the collective imagination, drawing on a selection of views that promote a clearly defined series of vantage points for panoramas.

For *The Italian Townscape*,[3] in search of the city's authentic and dynamic face,

Ivy de Wolfe instead photographed and documented its everyday life and the multiform possibilities of spatial experience, subverting the stereotypes in which tourists were apparently trapped. This approach can also be discerned in Monica Pidgeon's work.

As clearly appears in these visual exercises, the peculiar character of Rome's urban landscape is therefore defined not only by the reiteration of the subjects portrayed and the favoured vantage points but also by a series of approaches to composition and framing that are indebted to the specific topographical and morphological as well as social and cultural qualities of the city. In this tension between concrete, recognisable elements and the possibility of unconfined, fanciful representation, Rome invented an inexhaustible system of collective memories always open to renewal and reinterpretation.

The photographic image is indeed endowed with enormous power to inform and instruct our imagination, forcing us into a subjective apprehension and perception of the city. With particular reference to the composition of views in accordance with this tension between the real and the imaginary, it is possible to identify three recurrent themes found in variable combinations in most views of Rome's urban landscape from the dawn of photography to the present.

One is the dialogue between the urban panorama and the horizon. In this case, the dense and multiform structure of the architectonic and urban composition finds figurative resolution in definition as mass in space. The broad Roman sky with its bright, perpendicular light becomes a scenic canvas, not merely a neutral backdrop but an object laden with value that can, from case to case, impose different meanings on the underlying compositional plane, occupying variable proportions of the image. The broad horizon with its piercing light has the power to unite the various elements beneath it: ancient columns, baroque domes, medieval towers and heroes of the struggle for national liberation and unification. Each one is equitably juxtaposed with the Roman sky, responding with its individuality to the vast, unifying expanse. In this case, the natural elements involved in making up the panorama are treated on a par with pinnacles and sculptures as individual identities against the horizon. Distance thus comes to play a key part in suggesting the possibility of personal perception and visualization of the landscape. The dome of Saint Peter's provides the best example. A religious but also artistic and cultural symbol, it is the paramount subject of Roman views.

Set amongst countless other domes against the broad horizon, it is an always recognisable form, visible from countless angles and even serving as a landmark. The distance at which it is often represented makes it possible in any case to avoid complete revelation and to shroud its actual scale and presence in mystery.

Another, stemming from the first and more specific, is the use of natural elements as elements of the built landscape. In the various photographs of the Tiber, the countryside and urban vegetation, nature becomes timeless architecture, the quintessential *genius loci*. The pines are nearly always shown in the shade as solid masses, casting shadows in turn onto the buildings and thus creating additional mouldings confused with those of columns and obelisks. The Tiber is thus presented sometimes as a mirror, reflecting the city and the built environment, and sometimes as a solid surface, base and backdrop to enclose space and highlight the void created by the bridge.

In these images, nature is treated no differently from the ancient monuments and buildings of Rome to the point of confusion with the solid volumes of the city. The urban landscape thus manifests itself as crystallised instant, and the dynamic temporality usually attributed to the natural element is eliminated so as to emphasise the eternal dimension of timelessness. The duality of nature and artifice is condensed into a joint operation on the landscape in which the man-made and the natural are combined in a balanced synthesis of timeless acts.

Following on more precisely from the idea of urban dimension, a third recurrent theme is that of composition in spatial and temporal planes. As already stated, the complexity and variety of Rome's urban morphology makes it possible with the greatest ease to use natural and architectural elements as tools to frame the image and therefore to focus attention on the urban panorama. The background is enclosed and defined by an emphasised arch, tree or colonnade. Reference is clearly made here to time and an idea of eternity. Composition in planes becomes a method to define a spatial sequence that is automatically associated with a temporal sequence.

The panel is the means used to observe the past, contemplate the urban landscape and its history, and imagine what was once there. In the same way, the indefinite nature of the compositional forms and the ruins that frame them stimulate inventiveness and the imagination. Rome is a space of memory in which topography and morphology become

tools for the observation and visualisation of memories that are often ephemeral and intangible but represented so well in the composite landscape of the Eternal City.

All of these compositional themes highlight and fuel the tension between real and imaginary. The horizon as an imaginative canvas for individual elements of the architectural panorama, the crystallisation of natural elements, and finally the temporal value of planes in sequence all produce images corresponding to the typical representation of the city but also constitute fantastic, visionary representations themselves, thus leaving room for subjective interpretation and experience.

And so, when Dickens finally saw the Rome he had imagined, he unhesitatingly wrote: 'Here was Rome indeed at last; and such a Rome as no one can imagine in its full and awful grandeur!'[4] While clearly expressing satisfaction, his words emphasise at the same time that however prepared you may be, Rome as a whole, in all its greatness, cannot be imagined.

Carla Molinari

---

[1] Charles Dickens, *Pictures from Italy*, London: Bradbury & Evans, 1846, p. 80.
[2] Maria Elisa Tittoni and Anita Margiotta (eds.), *Scenari della Memoria. Roma nella fotografia 1850-1900*, Milan: Electa, 2002.
[3] Ivor de Wolfe, *The Italian Townscape*, London: Architecture Press, 1963.
[4] Charles Dickens, *op. cit.*, 1846, p. 81.

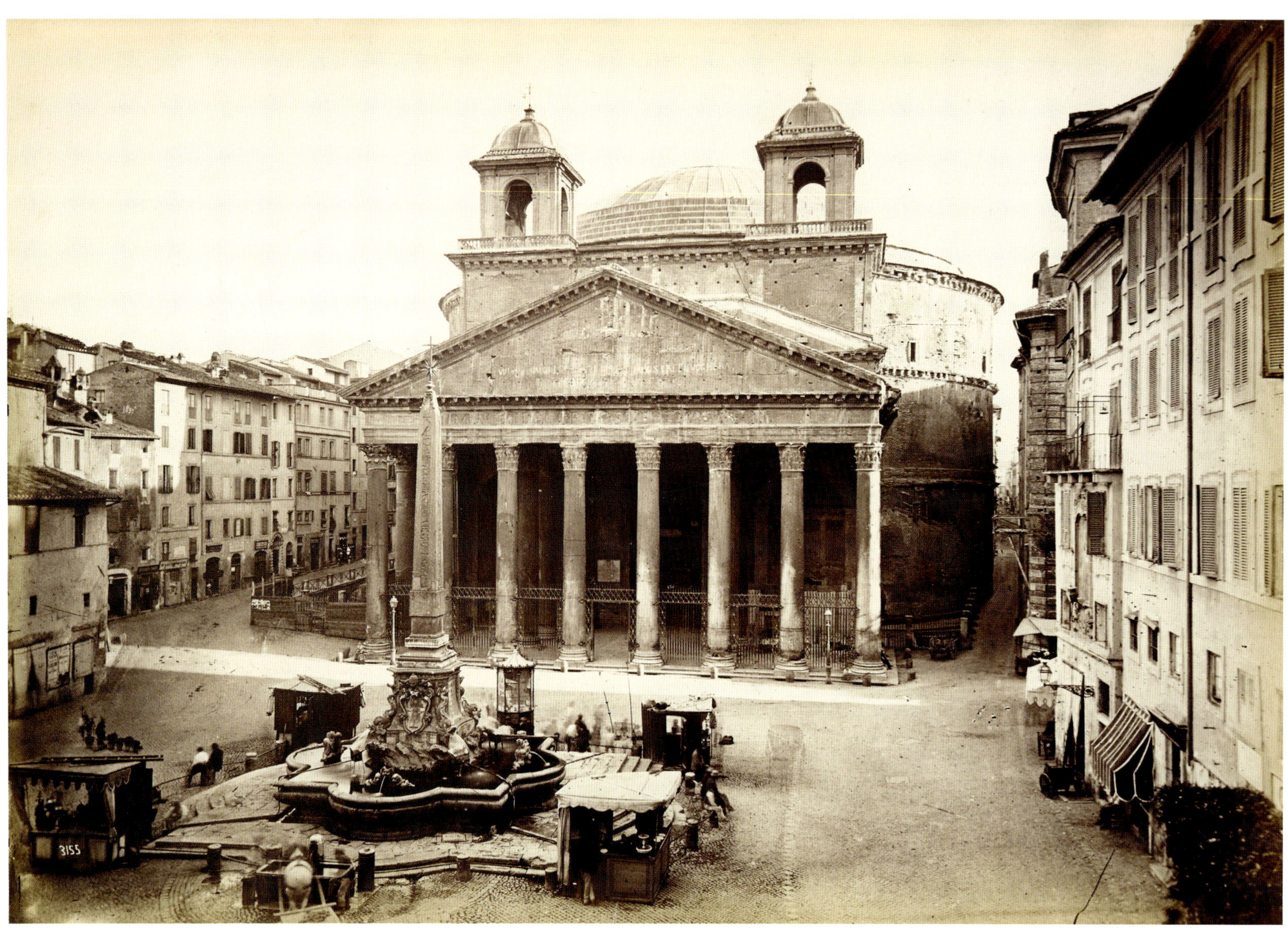

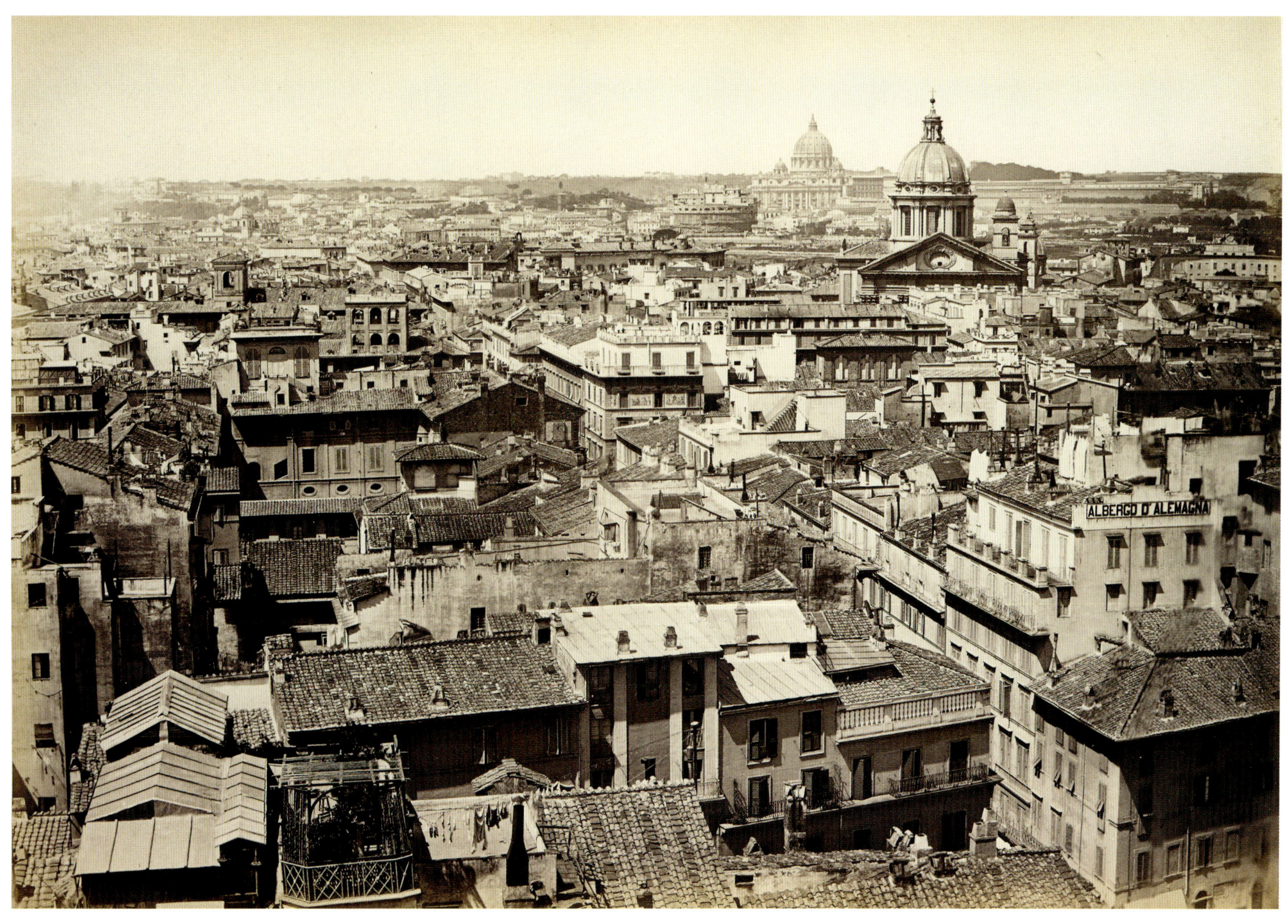

112. Unknown photographer
View from the Pincio, 1860s–1870s

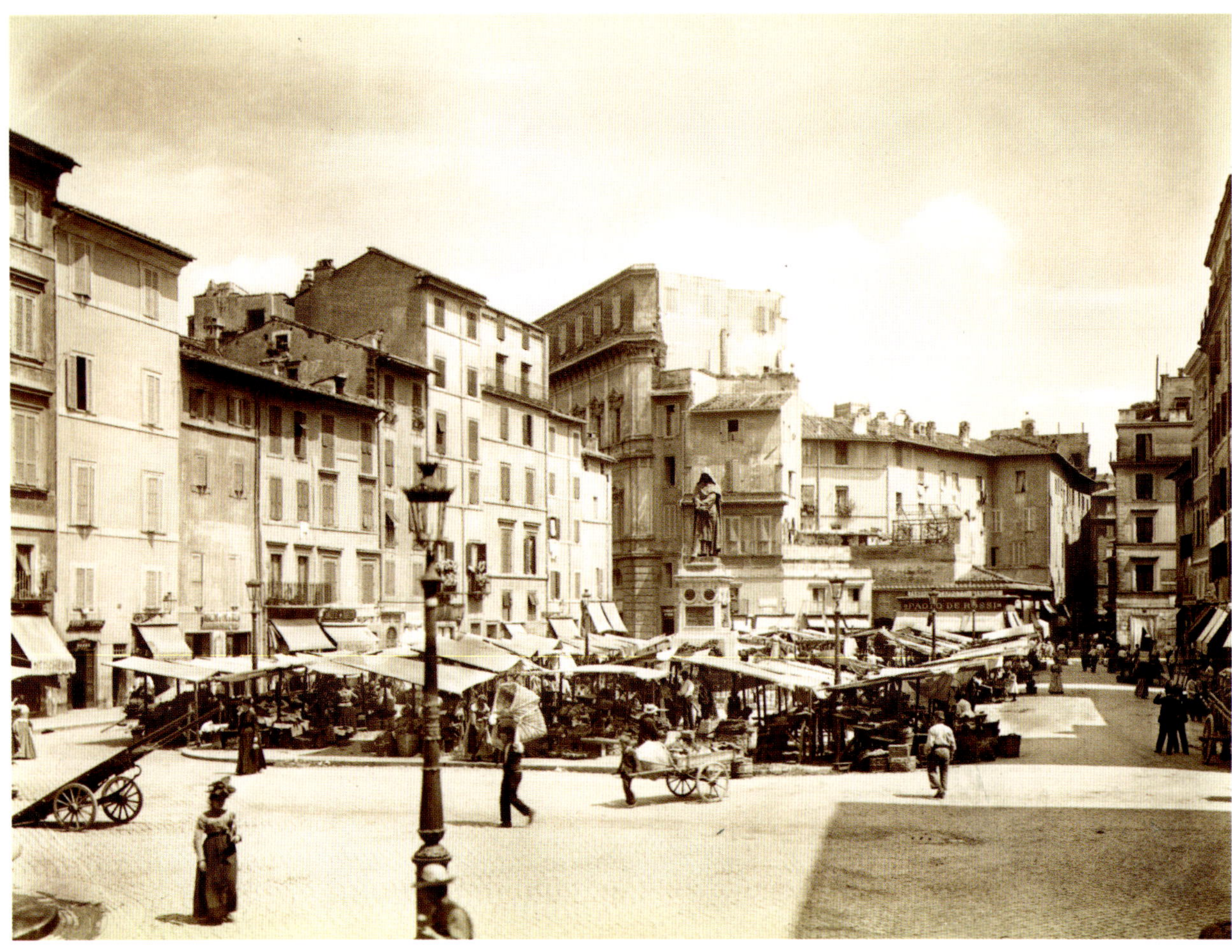

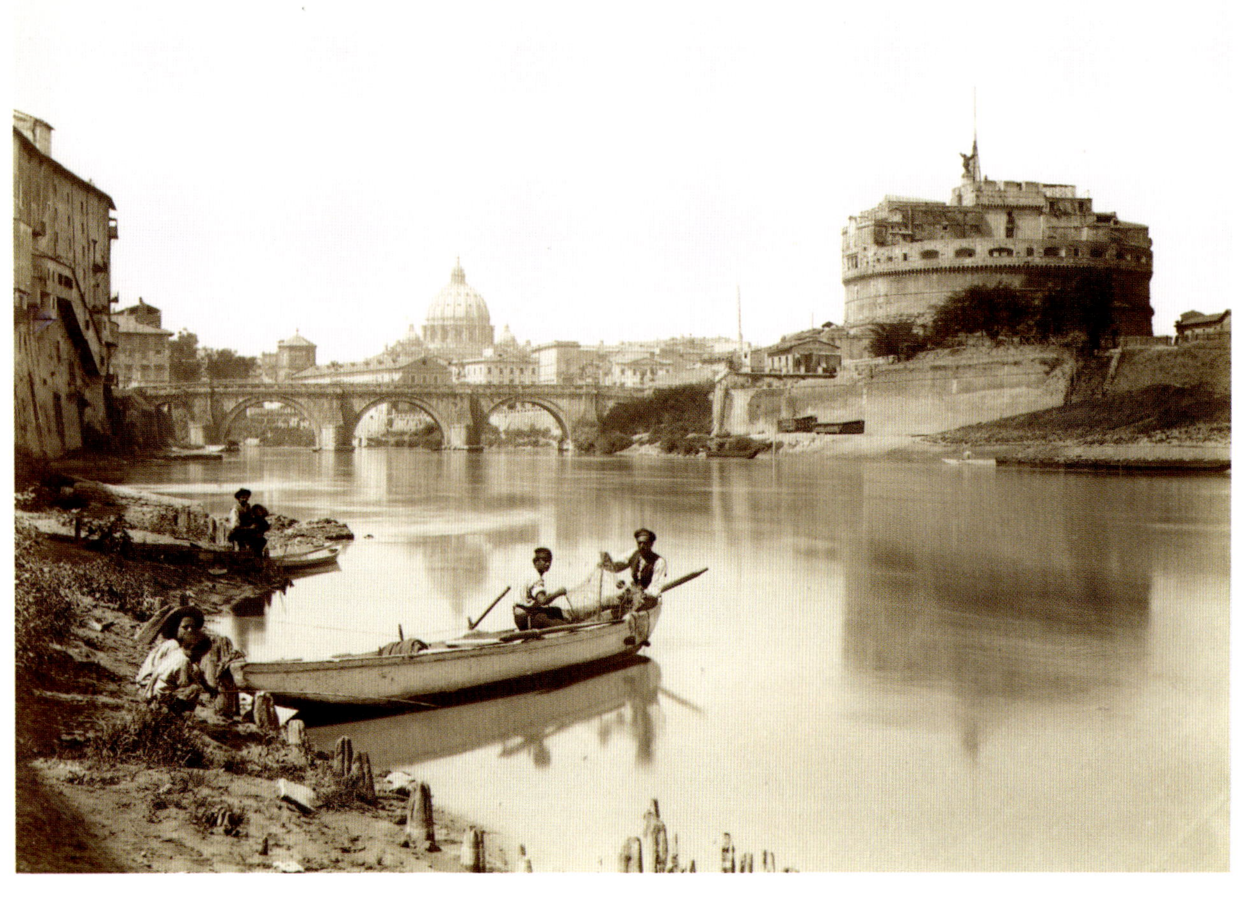

113. James Anderson
Campo dei Fiori, 1850s–1860s

114. James Anderson
*River Tiber with Saint Peter's
and Castel Sant'Angelo*, c. 1870

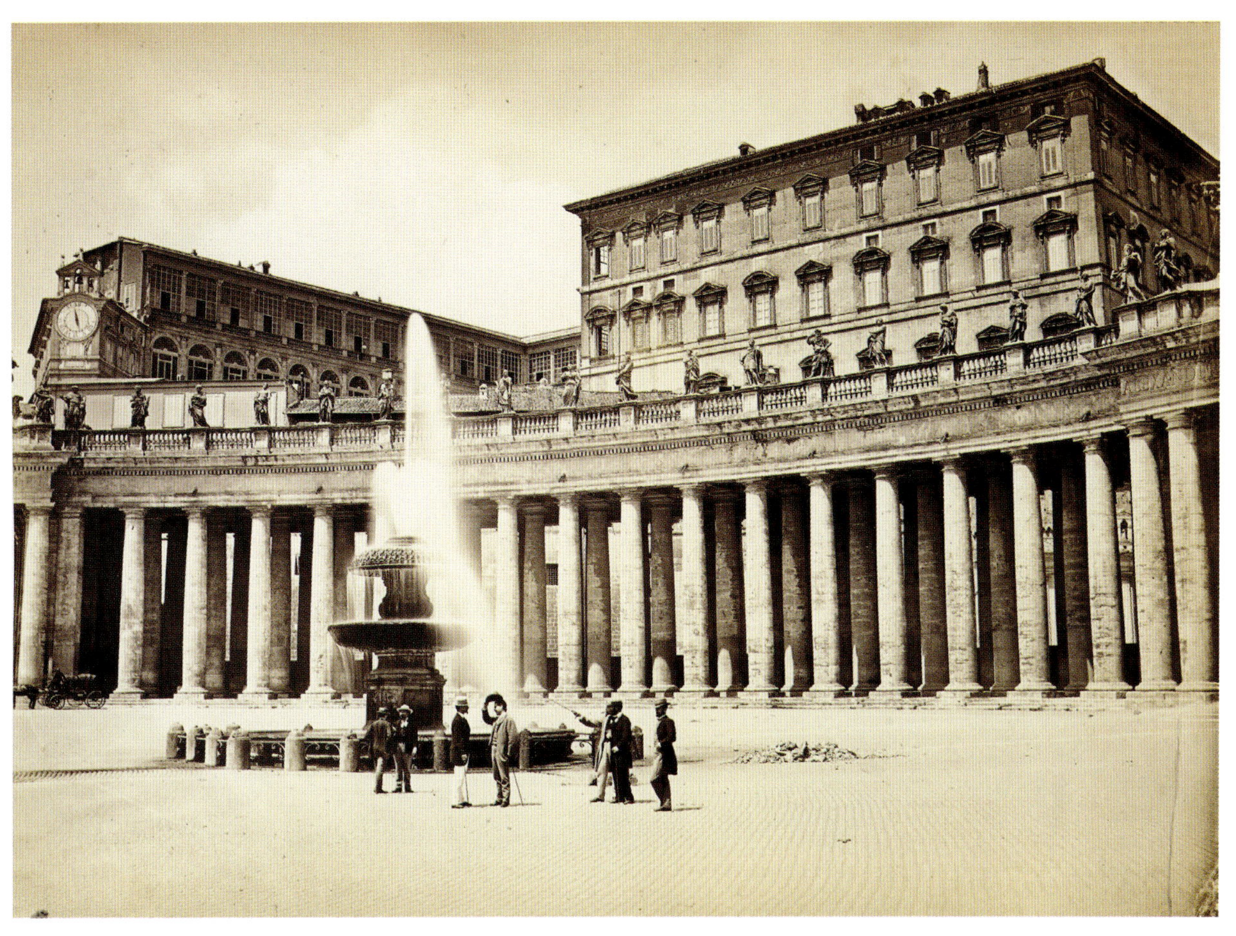

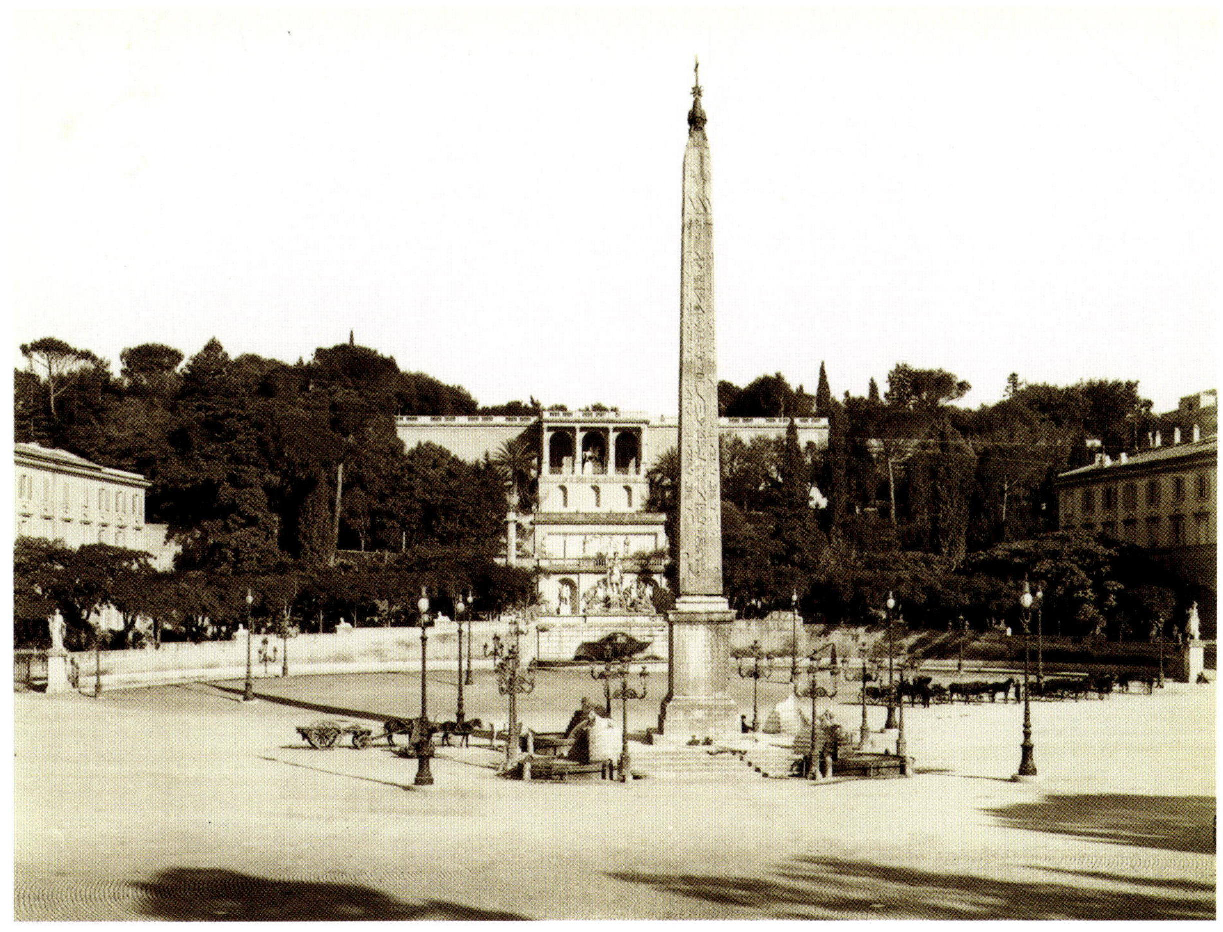

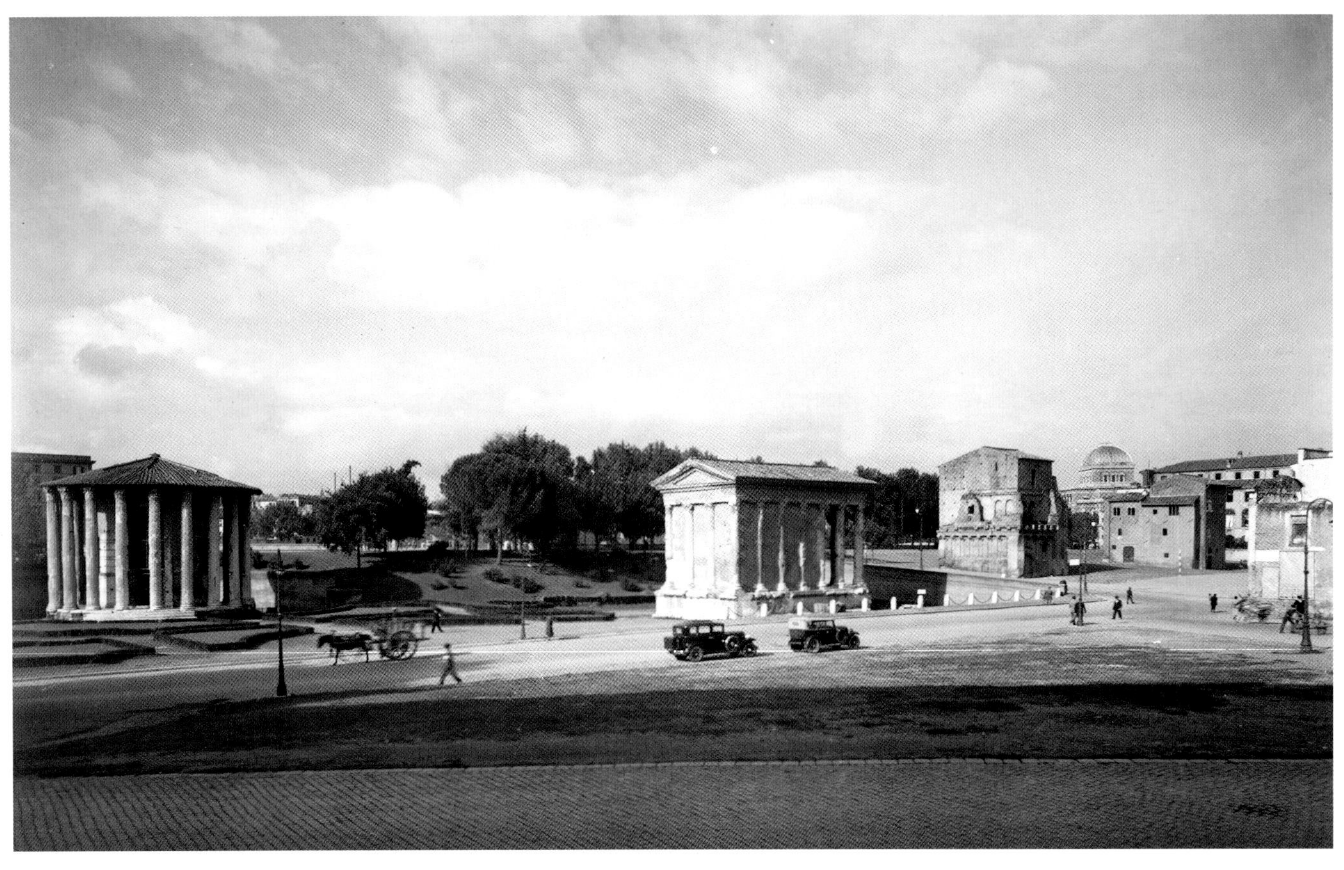

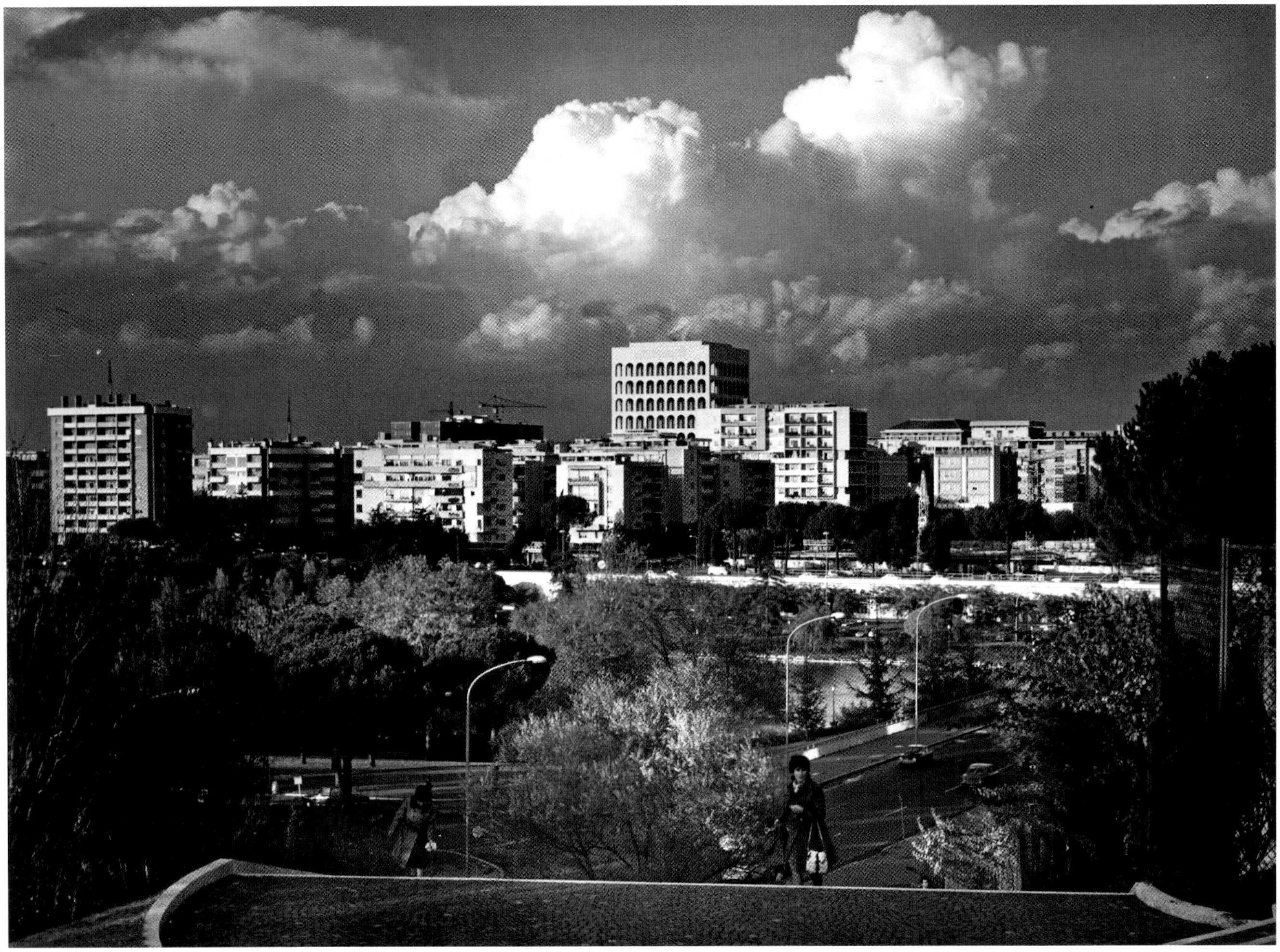

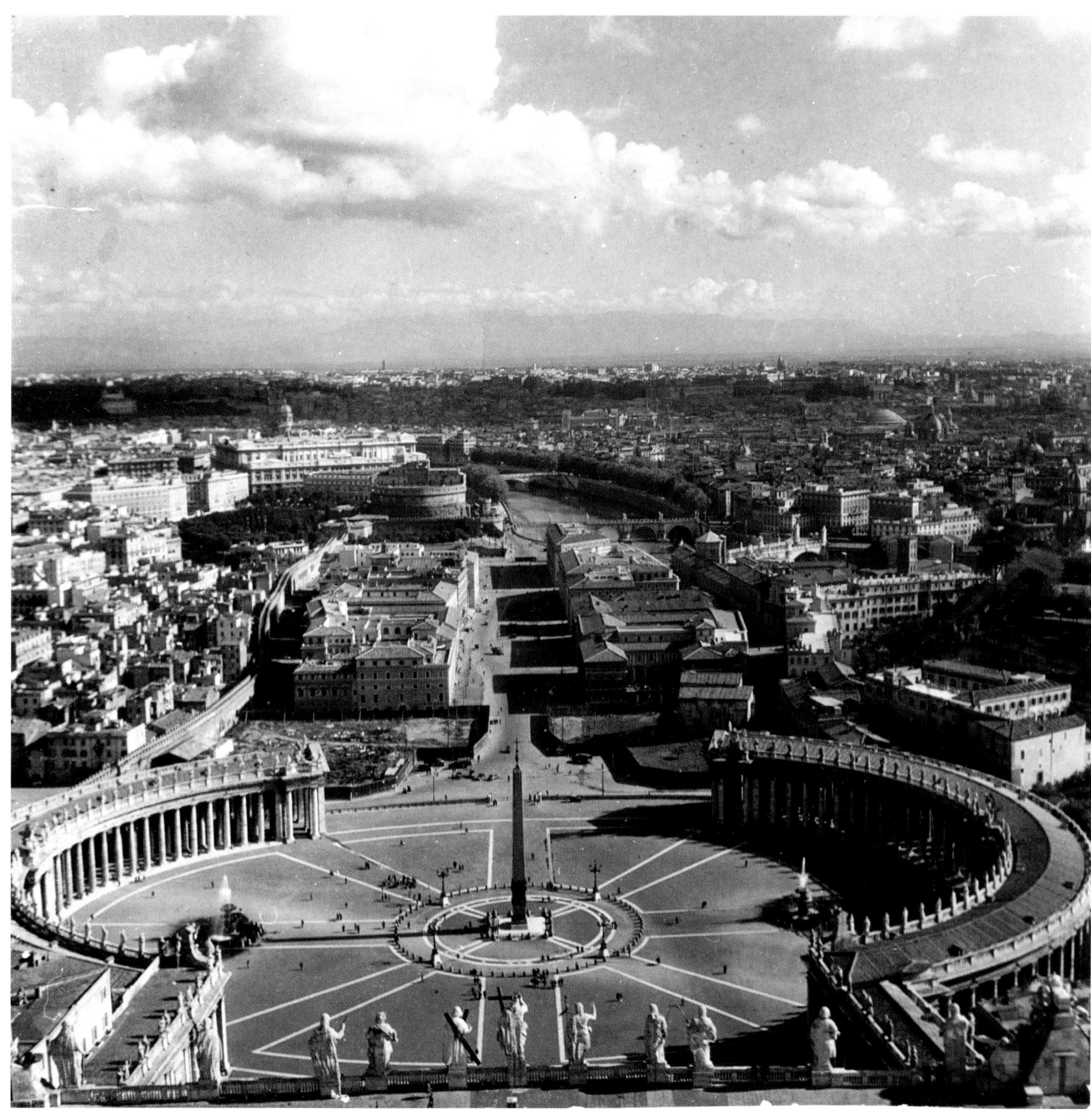

120. Ivy de Wolfe
*Dome of Saint Peter's Basilica
and Viale Vaticano Walls*, 1964

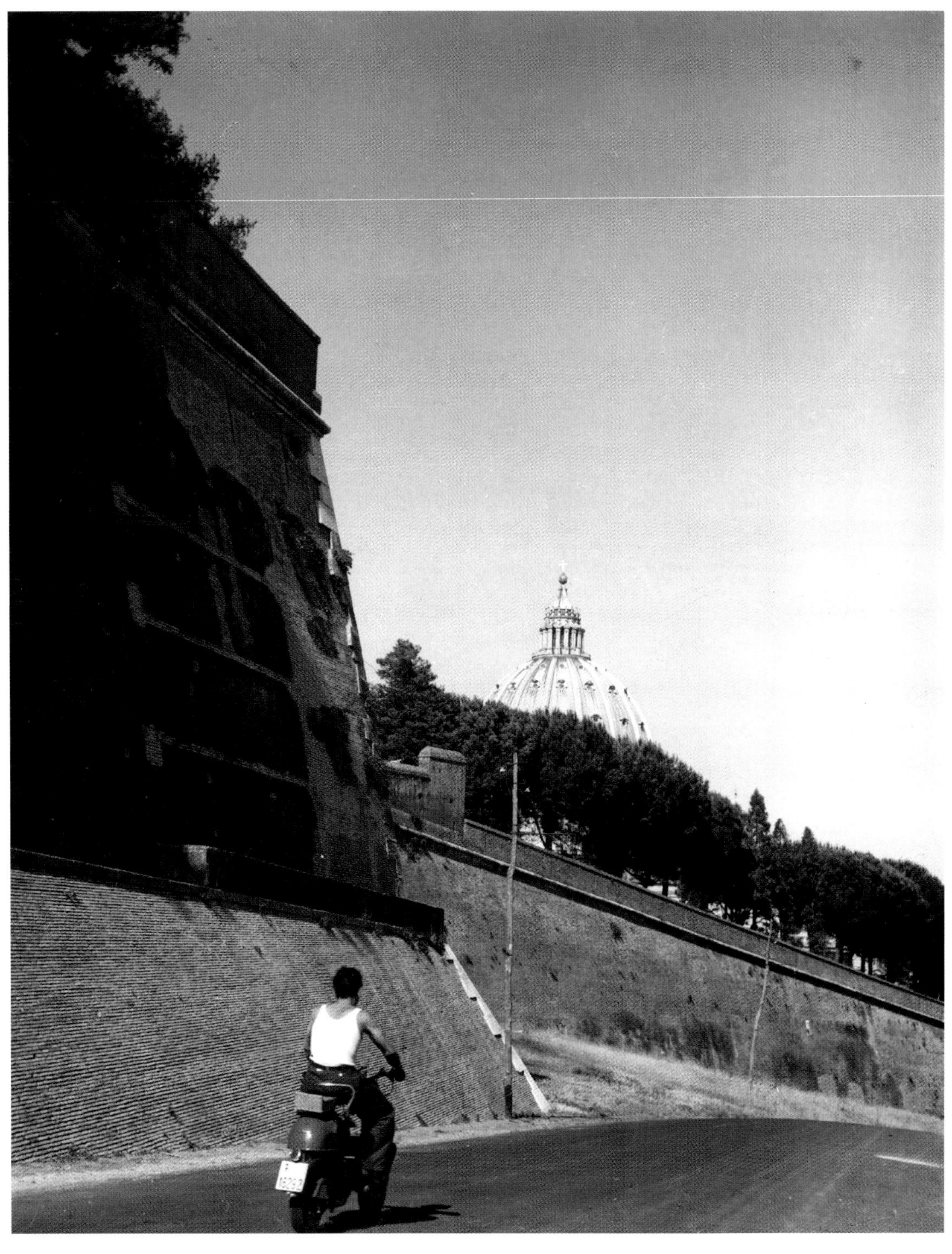

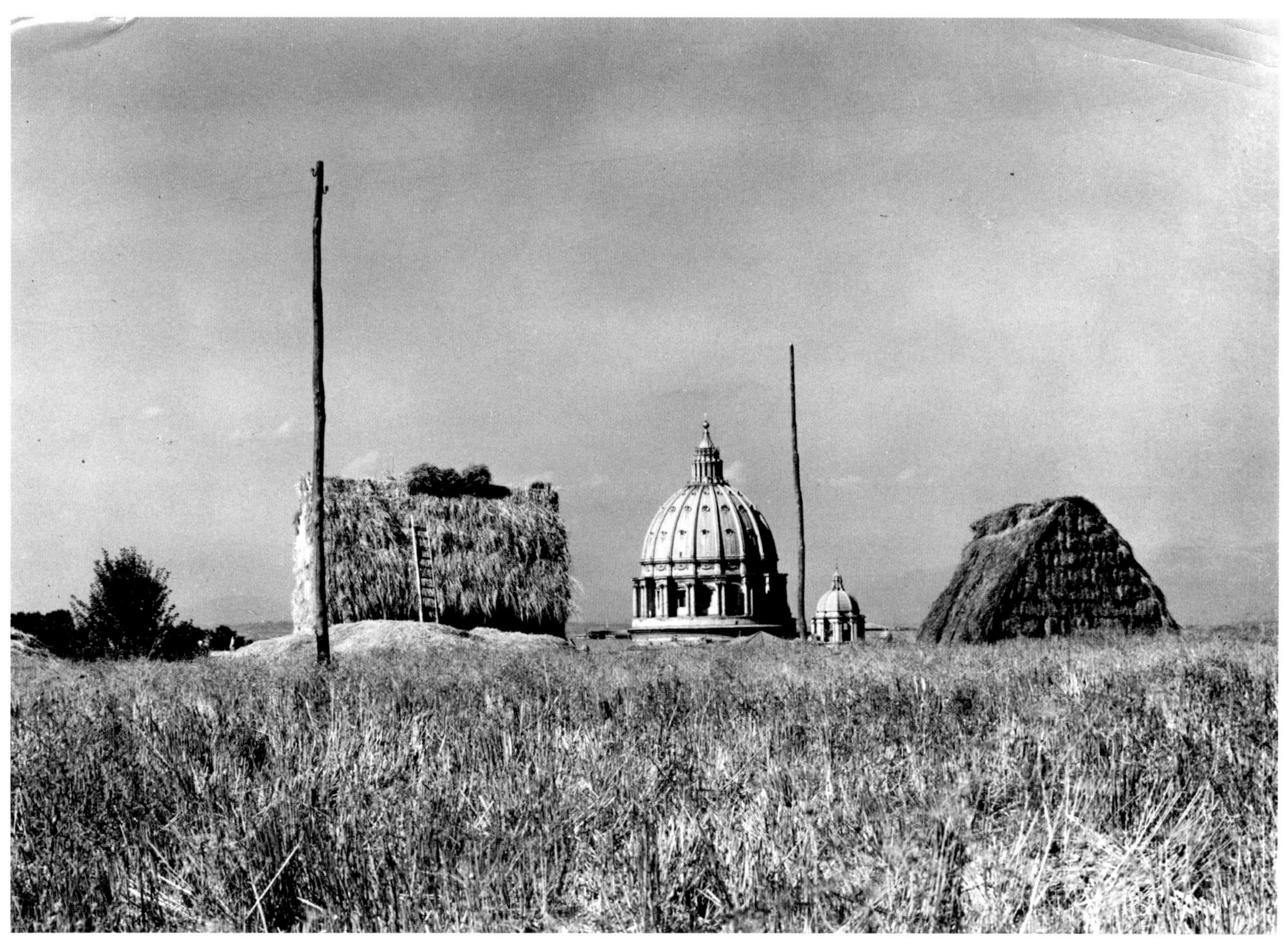

121. George Everard Kidder Smith
Dome of Saint Peter's Basilica,
1954

122. Edwin Smith
Aurelian Wall by Porta
San Sebastiano, 1970

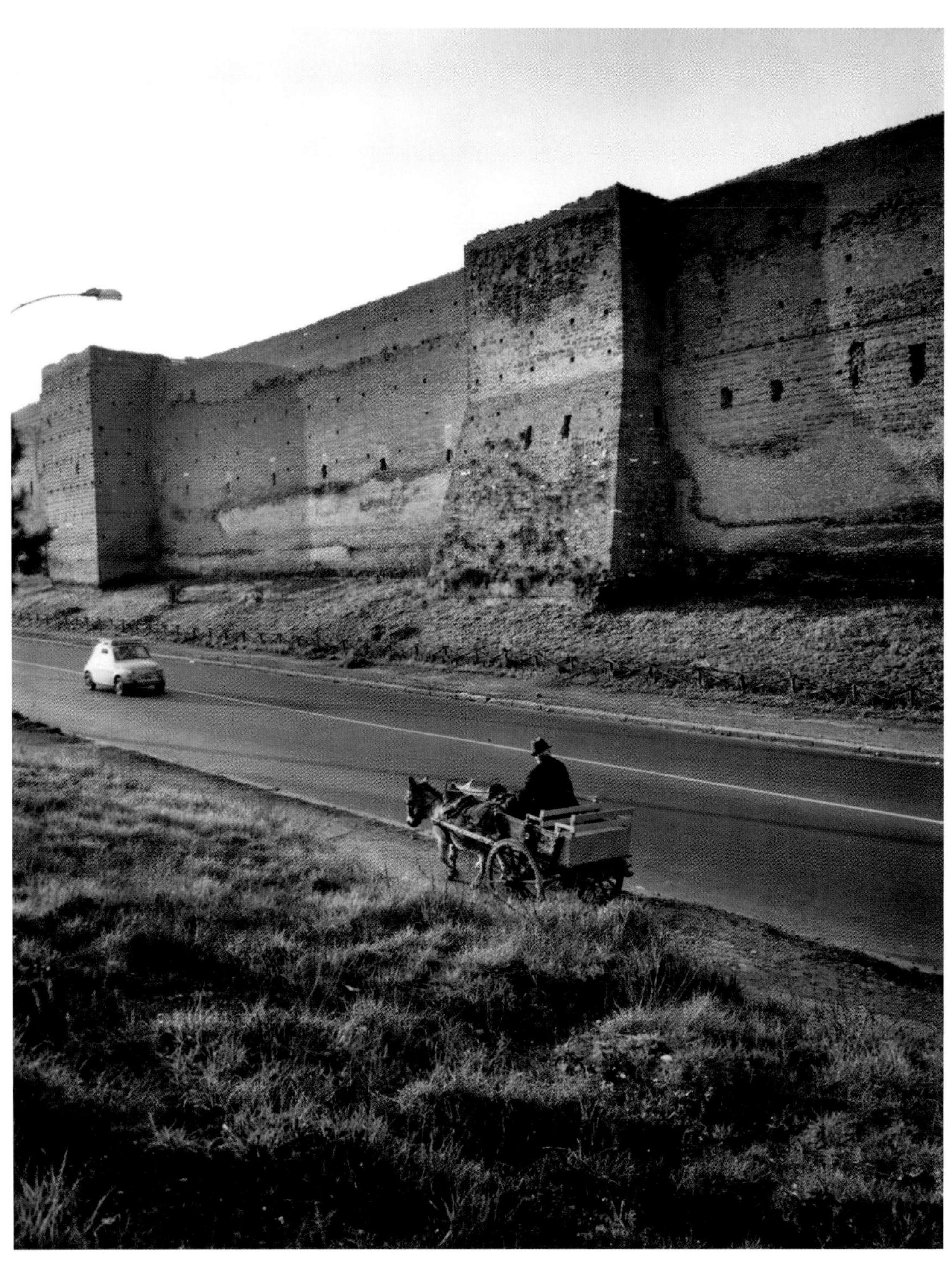

123. Unknown photographer
Piazza della Consolazione,
1930s

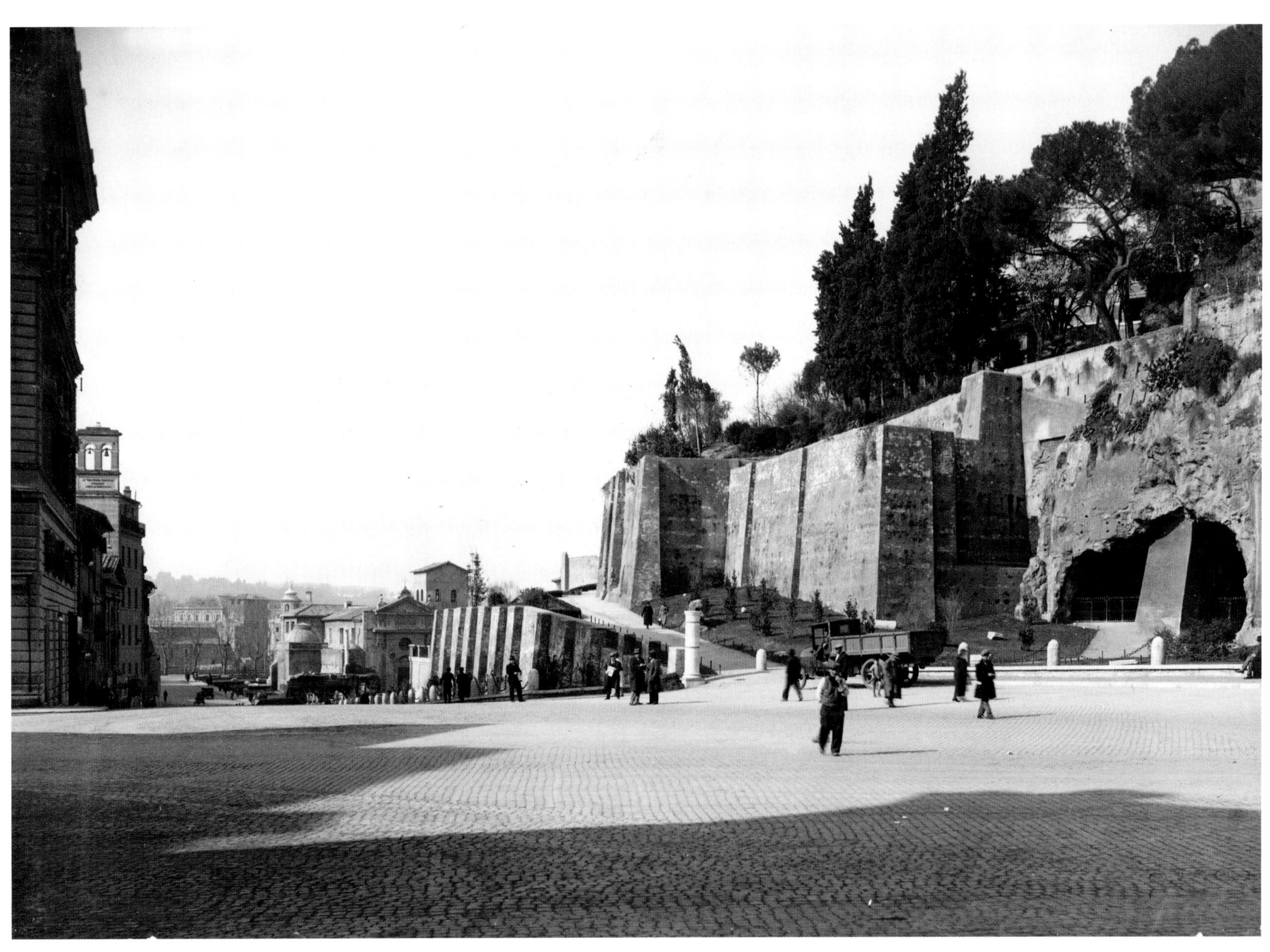

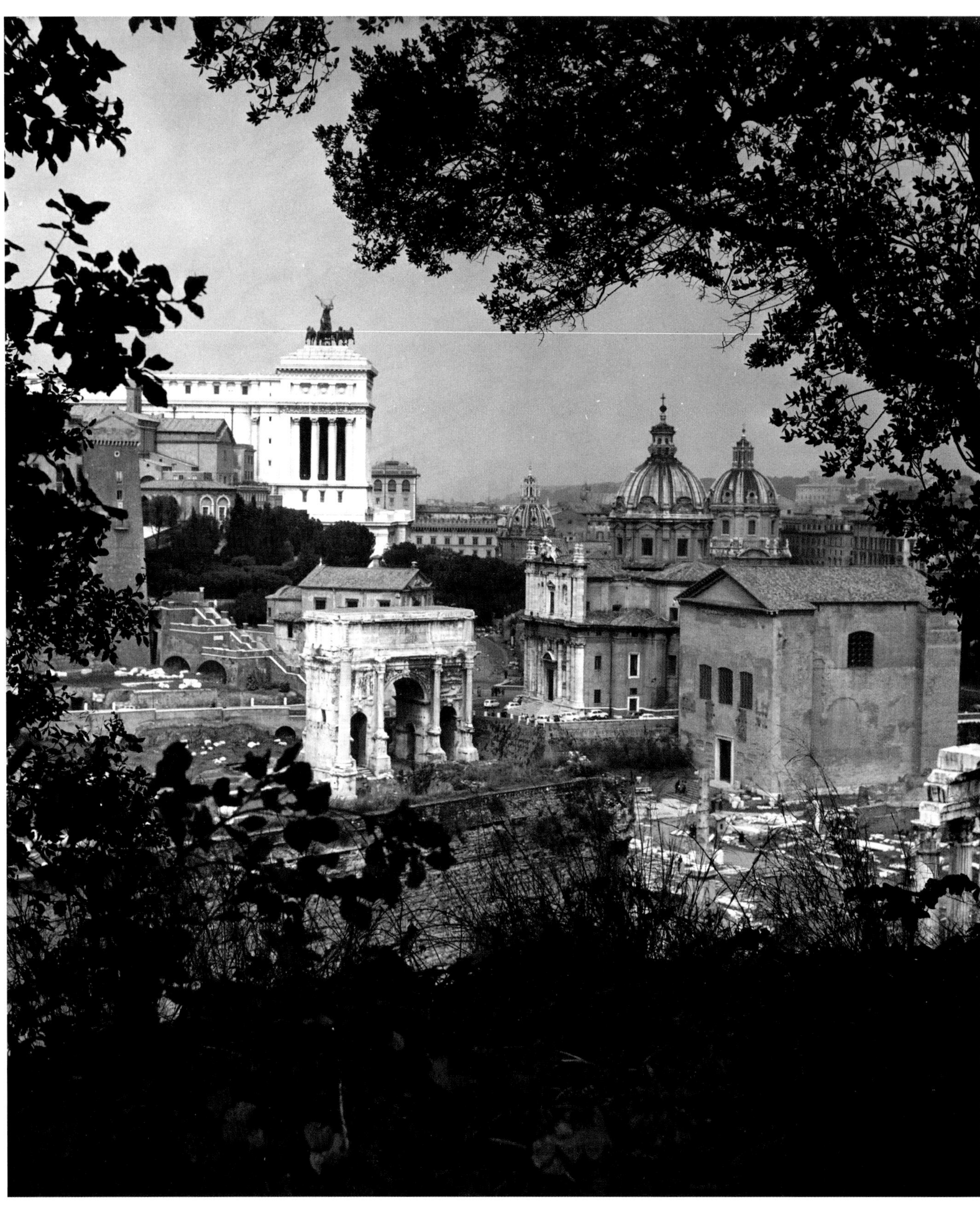

124. Edwin Smith
View from the Palatine Hill, 1963

125. Ralph Deakin
View from the Janiculum, 1930s

126. Ralph Deakin
*View from San Pietro
in Montorio*, 1930s

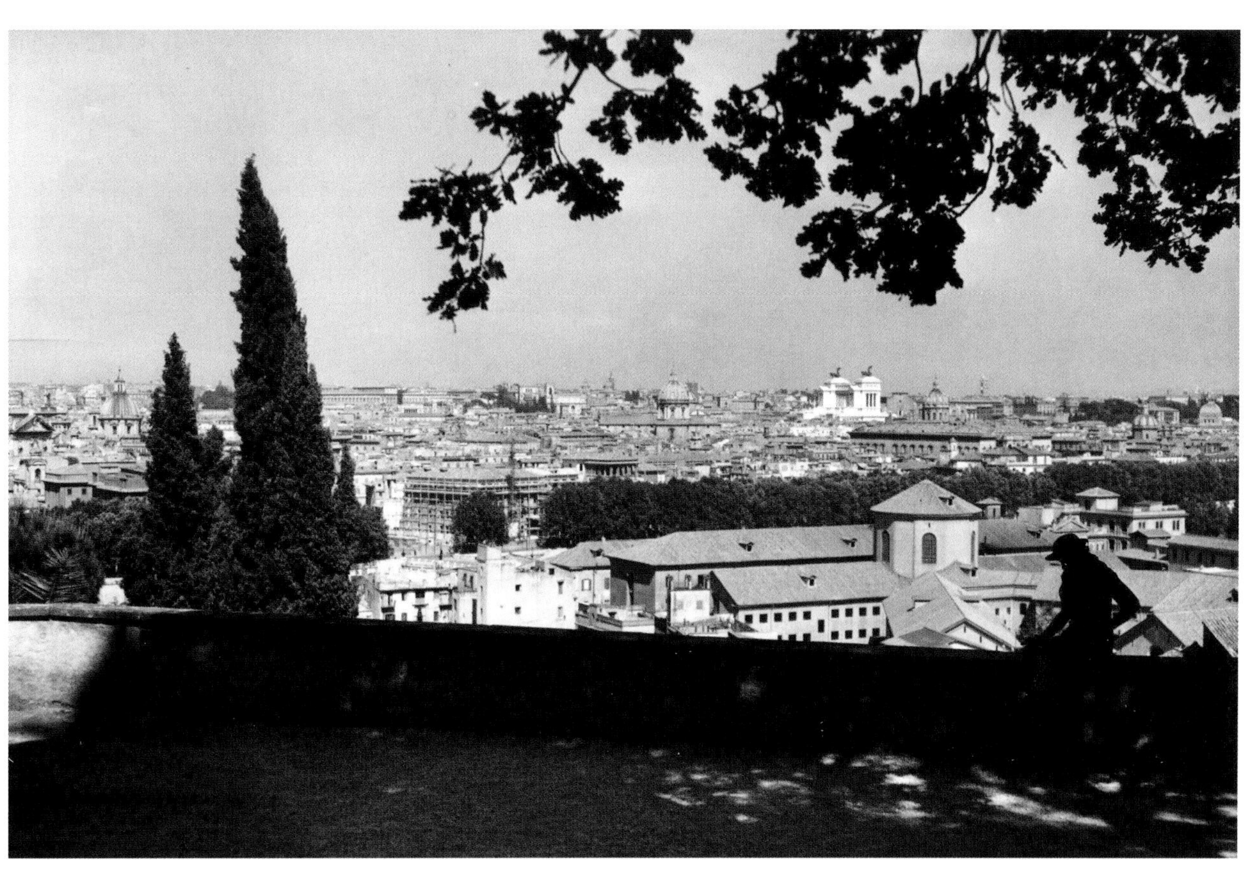

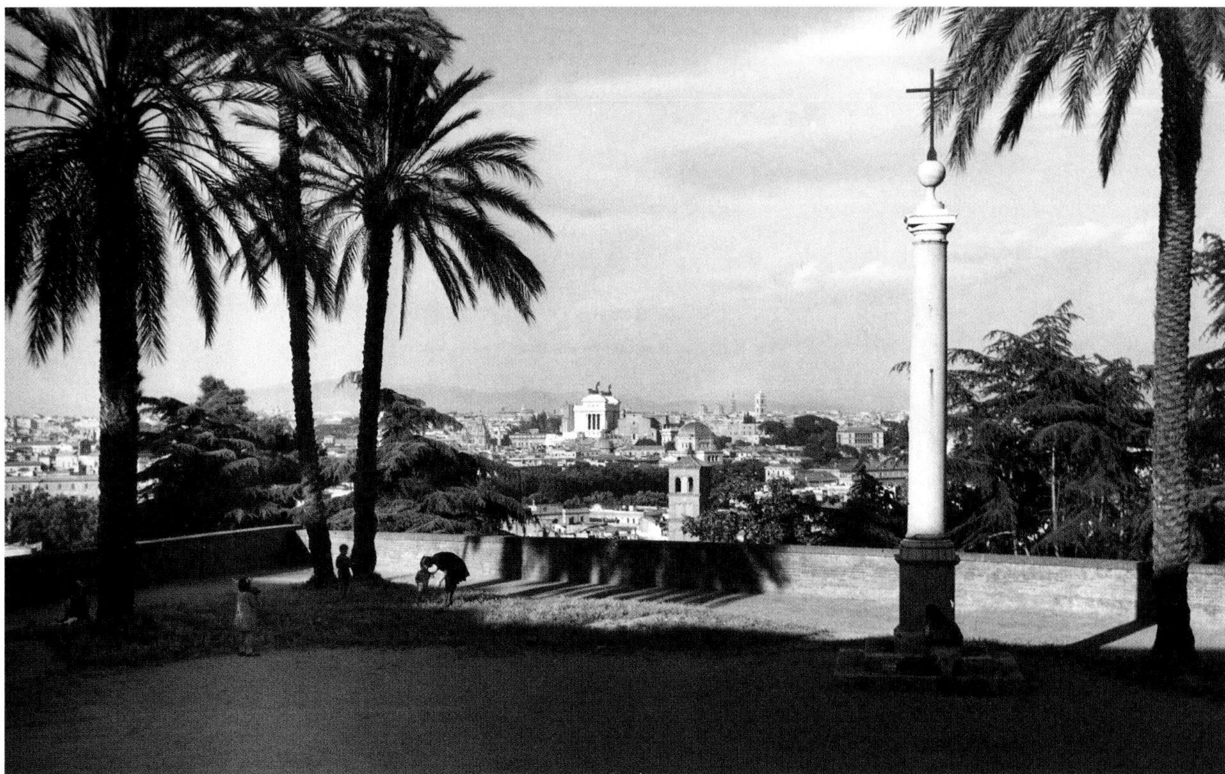

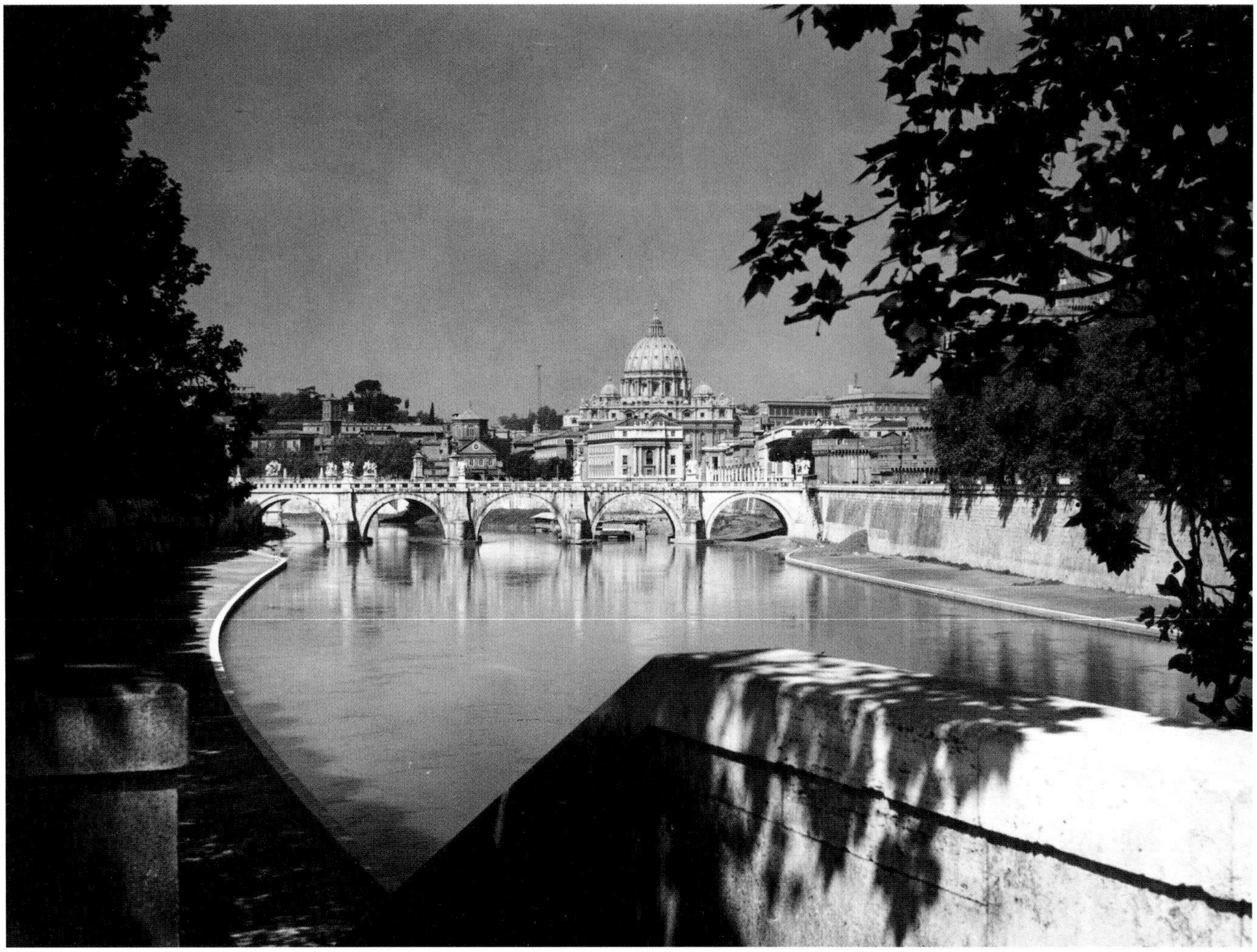

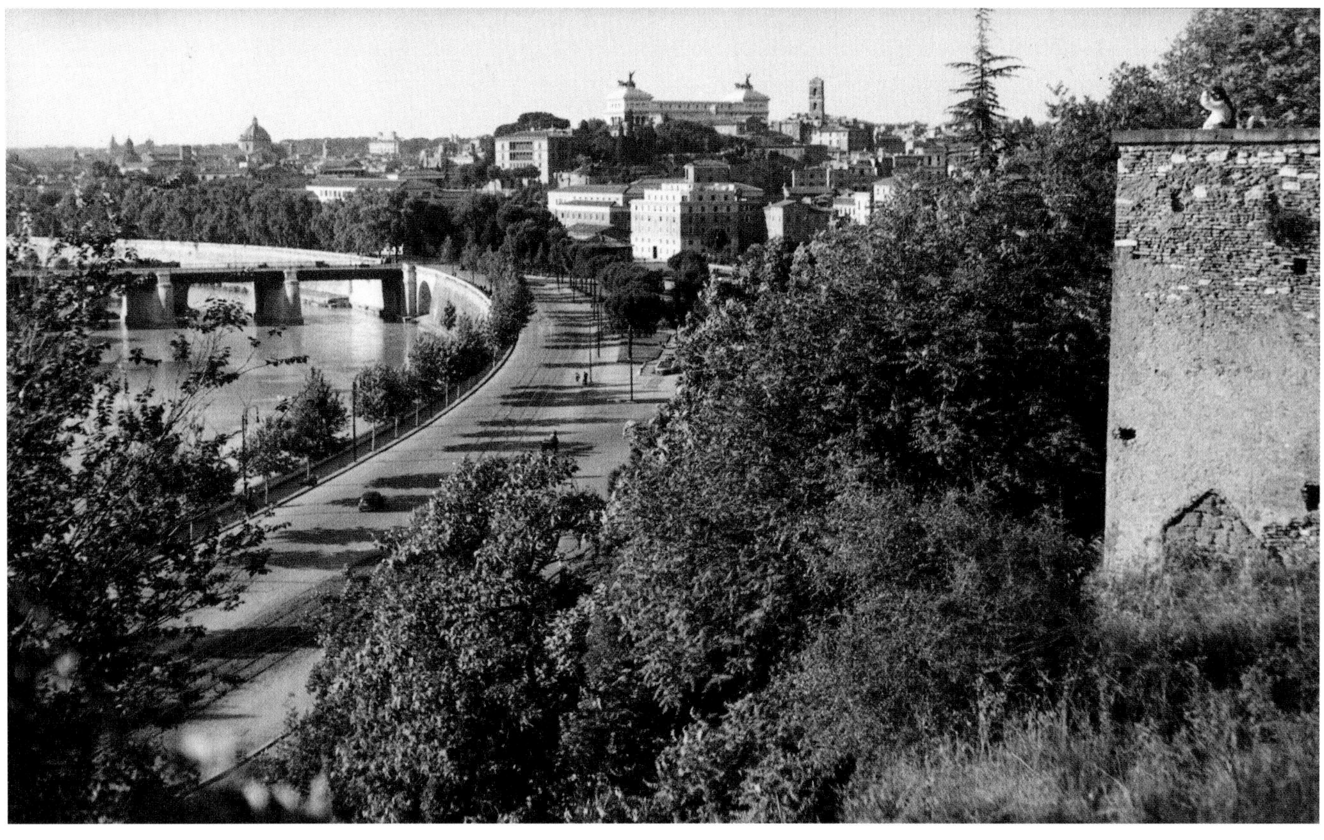

127. Edwin Smith
River Tiber and Ponte
Sant'Angelo, 1962

128. Ralph Deakin
View from the Aventine Hill,
1930s

129. Edwin Smith
Arco del Ponte Rotto
and Ponte Fabricio, 1963

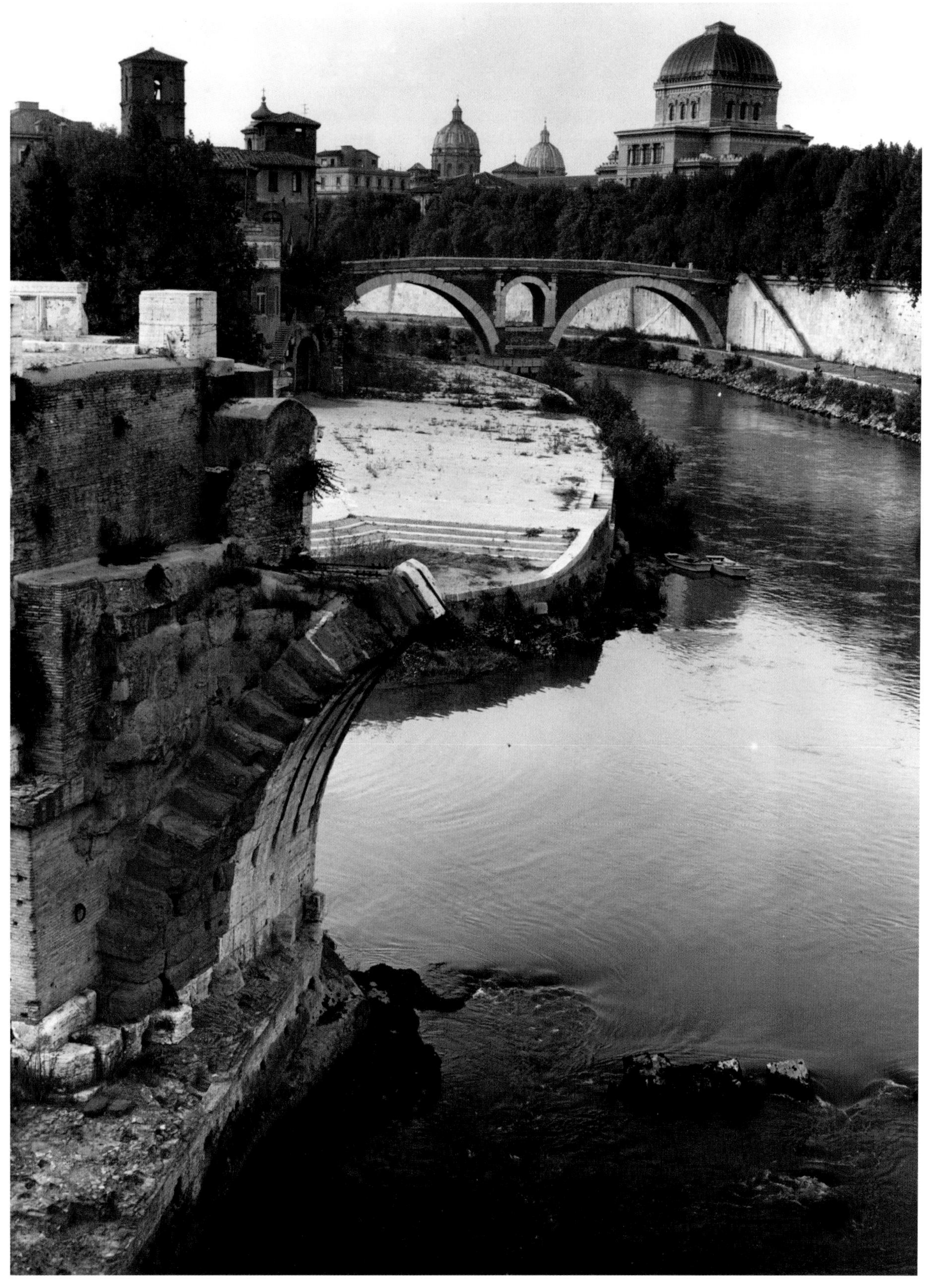

130. Ralph Deakin
*Castel Sant'Angelo
and Ponte Sant'Angelo*, 1930s

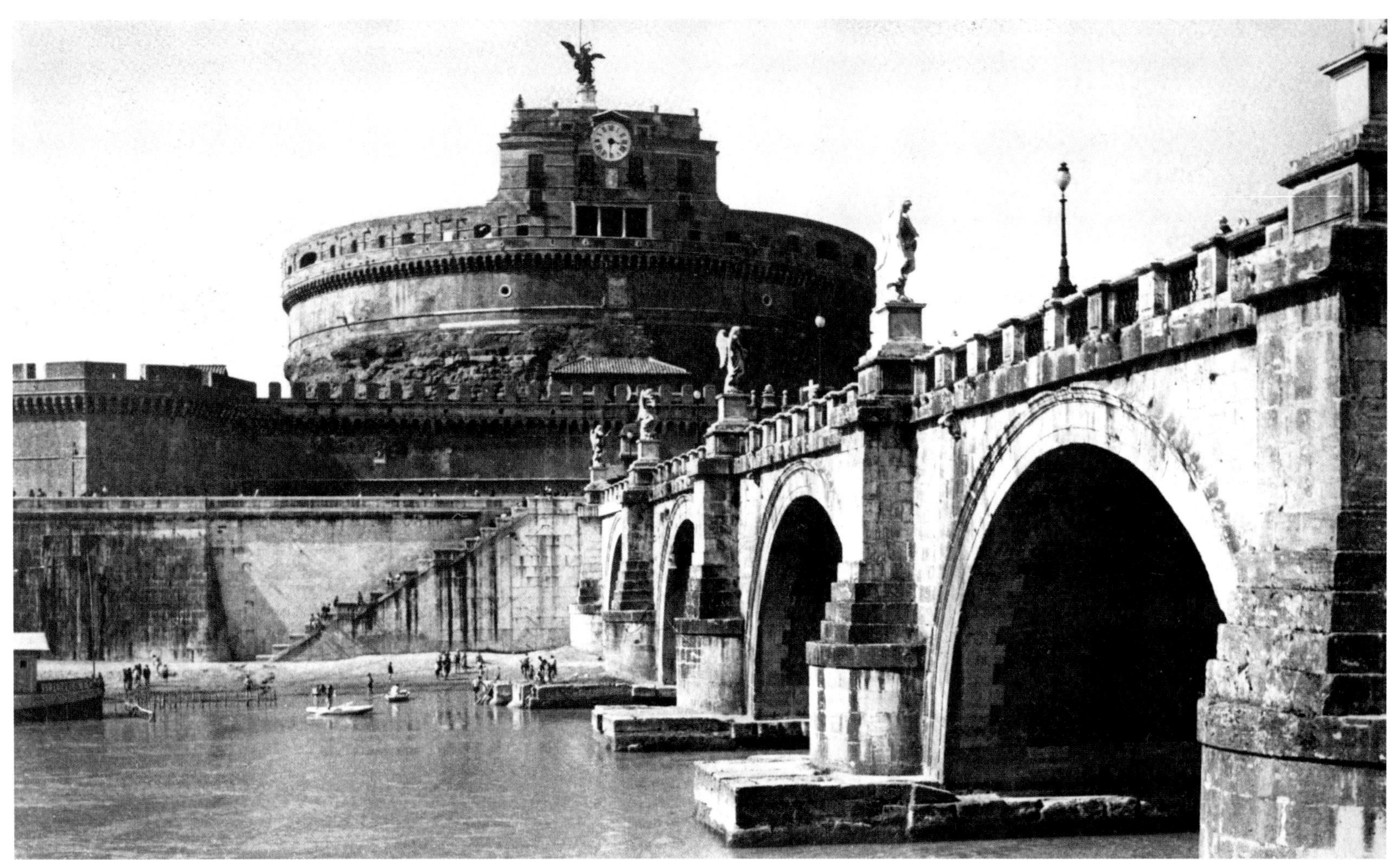

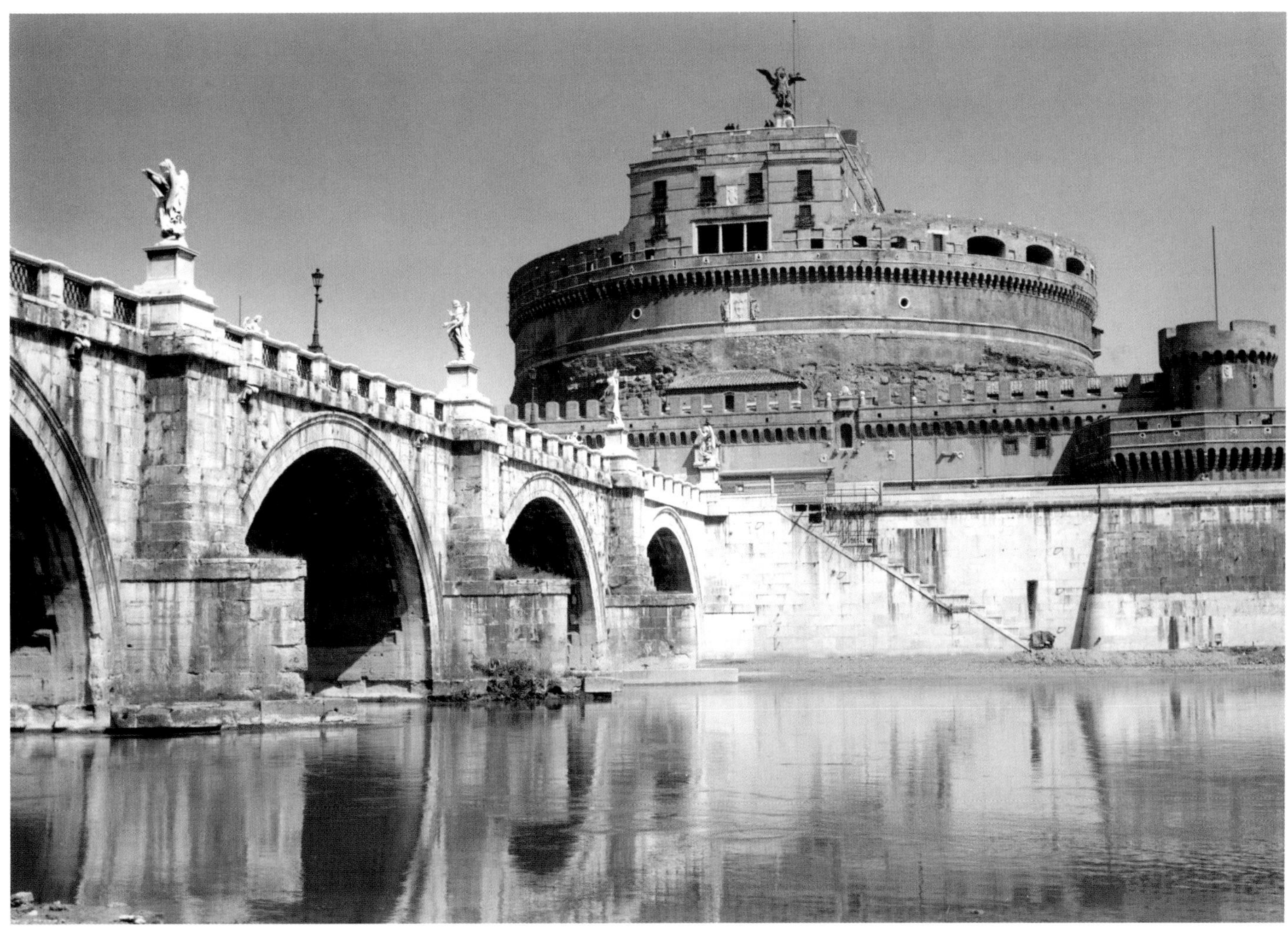

132. Ralph Deakin
Flavian Amphitheatre
(Colosseum), 1930s

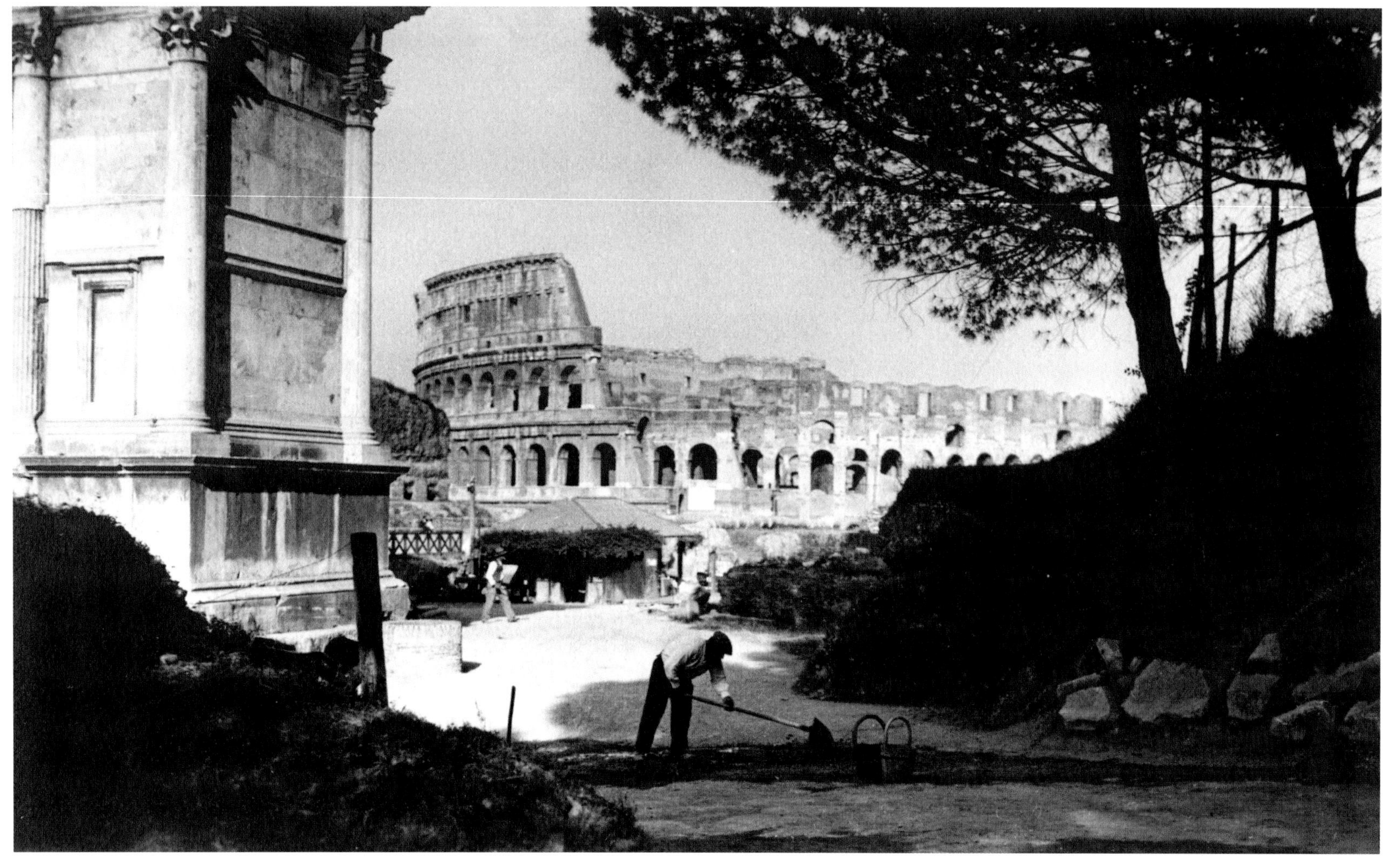

133. Monica Pidgeon
*View from Santa Maria
in Aracoeli*, 1961

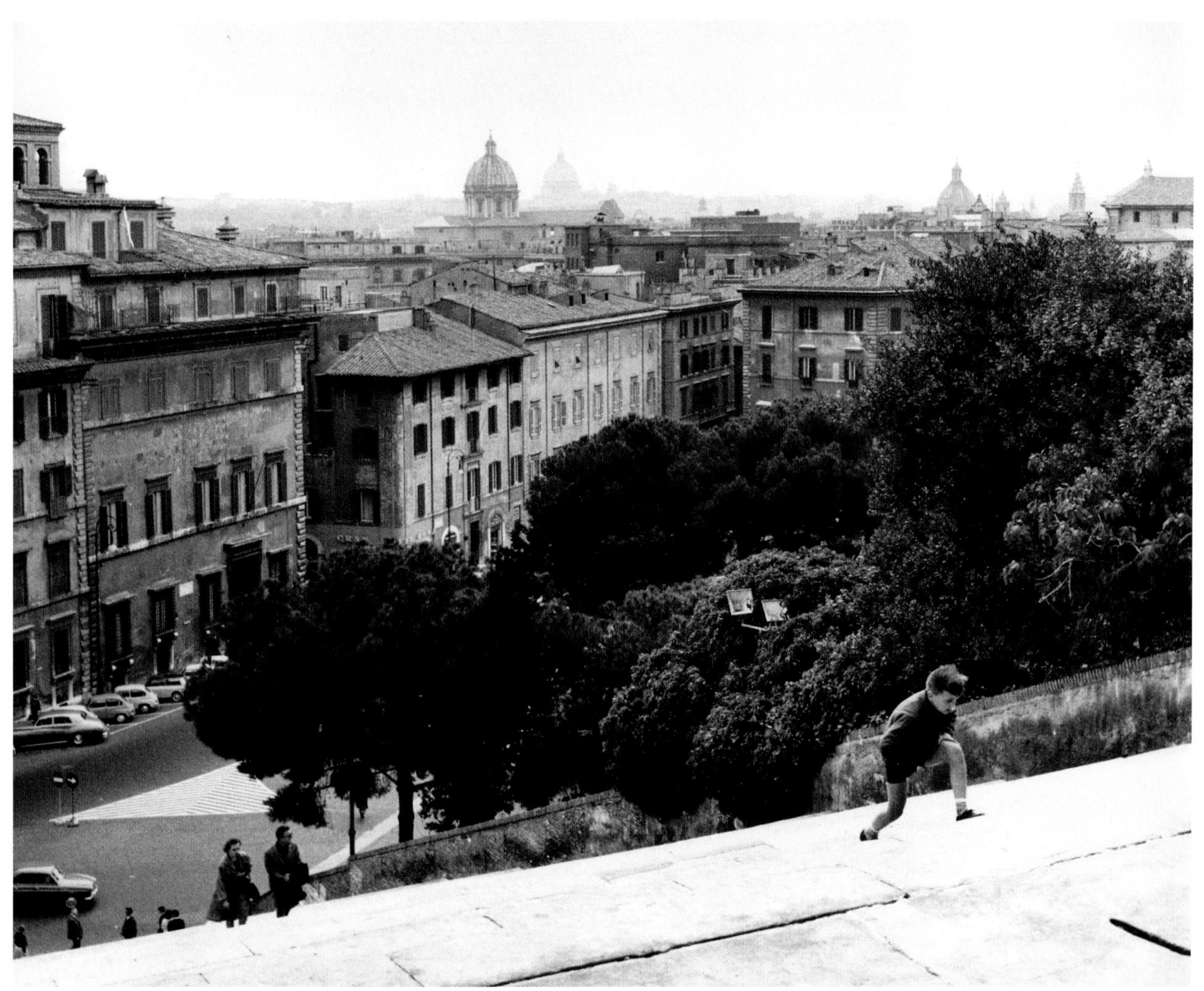

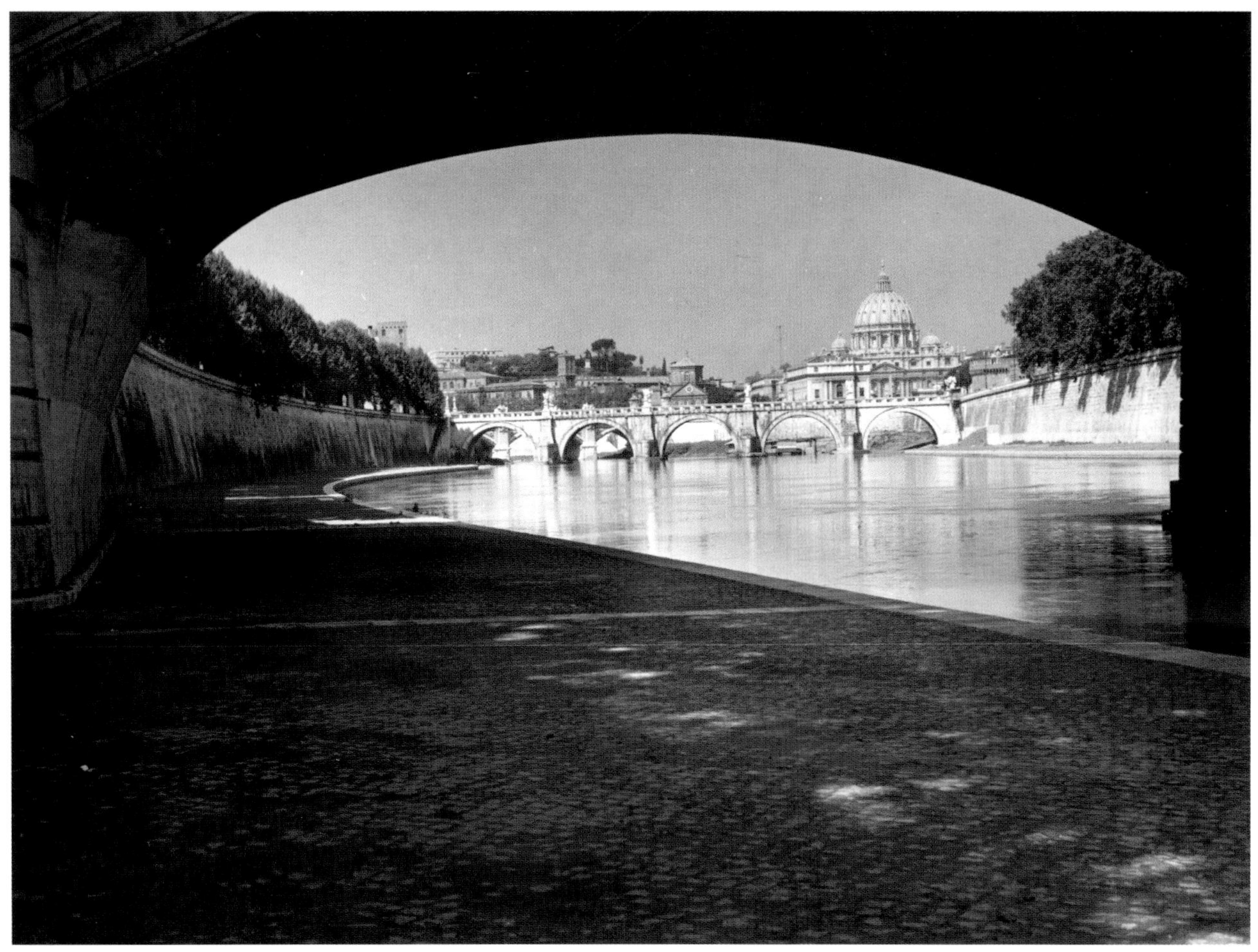

134. Edwin Smith
River Tiber and Ponte Sant'Angelo, 1962

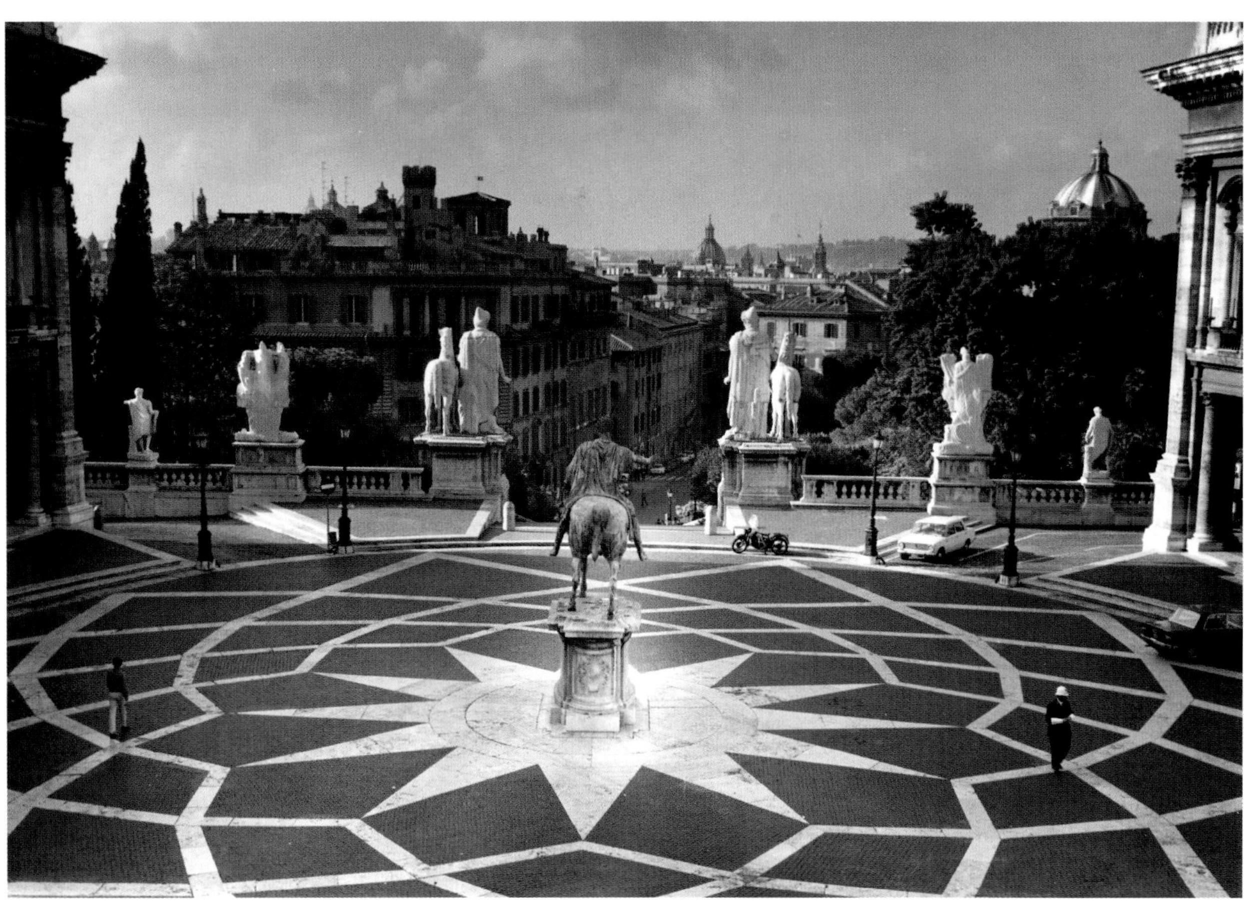

135. Edwin Smith
Piazza del Campidoglio, 1970

136. Edwin Smith
*View from Casa dei Cavalieri
di Rodi towards Torre
delle Milizie*, 1970

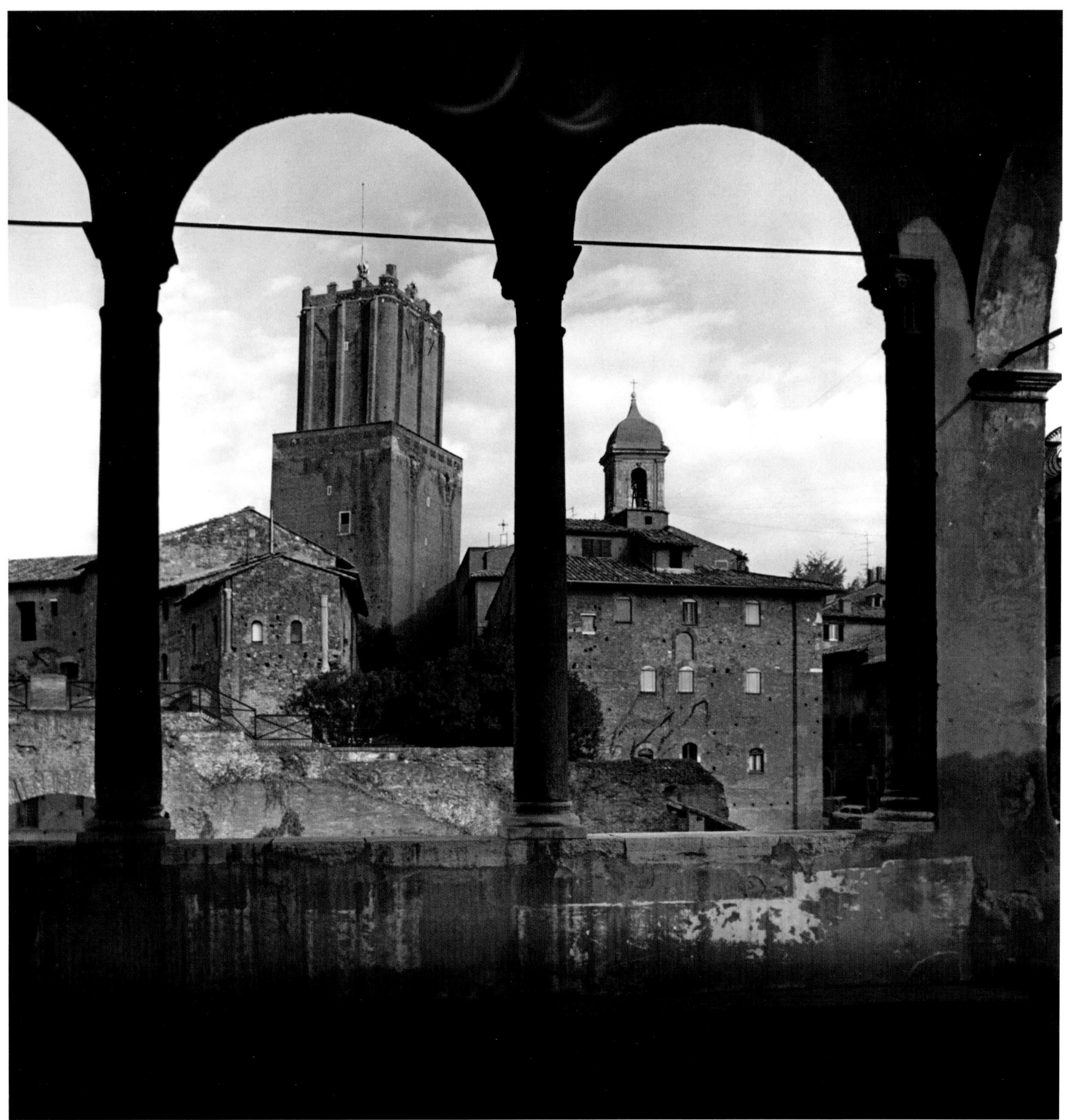

137. Edwin Smith
*Partial view of Via della
Conciliazione and of Saint
Peter's Basilica from Castel
Sant'Angelo*, 1970

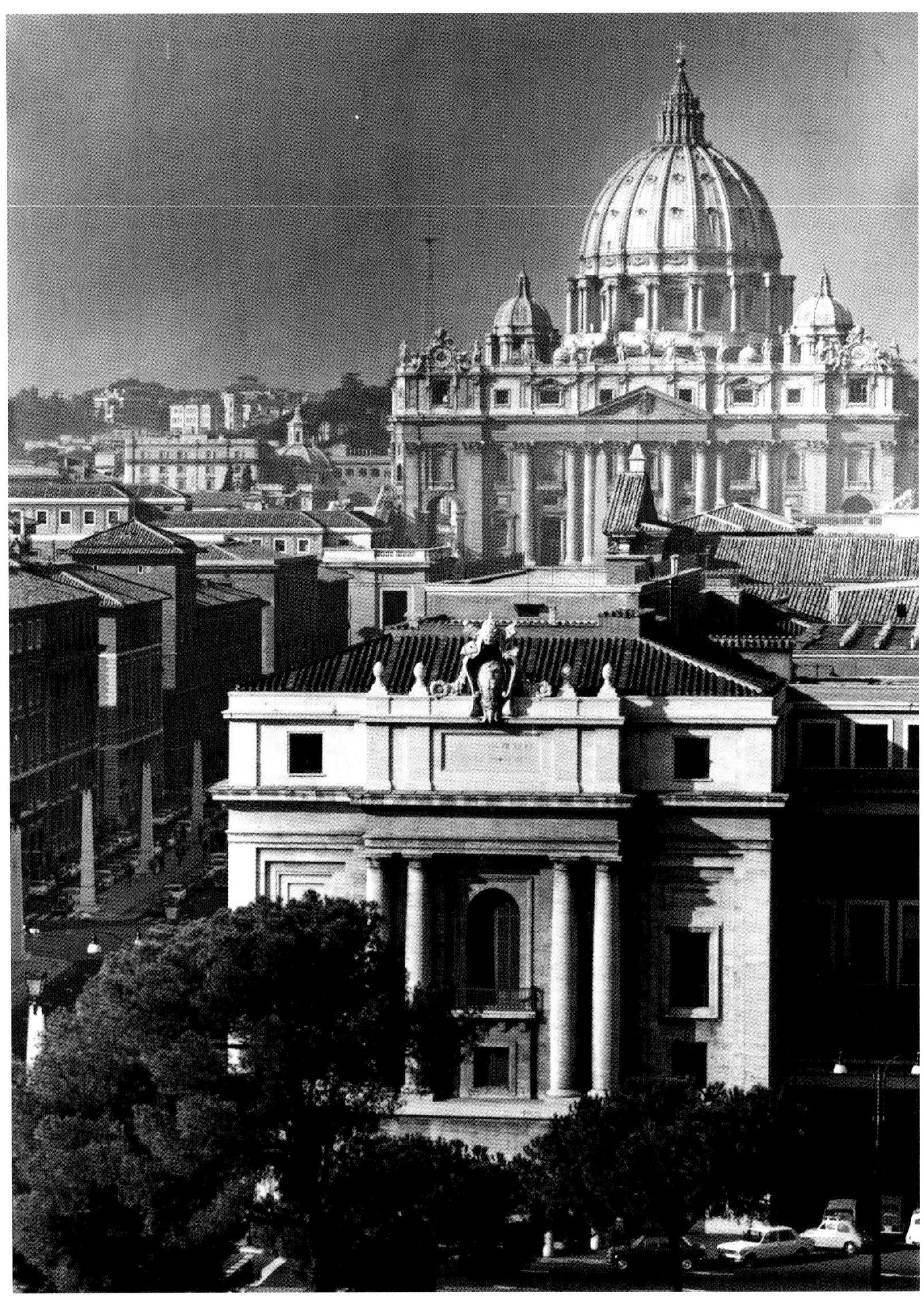

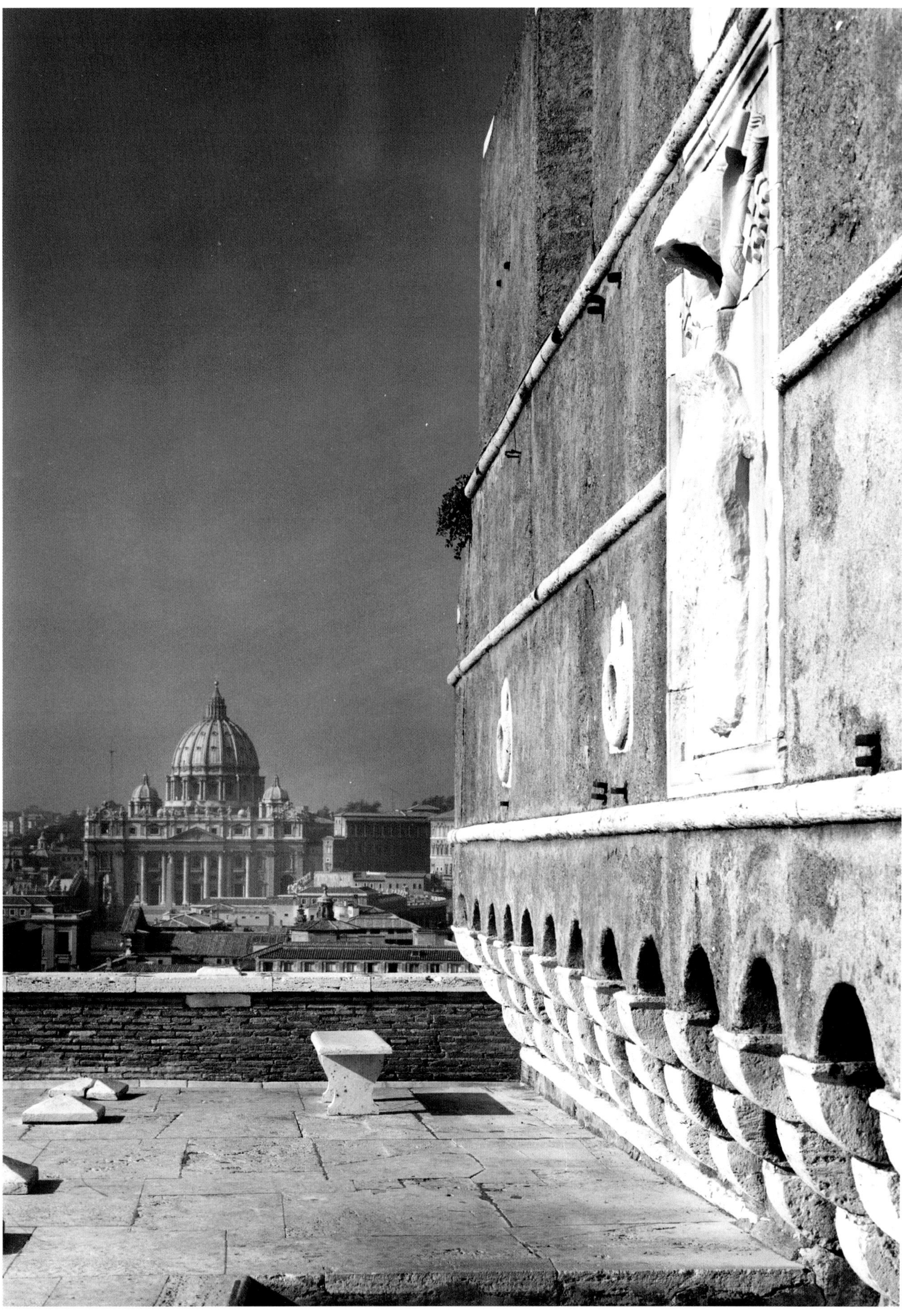

138. Edwin Smith
*Saint Peter's Basilica seen from
Castel Sant'Angelo*, 1957

139. Edwin Smith
Via dei Condotti and Trinità dei Monti, 1970

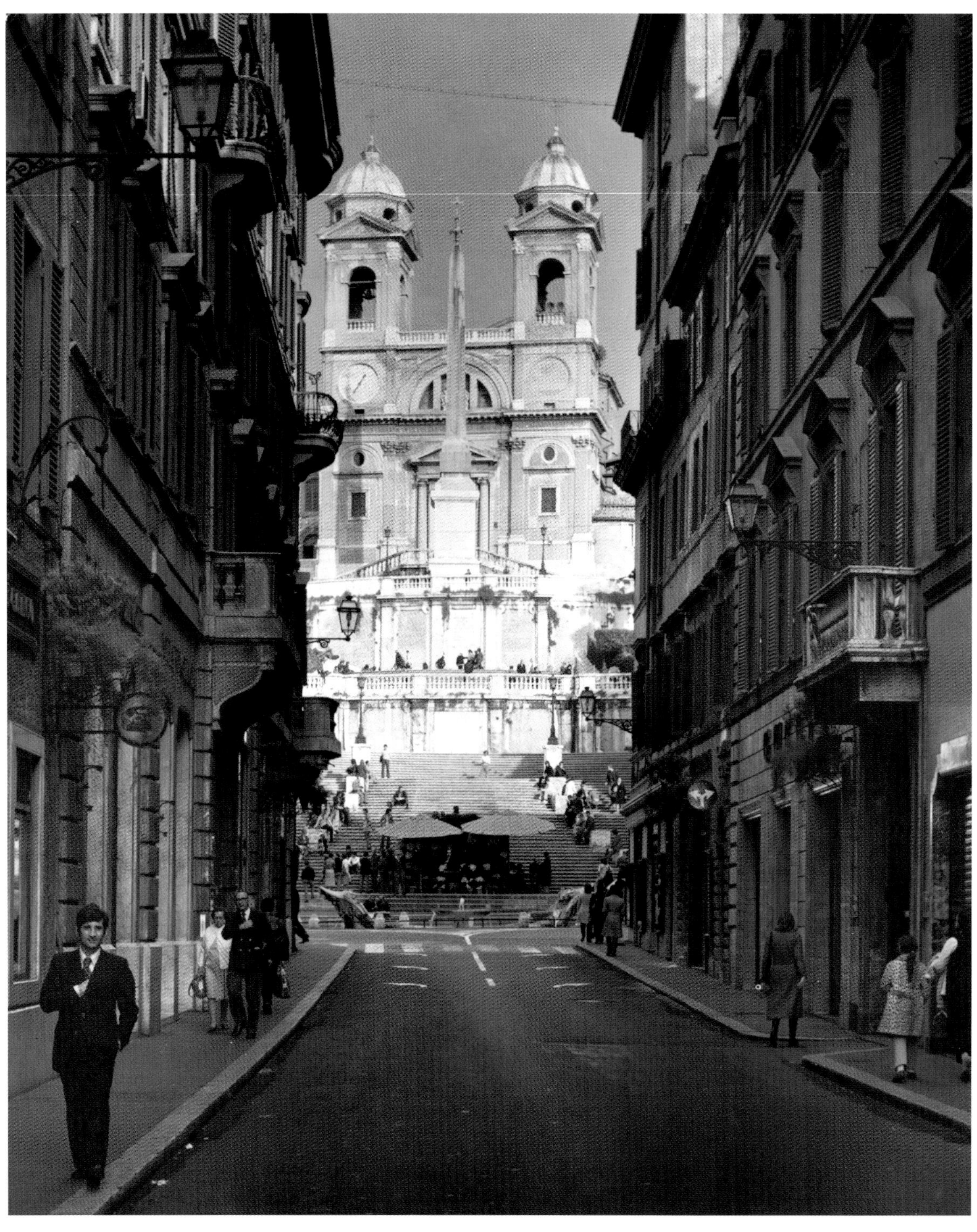

140. Stabilimento Fotografico
Domenico Anderson
Piazza di Spagna,
early twentieth century

141. Monica Pidgeon
Piazza di Spagna, 1961

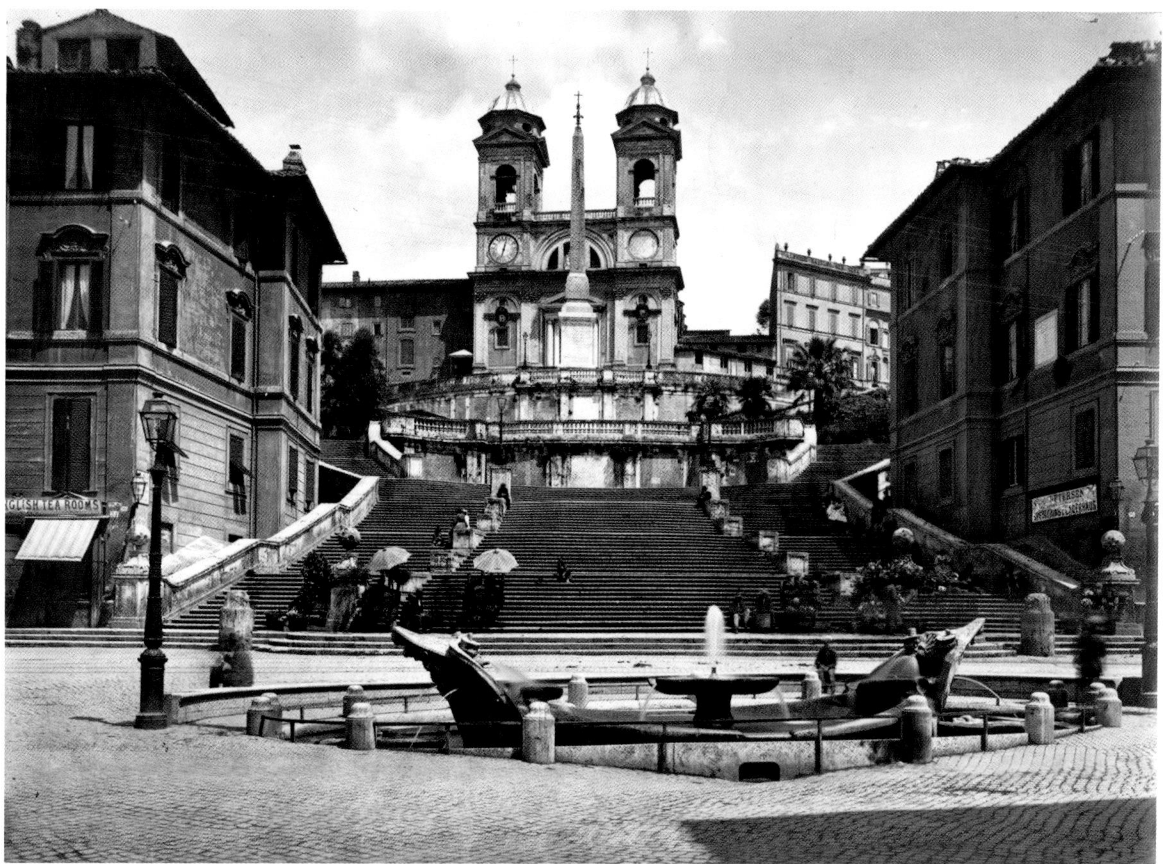

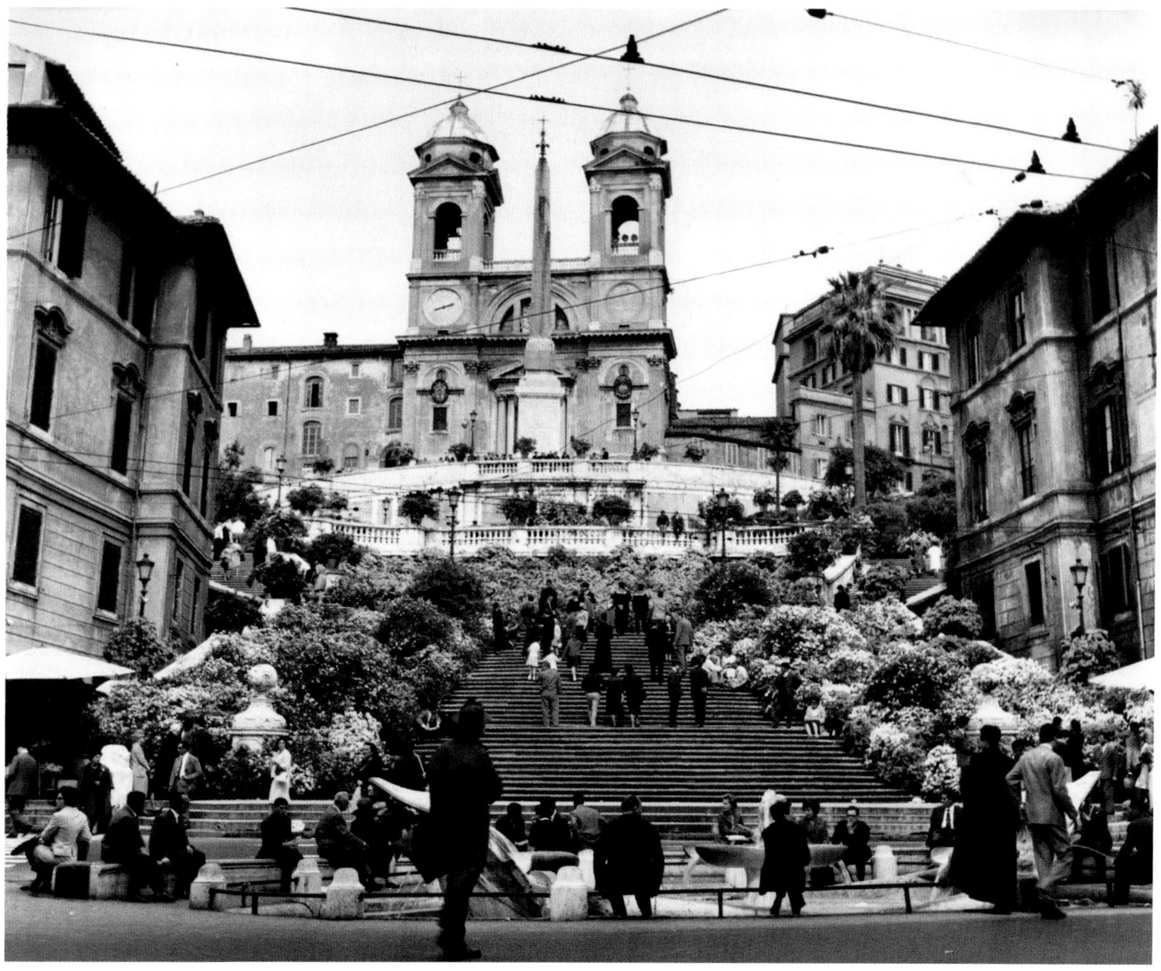

142. Unknown photographer
Spanish Steps,
Piazza di Spagna, 1950

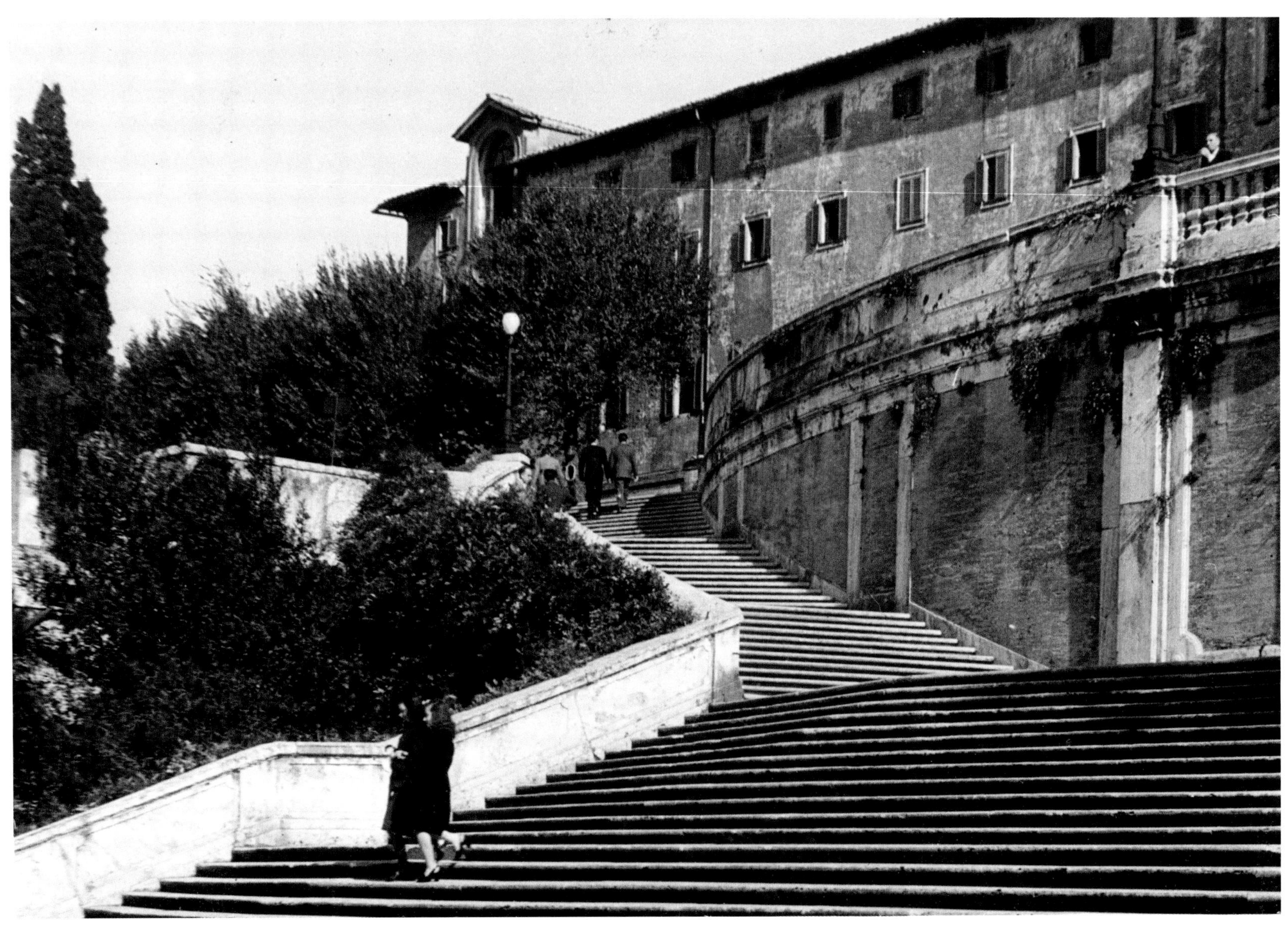

143. Ivy de Wolfe
*Church of Trinità dei Monti
and Spanish Steps,
Piazza di Spagna*, 1961

144. Ivy de Wolfe
*Church of Trinità dei Monti
and Spanish Steps,
Piazza di Spagna*, 1961

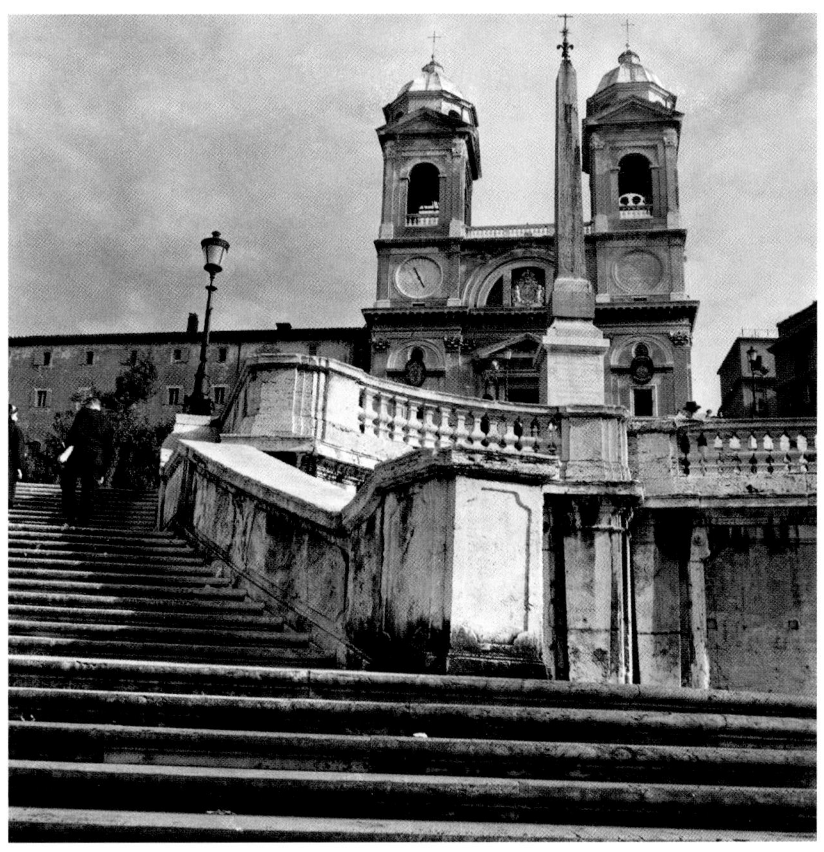

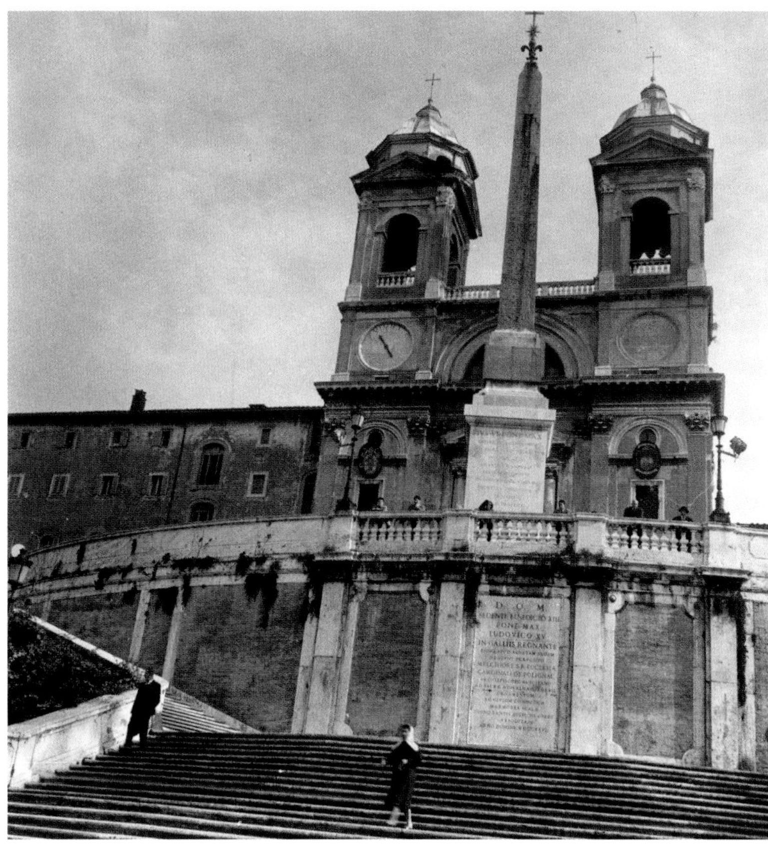

145. Ralph Deakin
Monument to Vittorio Emanuele II, or 'Vittoriano', 1930s

146. Ralph Deakin
View from Monument to Vittorio Emanuele II, 1930s

147. Ralph Deakin
Churches of Santa Maria di Loreto and Santissimo Nome di Maria seen from the Monument to Vittorio Emanuele II, 1930s

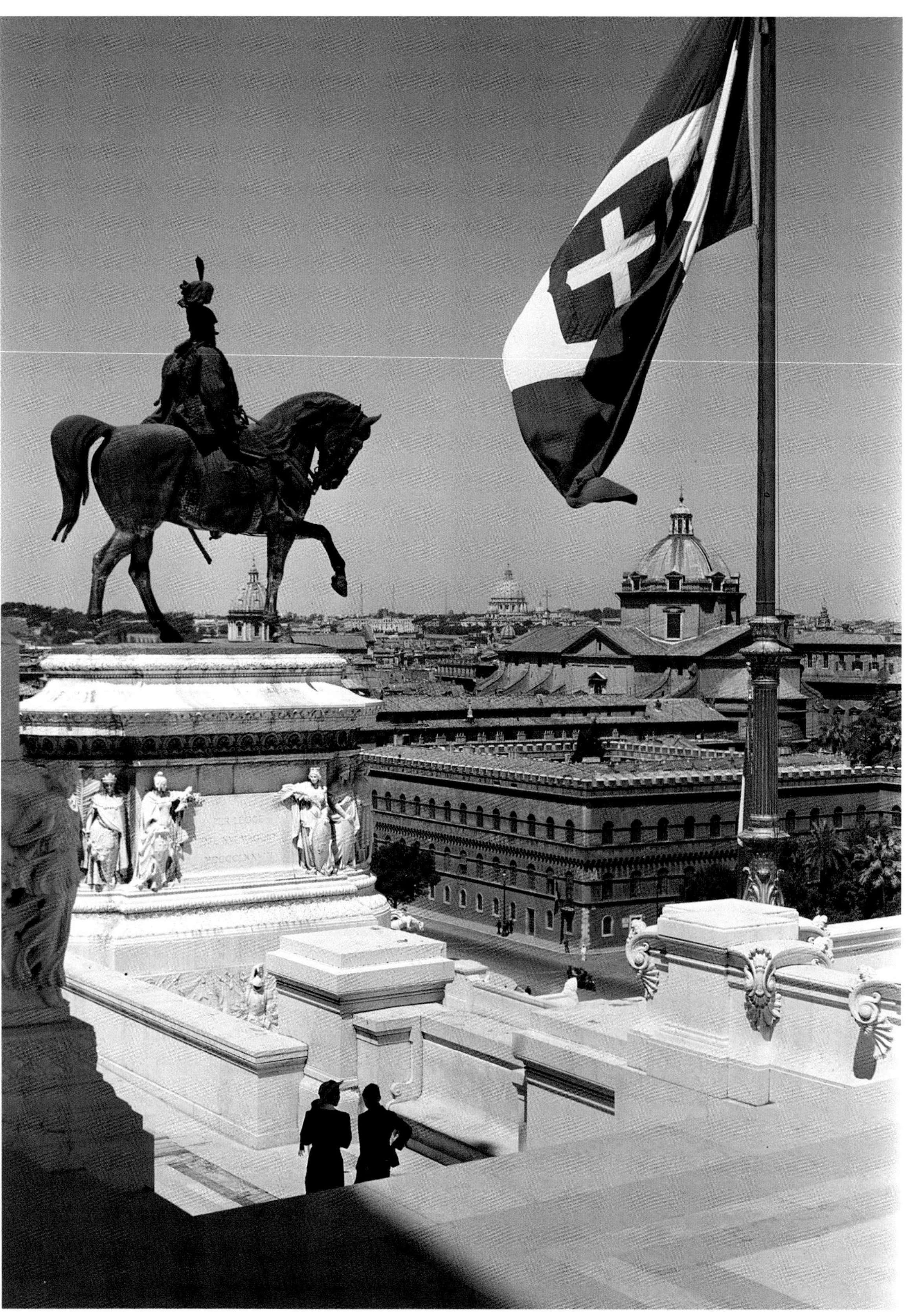

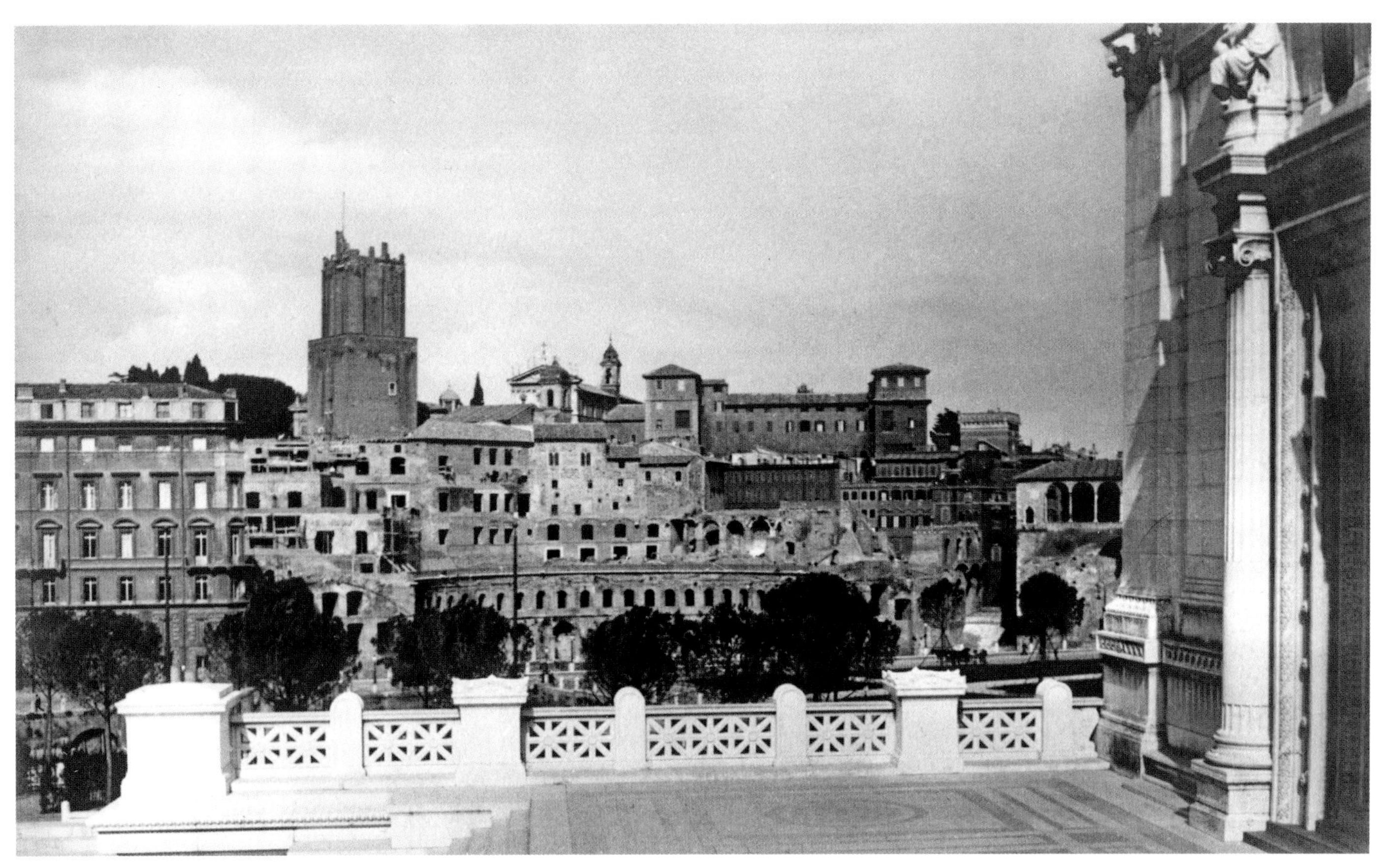

148. Tim Benton
*Portico linking the Palazzo
delle Arti e Tradizioni Popolari
and the Palazzo della Scienza
Universale, EUR, 1976*

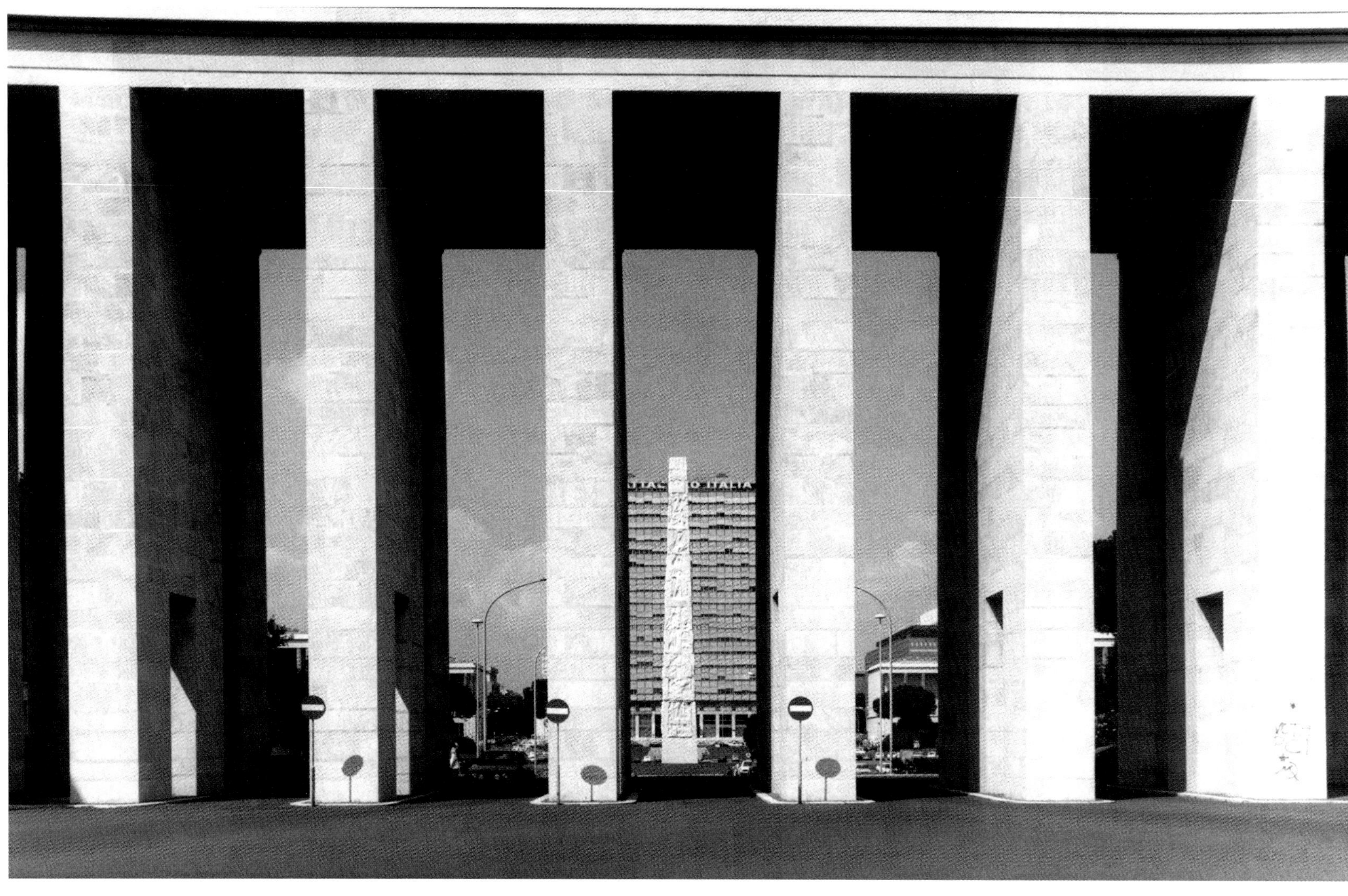

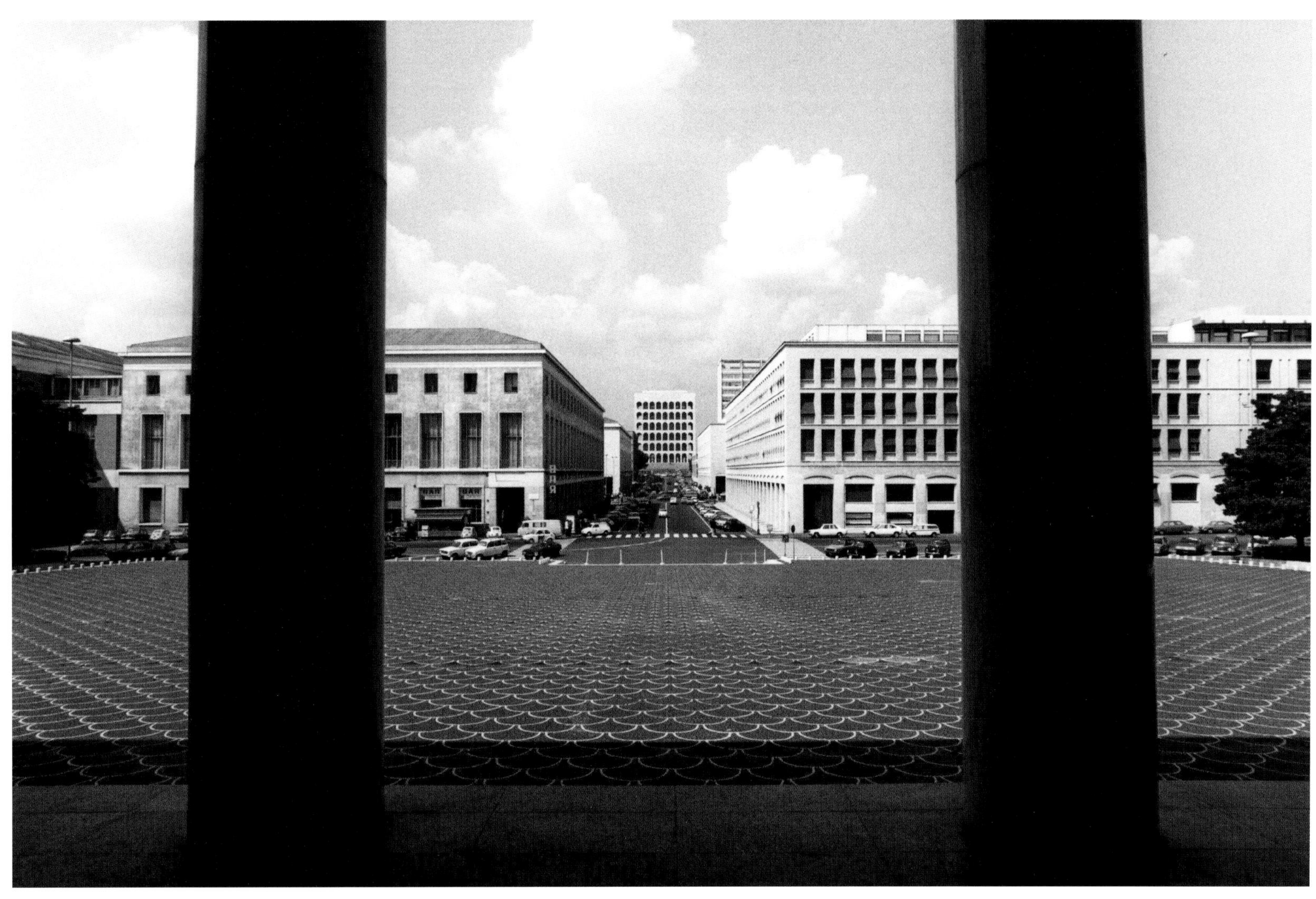

149. Tim Benton
*View from the Palazzo
dei Congressi to the Palazzo
della Civiltà, EUR*, 1976

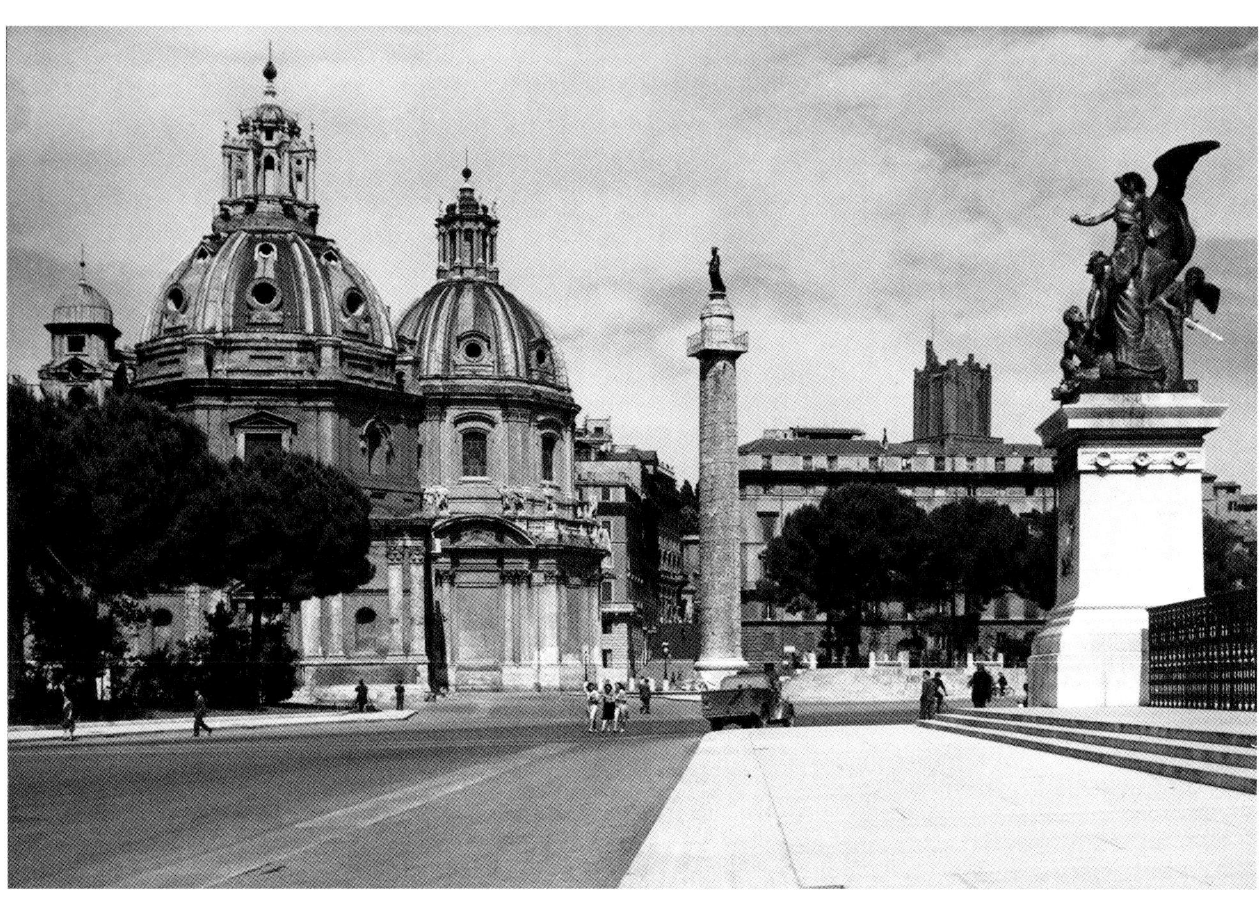

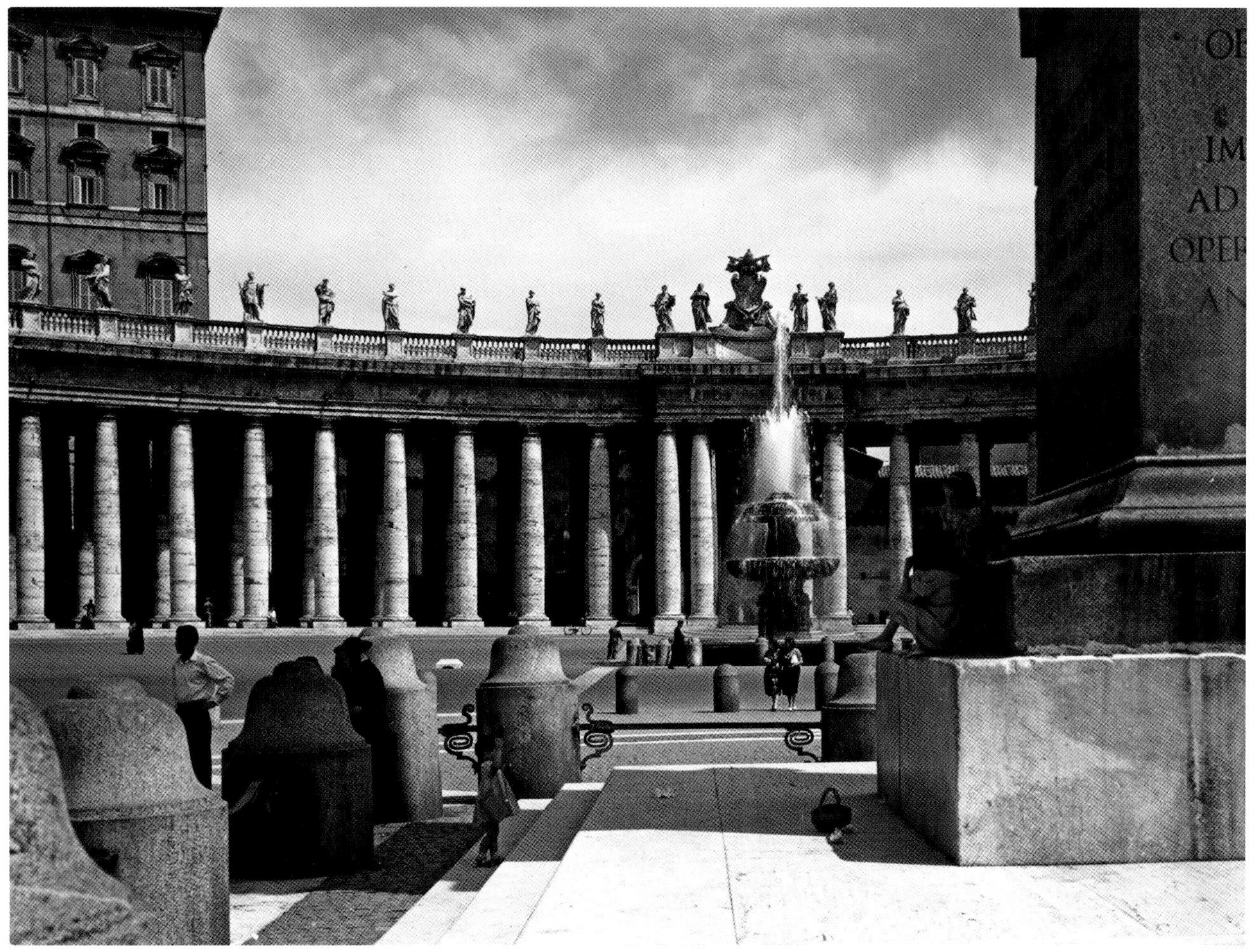

150. Ralph Deakin
*Santa Maria di Loreto,
Santissimo Nome di Maria
and Trajan's Column*, 1930s

151. George Everard Kidder Smith
Saint Peter's Square, 1954

152. Ralph Deakin
San Giovanni in Laterano,
1930s

153. Ralph Deakin
*Fontana dei Quattro Fiumi,
Piazza Navona*, 1930s

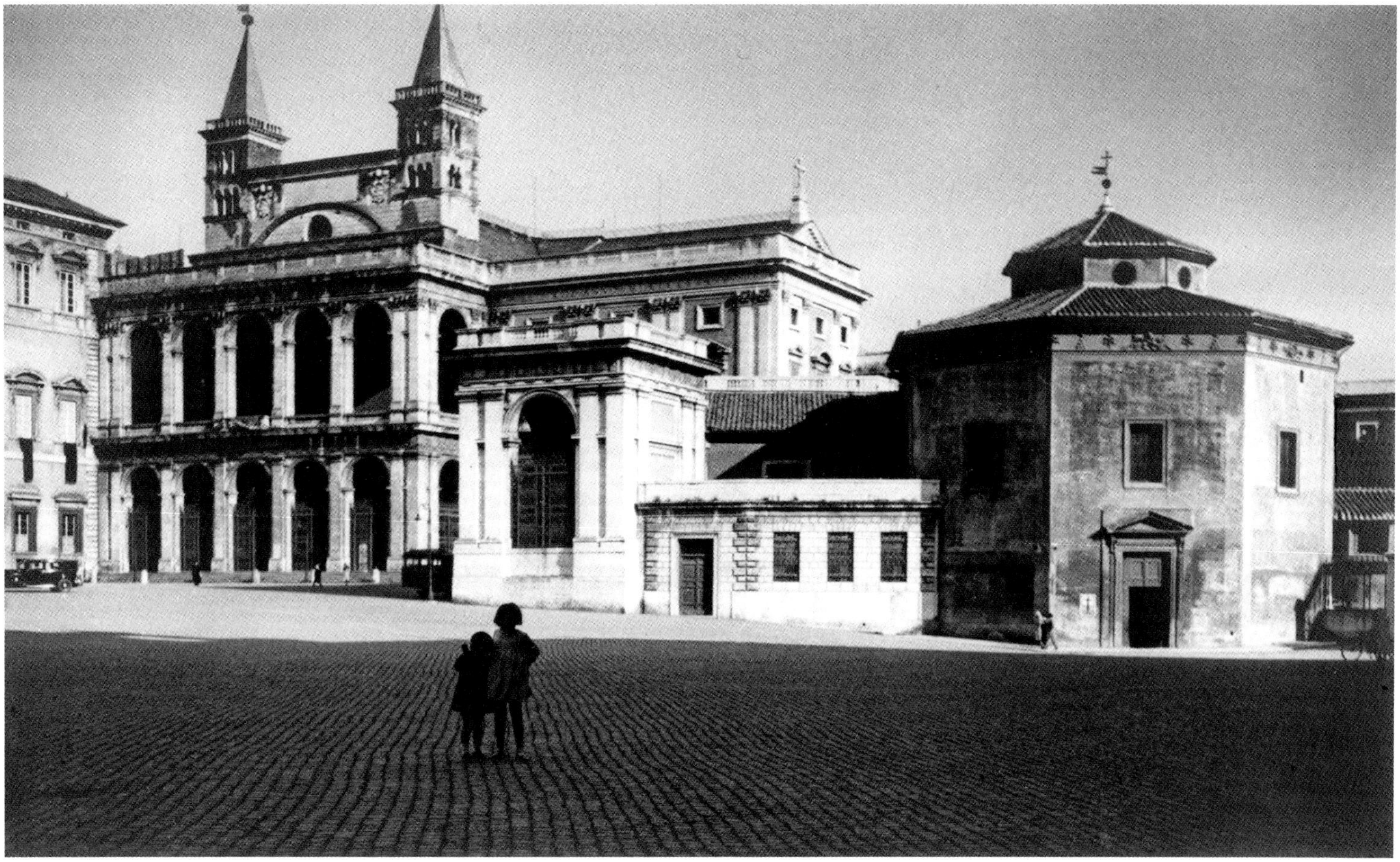

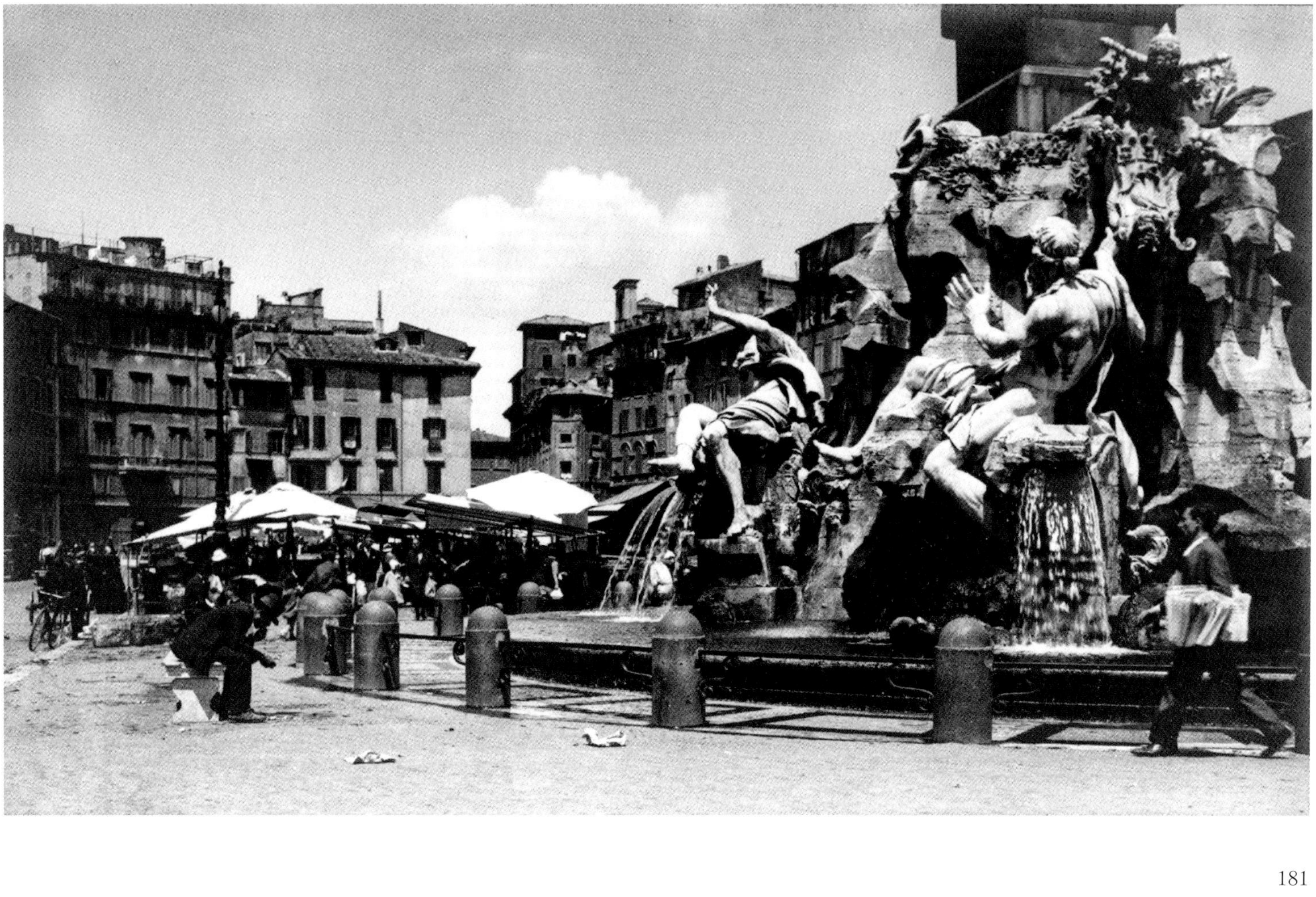

Atmospheres

It is no secret that the atmosphere at lunch is different to that at supper, that antique furniture have more atmosphere than modern ones, that even our appetite can be stimulated by an atmosphere of warmth and trust, that at times all it takes is a joke to transform an initial atmosphere of diffidence. Yet, despite our undoubted familiarity with all of this, the question of 'what is an atmosphere' has yet to find a satisfactory answer.
Tonino Griffero

Atmosphere is amorphous yet shapes the experience and appeal of a city, as scent supervenes on the materiality of a rose.[1] But how can one interrogate something so evasive as aura? A theory of atmosphere, as a 'quasi-thing', floats airily free of philosophical precision. Ancient antecedents, from *genius loci* to the numinous, explored the spirit or essence of location. German nineteenth-century thought advanced the idea that places possess a distinctive voice (*Stimmung*). Lately, scholars have explored the phenomenology of the city, and ways that an urban landscape articulates its own dialect. Most recently, Tonino Griffero penetrated the intellectual fog of 'ambiance'.[2] His analysis of the aesthetics of emotional spaces characterises the atmospheres emanating from built environments, and explores the role of ambiance in daily life, and its impact on emotion, behaviour and judgement.

Rome's voice is unique, roaring in its singular tongue, with the hoarse baritone of antiquity, warbling fountains or the shrill confidence of Baroque encrustations. But the sense of place and individuation distinguishing Rome are imparted by a range of cues beyond architecture and its historical context. Plays of light, shade and material; affects of geography, climate and topography; or conditions of society, culture and politics, each contribute to how people absorb and understand the individuality of their surroundings. Photography communicates atmospheric climates and affects, which can otherwise dissolve incoherently at the nib of the writer's quill. Using British post-war photographs alongside testimony from visitors, this section goes beyond discrete monuments, to the spaces in-between, to investigate how British eyes responded to Rome's special 'atmospheric skin', demonstrating that Rome's aura is a fundamental component of the city's eternal allure.

The image of the Eternal City has eclipsed our understanding of Rome's peculiar modernity.[3] Remaining unnervingly slow, and largely clerical not industrial, post-war Rome tarried by the criteria with which twentieth-century modernity is usually measured. Yet Rome was transforming in its own terms, and the face of the city was altered as urban clearances were hammered out on a massive scale. Rome's new urban spaces and its raw socio-political challenges caught the eye of British travellers, who were previously drawn to Rome by the perennial pull of Antiquity and the Old Masters. British post-war visitors increasingly swerved off-piste from Rome's eternal routes, squares and monuments in search of ulterior atmospheres, skirting the Aurelian walls, and adding visits to Fascist interventions or peripheral working-class quarters to the tourist's traditional bill of fayre.

One intriguing publication by the Anglo-Irish novelist Elizabeth Bowen, *A Time in Rome* (1960), less a guidebook than a collection of impressions, recounts her 'semi-psychogeographical' saunters into areas more familiar to Pasolini and proletariat labourers than to the prim tourist.[4] With sharp sense of 'place' and multi-sensorial receptiveness, Bowen's reactions capture the psycho-tropic effect of Rome's atmosphere, of which there are few more compelling evocations.

'I was really frightened by where I found myself: alone, so far as my eye could see, in the heart of the vast shell of this exhibition which had never taken place. What happened to be a tense, grey, gloomy and eerie March afternoon accorded with the spectral avenues, seeded along their cracks with desiccated grasses, and the Fascist-classical architecture looming around me. Heaved high on arcades, down which draughts wandered, the buildings were cases in marble white by nature but showed so thin as to let through a bluish death-hue… The horror of the whole mock-city, with its rows upon rows of square-cut, staring, unmeaning windows, was its emptiness […]'[5]

Photography, too, was exploring Rome's atmospheric qualities at a time of transition. Technical advances in fast film in the 1930s, and the success of Brassaï in Paris, bred a new direction in nocturnal photography and greater atmospheric effects. Theatre and the art of stage set remained a fundamental paradigm for the aesthetic of atmosphere. In painting, the eerie mood of the *scuola metafisica* and Giorgio De Chirico informed atmospheric views of Rome in British post-war photography. Neorealist cinema's take on poverty and its attachment to the real also crossed over media to preoccupy photographers. And after Cinecittà re-opened for business, following its requisitioning as a displaced persons' camp, its outputs rapidly shaped the British view of Rome.

Rome's aura was explored in the immensity of imperial Rome, the city's confounding modernism, the unresolved aftermath of Fascism, but also, increasingly, through the seduction of the *dolce vita*. The life and work of Marion Johnson (1912–1980), better known by her *nom de plume*, Georgina Masson, typify the British attraction to, and interpretation of, the aura of post-war Rome. Masson's *The Companion Guide to Rome* (1965) endures as the fundamental navigational tool to Rome. Her writing is marked by sensitivity to atmosphere, transmitting the travel experience by personal response to sites, their environment and their social contexts.[6] Masson also documented Rome exhaustively with her Rolleiflex camera. Prose and photography swing to the beat of the *dolce vita*.

The British photographer John Deakin (1912–1972) avidly documented street scenes and city lives in London, Paris and — his favourite city — Rome, where he spent long stints during the 1950s. In 1951, the travel writer Christopher Kininmonth published *Rome Alive,* which interspersed Deakin's Rome photographs with his own nostalgic effusions and observations. Here, text and image converge on a mutual chief focus — ordinary life — aiming to be 'something of a portrait of contemporary Rome'. As a *Vogue* photographer Deakin was versatile in subject matter, but was, above all, drawn to the streets. Like other contemporaries, he followed a genealogy rooted in the USA with the Farm Security Administration's social conscience photography of post-Depression rural challenges, and, more immediately, Alberto Lattuada's controversial images of Milanese flea markets deplored by the Fascist authorities for their demoralising depictions of Italian life. Deakin portrayed the homeless, braziers and tat merchants, wine carts and corner-shops, or a canopy of second-hand boots dangling above a market-stall in Campo de' Fiori. Kininmonth's *can-can* girls in a 'dingy and uncomfortable, dark and perpetually crowded' atmosphere, reflect the same funky Rome sucked up by Fellini, and fed back into the photography of the day. Kininmonth and Deakin also observed religious ceremony, which they saw as key to understanding Rome's particularity of place. Deakin's photographs grasp the atmosphere of Catholic Rome, exploring the visual possibilities of monochrome liturgical vestments — dog-collars and dark habits — against the capricious shadows of rippling Baroque façades.

Even if not present in the Royal Institute of British Architects photographs collection,

John Deakin's approach to the interpretation of the city closely recalls Monica Pidgeon's relationship to the 'representation' of reality. As British photographers were engrossed by the mood generated by human activity, so were they enchanted by the emotive qualities of Rome's climactic and aesthetic atmosphere. The Eternal City's distinctive golden light drenching its ruined grandeur made it a seedbed for photographers prone to a Keatsian flush. In *The Companion Guide*, Masson's balance of historical grip, anecdote and social observation is shot through with an acute sense of atmosphere. Opening on the Capitoline, she invites travellers to time their visit 'ideally, to coincide with the hour after sunset, when the sky on a fine night is a translucent shade of green and the monuments imperceptibly lit by a master hand are beginning to glow softly in the gathering darkness'. Sensibility to light, atmosphere and the picturesque in Masson's prose transfers to her photography. Many images are framed internally with picturesque foreground compositional elements, such as portals or trees, and photographs of buildings, whether ancient or freshly emerged from scaffolding, are articulated by the atmospheric disturbance of long shadows. This is epitomised by the portrayal of the newly constructed ticket hall at Termini Station (1951). The same sense of atmosphere, derived from foreground elements, unsettling shadow and a romantic eye, is at work in several views by Edwin Smith (1912–1971).

British photographers also explored atmosphere and the touch — the haptic quality of light against the texture of Rome's ageing fabric. Several photographers show Rome's distinctive pock-marked Travertine, the sheen of its ubiquitous *sanpietrini*, or the hatching of ancient exposed brick punctuated by black cavernous recesses at the Baths of Caracalla. Following Brassaï's Parisian street art photography, British photographers also studied Roman graffiti, recognising its surface, immediacy, ephemerality and vernacular voice as a contributor to urban atmosphere.

British cameras investigated Rome's atmospheres, but also saw atmospheric effects as instruments for creating social value, notably photographs by Ivy and Ivor de Wolfe (Hubert and Hazel de Cronin Hastings) furnishing their polemical publication, *The Italian Townscape* (1963). De Wolfe/Hastings, titans in architectural publishing, were disenchanted by the stifling of conviviality in British cities by standardisation, monotonous consumerism and the tyranny of traffic engineers. They produced atmospheric images of Rome,

exploring how picturesque nuances in Italian urbanism, by contrast to the UK, sustained a more humane city existence. Elements like 'foils, focal points, fluctuations, vistas closed and vistas open, truncation, change of level, perspective, silhouette, intricacy, anticipation, continuity, space, enclosure, exposure, the precinct, profile' created visual stimulation, atmospheric charge and, subsequently, better experience of lived-in spaces. The delights of vistas are shown by glimpses snatched through colonnades hugging Piazza San Pietro, or evening sun highlighting the Arch of Janus across the Forum Boarium. Intricacy abounds in the contours and materiality of the amphibious rock anchoring the Trevi fountain; and the use of silhouette in the formalist shadows cast by pedestrians across Termini Station rivals even the metaphysical master. De Wolfe/Hastings's photographs underpin the argument that townscape is the greatest artefact and, like a theatrical backdrop, its components collude to shape the ambiance of urban life.

If photography is the most atmospheric medium, Rome is the epitome of the atmospheric city, with its unique social and physical ambiance. Photographers observed the vast constellation of factors creating Rome's atmospheric in many ways. It is in these ghostly or intricate spaces, between and around, articulated by light and silhouette, material and climactic effects, where an important part of Rome's complex soul resides.

Tom True

[1] Thanks to Jacopo Benci and Marco Iuliano for their generous suggestions. The metaphor is from Jürgen Hasse in *Die Alte Stadt*, 35, 2008, 2, p. 103.
[2] Tonino Griffero, *Atmosferologia. Estetica degli spazi emozionali*, Rome-Bari: Laterza, 2010.
[3] See John David Rhodes, both forthcoming and published, including *Stupendous, miserable city: Pasolini's Rome*, Minneapolis: University of Minnesota Press, 2007.
[4] John David Rhodes, Elena Gorfinkel (eds.) *Taking place: location and the moving image*, Minneapolis and London: University of Minnesota Press, 2011, pp. 31–54.
[5] Elizabeth Bowen, *A Time in Rome*, London: Longmans, Green & Co., 1960, p. 161.
[6] Alessandra Capodiferro, Cornelia Lauf (eds.), *Georgina Masson: 1912-1980*, Milan: Charta, 2003.

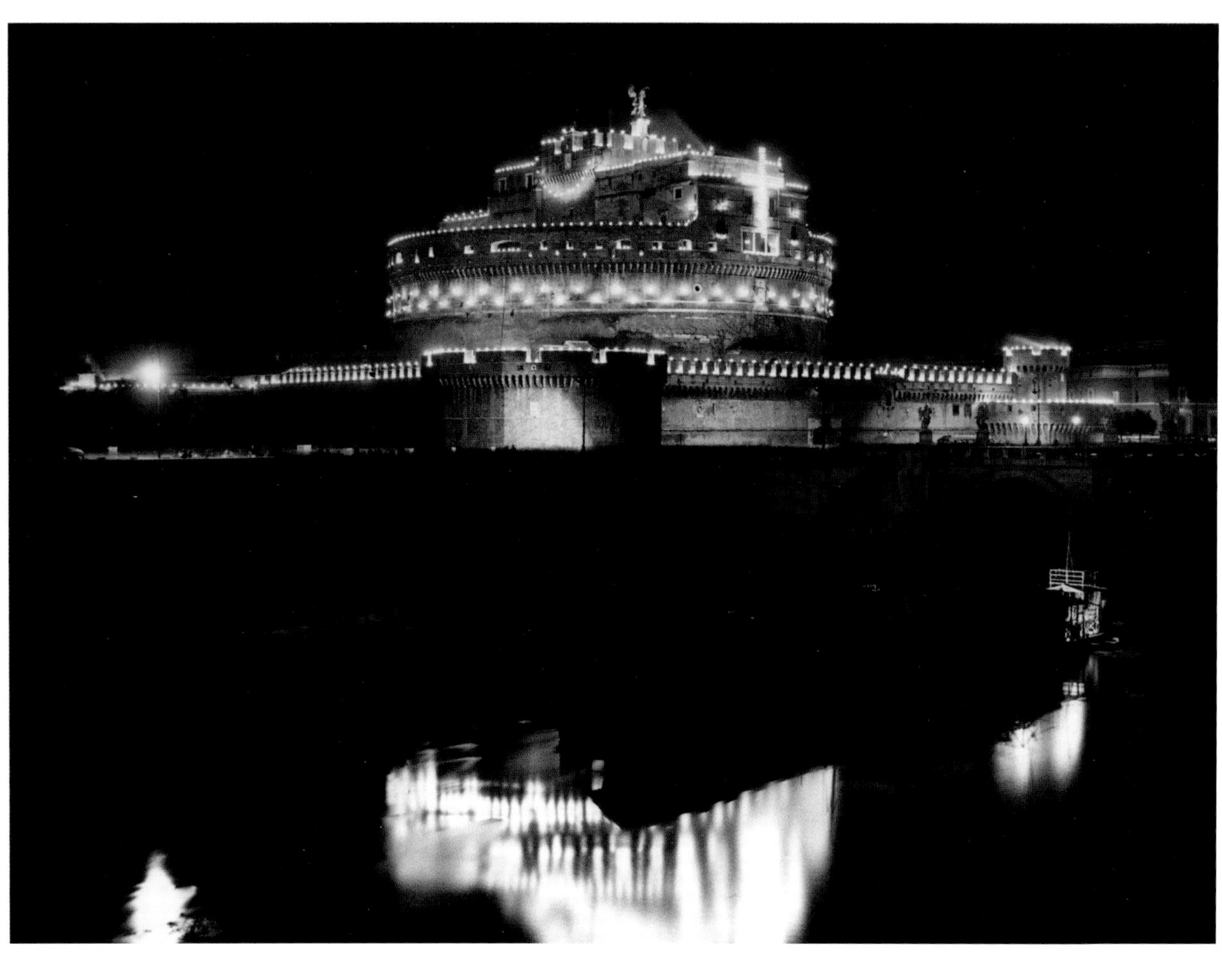

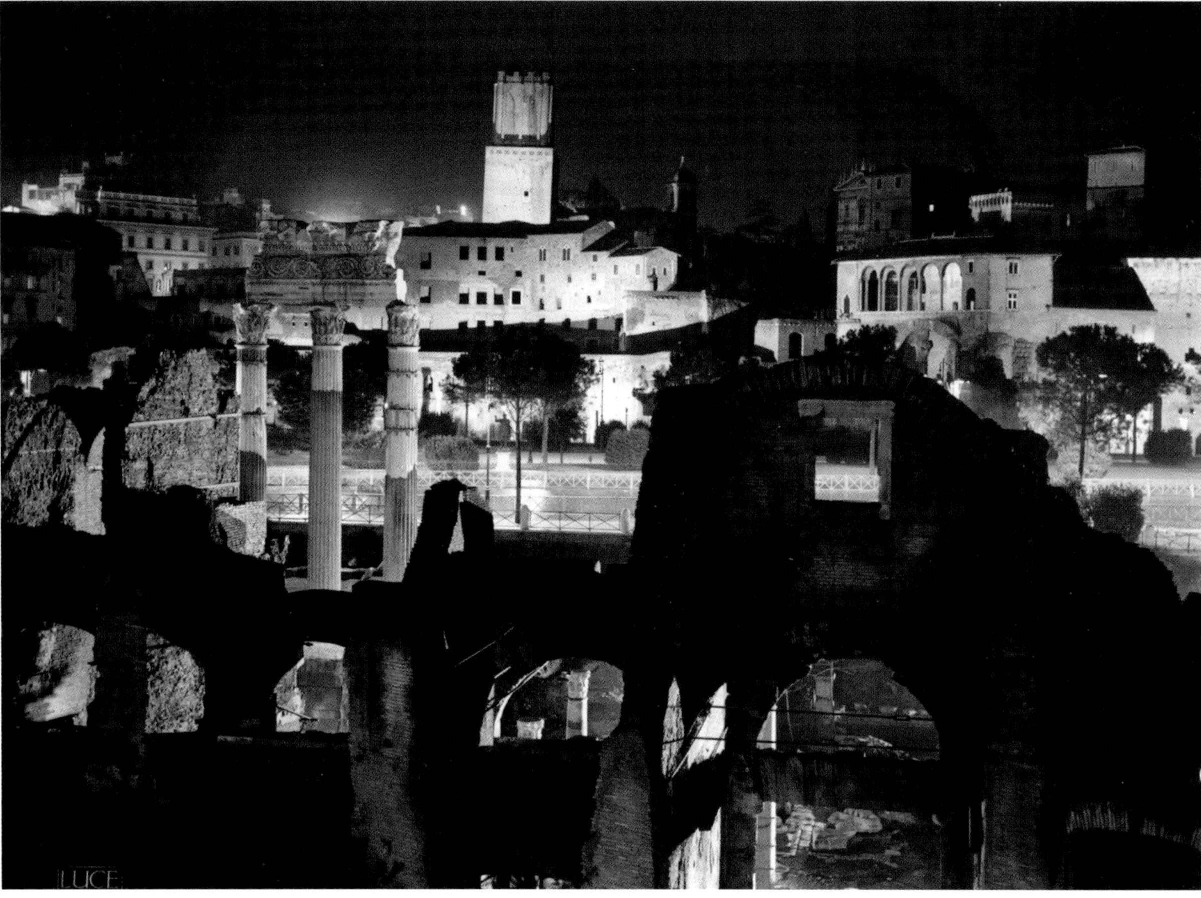

154. Spartaco Appetiti
Castel Sant'Angelo at night,
1950s

155. Istituto Luce
Roman Forum at night, 1960s

156. Unknown photographer
*Flavian Amphitheatre
(Colosseum) at night*, 1979

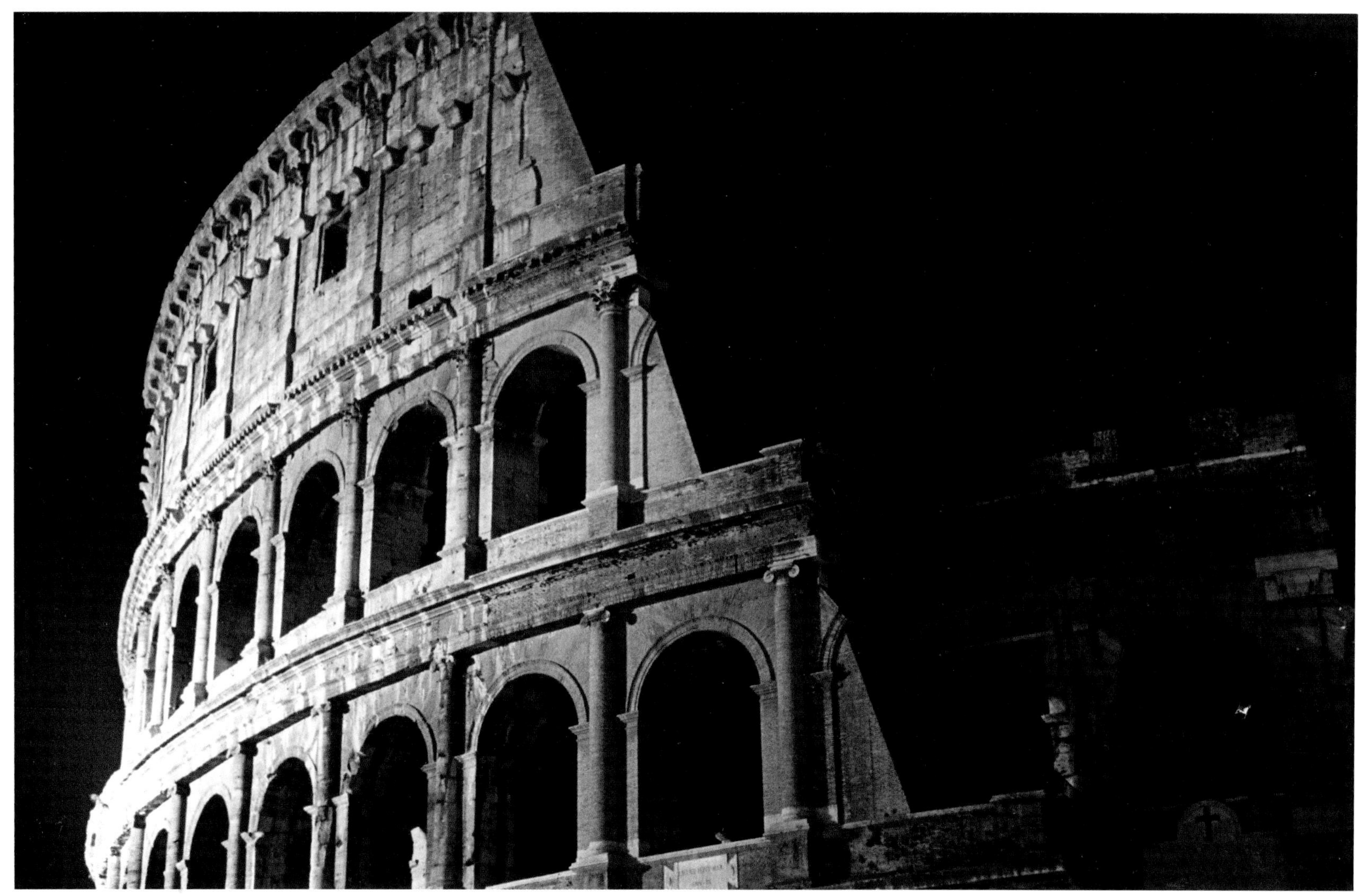

157. Unknown photographer
Café Doney, Via Veneto, 1950

158. Edwin Smith
Antico Caffè Greco,
Via dei Condotti, 1963

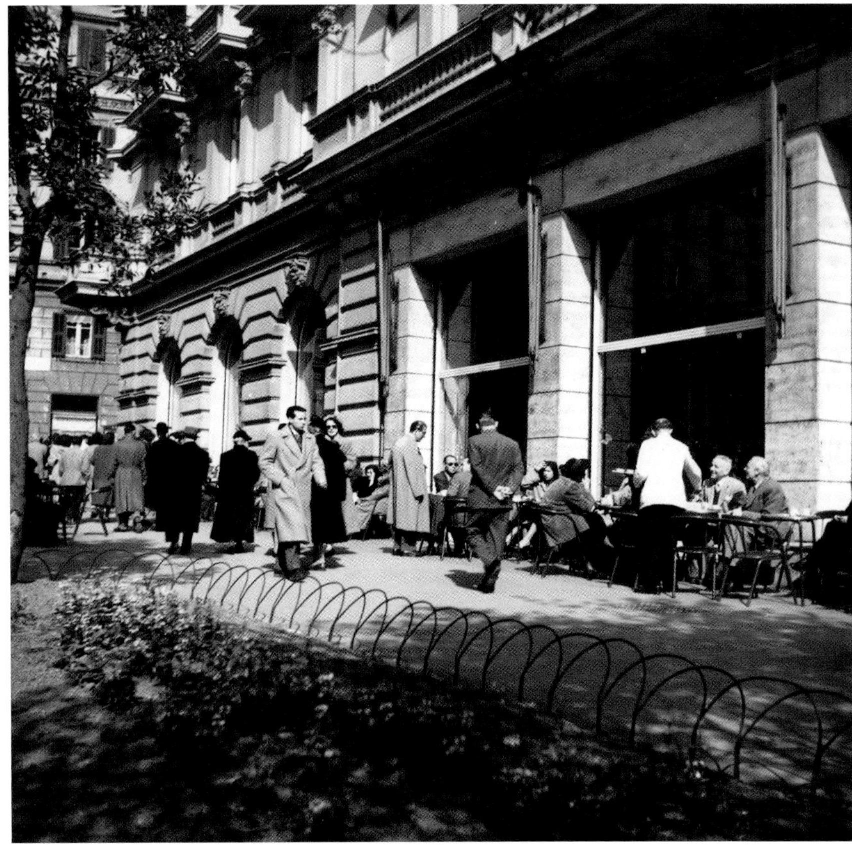

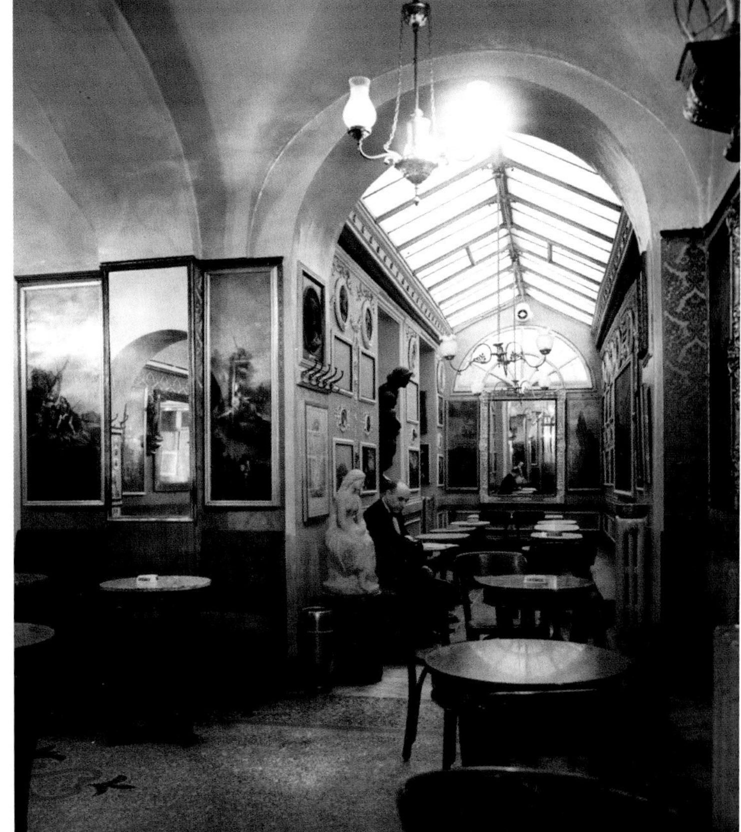

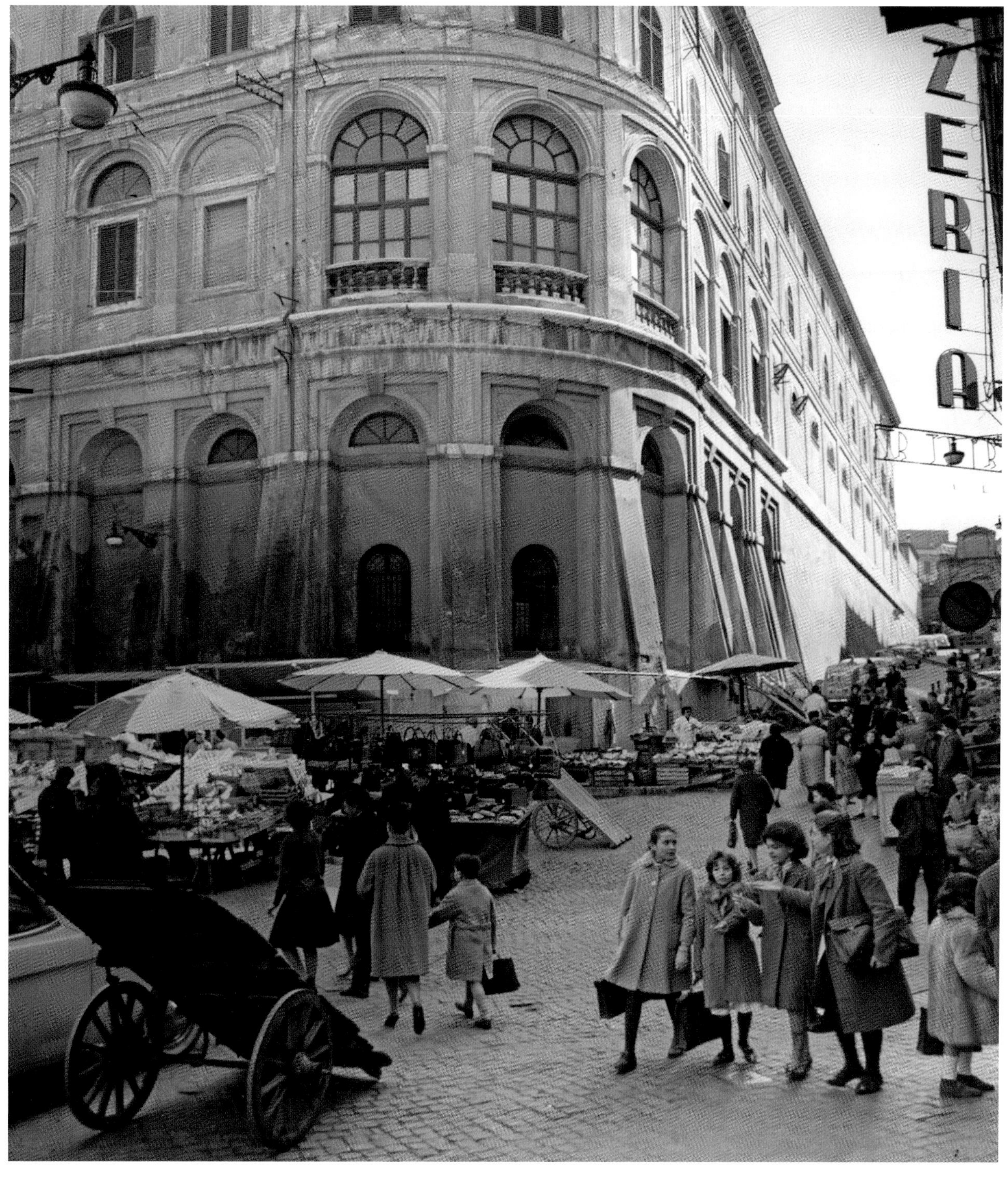

159. Edwin Smith
Market in Quirinale district,
1963

160. Monica Pidgeon
*Steps leading to the Palazzo
del Quirinale*, 1961

161. Edwin Smith
*Entrance to the Vatican
Apostolic Palace*, 1963

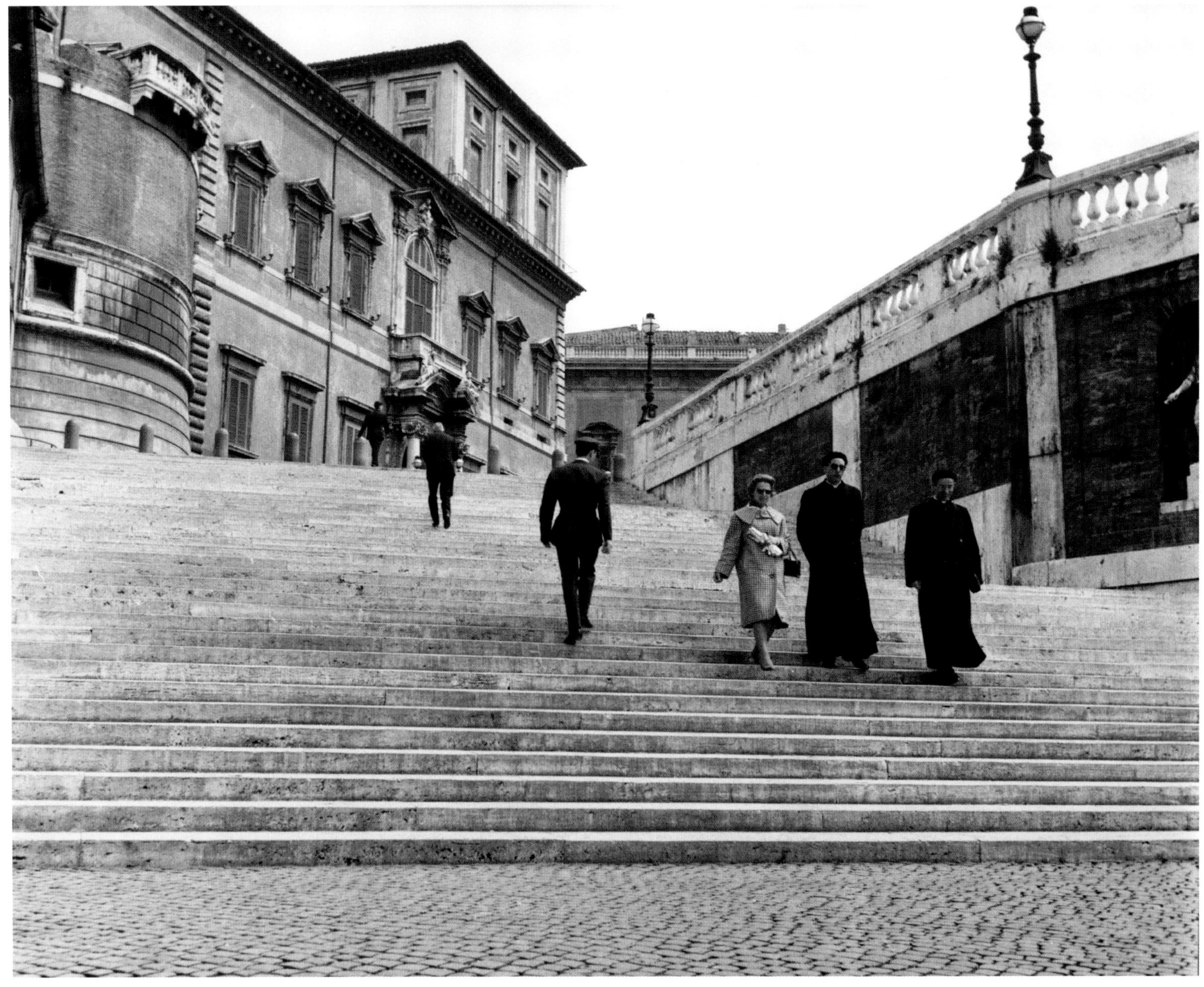

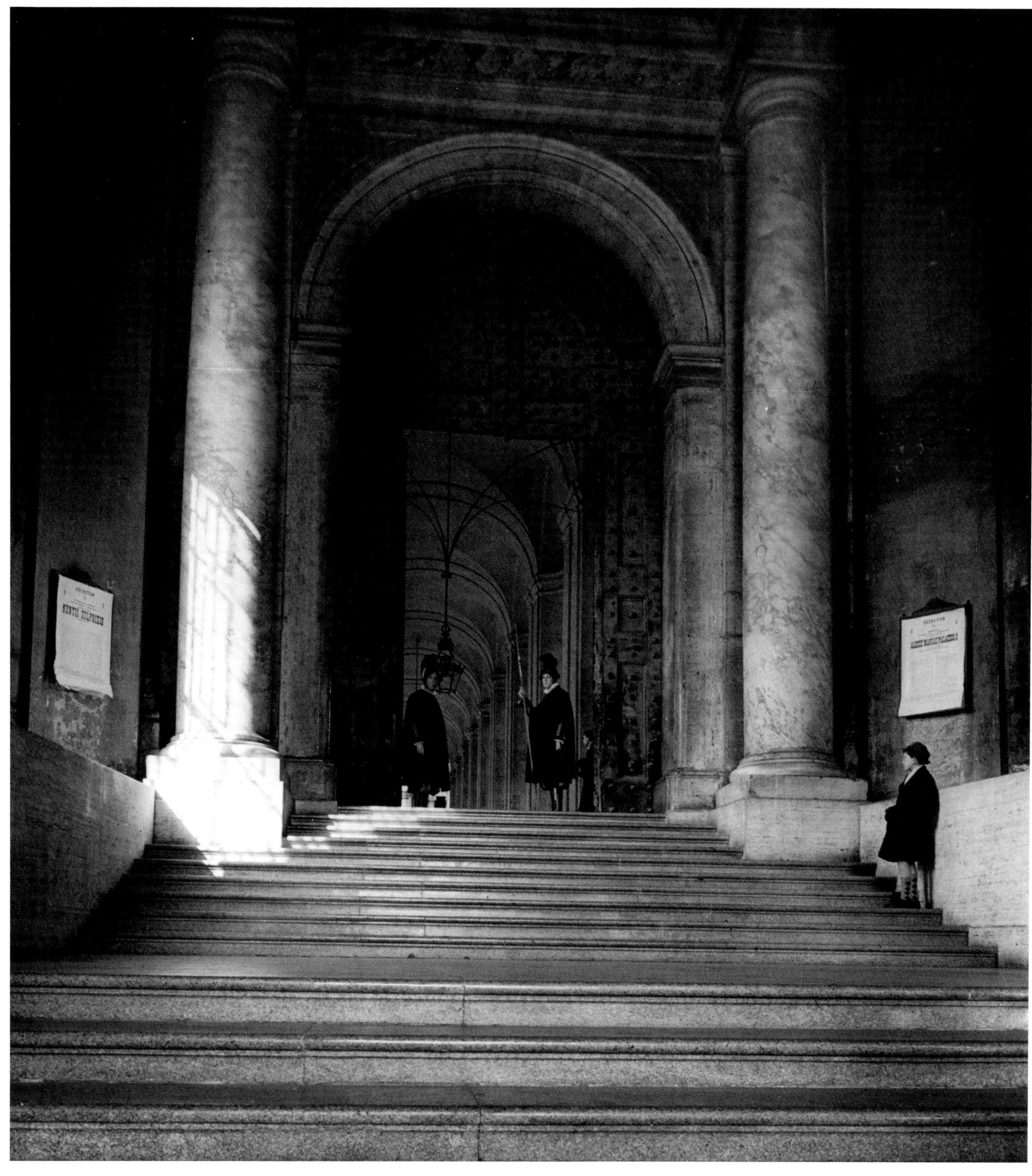

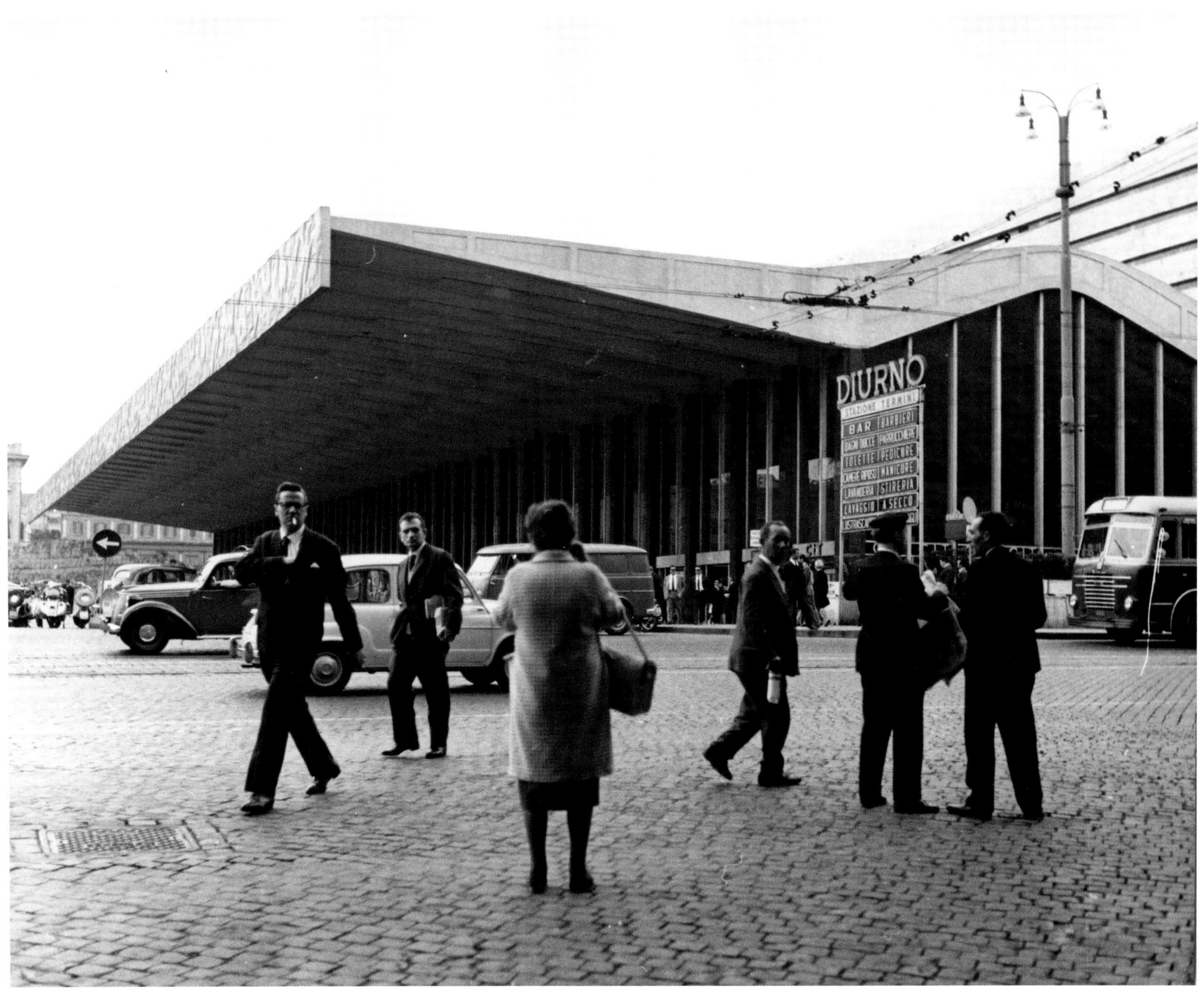

162. Monica Pidgeon
Termini Station, 1961

163. Monica Pidgeon
Termini Station, 1961

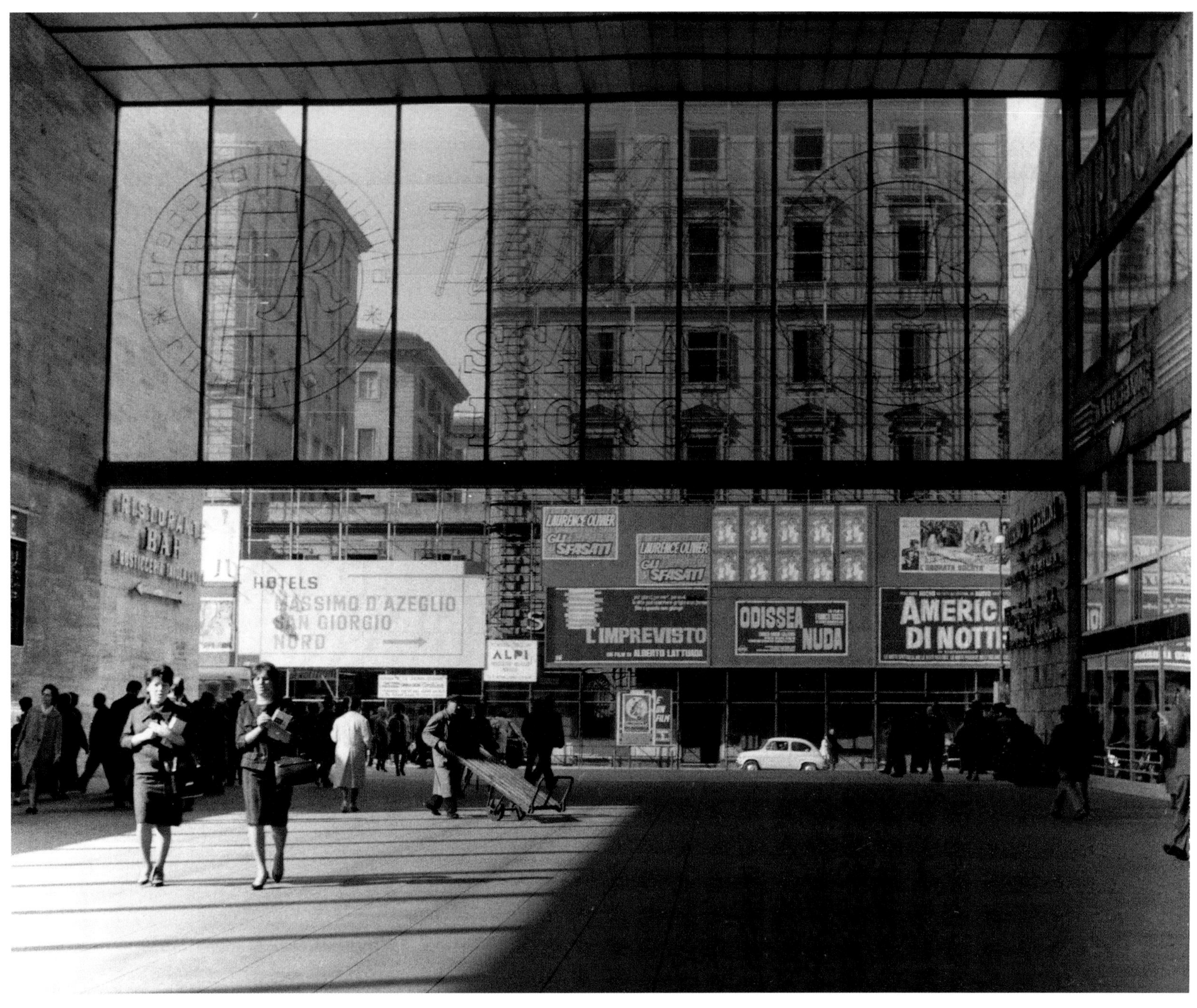

164. Ivy de Wolfe
Road markings,
Lungotevere, 1961

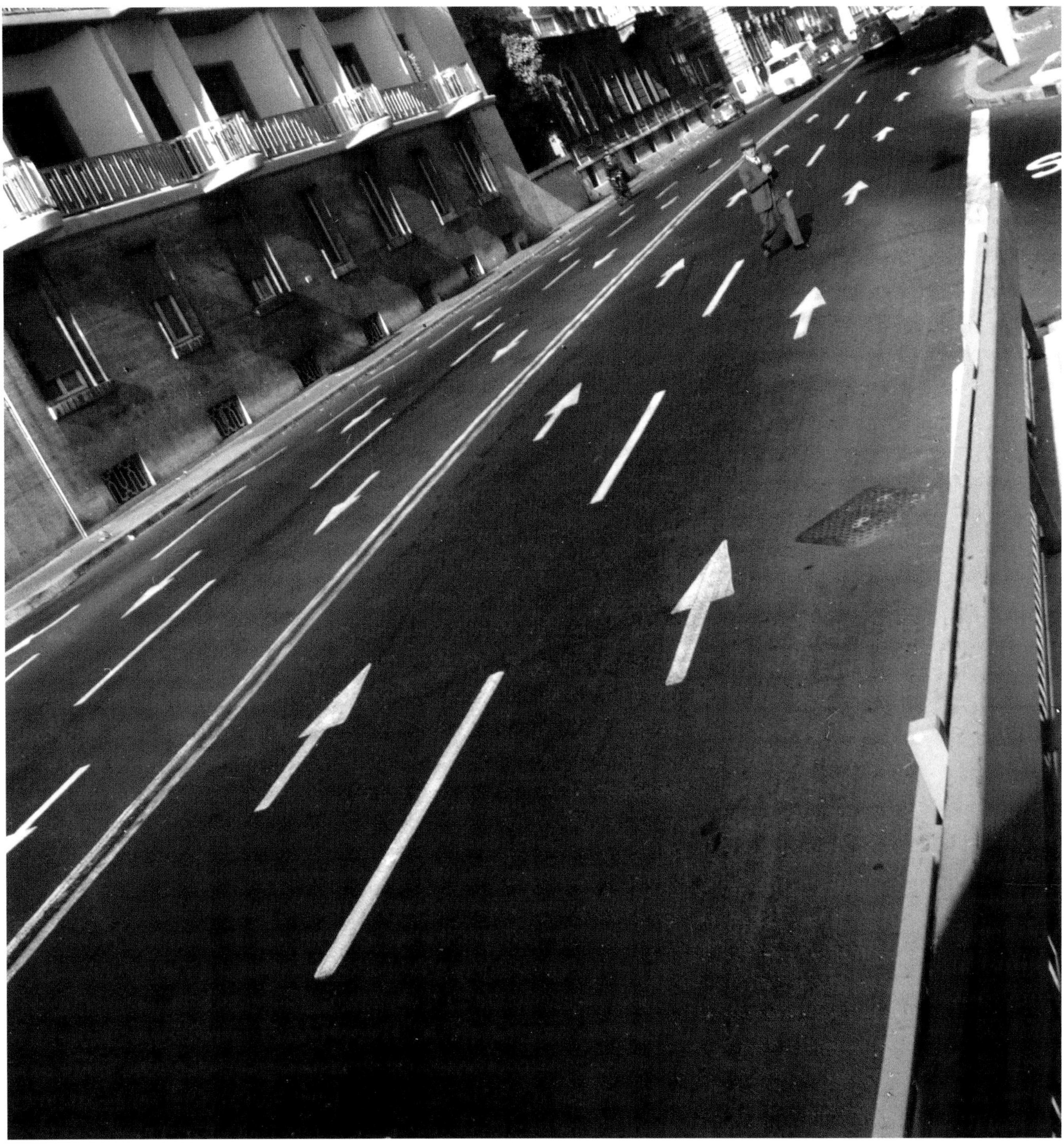

165. Ivy de Wolfe
Kerb with advertising, 1961

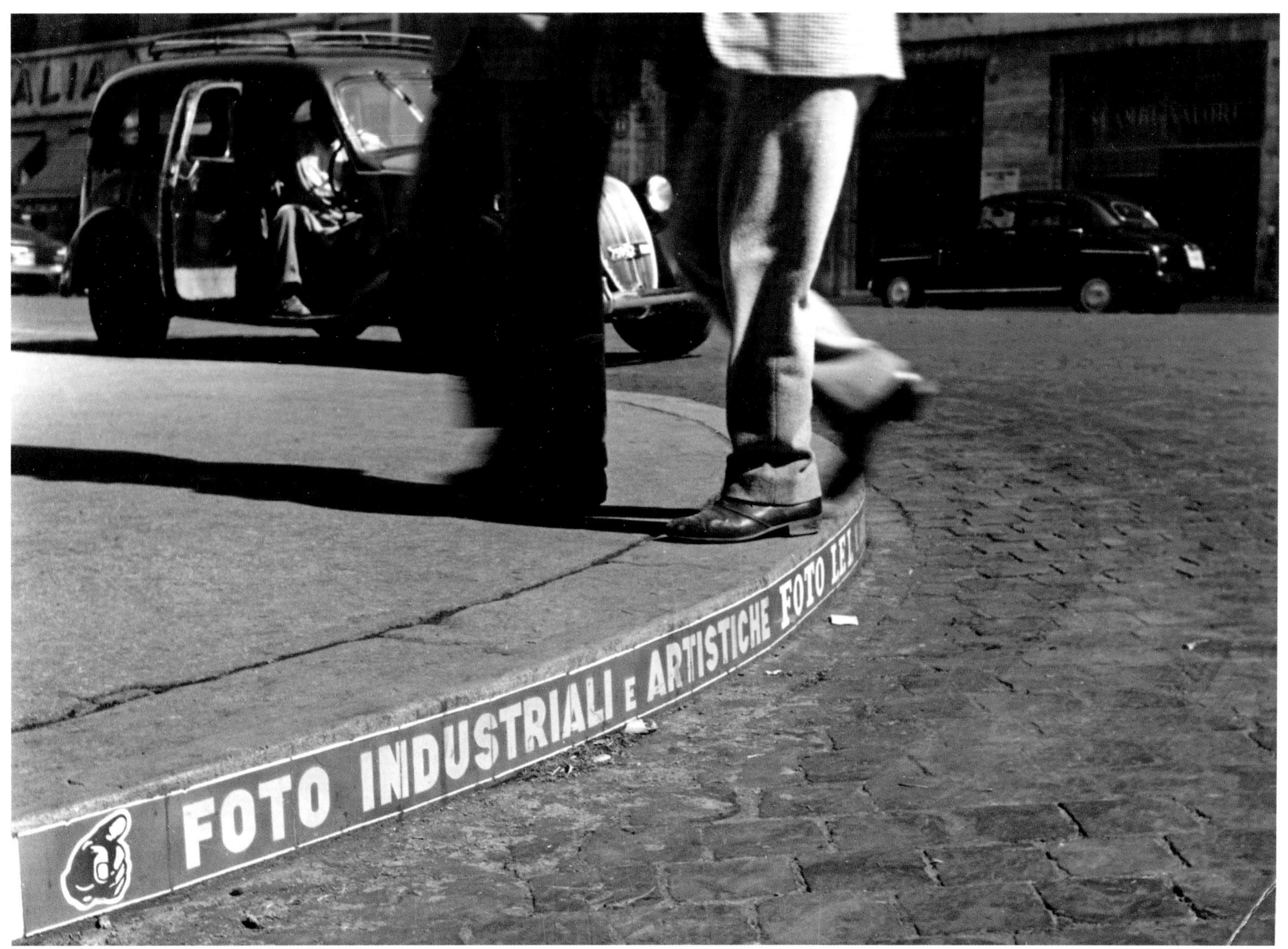

166. Monica Pidgeon
Spanish Steps,
Piazza di Spagna, 1961

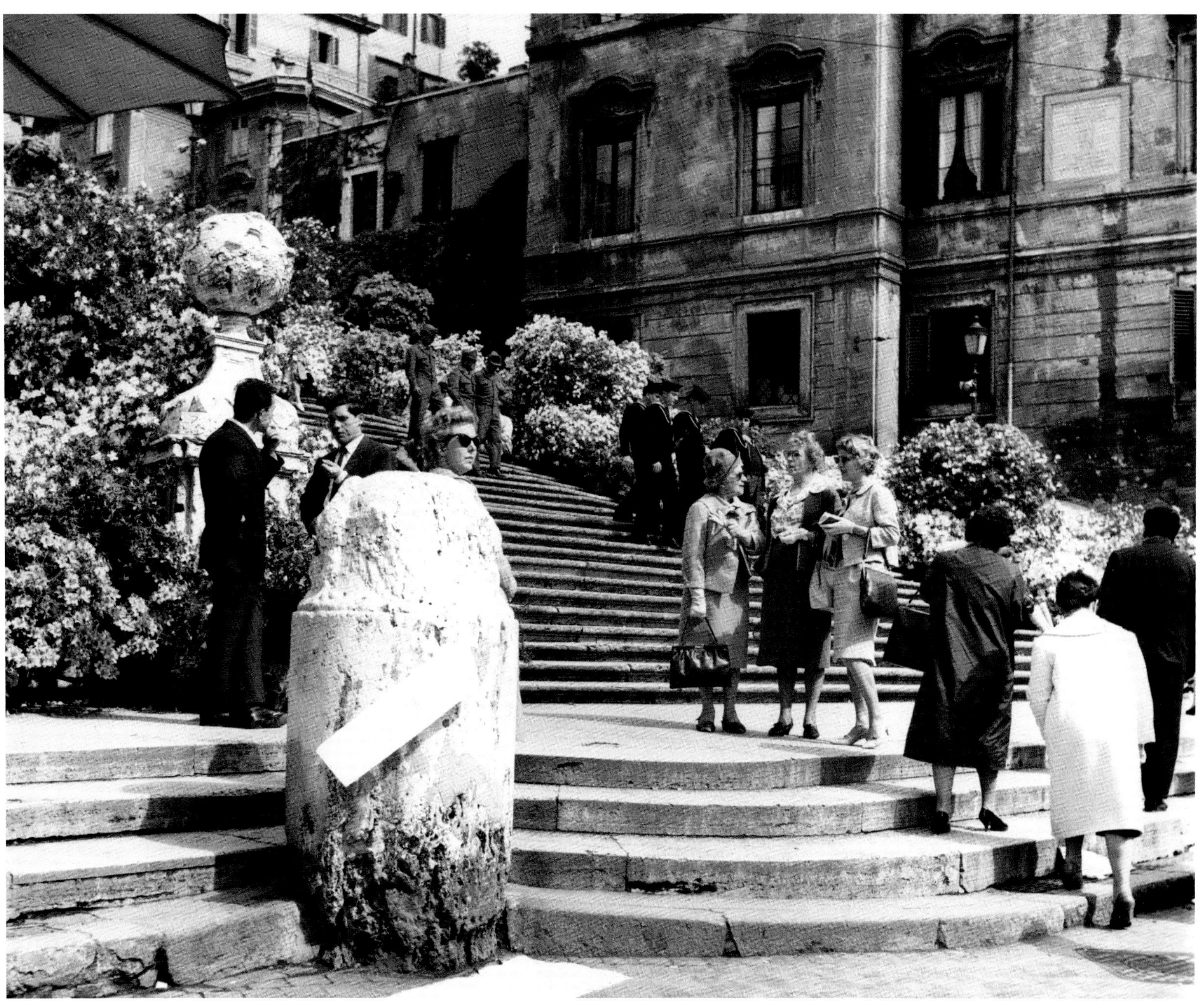

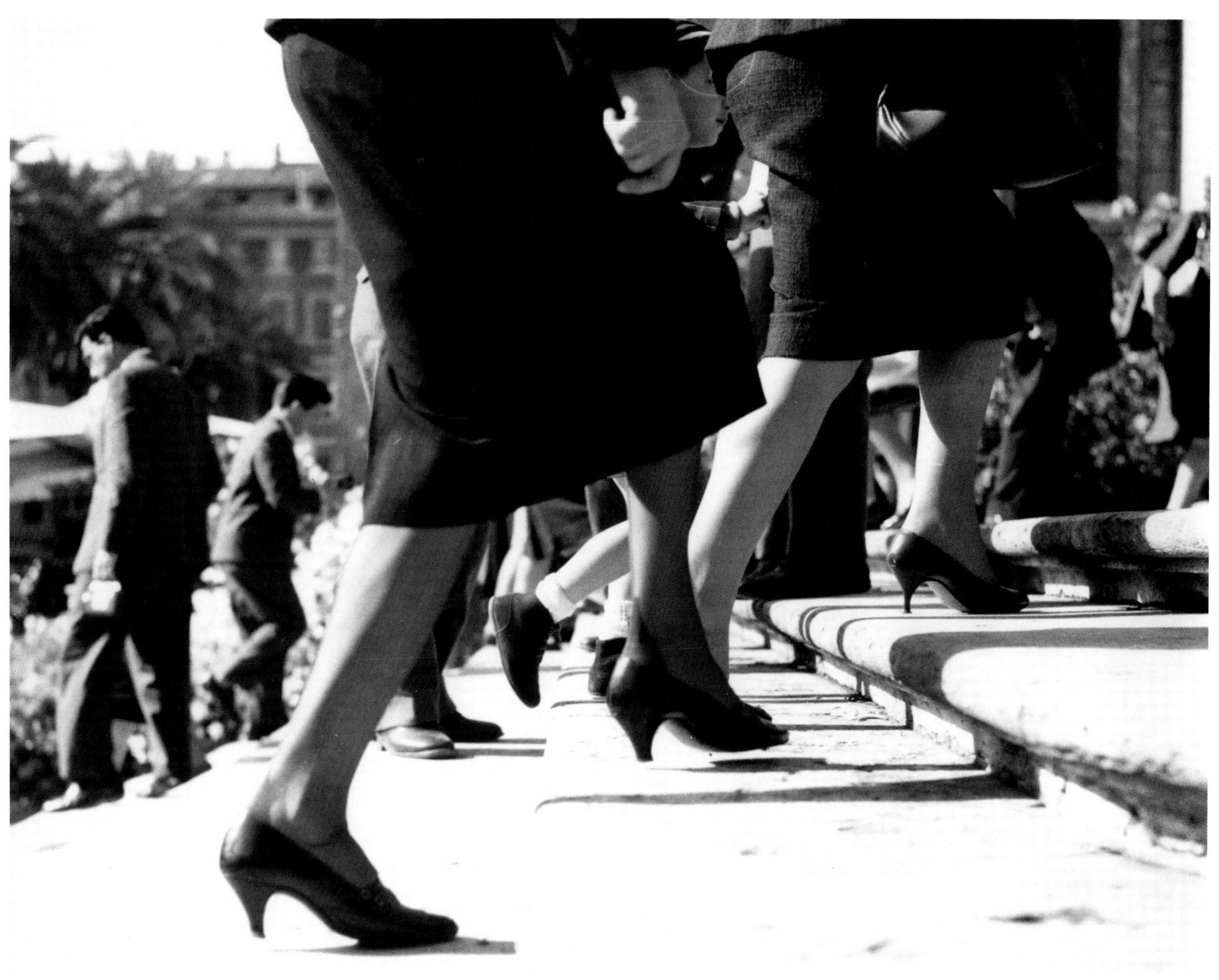

167. Monica Pidgeon
Spanish Steps,
Piazza di Spagna, 1961

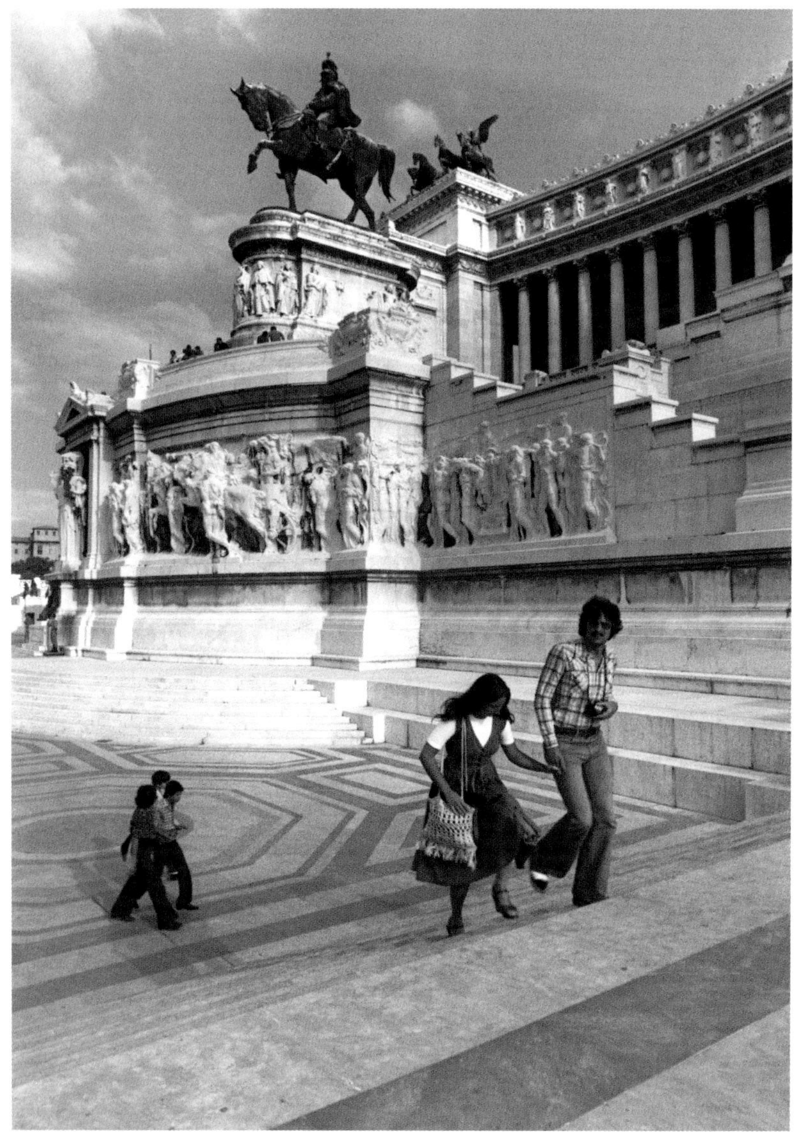

168. Tim Benton
Monument to Vittorio Emanuele II,
or 'Vittoriano', 1976

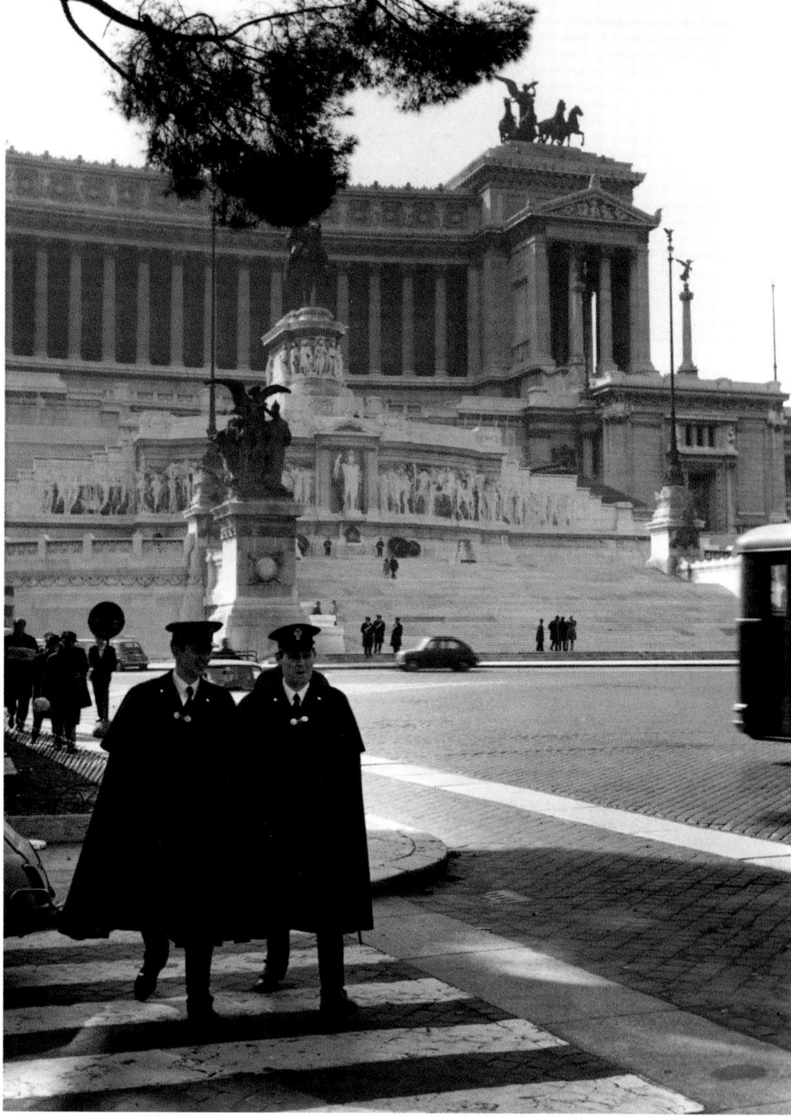

169. Edwin Smith
Piazza Venezia and the Monument
to Vittorio Emanuele II, 1970

170. Unknown photographer
Monument to Vittorio Emanuele II,
1958

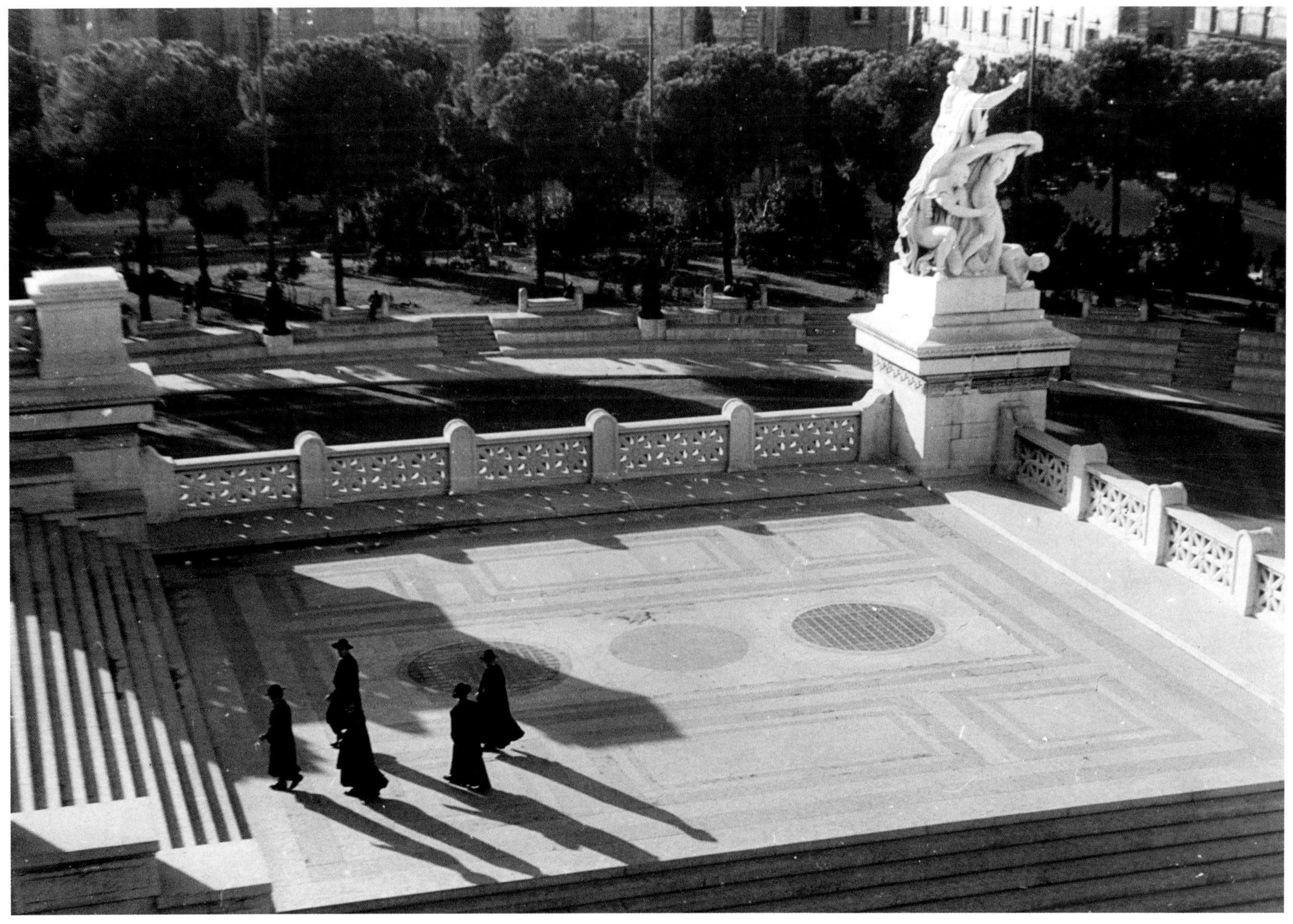

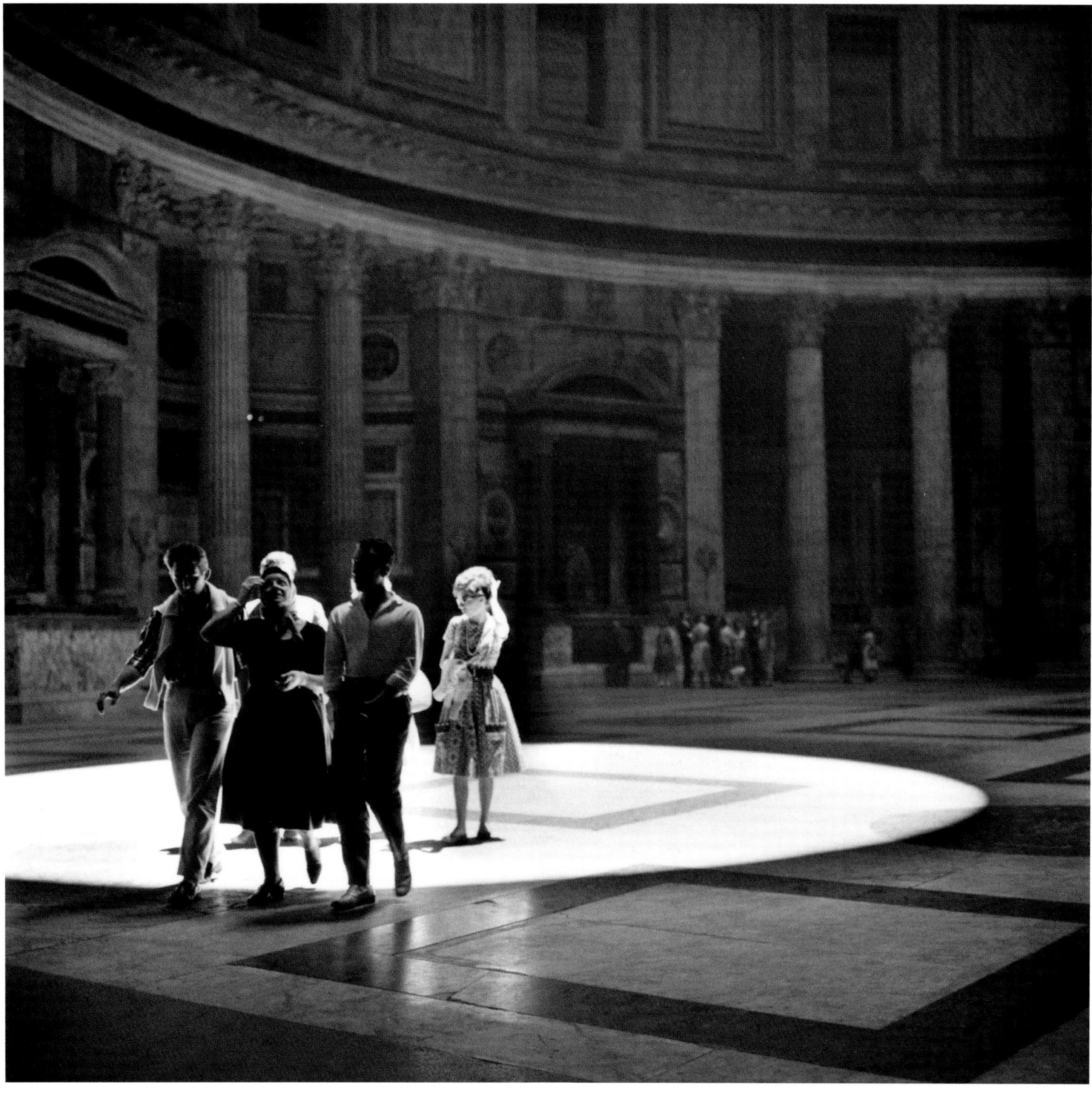

171. John Donat
Pantheon, 1960

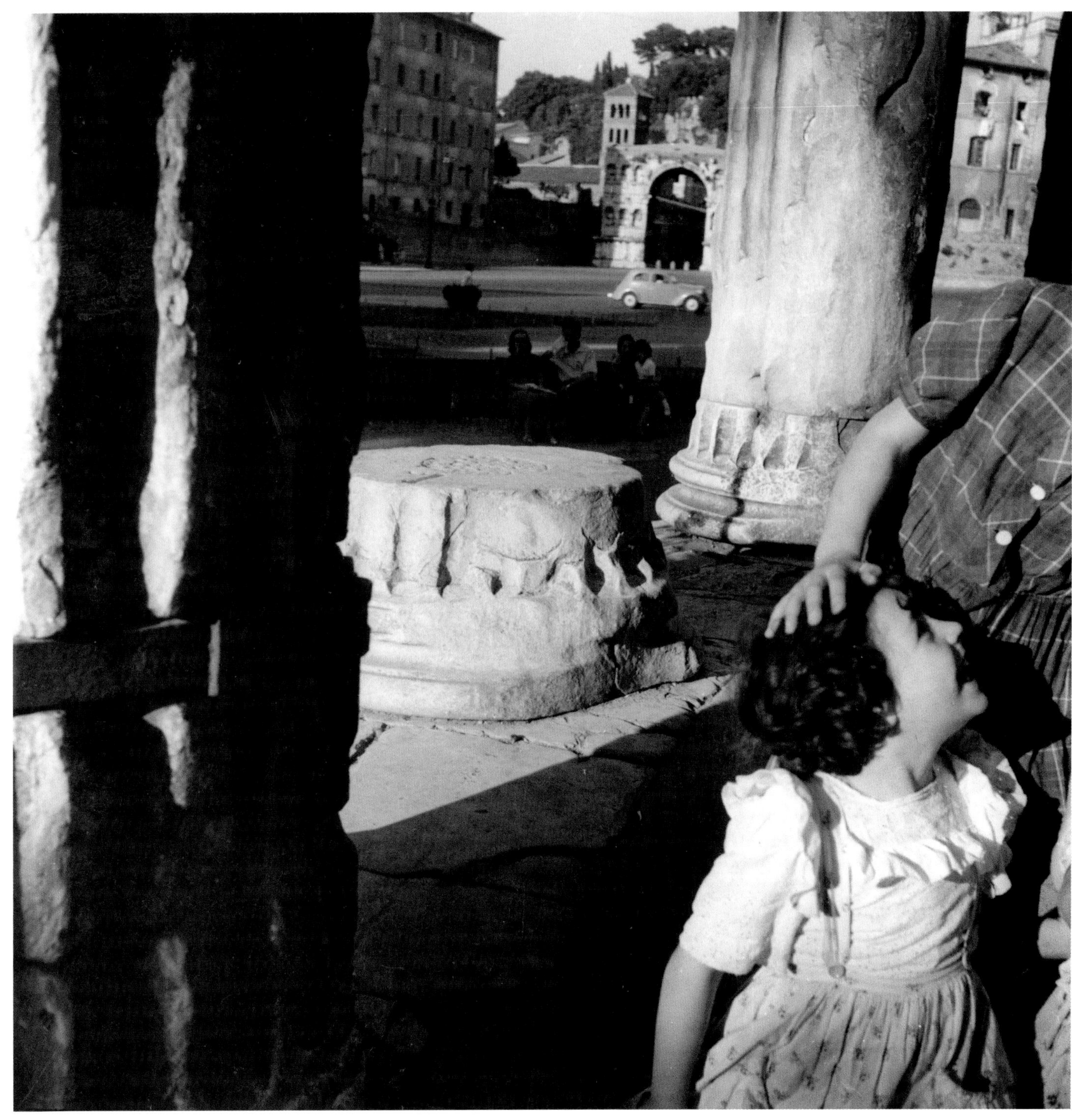

172. Ivy de Wolfe
*Columns of the Temple
of Hercules Victor
and Arch of Janus, 1962*

173. Studio Fotografico
Filippo Reale
Parco del Celio
and Flavian Amphitheatre
(Colosseum), 1930s

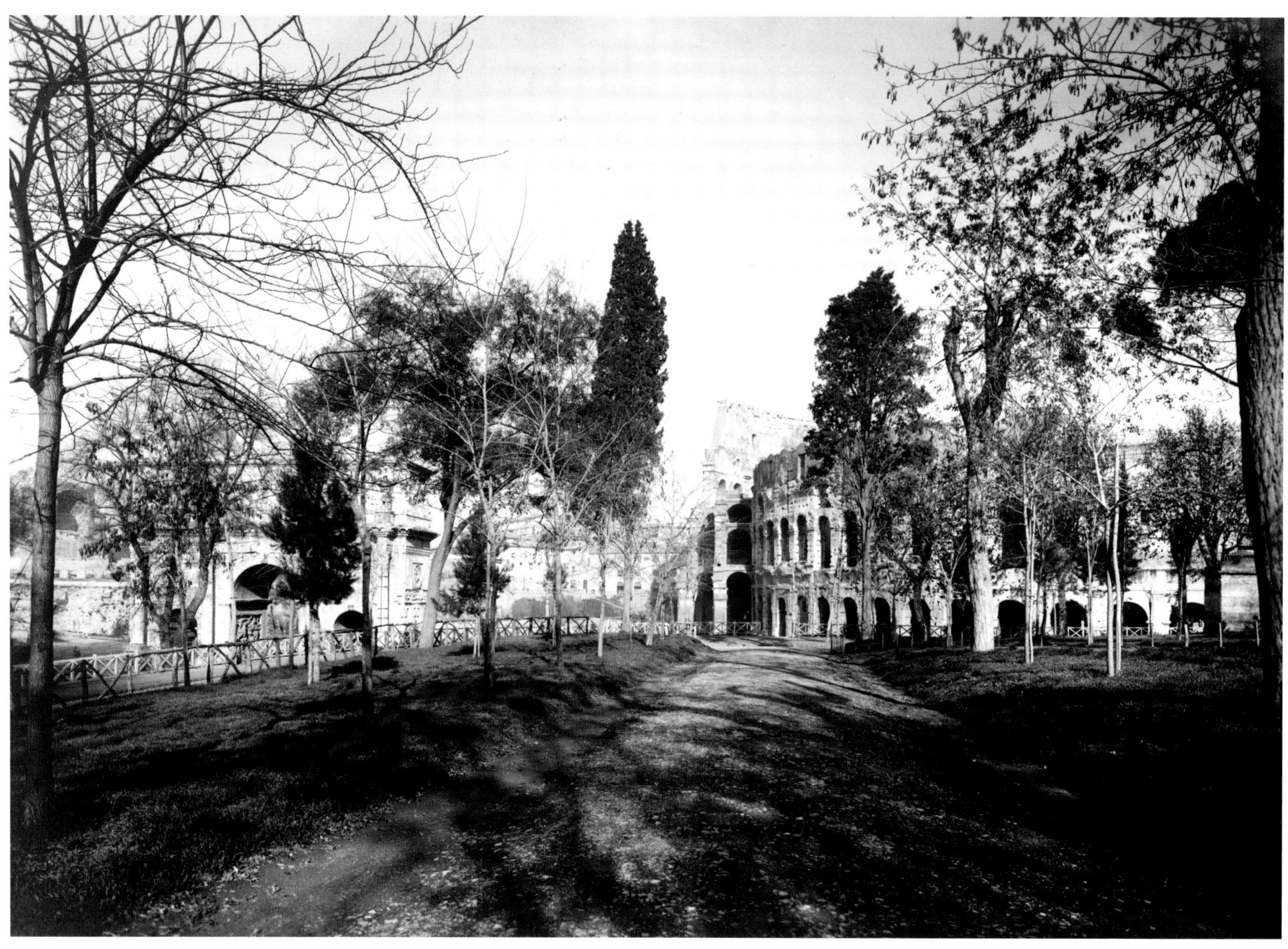

174. Monica Pidgeon
Flavian Amphitheatre, 1961

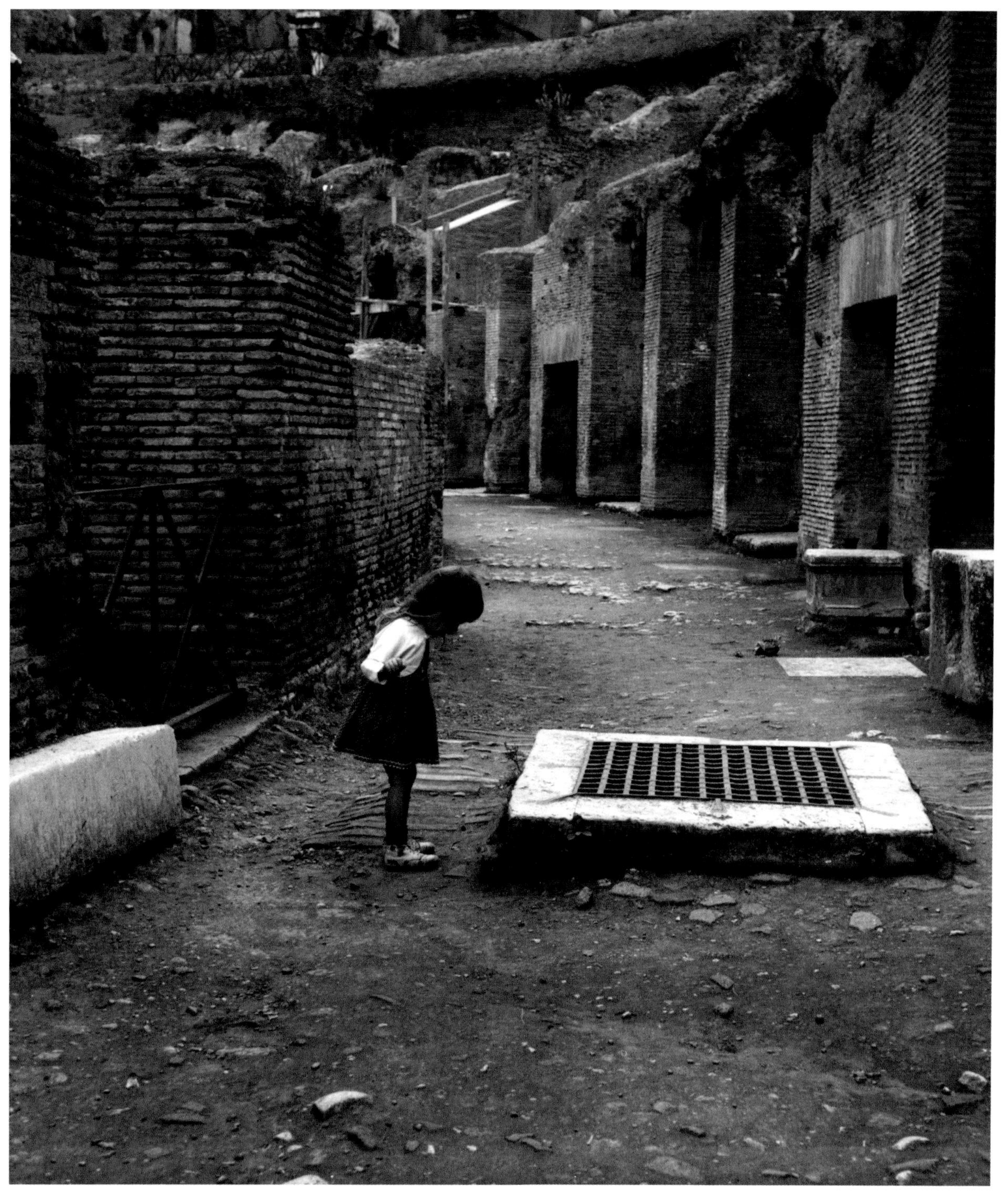

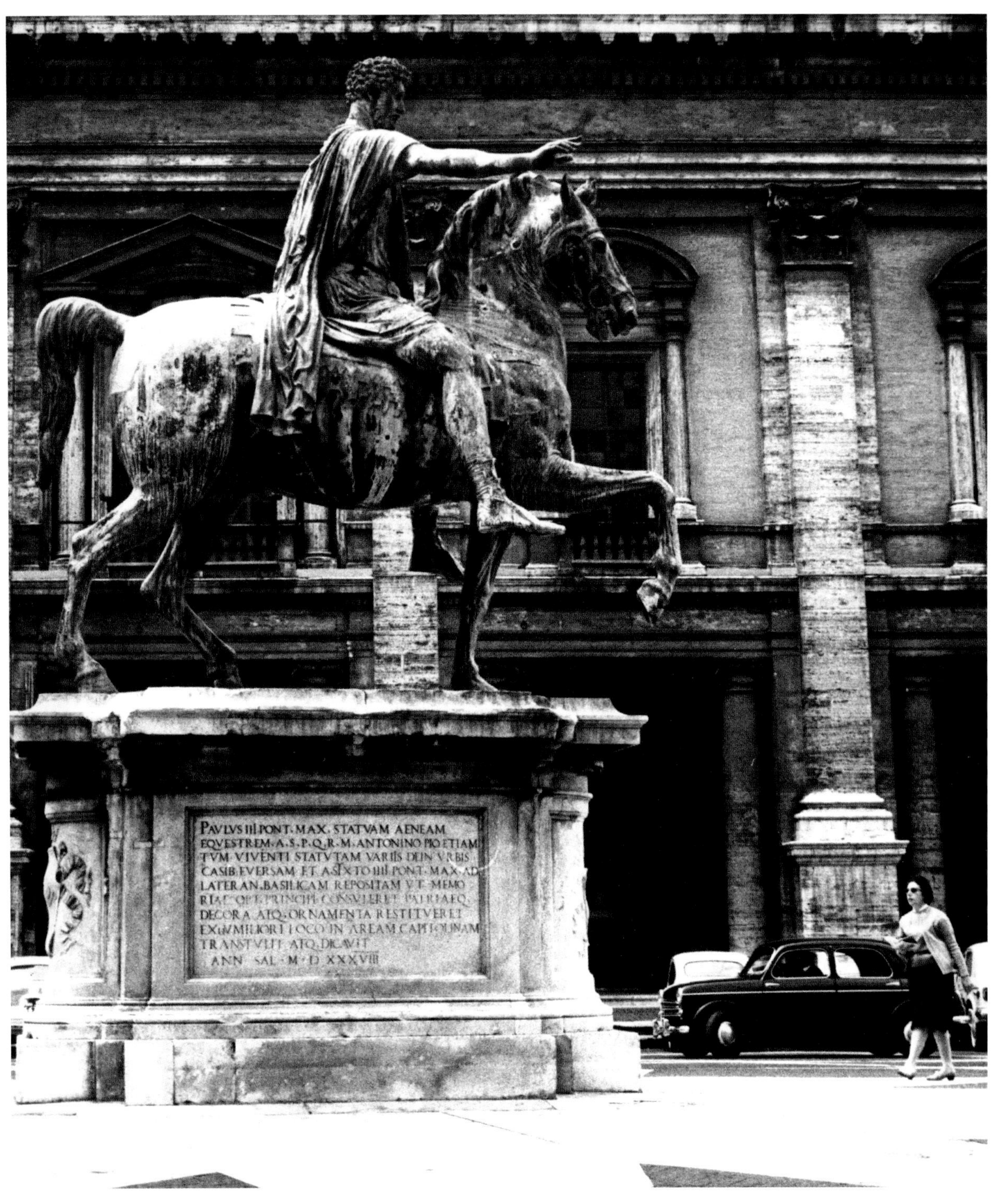

175. Monica Pidgeon
Statue of Marcus Aurelius,
Piazza del Campidoglio, 1961

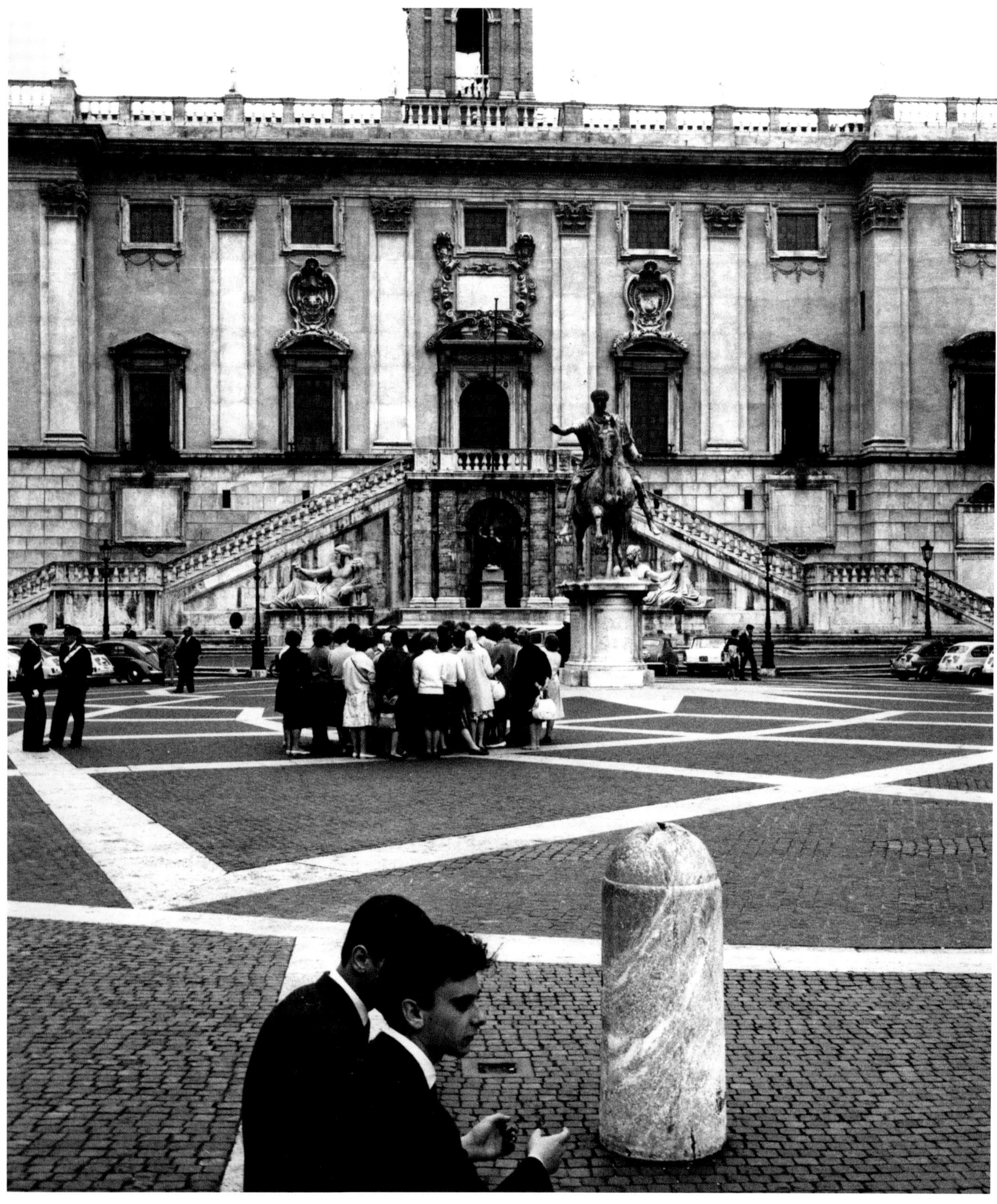

176. Monica Pidgeon
*Palazzo Senatorio, Piazza
del Campidoglio*, 1961

177. Ralph Deakin
Palazzo Senatorio,
Piazza del Campidoglio, 1930s

178. Edwin Smith
Palazzo Senatorio,
Piazza del Campidoglio, 1954

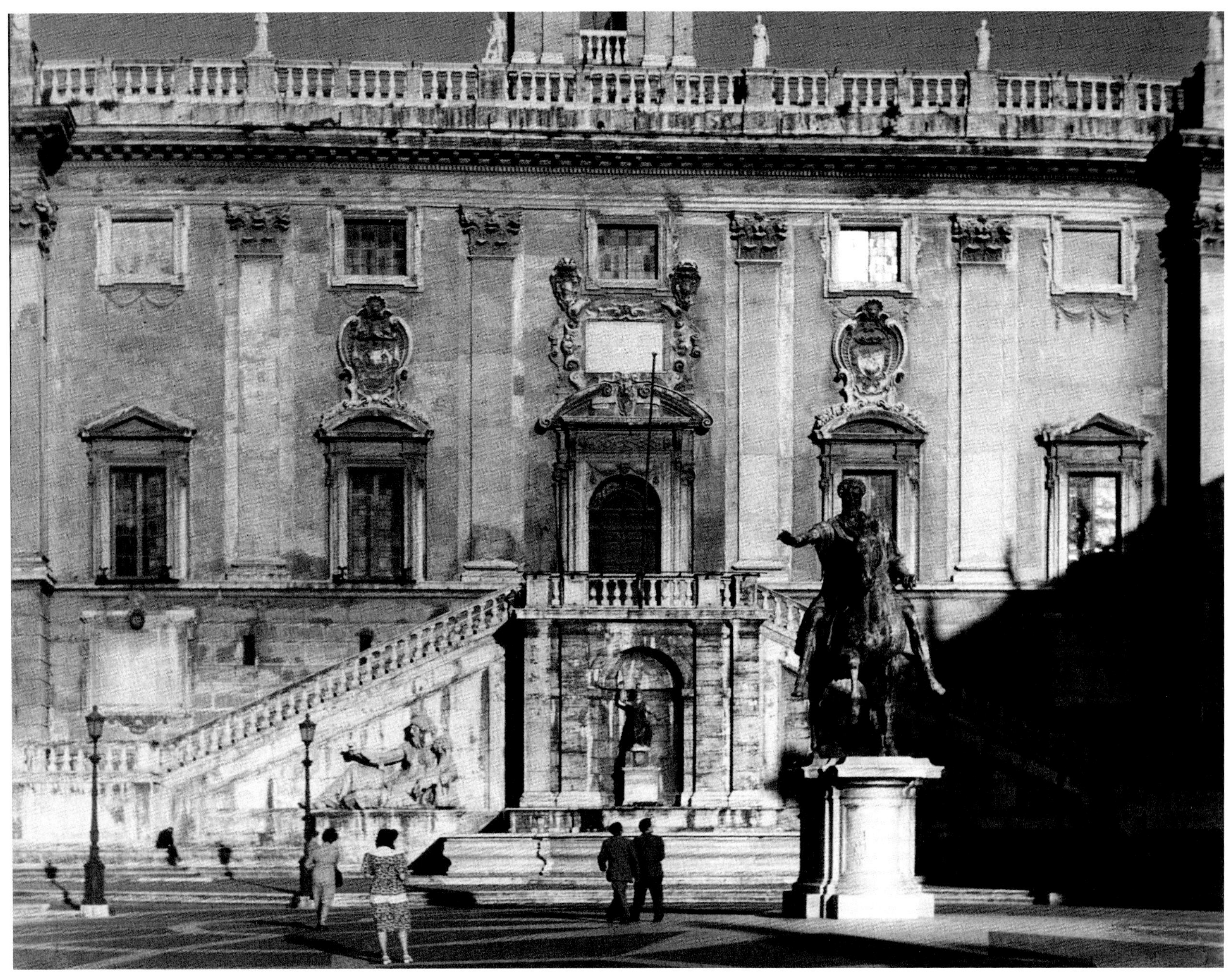

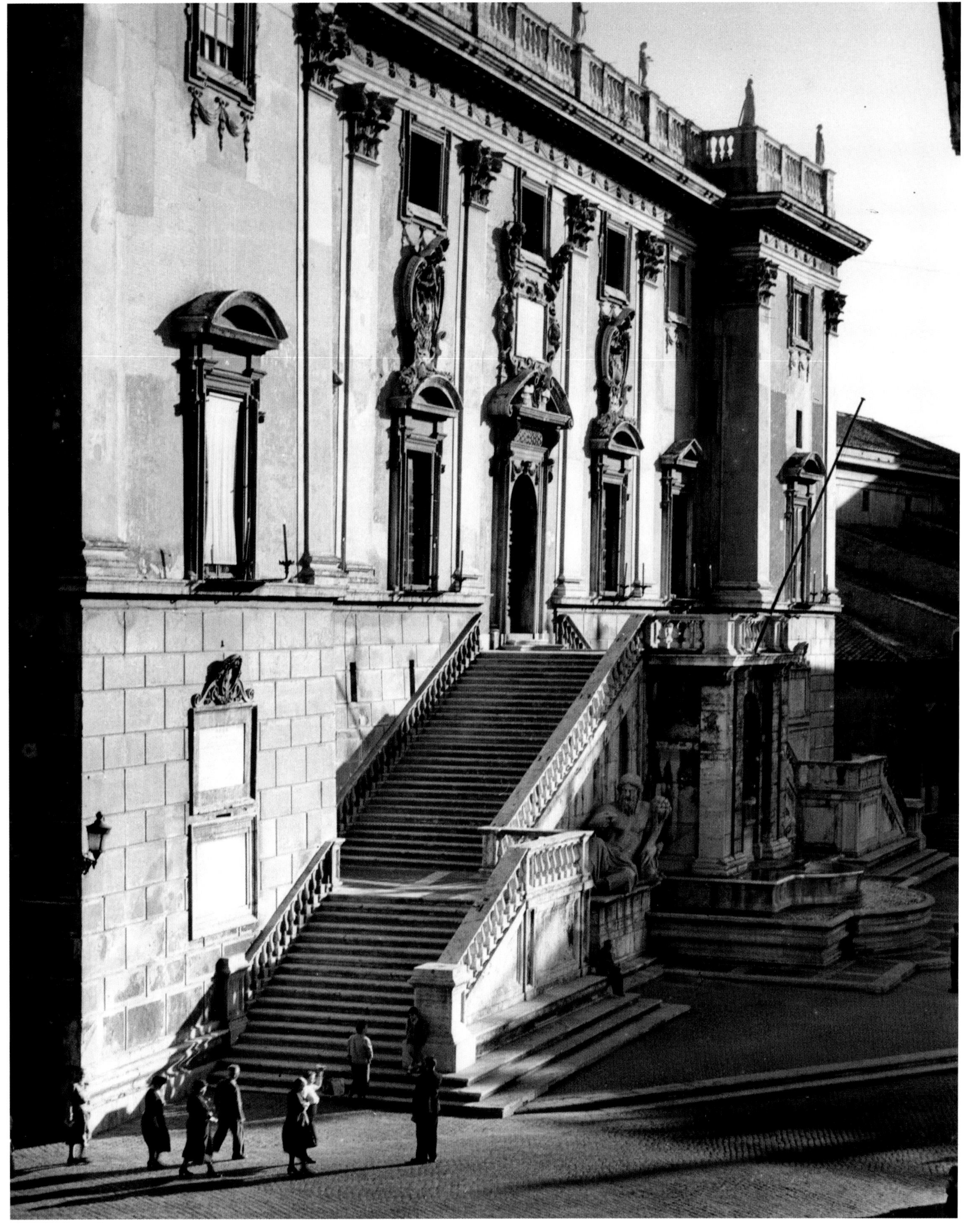

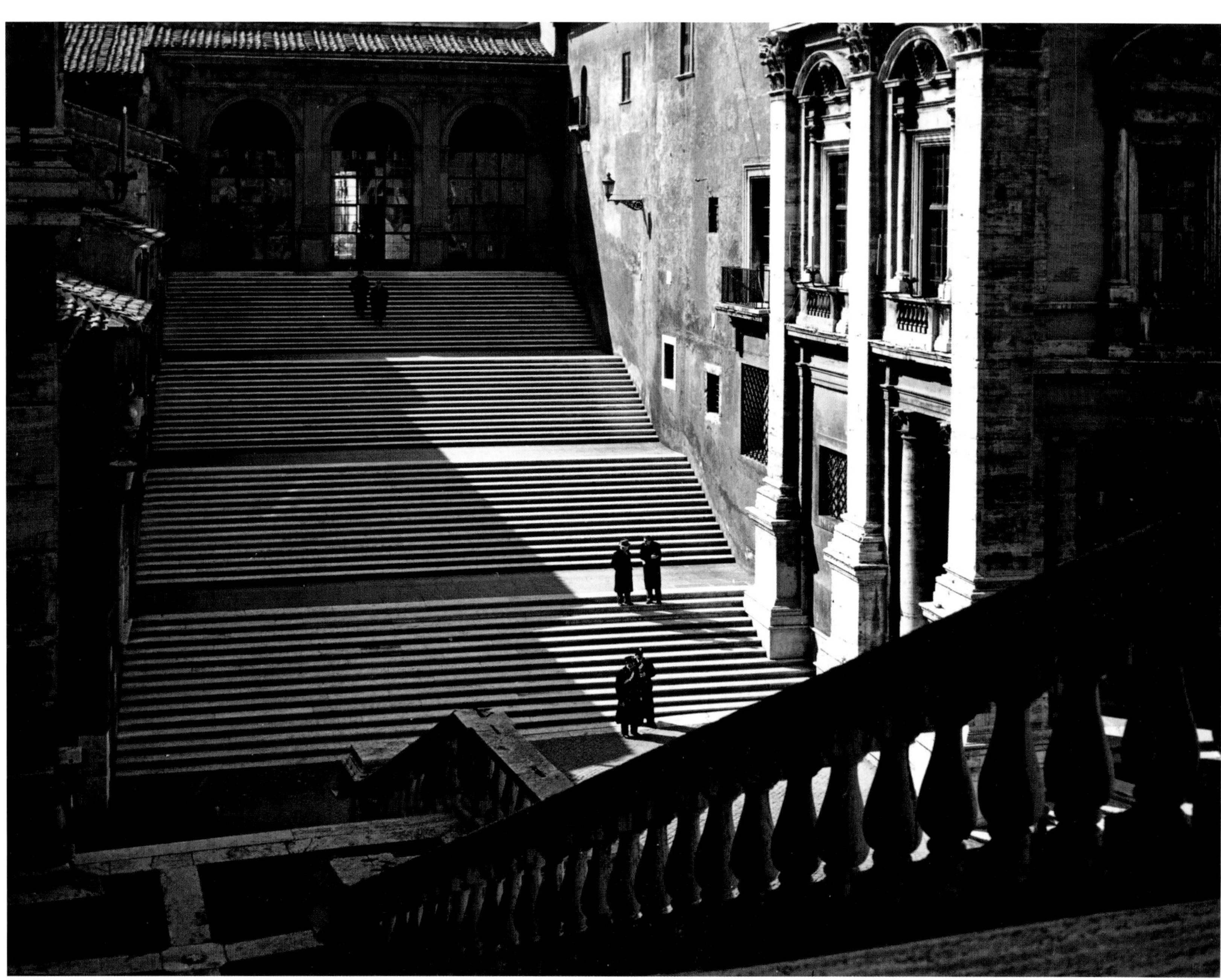

179. George Everard Kidder Smith
*Staircase adjacent to
the Palazzo dei Conservatori,
Piazza del Campidoglio, 1954*

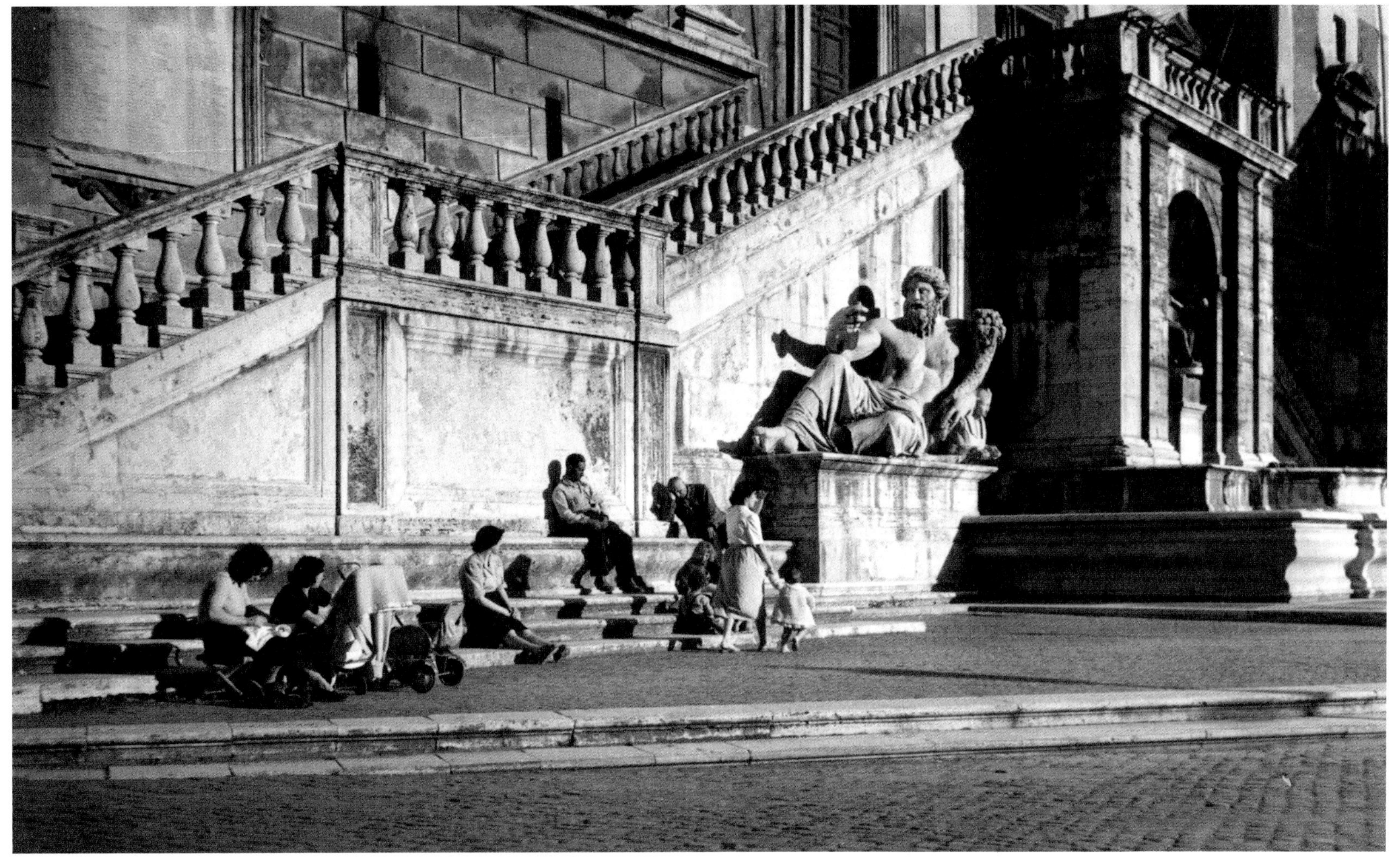

180. Ralph Deakin
Palazzo Senatorio,
*Piazza del Campidoglio,*1930s

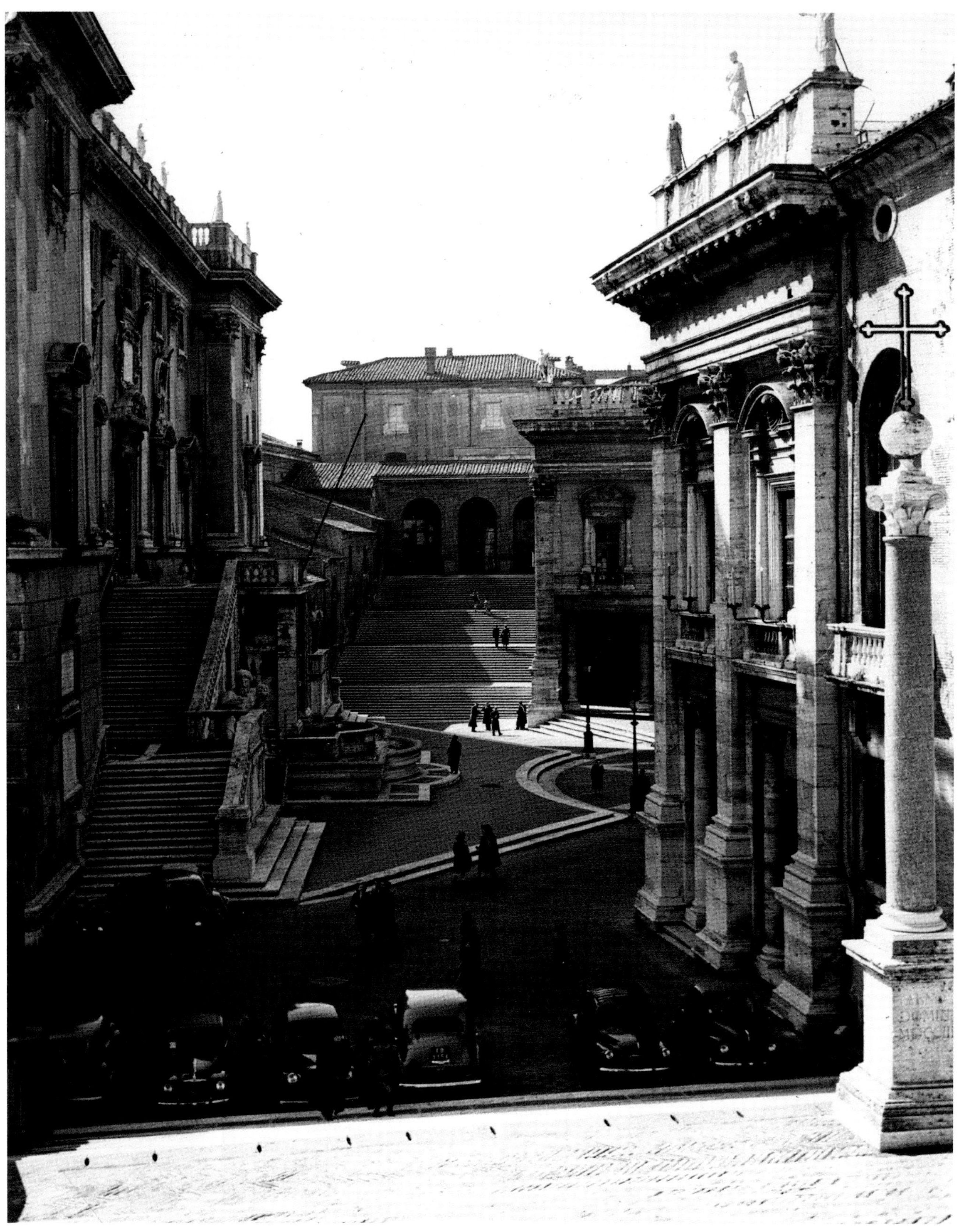

181. George Everard Kidder Smith
Piazza del Campidoglio, 1954

182. Monica Pidgeon
Saint Peter's Square, 1961

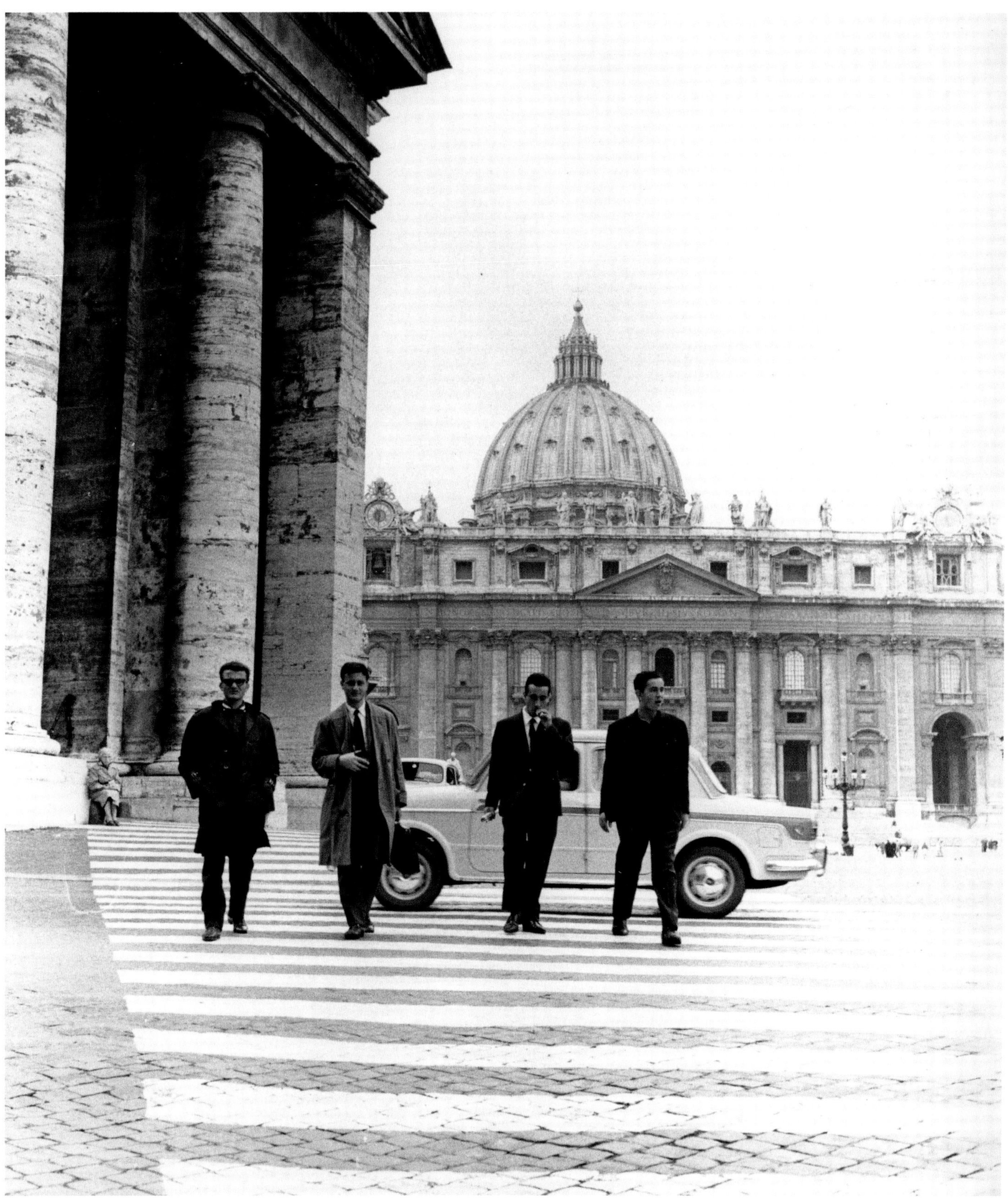

183. Edwin Smith
*Colonnade, Saint Peter's
Square*, 1960

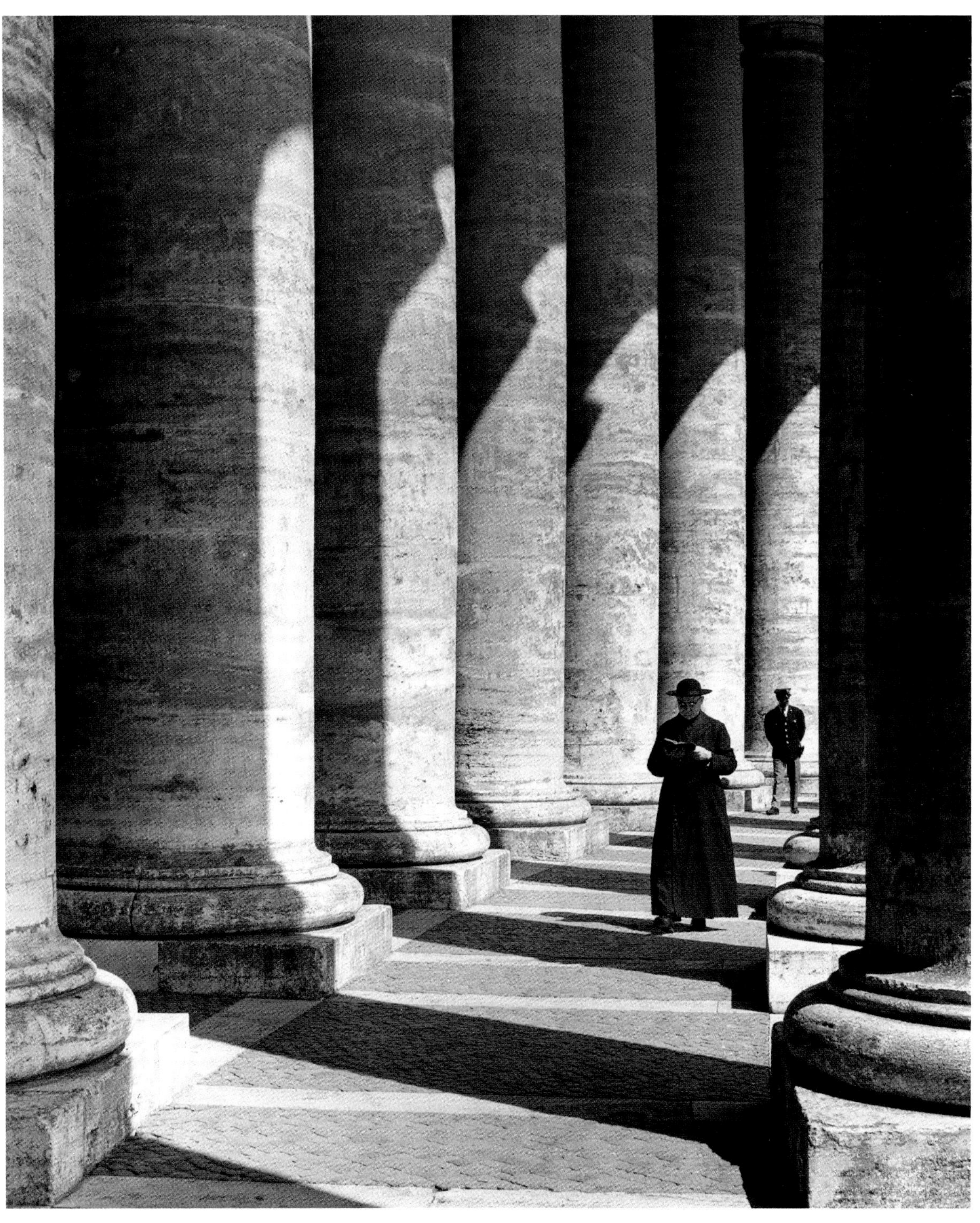

184. Monica Pidgeon
*Colonnade, Saint Peter's
Square*, 1961

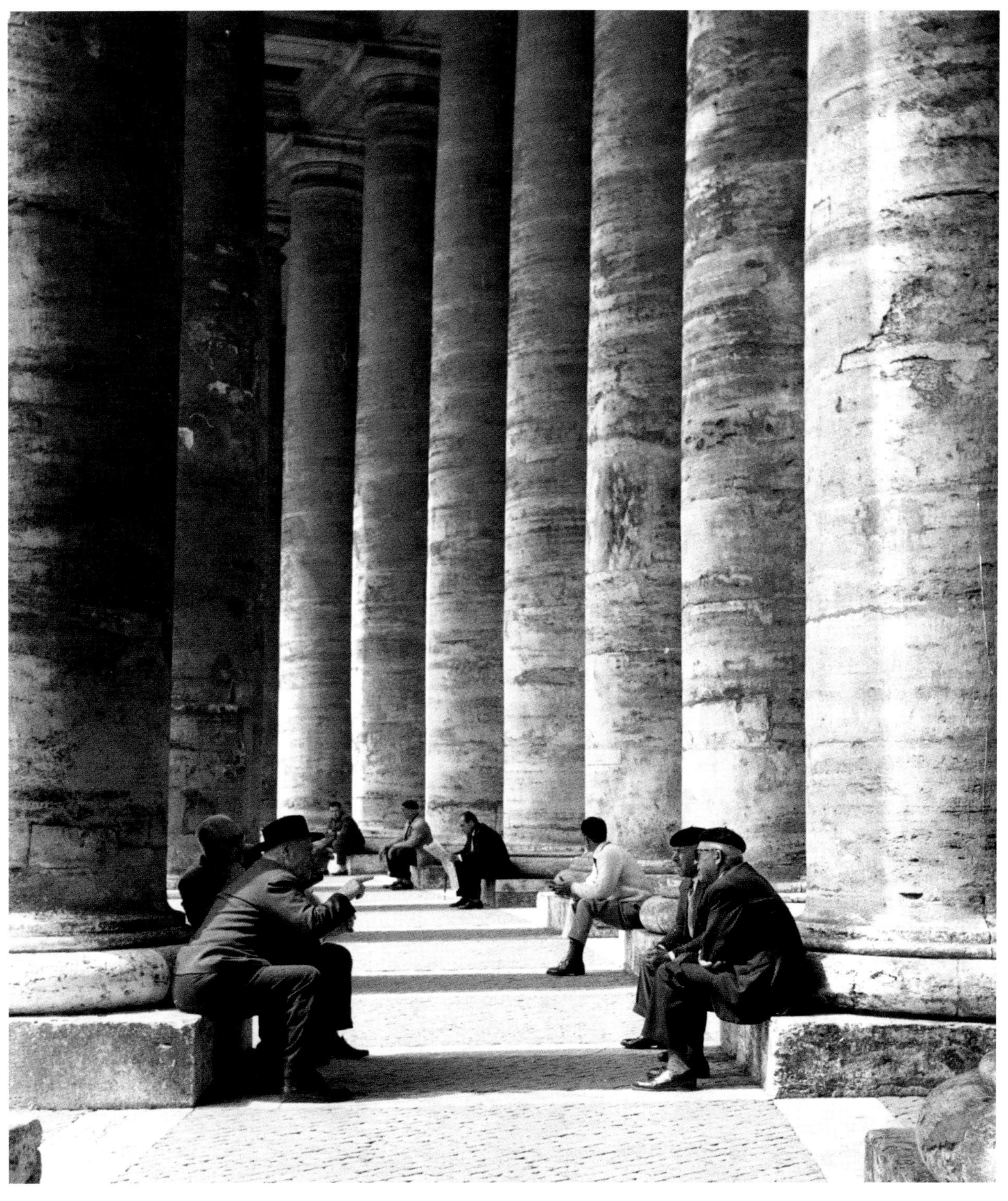

185. Monica Pidgeon
Food shop, 1961

186. Monica Pidgeon
Food shop, 1961

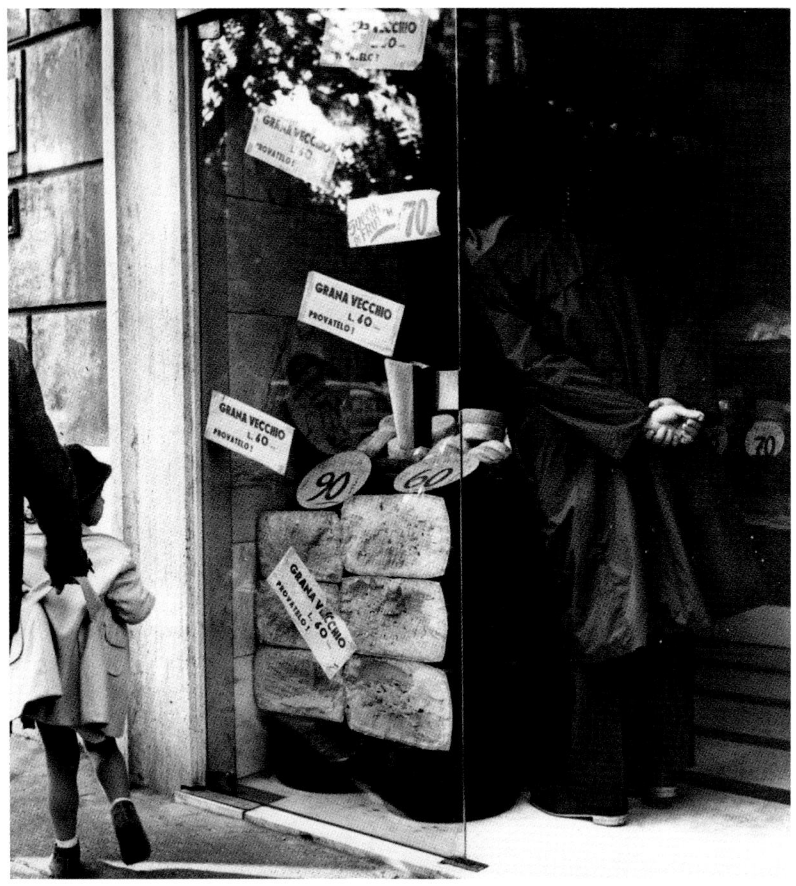
GRANA VECCHIO
L. 60
PROVATELO!
70
GRANA VECCHIO
L. 60
PROVATELO!
GRANA VECCHIO
L. 60
PROVATELO!
90
60
70
GRANA VECCHIO
L. 60
PROVATELO!

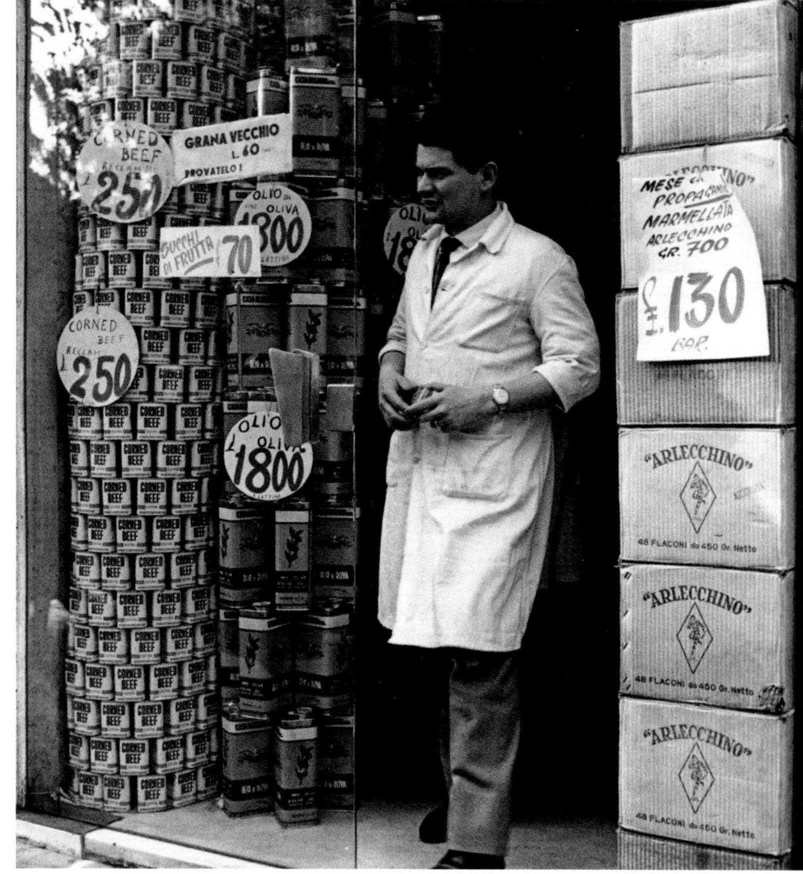
CORNED
BEEF
GRANA VECCHIO
L. 60
PROVATELO!
250
OLIVA
1800
70
CORNED
BEEF
250
OLIO
OLIVA
1800
MESE
PROPAGANDA
MARMELLATA
ARLECCHINO
GR. 700
L. 130
B.P.P.
"ARLECCHINO"
48 FLACONI da 450 Gr. Netto
"ARLECCHINO"
48 FLACONI da 450 Gr. Netto
"ARLECCHINO"
48 FLACONI da 450 Gr. Netto

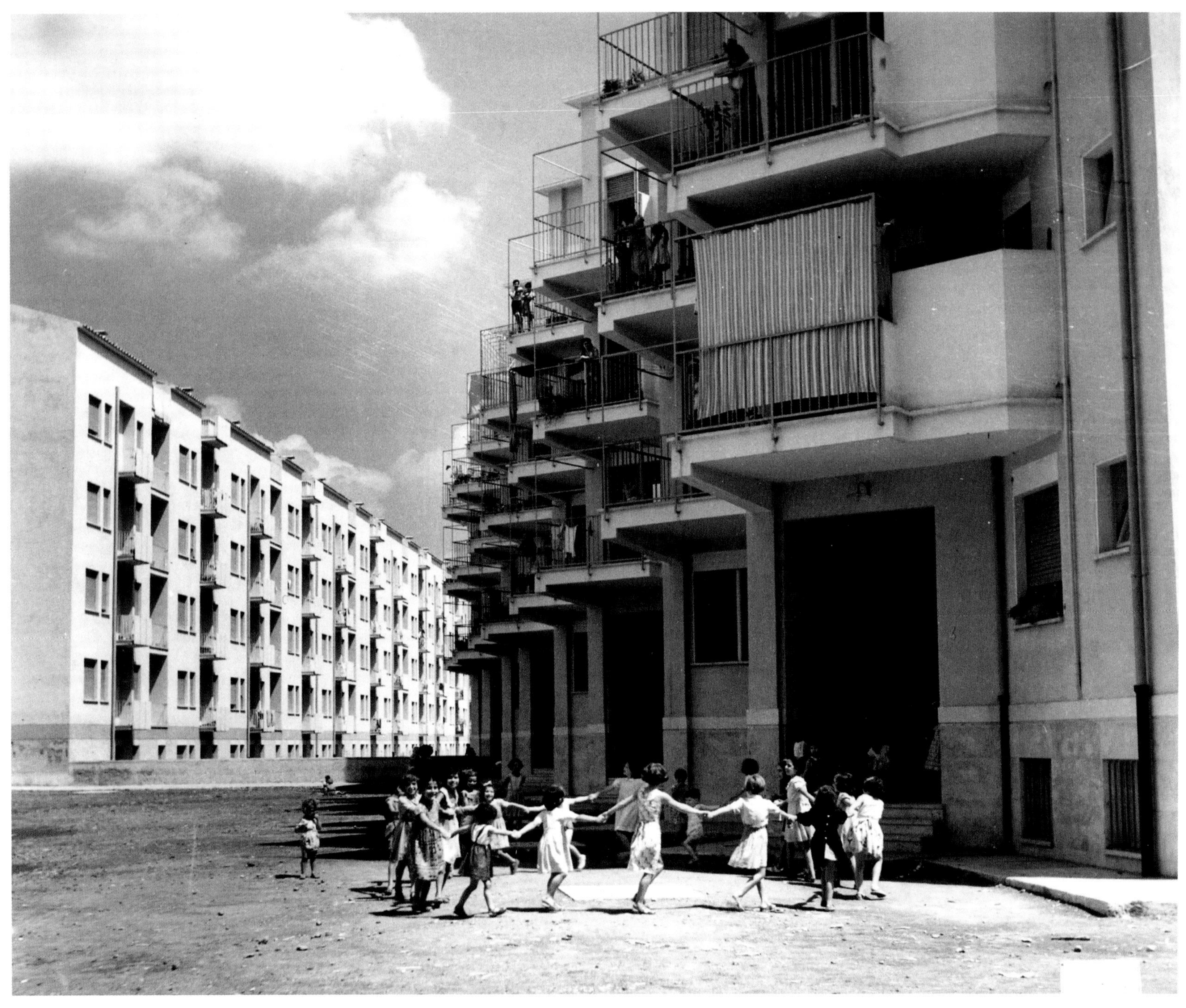

188. Monica Pidgeon
*Fontana della Barcaccia,
Piazza di Spagna*, 1961

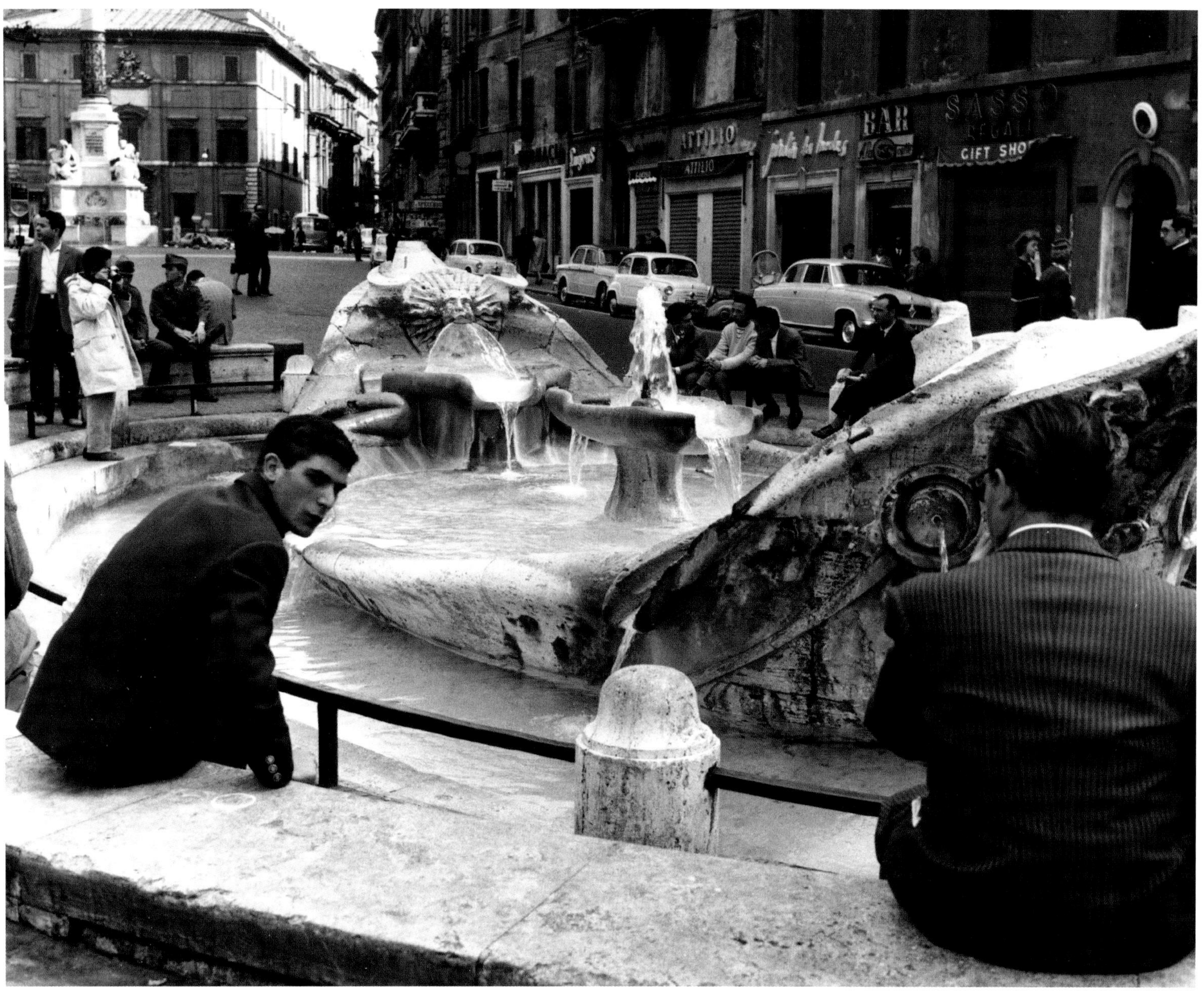

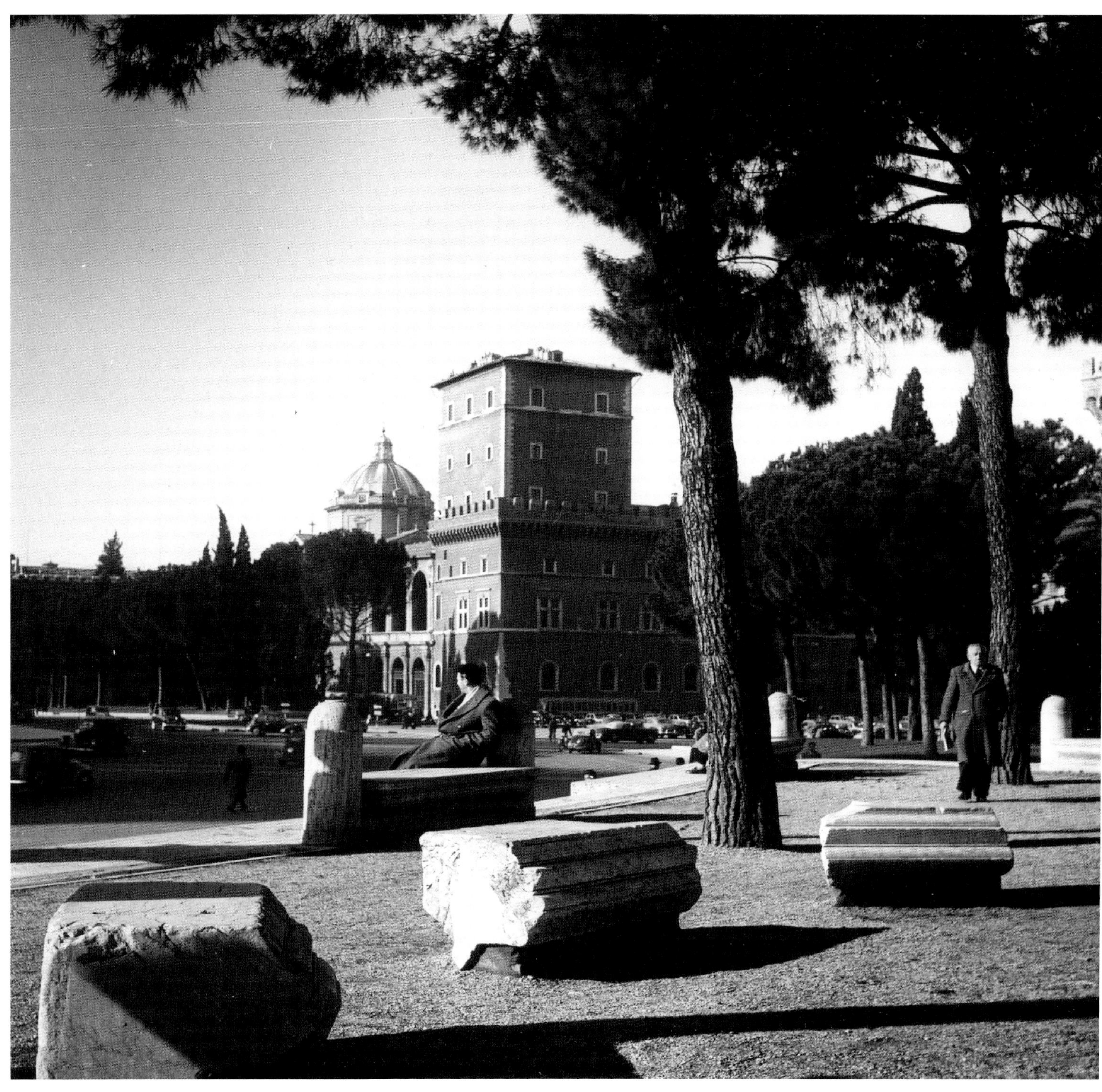

189. Marion Johnson
Piazza Venezia, 1953

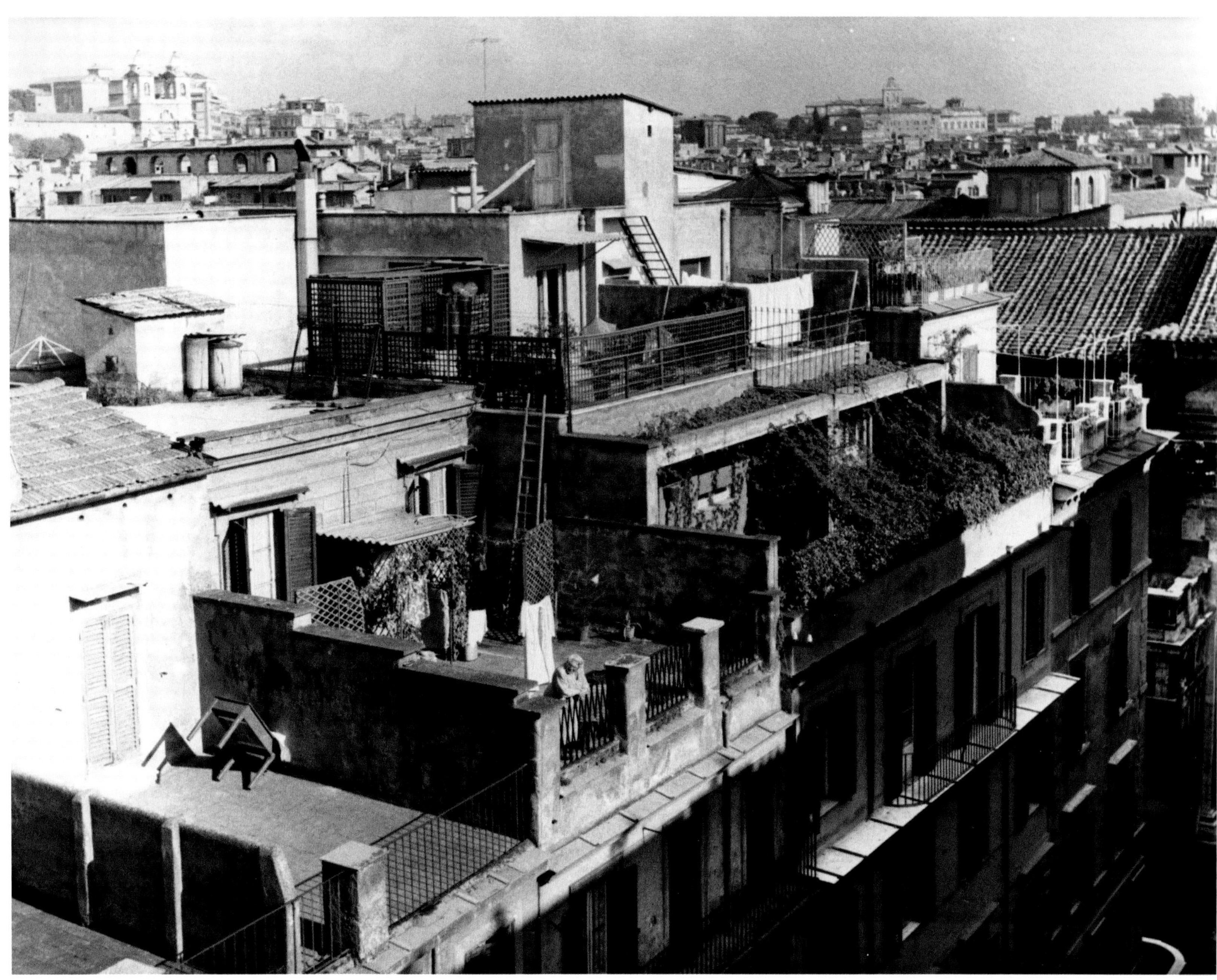

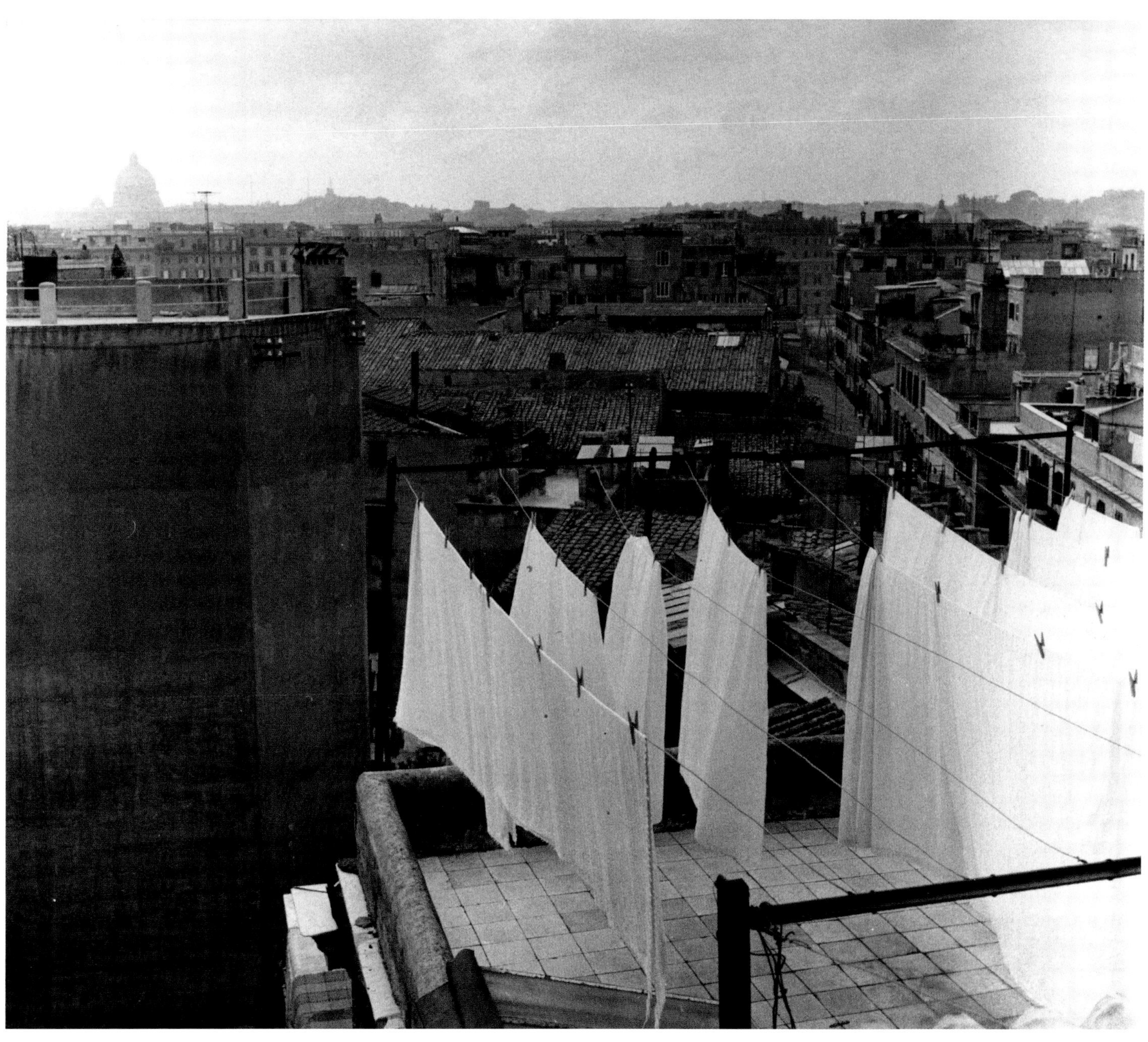

191. Monica Pidgeon
Roof terrace, 1961

192. Edwin Smith
Piazza di Sant'Ignazio, 1970

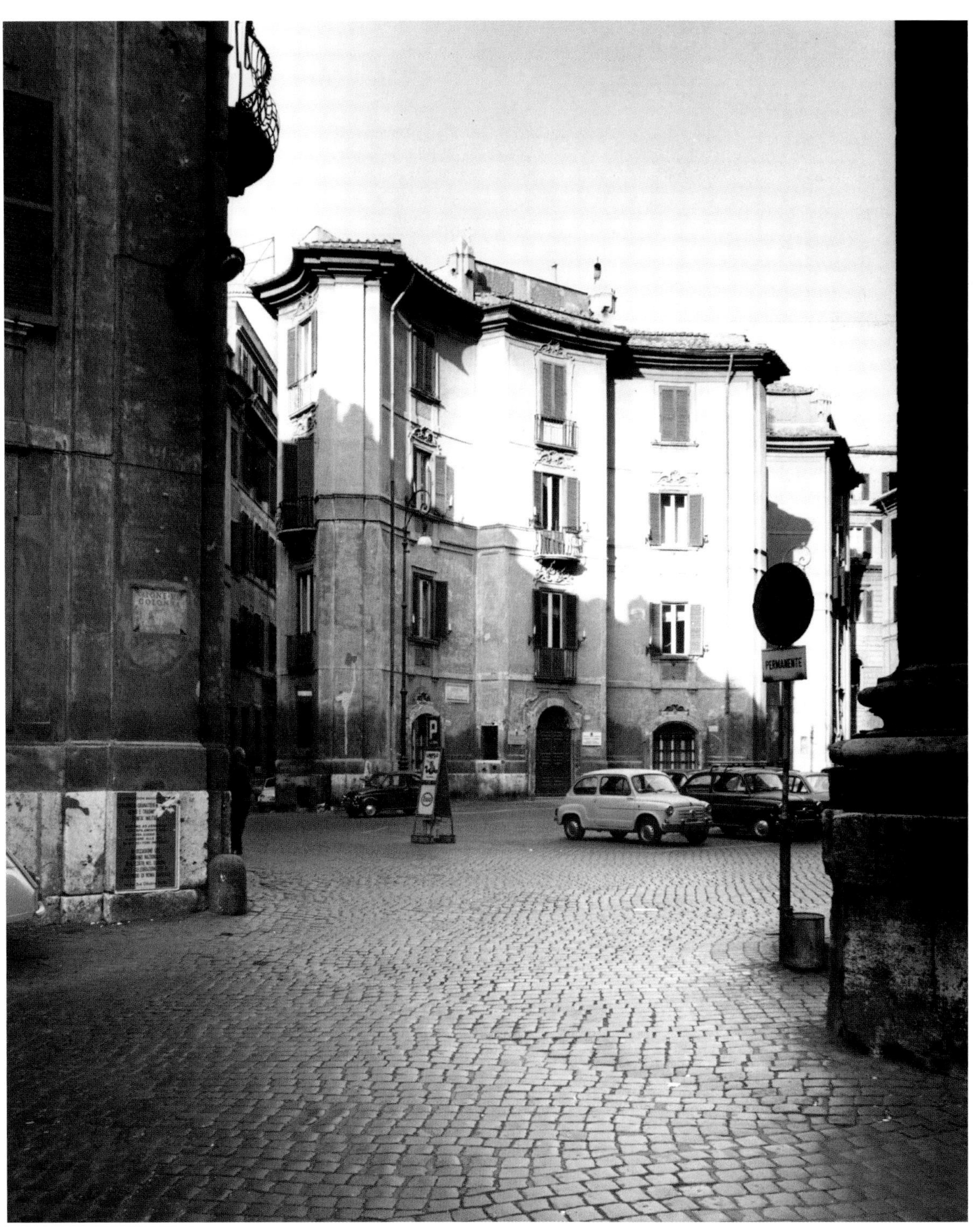

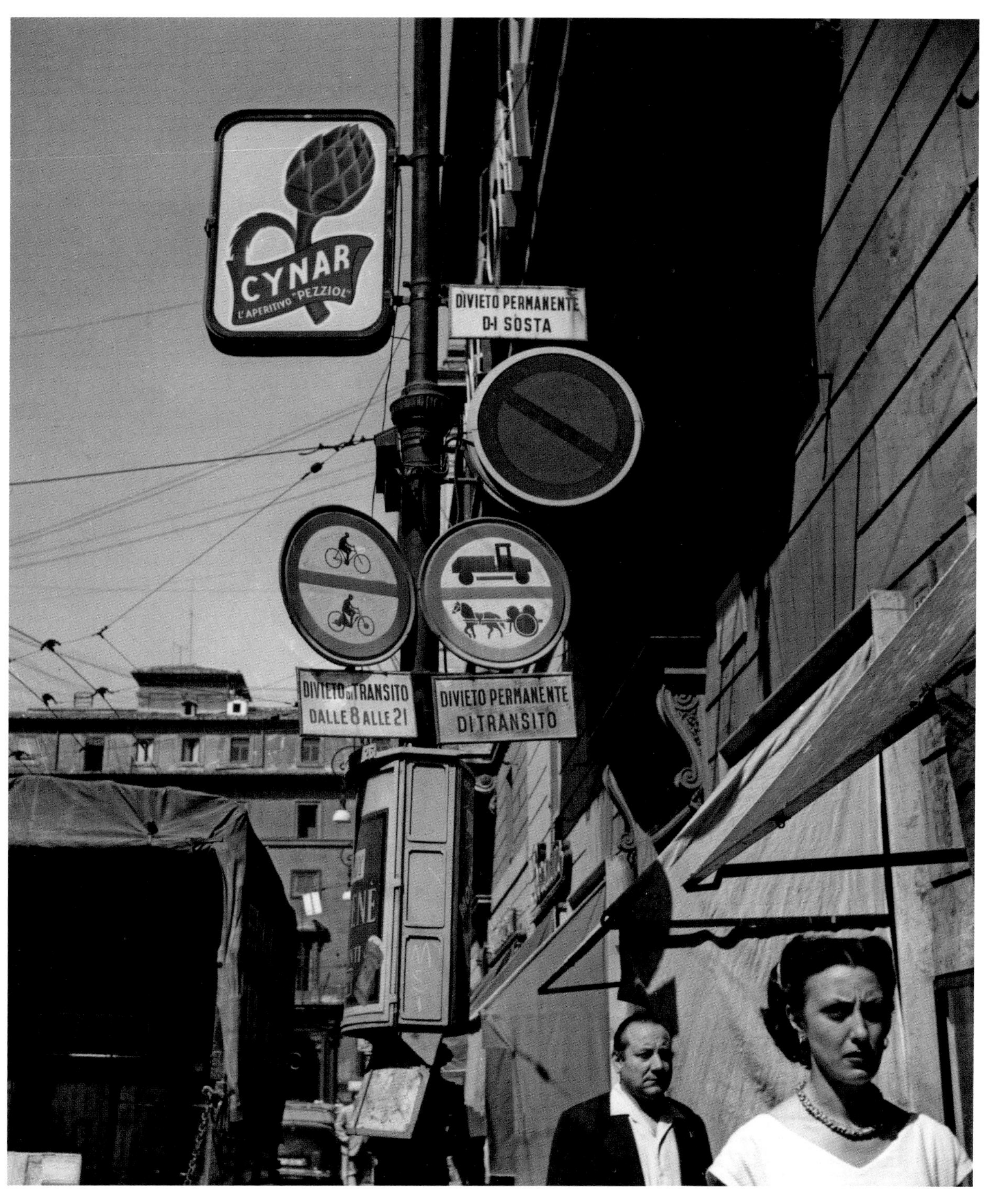

193. Ivy de Wolfe
Street and advertisement signs,
c. 1960

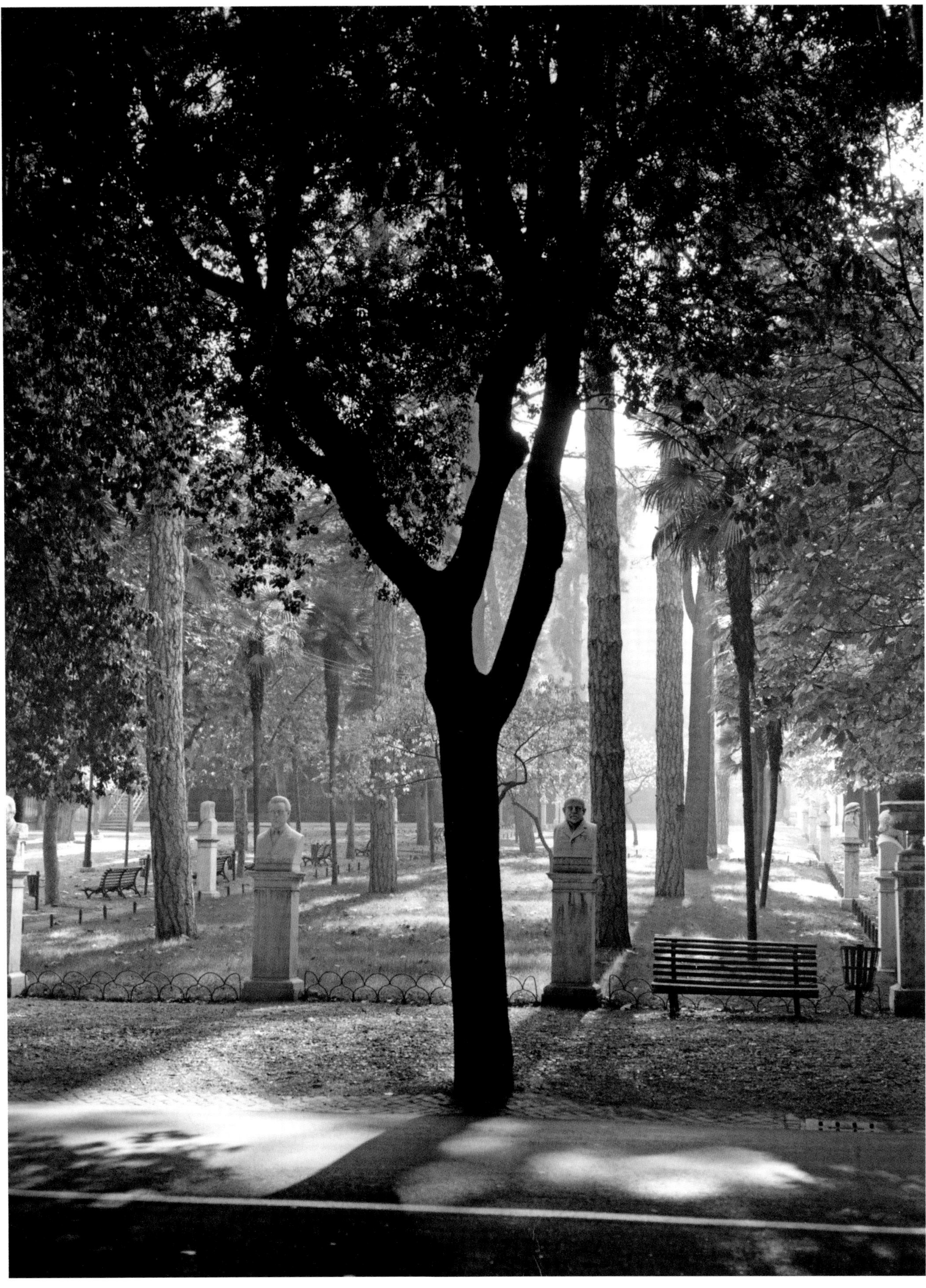

194. Edwin Smith
Pincio gardens, 1970

195. Edwin Smith
Pantheon, 1970

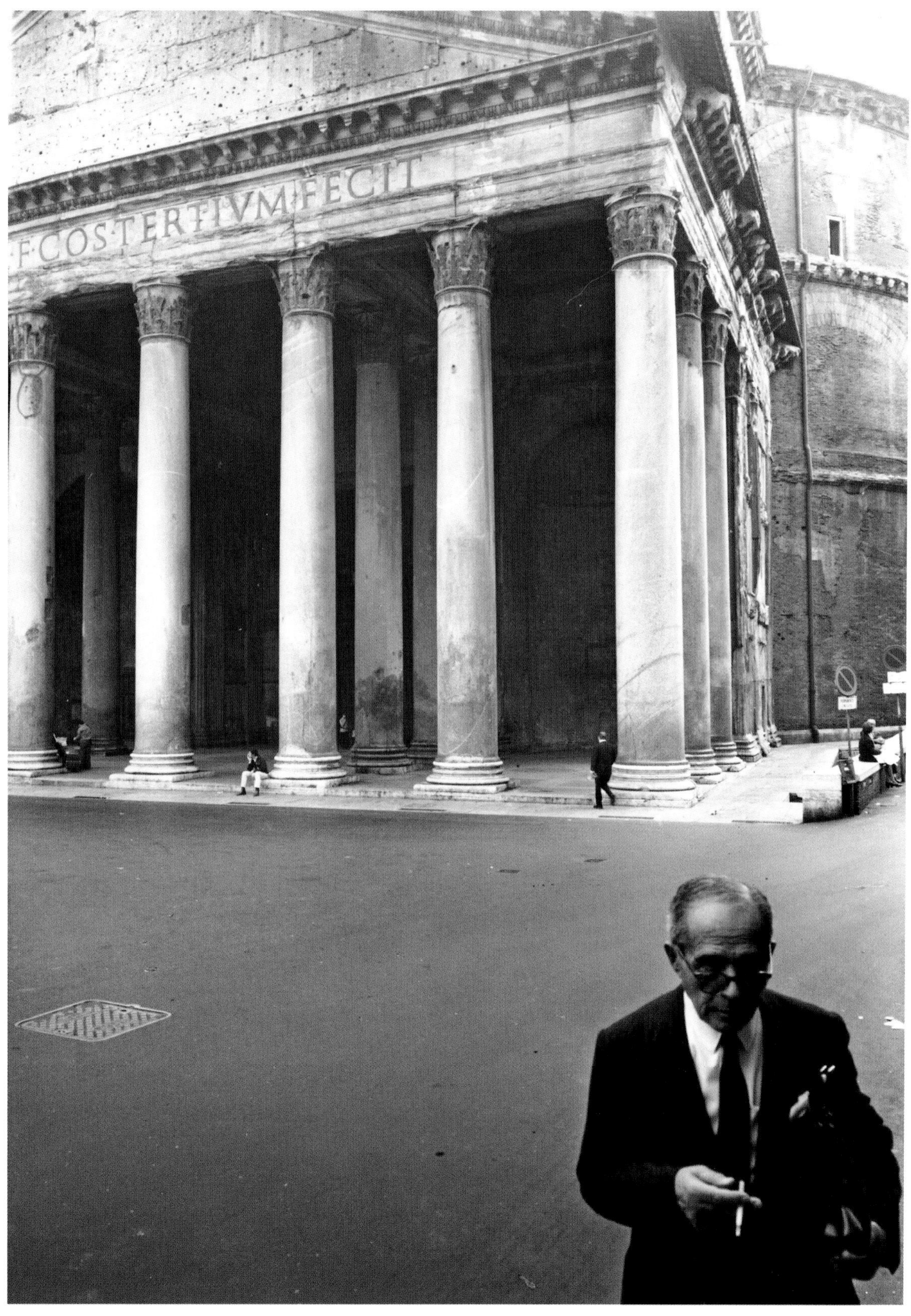

196. Ivy de Wolfe
Pavement plaque referring
to the city's water supply, 1960

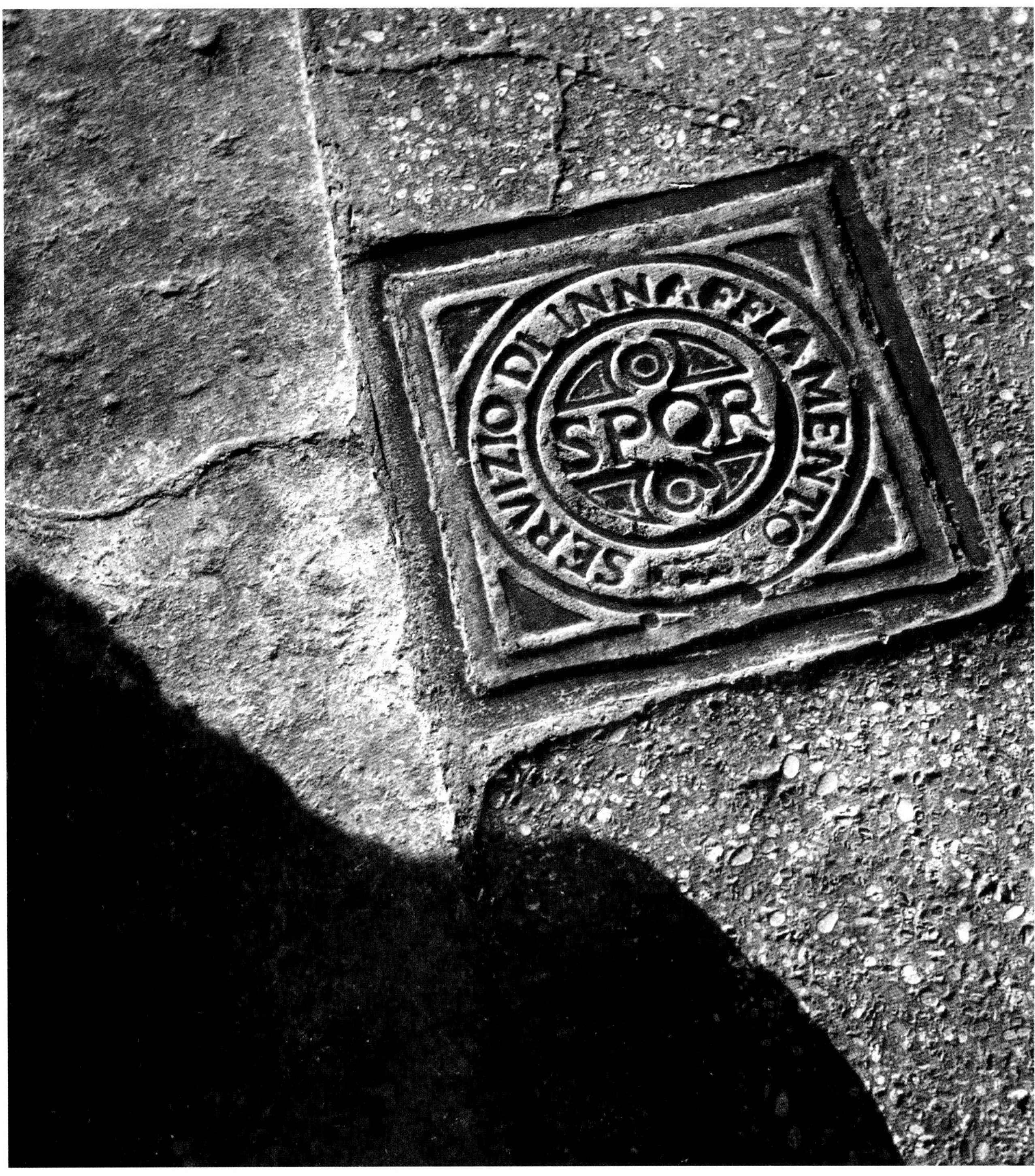

197. Ivy de Wolfe
Lungotevere, 1961

198. Ivy de Wolfe
Lungotevere, 1961

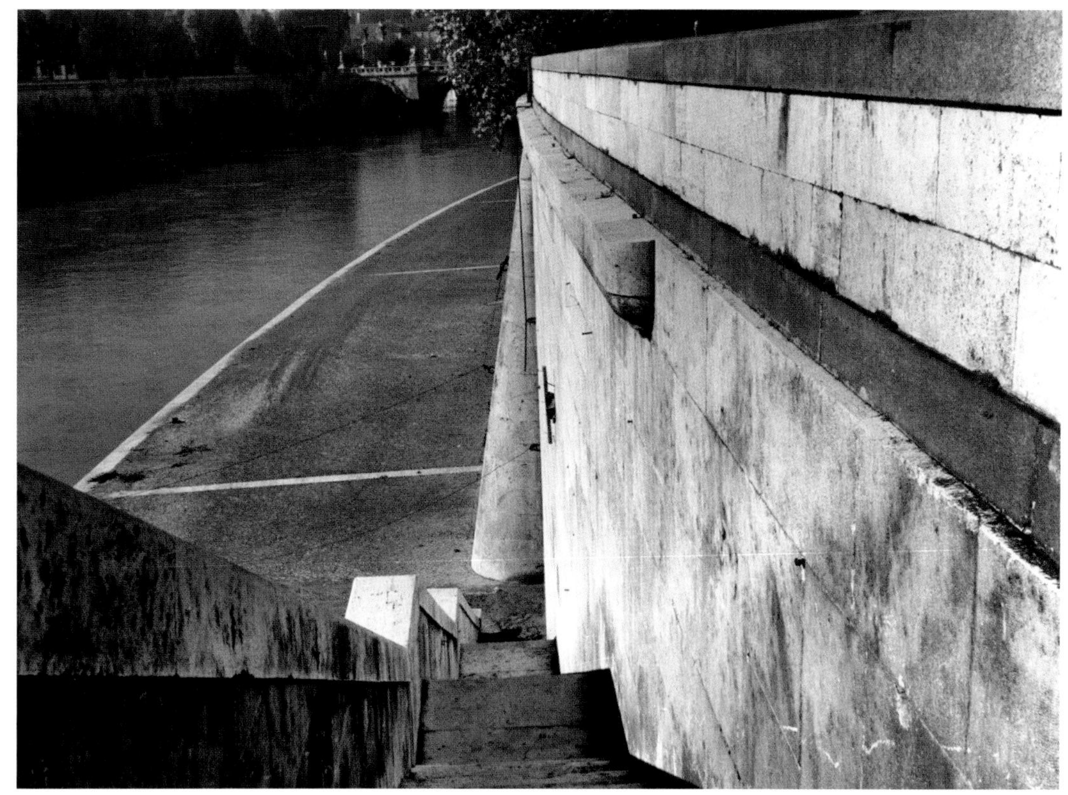

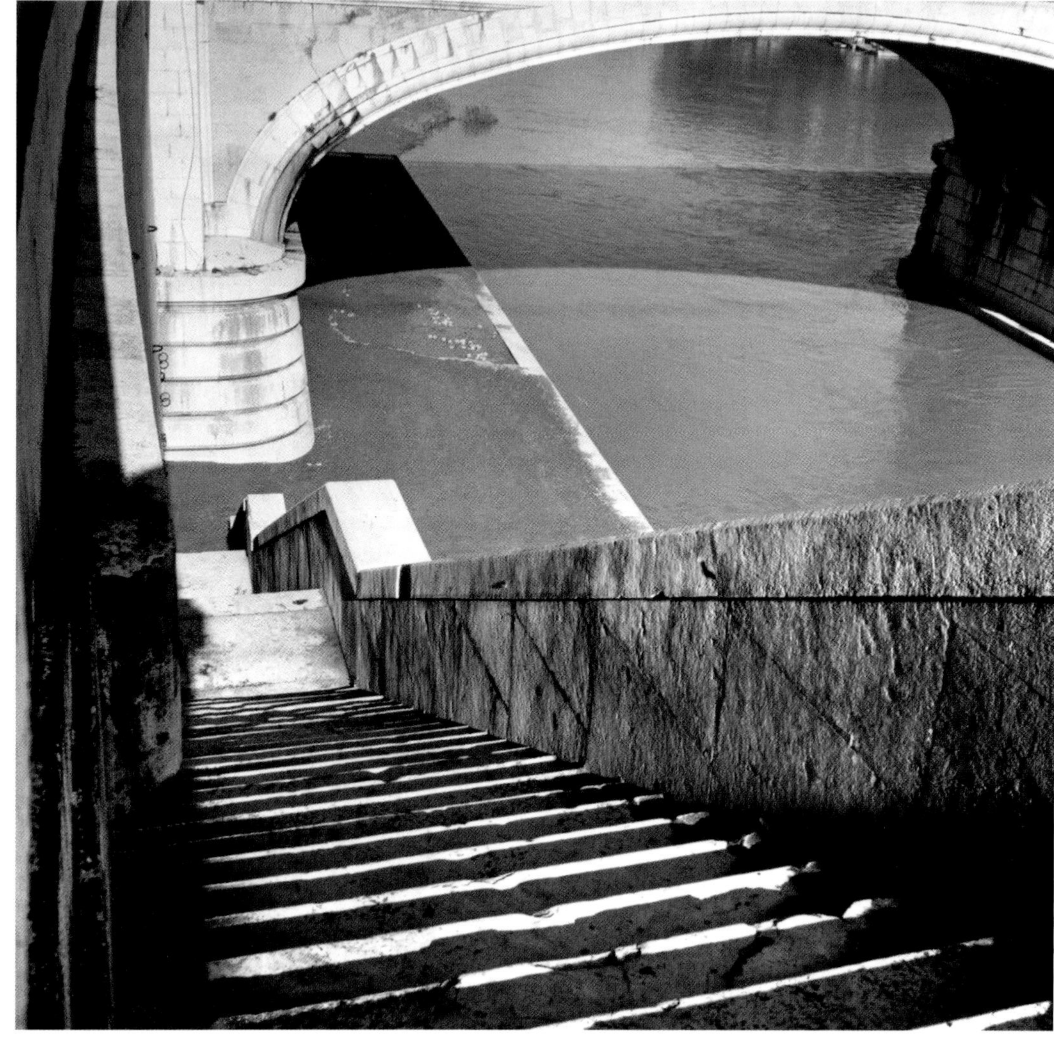

199. Edwin Smith
Pincio gardens, 1970

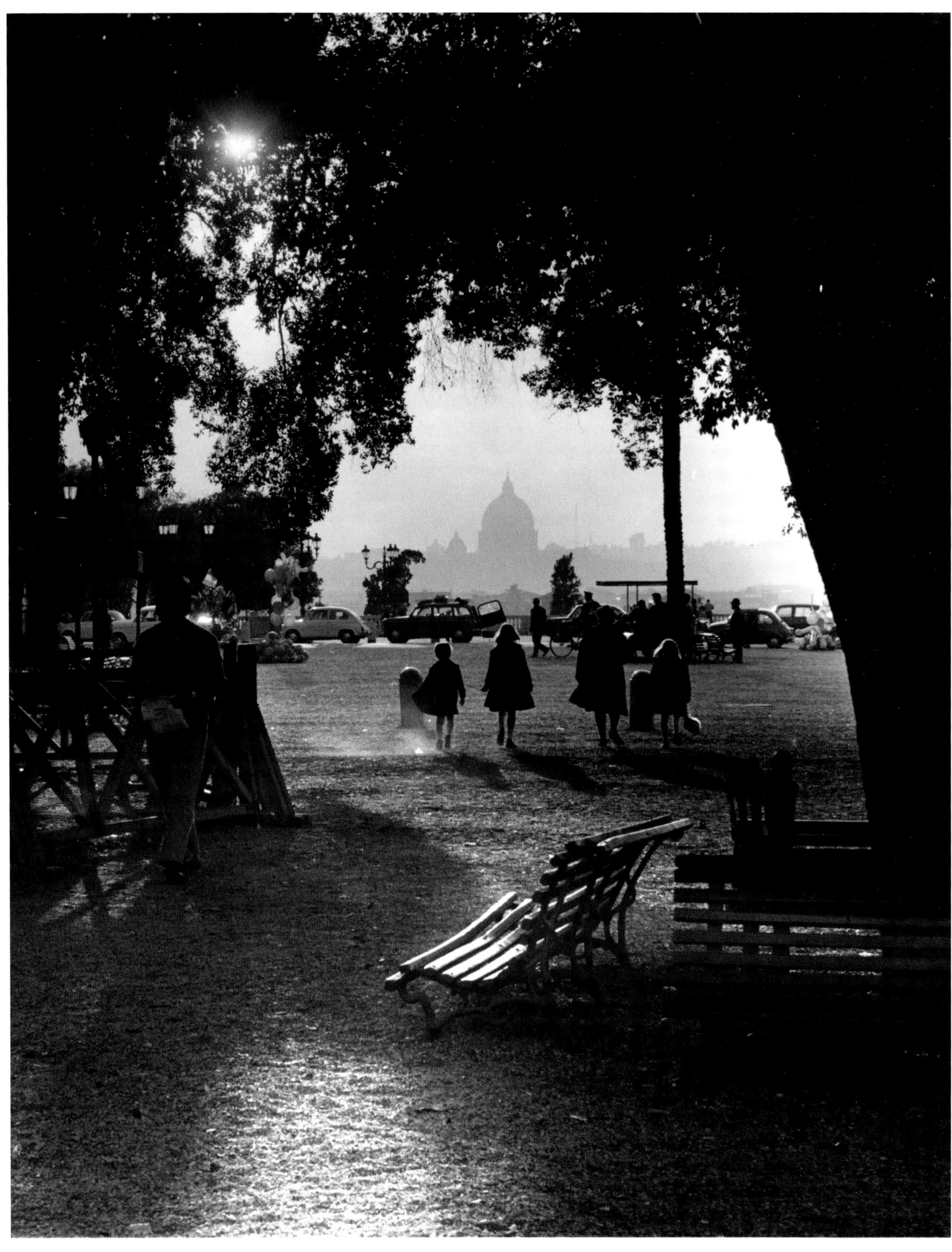

200. Edwin Smith
Piazza della Repubblica, 1970

201. Ivor de Wolfe
Termini Station, 1952

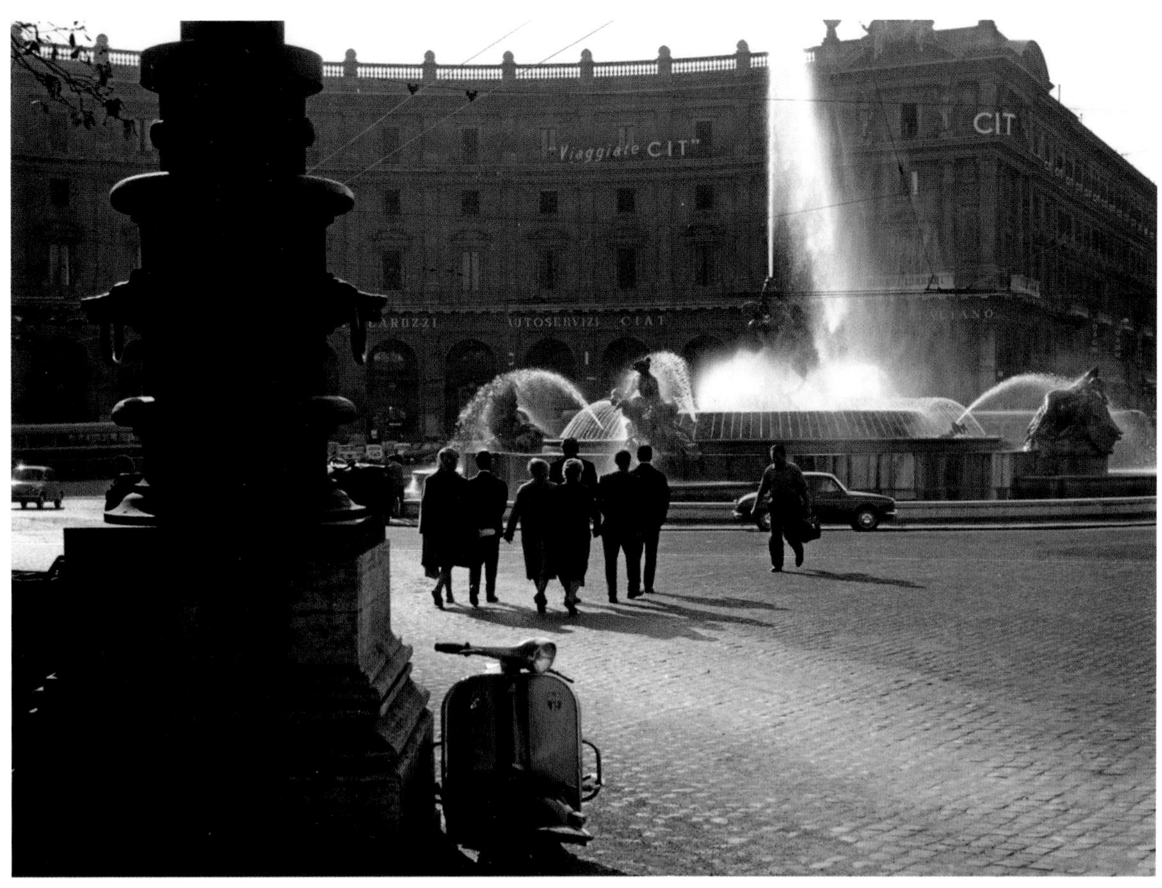

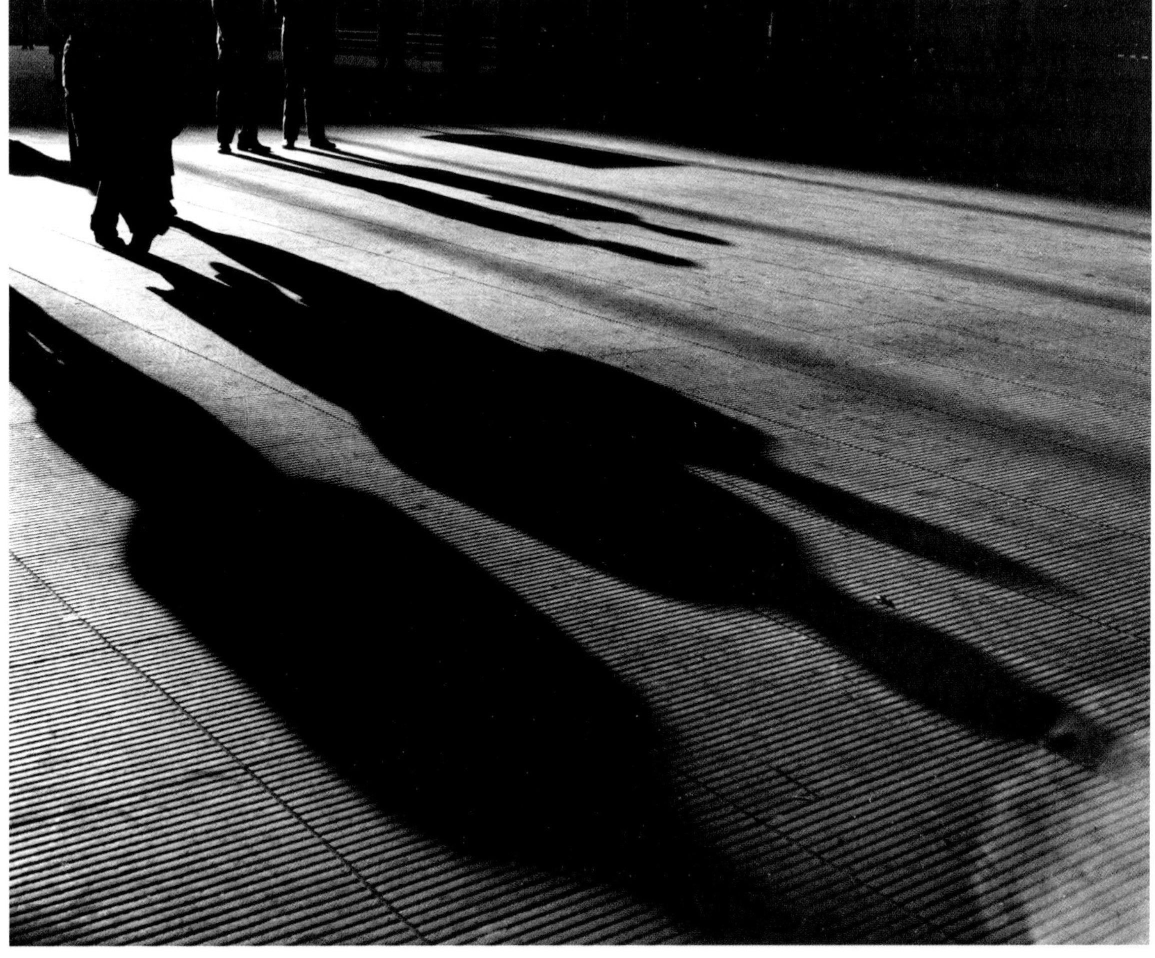

202. Edwin Smith
*Fontana delle Tartarughe,
Piazza Mattei, at night*, 1970

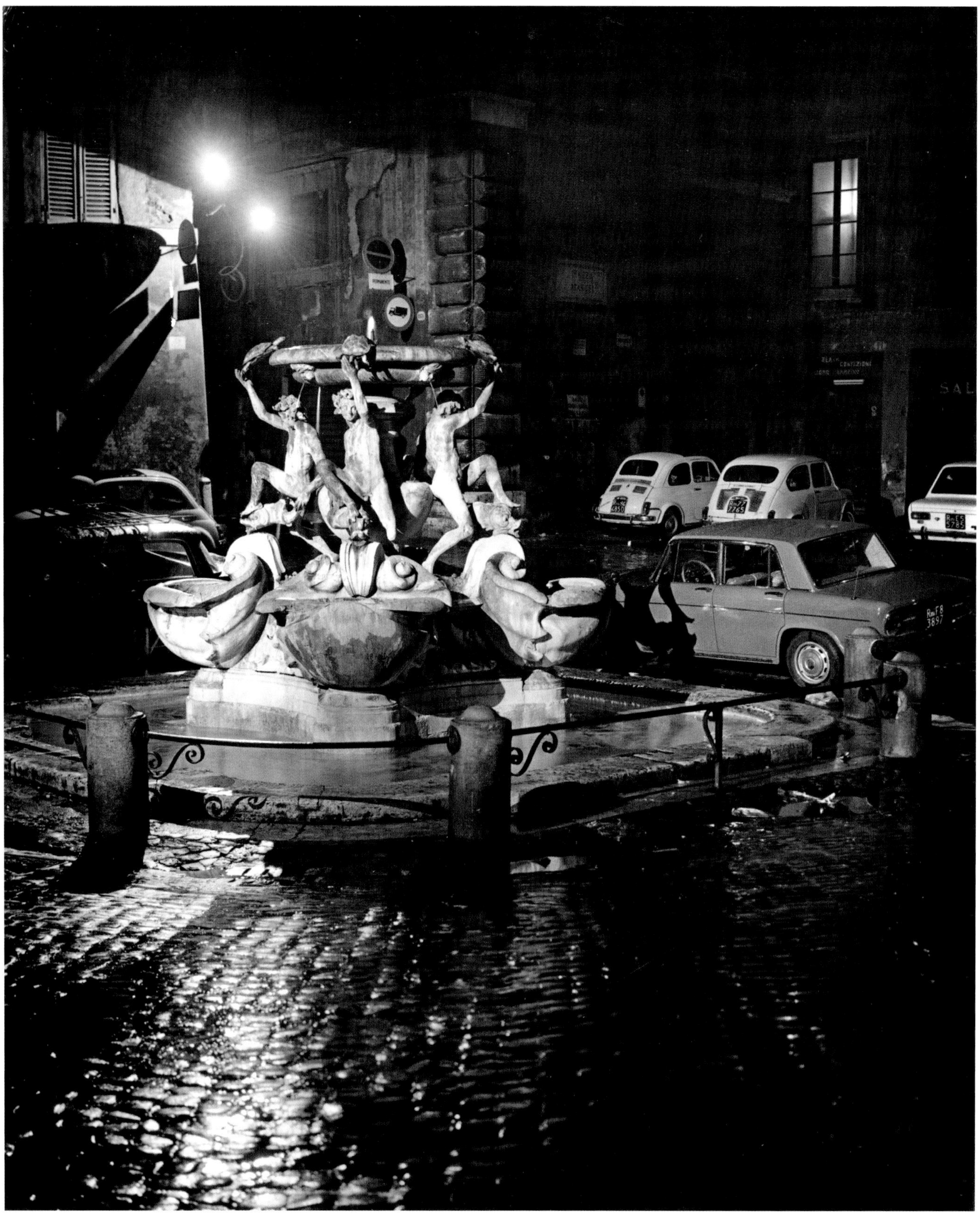

203. Edwin Smith
*Churches of Santissimo Nome
di Maria and Santa Maria
di Loreto at night, 1970*

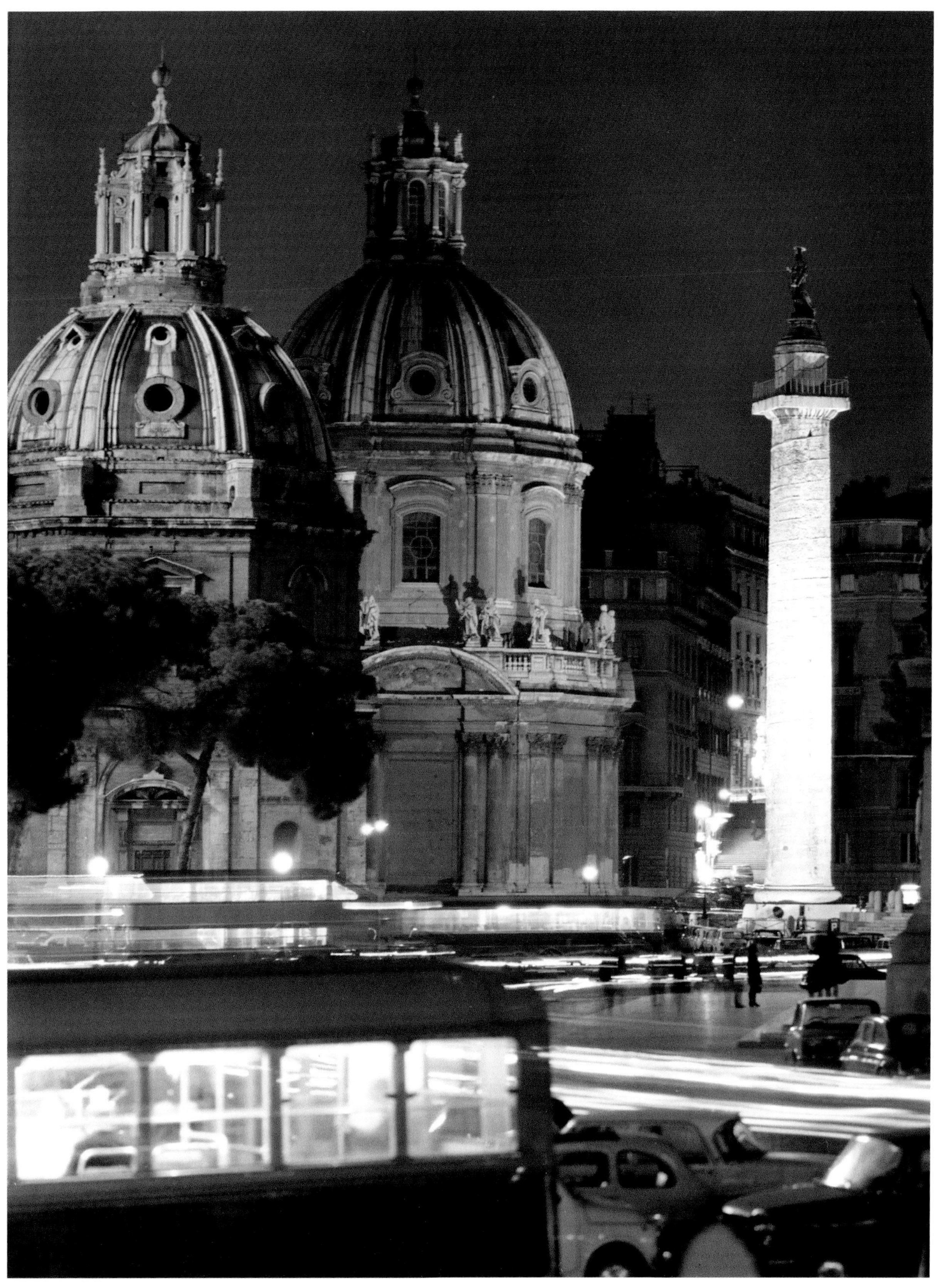

204. Unknown photographer
*Statue of the Nile, Fountain
of the Four Rivers,
Piazza Navona, at night*, 1950

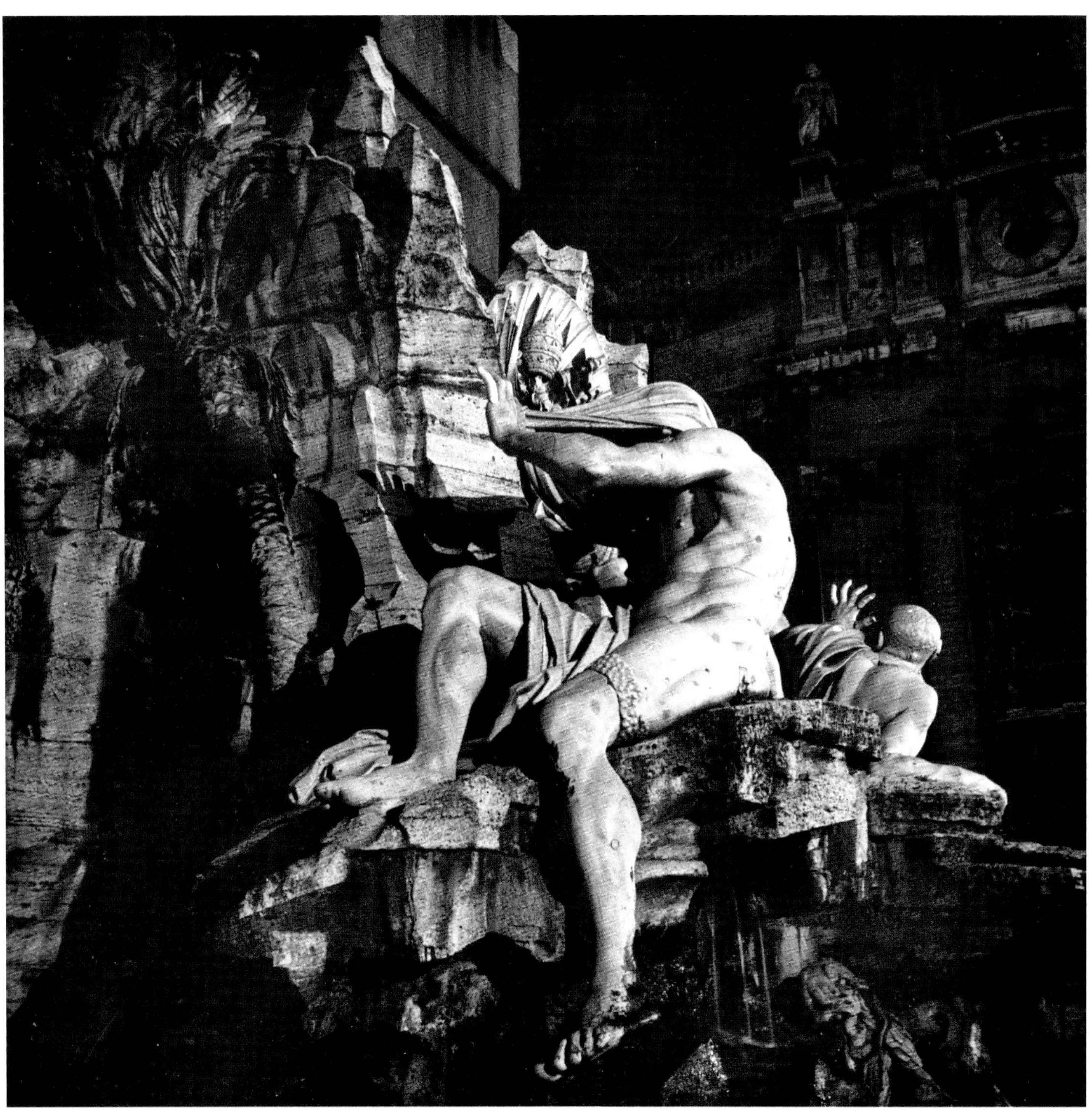

205. Monica Pidgeon
*Fontana della Barcaccia,
Piazza di Spagna, at night*, 1961

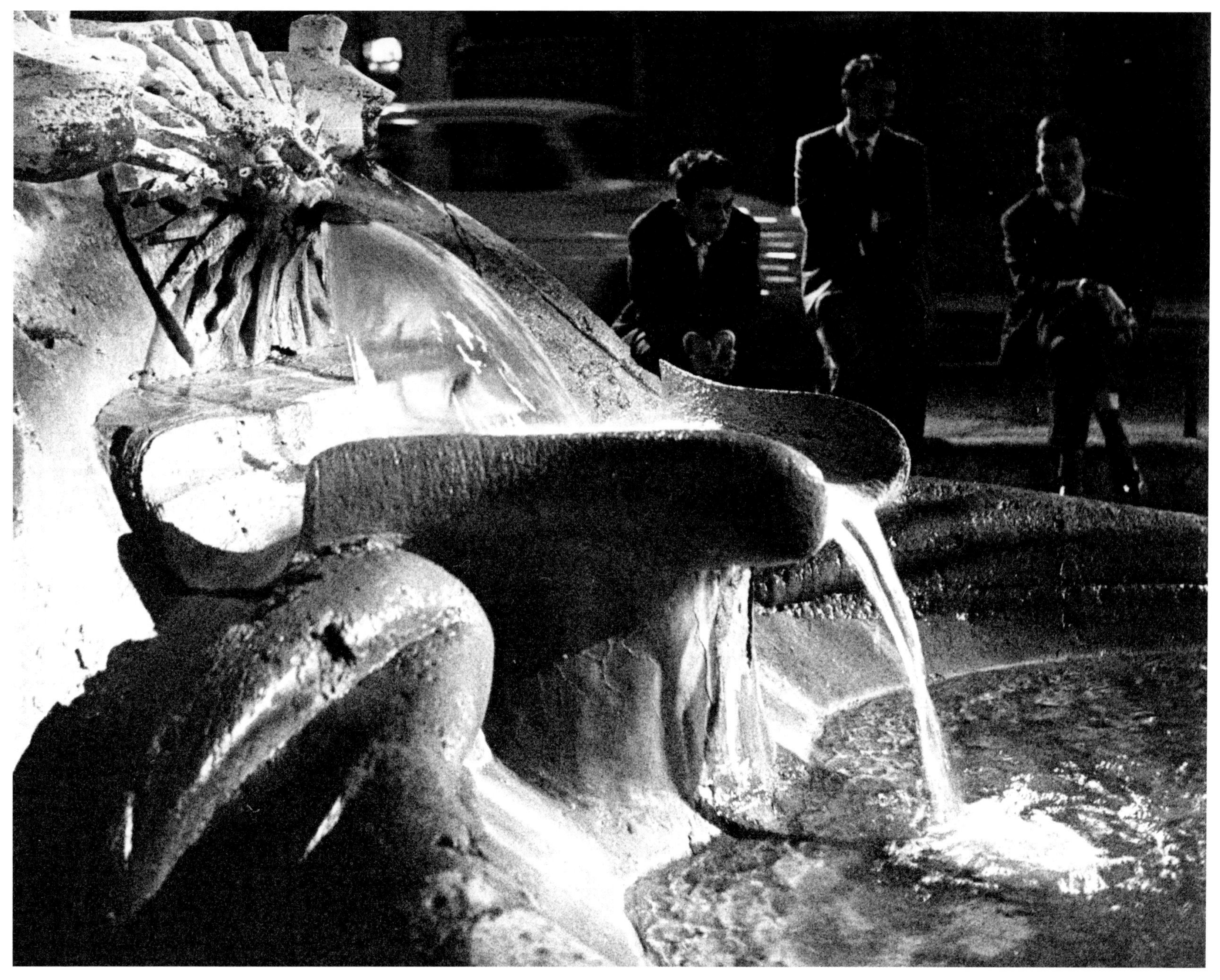

206. Monica Pidgeon
Via Frattina at night, 1961

207. Ivy de Wolfe
Neon signs at night, 1961

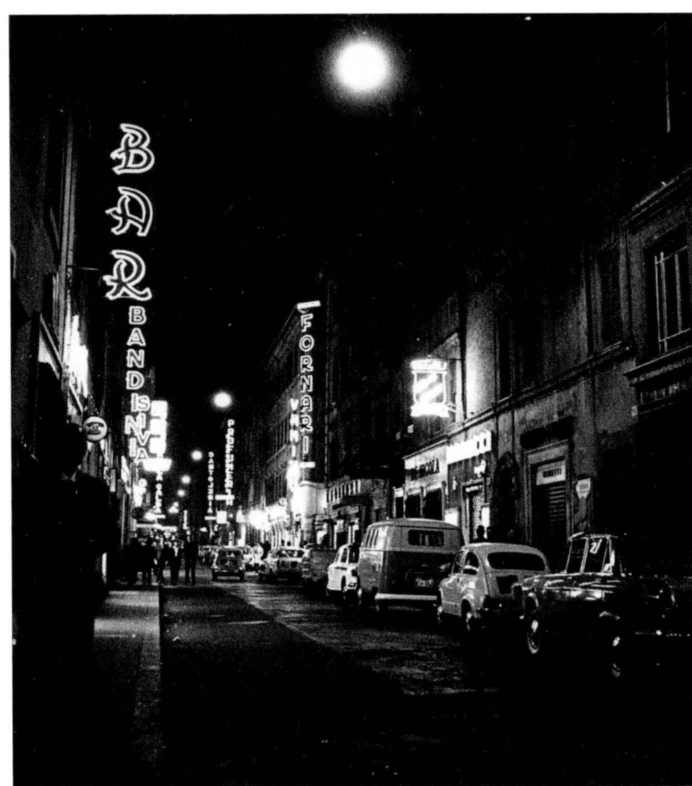

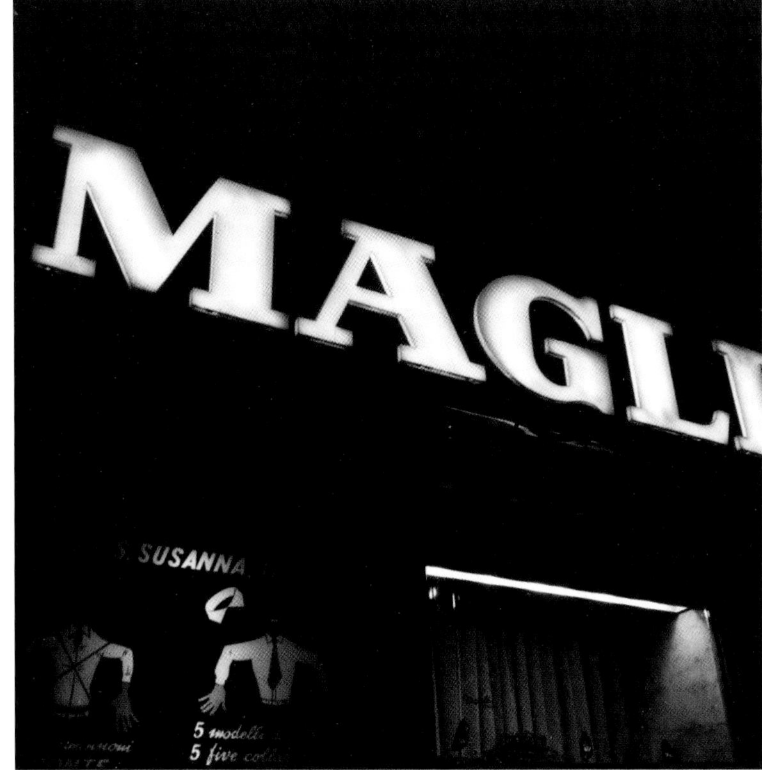

208. Ivy de Wolfe
Neon signs at night, 1961

209. Ivy de Wolfe
Neon signs at night, 1961

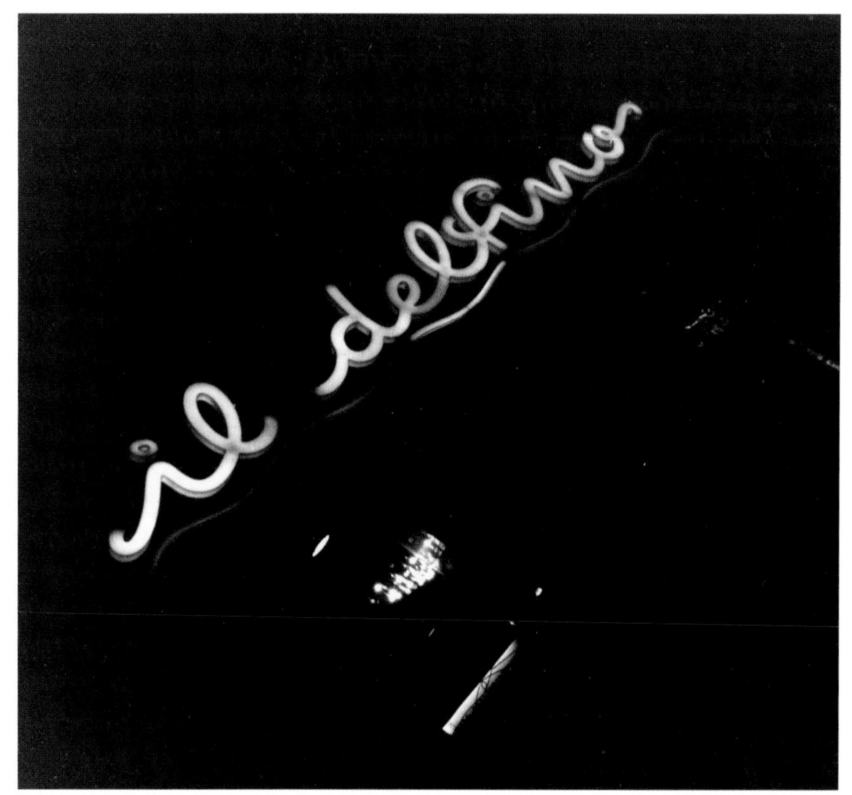

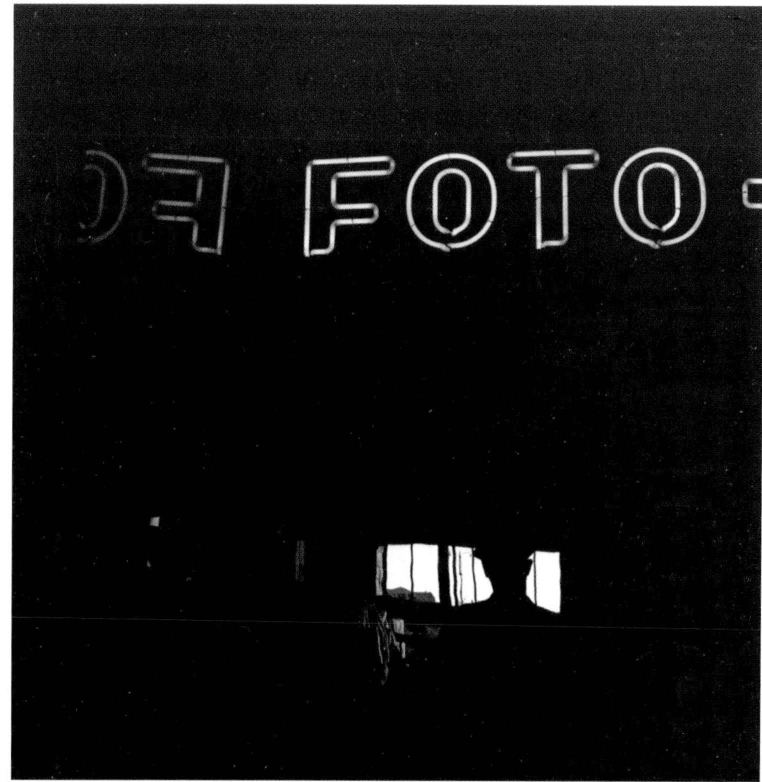

Appendix

James and Domenico Anderson

James Anderson, born Isaac Atkinson (1813–1877), was one of the first professional photographers to operate in Italy in the nineteenth century. Having left England to study painting in Paris, he then moved to Rome in 1838, where he began to practice photography professionally in 1845, specialising in reproductions of works of art, historical buildings and panoramic views. The studio he opened in 1853 soon became one of the most important in the city and his work was shown over the following decade in numerous exhibitions, including the World's Fairs of 1855 in Paris and 1862 in London. The studio continued to operate after his death under his son Domenico (1854–1938) and was subsequently run by his heirs until the 1940s. The Anderson archives of over 30,000 glass plate negatives was purchased in 1963 by the Fratelli Alinari firm, another important Italian dynasty of photographers.

Tim Benton

Tim Benton (b. 1945) is an architectural historian and photographer. He studied History and Art History at the University of Cambridge and holds a master's degree from the Courtauld Institute of Art. His photographs have been published in numerous books, including Anthony Blunt's *Sicilian Baroque* (1968) and *Neapolitan Baroque & Rococo Architecture* (1975). He is a noted scholar of the works of Le Corbusier but has also worked and published on Italian architecture of the 1930s and on Art Déco. He is emeritus professor of Art History at the Open University and has served as visiting professor at Williams College (2009), at the Department of Art History and Archaeology at Columbia University (2007) and at the Bard Graduate Center (2003). He was elected to the *conseil d'administration* of the Fondation Le Corbusier from 2008 to 2015. Benton has acted as associate curator in several major exhibitions including *Thirties England Between the Wars* (Hayward Gallery, London, 1979), *Le Corbusier, Architect of the Century* (Hayward Gallery, London, 1987), *Art and Power* (Hayward Gallery, London, 1995), *Art Deco 1910–1939* (Victoria and Albert Museum, London, 2003), *Modernism: Designing a New World 1918–1939* (Victoria and Albert Museum, London, 2006), *Modern Taste: Art Deco in Paris 1910–1935* (Fundación Juan March, Madrid, 2015).

Richard Bryant

Richard Bryant (b. 1947) is one of the world's leading contemporary photographers of architecture. Whilst studying architecture at Kingston University, Bryant quickly discovered how to combine the subject with a passion for photography cultivated since childhood. On graduating, he began to accept photographic commissions, initially for colleagues and friends, then for specialised journals, and finally for architects such as Norman Foster, Richard Rogers and James Stirling. He has worked all over the world since the 1980s, primarily capturing contemporary architecture but also photographing historical buildings. His photographs have appeared in numerous architectural magazines, including *Domus* and the *Architectural Review*. His great interest in the work of Carlo Scarpa led to the production of two books, one focusing on the Museo Canoviano, Possagno, in 2002 and the other on the Museo di Castelvecchio, Verona, in 2016. Attention should also be drawn to his monographic study of London published in 2008 with an introduction by Peter Ackroyd. Bryant received an honorary fellowship from the Royal Institute of British Architects in 1991 and was awarded an honorary doctorate in design from Kingston University in 1998.

Ralph Deakin

Ralph Deakin (1888–1952), Foreign Editor of *The Times* for thirty years from 1922 and the author of various essays, was also a talented amateur photographer. He photographed numerous European cities, including Rome, during the 1930s, focusing above all on historical architecture and the urban landscape, capturing an important historical moment before the continent was devastated by war. Director of the Reuters press agency from 1941 to 1945, Deakin was made an honorary associate of the Royal Institute of British Architects in 1950 in recognition of his interest in architecture.

Ivor and Ivy de Wolfe

Ivor and Ivy de Wolfe were the pseudonyms of Hubert de Cronin Hastings (1902–1986), the editor of the *Architectural Review* for nearly fifty years, and his wife Hazel (1902–?). Hastings helped to enhance the role of photography in the presentation of architecture during the 1930s by affording it great prominence in his journal. He and his wife made frequent trips to Italy, where they studied and photographed the urban landscape of cities large and small during the 1950s. Their work appeared in the *Architectural Review* in June 1962 and was then published the following year as *The Italian Townscape*, which not only examined the urban models of Italy but also developed a critique of contemporary British town planning. Hubert de Cronin Hastings received the Royal Gold Medal from the Royal Institute of British Architects in 1973 for his campaigning initiatives in the field of architecture.

Richard Pare

Richard Pare (b. 1948) studied photography and graphic design at Winchester and Ravensbourne College of Art before moving to the United States in 1971, where he studied photography at the School of the Art Institute of Chicago. Since then he has been working as a curator and photographer. He was the founding curator of the photography collection of the Canadian Centre for Architecture in Montreal from its inception in 1974 until 1989, when he became a consultant to the collection — a role he still fulfils. Pare continues to write and lecture on the history of photography. His exhibitions and publications include *Court House:*

A Photographic Document (1978), *Photography and Architecture: 1839–1939* (1982), *Tadao Ando, The Colours of Light* (1996, AIA monograph award) and *The Lost Vanguard: Architecture of the Russian Avant-garde* (2007). He contributed new photographic survey on the works of Le Corbusier for the 2013 exhibition at the Museum of Modern Art in New York, *Le Corbusier: An Atlas of Modern Landscapes*. He is currently concluding an extended project on the Swiss/French architect, having succeeded in photographing all but three of Le Corbusier's extant buildings.

Monica Pidgeon

Monica Pidgeon (1913–2009), the editor of *Architectural Design* from 1946 to 1975, was also a highly talented photographer. Born in Chile, Monica Lehmann (her maiden name before marriage to the architect Raymond Pidgeon) moved to London with her family in 1929 and went on to study architecture and interior design at the Bartlett School of Architecture, University College London. After graduating and working as a writer and illustrator, she became assistant to the editor of *Architectural Design* in 1941. A member of the Union International des Architectes (UIA) and of the Congrès International des Architectes (CIAM), Pidgeon took over as editor and made *Architectural Design* an international point of reference in the debate on modern architecture. This readiness to look beyond Britain is also reflected in her photographic work, which includes contemporary and historical works of architecture in North and South America (including some remarkable photographs of Brasilia), India (especially Chandigarh), Japan and of course Europe. An honorary fellow of the Royal Institute of British Architects as from 1970, she was the editor of the *RIBA Journal* from 1975 to 1979. The Pidgeon Audiovisual Collection, created by Pidgeon with Stephen Albert and World Microfilm in 1979, comprises 25 years of interviews with leading architects designed for students in the form of cassettes accompanied by slides. Digitised in 2006, the interviews are now accessible online.

Edwin Smith

Edwin Smith (1912–1971) was one of the leading British photographers of architecture and landscape in the twentieth century. His interest in photography developed early and although he initially studied architecture at the Architectural Association in London he also hoped to become a painter. In the mid-1930s, while working as a draughtsman for various architectural firms, he also began to work as a photographer on a broad range of subjects including fashion, advertising, portraiture and documentary photography. It was only after the war, having been commissioned to illustrate the book *English Parish Churches* (1952), that he began to specialise in architecture and above all historical buildings. The large number of books he produced, many of which were published by Thames & Hudson, made him known to the general public and established his reputation as a photographer. His fascination with Italy is reflected in *The Wonders of Italy* (1965) and *Rome: From its Foundation to the Present* (1971). Smith is the subject of Robert Elwall's *Evocations of Place* (2007) and of the retrospective exhibition *Ordinary Beauty* held by the RIBA in 2012.

Architectural Press

The Architectural Press published the *Architectural Review* and *Architects' Journal*, two of the most important architectural periodicals at both national and international levels, for over a century. Founded in 1896, they both made use of photography, like many other architectural magazines in other countries, as a fundamental medium for the presentation of architecture. In addition to official photographers such as Dell & Wainwright in the 1930s, followed by Sam Lambert, Hugh de Burgh Galwey, Bill Toomey and others in the second half of the century, they also commissioned professionals for specific jobs and purchased images from architects and other publications. The *Architectural Review* in particular often gave pride of place to photography in its page layout. It also made use on occasion of photographs taken by non-professionals like its editor Hubert de Cronin Hastings, the artist John Piper and the critic Iain Nairn. The Architectural Press also published a considerable number of books on a variety of subjects related to the discipline. Its photographic archives of over 500,000 images constitutes an extraordinary resource for research and documentation on British and world architecture in the twentieth century.

Antiquity

1. James Anderson
Colosseum
Albumen print, c. 1860
A134/1
RIBA Collections

2. Unknown photographer
*Colosseum seen from
the Domus Aurea*
Albumen print, 1860s–1870s
A109/20
RIBA Collections

3. Enrico Verzaschi
Roman Forum
Albumen print, after 1860
A109/14
RIBA Collections

4. Enrico Verzaschi
Roman Forum
Albumen print, after 1860
A109/16
RIBA Collections

5. Stabilimento Fotografico
Domenico Anderson
Friezes in the Roman Forum
Gelatine silver print,
early twentieth century
6145
RIBA Collections

6. Stabilimento Fotografico
Domenico Anderson
*Arch of Septimius Severus,
Roman Forum*
Gelatine silver print,
early twentieth century
6391
RIBA Collections

7. Unknown photographer
*Ruins of the House of Augusta,
Palatine Hill*
Gelatine silver print, 1950s
30807/16
RIBA Collections

8. Edwin Smith
*Roman Forum, with the Arch
of Septimius Severus
in the foreground*
Gelatine silver print, 1970
ESP/ROM/499
Edwin Smith / RIBA Collections

9. Ralph Deakin
*Atrium of Vesta's House, with
the Basilica of Maxentius
on the left, Roman Forum*
Gelatine silver print, 1930s
DK/I/340
Ralph Deakin / RIBA Collections

10. Edwin Smith
Roman Forum
Gelatine silver print, 1963
ESP/ROM/641
Edwin Smith / RIBA Collections

11. Edwin Smith
*Tomb of Marcus Vergilius
Eurysaces, Porta Maggiore*
Gelatine silver print, 1970
ES4056.8
Edwin Smith / RIBA Collections

12. Ralph Deakin
Temple of Portunus
Gelatine silver print, 1930s
DKN/I/471
Ralph Deakin / RIBA Collections

13. Edwin Smith
*Temple of Hercules Victor
and Temple of Portunus*
Gelatine silver print, 1962
ESP/ROM/659
Edwin Smith / RIBA Collections

14. Edwin Smith
*Arch of Septimius Severus,
Roman Forum*
Gelatine silver print, 1970
ESP/ROM/506
Edwin Smith / RIBA Collections

15. Edwin Smith
*Temple of Hadrian,
Piazza di Pietra*
Gelatine silver print, 1963
ESP/ROM/430
Edwin Smith / RIBA Collections

16. Edwin Smith
Pantheon
Gelatine silver print, 1963
ESP/ROM/391
Edwin Smith / RIBA Collections

17. Edwin Smith
Pantheon
Gelatine silver print, 1970
ESP/ROM/400
Edwin Smith / RIBA Collections

18. Ralph Deakin
Pantheon
Gelatine silver print, 1930s
DK/I/309
Ralph Deakin / RIBA Collections

19. Edwin Smith
*Fragments of the colossal
statue of Constantine the
Great, Palazzo dei Conservatori*
Gelatine silver print, 1954
ESP/ROM/631
Edwin Smith / RIBA Collections

20. Edwin Smith
*Fragments of the colossal
statue of Constantine the
Great, Palazzo dei Conservatori*
Gelatine silver print, 1954
ESP/ROM/664
Edwin Smith / RIBA Collections

21. Unknown photographer
*Fragments of the colossal
statue of Constantine the
Great, Palazzo dei Conservatori*
Gelatine silver print, 1950s
30807/15
RIBA Collections

22. Edwin Smith
Baths of Caracalla
Gelatine silver print, 1970
ESP/ROM/459
Edwin Smith / RIBA Collections

23. Edwin Smith
Baths of Caracalla
Gelatine silver print, 1970
ESP/ROM/460
Edwin Smith / RIBA Collections

24. Edwin Smith
Baths of Caracalla
Gelatine silver print, 1970
ESP/ROM/458
Edwin Smith / RIBA Collections

25. Monica Pidgeon
Basilica of Maxentius
Gelatine silver print, 1961
MP uncatalogued
Monica Pidgeon / RIBA
Collections

26. Edwin Smith
Baths of Diocletian
Gelatine silver print, 1970
ESP/ROM/476
Edwin Smith / RIBA Collections

27. Ralph Deakin
*Remains of the Palace
of Caligula, Palatine Hill*
Gelatine silver print, 1930s
DK/I/381
Ralph Deakin / RIBA Collections

28. Ralph Deakin
Arch of Drusus, Via Appia
Gelatine silver print, 1930s
DK/I/313
Ralph Deakin / RIBA Collections

29. Edwin Smith
Tabularium, Roman Forum
Gelatine silver print, 1970
ESP/ROM/541
Edwin Smith / RIBA Collections

30. Photographer unknown
*Remains of the Temple of Mars
Ultor, Forum of Augustus,
in the Convent of Santa Maria
Annunziata ai Monti*
Gelatine silver print, 1930s
AP13 uncatalogued
Architectural Press Archive /
RIBA Collections

31. Photographer unknown
*Temple of Venus and Roma,
Roman Forum after the 1932
fitting out*
Gelatine silver print, 1930s
AP13 uncatalogued
Architectural Press Archive /
RIBA Collections

32. Edwin Smith
*Circus Maximus, with the
Palatine Hill in the background*
Gelatine silver print, 1970
ESP/ROM/592
Edwin Smith / RIBA Collections

33. Edwin Smith
*Temple of Venus and Roma,
Roman Forum*
Gelatine silver print, 1970
ESP/ROM/431
Edwin Smith / RIBA Collections

34. Ralph Deakin
Colosseum
Gelatine silver print, 1930s
DK/I/318
Ralph Deakin / RIBA Collections

35. Ralph Deakin
Roman Forum
Gelatine silver print, 1930s
DK/I/332
Ralph Deakin / RIBA Collections

36. Monica Pidgeon
Colosseum from the north-west
Gelatine silver print, 1961
MP uncatalogued
Monica Pidgeon / RIBA
Collections

37. Monica Pidgeon
Temple of Vespasian
Gelatine silver print, 1961
MP uncatalogued
Monica Pidgeon / RIBA
Collections

38. Ralph Deakin
*Arch of Constantine, with a
glimpse of the Colosseum*
Gelatine silver print, 1930s
DK/I/316
Ralph Deakin / RIBA Collections

39. Unknown photographer
Colosseum
Gelatine silver print, 1950s
30807/18
RIBA Collections

40. Stabilimento Fotografico
Domenico Anderson
Colosseum
Gelatine silver print,
early twentieth century
LS uncatalogued
RIBA Collections

41. Edwin Smith
Colosseum
Gelatine silver print, 1970
ESP/ROM/445
Edwin Smith / RIBA Collections

Modernity

42. Stabilimento Fotografico
Vasari
Termini Station
(Eugenio Montuori, Leo Calini,
Annibale Vitellozzi, Massimo
Castellazzi, Vasco Fadigati,
Achille Pintonello)
Gelatine silver print, 1950
AP229/61A
Architectural Press Archive /
RIBA Collections

43. Marion Johnson
(aka Georgina Masson)
Termini Station
(Eugenio Montuori, Leo Calini,
Annibale Vitellozzi, Massimo
Castellazzi, Vasco Fadigati,
Achille Pintonello)
Gelatine silver print, 1951
AP229/57
Architectural Press Archive /
RIBA Collections
Courtesy of the American
Academy in Rome

44. Marion Johnson
(aka Georgina Masson)
Termini Station
(Eugenio Montuori, Leo Calini,
Annibale Vitellozzi, Massimo
Castellazzi, Vasco Fadigati,
Achille Pintonello)
Gelatine silver print, 1950
AP229/41
Architectural Press Archive /
RIBA Collections
Courtesy of the American
Academy in Rome

45. Marion Johnson
(aka Georgina Masson)
Termini Station
(Eugenio Montuori, Leo Calini,
Annibale Vitellozzi, Massimo
Castellazzi, Vasco Fadigati,
Achille Pintonello)
Gelatine silver print, 1950
AP229/63
Architectural Press Archive /
RIBA Collections
Courtesy of the American
Academy in Rome

46. Marion Johnson
(aka Georgina Masson)
Termini Station
(Eugenio Montuori, Leo Calini,
Annibale Vitellozzi, Massimo
Castellazzi, Vasco Fadigati,
Achille Pintonello)
Gelatine silver print, 1950
AP229/77
Architectural Press Archive /
RIBA Collections
Courtesy of the American
Academy in Rome

47. Marion Johnson
(aka Georgina Masson)
Termini Station
(Eugenio Montuori, Leo Calini,
Annibale Vitellozzi, Massimo
Castellazzi, Vasco Fadigati,
Achille Pintonello)
Gelatine silver print, 1951
AP229/42
Architectural Press Archive /
RIBA Collections
Courtesy of the American
Academy in Rome

48. Stabilimento Fotografico
Domenico Anderson
Palazzo Farnese
(Michelangelo, Antonio
da Sangallo il Giovane)
Gelatine silver print,
early twentieth century
6190
RIBA Collections

49. Stabilimento Fotografico
Domenico Anderson
Palazzo Massimo alle Colonne
(Baldassarre Peruzzi)
Gelatine silver print,
early twentieth century
221
RIBA Collections

50. Edwin Smith
*Tempietto, San Pietro in
Montorio*
(Donato Bramante)
Gelatine silver print, 1966
ESP/ROM/193
Edwin Smith / RIBA Collections

51. Edwin Smith
Sant'Ivo alla Sapienza
(Francesco Borromini)
Gelatine silver print, 1962
LS ESP/ROM/303
Edwin Smith / RIBA Collections

52. Stabilimento Fotografico
Domenico Anderson
*Model of the dome
of Saint Peter's Basilica*
(mock-up by Antonio
da Sangallo il Giovane)
Gelatine silver print,
early twentieth century
41699/145
RIBA Collections

53. Stabilimento Fotografico
Domenico Anderson
Dome of Saint Peter's Basilica
(Michelangelo,
Giacomo della Porta)
Gelatine silver print,
early twentieth century
7758
RIBA Collections

54. Edwin Smith
*Sala dei Parati Piemontesi,
Palazzo del Quirinale*
Gelatine silver print, 1963
ESP/ITA/505
Edwin Smith / RIBA Collections

55. Ralph Deakin
*Chiesa Nuova, or Santa Maria
in Vallicella*
(Matteo di Città di Castello,
Martino Longhi the Elder)
Gelatine silver print, 1930s
DKN/I/533
Ralph Deakin / RIBA Collections

56. Stabilimento Fotografico
Domenico Anderson
Saint Peter's Basilica
Gelatine silver print,
early twentieth century
101
RIBA Collections

57. Stabilimento Fotografico
Domenico Anderson
*Dome of the Avila Chapel,
Santa Maria in Trastevere*
(Antonio Gherardi)
Gelatine silver print,
early twentieth century
46199/128
RIBA Collections

58. Edwin Smith
*Dome and baldacchino,
Saint Peter's Basilica*
(Michelangelo,
Gian Lorenzo Bernini)
Gelatine silver print, 1970
ESP/ROM/232
Edwin Smith / RIBA Collections

59. Edwin Smith
Saint Peter's Basilica
Gelatine silver print, 1970
ESP/ROM/231
Edwin Smith / RIBA Collections

60. Edwin Smith
Santa Maria Maggiore
(Carlo Rinaldi)
Gelatine silver print, 1970
ESP/ROM/313
Edwin Smith / RIBA Collections

61. Edwin Smith
Façade of Saint Peter's Basilica
(Carlo Maderno)
Gelatine silver print, 1970
ESP/ROM/208
Edwin Smith / RIBA Collections

62. Stabilimento Fotografico
Domenico Anderson
Palazzo in Via Monserrato
Gelatine silver print,
early twentieth century
30371
RIBA Collections

63. Stabilimento Fotografico
Domenico Anderson
Palazzo Falconieri
(Francesco Borromini)
Gelatine silver print,
early twentieth century
41699/28
RIBA Collections

64. Stabilimento Fotografico
Domenico Anderson
*Sant'Agnese in Agone, Piazza
Navona*
(Francesco Borromini)
Gelatine silver print,
early twentieth century
RIBA112809
RIBA Collections

65. Stabilimento Fotografico
Domenico Anderson
Sant'Andrea delle Fratte
(Francesco Borromini)
Gelatine silver print,
early twentieth century
41699/95
RIBA Collections

66. Stabilimento Fotografico
Domenico Anderson
San Carlo alle Quattro Fontane
(Francesco Borromimi)
Gelatine silver print,
early twentieth century
41699/99
RIBA Collections

67. Edwin Smith
*Fountain of the Four Rivers,
Piazza Navona*
(Gian Lorenzo Bernini)
Gelatine silver print, 1970
ESP/ROM/60
Edwin Smith / RIBA Collections

68. Edwin Smith
*Fontana della Barcaccia,
Piazza di Spagna*
(Pietro and Gian Lorenzo
Bernini)
Gelatine silver print, 1962
ESP/ROM/116A
Edwin Smith / RIBA Collections

69. Ivy de Wolfe
Trevi Fountain
(Nicola Salvi)
Gelatine silver print, 1961
33570/1
RIBA Collections

70. Ivy de Wolfe
Trevi Fountain
(Nicola Salvi)
Gelatine silver print, 1961
33638/7
RIBA Collections

71. Tim Benton
Fencing Academy, Foro Italico
(Luigi Moretti)
Gelatine silver print, 1976
RIBA107451*
Tim Benton / RIBA Collections

72. Stabilimento Fotografico
Domenico Anderson
*Industrial school for the
daughters of post office
employees, Garbatella*
(Angiolo Mazzoni)
Gelatine silver print, 1936
Ra6/4
RIBA Collections

73. Stabilimento Fotografico
Domenico Anderson
*Industrial school for the
daughters of post office
employees, Garbatella*
(Angiolo Mazzoni)
Gelatine silver print, 1936
Ra6/1
RIBA Collections

74. Tim Benton
*Portico of the Santi Pietro
e Paolo Basilica, EUR*
(Arnaldo Foschini)
Gelatine silver print, 1976
RIBA107400*
Tim Benton / RIBA Collections

75. Tim Benton
*Palazzo della Civiltà Italiana,
EUR*
(Giovanni Guerrini, Ernesto
La Padula, Mario Romano)
Gelatine silver print, 1976
RIBA107438*
Tim Benton / RIBA Collections

76. George Everard Kidder Smith
*Palazzo dello Sport under
construction, EUR*
(Marcello Piacentini,
Pier Luigi Nervi)
Gelatine silver print, 1954
AP475/214
Architectural Press Archive /
RIBA Collections
Courtesy of IUAV, Venice

77. Edwin Smith
Palazzetto dello Sport
(Annibale Vitellozzi,
Pier Luigi Nervi)
Gelatine silver print, 1970
ESP/ROM/375
Edwin Smith / RIBA Collections

78. Oscar Savio
*Staircase, Grandi Magazzini
la Rinascente*
(Franco Albini, Franca Helg)
Gelatine silver print, 1961
AP13 uncatalogued
Architectural Press Archive /
RIBA Collections

79. Oscar Savio
*Staircase, Grandi Magazzini
la Rinascente*
(Franco Albini, Franca Helg)
Gelatine silver print, 1961
AP375/54
Architectural Press Archive /
RIBA Collections

80. Alberto Cartoni
Casa del Girasole
(Luigi Moretti)
Gelatine silver print, 1950
AP671 uncatalogued
Architectural Press Archive /
RIBA Collections
Courtesy of Archivio Cicconi,
Roma

81. Alberto Cartoni
Casa del Girasole (Luigi
Moretti)
Gelatine silver print, 1950
AP671 uncatalogued
Architectural Press Archive /
RIBA Collections
Courtesy of Archivio Cicconi,
Roma

82. Tim Benton
*Palazzina Nebbiosi, lungotevere
Arnaldo da Brescia*
(Giuseppe Capponi)
Gelatine silver print, 1976
RIBA107368*
Tim Benton / RIBA Collections

83. Ludovico Canali
*Multi-purpose office building
between Via Campania
and Via Romagna*
(Vincenzo, Fausto
and Lucio Passarelli)
Gelatine silver print, 1966
AP14 uncatalogued
Architectural Press Archive /
RIBA Collections

84. Ralph Deakin
*Monument to Vittorio
Emanuele II, or 'Vittoriano'*
(Giuseppe Sacconi, Gaetano
Koch, Manfredo Manfredi,
Pio Piacentini)
Gelatine silver print, 1930s
DK/I/482
Ralph Deakin / RIBA Collections

85. Bruno De Hamel
*Chancery Building, British
Embassy* (Basil Spence)
Gelatine silver print, 1971
AP318/27
Architectural Press Archive /
RIBA Collections

86. Edwin Smith
*Palazzo Nuovo, Piazza del
Campidoglio*
(Michelangelo, Girolamo
Rainaldi, Carlo Rainaldi)
Gelatine silver print, 1954
ESP/ROM/167
Edwin Smith / RIBA Collections

87. Tim Benton
*Staircase, Palazzo Senatorio,
Piazza del Campidoglio*
(Michelangelo,
Giacomo della Porta)
Gelatine silver print, 1976
RIBA107387*
Tim Benton / RIBA Collections

88. Richard Pare
*Statue of the Nile, Fountain
of the Four Rivers,
and Sant'Agnese in Agone,
Piazza Navona*
(Gian Lorenzo Bernini –
fountain; Girolamo Rainaldi,
Francesco Borromini, Carlo
Rainaldi – church)
Colour transparency, 1985
RIBA113960*
Richard Pare / RIBA Collections

89. Richard Pare
*Statue of the Ganges,
Fountain of the Four Rivers,
Piazza Navona*
(Gian Lorenzo Bernini)
Colour transparency, 1985
RIBA113957*
Richard Pare / RIBA Collections

90. Richard Pare
*14 Piazza dei Mercanti,
Trastevere*
Colour transparency, 1985
RIBA113956*
Richard Pare / RIBA Collections

91. Richard Pare
*Spanish Steps, towards
Trinità dei Monti*
(Francesco De Sanctis)
Colour transparency, 1985
RIBA113955*
Richard Pare / RIBA Collections

92. Richard Pare
Pyramid of Caius Cestius
Colour transparency, 1985
RIBA113961*
Richard Pare / RIBA Collections

93. Richard Pare
Pantheon
Colour transparency, 1985
RIBA 114070*
Richard Pare / RIBA Collections

94. Richard Pare
Arco del Ponte Rotto
Colour transparency, 1985
RIBA113964*
Richard Pare / RIBA Collections

95. Richard Pare
Pincio gardens
Colour transparency, 1985
RIBA113958*
Richard Pare / RIBA Collections

96. Richard Pare
Isola Tiberina
Colour transparency, 1985
RIBA113963*
Richard Pare / RIBA Collections

97. Richard Pare
EUR
Colour transparency, c. 2000
RIBA113959*
Richard Pare / RIBA Collections

98. Richard Pare
*Palazzo della Civiltà Italiana,
EUR*
(Giovanni Guerrini, Ernesto
La Padula, Mario Romano)
Colour transparency, 1985
RIBA113962*
Richard Pare / RIBA Collections

99. Richard Bryant
Palazzetto dello Sport
(Annibale Vitellozzi,
Pier Luigi Nervi)
Digital image, 2009
RIBA113690*
Richard Bryant / RIBA
Collections

100. Richard Bryant
Ara Pacis Museum, Rome
(Richard Meier)
Digital image, 2009
RIBA112906*
Richard Bryant / RIBA
Collections

101. Richard Bryant
Parco della Musica
(Renzo Piano Building
Workshop)
Colour transparency, 2002
RIBA112894*
Richard Bryant / RIBA
Collections

102. Richard Bryant
Parco della Musica
(Renzo Piano Building
Workshop)
Colour transparency, 2002
RIBA113683*
Richard Bryant / RIBA
Collections

103. Richard Bryant
Parco della Musica
(Renzo Piano Building
Workshop)
Colour transparency, 2002
RIBA113682*
Richard Bryant / RIBA
Collections

104. Richard Bryant
Parco della Musica
(Renzo Piano Building
Workshop)
Colour transparency, 2002
RIBA113680*
Richard Bryant / RIBA
Collections

105. Richard Bryant
*Chiesa del Dio Padre
Misericordioso, Tor Tre Teste*
(Richard Meier)
Colour transparency, 2003
RIBA112897*
Richard Bryant / RIBA
Collections

106. Richard Bryant
*Chiesa del Dio Padre
Misericordioso, Tor Tre Teste*
(Richard Meier)
Colour transparency, 2003
RIBA112902*
Richard Bryant / RIBA
Collections

107. Richard Bryant
*Chiesa del Dio Padre
Misericordioso, Tor Tre Teste*
(Richard Meier)
Colour transparency, 2003
RIBA112899*
Richard Bryant / RIBA
Collections

108. Richard Bryant
*MAXXI, National Museum
of 21st Century Arts*
(Zaha Hadid Architects)
Digital image, 2009
RIBA113687*
Richard Bryant / RIBA
Collections

109. Richard Bryant
*MAXXI, National Museum
of 21st Century Arts*
(Zaha Hadid Architects)
Digital image, 2009
RIBA113688
Richard Bryant / RIBA
Collections

110. Richard Bryant
*MAXXI, National Museum
of 21st Century Arts*
(Zaha Hadid Architects)
Digital image, 2009
RIBA113686*
Richard Bryant / RIBA
Collections

Urban Landscapes

111. Enrico Verzaschi
*Pantheon and Piazza
della Rotonda*
Albumen print, after 1860
A109/10
RIBA Collections

112. Unknown photographer
View from the Pincio
Albumen print, 1860s–1870s
A109/26
RIBA Collections

113. James Anderson
Campo dei Fiori
Albumen print, 1850s–1860s
RIBA112802
RIBA Collections

114. James Anderson
*River Tiber with Saint Peter's
and Castel Sant'Angelo*
Albumen print, c. 1870
41699/4
RIBA Collections

115. Unknown photographer
Saint Peter's Square
Albumen print, before 1865
A109/2
RIBA Collections

116. James Anderson
Piazza del Popolo
Albumen print, 1850s–1860s
41699/6
RIBA Collections

117. Unknown photographer
*Temple of Hercules Victor
and the Temple of Portunus,
Piazza Bocca della Verità*
Gelatine silver print, 1930s
AP13 uncatalogued
Architectural Press Archive /
RIBA Collections

118. Edwin Smith
*EUR from the Palazzo
dello Sport*
Gelatine silver print, 1970
ESP/ROM/365
Edwin Smith / RIBA Collections

119. Unknown photographer
View from Saint Peter's Dome,
Gelatine silver print, 1950
AP13 uncatalogued
Architectural Press Archive /
RIBA Collections

120. Ivy de Wolfe
*Dome of Saint Peter's Basilica
and Viale Vaticano Walls*
Gelatine silver print, 1964
33638/3
RIBA Collections

121. George Everard Kidder Smith
Dome of Saint Peter's Basilica
Gelatine silver print, 1954
AP123/137
Architectural Press Archive /
RIBA Collections
Courtesy of IUAV, Venice

122. Edwin Smith
*Aurelian Wall by Porta
San Sebastiano*
Gelatine silver print, 1970
ESP/ROM/35
Edwin Smith / RIBA Collections

123. Unknown photographer
Piazza della Consolazione
Gelatine silver print, 1930s
AP13 uncatalogued
Architectural Press Archive /
RIBA Collections

124. Edwin Smith
View from the Palatine Hill
Gelatine silver print, 1963
ESP/ROM/593
Edwin Smith / RIBA Collections

125. Ralph Deakin
View from the Janiculum
Gelatine silver print, 1930s
DK/I/455
Ralph Deakin / RIBA Collections

126. Ralph Deakin
*View from San Pietro
in Montorio*
Gelatine silver print, 1930s
DK/I/450/1
Ralph Deakin / RIBA Collections

127. Edwin Smith
*River Tiber and Ponte
Sant'Angelo*
Gelatine silver print, 1962
ESP/ROM/8
Edwin Smith / RIBA Collections

128. Ralph Deakin
View from the Aventine Hill
Gelatine silver print, 1930s
DK/I/450
Ralph Deakin / RIBA Collections

129. Edwin Smith
*Arco del Ponte Rotto
and Ponte Fabricio*
Gelatine silver print, 1963
ESP/ROM/28
Edwin Smith / RIBA Collections

130. Ralph Deakin
*Castel Sant'Angelo
and Ponte Sant'Angelo*
Gelatine silver print, 1930s
DK/I/308
Ralph Deakin / RIBA Collections

131. Edwin Smith
*Castel Sant'Angelo
and Ponte Sant'Angelo*
Gelatine silver print, 1962
ESP/ROM/12
Edwin Smith / RIBA Collections

132. Ralph Deakin
Colosseum
Gelatine silver print, 1930s
DK/I/322
Ralph Deakin / RIBA Collections

133. Monica Pidgeon
*View from Santa Maria
in Aracoeli*
Gelatine silver print, 1961
MP uncatalogued
Monica Pidgeon / RIBA
Collections

134. Edwin Smith
*River Tiber and Ponte
Sant'Angelo*
Gelatine silver print, 1962
ESP/ROM/8c
Edwin Smith / RIBA Collections

135. Edwin Smith
Piazza del Campidoglio
Gelatine silver print, 1970
ESP/ROM/169
Edwin Smith / RIBA Collections

136. Edwin Smith
*View from Casa dei Cavalieri di
Rodi towards Torre delle Milizie*
Gelatine silver print, 1970
ESP/ROM/422
Edwin Smith / RIBA Collections

137. Edwin Smith
*Partial view of Via della
Conciliazione and of
Saint Peter's Basilica from
Castel Sant'Angelo*
Gelatine silver print, 1970
ESP/ROM/197
Edwin Smith / RIBA Collections

138. Edwin Smith
*Saint Peter's Basilica seen
from Castel Sant'Angelo*
Gelatine silver print, 1957
ESP/ROM/196
Edwin Smith / RIBA Collections

139. Edwin Smith
*Via dei Condotti and Trinità
dei Monti*
Gelatine silver print, 1970
ESP/ROM/110
Edwin Smith / RIBA Collections

140. Stabilimento Fotografico
Domenico Anderson
Piazza di Spagna
Gelatine silver print,
early twentieth century
7800
RIBA Collections

141. Monica Pidgeon
Piazza di Spagna
Gelatine silver print, 1961
MP uncatalogued
Monica Pidgeon / RIBA
Collections

142. Unknown photographer
Spanish Steps, Piazza di Spagna
(Francesco De Sanctis)
Gelatine silver print, 1950
AP13 uncatalogued
Architectural Press Archive /
RIBA Collections

143. Ivy de Wolfe
*Church of Trinità dei Monti and
Spanish Steps, Piazza di Spagna*
(Francesco De Sanctis)
Gelatine silver print, 1961
33575/2
RIBA Collections

144. Ivy de Wolfe
*Church of Trinità dei Monti and
Spanish Steps, Piazza di Spagna*
(Francesco De Sanctis)
Gelatine silver print, 1961
33575/2
RIBA Collections

145. Ralph Deakin
*Monument to Vittorio
Emanuele II, or 'Vittoriano'*
*(Giuseppe Sacconi,
Gaetano Koch, Manfredo
Manfredi, Pio Piacentini)'*
Gelatine silver print, 1930s
DKN/I/640
Ralph Deakin / RIBA Collections

146. Ralph Deakin
*View from Monument to
Vittorio Emanuele II,
or 'Vittoriano'*
*(Giuseppe Sacconi,
Gaetano Koch, Manfredo
Manfredi, Pio Piacentini)*
Gelatine silver print, 1930s
DK/I/329
Ralph Deakin / RIBA Collections

147. Ralph Deakin
*Churches of Santa Maria
di Loreto and Santissimo
Nome di Maria seen from
the Monument to Vittorio
Emanuele II, or 'Vittoriano'*
*(Antoine Dérizet; Antonio
da Sangallo the Younger,
Jacopo del Duca)*
Gelatine silver print, 1930s
FH/PUBL/12/A
Ralph Deakin / RIBA Collections

148. Tim Benton
*Portico linking the Palazzo
delle Arti e Tradizioni Popolari
and the Palazzo della Scienza
Universale, EUR*
Gelatine silver print, 1976
RIBA107405*
Tim Benton / RIBA Collections

149. Tim Benton
*View from the Palazzo
dei Congressi to the Palazzo
della Civiltà, EUR*
Gelatine silver print, 1976
RIBA107396*
Tim Benton / RIBA Collections

150. Ralph Deakin
*Santa Maria di Loreto,
Santissimo Nome di Maria
and Trajan's Column*
Gelatine silver print, 1930s
DK/I/410
Ralph Deakin / RIBA Collections

151. George Everard Kidder Smith
Saint Peter's Square
(Gian Lorenzo Bernini)
Gelatine silver print, 1954
AP121/183
Architectural Press Archive /
RIBA Collections
Courtesy of IUAV, Venice

152. Ralph Deakin
San Giovanni in Laterano
(Francesco Borromini,
Alessandro Galilei))
Gelatine silver print, 1930s
DK/I/393/2
Ralph Deakin / RIBA Collections

153. Ralph Deakin
*Fontana dei Quattro Fiumi,
Piazza Navona*
(Gian Lorenzo Bernini)
Gelatine silver print, 1930s
DK/I/470
Ralph Deakin / RIBA Collections

Atmospheres

154. Spartaco Appetiti
Castel Sant'Angelo at night
Gelatine silver print, 1950s
AP13 uncatalogued
Architectural Press Archive /
RIBA Collections
Courtesy of Archivio Cicconi,
Roma

155. Istituto Luce
Roman Forum at night
Gelatine silver print, 1960s
AP13 uncatalogued
Architectural Press Archive /
RIBA Collections
© Istituto Luce

156. Unknown photographer
Colosseum at night
Gelatine silver print, 1979
AP13 uncatalogued
Architectural Press Archive /
RIBA Collections

157. Unknown photographer
Café Doney, Via Veneto
Gelatine silver print, 1950
AP13 uncatalogued
Architectural Press Archive /
RIBA Collections

158. Edwin Smith
*Antico Caffè Greco,
Via dei Condotti*
Gelatine silver print, 1963
LS ESP/ROM/357
Edwin Smith / RIBA Collections

159. Edwin Smith
Market in Quirinale district
Gelatine silver print, 1963
Edwin Smith / LS ESP/ROM/355
RIBA Collections

160. Monica Pidgeon
*Steps leading to the Palazzo
del Quirinale*
Gelatine silver print, 1961
MP uncatalogued
Monica Pidgeon / RIBA
Collections

161. Edwin Smith
*Entrance to the Vatican
Apostolic Palace*
Gelatine silver print, 1963
LS ESP/ROM/230
Edwin Smith / RIBA Collections

162. Monica Pidgeon
Termini Station
(Eugenio Montuori, Leo Calini,
Annibale Vitellozzi, Massimo
Castellazzi, Vasco Fadigati,
Achille Pintonello)
Gelatine silver print, 1961
MP uncatalogued
Monica Pidgeon / RIBA
Collections

163. Monica Pidgeon
Termini Station
(Eugenio Montuori, Leo Calini,
Annibale Vitellozzi, Massimo
Castellazzi, Vasco Fadigati,
Achille Pintonello)
Gelatine silver print, 1961
MP uncatalogued
Monica Pidgeon / RIBA
Collections

164. Ivy de Wolfe
Road markings, Lungotevere
Gelatine silver print, 1961
33638/13
RIBA Collections

165. Ivy de Wolfe
Kerb with advertising
Gelatine silver print, 1961
33638/2
RIBA Collections

166. Monica Pidgeon
Spanish Steps, Piazza di Spagna
(Francesco De Sanctis)
Gelatine silver print, 1961
MP uncatalogued
Monica Pidgeon / RIBA
Collections

167. Monica Pidgeon
Spanish Steps, Piazza di Spagna
(Francesco De Sanctis)
Gelatine silver print, 1961
MP uncatalogued
Monica Pidgeon / RIBA
Collections

168. Tim Benton
*Monument to Vittorio
Emanuele II, or 'Vittoriano'*
(Giuseppe Sacconi,
Gaetano Koch, Manfredo
Manfredi, Pio Piacentini)
Gelatine silver print, 1976
RIBA107385*
Tim Benton / RIBA Collections

169. Edwin Smith
*Piazza Venezia and the
Monument to Vittorio
Emanuele II, or 'Vittoriano'*
(Giuseppe Sacconi,
Gaetano Koch, Manfredo
Manfredi, Pio Piacentini)
Gelatine silver print, 1970
ESP/ROM/104
Edwin Smith / RIBA Collections

170. Unknown photographer
*Monument to Vittorio
Emanuele II, or 'Vittoriano'*
(Giuseppe Sacconi,
Gaetano Koch, Manfredo
Manfredi, Pio Piacentini)
Gelatine silver print, 1958
AP14 uncatalogued
Architectural Press Archive /
RIBA Collections

171. John Donat
Pantheon
Gelatine silver print, 1960
JD uncatalogued
John Donat / RIBA Collections

172. Ivy de Wolfe
*Colums of the Temple
of Hercules Victor
and Arch of Janus*, 1962
Gelatine silver print, 1962
33638
RIBA Collections

173. Studio Fotografico Filippo
Reale
Parco del Celio and Colosseum
Gelatine silver print, 1930s
AP13 uncatalogued
Architectural Press Archive /
RIBA Collections

174. Monica Pidgeon
Colosseum
Gelatine silver print, 1961
MP uncatalogued
Monica Pidgeon / RIBA
Collections

175. Monica Pidgeon
*Statue of Marcus Aurelius,
Piazza del Campidoglio*
Gelatine silver print, 1961
MP uncatalogued
Monica Pidgeon / RIBA
Collections

176. Monica Pidgeon
*Palazzo Senatorio,
Piazza del Campidoglio*
(Michelangelo,
Giacomo della Porta)
Gelatine silver print, 1961
MP uncatalogued
Monica Pidgeon / RIBA
Collections

177. Ralph Deakin
*Palazzo Senatorio,
Piazza
del Campidoglio*
(Michelangelo,
Giacomo della Porta)
Gelatine silver print, 1930s
DK/I/463
Ralph Deakin / RIBA Collections

178. Edwin Smith
*Palazzo Senatorio,
Piazza del Campidoglio*
(Michelangelo,
Giacomo della Porta)
Gelatine silver print, 1954
ESP/ROM/163A
Edwin Smith / RIBA Collections

179. George Everard Kidder Smith
*Staircase adjacent to the
Palazzo dei Conservatori,
Piazza del Campidoglio*
Gelatine silver print, 1954
AP121/173
Architectural Press Archive /
RIBA Collections
Courtesy of IUAV, Venice

180. Ralph Deakin
*Palazzo Senatorio,
Piazza del Campidoglio*
(Michelangelo,
Giacomo della Porta)
Gelatine silver print, 1930s
DK/I/462
Ralph Deakin / RIBA Collections

181. George Everard Kidder Smith
Piazza del Campidoglio
Gelatine silver print, 1954
AP121/171
Architectural Press Archive /
RIBA Collections
Courtesy of IUAV, Venice

182. Monica Pidgeon
Saint Peter's Square
Gelatine silver print, 1961
MP uncatalogued
Monica Pidgeon / RIBA
Collections

183. Edwin Smith
*Colonnade, Saint Peter's
Square*
(Gian Lorenzo Bernini)
Gelatine silver print, 1960
ESP/ROM/216
Edwin Smith / RIBA Collections

184. Monica Pidgeon
*Colonnade, Saint Peter's
Square*
(Gian Lorenzo Bernini)
Gelatine silver print, 1961
MP uncatalogued
Monica Pidgeon / RIBA
Collections

185. Monica Pidgeon
Food shop
Gelatine silver print, 1961
MP uncatalogued
Monica Pidgeon / RIBA
Collections

186. Monica Pidgeon
Food shop
Gelatine silver print, 1961
MP uncatalogued
Monica Pidgeon / RIBA
Collections

187. Unknown photographer
INA-Casa housing,
Valco San Paolo
(Mario De Renzi,
Saverio Muratori et al.)
Gelatine silver print, 1951
AP13 uncatalogued
Architectural Press Archive /
RIBA Collections

188. Monica Pidgeon
Fontana della Barcaccia,
Piazza di Spagna
(Pietro Bernini,
Gian Lorenzo Bernini)
Gelatine silver print, 1961
MP uncatalogued
Monica Pidgeon / RIBA
Collections

189. Marion Johnson
(aka Georgina Masson)
Piazza Venezia
Gelatine silver print, 1953
AP88/106
Architectural Press Archive /
RIBA Collections
Courtesy of the American
Academy in Rome

190. Monica Pidgeon
Roof terraces
Gelatine silver print, 1961
MP uncatalogued
Monica Pidgeon / RIBA
Collections

191. Monica Pidgeon
Roof terrace
Gelatine silver print, 1961
MP uncatalogued
Monica Pidgeon / RIBA
Collections

192. Edwin Smith
Piazza di Sant'Ignazio
(Filippo Raguzzini)
Gelatine silver print, 1970
ESP/ROM/52
Edwin Smith / RIBA Collections

193. Ivy de Wolfe
Street and advertisement signs
Gelatine silver print, c. 1960
33587/35
RIBA Collections

194. Edwin Smith
Pincio gardens
Gelatine silver print, 1970
ESP/ROM/128
Edwin Smith / RIBA Collections

195. Edwin Smith
Pantheon
Gelatine silver print, 1970
ESP/ROM/386
Edwin Smith / RIBA Collections

196. Ivy de Wolfe
Pavement plaque referring
to the city's water supply
Gelatine silver print, 1960
33587/39
RIBA Collections

197. Ivy de Wolfe
Lungotevere
Gelatine silver print, 1961
33638/9
RIBA Collections

198. Ivy de Wolfe
Lungotevere
Gelatine silver print, 1961
33638/8
RIBA Collections

199. Edwin Smith
Pincio gardens
Gelatine silver print, 1970
ESP/ROM/124
Edwin Smith / RIBA Collections

200. Edwin Smith
Piazza della Repubblica
Gelatine silver print, 1970
ESP/ROM/78
Edwin Smith / RIBA Collections

201. Ivor de Wolfe
Termini Station
(Eugenio Montuori, Leo Calini,
Annibale Vitellozzi, Massimo
Castellazzi, Vasco Fadigati,
Achille Pintonello)
Gelatine silver print, 1952
33569/33
RIBA Collections

202. Edwin Smith
Fontana delle Tartarughe,
Piazza Mattei, at night
(Giacomo della Porta,
Taddeo Landini)
Gelatine silver print, 1970
ESP/ROM/84
Edwin Smith / RIBA Collections

203. Edwin Smith
Churches of Santissimo Nome
di Maria and Santa Maria
di Loreto at night
(Antoine Dérizet; Antonio
da Sangallo the Younger,
Jacopo del Duca)
Gelatine silver print, 1970
ESP/ROM/307
Edwin Smith / RIBA Collections

204. Unknown photographer
Statue of the Nile, Fountain of
the Four Rivers, Piazza Navona,
at night
(Gian Lorenzo Bernini)
Gelatine silver print, 1950
AP13 uncatalogued
Architectural Press Archive /
RIBA Collections

205. Monica Pidgeon
Fontana della Barcaccia,
Piazza di Spagna, at night
(Pietro Bernini,
Gian Lorenzo Bernini)
Gelatine silver print, 1961
MP uncatalogued
Monica Pidgeon / RIBA
Collections

206. Monica Pidgeon
Via Frattina at night
Gelatine silver print, 1961
MP uncatalogued
Monica Pidgeon / RIBA
Collections

207. Ivy de Wolfe
Neon signs at night
Gelatine silver print, 1961
33572/8
RIBA Collections

208. Ivy de Wolfe
Neon signs at night
Gelatine silver print, 1961
33572/2
RIBA Collections

209. Ivy de Wolfe
Neon signs at night
Gelatine silver print, 1961
33572/6
RIBA Collections

* digital image in the
RIBA Collections

Bibliography

Rome as Eternal City has long existed within the British consciousness both as imagined construct and experienced reality. Forming the intersection of ancient history, art, aesthetic taste, memory, myth and archaeology, the city has provided a rich source of inspiration for artists and writers for centuries. Consequently, a wealth of literature examining Rome as explored by British visitors and residents has been published across a range of disciplines, providing insights into the architectural and urban evolution of the city, as seen through the eyes of artists and photographers from the fifteenth to the twentieth centuries.

In particular, photographic imagery (both its creation and consumption) played an increasingly central role in the experience of the nineteenth-century traveller to Rome, with early photography and the written word becoming enmeshed to both reflect the reality and perpetuate the imagined romance of the city. As explored in a number of recent books and exhibitions, the prevailing fascination with ancient sites, monuments and architecture however, owed as much to the constructed concept of an idealised, 'timeless' landscape of the imagination as it did to the accurate representation of history. Seen through a very particular lens, a specific interpretation of ancient culture was generated to suit contemporary tastes, with early photographers attempting to depict a sense of the antique, in line with their own cultural preoccupations. Ruined architecture and monuments could therefore be seen as the embodiment of the history, myths, noble values and moral teachings of ancient civilisations, whilst crucially providing a suitably fashionable, picturesque visual aesthetic.

The most successful and influential of the early British photographers exploring the city's ancient built heritage were mid-nineteenth-century rivals and pioneers of the 'Roman School of Photography', Robert Macpherson and James Anderson. The cultural climate which saw increased numbers of British visitors travelling to Rome in the nineteenth to early twentieth centuries is described in a number of recent texts focusing on the growth of tourism and travel. These illustrate how the growing appetite for easily portable visual souvenirs was both encouraged and satiated by the Rome-based photographers and photographic studios of the time, whilst a growing fashion for amateur photography as a hobby saw visitors seeking to capture the visual wonders of the city for themselves.

Increasingly, tourists and amateur photographers were seeking out what were considered the 'essential' sights of ancient Rome as prescribed by their Baedeker or Murray guidebooks. Particular monuments and panoramas of the city were captured for posterity and marketed for mass consumption as the tourist trade continued to burgeon. Certain buildings and sites therefore achieved almost totemic status, perpetuating the city's romantic mystery and allure for foreign travellers. In addition, the inclusion of previously overlooked buildings in publications by successful resident photographers such as Robert Macpherson essentially 'legitimised' them as worthy subjects on the tourist itinerary: a demonstration of how photography holds the power to elevate architecture to iconic status.

At the dawn of the twentieth century, however, photography was becoming increasingly commonplace, whilst the advent of the picture postcard was providing tourists with cheap, mass-produced images. The novelty of merely recording a view or historic site was no longer enough, and advances in technology saw photographers seeking to experiment with the more expressive qualities of the camera. Increasingly, it was possible to focus on particular details, playing with ideas of perspective and light to purposefully emphasise certain elements and distort others, looking to the architecture of the future as much as that of the past. By 're-framing' the city in new ways, they sought not merely to record its topography, architecture and ancient ruins, but to capture and distil the particular qualities and atmosphere of this unique city.

Architectural journals and magazines came into their own in between nineteenth and twentieth century with the resulting demand for architectural photography seeing increased collaboration between the photographers and architects of the Modernist period. This symbiotic relationship between the published image and the built environment both reflected and shaped the stylistic preoccupations of the time, with photography actively influencing the perception of Rome's modern architecture. Literature on the subject has explored how architects and photographers increasingly sought to create and disseminate a distinct architectural language and sense of national identity through visual means — one which both celebrated the glories of the ancient past and pronounced the aspirations of twentieth-century Italy.

Eminently photogenic, iconic buildings such the Palazzo della Civiltà Italiana incorporated the clean lines of the Modernist aesthetic with visual references to Rome's architectural past, adding to the allure of the city's complex urban landscape for photographers.

Following the destruction of World War II, the 1950s and 1960s eventually saw 'rebirth' of Italy's economy, with the city of Rome again becoming a hive of tourist activity at the perceived epicentre of a newly-marketed *dolce vita* of glamour and culture. Expressed through post-war photography and cinema, this renewed fascination with the Eternal City was once again interpreted through a romantic lens, capturing the imagination and proving irresistible for foreign visitors. Increasingly, popular photography depicted Rome as a peopled city of contrasts, contradictions and juxtapositions, with the ancient heritage of the city providing a visual foil for the clean lines and aesthetics of mid-twentieth-century architecture, design and fashion.

In 1955 however, American photographer G. E. Kidder-Smith published his seminal book *Italy Builds* for London's Architectural Press, which through words and images examined the impact of modern architecture in Italy. Kidder-Smith's photography and the book's accompanying essays explore the notion of 'urban inheritance' for the modern architect in post-Fascist Italy, the interpretation of historical precedent, and architecture's close relationship with contemporary social and cultural forces, whilst demonstrating the ongoing relevance of urban elements such as the piazza in the Italian way of life.

Eight years later, Hubert and Hazel de Cronin Hastings, working under the pseudonyms of Ivor and Ivy de Wolfe, published *The Italian Townscape*, a remarkable book replete with their own photographic illustrations. The book's lyrical imagery and eccentrically engaging text traces the visual rhythms of the Italian urban environment (including those of Rome itself), whilst interpreting the word 'townscape' in its broadest, most holistic sense. Through the play of light and shadow, space and form, the book's imagery explores the many facets of the Italian city, both tangible and intangible, grandiose and mundane, whilst demonstrating how a place is inevitably shaped by the everyday human interventions of its inhabitants.

Rome's unique sense of place and its dichotomies of old and new are further explored in Stewart Perowne's book of 1971 entitled *Rome: From its Foundation to the Present*, which is richly illustrated with images by the British photographer Edwin Smith. Smith's empathetic evocations of the architecture and environs of Rome are beguilingly poetic in their sense of atmosphere and yet are firmly rooted in a particular time and place. In this publication, the city's ancient monuments and modern architecture are not depicted as historical specimens shown in splendid isolation from their environment, but rather as elements within the context of the modern city, creating a multi-dimensional sense of place. As Perowne's book demonstrates, Smith's Rome is a populous, living city of contrasts, where ancient and modern exist side by side.

To summarise then, the desire to express the unique character of Rome through photography has existed since the very birth of the medium itself. Literature on the subject has consequently served two purposes: to either provide a narrative historical survey of the varied approaches taken by photographers in Rome, or to exploit photography in its published form as a means of actively shaping, challenging and influencing our perceptions of the city in a more expressive sense. Positioned somewhere between the realms of imagination and reality in the British consciousness, Rome continues to inspire and fascinate photographers, artists and writers today. This brief survey of literature — together with the select bibliography that follows — demonstrates photography's ongoing ability to both raise questions and offer insights into the heritage and ambitions of a modern city grappling with issues of preservation and progress.

Jemma Street

1846
Dickens, C., *Pictures from Italy*, London: Bradbury & Evans.

1852
Thomas, R. W., 'Photography in Rome', in *The Art Journal*, May, pp. 159–160.

1857
Murray, J., *A Handbook for Travellers in Central Italy, Part 2: Rome and Its Environs*, fourth edition, London: J. Murray.

1859
Anderson, J., *Catalogue des photographies de Rome de James Anderson, en vente chez J. Sphitöver*, Rome.

1863
Macpherson, R., *Vatican Sculptures, Selected and Arranged in the Order in which They are Found in the Galleries, Briefly Explained*, Glasgow and London: William Mackenzie and Chapman & Hall.

1879
Parker, J. H., *Historical photographs: A catalogue of three thousand three hundred photographs of antiquities in Rome and Italy*, London: E. Stanford.

1882
Boito, C., 'Il Monumento Nazionale a Vittorio Emanuele', in *Nuova Antologia*, vol. LXIV, August.

1900
Brettingham, M., 'The Forum today', in *Architectural Review*, November, pp. 229–231, 280.

1909
Latham, C., March Phillipps, E., *The Gardens of Italy*, London and New York: Country Life Ltd. & Charles Scribner's Sons, vol. I.
Potter, O. M., *The Colour of Rome: Historic, Personal & Local*, London: Chatto & Windus.

1911
Acciaresi, P., *Giuseppe Sacconi e l'opera sua massima. Cronaca dei lavori del Monumento Nazionale a Vittorio Emanuele II*, Rome: Tipografia dell'Unione Editrice.

1912
Judge, M., 'New Interpretations of Rome', in *Architectural Review*, February, pp. 80–89.
Ward, W. H., 'Rome under the Renaissance Popes', in *Architectural Review*, April, pp. 214–218.

1923
Lubbock, P., *Roman Pictures*, London: Cape.
Reddie, Lilias A., *Roman recollections; the Forum and the Palatine, with ninety-three illustrations from photographs taken by the author*, London: Sands & Co.

1926
Lucas, E. V., *A Wanderer in Rome*, London: Methuen.

1930
Angeli, D., *Le cronache del Caffè Greco*, Milan: Treves.

1933
Yerbury, F. R., 'The A.A. Excursion 1933 – Italy, Old and New', in *Architectural Association Journal*, vol. 49, no. 557, pp. 207–233.

1950
Reed, H. H., 'Rome: the third sack', in *Architectural Review*, February, pp. 91–110.

1951
'Railway terminus', in *Architectural Review*, April, pp. 208–215.
Rudofsky, B., 'The third Rome: Mussolini's project', in *Architectural Review*, no. 655, July, pp. 2, 30–37.

1952
Kidder-Smith, G. E., 'Contemporary Italian Architecture and the Italian Heritage', in *RIBA Journal*, vol. 59, no. 4.

1955
Kidder-Smith, G. E., *Italy Builds*, London: Architectural Press.

1956
Klein, W., *William Klein: Rome*, Paris: Editions du Seuil.

1958
Santiago, M., 'Palazzetto dello Sport, Rome', in *Architectural Review*, February, pp. 90, 140–41.

1960
Menen, A., *Rome Revealed*, London: Thames & Hudson.
'Modern architecture in Rome. Selection of buildings made in consultation with Carlo Pouchain and Bruno Zevi', in *Architectural Design*, July, pp. 280–281.

1962
'The Italian Townscape', in *Architectural Review*, special issue, June.
Atkinson, F., 'La Rinascente Store, Rome', in *Architectural Review*, October, vol. 132, no. 788, pp. 268–274.
Rogers, E., 'Department store "La Rinascente", Rome', in *Architectural Design*, June, pp. 286–289.

1963
De Wolfe, I. & De Wolfe, I. [pseuds.], *The Italian Townscape*, London: Architectural Press.

1965
Masson, G., *The Companion guide to Rome*, London: Collins.
Negro, S., *Nuovo Album Romano*, Vicenza: Neri Pozza Editore.

1969
Masson, G., 'Rome and the Villa Pamphilj', in *Architectural Review*, August, pp. 131–35.

1971
Perowne, S., *Rome: From its Foundation to the Present*, London: P. Elek Productions.
Zevi, B., 'British Embassy in Rome', in *Architectural Review*, September, pp. 152–170.

1975
Brizzi, B., *Roma cento anni fa nelle fotografie della raccolta Parker*, Rome: Edizioni Quasar.
Patetta, L., *Storia dell'architettura. Antologia critica*, Milan: Etas libri.

1976
Rykwert, J., *The Idea of a Town: The Anthropology of Urban Form in Rome, Italy and the Ancient World*, Princeton, N.J.: Princeton University Press.

1978
Becchetti, P., *Fotografi e Fotografia in Italia, 1839–1880*, Rome: Edizioni Quasar.
Marder, T. A., 'Roma interrotta: modern architects on [Giambattista] Nolli', in *Architectural Review*, August, pp. 64–66.
Paczowski, B., 'The Trevi Fountain: on the ambiguity of the concept of nature', in *Architectural Review*, January, pp. 72–78.
Helsted, D., 'Rome in Early Photographs', in *The History of Photography 2*, no. 4, pp. 335–346.

1979
Becchetti, P., Pietrangeli, C., *Roma in dagherrotipia*, Rome: Edizioni Quasar.
Bertelli, C., Bollati, G., 'L'immagine fotografica 1845–1945', in *Storia d'Italia, Annali*, 2 vols., vol. 2, Turin: Einaudi.
Constant, C., 'Mannerist Rome: map guide to Rome in the 16th century', in *Architectural Design*, vol. 49, no. 3/4, pp. 19–26, 106–107.
Lucas, U. (ed.), *L'immagine fotografica 1945–2000*, in *Storia d'Italia, Annali*, 2 vols., vol. 20, Turin: Einaudi.

1980
Hershkowitz, R., *The British photographer abroad. The first thirthy years*, London: Robert Hershkowitz.
Insolera, I., *Le Città nella Storia d'Italia: Roma*, Rome-Bari: Laterza.

1981
Einaudi, K., 'The Fototeca Unione Archive and Archaeological Photography', in *Visual Resources, an International Journal on Images and their Uses*, vol. 2, no. 1–3, pp. 7–17.
Miraglia, M., 'Note per una storia della fotografia italiana (1839–1911)', in *Storia dell'arte Italiana*, vol. 9, tome II, Turin: Einaudi, pp. 421–544.

1983

Becchetti, P., *La fotografia a Roma dalle origini al 1915*, Rome: Editore Colombo.
MacKenzie, R., 'The Cradle and Grave of Empires: Robert Macpherson and the Photography of Nineteenth Century Rome', in *The Photographic Collector*, vol. 4, no. 2, pp. 215–232.

1984

Guidoni, E., *Roma in cartolina. I monumenti e la città fra cronaca e immagine (1895–1945)*, Rome: Edizioni Kappa.
Smith, E., Cook, O., *Edwin Smith: Photographs 1935–1971*, London: Thames & Hudson.

1986

Becchetti, P., 'Una dinastia di fotografi romani: gli Anderson', in *Archivio Fotografico Toscano*, II, no. 4, pp. 56–67.
Munsterberg, M., 'A biographical sketch of Robert Macpherson', in *The Art Bulletin*, vol. 68, no. 1, pp.142–153.
Porzio, P. L. (ed.), *Il Vittoriano. Materiali per una storia*, Rome: Palombi Editori.

1987

Becchetti, P., Pietrangeli C., *Un inglese fotografo a Roma, Robert MacPherson*, Rome: Edizioni Quasar.

1990

Buckman, R., *The Photographic Work of Calvert Richard Jones*, London: Science Museum.

1991

La fotografia a Roma nel secolo XIX. La veduta, il ritratto, l'archeologia (conference proceedings, Palazzo Braschi, Rome,12–13 December 1989), Rome: Artemide.
Margiotta, A., '"Rome 1857": un album di antiche vedute fotografiche romane', in *Bollettino dei Musei Comunali di Roma*, special issue, 5, pp. 83–90.
Zannier, I. (ed.), *Segni di luce. Alle origini della fotografia in Italia*, Ravenna: Longo Editore.

1992

Benevolo, L., *Roma dal 1870 al 1990*, Rome-Bari: Laterza.
Szegedy-Maszak, A., 'A Perfect Ruin: Nineteenth-Century Views of the Colosseum', in *Arion: A Journal of Humanities and the Classics*, third series, vol. 2, no. 1, pp. 115–142.

1993

Barefoot, B., *The English Road to Rome*, Upton-upon-Severn: Images Publishing (Malvern).
Becchetti, P., *Roma nelle fotografie della fondazione Marco Besso 1850–1920*, Rome: Editore Colombo.

1994

Romano, S. (ed.), *L'immagine di Roma 1848–1895, la città, l'archeologia, il medioevo nei calotipi del Fondo Tuminello*, Naples: Electa Napoli.

1996

Becchetti, P., *Roma nelle fotografie dei fratelli D'Alessandri 1858–1930*, Rome: Editore Colombo.
Davey, P., 'Outrage. Rome sick: monument to Vittorio Emanuele II, Rome, Italy', in *Architectural Review*, October, p. 25.
MacKenzie, R., 'Scottish photographers in nineteenth century Italy', in *History of Photography*, vol. 20, no. 1, pp. 33–40.
Maffioli, M., *Il bel vedere: fotografi e architetti nell'Italia dell'Ottocento*, Turin: Società Editrice Internazionale.
Pelizzari, M. A. (ed.), 'Nineteenth-century Photography in Italy', in *History of Photography*, vol. 20, no. 1.

1997

Bass, D., 'Insiders and Outsiders – Latent Urban Thinking in Movies of Modern Rome', in François Penz, Maureen Thomas (eds.), *Cinema & Architecture: Méliès, Mallet-Stevens, Multimedia*, London: British Film Institute, pp. 84–99.
Conforti, C., 'Roma, Napoli, Sicilia', in Dal Co, F. (ed.), *Storia dell'architettura italiana. Il secondo Novecento*, Milan: Electa, pp. 176–241.

1999

Crawford, A., 'Robert Macpherson 1814–72, the Foremost Photographer of Rome', in *Papers of the British School at Rome*, 67, pp. 353–403.
Szegedy-Maszak, A., 'Roman Views', in *Six Exposures: Essays in Celebration of the Opening of the Harrison D. Horblit Collection of Early Photography*, Cambridge, MA: Houghton Library, pp. 89–106.

2000

Bertozzi, M., Bertellini, G., 'Visualising the Past: The Italian City in Early Cinema', in *Film History*, vol. 12, no. 3, Early Italian Cinema, pp. 322–329.
Salmon, F., 'The Impact of the Archaeology of Rome on British Architects and Their Work c. 1750–1840', in *The Impact of Italy: The Grand Tour and Beyond*, London: British School at Rome.

2001

Bruscolini, E., *Rome in Cinema between Fiction and Reality*, Venice: Marsilio.
Forgacs, D., 'Urban legends: Ten cities that shook cinema – Rome – The in-crowd', in *Sight and Sound*, vol. 11, no. 9, pp. 30–33.
Insolera, I., *Roma fascista nelle fotografie dell'Istituto Luce*, Rome: Editori Riuniti.
Szegedy-Maszak, A., 'Rambles in Rome', in Richardson, C., Smith, G. (eds.), *Britannia, Italia, Germania: Taste and Travel in the Nineteenth Century*, Edinburgh: VARIE, pp. 6–22.
Vidotto, V., *Roma contemporanea*, Rome-Bari: Laterza.

2002

Ackerman, J. S., 'On the origins of architectural photography', in Kester Rattenbury (ed.), *This is not architecture: media constructions*, London and New York: Routledge, pp. 24–35.
Bevilacqua, P., *Il Paesaggio italiano nelle fotografie dell'Istituto Luce*, Rome: Editori Riuniti.
Tittoni, M. E., Margiotta, A. (eds.), *Scenari della memoria. Roma nella fotografia 1850–1900*, Milan: Mondadori Electa.

2003

Black, J., *Italy and the Grand Tour*, New Haven: Yale University Press.
Dossi, C., *I mattoidi al concorso pel Monumento a Vittorio Emanuele*, Milan: Lampi di stampa.
Pelizzari, M. A., 'Retracing the Outlines of Rome: Intertextuality and Imaginative Geographies in Nineteenth-Century Photographs', in J. M. Schwartz, J. R. Ryan (eds.), *Picturing Place: Photography and the Geographical Imagination*, London and New York: I. B. Tauris.

2004

Becchetti, P., Brizzi, B., *Roma in tre dimensioni. La fotografia stereoscopica*, Rome: Editore Colombo.
Borm, J., 'Defining Travel: On the Travel Book, Travel Writing and Terminology', in G. Hooper, T. Youngs (eds.), *Perspectives on Travel Writing*, Aldershot: Ashgate.
Cresti, C. (ed.), *Fotografia e architettura*, Florence: Pontecorboli.
Cresti, C., Gravagnuolo, B., Gurrieri, F., 'Architettura e città negli anni del fascismo in Italia e nelle colonie', in *Architettura e Arte*, Quaderni semestrali 3/4, Florence: Pontecorboli.
Gregory, R., 'Delight. Pantheon, Rome, Italy', in *Architectural Review*, April, p. 98.

2005

Russo, A., *Viewpoints: Italy in Black and White*, Milan: Skira.

2006

Davey, P., 'Pax Romana', in *Architectural Review*, October, pp. 54–61.
Jolivet, V., *Ruines italiennes. Photographies des collections Alinari*, Paris: Gallimard.
Pfister, M., 'Enchantment and Disenchantment: English Romantic Visions of Italy', in *Journal of Anglo-Italian Studies*, no. 8, pp. 59–73.
Slessor, C., 'Roman remains', in *Architectural Review*, January, pp. 18–19.

2007

Leone, R., Margiotta, A., *Fori Imperiali. Demolizioni e scavi: Fotografie 1924/1940*, Milan: Electa.

2008

Kirk, T., 'Monumental Monstrosity, Monstrous Monumentality', in *Perspecta*, no. 40.
Wrigley, R. (ed.), *Cinematic Rome*, Leicester: Troubador.

2009

Erwitt, E., *Elliott Erwitt's Rome*, Kempen: teNeues Publishing.
Fanelli, G., *Per una storia dell'iconografia fotografica del Foro Romano nell'Ottocento*, Paris: privately printed.
Fanelli, G., *Storia della fotografia di architettura*, Rome-Bari: Laterza.
Tittoni, M. E., Betti, F., D'Amelio, A. M., Leone, R., Margiotta, A. (eds.), *Via dell'Impero: demolizioni e scavi; Fotografie 1930/1943*, Milan: Electa.

2010

Hom, S. M., 'Consuming the View: Tourism, Rome, and the Topos of the Eternal City', in *Annali d'Italianistica*, vol. 28, special issue on *Capital City: Rome 1870–2010*, pp. 91–116.
Muntoni, A., *Roma tra le due guerre, 1919–1944: architettura, modelli urbani, linguaggi della modernità*, Rome: Kappa.
Paulicelli, E., 'Fashioning Rome: Cinema, Fashion and the Media in the Post War Years', in *Annali d'Italianistica*, vol. 28, special issue on *Capital City: Rome 1870–2010*, pp. 257–278.
Pelizzari, M. A., *Photography and Italy*, London: Reaktion Books Ltd.
Sachs, J., *Romantic Antiquity: Rome in the British Imagination, 1789–1832*, Oxford and New York: Oxford University Press.
Slessor, C., 'MAXXI, Rome, Italy', in *Architectural Review*, January, pp. 44–53, 106.

2011

Bosworth, R. J. B., *Whispering City: Rome and its histories*, New Haven, CT, and London: Yale University Press.
Wester, S., 'Three Nineteenth-Century Photographers of the Ruins of Ancient Rome', in *Visual Resources*, no. 8:4, pp. 343–354.

2012

Pinto, J., *Speaking Ruins: Piranesi, Architects and Antiquity in Eighteenth-Century Rome (Thomas Spencer Jerome Lectures)*, Ann Arbor, MI: University of Michigan Press.

2013
Mailloux, S., 'Narrative as Embodied Intensities: The Eloquence of Travel in 19th Century Rome', in *Narrative*, vol. 21, no. 2, pp. 125–139.
Wrigley, R., *Roman fever: influence, infection and the image of Rome, 1700–1870*, New Haven, CT: Yale University Press.

2014
Elwall, R., *Evocations of Place: The Photography of Edwin Smith*, London: Merrell.
Hill, S. P., Minghelli, G., *Stillness in Motion: Italy, Photography, and the Meanings of Modernity*, Toronto: Toronto University Press.
Russell, A., 'Memory and movement in the Roman Fora from antiquity to Metro C.', in *Journal of the Society of Architectural Historians*, vol. 73, no. 4, pp. 478–506.

2015
Agazarian, D., 'Victorian Roads to Rome: historical travel in the wake of the Grand Tour', in *Nineteenth-Century Contexts*, vol. 37, no. 5, pp. 391–409
Harris, L. et al., 'Imagining a Nation's Capital: Rome and the John Henry Parker Photography Collection, 1864–1879', in *Nineteenth-Century Art Worldwide, a journal of nineteenth-century visual culture*, vol. 14, no. 1, Spring.

2016
Maggi, A., 'Capturing the Italian Townscape: from the beginnings of Italian landscape photography to the anti-idyllic images of Ivor and Ivy de Wolfe', in *The Journal of Architecture*, vol. 21, no. 6.

2017
Bonetti, M. F., 'La Mostra della fotografia a Roma dal 1840 al 1915: collezionisti, studiosi e conoscitori intorno al 1953', in *Rivista di Studi di Fotografia*, no. 6, pp. 50–70.
Fanelli, G., *Rome: Portrait of a city*, Cologne: Taschen.
Pemble, J., *The Rome We Have Lost*, Oxford: Oxford University Press.
Rhodes, J. D., 'Balsdon Fellowships. The Uneternal City: Modern Rome According to the Cinema', in *Papers of the British School at Rome*, vol. 85, Cambridge: Cambridge University Press, pp. 335–354.
Settis, S., *Architettura e democrazia. Paesaggio, città, diritta civili*, Turin: Einaudi.
Slessor, C., 'Reading the Ruins: a Catastrophic History of Architecture', in *Architectural Review*, December, pp. 80–86.
Weststeijn, A., Whitling, F., *Termini. Cornerstone of modern Rome*, Papers of the Royal Netherlands Institute in Rome, Rome: Quasar.

2018
Furini, G., Gambetta G., 'Le fotografie di Rodrigo Pais come documentazione dello sviluppo urbano di Roma nella seconda metà del Novecento', in Crippa, M. A., Zanzottera, F. (eds.), *Fotografia per l'Architettura del XX secolo in Italia. Costruzione della storia, progetto, cantiere*, Cinisello Balsamo: Silvana Editoriale, pp. 195–198.

Exhibition catalogues

1953
Mostra della fotografia a Roma, dal 1840 al 1915 (Rome, Palazzo Braschi), Associazione Amici dei Musei di Roma, Ente Provinciale per il Turismo, Rome: U. Quintily Tip.

1971
Becchetti, P., Cavazzi, L., Della Rocchetta, G. I., Pietrangeli, C., *Roma cento anni fa nelle fotografie del tempo* (Rome, Palazzo Braschi, 17 December 1970 – 17 March 1971), Rome: Amici dei Musei di Roma.

1977
Rome in Early Photographs, the Age of Pius IX, Photographs 1846–1878 from Roman and Danish Collections, translated by Ann Thornton (Copenhagen, The Thorvaldsen Museum, 1977), Copenhagen: The Thorvaldsen Museum, 1977; Becchetti, P., Helsted, D., Henschen, E., Jörnaes, B., *Roma dei fotografi al tempo di Pio IX 1846–1878. Fotografie da collezioni danesi e romane* (Rome, Palazzo Braschi, 1978), Rome: Multigrafica.

1979
Fotografia italiana dell'Ottocento (Florence, Palazzo Pitti, October–December 1979; Venice, Ala Napoleonica, January–March 1980), Milan: Electa and Firenze: Alinari.

1980
Keller, J., Breisch, K. A., *A Victorian View of Ancient Rome. The Parker Collection of Historical Photographs in the Kelsey Museum of Archaeology* (Kelsey Museum of Archaeology, September–December 1980), Ann Arbor, MI: Kelsey Museum of Archaeology, The University of Michigan.
Watson, W. M., *Images of Italy, Photography in the nineteenth century* (Mount Holyoke College Art Museum, 8 February – 14 March 1980), South Hadley, MA: Mount Holyoke College Art Museum.

1982
Pare, R., *Photography and Architecture: 1839–1939* (Chicago, Art Institute of Chicago, 9 May – 26 June 1983; New York, Cooper-Hewitt Museum, 26 July – 16 October 1983; Paris, Musée National d'Art Moderne – Centre Georges Pompidou, 22 February – 8 April 1984; Ottawa, National Gallery of Canada, 13 September – 11 November 1984), Montreal: Callaway Editions / Canadian Centre for Architecture.

1984
Brettell, R. R., *Paper and Light, the Calotype in France and Great Britain, 1839–1870* (Houston, The Museum of Fine Arts, and Chicago, The Art Institute of Chicago, Fall–Winter 1982–83), Boston: D. R. Godine, and London: Kudos & Godine, in association with the Museum of Fine Arts, Houston, and the Art Institute of Chicago.

1987
Cavazzi, L., Tozzi, S., Margiotta, R., *Pittori fotografi a Roma, 1845–1870, Immagini raccolta fotografica Comunale* (Rome, Palazzo Braschi, 25 June – 27 September 1987), Rome: Multigrafica.

1988
Lassam, R. E., Gray, M., *The Romantic Era – La Calotipia in Italia 1845–1860: Reverendo Calvert Richard Jones, 1804–1877; Reverendo George Wilson Bridges, 1788–1863; William Robert Baker di Bayfordbury, 1810–1896*, Florence: Alinari.
Wester, S. (ed.), *This present, which is still the past: nineteenth century photographs of classical monuments*, Santa Monica, CA.: Photo Archive, Getty Center for the History of Art and the Humanities.

1989
Cavazzi, L., Margiotta, A., Tozzi, A., *Un Inglese a Roma, 1864–1877: La raccolta Parker nell'Archivio Fotografico Comunale*, Rome: Artemide Editoriale.

1993
Biblioteca Vallicelliana, Soprintendenza Archeologica di Roma, *Archeologia in posa, cento anni di fotografia del Foro Romano* (Rome, Biblioteca Vallicelliana, Salone borrominiano, 1993), Rome: Editori De Luca.

1996
Liversidge, M., Edwards, C. (eds.), *Imagining Rome: British Artists and Rome in the Nineteenth Century* (Bristol, City Museum and Art Gallery, 3 May – 23 June 1996), London: Merrell Holberton.

1999
Margiotta, A., Tozzi, S., *Rome au XIX siècle: Photographies inedites 1852–1890* (Paris, Musée Carnavalet, 19 June – 5 September 1999), Rome: Palombi Editori.

2002
Leone, R., Museo di Roma (eds.), *Il Museo di Roma racconta la città* (Rome, Palazzo Braschi, from 4 May 2002), Rome: Gangemi editore.

2003
Bonetti, M. F., Maffioli, M. (eds.), *L'Italia d'argento. 1839–1859. Storia del dagherrotipo in Italia* (Florence, Sala d'arme di Palazzo Vecchio, 30 May – 13 July 2003; Rome, Palazzo Fontana di Trevi, 26 September – 16 November 2003), Florence: Fratelli Alinari.
Capodiferro, A., Lauf C. (eds.), *Georgina Masson 1912–1980* (Rome, American Academy in Rome Gallery, 29 April – 28 June 2003), Milan: Charta.
Cartier-Bresson, A., Margiotta, A. (eds.), *Roma 1850. Il Circolo dei pittori fotografi del Caffè Greco* (Rome, Musei Capitolini, Palazzo Caffarelli, 29 November 2003 – 25 January 2004; Paris, Maison Européenne de la Photographie, 11 February – 18 April 2004), Milan: Electa.

2004
Cartier-Bresson, A., Maffioli, M., Riottot El-Habib B. (eds.), *Vu d'Italie 1841–1941. La photographie italienne dans les collections du Musée Alinari* (Paris, Pavillon des Arts, 10 November 2004 – 6 March 2005), Florence: Fratelli Alinari.

2005
Ritter, D., *Rom 1846–1870: James Anderson und die Maler-Fotografen: Sammlung Siegert* (Munich, Neue Pinakothek, 4 May – 11 September 2005), Bönningheim: Edition Braus.
De Seta, C., *Imago urbis Romae: l'immagine di Roma in età moderna* (Rome, Musei Capitolini, 11 February – 15 May 2005), Milan: Electa.
Lyons, C. L., Papadopoulos, J. K., Stewart, L. S., Szegedy-Maszak, A., *Antiquity & Photography: Early Views of Ancient Mediterranean Sites* (Malibu, Getty Villa, Winter 2005 and Spring 2006), Los Angeles: Getty Publications.

2006
Boemi, M. F., Travaglini, C. M. (eds.), *Roma dall'alto*: (Rome, Casa dell'architettura, Acquario romano, 25 October – 30 November 2006), Rome: Università degli Studi Roma Tre.

2007
Lundberg, W. B., Pinto, J. A. (eds.), *Steps Off the Beaten Path: Nineteenth Century Photographs of Rome and Its Environs – Sentieri smarriti e ritrovati: Roma e dintorni nelle fotografie del secondo Ottocento: immagini della collezione di Delaney e W. Bruce Lundberg* (New York, American Academy in Rome, December 2006 – June 2007; Rome, American Academy in Rome Gallery, 24 November 2007 – 11 January 2008), Milan: Charta.
Taylor, R. (ed.), *Impressed by Light: British Photographs from Papers Negatives, 1840–1860* (New York, The Metropolitan Museum of Art, 24 September – 30 December 2007; Washington, National Gallery of Art, 3 February – 4 May 2008; Paris, Musée d'Orsay, 26 May – 7 September 2008), New Haven, London: Yale University Press.

2008
Bonetti, M. F., Dall'Olio, C., Prandi, A., *Roma, 1840–1870: La fotografia, il collezionista, e lo storico* (Rome, Calcografia, 18 January – 9 March 2008; Modena, Fotomuseo Giuseppe Panini, 15 March – 4 May 2008), Rome: Peliti.

2009
Coates-Stephens, R., *Immagini e memoria: Rome in the photographs of Father Peter Paul Mackey 1890–1901* (London, Sir John Soane's Museum, 19 June – 12 September 2009), London: British School at Rome.
Elwall, R., Carullo, V., *Framing Modernism: Architecture and Photography in Italy 1926–1965* (London, Estorick Collection of Modern Italian Art, 29 April – 21 June 2009; Rome, MAXXI, 24 March – 22 May 2011), London: Estorick Foundation.

2011
Barbero, L. M. (ed.), *Roma '50–'60. Guida alle architetture nelle fotografie di Oscar Savio* (Rome, MACRO – Museo d'Arte Contemporanea Roma, 23 January – 19 September 2010), Milan: Mondadori Electa.

2015
Mina, G. A. M., *Con la luce di Roma – In Rome's Light: Fotografie dal 1840 al 1870 nella Collezione Marco Antonetto* (Ligornetto, Museo Vincenzo Vela, 22 November 2015 – 10 April 2016), Bern: Cataloghi del museo Vela.

2016
Furini, G., Gambetta, G. (eds.), *Abitare a Roma in periferia. Fotografie di Rodrigo Pais* (Rome, Museo di Roma in Trastevere, 21 September 2016 –15 January 2017), Rome: Gangemi.
Parisi Presicce, C., Danti, A. (eds.), *Campidoglio. Mito, memoria, archeologia* (Rome, Musei Capitolini, 1 March – 19 June 2016), Rome: Campisano.
Pinto, J. A., *City of the Soul: Rome and the Romantics* (New York, Morgan Library & Museum, 17 June – 11 September 2016), New York: Morgan Library & Museum, Foundation for Landscape Studies; Hanover, N.H.: University Press of New England.

2017
Beth Saunders, *The Rise of Paper Photography in Italy*, online essay accompanying the exhibition *Paradise of Exiles: Early Photography in Italy* (New York, The Met Fifth Avenue, Gallery 852, The Howard Gilman Gallery, 13 March – 13 August 2017).